Do Not
Disturb

AAA to ZZZ.
Save at over 1800 Days Inns.

Rest easy. Just show your AAA card at check-in for a clean, comfortable room and savings of 10% or more.*

For service exceeding your expectations, Days Inn proudly offers reliable in-room communications from AT&T.**So you'll stay better connected to family, friends and work anywhere, anytime.

For reservations, call 1-800-AAA DAYS or visit www.daysinn.com.

There you go.SM

*Discount applies to standard rate and may not be combined with any other discounts or special offers. Discounts vary by property. Some restrictions may apply.
**Available at most locations.
© 1998 Days Inns of America, Inc.

AT&T
It's all within your reach.

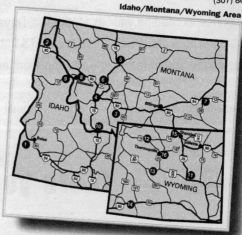

Idaho
Montana
Wyoming

Valid through February 2000

Published by:
AAA Publishing
1000 AAA Drive
Heathrow, FL 32746-5063
Copyright AAA 1999.

Send Written Comments to:
AAA Member Comments
Box 61, 1000 AAA Drive
Heathrow, FL 32746-5063

Advertising Rate and Circulation Information
Call: (407) 444-8280

Printed in the USA by Quebecor Printing, Buffalo, NY

Stock #4611

Idaho
Montana
Wyoming

TourBook Navigator

Comprehensive City Index

■ Idaho

■ Montana

■ *Wyoming*

Featured Information

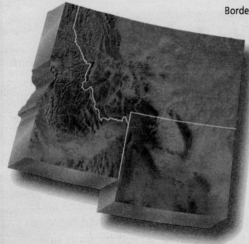

When traveling away from home...

Member Services Call Center
SUPERNUMBER ®
1-800-AAA-HELP
1-800-955-4TDD (Hearing Impaired)

a 24-hour, toll-free, Emergency Road Service information system.

It's easy to use:

Look in the white pages of the telephone book for a listing under "AAA" in the United States or "CAA" in Canada, since road service is dispatched by the local club in many communities.

If there is no listing, have your membership card handy and call **SUPERNUMBER®**, **1-800-AAA-HELP,** for the nearest road service facility. *Hearing Impaired call* **1-800-955-4TDD.**

SUPERNUMBER®, is available in the United States and Canada 24 hours a day, but **only** for Emergency Road Service and only when traveling outside the area served by your home club. Contact the nearest club office regarding other services you may require.

NOTE: NOT AVAILABLE WHEN TRAVELING IN MEXICO.

When it comes to personal trip planning, nobody beats trained AAA travel counselors.

Our highly trained counselors can assist you with all facets of planning your trip, from designing the route to making reservations. In addition, only AAA travel counselors can provide our exclusive collection of travel materials selected especially for you.

TourBook® guides are comprehensive travel guides listing AAA-approved attractions, lodgings and restaurants. In addition to the coveted diamond ratings, you'll find descriptions of towns and cities and information on discounts available only to AAA members. TourBooks are updated annually and cover every state and province in the United States and Canada.

TripTik® routings trace your route mile-by-mile and are clearly marked with the vital information you need while on the road, such as highway exits and rest stops. These handy spiral-bound maps are custom-configured by your AAA travel counselor and can highlight the quickest, shortest or most scenic routes, as well as highway construction projects along the way.

Only AAA offers an integrated travel information system that is tailored to your individual needs.

Sheet maps are updated annually and cover every state and province, plus regional areas throughout North America. An extensive network of road reporters and club staff work with AAA cartographers to ensure that AAA maps are the most detailed and accurate maps available.

CampBook® guides list AAA-approved camping and RV facilities, both public and private, throughout the United States and Canada.

So the next time you're planning a trip, remember to visit your local AAA travel counselor, and ***Travel With Someone You Trust.***®

Congratulations. You made it.

It's a place where you can kick off your shoes and take it easy.

Where you can take a load off your mind as well as your feet.

Where you can relax, because you know we don't.

Call 1-800-HAMPTON® or visit us at hampton-inn.com.

We make it easy to take it easy.℠

TRUST the AAA TourBook for objective travel information. Follow the pages of TourBook Navigator to thoroughly understand this unique member benefit.

Each attraction, lodging and restaurant is listed on the basis of merit alone after careful evaluation, approval and rating by one of our full-time inspectors or, in rare cases, a designated representative.

Annual lodging inspections are unannounced and conducted on site by random room sample. Learn how to use the diamonds on pages 14-15.

An establishment's decision to advertise in TourBooks has no bearing on its inspection, evaluation or rating. Advertising for services or products does not imply AAA endorsement.

Casino gambling establishments not contained within hotels, as well as recreational activities of a participatory nature (requiring physical exertion or special skills), are not inspected but are presented in a bulleted format for informational purposes.

All information in this TourBook was reviewed for accuracy before publication. However, since changes inevitably occur between annual editions, we suggest you contact establishments directly to confirm prices and schedules.

How the TourBook is Organized

Geographic listing is used for accuracy and consistency. This means attractions, lodgings and restaurants are listed under the city or town in which they physically are located—or in some cases under the nearest recognized city or town. See the comprehensive City Index on page 338 for an A-to-Z list of towns in this TourBook.

Most listings are alphabetically organized by state or province, city, and establishment name. Reflecting contemporary travel patterns, TourBooks cluster information in two additional ways that illustrate geographic relationships among major travel targets:

- **Destination cities** are metro areas we define with local expertise supplementing government models. Our defined metro areas comprise core cities along with vicinity communities.

- **Destination areas** are regions with broad tourist appeal beyond the local. Several cities will comprise the area.

Note: If a city is grouped in a destination vicinity section, the city name will still appear at its alphabetical location in the book—and a handy cross reference will give the exact page on which listings for that city begin.

Map illustrations at the beginning of their sections orient you to these major destinations. A color bar across the top of the page indicates you are in a destination section.

Additional color tabs on the sides of pages are coded to a state or province. Match the color tabs to easily switch from attractions to lodgings and restaurants.

Sample Lodging Listing

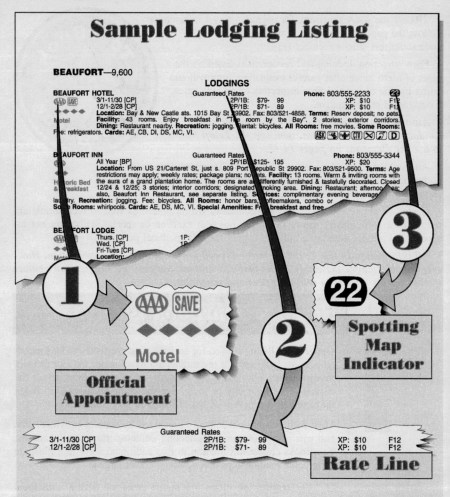

BEAUFORT—9,600

LODGINGS

BEAUFORT HOTEL — Guaranteed Rates — Phone: 803/555-2233 — 22
3/1-11/30 [CP] — 2P/1B: $79- 99 — XP: $10 — F12
12/1-2/28 [CP] — 2P/1B: $71- 89 — XP: $10 — F12
Location: Bay & New Castle sts. 1015 Bay St 29902. Fax: 803/521-4858. **Terms:** Reserv deposit; no pets. **Facility:** 43 rooms. Enjoy breakfast in "The room by the Bay". 2 stories; exterior corridors. **Dining:** Restaurant nearby. **Recreation:** jogging. Rental: bicycles. **All Rooms:** free movies. **Some Rooms:** Fee: refrigerators. **Cards:** AE, CB, DI, DS, MC, VI.

BEAUFORT INN — Guaranteed Rates — Phone: 803/555-3344
All Year [BP] — 2P/1B: $125- 195 — XP: $20
Location: From US 21/Carteret St, just s. 809 Port Republic St 29902. Fax: 803/521-9500. **Terms:** Age restrictions may apply; weekly rates; package plans; no pets. **Facility:** 13 rooms. Warm & inviting rooms with the aura of a grand plantation home. The rooms are all differently furnished & tastefully decorated. Closed 12/24 & 12/25; 3 stories; interior corridors; designated smoking area. **Dining:** Restaurant; afternoon tea; also, Beaufort Inn Restaurant, see separate listing. **Services:** complimentary evening beverage; laundry. **Recreation:** jogging. Fee: bicycles. **All Rooms:** honor bars, coffeemakers, combo or Some Rooms: whirlpools. **Cards:** AE, DS, MC, VI. **Special Amenities:** Free breakfast and free

BEAUFORT LODGE
Thurs. [CP] — 1P:
Wed. [CP] — 1P
Fri-Tues [CP]
Location:

1 — **Official Appointment**

2 — **Rate Line**

22 — **Spotting Map Indicator**

	Guaranteed Rates		
3/1-11/30 [CP]	2P/1B:	$79- 99	XP: $10 — F12
12/1-2/28 [CP]	2P/1B:	$71- 89	XP: $10 — F12

1 ◆◆◆ or ◆◆◆ The number of diamonds—not the color—informs you of the overall level of quality in a lodging's amenities and service. More diamond details on pages 14-15.

Motel or Motel Diamond ratings are applied in the context of lodging type, or classification. See pages 16-17 for our Lodging Classifications.

⊕ or ⊕ indicates our Official Appointment (OA) lodgings. The OA Program permits properties to display and advertise the ⊕ or ⊕ emblem. **We highlight these properties with red diamonds and classification**. OAs have a special interest in serving members like you. Some OA listings include special amenities such as free breakfast; early check-in/late check-out; free room upgrade or preferred room, such as ocean view or poolside (subject to availability); free local phone calls; and free daily newspaper. This does not imply that only these properties offer these amenities. The ⊕ or ⊕ sign helps traveling members find accommodations that want member business.

Discounts

SAVE is used to highlight Official Appointment properties that guarantee members a minimum 10% discount off the published TourBook rates.

SAVE appears in "icon row" below the listing and indicates that the following Show Your Card & Save® chain partners provide special values to our members: Choice Hotels, Days Inn, Hilton, Hyatt and La Quinta. Individual properties in these chains appearing in the TourBook have been inspected and approved by AAA. Be sure to read "How to Get the Best Room Rates," page 12.

S$ identifies establishments offering a senior discount with either the Guaranteed Rates or Rates Subject to Change options (see below). Where S$ appears in "icon row," a minimum discount of 10% off the prevailing or guaranteed rates is available to members who are 60 or older.

ASK in "icon row" below the listing points out the many TourBook properties that offer discounts to members even though the lodgings do not participate in a formal discount program. The ASK is another reminder to *ask* about available discounts when making your reservations or at check-in.

NOTE: Discounts normally offered at some lodgings may not apply during special events or holiday periods. Special rates and discounts may not apply to all room types.

Rate Lines and Rate Options

Rate Lines

Shown from left to right: dates the rates are effective, any meal plan included, the number of Persons/Beds allowed/provided, the rates charged, the extra person (XP) charge and any applicable family plan indicator. (See next page for meal and family plan codes.) Rates are for typical or standard rooms, not special units.

Rate Options

If a lodging chooses not to offer a discount to our members, then it must select one of the following rate options:

> **Guaranteed Rates**—The establishment guarantees our members will not be charged more than the maximum rates printed in the TourBook.

> **Rates Subject to Change**—Rates may vary for the life of the TourBook but are guaranteed not to exceed a 15% increase on the printed rates.

Printed rates are based on rack rates and last room availability and are rounded to the nearest dollar. Rates do not include taxes and discounts. U.S. rates are in U.S. dollars; rates for Canadian lodgings are in Canadian dollars. Lodgings may temporarily increase room rates or modify policies during a special event or holiday.

Always Verify Rates and Discounts

To obtain published rates or discounts, you must identify yourself as a AAA or CAA member and request them when making reservations. The SAVE or senior discounts may not be used in conjunction with other discounts. Show your card at registration and verify the room rate.

22 are numerals used to locate, or "spot," lodgings on maps we provide for larger cities. We spot restaurants with black numerals on white background ovals **22** .

What the Icons Mean

Member Services

- Ⓨ Cocktail Lounge
- Ⓘ Restaurant on Premises
- Ⓘ▸ Restaurant off Premises (walking distance)
- Ⓔ 24 Hour Room Service
- 🞐 Nightclub
- Ⓔ Entertainment
- ✚ Transportation to Airport
- Ⓗ Pets Allowed

Special Features

- Ⓓ Child Care
- 🖐 Business Services
- Ⓐ Laundry Service
- Ⓖ Fully Accessible
- Ⓕ Semi-Accessible
- Ⓖ Roll-in Showers
- Ⓐ Hearing Impaired
- 🖐 Valet Parking

Room Amenities

- Ⓟ Coffee Maker in Room
- Ⓘ Honor Bar
- Ⓟ Data Port/Modem Line
- Ⓝ No Cable TV
- Ⓧ Movies
- Ⓥ VCR
- Ⓡ Radio
- Ⓧ Non-Smoking Rooms
- Ⓜ Microwaves
- Ⓡ Refrigerator
- Ⓐ No Air Conditioning
- Ⓩ No Telephones

Sports/Recreation

- Ⓢ Pool
- Ⓕ Fitness Center
- Ⓧ Recreation Facilities

Safety Features

- Ⓢ Sprinklers
- Ⓓ Smoke Detectors
- Ⓘ Safe

Fees may be charged for some of the services represented by the icons listed above; please inquire when making reservations. Check-in times are shown in the listing only if they are after 3 p.m.; check-out times are shown only if they are before 10 a.m. Parking is on the premises and free unless otherwise noted. If a pet icon is not present, assume that the property does not accept pets; although deposits and fees are stated in the listing, check policies and restrictions when making reservations.

Meal Plan Indicators

CP = Continental Plan of pastry, juice and another beverage or may offer expanded breakfast items
BP = Breakfast Plan of full hot breakfast
AP = American Plan of three meals daily
MAP = Modified American Plan of two meals daily
EP = European Plan, where rate includes only room

Family Plan Indicators

The establishment may limit the number of children to whom the family plan applies.
F17 = children 17 and under stay free (age displayed will reflect property's policy)
D17 = discount for children 17 and under
F = children stay free
D = discounts for children

Access for Disabled Travelers

Qualified properties listed in this book have symbols indicating they are either *Fully Accessible or Semi-Accessible*. This two-tiered standard was developed to meet members' varying degrees of accessibility needs.

Fully Accessible properties meet the needs of those who are significantly disabled and primarily confined to a wheelchair. A fully accessible lodging will provide at least one guest room meeting the designated criteria. A traveler with these disabilities will be able to park and access public areas, including restrooms, check-in facilities and at least one food and beverage outlet. A *Fully Accessible* restaurant indicates that parking, dining rooms and restrooms are accessible.

Semi-Accessible properties meet the needs of those who are disabled but have some mobility and are not confined to a wheelchair. Such travelers would include people using a cane or walker, or a disabled individual with good mobility but a limited arm or hand range of motion. A *Semi-Accessible* lodging will provide at least one guest room meeting the designated criteria. A traveler with these disabilities will be able to park and access public areas, including restrooms, check-in facilities and at least one food and beverage outlet. A *Semi-Accessible* restaurant indicates that parking, dining rooms and restrooms are accessible.

This symbol indicates a property with the following equipment available for *Hearing Impaired* travelers: TDD at front desk or switchboard; visual notification of fire alarm, incoming telephone calls, door knock or bell; closed caption decoder available; text telephone or TDD available for guest room use; telephone amplification device available, with shelf and electric outlet next to guest room telephone.

AAA/CAA urges members with disabilities to always phone ahead to fully understand the accommodation's offerings. Some properties do not fully comply with AAA/CAA's exacting accessibility standards but may offer some property design standards that meet the needs of some guests with disabilities.

AAA/CAA does not evaluate recreational facilities, banquet rooms or convention and meeting facilities for accessibility. Call a property directly to inquire about your needs for these areas.

The criteria used by AAA/CAA do not represent the full scope of the Americans With Disabilities Act of 1990 Accessibility Guidelines (ADAAG); they are, however, consistent with the ADAAG. Members can obtain from their local AAA/CAA club the AAA brochure "Accessibility Criteria for Travelers With Disabilities," which describes the specific criteria pertaining to the *Fully Accessible* and *Semi-Accessible* standards.

The Americans With Disabilities Act (ADA) prohibits businesses that serve the public from discriminating against persons with disabilities who are aided by service animals. Some businesses have mistakenly denied access to their properties to persons with disabilities who use service animals. ADA has priority over all state and local laws, as well as a business owner's standard of business, that might bar animals from the premises. Businesses must permit guests and their service animal entry, as well as allow service animals to accompany guests to all public areas of a property. A property is permitted to ask whether the animal is a service animal or a pet, or whether a guest has a disability. The property may not, however, ask questions about the nature of a disability or require proof of one.

How to Get the Best Room Rates

You'll find the best room rate if you book your reservation in advance with the help of a travel counselor or agent at your local AAA/CAA office.

If you're not yet ready to make firm vacation plans or if you prefer a more spontaneous trip, take advantage of the partnerships that preferred hotel chains have arranged with AAA. Call the toll-free numbers on the opposite page that have been set up exclusively for the purpose of reserving with these *Show Your Card & Save*® chain partners.

Even if you were unable to make a reservation, be sure to show your membership card at the desk and ask if you're being offered the lowest rate available for that time. Many lodgings offer reduced rates to members.

Making Reservations

Give Proper Identification

When making reservations, you must identify yourself as a AAA/CAA member. Give all pertinent information about your planned stay. Request written confirmation to guarantee: type of room, rate, dates of stay, and cancellation and refund policies. **Note:** Age restrictions may apply.

Confirm Deposit, Refund and Cancellation Policies

Most establishments give full deposit refunds if they have been notified at least 48 hours before the normal check-in time. However, when making reservations, confirm the property's deposit, cancellation and refund policies. Some properties may charge a cancellation or handling fee. When this applies, "handling fee imposed" will appear in the listing. If you cancel too late, you have little recourse if a refund is denied. When an establishment requires a full or partial payment in advance, and your trip is cut short, a refund may not be given.

When canceling reservations, call the lodging immediately. Make a note of the date and time you called, the cancellation number if there is one, and the name of the person who handled the cancellation. If your AAA/CAA club made your reservation, allow them to make the cancellation for you as well so you will have proof of cancellation.

Review Charges for Appropriate Rates

When you are charged more than the rate listed in the TourBook, under the option **Guaranteed Rates,** or you qualify for the **Senior Discount** and did not receive it, question the additional charge. If management refuses to adhere to the published rate, pay for the room and submit your receipt and membership number to AAA/CAA *within 30 days*. Include all pertinent information: dates of stay, rate paid, itemized paid receipts, number of persons in your party, the room number you occupied, and list any extra room equipment used. A refund of the amount paid in excess of the stated maximum will be made if our investigation indicates that unjustified charging has occurred.

Get the Room You Reserved

When you find your room is not as specified, and you have written confirmation of reservations for a certain type of accommodation, you should be given the option of choosing a different room or finding one elsewhere. Should you choose to go elsewhere and a refund is refused or resisted, submit the matter to AAA/CAA *within 30 days* along with complete documentation, including your reasons for refusing the room and copies of your written confirmation and any receipts or canceled checks associated with this problem.

Preferred Lodging Partners

Call the member-only toll-free numbers or your club to get these member benefits.

Choice Hotel brands
(800) 228-1222

◀

- **SAVE** Save 10% at Sleep, Comfort, Quality and Econo Lodge
- **SAVE** Save 20% at Clarion Hotels and Clarion Carriage House Inns
- **SAVE** Guaranteed stay - If you're not satisfied with your stay, it's free

Days Inn
(800) 432-9755

◀

- **SAVE** Guaranteed lowest rates available for dates of stay when booked in advance

Hilton Worldwide
(800) 916-2221

◀

- **SAVE** Guaranteed lowest rates available for dates of stay when booked in advance

Hyatt Hotels
(800) 532-1496

◀

- **SAVE** Guaranteed lowest rates available for dates of stay when booked in advance
- **SAVE** Receive second dinner entree at half-price in Hyatt dining room when staying at the hotel

La Quinta Inns
(800) 221-4731

◀

- **SAVE** Guaranteed lowest public rate for dates of stay for standard room
- **SAVE** Children under 18 and spouse sharing room stay free
- **SAVE** Guaranteed stay - If you're not satisfied with your stay, it's free

Red Roof Inns
(877) 222-7663

◀

- **SAVE** Save 10% at all Red Roof Inns
- **SAVE** Guaranteed stay - If you're not happy with your night's stay and the problem can't be corrected, it's free

Special rates and discounts may not apply to all room types. Not available to groups and cannot be combined with other discounts. Restrictions apply to stay guarantees. Valid AAA/CAA membership card must be presented at check-in. Offers good at time of publication; chains and offers may change without notice.

Show Your Card & Save

The Lodging Diamonds

AAA-RATED® lodgings are evaluated annually during unannounced visits by full-time inspectors. Properties must satisfy a set of minimum requirements that reflect the basic lodging needs members have identified. An increased number of diamonds reflects higher levels of quality in service and amenities.

The few lodgings with ⒤ in place of diamonds are included as an "informational only" service for members. It indicates that a property has not been rated for one or more of the following reasons: too new to rate; under construction; under major renovation; not inspected; or may not meet all AAA requirements.

Properties meet all Listing Requirements. They are clean and well-maintained.

Properties maintain the attributes offered at the one diamond level while showing noticeable enhancements in room decor and quality of furnishings.

Properties show a marked upgrade in physical attributes, services and comfort. Additional amenities, services and facilities may be offered.

Properties reflect an exceptional degree of hospitality, service and attention to detail, while offering upscale facilities and a variety of amenities.

Property facilities and operations exemplify an impeccable standard of excellence while exceeding guest expectations in hospitality and service. These renowned properties are both striking and luxurious, offering many extra amenities.

The Restaurant Diamonds

Diamond ratings are assigned based on conditions noted at the time of the evaluation. Food quality is the most critical to the overall rating, but other factors also are considered, such as service and atmosphere. Restaurants are classified by cuisine type. Some listings include additional information, such as the availability of a senior citizen menu, children's menu or "early bird specials," if offered at least 5 days a week. The dinner price range is approximate and includes a salad or appetizer, an entree, a vegetable and a non-alcoholic beverage for one person. Taxes and tip are not included. *Note: Major restaurant chains are not listed due to their widespread recognition.*

Provides a simple, family or specialty meal in clean, pleasant surroundings. Food is basic and wholesome. Service is casual, limited or self-serve. Decor is informal.

More extensive menus for family or adult dining. Food is prepared with standard ingredients. Service is attentive but may be informal, casual, limited or self-serve. The decor presents a unified theme that is comfortable but also may be trendy, casual or upbeat.

An upscale or special family dining experience. Food is cooked to order and creatively prepared with quality ingredients. A wine list is available. A skilled, often uniformed staff provides service. The usually professional and inviting decor projects a trendy, upbeat, casual or formal atmosphere.

A high degree of sophistication, thus creating an adult dining experience. Complex food is creatively presented. An extensive wine list is offered. The service staff, often formally attired, is professionally trained. The decor is distinctive, stylish and elegant; some establishments are casual while still offering refinement or formality.

A memorable occasion—the ultimate in adult dining. Food shows the highest culinary skills, evident in all areas of preparation and presentation. An extensive wine list is available. A professional staff—often in formal attire—provides flawless and pampering service. The decor has classic details, often formal, and reflects comfort and luxury.

Lodging Classifications

AAA inspectors evaluate lodgings based on classification, since all lodging types by definition do not provide the same level of service and facilities. Thus, hotels are rated in comparison to other hotels—and so on. A lodging's classification appears beneath its diamond rating in the listing.

Motel
(limited service)

Low-rise or multistory establishment offering limited public and recreational facilities.

Hotel
(full service)

Usually high-rise establishments, offering a full range of on-premises food and beverage service, cocktail lounge, entertainment, conference facilities, business services, shops and recreational activities. Wide range of services provided by uniformed staff on duty 24 hours. Parking arrangements vary.

Motor Inn
(moderate service)

Single or multistory establishment offering on-premises food and beverage service. Meeting and banquet facilities and some recreational activities. Usually complimentary on-site parking.

Bed and Breakfast
(limited service)

Usually smaller establishments emphasizing a more personal relationship between operators and guests, leading to an "at home" feeling. Guest units tend to be individually decorated. Rooms may not include some modern amenities such as televisions and telephones, and may have a shared bathroom. Usually owner-operated, with a common room or parlor, separate from the innkeeper's living quarters, where guests and operators can interact during evening and breakfast hours. Evening office closures are normal. A continental or full, hot breakfast is served and is included in the room rate.

Country Inn
(moderate service)

Although similar in definition to a bed and breakfast, country inns are usually larger in size, provide more spacious public areas and offer a dining facility that serves at least breakfast and dinner. May be located in a rural setting or downtown area.

Apartment
(limited service)

Establishments that primarily offer transient guest accommodations with one or more bedrooms, a living room, a full kitchen and an eating area. Studio-type apartments may combine the sleeping and living areas into one room.

Condominium
(limited service)

Establishments that primarily offer guest accommodations that are privately owned by individuals and available for rent. These can include apartment-style units or homes. A variety of room styles and decor treatments as well as limited housekeeping service is typical. May have off-site registration.

Lodging Classifications

Complex
(service varies depending on type of lodgings)

A combination of two or more types of lodging classifications.

Cottage
(limited service)

Establishments that primarily provide individual housing units that may offer one or more separate sleeping rooms, a living room and cooking facilities. Usually incorporate rustic decor treatments and are geared to vacationers.

Lodge
(moderate service)

Typically two or more stories with all facilities in one building, rustic decor. Located in vacation, ski, fishing areas, etc. Usually has food and beverage service.

Ranch
(moderate service)

Often offers rustic decor treatments and food and beverage facilities. Entertainment and recreational activities are geared to a Western-style adventure vacation. May provide some meeting facilities.

Resort
(full service)

Geared to vacation travelers. It is a destination offering varied food and beverage outlets, specialty shops, meeting or conference facilities, entertainment, and extensive recreational facilities for special interests such as golf, tennis, skiing, fishing and water sports. Assorted social and recreational programs are typically offered in season, and a variety of package plans are usually available, including meal plans incorporated into the rates. Larger resorts may offer a variety of guest accommodations.

Subclassifications

The following are subclassifications that may appear along with the classifications listed above to provide a more specific description of the lodging:

Suite

One or more bedrooms and a living room/sitting area, which is closed off by a full wall. *Note:* May not have a partition bedroom door.

Extended Stay

Properties catering to longer-term guest stays. Will have kitchens or efficiencies. May have a separate living room area, evening office closure and limited housekeeping services.

Historic

Accommodations in restored structures built prior to 1920, reflecting the ambiance of yesteryear and the surrounding area. Antique furnishings complement the overall decor of the property. Rooms may lack some modern amenities and may have shared bathrooms.

Guest Safety

Precautions Can Save A Vacation!

Travelers are faced with the task of protecting themselves while in a strange environment. Although there is no way to guarantee absolute protection from crime, the experts—law enforcement officials—advise travelers to take a pro-active approach to securing their property and ensuring their safety.

1 Make sure the hotel desk clerk does not announce your room number; if so, quietly request a new room assignment.

2 Ask front desk personnel which areas of town to avoid and what, if any, special precautions should be taken when driving a rental car (some criminals target tourists driving rental cars).

3 Never open the door to a stranger; use the peephole and request identification. If you are still unsure, call the front desk to verify the identity of the person and the purpose of his/her visit.

4 Carry money separately from credit cards or use a "fanny pack." Carry your purse close to your body and your wallet in an inside coat or front trouser pocket. Never leave luggage unattended, and use your business address, if possible, on luggage tags.

5 Beware of distractions staged by would-be scam artists, especially groups of children that surround you or a stranger who accidentally spills something on you. They may be lifting your wallet.

6 If using an automatic teller machine (ATM), choose one in a well-lit area with plenty of foot traffic, such as one at a grocery store. Law enforcement officials suggest that machines inside establishments are generally safer to use.

7 Use room safes or safety deposit boxes provided by the hotel. Store all valuables out of sight, even when you are in the room.

8 Law enforcement agencies consider card-key (electronic) door locks the most secure.

Guest Safety

In order to be approved for listing in AAA/CAA TourBook® guides for the United States and Canada, all lodgings must comply with AAA's guest room security requirements.

In response to AAA/CAA members' concern about their safety at properties, AAA RATED® accommodations must have deadbolt locks on all guest room entry doors and connecting room doors.

If the area outside the guest room door is not visible from inside the room through a window or door panel, viewports must be installed on all guest room entry doors. Bed and breakfast properties and country inns are not required to have viewports. Ground floor and easily accessible sliding doors must be equipped with some other type of secondary security locks.

Field inspectors view a percentage of rooms at each property. It is not feasible for the inspectors to evaluate every room in every lodging establishment. So, AAA cannot guarantee that there are working locks on all doors and windows in all guest rooms.

Because of the highly specialized skills needed to conduct professional fire safety inspections, AAA/CAA inspectors cannot assess fire safety. However, guest rooms in U.S. lodging properties must be equipped with an operational, single-station smoke detector, and all public areas must have operational smoke detectors or an automatic sprinkler system. **Note:** Some Canadian lodgings are an exception to this requirement. There may be some Canadian properties that were approved prior to 1988 that use heat sensors in place of smoke detectors and/or automatic sprinkler systems.

Since all U.S. lodgings must be equipped as described above, no special notation is made in the U.S. listings. Canadian listings reflect with icons (shown on page 8) the type of fire safety equipment provided. A AAA/CAA inspector has evaluated a sampling of the rooms to verify this equipment is in place. For additional fire safety information read the page posted on the back of your guest room door, or write:

National Fire Protection Association,
1 Batterymarch Park, P.O. Box 9101,
Quincy, MA 02269-9101.

TourBook Maps

Attractions Section

Orientation maps

These maps near the start of each Attractions section show only those places we call points of interest. Stars accent towns with "must see" attractions. And the black ovals with white numerals locate items listed in the nearby Recreation Areas chart.

Defined metro and destination area maps

These maps illustrate key travel areas defined by local travel experts. Communities shown have listings for AAA approved attractions.

National park maps

These maps represent the area in and around the park. Some campground sites and lodges spotted on the maps do not meet AAA/CAA criteria, but are shown for members who nevertheless wish to stay there.

City maps

These maps show areas where numerous points of interest are concentrated and indicate their location in relation to major roads, parks, airports and other landmarks.

Walking or self-guiding tour maps

These maps correspond to specific routes described in TourBook text.

Driving Distance Maps

Driving distance maps

These maps located in the Featured Information section of the book are intended to be used only for trip-distance and driving-time planning.

TourBook Maps

Lodgings & Restaurants Section

State or province orientation maps

These maps appear before the property listings in the Lodgings & Restaurants section of selected TourBooks. These maps show the relative positions of major metropolitan areas and the vicinity towns in those areas.

Area maps

These maps denote large geographical areas in which there are many towns containing lodgings and/or restaurants. Due to these maps' small scale, lodgings and restaurants are not shown; towns with lodgings and/or restaurants are printed in magenta type.

Defined metro and destination area maps

These maps illustrate key travel areas defined by local travel experts. Communities shown have listings for AAA RATED® lodgings and/or restaurants.

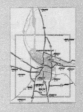

Spotting maps

These maps show the location of lodgings and restaurants. Lodgings are spotted with a black-background numeral (⑳, for example); restaurants are spotted with a white-background numeral (⑳ for example). Spotting map indexes have been placed after the main city heading to provide the user with a convenient method to identify what an area has to offer at a glance. The index references the map page number where the property is spotted, indicates if a property is an Official Appointment and contains an advertising reference if applicable. It also lists the property's diamond rating, high season rate range and listing page number.

Downtown/city spotting maps

These maps are provided when spotted facilities are very concentrated. Starred points of interest also appear on these maps.

Vicinity spotting maps

These maps spot those properties that are outside the downtown or city area. Major roads, landmarks, airports and starred points of interest are shown on vicinity spotting maps as well. The names of suburban communities that have AAA RATED® accommodations are shown in magenta type.

Sample Attraction Listing

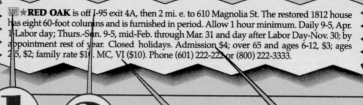

SAVE ★RED OAK is off I-95 exit 4A, then 2 mi. e. to 610 Magnolia St. The restored 1812 house has eight 60-foot columns and is furnished in period. Allow 1 hour minimum. Daily 9-5, Apr. 1-Labor day; Thurs.-Sun. 9-5, mid-Feb. through Mar. 31 and day after Labor Day-Nov. 30; by appointment rest of year. Closed holidays. Admission $4; over 65 and ages 6-12, $3; ages 2-5, $2; family rate $10. MC, VI ($10). Phone (601) 222-222 or (800) 222-3333.

SAVE ★

off I-95 exit

year. Closed
D. MC, VI ($

gh Mar. 31 and day after Labor Day-Nov. 30;
Admission $4; over 65 and ages 6-12, $3; a
(601) 222-222 or (800) 222-3333.

① **SAVE** participants offer AAA/CAA cardholders and up to six family members at least 10% off admission for the validity period of the TourBook. Present your card at the admissions desk. A list of participating attractions appears in the Indexes section of the book. The SAVE discount may not be used in conjunction with other discounts. Discounts may not apply during special events or particular days or seasons.

★—Attraction is of exceptional interest and quality.

② Unless otherwise specified, directions are given from the center of town, using the following highway designations: I (interstate highway), US (federal highway), Hwy. (Canadian highway), SR (state route), CR (county road), FM (farm to market road), FR (forest road), MM (mile marker).

③
AE=American Express	DS=Discover	MC=MasterCard
CB=Carte Blanche	JC=Japanese Credit Bureau	VI=VISA
DI=Diners Club		

Minimum amounts that may be charged appear in parentheses when applicable.

④ Admission prices are quoted *without* sales tax. Children under the lowest age specified are admitted free when accompanied by an adult. Days, months and age groups written with a hyphen are *inclusive*. Prices pertaining to attractions in the United States are quoted in U.S. dollars; Canadian province and territory attraction prices are quoted in Canadian dollars.

Confirm Prices and Schedules

All information was reviewed for accuracy before publication. However, since changes often occur between annual editions, please use the phone numbers in the listings to confirm prices and schedules.

Attraction Partners

These Show Your Card & Save® attraction partners provide the listed member benefits. Admission tickets that offer greater discounts may be available for purchase at the local AAA club.

Universal Studios (Florida and Hollywood)

SAVE Save $3 on admission at the gate

SAVE Save 10% on selected souvenirs and dining

SeaWorld/Busch Gardens

Save at SeaWorld, Busch Gardens, Sesame Place, Water Country U.S.A. and Adventure Island

SAVE Save 10% on general admission

SAVE Save 10% at a selected restaurant and retail shops inside the park

Offers at the attractions listed above are good at the time of publication and are subject to change without notice.

Show Your Card & Save

Golden Passports

Citizens or permanent residents of the United States who are 62 and older can obtain Golden Age Passports for a one-time $10 fee. Golden Access Passports are free to citizens or permanent residents of the United States (regardless of age) who are medically blind or permanently disabled. Both cover entrance fees for the holder and accompanying private party to all national parks and historic sites, monuments and battlefields within the U.S. national park system, plus half off camping and other fees. Apply in person at most federally operated areas.

WE'RE WITH YOU ALL THE WAY

When you belong to AAA, you're never alone. You have the security of AAA's Emergency Road Service behind you, *plus the world's largest travel organization on hand.* AAA does everything from booking airline tickets and lodgings to providing special member discounts on cruises, escorted tours, tour packages, car rentals, hotels and attractions, fee-free American Express® Travelers Cheques and free TripTik® maps, TourBook® guide and CampBook® guides. *As a AAA member—you're in good company.*

Contact your local AAA Club for more information.

 Travel With Someone You Trust®

Idaho

Ride the Wild Ones

Idaho's rivers are paradise for white-water rafting enthusiasts

Lewis and Clark Revisited

Millions of acres of wilderness await exploration by land, horseback and water

Idaho's Seaport

The Columbia River connects the inland port of Lewiston to the Pacific Ocean

The Renowned Potato

When you think of Idaho, its number one crop comes to mind

World Class Skiing

Sun Valley was America's first resort designed specifically for skiing

wild at heart

V isit Idaho and you'll need an oxygen mask; the scenery is *that* breathtaking. From the serrated granite peaks of the Sawtooth Mountains in the center of the state to the towering Seven Devils near Hells Canyon, Idaho features some of the country's most stunning high-altitude panoramas. And if the views don't steal your breath away, the thin air at these lofty elevations just might.

Fortunately, there's no better place to deeply inhale than within the state's numerous unspoiled wilderness areas. Clean air and peaceful solitude attract pollution- and stress-weary urbanites from around the country to places like the Selway-Bitterroot Wilderness or Craters of the Moon National Monument.

You can expel that fresh air again in a shout of triumph as you conquer exhilarating white water along the Snake, Selway or Salmon rivers. Whoop with excitement as you fly down a powder-covered slope in Sun Valley or on Schweitzer Mountain. Scream with delight at the discovery of a star garnet near Coeur d'Alene, the only place outside of India you can find such treasure and just one reason Idaho's nickname—the Gem State—is appropriate.

Whatever you do, take a deep breath first; you'll want to be ready to enjoy Idaho.

"Tab-ba-bone!" When that word, thought to mean "white man" in Shoshone, was first shouted in 1805, it referred to Meriwether Lewis and William Clark. After gaining the Louisiana Territory in 1803, Thomas Jefferson sent Lewis and Clark to explore the area west of the Rocky Mountains. They crossed the Lolo Pass 2 years later and followed the Lochsa and Clearwater drainages to the Snake River, becoming the area's first white settlers. Shortly thereafter a change in European fashion caused thousands of trappers to follow these initial trails into the Snake River area.

In the early 1800s European fashion was tall, fancy fur hats, making beaver skins valuable. American and British trappers cut new paths in search of furs. David Thompson of Britain quickly established the first white settlement in Idaho: a trading post for the North West Co. on Lake Pend Oreille where guns, knives and pots were exchanged for beaver pelts.

Throughout this joint occupancy, which terminated with the Treaty of 1846, British fur trade dominated the region. Then overtrapping and a shift of fashion from fur to silk hats depleted both supply and demand. Fur traders moved out and missionaries moved in to convert the Indian population.

Notable were Henry Spalding, who established missions among the Nez Perce, and Father Pierre Jean De Smet, who worked among the Coeur d'Alenes. Mormons emigrating from Utah established Idaho's first permanent settlement in Franklin in 1860. Meanwhile immigration along the Oregon Trail increased as Oregon fever gripped more Easterners and the discovery of gold in California increased traffic on the road.

Still most travelers did not consider settling in Idaho until gold was discovered by Elias D. Pierce. Pierce sneaked a group of prospectors near the Clearwater River, where they "Found gold in every place in the stream-I never saw a party of men so excited; they made the hills and mountains ring with joy." Prospectors from Oregon and California quickly followed, and in 1863 President Lincoln organized the Idaho Territory with Lewiston as the first capital. Boise was designated as the capital in 1864, and Idaho's present boundaries were fixed in 1868.

The expanding mining economy needed goods and services, and the encroachment of ranchers, miners and farmers onto American Indian lands undermined the last goodwill efforts created by Lewis and Clark. Skirmishes between the miners and American Indians soon

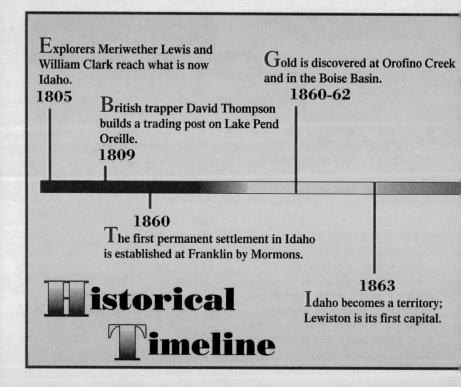

Explorers Meriwether Lewis and William Clark reach what is now Idaho.
1805

British trapper David Thompson builds a trading post on Lake Pend Oreille.
1809

Gold is discovered at Orofino Creek and in the Boise Basin.
1860-62

1860
The first permanent settlement in Idaho is established at Franklin by Mormons.

1863
Idaho becomes a territory; Lewiston is its first capital.

Historical Timeline

escalated into the Nez Perce, Bannock, and Sheepeater wars, where American Indians were eventually driven onto barren reservations. The great Nez Perce leader Chief Joseph echoed the sentiments of his tribe and others when he announced in defeat, "My heart is sick and sad. From where the sun now stands, I will fight no more forever."

The extension of the railroads into the territory in the early 1880s allowed the development of the newly discovered lead and silver lodes in the Coeur d'Alene and Wood River districts, spurring a huge growth in population. On July 3, 1890, Idaho became a state.

But Colorado almost became Idaho. "Idaho" was first proposed for the territory centered around Pike's Peak in the 1860s. When the U.S. Senate could not verify the word's Indian origins, it chose "Colorado" for its new state name. More than 20 years later, "Idaho" was applied to the 43rd state in the union.

In the early 1900s farming expanded as state and federal governments initiated irrigation projects; much of Idaho's soil produced valuable crops like wheat, alfalfa and sugar beets.

Bitter miners' strikes and labor upheavals in the 1890s culminated in the 1905 assassination of ex-Gov. Frank Steunenberg. During the investigation and trials William E. Borah became an important force in state politics, serving as U.S. senator 1907-40 and gaining national prominence as the "Lion of Idaho."

The protection of natural resources dominates the thoughts of contemporary Idahoans. Population and economic pressures as well as toxic waste contamination posed by the Federal Government's investment in nuclear power pose threats to the state's pristine wilderness.

Geography

Although it is unlikely "Idaho" ever meant "gem of the mountains," huge ranges dominate the state's topography. The northern part of the state holds a mountain massif interrupted by rivers and two prairies: the Palouse Country around Moscow and Big Camas Prairie near Grangeville. The southeastern corner hosts high ranges, while the rest of the southern border consists of dry, low peaks. Out of Idaho's 81 distinct ranges, more than 42 mountains top 10,000 feet.

Ribboned around these ranges are more than 16,000 miles of rivers and streams. Shaped like a question mark lying on its back, the most imposing river is the Snake. Starting in Yellowstone National Park, it flows westward for more than 1,000 miles through Idaho. With 11 dams

Miners' strikes and labor upheaval culminate in the assassination of former governor Frank Steunenberg. **1905**

Northern Idaho is covered with volcanic ash following the eruption of Washington's Mount St. Helens. **1980**

The railroad first reaches Idaho at Franklin. **1874**

Engineers complete a series of three dams to harness the power of the Snake River. **1968**

1890
Idaho becomes the 43rd state.

1951
An Atomic Energy Commission testing station near Idaho Falls is the site where nuclear fission first produces electricity.

1995
Olympic medalist and Idaho native Picabo Street becomes the first American to win the World Cup downhill skiing championship.

FAST FACTS

POPULATION: 1,210,200.

AREA: 83,557 square miles; ranks 13th.

CAPITAL: Boise.

HIGHEST POINT: 12,662 ft., Borah Peak.

LOWEST POINT: 710 ft., Snake River.

TIME ZONES: Mountain/Pacific. DST.

MINIMUM AGE FOR DRIVERS: with driver's education training, 16 (restricted to daylight hours, 15); otherwise 17.

SEAT BELT/CHILD RESTRAINT LAWS: Seat belts required for driver and front-seat passengers; child restraints required for under 4.

HELMETS FOR MOTORCYCLISTS: Required for persons under 18.

RADAR DETECTORS: Permitted.

FIREARMS LAWS: Vary by state and/or county. Contact Idaho State Police, 2700 N. South Hwy., Lewiston, ID 83501; phone (208) 743-9546.

HOLIDAYS: Jan. 1; Martin Luther King Jr.'s Birthday, Jan. (3rd Mon.); Washington's Birthday, Feb. (3rd Mon.); Memorial Day, May (last Mon.); July 4; Labor Day, Sept. (1st Mon.); Columbus Day, Oct. (2nd Mon.); Veterans Day, Oct. (4th Mon.); Thanksgiving; Dec. 25.

TAXES: Idaho's statewide sales tax is 5 percent. There is a 2-percent Travel & Convention Tax on lodgings, with local options to levy up to an additional 5 percent.

STATE INFORMATION CENTERS: Welcome centers that provide details on state attractions, accommodations, historic sites, parks and events as well as road and ski reports are at Fruitland I-84E, Milepost 1; 6 miles south of Malad on I-15N; and along I-90E at Post Falls.

checking its speed, the river provides hydroelectric power and irrigation for three-fourths of all Idahoans.

Rivaling the Snake River in power, the Salmon River is aptly nicknamed the "River of No Return." Swift, and in spots dangerous, the salmon-spawning stream separates northern and southern Idaho.

At more than 148 square miles, the Pend Oreille is the largest of the state's more than 2,000 lakes. In the southeast is Bear Lake, half of which is in Utah. In the north are Priest, Coeur d'Alene and Hayden lakes.

Economy

Idaho's major industries include agriculture, food processing, forestry, high-tech manufacturing, tourism and mining. The most heavily developed agricultural area is southern Idaho, in the valley of the Snake River and its tributaries.

Potatoes and wheat, grown copiously in the Palouse country, and hay, oats, barley, onions, beans, peas, sugar beets and fruits are the most important crops. Seed production is a leading industry; others are sugar refining and potato processing. Cattle and sheep raising, trout and dairying support the major industries of meatpacking and wool, milk and cheese production.

A large portion of the valuable timberland that covers approximately 40 percent of the land area in Idaho is within national forests. Lumbering of white fir, Douglas fir and red cedar produces millions annually.

In order of value the chief minerals are phosphate, silver, gold, molybdenum and zinc. Silver, gold and zinc come mainly from the great Coeur d'Alene mining district. Some of the largest phosphate deposits in the world lie in the southeast; phosphoric acid and phosphate fertilizer are important byproducts.

The manufacturing of high-tech electronics is playing an increasingly important role in Idaho's economy. Also, Boise is the home of one of the country's highest concentrations per capita of national and world business headquarters.

Tourism is Idaho's third largest and fastest growing industry. Federal and state assistance has helped develop tourist areas such as Lava Hot Springs Resort near Pocatello. Other popular destinations include Sun Valley, Coeur d'Alene, Hells Canyon, McCall and the state's rivers, lakes, mountains and recreational areas.

Recreation

Inspiring scenery and varied recreational opportunities make Idaho an ideal vacation state. The traditional strongholds are Sun Valley in central Idaho and Coeur d'Alene in the north.

Boating, fishing and other outdoor activities are popular at Coeur d'Alene, Pend Oreille and Priest Lake in the north. These same pastimes are enjoyed on the reservoirs along the Snake River and its tributaries in the south. Idaho's anglers reel in champion-size trout and load stringers with whitefish, bass and crappie. The state's wild rivers provide white-water float trips down the Salmon River and jet boat excursions into lower Hells Canyon.

Hunting for deer and elk is popular. Moose, pronghorn antelopes, bears, bighorn sheep and mountain goats also are hunted, but on a carefully controlled basis. Acres of farmland, riverbottom and marshland provide hunting grounds for grouse, partridges, pheasants and ducks.

Skiing is available in areas usually within national forests. Prominent areas are the Schweitzer Mountain Ski Resort near Sandpoint; Silver Mountain south of Kellogg; Brundage Mountain near McCall; Bogus Basin north of Boise; Pomerelle south of Burley; Pebble Creek near Pocatello; and Sun Valley.

Camping, picnicking and fishing are available at developed areas in Idaho's national forests. More than 2 million acres of unspoiled natural beauty are preserved in the Selway-Bitterroot Wilderness Area, the Frank Church National Recreation Area, the River of No Return Wilderness and the Sawtooth Wilderness. Only pack trains and hikers penetrate these regions—outfitters can be found in surrounding towns. More than 31,000 acres in the Snake River Birds of Prey Natural Area provide glimpses of eagles, falcons, ospreys, owls and hawks.

History, scenery and recreation often combine in the various units of the state park system. For information on campgrounds *see the AAA Northwestern CampBook.*

Throughout the TourBook, you may notice a Recreational Activities heading with bulleted listings of recreation-oriented establishments listed underneath. Since normal AAA inspection criteria cannot be applied, these establishments are presented for information only. Age, height and weight restrictions may apply. Reservations are often recommended and sometimes required. Visitors should phone or write the attraction for additional information, and the address and phone number are provided for this purpose.

FOR YOUR INFORMATION

FURTHER INFORMATION FOR VISITORS:
Idaho Travel Council
Box 83720
Boise, ID 83720-0093
(800) 635-7820

RECREATION INFORMATION:
Idaho Parks and Recreation Department
State House Mail
Boise, ID 83720-8000
(208) 327-7444
(800) 635-7820

FISHING AND HUNTING REGULATIONS:
Idaho Fish and Game Department
Box 25
600 S. Walnut St.
Boise, ID 83707
(208) 334-3700

NATIONAL FOREST INFORMATION:
U.S. Forest Service
Northern Region (Northern Idaho)
Federal Building
P.O. Box 7669
Missoula, MT 59807
(406) 329-3511
(800) 280-2267 (reservations)
TDD (800) 879-4496

U.S. Forest Service
Intermountain Region (Southern Idaho)
2501 Wall Ave.
Ogden, UT 84401
(801) 625-5306
(800) 280-2267 (reservations)
TDD (800) 879-4496

DID YOU KNOW?

The world's largest potato chip resides at the Idaho Potato Expo in Blackfoot.

There are many caves in Idaho, including a cave of ice near Shoshone.

The name Idaho means "gem of the mountains."

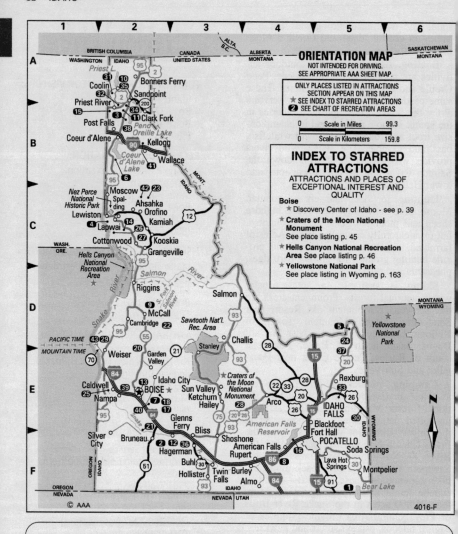

| | 1 | 2 | 3 | 4 | 5 | 6 |

ORIENTATION MAP
NOT INTENDED FOR DRIVING.
SEE APPROPRIATE AAA SHEET MAP.

ONLY PLACES LISTED IN ATTRACTIONS
SECTION APPEAR ON THIS MAP
★ SEE INDEX TO STARRED ATTRACTIONS
2 SEE CHART OF RECREATION AREAS

0   Scale in Miles   99.3
0   Scale in Kilometers   159.8

INDEX TO STARRED ATTRACTIONS
ATTRACTIONS AND PLACES OF
EXCEPTIONAL INTEREST AND
QUALITY

Boise
★ Discovery Center of Idaho - see p. 39
★ **Craters of the Moon National Monument**
See place listing p. 45
★ **Hells Canyon National Recreation Area** See place listing p. 46
★ **Yellowstone National Park**
See place listing in Wyoming p. 163

© AAA

4016-F

RECREATION AREAS

	MAP LOCATION	CAMPING	PICNICKING	HIKING TRAILS	BOATING	BOAT RAMP	BOAT RENTAL	FISHING	SWIMMING	PETS ON LEASH	BICYCLE TRAILS	WINTER SPORTS	VISITOR CENTER	LODGE/CABINS	FOOD SERVICE
NATIONAL FORESTS *(See place listings)*															
Boise 2,648,468 acres. South-central Idaho.		•	•	•	•	•		•	•	•		•	•		
Caribou 972,407 acres. Southeastern Idaho.		•	•	•				•	•	•		•			
Clearwater 1,739,353 acres. Northeastern Idaho.		•	•	•	•	•		•	•	•		•	•		
Idaho Panhandle 2,495,517 acres. Northern and north-western Idaho.		•	•	•	•	•	•	•	•	•	•	•	•	•	•
Nez Perce 2,223,594 acres. North-central Idaho.		•	•	•	•	•	•	•	•	•		•	•	•	
Payette 2,307,897 acres. West-central Idaho.		•	•	•	•	•		•	•	•		•	•		
Salmon-Challis 4,300,000 acres. East-central Idaho.		•	•	•	•	•		•	•	•		•	•	•	•
Sawtooth 2,101,422 acres. South-central Idaho. Horse rental.		•	•	•	•	•	•	•	•	•		•	•	•	•
Targhee 1,800,000 acres. Southeastern Idaho.		•	•	•	•	•		•	•	•		•	•	•	•
NATIONAL RECREATION AREAS *(See place listings)*															
Hells Canyon (C-1) 652,977 acres.		•	•	•	•	•	•	•	•	•		•	•	•	•
Sawtooth (D-3) 756,000 acres.		•	•	•	•	•	•	•	•	•	•	•	•	•	•
ARMY CORPS OF ENGINEERS															
Albeni Cove (B-1) 20 acres 1 mi. e. of Oldtown on a county road. Water skiing.	⑮	•	•		•	•		•	•	•					
Dworshak Reservoir (C-2) 19,823 acres 7 mi. n. of Orofino. Birdwatching, water skiing.	㉓	•	•	•	•	•	•	•	•	•					•
Lucky Peak (E-2) 237 acres 9 mi. s.e. of Boise on SR 21. Water skiing.	⑦		•	•	•	•	•	•	•	•	•				•
STATE															
Bear Lake (F-5) 52 acres 20 mi. s. of Montpelier off US 89. Water skiing.	❶	•	•		•		•		•	•					•
Bruneau Dunes (F-2) 4,800 acres 8 mi. n.e. of Bruneau off SR 51. Sand dunes. No motorized boats.	❷	•	•	•	•			•	•	•		•	•		
Dworshak (C-2) 1,000 acres 26 mi. n.w. of Orofino.	㊷	•	•	•	•			•					•		•
Eagle Island (E-2) 547 acres 8 mi. w. of Boise off SR 44 or US 20/26. Water slide.	㊴		•						•	•					
Farragut (B-2) 4,733 acres 4 mi. e. of Athol on SR 54. Historic. Cross-country skiing, snowmobiling.	❸	•	•	•	•	•		•	•	•		•	•		
Harriman Historic (E-5) 4,300 acres 18 mi. n. of Ashton on US 20. Cross-country skiing; horse rental.	㊲	•	•					•			•	•	•		
Hells Gate (C-1) 960 acres 4 mi. s. of Lewiston on Snake River Ave. Water skiing; horse rental.	❹	•	•	•	•	•		•	•	•		•	•		
Henry's Lake (D-5) 586 acres 15 mi. w. of West Yellowstone off US 20. Birdwatching, water skiing.	❺	•	•		•	•	•	•							
Heyburn (B-2) 7,825 acres 5 mi. e. of Plummer on SR 5. Cross-country skiing, snowmobiling.	❻	•	•	•	•	•	•	•	•	•		•			•
Lucky Peak (E-2) 237 acres 10 mi. s.e. of Boise off SR 21.	㊵	•	•	•	•	•		•	•	•					
Malad Gorge (F-3) 652 acres .25 mi. s. off I-84 exit 147, then .25 mi. w. following signs. *(See Bliss p. 37)*	㊱		•	•				•		•					
Massacre Rocks (F-4) 565 acres 10 mi. s.w. of American Falls off I-86. Historic.	❽	•	•	•	•			•		•			•		
Old Mission (B-2) 18 acres 11 mi. w. off I-90 exit 39. Historic. *(See Kellogg p. 50)*	㊶	•	•	•	•			•		•			•		
Ponderosa (D-2) 1,280 acres 2 mi. n.e. of McCall on E. Lake Dr. Cross-country skiing.	❾	•	•	•	•	•	•	•	•	•		•	•		
Priest Lake (A-2) 463 acres 11 mi. n. of Coolin. Cross-country skiing, snowmobiling.	❿	•	•	•	•	•	•	•	•	•		•			
Round Lake (B-2) 142 acres 10 mi. s. of Sandpoint off US 95 on Dufort Rd. Cross-country skiing, ice fishing, ice skating, sledding, snowshoeing. No motorized boats.	⓫	•	•	•	•	•	•		•	•	•		•	•	
Three Island Crossing (F-3) 513 acres 1 mi. w. of Glenns Ferry via Commercial St. s. and Madison w. Historic.	⓬	•	•	•				•		•					

RECREATION AREAS

	MAP LOCATION	CAMPING	PICNICKING	HIKING TRAILS	BOATING	BOAT RAMP	BOAT RENTAL	FISHING	SWIMMING	PETS ON LEASH	BICYCLE TRAILS	WINTER SPORTS	VISITOR CENTER	LODGE/CABINS	FOOD SERVICE
Veterans Memorial (E-2) 80 acres on SR 44 at 36th St. in Boise. Birdwatching. No motorized boats.	13		•	•	•			•		•	•	•			
Winchester Lake (C-2) 318 acres 1 mi. s.w. of Winchester on US 95 Bus. Rte. Cross-country skiing, ice fishing, ice skating, sledding. No motorized boats (except with electric motors).	14	•	•	•	•	•		•		•	•	•	•		
OTHER															
American Falls Reservoir (F-4) 59,893 acres .25 mi. n. of American Falls on I-15. Historic.	16	•	•		•	•		•	•	•			•		
Anderson Ranch Reservoir (E-2) 5,000 acres 30 mi. n.e. of Mountain Home on SR 20 and FR 61.	17	•	•	•	•	•	•	•	•	•		•		•	•
Arrowrock Reservoir (E-2) 4,000 acres 16 mi. e. of Boise on SR 21 and FR 268.	18	•	•		•	•		•	•	•		•		•	
Black Canyon Reservoir (E-2) 2,364 acres 8 mi. n.e. of Emmett on SR 52.	19		•		•	•		•	•	•					
Cascade Reservoir (D-2) 33,788 acres 20 mi. s. of McCall on SR 55. Ice fishing, snowmobiling.	20	•	•		•	•	•	•	•	•		•			•
C.J. Strike Reservoir (E-2) 7,500 acres. (See Bruneau p. 41)	21	•	•		•	•		•	•	•					
Deadwood Reservoir (D-2) 3,000 acres 34 mi. n.e. of Garden Valley on FR 555.	22	•	•		•	•		•	•	•		•			
Island Park Reservoir (D-5) 7,800 acres 27 mi. n. of Ashton off US 20. Snowmobiling.	24	•	•		•	•		•	•	•		•		•	•
Lake Lowell (E-1) 10,587 acres 8 mi. s. of Caldwell via 10th Ave. or SR 55. Water skiing.	25		•		•	•		•	•	•		•	•		
Lake Waha (C-2) 100 acres 18 mi. s.e. of Lewiston on Thain Rd.	26	•	•	•	•	•		•	•	•					
Little Wood River Reservoir (E-3) 976 acres 11 mi. n. of Carey on access road.	28	•	•		•	•		•	•	•					
Mann Creek Reservoir (D-2) 4 acres 9 mi. n. of Weiser on US 95. Water skiing.	29	•	•		•	•		•	•	•					
Palisades Reservoir (E-5) 27,845 acres 50 mi. s.e. of Idaho Falls on US 26.	30	•	•		•	•		•	•	•			•		
Pend Oreille Lake (B-2) 94,600 acres. (See Sandpoint p. 58)	38	•	•		•	•		•	•	•					
Priest River (A-2) 20 acres .5 mi. e. of Priest River off US 2. Water skiing.	31	•	•		•	•		•	•	•					
Riley Creek (A-2) 45 acres 1 mi. s. of Laclede on Riley Creek Rd. Water skiing.	32	•	•		•	•		•	•						
Ririe Reservoir (E-5) 6,069 acres 20 mi. n.e. of Idaho Falls on US 26.	33	•	•		•	•		•	•	•			•		
Springy Point (B-2) 13 acres 3.25 mi. w. of Sandpoint on US 95. Water skiing.	34	•	•		•	•		•	•	•					
Steck Park (D-1) 20 mi. n.w. of Weiser via SR 70 on the Snake River.	43	•	•			•		•		•					
Trestle Creek (A-2) 2 acres n.w. of Hope on SR 200. Water skiing.	35		•		•	•		•	•	•					

Fascinated by Fossils?
Galvanized by Gardens?
Wild about Waterfalls?
Intrigued by Islands?

The Points of Interest Index will lead you to them.

Points of Interest

AHSAHKA (C-2) elev. 1,001'

DWORSHAK DAM VISITOR CENTER is 3 mi. e. on SR 7, following signs, on the North Fork of the Clearwater River. The visitor center overlooks the 717-foot dam, one of the highest straight-axis concrete gravity dams in the world. Behind the dam, Dworshak Reservoir *(see Recreation Chart)* extends 54 miles into wild, rugged timberland.

Free guided tours of the dam are available. Movies and slide presentations are shown on request. Daily 10-4. Free. Phone (208) 476-1261 or 476-1255.

DWORSHAK NATIONAL FISH HATCHERY, s.e. on SR 7 at the confluence of the two forks of the Clearwater River, is one of the largest steelhead trout hatcheries in the world. About 3 million steelhead trout and 1 million chinook salmon are raised annually in environmentally controlled ponds. The best time to see the adult steelhead is March through May; the returning salmon brood stock June through August.

The hatchery building has displays, a viewing balcony above the spawning room, incubators and nursery tank facilities. There are 126 outdoor ponds. A self-guiding tour map is available. Allow 30 minutes minimum. Daily 7:30-4; hatchery building closed major holidays. Free. Phone (208) 476-4591.

ALMO (F-4) elev. 5,390'

CITY OF ROCKS NATIONAL RESERVE is .5 mi. s. on HC 61 and 4 mi. w. on an unpaved road. Within the 14,300-acre reserve are massive granite rocks, some 2.5 billion years old, eroded into shapes resembling the ruins of an ancient city. Inscriptions written in axle grease and scratched into the rocks by pioneers traversing the Oregon and California trails afford insights into immigrant trail history.

Picnicking, rock climbing, sightseeing and hiking through high deserts are possible. The reserve offers 78 primitive campsites. Potable water and restroom facilities are available. For information write to the Park Manager, City of Rocks National Reserve, P.O. Box 169, Almo, ID 83312. The overnight fee is $7 for one vehicle, $12 for more than one vehicle. Only eight persons per site are permitted. Phone (208) 824-5519.

AMERICAN FALLS (F-4) pop. 3,800, elev. 4,330'

The "Idaho Gem Community" of American Falls, an early campsite on the old Oregon Trail,

STARRED ATTRACTIONS

Craters of the Moon National Monument—The lunar-like volcanic landscape at this national monument can be viewed from a drive along a 7-mile-long loop road. See place listing p. 45.

Discovery Center of Idaho—This family-oriented science museum has hands-on exhibits for all ages. See Boise p. 39.

Hells Canyon National Recreation Area—North America's deepest gorge is the standout of this ruggedly scenic wilderness region in western Idaho. See place listing p. 46.

Yellowstone National Park—The more than 3,400 acres of America's first national park are home to buffaloes, bighorn sheep, elk, moose and pronghorn antelopes as well as thousands of thermal pools and springs. See place listing in Wyoming p. 163.

DID YOU KNOW?

Idaho's ghost towns, such as DeLamar, Idaho City and Silver City, are reminders of once-thriving mining operations.

The Snake River's Shoshone Falls is known as the "Niagara of the West," falling from cliffs that are higher than its Eastern counterpart.

Lava Hot Springs has 110 degree F mineral springs that geologists believe have been at that temperature for 50 million years.

Idaho was the name first suggested for what was to become know as the Colorado Territory.

The town of Buhl claims to be the rainbow trout capital of the United States.

Idaho has about 50 mountains that stand more than 10,000 feet tall.

LAKES SUPERIOR.

IDAHO
1-800-VISIT ID   www.visitid.org

Redfish Lake

is the center of irrigation projects that enable the cultivation of thousands of acres of farmland. The American Falls Reservoir *(see Recreation Chart)*, the largest on the Snake River, provides excellent opportunities for boating, sailing, water skiing and rainbow trout fishing. Free tours of the dam are offered; phone (208) 226-2434.

American Falls Chamber of Commerce: 258 Idaho St., P.O. Box 207, American Falls, ID 83211; phone (208) 226-7214.

ARCO (E-4) pop. 1,000, elev. 5,320'

EXPERIMENTAL BREEDER REACTOR #1 is 20 mi. e. on US 20 at the Idaho National Engineering Laboratory. On Dec. 20, 1951, the reactor became the first atomic reactor to generate a usable amount of electricity. In 1966 President Lyndon Johnson dedicated this facility as a registered national historic landmark. Videotape presentations and exhibits are available to visitors. Free guided tours through the facility are conducted by trained guides. Pamphlets explaining four nuclear reactors, a reactor control room and detection devices are available upon request.

Allow 1 hour minimum. Daily 9-5, Memorial Day weekend-Labor Day; by appointment rest of year. Free. Phone (208) 526-0050.

BEAVERHEAD DEARLODGE NATIONAL FOREST—
see Montana p. 77.

BITTERROOT NATIONAL FOREST—
see Montana p. 81.

BLACKFOOT (E-4) pop. 9,600, elev. 4,497'

BINGHAM COUNTY HISTORICAL MUSEUM, 190 N. Shilling Ave., is in a renovated 1905 Southern mansion built of lava rock and lumber. The museum displays period furnishings, clothing, photographs and other historical items. Allow 30 minutes minimum. Wed.-Fri. 1-4:30, Apr.-Oct. Free. Phone (208) 785-4788 or 785-8040.

IDAHO POTATO EXPO, 130 N.W. Main St., presents a variety of exhibits related to the potato, including antique machinery and tools, gunny sacks and, at 24 by 14 inches, the "Guinness Book of World Records" world's largest potato chip. Each visitor is offered a free baked potato. Videotapes about the potato industry and production processes are shown. Phone for special tour arrangements.

Allow 1 hour minimum. Mon.-Sat. 10-7, Sun. 10-5, May-Sept. Admission $3; over 55, $2.50; ages 6-12, $1. Phone (208) 785-2517. *See color ad.*

BLISS (E-3) pop. 200, elev. 3,261'

MALAD GORGE STATE PARK is .25 mi. s. off I-84 exit 147, then .25 mi. w., following signs. Markers indicate the park's points of interest that can be seen from a car on a 2.5-mile loop road. From the park's footbridge visitors can see the bottom of the 250-foot-deep gorge where the Emerald Pool waterfall plunges into the Devil's Washbowl. Hiking trails take the more adventurous along the edge of the gorge and into the interior of the park.

Eagles, hawks, waterfowls, coyotes, rockchucks (marmots) and mule deer can be seen throughout the park. The park contains prehistoric American Indian hunting blinds—a series of rock walls along a V-shaped cliff behind which hunters once hid; big game was driven toward the cliff's edge where the hunters would rise and attack.

The Kelton Wagon Road bridge site shows wagon wheel grooves in the lava bed of a runoff channel of the Malad Gorge. Other features of the park include a portion of the Oregon Trail, volcanic collapse features, underground springs and waterfalls. Picnicking is permitted. Allow 30 minutes minimum. Daily dawn-dusk. Free. Phone (208) 837-4505. *See Recreation Chart.*

BOISE (E-2) pop. 125,600, elev. 2,739'

The woods lining the Boise River were a welcome sight for French-Canadian trappers who were grateful to reach a forest again after trudging across the territory's semiarid plain. As a result, they named the area *Boisé,* meaning "wooded." The city, however, was not founded until 1863, a year after the gold rush reached the Boise Basin.

"The City of Trees," Boise is Idaho's capital and largest metropolitan area. The first sessions of the territorial government were held during 1863 in Lewiston, then moved to this population center the following year. The new territorial capital was the center of commerce and culture for miners and traders from nearby mountain boom towns.

The quality of life, low cost of living and liberal tax advantages as well as the city's role as state capital and transportation hub, account for Boise's steady economic growth. Many national and multinational firms have their headquarters in Boise, and light industry flourishes. The city also is the home of Boise State University and Regional Medical Centers. Built in 1863, the O'Farrell Cabin on Fort Street is one of the city's oldest buildings.

Boise is the southwest terminus of SR 21, the Ponderosa Pine Scenic Route. The route passes through part of Sawtooth National Forest before ending in Stanley; portions of SR 21 are closed in winter.

Protected from unduly harsh winter weather by the Owyhee Mountains, the capital enjoys year-round opportunities for leisure and recreation. Ann Morrison Park, 153 acres between Americana and Capitol boulevards, offers picnicking, playgrounds, ballfields and tennis courts. Skates and bicycles can be rented at Wheels-R-Fun at the south end of 13th Street. A novel way to reach Ann Morrison Park is by rental raft or inner tube from Barber Park, which is on the southeast edge of town; at the junction of Warm Springs Avenue and SR 21 turn onto Eckert, the street on which the park is. Rentals

are available daily Memorial Day through Labor Day; a return shuttle bus is available.

The Boise Greenbelt, a 25-mile bicycle and pedestrian path, follows the Boise River. Pari-mutuel horse racing takes place at Les Bois Park from early May through August on the Western Idaho Fairgrounds; phone (208) 376-7223.

Note: Policies concerning admittance of children to pari-mutuel betting facilities vary. Phone for information.

Once used as an American Indian lookout, Table Rock rises 1,100 feet above the valley east of Boise. Its flat summit, surmounted by an illuminated cross that can be seen for miles, affords a view of the city and a pioneer route south of the river.

To the southeast, 12 miles south of Kuna, the Snake River Birds of Prey Natural Area provides a haven for a number of species of birds and other wildlife. It is home to one of the largest concentrations of birds of prey in the world.

Boise Convention and Visitors Bureau: 168 N. 9th St., #200, Boise, ID 83702; phone (208) 344-7777 or (800) 635-5240. *See color ad.*

Shopping areas: Boise Factory Outlets, I-84 exit Gowen Road, offers more than 40 factory stores. Boise Towne Square, Milwaukee and Franklin sts., features The Bon Marche, Dillard's, JCPenney, Mervyn's and Sears. Downtown shopping includes 8th Street Marketplace, a former late 1890s warehouse district at 8th and Front streets; Hyde Park on N. 13th Street; and Old Boise Historic District on Main Street between Capitol and 4th streets.

BASQUE MUSEUM AND CULTURAL CENTER, 611 Grove St., next to the convention center downtown, celebrates the legacy of the Basques. Exhibits focus on traditional music, dance, sports, food and homes. Basque history and culture is further depicted through a cultural center, library and genealogy research room. Staff and volunteers are Basques who are knowledgeable about the heritage. Allow 30 minutes minimum.

Tues.-Fri. 10-4, Sat. 11-3; closed holidays. Admission $1, under 13 free. Phone (208) 343-2671.

BOISE STATE UNIVERSITY, 1910 University Dr. along the Boise River, is an important educational, cultural, theatrical, musical and athletic center. Established in 1932, the university has 15,300 students enrolled in eight schools and colleges.

Highlights of the campus include the Simplot/Micron Technology Center, Christ Chapel, the Boise State University Pavilion entertainment complex and the Morrison Center for the Performing Arts, home of the Boise Philharmonic Orchestra. Bronco Stadium is noted for the blue artificial turf of its football field. Public tours are offered Mon.-Fri.; reservations are required. Phone the New Student Information Center at (208) 385-1820.

SAVE BOISE TOUR TRAIN, leaving from the tour train depot across from the rose garden in Julia Davis Park off Capitol Blvd., offers 1-hour narrated tours of the historic and downtown areas of Boise. An enclosed trolley-style bus is used during inclement weather.

Mon.-Sat. at 10, 11:15, 12:30, 1:45 and 3, Sun. at noon, 1:15, 2:30 and 3:45, June 1-Labor Day; Sat.-Sun. and holidays at noon, 1:30 and 3, in May; Wed.-Fri. at noon and 1:30, Sat. at 10:30, noon, 1:30 and 3, Sun. at noon, 1:30 and 3, day after Labor Day-Sept. 30; Sat.-Sun. at noon, 1:30 and 3, in Oct.; Sat. at 1:30, rest of year. Arrive for boarding at least 15 minutes prior to departure. Fare $6.50; over 62, $6; ages 13-17, $5; ages 4-12, $3.50. Phone (208) 342-4796.

★ **DISCOVERY CENTER OF IDAHO,** 131 Myrtle St., is a science museum with hands-on displays. More than 200 permanent exhibits invite persons of all ages to touch, explore and discover by doing. Allow 1 hour minimum. Tues.-Fri. 9-5, Sat. 10-5, Sun. noon-5, Sept.-May; Tues.-Sat. 10-5, Sun. noon-5, rest of year. Closed Jan. 1, Thanksgiving and Dec. 25. Admission $4; over 59, $3; ages 3-18, $2.50. Phone (208) 343-9895.

FIRST UNITED METHODIST CHURCH (Cathedral of the Rockies) occupies a city block bordered by 11th, 12th, Franklin and Hay sts.; enter through the office at 1110 W. Franklin St. The church dates from 1872; the present Gothic structure, the third building used by the congregation, contains impressive stained-glass windows. Self-guiding tours are available. Open Mon.-Fri. 8:30-5. Free. Phone (208) 343-7511.

IDAHO BOTANICAL GARDEN, 2.5 mi. e. on Main St. and Warm Springs Rd. to 2355 Old Penitentiary Rd., offers 10 themed gardens. The Herb Garden displays a variety of culinary and

medicinal herbs as well as herbs used in insect repellents, soaps, perfumes and potpourri. The Iris Garden features most Dyke's Medal winning varieties dating back to the 1920s. Tiger swallowtail and morning cloak butterflies and black-chinned and Rufous hummingbirds visit the Butterfly/Hummingbird Garden.

Printed information is provided for a self-guiding tour. Allow 1 hour minimum. Mon.-Fri. and holidays 9-5, Sat.-Sun. 10-6, mid-Apr. to mid-Oct. Admission $3; over 60 and ages 6-18, $2. Phone (208) 343-8649.

JULIA DAVIS PARK, with entrances on Capitol Blvd. or Myrtle St., contains a lagoon, rose garden, playground and a bandshell where concerts are given in the summer. Picnicking is permitted and boat rentals are available. A large portion of the Boise River Greenbelt is accessible from the park. The Discovery Center of Idaho *(see attraction listing)* offers hands-on exhibits for all ages. Daily dawn-dusk. Free. Phone (208) 384-4240.

Boise Art Museum, 670 S. Julia Davis Dr. at the park entrance, displays the Janss Collection of American Realism and presents more than 15 changing art exhibits annually. Guided tours are available by appointment. Allow 1 hour minimum. Mon.-Fri. 10-5, Sat.-Sun. noon-5, June-Aug.; Tues.-Fri. 10-5, Sat.-Sun. noon-5, rest of year. Admission $4; over 59 and college students $2; grades 1-12, $1. Phone (208) 345-8330.

Idaho Historical Museum, 610 N. Julia Davis Dr., provides an overview of the state's history. Displays include a 19th-century saloon and bank as well as relics of early Idaho. Allow 1 hour minimum. Mon.-Sat. 9-5, Sun. and holidays 1-5. Free. Phone (208) 334-2120.

Zoo Boise, .5 mi. s. off Capitol Blvd., has a variety of animals from around the world. Food is available. Daily 10-5 (also Thurs. 5-9, June-Aug.). Admission $4; over 61, $2; ages 4-11, $1.75. Thurs. admission $2; over 61, $1.75; ages 4-11, $1. Phone (208) 384-4260.

MORRISON KNUDSEN NATURE CENTER is 2.5 mi. off I-84 exit 54 (Broadway St.); cross the Boise River, turn e. onto Park Blvd. then .5 mi. e. to 600 S. Walnut Ave., following signs. This 4.5-acre area features a sampling of the ecosystems present in Idaho. Walking trails pass a mountain stream with logjams and waterfalls, a wetlands pond and a high desert plain with sagebrush and lava rock. Along the way are plants and wildlife indigenous to each area. Windows along the path show how fish are born and how a stream receives oxygen.

Use Your Safety Belts!

The visitor center offers exhibits and occasional lectures. Allow 1 hour minimum. Outdoor area open daily dawn-dusk. Visitor center hours vary; phone ahead. Outdoor area free. Visitor center by donations. Phone (208) 334-2225, or 368-6060 for recorded hours information.

SAVE **OLD IDAHO PENITENTIARY,** 2.5 mi. e. via Main St. and Warm Springs Ave. at 2445 Old Penitentiary Rd., was used 1870-1973 as a territorial prison and then as Idaho's only state penitentiary. The grounds and a rose garden are maintained as they were by the inmates in the early 1900s. Additions to the original building were constructed by the prisoners with sandstone they quarried and cut. An exhibit about prison tattoos is housed in the old barber shop. The women's ward provides insight into prison life for female inmates. A film and a self-guiding walking tour map also are offered. Guided tours are available during summer hours. Picnicking is permitted.

Allow 2 hours minimum. Daily 10-5, Memorial Day-Labor Day; noon-5, rest of year. Closed state holidays except Memorial Day, July 4 and Labor Day. Admission $4; senior citizens and ages 6-12, $3. Phone (208) 368-6080 or 334-2844.

STATE CAPITOL, bordered by Jefferson, W. State, 6th and 8th sts., is the most impressive of Boise's public buildings. Built of sandstone from Idaho and marble from Alaska, Georgia, Vermont and Italy, the Capitol was begun in 1905 and completed in 1920. A 5-foot statue of a golden eagle tops the dome of the classical-style building.

Agricultural, mineral, gemstone and timber products are displayed on the first floor. A replica of the Winged Victory of Samothrace, a gift from France, and an equestrian statue of George Washington, carved from yellow pine and coated in gold, are of particular interest. Guided tours can be arranged Mon.-Fri. 8-4; closed holidays. Free. Phone (208) 334-2844.

WORLD CENTER FOR BIRDS OF PREY is 7 mi. s. at 5666 W. Flying Hawk Ln. Take I-84 exit 50 to S. Cole Rd., about 6 mi. s. the road ends and Flying Hawk Ln. begins; then w. on Flying Hawk Ln. to the top of the hill. This 7,200 square-foot interpretive center features exhibits about birds of prey, biology, ecology and conservation as well as a tropical forest. Live falcons and eagles are available for viewing. Staff is available to answer questions.

Daily 9-5, Mar.-Oct.; 10-4, rest of year. Closed Jan. 1, Thanksgiving and Dec. 25. Admission $4; over 62, $3; ages 4-16, $2. Phone (208) 362-8687.

BOISE NATIONAL FOREST

Elevations in the forest range from 2860 ft. at Lucky Peak Reservoir to 10,776 ft. at Thomason Peak. Refer to AAA maps for additional elevation information.

Lakes, abandoned mines and ghost towns amid ponderosa pine and Douglas fir dot the 2,648,468 acres of mountainous terrain that make up the Boise National Forest. Large areas of the forest serve as summer range for big game. Black bears, wolves, mountain goats, bighorn sheep, deer and elk inhabit the woods. Upland game birds including chukars, sage grouse, Hungarian partridges and turkeys roam the back country. Salmon, trout and bass thrive in the cold, clear rivers, streams and reservoirs.

Deep canyons, rugged peaks exceeding 9,000 feet and high meadows offer an abundance of recreation opportunities year-round. Cross-country skiing and snowmobiling are popular during the winter. The forest offers more than 900 miles of hiking trails.

Scenic drives wind through the canyons and along the edge of the Sawtooth Wilderness; only trails enter the Frank Church-River of No Return Wilderness in the northeast section. The development of the Cascade Reservoir recreation facilities continues; phone for more recent information on special facilities and amenities.

Additional information can be obtained from the Public Affairs Office, Boise National Forest, 1387 S. Vinnell Way, Boise, ID 83709; phone (208) 373-4007. *See Recreation Chart and the AAA Northwestern CampBook.*

BONNERS FERRY (A-2) pop. 2,200, elev. 1,773'

Although trappers David Thompson and Finan McDonald were drawn to the banks of the Kootenai River and established a fur trading post in 1808, it was not until 1864 that a permanent settlement was founded. It was in that year that E.L. Bonner's ferry replaced the canoes of American Indians, who the previous year had carried gold miners rushing to the Canadian Wild Horse lode.

Trapping and river transportation no longer dominate the commerce of Bonners Ferry; today the town, 25 miles south of Canada, maintains a resource-oriented economy of lumbering and farming. Several large hops farms are in the community.

The mountainous terrain of northern Idaho and the gorge cut by the Kootenai River make the Bonners Ferry region popular for its beauty.

Katka View Point, 9 miles east on CR 24, provides a view of the Kootenai Valley, the Selkirk Mountains and the proposed Selkirk Crest National Wilderness area. At Smith Creek Falls and View Point, approximately 25 miles north of Bonners Ferry on CR 45 via US 95 and SR 1, a trail leads to an overlook and the falls.

Another scenic trip is provided by traveling US 2 to a point between mileposts 70 and 71, where an overlook affords a view of the Moyie River canyon, waterfalls and the Big Moyie Canyon Bridge. At 600 feet above the canyon, the span is one of Idaho's highest bridges.

A final route leaves US 2 at Moyie Springs, about 7 miles east of Bonners Ferry, and proceeds through a portion of the Idaho Panhandle National Forests *(see place listing p. 49)* to US 95.

Greater Bonners Ferry Chamber of Commerce: P.O. Box X, Bonners Ferry, ID 83805; phone (208) 267-5922.

KOOTENAI NATIONAL WILDLIFE REFUGE is 5 mi. w. on the dike road along the south shore of the Kootenai River; be alert for logging trucks. Almost 3,000 acres along the river provide feeding, resting and breeding areas for migratory birds. Tundra swan are common in spring; Canada geese and duck are most numerous in fall. White-tailed and mule deer, moose, black bears and coyotes also use the refuge.

One vehicle route, three observation areas and several foot trails are maintained for visitors. Picnicking is permitted. For other recreation information contact the Refuge Headquarters, HCR 60, Box 283, Bonners Ferry, ID 83805. Refuge open daily dawn-dusk, but entry limited during Oct.-Dec. hunting season. Free. Phone (208) 267-3888.

BRUNEAU (F-2) pop. 700, elev. 2,525'

Bruneau, the French name first given the brown-water river that skirts the northern edge of the Great Basin Desert, was founded by 19th-century French-Canadian trappers. The town is the community nearest Bruneau Dunes State Park *(see Recreation Chart).* The park's dunes, which rise to 470 feet, are considered the tallest single-structured sand dunes in North America.

BRUNEAU CANYON OVERLOOK is 15 mi. s.e. via a paved and gravel road, then 3 mi. w. on a dirt road, following signs. The Bruneau River courses through a narrow canyon whose vertical walls are 800 feet high in places.

C.J. STRIKE DAM, n.w. via SR 78 on the Snake River, has created a 7,500-acre reservoir. Boating, swimming, fishing, picnicking and camping are permitted. Park open daily 24 hours. Dam open daily 8-4. Free. Phone (208) 834-2295. *See Recreation Chart.*

BUHL (F-3) pop. 3,500, elev. 3,800'

Buhl (BEWL) is on the Snake River, at the western end of a valley that grew little but sagebrush until 1906, when irrigation transformed the desert into lush farmland. Agriculture and aquaculture are the bases of Buhl's present economy. Tourism and the raising of sheep and beef and dairy cattle are important. The surrounding area produces barley, sugar beets, corn, dry beans, alfalfa, grains, sugar snap peas, seed crops and potatoes.

Buhl is said to be the rainbow trout capital of the United States, since the town is a leader in trout research and production. Trout farms raise and process rainbow trout that are shipped throughout the world; similar farms produce catfish, tilapia and salmon. The products of dirt farms and local craftsmen are available at the farmers' market at the visitor center at 716 US 30E Wed. 5-8 p.m., mid-June through September.

An oddity of nature called the Balanced Rock can be seen by taking a short drive south to Castleford, then 6 miles west. The 40-foot-high rock is perched on a base only a few feet in diameter.

Buhl Chamber of Commerce: 716 US 30E, Buhl, ID 83316; phone (208) 543-6682.

THOUSAND SPRINGS, n. on US 30 in Snake River Canyon, appears over a 2-mile area, gushing in beautiful cascades from the sides of the canyon. The springs are believed to be the reappearance of Lost River, which vanishes into the lava fields near Arco, about 90 miles northeast. Three pools are in an area of hot mineral baths.

BURLEY (F-3) pop. 8,700, elev. 4,165'

Hydroplanes, super stock and other powerful racing craft churn up Burley's Snake River waterfront during the month of June, when such national speedboat championships as the Idaho Regatta take place.

Mini-Cassia Chamber of Commerce: 324 Scott Ave., Rupert, ID 83350; phone (208) 436-4793 or (800) 333-3408 out of state.

CASSIA COUNTY HISTORICAL SOCIETY MUSEUM, E. Main St. and Highland Ave., contains collections of fossils, an early railroad car and caboose, local history items, and tools and wagons of the miners, trappers, loggers and farmers who settled southern Idaho. Audiovisual displays chart the pioneer trails that led immigrants to the Pacific Northwest.

On the museum grounds are furnished replicas of a one-room cabin, general store, schoolhouse, barbershop and a sheepherder's wagon. Allow 1 hour minimum. Tues.-Sat. 10-5, Apr. 1-Nov. 15; closed holidays. Donations. Phone (208) 678-7172.

CALDWELL (E-1) pop. 18,400, elev. 2,367'

Situated on the Boise River, Caldwell was established in the late 19th century. The community, which began as a construction camp for the Oregon Short Line Railroad, is now associated with the processing and distribution of farm products. Boone Science Hall, near the corner of 20th and Fillmore streets on the Albertson College of Idaho campus, houses the Orma J. Smith Museum of Natural History, the Evans Gem and Mineral Collection and the Whittenberger Planetarium; phone (208) 459-5211 ext. 215.

Caldwell Chamber of Commerce: 300 Frontage Rd., P.O. Box 819, Caldwell, ID 83606; phone (208) 459-7493.

WINERIES

- **Ste. Chapelle Winery,** 8 mi. s.w. on SR 55, then .5 mi. e., following signs. Mon.-Sat. 10-5, Sun. noon-5; closed Easter, Thanksgiving and Dec. 25. Phone (208) 459-7222.

CAMBRIDGE (D-2) pop. 400, elev. 2,739'

CAMBRIDGE MUSEUM, jct. US 95 and SR 71, provides information on the area's heritage from the arrival of the first settlers in 1869 until the 1930s. Displays focus on geology and farming relics, American Indian life and pioneer days in the community. Visitors can see a blacksmith shop and a replica of a schoolroom with historic items. A reproduction of a mine entrance includes illustrations that demonstrate dynamiting techniques.

Allow 30 minutes minimum. Wed.-Sat. 10-4, Sun. 1-4, mid-May to mid-Sept. Donations. Phone (208) 257-3541.

RECREATIONAL ACTIVITIES

White-water Rafting

- **Hughes River Expeditions,** location departures vary with trip. Write P.O. Box 217, Cambridge, ID 83610. Expeditions offered May-Sept. Phone (208) 257-3477 or (800) 262-1882.

CARIBOU NATIONAL FOREST

Elevations in the forest range from 4,850 ft. at Mink Creek to 9,957 ft. at Mead Peak. Refer to AAA maps for additional elevation information.

Extending into Wyoming and Utah, the 972,407-acre Caribou National Forest is noted for rugged scenery marked by towering mountain ranges and beautiful valleys. Drives along the Snake River and through the many canyons provide scenic vistas. A few traces of the ghost towns of Keenan and Caribou City recall the gold rush days. *See Recreation Chart and the AAA Northwestern CampBook.*

CHALLIS (D-4) pop. 1,100, elev. 5,288′

LAND OF THE YANKEE FORK HISTORIC AREA, has its interpretive center on SR 75 just s. of jct. US 93. The center offers an 18-minute slide program about the history of the mines and ghost towns in the area, and dioramas and photographs telling the story of the mines and miners 1860-1910. Self-guiding tour maps and brochures are available here.

The center is the starting point for a 91-mile, 3-hour scenic interpretive loop which goes west and south on a narrow, gravel and dirt forest road, the Custer Motorway Adventure Road (FR 70), which is not recommended for vehicles with low clearance, trailers or large motorhomes. This road runs past stage stations, ghost towns, abandoned mines and mills, a gold dredge and dredge tailings. In season the dredge is open for tours.

At Sunbeam Dam Interpretive Site, where information on the Historic Area, the Sawtooth National Recreation Area *(see place listing p. 59),* and the dam is available, the return portion of the loop becomes paved SR 75 (the Salmon River Scenic Byway), which parallels the Salmon River.

Allow 30 minutes for the interpretive center. Allow 3 hours for the loop. Interpretive center open daily 8-6, May-Sept.; 9-5, rest of year. The Custer Motorway Adventure Road (FR 70) is closed by snow late Oct.-June 30. Park and interpretive centers free. Gold dredge tour $2.50, children $1.50. Phone (208) 879-5244.

CHALLIS NATIONAL FOREST—
See Salmon-Challis National Forest p. 58.

CLARK FORK (B-2) pop. 400, elev. 2,084′

Clark Fork lies at the foot of the Cabinet Mountains, just northeast of Lake Pend Oreille. The town is on the lake's main tributary, the Clark Fork River, just before it flows into the lake. This location experiences unusually warm winters and cool summers.

The town sprang up in the 1880s when the main line of the Northern Pacific Railroad cut through the Bitterroot and Cabinet mountains. The railroad made lumbering profitable, and lumberjacks began arriving on the area's first steam tugboats. Soon nearby trappers were giving up their trade and joining the timber camps. Today the area attracts hikers, anglers and other outdoor enthusiasts.

Hope, Clark Fork & Trestle Creek Chamber of Commerce: P.O. Box 304, Hope, ID 83836.

CABINET GORGE DAM, 8 mi. e. on SR 200, on the Clark Fork River, is a horseshoe-shaped dam in a scenic setting. A lookout point affords an excellent view of the project.

CLEARWATER NATIONAL FOREST

Elevations in the forest range from 1,200 ft. to 8,820 ft. at Ranger Peak. Refer to AAA maps for additional elevation information.

Large stands of tall trees and many miles of clear, fast-running streams and rivers characterize the rugged, mountainous Clearwater National Forest. Scenic Lewis and Clark Highway (US 12) runs a few miles south of but roughly parallel to the Lolo Trail, the American Indian route across the Bitterroots to buffalo-hunting country.

A portion of the Selway-Bitterroot Wilderness, the second largest wilderness area in the continental United States, makes up part of Clearwater's 1,739,353 acres. US 12 follows the rugged Lochsa Wild and Scenic River, where kayak and raft enthusiasts challenge the stream's whitewater.

Lolo Pass Visitors Center, along US 12 at the crest of the Bitterroots on the Idaho-Montana border, and the restored Lochsa Historical Ranger Station, halfway between Powell and Kooskia on US 12, are open Memorial Day weekend through Labor Day. *See Recreation Chart and the AAA Northwestern CampBook.*

COEUR D'ALENE (B-1) pop. 24,600, elev. 2,157′

Once a frontier outpost, Coeur d'Alene (CORE-dah-LANE) received its name after French traders attempted to bribe local American Indians with trinkets in exchange for valuable pelts. Unimpressed, the American Indians refused. The French thought them hard-hearted or, in their vernacular, sharp as an awl. Coeur d'Alene translates to mean "heart of the awl."

Coeur d'Alene is now a recreational retreat with a busy waterfront and luxurious resorts. North Idaho College occupies the old fort site and Fort Sherman Chapel survives at the corner of Hubbard Street and Woodland Drive. For a broader perspective of the area, visitors can take a tour in a horse-drawn carriage or on a double-decker bus.

Greater Coeur d'Alene Convention & Visitor Bureau: P.O. Box 850, Coeur d'Alene, ID

83816-1088; phone (208) 773-4080 or (800) 292-2553. *See color ad p. 56.*

Shopping areas: Silver Lake Mall, 3.5 miles north on US 95, offers Emporium, JCPenney and Sears. The Factory Outlets Mall, 10 miles west off I-90 exit 2 in Post Falls *(see place listing p. 56),* contains some 60 outlet stores.

AERIAL RETARDANT PLANT, 6 mi. n. on US 95 then w. on Wyoming Rd. to the airport, prepares chemical fire retardants for aerial tankers that extinguish fires in the surrounding forests. Visitors can see the planes being loaded in the event of a forest fire. Allow 1 hour minimum. Tours daily 9-4, July-Sept. Free. Phone (208) 772-3283.

LAKE COEUR D'ALENE, once called one of the five most beautiful lakes in the world by *National Geographic,* is surrounded by mountains and a lush forest. Twenty-five miles long, it averages 2.5 miles in width. One of the nation's largest populations of osprey nest at the lake, and during the winter American bald eagles dive into the lake to catch salmon.

Power boating, sailing and fishing are popular during the warm months; seaplane flights are available. The lake offers a number of public access points, including Mowry State Park, which is accessible only by boat.

LAKE COEUR D'ALENE CRUISES depart from the Coeur d'Alene city dock at Independence Point. Allow 2 hours minimum. Cruises daily at 1:30, 3:30 and 5:30. Sunday brunch, Monday Sunset, charter and full-day cruises are available. Departure times vary; phone ahead. Fare $12.75; senior citizens $11.75; under 12, $7.75. AE, DS, MC, VI. Phone (208) 765-4000.

MUSEUM OF NORTH IDAHO, 115 Northwest Blvd., explores the history of the Coeur d'Alene region. Exhibits include mining, exploration, transportation and early settler displays, as well as fire fighting, logging, lumbering and rotating seasonal exhibits. Allow 30 minutes minimum. Tues.-Sat. 11-5, Apr. -Oct.; closed July 4. Admission $1.50; ages 6-16, 50c; family rate $4. Phone (208) 664-3448.

Fort Sherman Museum, behind the Museum of North Idaho, displays artifacts from U.S. military personnel and Coeur d'Alene Indians at Fort Sherman. It also houses an original forest service smoke chasers' cabin. Allow 30 minutes minimum. Tues.-Sat. 1-4:45, Apr.-Oct.; closed holidays. Free.

SILVERWOOD, 15 mi. n. on US 95, is a late-1800s mining town theme park. The Victorian-styled park features three roller coasters, including the wooden coaster Tremors; a log flume; a steam train; and other rides, shows and midway games. Music and entertainment are offered. Food is available.

Allow 3 hours minimum. Daily 11-8, June-Aug.; Sat.-Sun. 11-6, May 8-Memorial Day

weekend and Sept.-Oct. (also 6-8 p.m. Memorial Day and Labor Day weekends). Admission $21.99; over 65 and ages 3-7, $13.99. Phone (208) 683-3400.

WILD WATERS is off I-90 exit 12, then s. on Lincoln, e. on Ironwood Dr. and n. on Government Way. The park offers a variety of amusements, including waterslides, spas and inner tube river rides. Children's waterslides, an arcade and a playground also are available. Allow 1 hour minimum. Daily 11-9, Memorial Day-Aug. 25; 11-7, Aug. 26-Labor Day. All-day pass $13.95; ages 4-11, $11.95; over 65, $3.95. After 3 p.m. $7.95. Phone (208) 667-6491.

☀❄ RECREATIONAL ACTIVITIES

White-water Rafting

- **River Odysseys West,** 314 E. Garden St., P.O. Box 579, Coeur d'Alene, ID 83816. Trips depart daily at 9, May 1-Sept. 15. Phone (800) 451-6034.

COOLIN (A-2) pop. 200, elev. 2,147'

Coolin is the headquarters for the Priest Lake resort area. Priest Lake, with its 80-mile shoreline, is known for its big Mackinaw trout. The 25-mile-long lake is two lakes connected by a river. Of the lake's seven islands, Kalispell, Bartoo, Four Mile and Eight Mile islands are available for camping. The Roosevelt Grove of Ancient Cedars, a virgin forest, is on the west side of Priest Lake, northwest of Nordman via FS 302 in Washington. Priest Lake State Park, on the east shore of Priest Lake, offers trails through cedar-hemlock forests *(see Recreation Chart).*

Priest Lake Chamber of Commerce: Steamboat Bay Rd., #21, P.O. Box 174, Coolin, ID 83821-0174; phone (208) 443-3191 or (888) 774-3785.

COTTONWOOD (C-2) pop. 800, elev. 3,411'

During July 3-5, 1877, the area southeast of Cottonwood was the scene of several skirmishes between the Nez Perce and U.S. Cavalry troops and scouts. State interpretive markers give details of the battles. *See Nez Perce National Historical Park p. 54.*

St. Gertrude's Priory and Museum, on the grounds of the Priory of Saint Gertrude, houses collections about local history including mining artifacts, American Indian memorabilia, ceramics and art. The hand-carved wooden high altar was constructed with mortise and glue; not a single nail was used. Near the northern entrance to the town is a large statue of a dog known as the World's Biggest Beagle.

WEIS ROCKSHELTER is 7 mi. s. in Grave's Creek Canyon. Archeological excavations of this cliff recess have revealed almost continuous human occupation between 5500 B.C. and A.D. 1400.

★CRATERS OF THE MOON NATIONAL MONUMENT (E-4)

Craters of the Moon National Monument, at the base of the Pioneer Mountains, is 18 miles west of Arco (see place listing p. 37) via US 20/26 and US 93.

This 83-square-mile area contains more basaltic volcanic features than any other area of its size in the continental United States. Lava rivers once flooded the surrounding countryside, leaving vast lava fields covered by cinder cones with large central vents that were thought by early observers to resemble the craters on the moon. The volcanic activity dates back about 15,000 years, with the last eruptions occurring about 2,000 years ago.

The area's variety of surface patterns and formations is typical of the world's other basaltic lava sites. Visitors should be cautious of sharp lava formations.

A 7-mile loop drive, open from mid-April to early November, leads past the monument's main points of interest and takes about 2 to 3 hours to complete. The view from the summit of Inferno Cone takes in the cinder cone chain along the Great Rift, a weakened zone of fissures in the Earth's crust.

The cones formed when fountains of molten, gas-charged rock shot into the air. The frothy lava then cooled and hardened into cinders that fell around the vent, producing symmetrical cones. Numerous lava bombs, ejected blobs of less frothy lava that range from an inch to several feet in diameter, are scattered over the slopes. Big Cinder, 700 feet high, is one of the world's largest purely basaltic cinder cones.

Nearby is the Big Craters-Spatter Cone Area. These cones formed when clots of pasty lava stuck together as they fell back to Earth. A trail leads from the drive to the Cave Area, a series of lava tubes that range up to 50 feet in diameter and hundreds of feet in length. The largest is 830-foot Indian Tunnel; Boy Scout Cave has a floor of ice, even in summer. Some of the tubes can be explored; wear sturdy shoes and carry a flashlight.

Other trails lead to Devil's Orchard, cinder fields scattered with fragments of a crater wall, and the Tree Mold Area, where lava slowly enveloped a group of living trees.

More than 300 species of plants and many different species of animals live in this seemingly desolate terrain. In early summer wildflowers burst into bloom on the cinder fields and slopes of the cones.

Near the monument entrance are a visitor center and campground-picnic area (see the AAA Northwestern CampBook). Guided walks and evening programs are provided during summer months; phone for schedule. The entrance fee is $4 per private vehicle; a season pass limited to Craters of the Moon is available for $10.

VISITOR CENTER is at the start of the 7-mile loop drive. Exhibits explain the geology, plants, animals and history of the monument. Daily 8-6, mid-June through Labor Day; 8-4:30, except holidays, rest of year. Phone (208) 527-3257.

FORT HALL (E-5) pop. 2,700, elev. 4,754'

One of the first permanent settlements in Idaho, Fort Hall was established as a trading post on the banks of the Snake River in 1834. Later owned by the Hudson Bay Co., the trading post was abandoned in 1856 due to increased hostility with the American Indians and a decline in fur trading.

In 1864 a stage station was constructed a short distance southeast of Fort Hall. Built on the banks of Spring Creek with materials from this original fort, this post also was known as Fort Hall. In 1868 a treaty established the Fort Hall Indian Reservation and agency offices some 20 miles east of the original post also were identified as Fort Hall. Today the Fort Hall Indian Reservation has its headquarters east of the townsite on US 91.

GARDEN VALLEY (E-2) elev. 3,143'

 RECREATIONAL ACTIVITIES

White-water Rafting

- **Cascade Raft Co. and Kayak School**, on SR 55 near Horseshoe Bend or the Garden Valley Outpost office in Garden Valley. Write R.R. 1, Box 117A, Horseshoe Bend, ID 83629. Other activities are offered. Departures daily at 8:30, 9:30 and 1:30, May 1 to mid-Sept. Phone (800) 292-7238. See ad p. 39.

GLENNS FERRY (E-3) pop. 1,300, elev. 2,560'

 WINERIES

- **Carmela Vineyards**, I-84 Glenns Ferry exit, next to Three Islands State Park following signs. Daily 9-9; closed Jan. 1 and Dec. 25. Phone (208) 366-2313.

GRANGEVILLE (C-2) pop. 3,200, elev. 3,323'

A boom town in gold rush days, Grangeville is a light industry and agricultural center and the largest town on the fertile Camas Prairie, one of the leading wheat-producing areas in the country. The town also is an outfitting point for wilderness and float trips.

South of Grangeville on scenic US 95 is the Camas Prairie, where groups of Nez Perce Indians once gathered in summer to dig camas roots, an important part of their diet. Today it is a site for an archaeological excavation for mammoth bones. *See Nez Perce National Historical Park p. 54.*

Grangeville Chamber of Commerce: US 95 at Pine, Grangeville, ID 83530; phone (208) 983-0460.

Self-guiding tours: A brochure for a driving tour of White Bird Battlefield is available at the Nez Perce National Historical Park *(see place listing p. 54)* headquarters in Spalding and at the Forest Service office in Grangeville as well as the Grangeville Chamber and Visitor Center. The battlefield, 16 miles south of Grangeville on US 95, was the site of the first confrontation of the Nez Perce War. The American Indians won the 1877 battle.

HAGERMAN (F-3) pop. 600

HAGERMAN FOSSIL BEDS NATIONAL MONUMENT is directly w. across the Snake River; take US 30 5 mi. s., then go w. on first road (gravel) immediately s. of the bridge. The monument is undeveloped and has limited facilities. A parking lot with a boardwalk overlook includes exhibits to the right after entering the monument. Other vehicle and on-foot access to the monument is difficult. The visitor center, with exhibits and audiovisual programs, is a good place to start your visit. It is on US 30 across from the high school.

Encompassing more than 4,000 acres, the monument includes several miles of cliffs along the river. The 3.5-million-year-old fossil beds, which constitute one of the best freshwater fish and small-mammal fossil sites in North America, also have yielded remains of early forms of horses, camels, peccary, beavers and turtles. An accessible trail overlooks primitive ruts of the Oregon Trail. For further information write the Superintendent, Hagerman Fossil Beds National Monument, P.O. Box 570, Hagerman, ID 83332.

Visitor center open daily 9-5, but days and hours may vary Oct.-May; phone to verify schedule. Phone (208) 837-4793.

1000 SPRINGS TOURS, departing from Sligar's 1000 Springs Resort 7 mi. s. on US 30, offers boat trips through the Snake River Canyon and the 1000 Springs area. Waterfalls, wildflowers and waterfowls can be seen as guides provide area history and geography. A dinner cruise also is available. Two-hour tours depart daily at 10, 1 and 4, Apr.-Oct. Departure times may vary; phone ahead. Fare $19-$24; under 12, $12-$17. Reservations are required. MC, VI. Phone (208) 837-9006 or (800) 838-1096.

 RECREATIONAL ACTIVITIES

White-water Rafting

- ⓈⒶⓋⒺ **High Adventure River Tours,** off I-84 exit 147 at 1211 E. 2350 S., Hagerman, ID 83332. Daily Apr.-Sept. Phone (208) 837-9005, or (800) 286-4123 in Idaho.

WINERIES

- **Rose Creek Vineyards,** off SR 30 traveling e. on Reed St. 3 blks. to 226 E. Ave. N. Daily 11:30-5:30; closed Easter, Thanksgiving and Dec. 25. Phone (208) 837-4413.

HAILEY (E-3) pop. 3,700, elev. 5,330'

Hailey, laid out in the spring of 1881 by John Hailey, was the center of a rich mining district in its early days. An early Northwest pioneer, Hailey had previously taken part in the Boise Basin Gold Rush in 1862 and had established a name for himself as the owner of a stage and freight line. Fortunes in gold, silver and lead were extracted from mines with such names as Black Cinder, Star, Hope, Climax, Democrat and Big Camas until the mining boom played out in the late 1890s.

On May 7, 1883, Hailey residents witnessed the driving of the last spike of the Wood River branch of the Oregon Short Line. In October of that year the Idaho Territory's first telephone exchange went into use at Hailey. Hailey also was the first to have an electric light plant.

Hailey Chamber of Commerce: 14 W. Bullion, P.O. Box 100, Hailey, ID 83333; phone (208) 788-2700.

BLAINE COUNTY HISTORICAL MUSEUM, N. Main St. (SR 75), displays early pioneer relics and memorabilia of local interest, including a replica of a mine tunnel. The American Political Items collection contains articles from political campaigns since the late 1800s. Allow 30 minutes minimum. Mon. and Wed.-Sat. 11-5, Sun. 1-5, Memorial Day weekend-Labor Day. Donations. Phone (208) 788-1801 or 788-4185.

★ HELLS CANYON NATIONAL RECREATION AREA (C-1)

The 652,977-acre Hells Canyon National Recreation Area straddles the Snake River Canyon

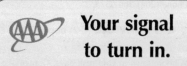

Your signal to turn in.

and encompasses parts of national forests in western Idaho and northeastern Oregon. The area is reached via SRs 82 and 86 in Oregon and US 95 in Idaho.

Confined within steep, eroded black basalt walls, the surging Snake River has carved North America's deepest gorge, measuring 7,913 feet from He Devil Mountain to Granite Creek below. White-water rapids alternating with deep pools characterize this 71-mile portion of the Snake River as it races north to meet the Columbia River.

The varied elevations of Hells Canyon support mixed plant communities sheltering such wildlife as bears, bobcats, bighorn sheep, cougars, elk, mule deer, mountain goats and many smaller birds, mammals and reptiles. Sturgeon, reputedly growing up to 11 feet long, inhabit the Snake River, sharing it with bass, catfish, salmon and steelhead and rainbow trout.

From the desertlike canyon floor to the alpine lakes of the Seven Devils region, the area presents a variety of recreational opportunities, including boating, float trips and backpacking. From Pittsburg Landing the Kirkwood Historic Ranch and Museum, once the home of Idaho governor and U.S. senator Len B. Jordan, is accessible by powerboat, floatboat or pack trail.

The Rapid River originates in the Seven Devils Mountains and eventually joins the lower Salmon River. The forks of the Rapid River provide quality water for raising Chinook salmon and therefore house the Rapid River Fish Hatchery.

The 214,000-acre Hells Canyon Wilderness, with its extensive trail system, protects a large portion of the canyon along the Oregon-Idaho border. If you plan to fish the lakes and the Snake River shoreline, you must acquire the appropriate state licenses *(see For Your Information box);* both Oregon and Idaho licenses are valid for boat fishing on the river.

The Hells Canyon Scenic Byway is a series of routes to and through the Hells Canyon National Recreation Area. **On the Oregon side,** the best route is a two-lane paved loop which originates in Baker City. From Baker City follow SR 86 to Richland for approximately 41 miles. From Richland continue on SR 86 north for 11 miles to Halfway. Nine miles north of Halfway, SR 86 will intersect with FS 39N. Take FS 39N through the heart of Hells Canyon, high mountain country and through the town of Joseph to Enterprise. One mile west of Enterprise on SR 82 is the Wallowa Mountain Visitors Center. Continue along SR 82 west for approximately 64 miles to arrive back at I-84 at La Grande. The entire loop will take approximately 5 hours.

Another possible route from the Oregon side to the recreation area is via SR 82 to Enterprise and Joseph. From Joseph it is possible to go to Hat Point, a 6,982-foot ridge overlooking Hells Canyon, via Imnaha. The route to Hat Point follows FS 4240, a gravel, narrow road with steep grades.

Another route from Imnaha, FS 3955, parallels the Imnaha River as it meanders through rims and benches similar to those along the Snake River. This route connects with the Wallowa Mountain Loop (FS 39), which leads back to Joseph or Halfway. Both FS 3955 and FS 39 are maintained for cars and trailers. FS 39 can be followed east to FS 3965 which leads to the Hells Canyon overlook. With an elevation of 6,000 feet, the overlook provides a spectacular view of the Wallowa Mountains in Idaho and Oregon.

For maps and brochures of different drives contact the Baker County Visitors and Convention Bureau, 490 Campbell, Baker City, OR 97814; phone (541) 523-3356 or (800) 523-1235.

Buckhorn Springs, a scenic area overlooking the Imnaha drainage, can be reached from FS 46 off SR 3, a mostly gravel logging road.

On the Idaho side the best route to the canyon is SR 71. From Cambridge the road runs 29 miles northwest to Oxbow, Ore., crossing the Snake River near Brownlee Dam. It crosses back into Idaho at Oxbow, then follows the river north to Hells Canyon Dam. The total distance is about 55 miles.

Note: It is advisable to check with the Hells Canyon Recreation Area regarding road conditions and construction. Some roads are gravel and caution should be exercised. Phone (541) 426-4978 or (800) 523-1235.

More than 30 outfitters provide float and jet boat trips down the Snake River from Hells Canyon Dam and jet boat trips upstream from Lewiston. For a list of local outfitters contact the Supervisor, Hells Canyon National Recreation Area, 2535 Riverside Dr., P.O. Box 699, Clarkston, WA 99403; phone (509) 758-0616 or (509) 758-1957 for river information. *See Recreation Chart and the AAA Northwestern CampBook.*

BEAMERS HELLS CANYON TOURS, departing from the Port of Clarkston dock in Washington at 700 Port Dr., offers jet boat excursions through Hells Canyon—North America's deepest river gorge. One- and 2-day excursions are available. Allow 8 hours minimum. Daily 6-6, May-Sept.; Mon.-Fri. 8-4, rest of year. Closed Jan. 1, Thanksgiving and Dec. 25. Fare $90; ages 6-12, $45. DS, MC, VI. Phone (800) 522-6966. *See color ad p. 47.*

HELLS CANYON ADVENTURES, SR 86 to Hells Canyon Dam, offers guided 2-, 3- and 6-hour jetboat trips. White-water rafting trips as well as fishing and hunting excursions on the Snake River also are available. Contact Hells Canyon Adventures, P.O. Box 159, Oxbow, OR 97840.

Tours depart daily May 15-Sept. 15. Two-hour trip departs at 2. Three-hour trip departs at 10. Six-hour and white-water trips depart at 9. Two-hour trip $30; under 12, $10; family rate $90. Three-hour trip $40; under 12, $15. Six-hour trip $95; under 12, $50. Reservations are required. Phone (541) 785-3352, or (800) 422-3568 out of Ore. *See ad.*

HOLLISTER (F-3) pop. 100 , elev. 4,525'

IDAHO HERITAGE MUSEUM, 2.5 mi. s. on US 93, claims one of the largest private collections of American Indian artifacts and wildlife specimens of the American West. Over 12,000 American Indian artifacts are exhibited, including arrowheads. Big game animals, game birds and fish, all displayed in their natural habitats, are among the 300 mounted animals on display.

Allow 1 hour minimum. Tues.-Sun. 10-4. Admission $4; over 55, $3.50; ages 6-16, $2.50. Phone (208) 655-4444.

IDAHO CITY (E-2) pop. 300, elev. 4,000'

Soon after gold was discovered in the Boise Basin in 1862, Idaho City became one of the largest cities in the Pacific Northwest. By 1865 it was home to some 7,000 goldseekers; nearly one quarter were Chinese. At its peak the basin was home to 15,000-20,000 miners. The mining district around Idaho City, including nearby Placerville and Centerville, was one of the largest sources of gold ever discovered.

More than 20 pioneer buildings from the 1860s and miles of dredge workings are still visible. The First Masonic Hall, built in 1865 to house Idaho's first Grand Lodge of Masons, displays Masonic items. Idaho City was the site of the territory's first prison, a portion of which has been restored.

Boise National Forest *(see place listing p. 41)* surrounds the town. Idaho City lies on scenic SR 21, also known as the Ponderosa Pine Scenic Route. SR 21 heads northeast through Sawtooth National Forest *(see place listing p. 59)* and ends in Stanley.

BOISE BASIN MUSEUM, Montgomery St. at Wall St., was erected as a post office in 1867 and served as a Wells Fargo station before being renovated for its present use. Exhibits commemorate the town's origin with memorabilia from its days as a mining boom town. Guided walking tours of the town are available by prior arrangement.

Daily 11-4, Memorial Day weekend-Labor Day; Sat.-Sun. 11-4, May 1-day before Memorial Day and day after Labor Day-Sept. 30. Museum admission $2. Town walking tours $3, senior citizens $1.50, under 13 free with an adult. There is a $30 minimum per group for walking tours. Phone (208) 392-4550.

WARM SPRINGS RESORT, 1.5 mi. s.w. on SR 21, contains a series of hot springs averaging 110 degrees F and a thermal-water swimming pool. Picnic area, cabins, campground and RV hookups are available. Bathing equipment rentals are available. Plastic pants are required for under 2. Wed.-Mon. 10-10, May 1-Labor Day; Wed.-Sun. noon-9, rest of year. Closed Thanksgiving and Dec. 25. Admission $5; under 13, $2.50. Phone (208) 392-4437.

IDAHO FALLS (E-5) pop. 43,900, elev. 4,742'

Although it lies miles from the silver and gold lodes discovered in the region during the mid-1800s, Idaho Falls owes its formation to these riches. The settlement—originally called Taylor's Crossing—was established about 1860 along one of the few fording points on the upper Snake River. J.M. Taylor's ferry attracted many miners en route to Montana from Salt Lake City.

As the veins of precious metal diminished, transients and disillusioned residents abandoned the area. The few remaining settlers, faced with either adopting a new livelihood or adding the community to the growing list of Western ghost towns, dug channels to irrigate the arid land. Soon the town flourished along with the newly established agriculture. The irrigation system that saved the town now provides water to more than 1 million acres of farmland.

Tautphaus Park has tennis courts, picnic grounds, rides and a zoo. Sandy Downs, 2 miles south of 17th Street on St. Clair Road, is the site of various recreational activities.

Greater Idaho Falls Chamber of Commerce: 505 Lindsay Blvd., P.O. Box 50498, Idaho Falls, ID 83405-0498; phone (208) 523-1010 or (800) 634-3246.

BONNEVILLE MUSEUM, 2 mi. e. off I-15 Broadway exit at 200 N. Eastern Ave., presents the story of Bonneville County from prehistoric times to the Atomic Age. The museum offers permanent displays about natural history, early inhabitants and explorers, agriculture, mining and nuclear energy. A reference room is available for research. Eagle Rock USA is a replica of the 19th century community that later became Idaho Falls.

Allow 1 hour minimum. Mon.-Fri. 10-5, Sat. 1-5; closed holidays. Admission $1; ages 4-17, 25c. Phone (208) 522-1400.

IDAHO FALLS is .5 mi. e. off I-15 Broadway exit, then n. on River Pkwy. The low but picturesque and turbulent waterfall on the Snake River is 1,500 feet wide. Next to the scenic falls is a landscaped picnic area and a 2.5-mile greenbelt.

IDAHO PANHANDLE NATIONAL FORESTS

Elevations in the forest range from 2,060 ft. at Pend Oreille Lake to 7,705 ft. at Northwest Peak. Refer to AAA maps for additional elevation information.

Encompassing nearly 2.5 million acres in northern Idaho and adjoining parts of Montana and Washington, the many-segmented Idaho Panhandle National Forests have rugged peaks, canyons and valleys. The area includes the former St. Joe, Kaniksu and Coeur d'Alene national forests.

Of particular interest are the stands of old-growth cedars at Hanna Flats and Roosevelt Grove near Priest Lake, the Settlers Grove of Ancient Cedars near Prichard and the Hobo Cedar Grove near Clarkia.

Information is available at the headquarters in Coeur d'Alene and at ranger stations at Avery, Bonners Ferry, Fernan, Priest Lake, St. Maries, Sandpoint and Wallace; phone (208) 765-7223.

Fishing is available at Priest Lake, Lake Coeur d'Alene and Lake Pend Oreille; nature trails traverse these areas. Float trips are popular on the Coeur d'Alene, St. Joe and Priest rivers. Winter sports areas are off SR 6 between St. Maries and Moscow, at Lookout Pass just off I-90 on the Idaho-Montana border and at 4th of July Pass off I-90.

For a fee, modern-day fortune seekers can collect gem-quality garnets in an area on the East Fork of Emerald Creek, 8 miles southeast of SR 3 between Clarkia and Fernwood. *See Recreation Chart and the AAA Northwestern CampBook.*

KAMIAH (C-2) pop. 1,200, elev. 1,196'

Lewis and Clark camped on the north bank of the Clearwater River north of Kamiah in the spring of 1806 on their homeward journey. Today a sawmill occupies the site of their month-long encampment. A pasture about a half mile northwest of Kamiah is supposedly the location of the mission that Asa and Sarah Smith started in 1839. They stayed only 2 years, and their work in this area was not resumed until 30 years later.

Kamiah Chamber of Commerce: 516 Main St., P.O. Box 1124, Kamiah, ID 83536; phone (208) 935-2290.

EAST KAMIAH, 2 mi. e. on US 12, contains a volcanic rock formation called Heart of the Monster, the place of creation in Nez Perce mythology.

According to American Indian folklore, during the prehuman animal years a great monster was devouring all the animals. Coyote, the legendary chief animal of this age, slew the monster, cut him into many pieces and scattered these bits to the four winds. Legend has it that where each piece of the monster landed, a new Indian tribe arose. The Nez Perce tribe arose from drops of blood from the monster's heart. An interpretive center is available. Daily dawn-dusk.

KELLOGG (B-2) pop. 2,600, elev. 2,305'

Kellogg has made a major transition from mining community to alpine village. Kellogg is in the billion-dollar Coeur d'Alene mining district, which yields silver, lead, gold and zinc; the Sunshine Silver Mine is the largest in the United States. The Shoshone County Mining and Smelting Museum chronicles the colorful history of Silver Valley.

Greater Kellogg Area Chamber of Commerce: 608 Bunker Ave., Kellogg, ID 83837; phone (208) 784-0821.

OLD MISSION STATE PARK, 11 mi. w. off I-90 exit 39, is named for the restored Old Sacred Heart Mission built in the 1850s by Coeur d'Alene Indians under the guidance of Jesuit priest Father Antonio Ravalli. The foot thick mission walls were built of woven straw and adobe mud without nails. Slide shows, church tours and a visitor center are available. Daily 8-6, June-Aug.; 9-5, rest of year. Admission $3 per private vehicle. Phone (208) 682-3814. *See Recreation Chart.*

SILVER MOUNTAIN GONDOLA is off I-90 exit 49, then .25 mi. e. to 610 Bunker Ave. Visitors travel 3.1 miles in what is said to be the world's longest single-stage gondola. The enclosed tram takes about 19 minutes to rise 3,400 feet from the base village at Kellogg to the Mountain Haus upper terminal.

From the Mountain Haus, visitors can take a chair lift to 6,300-foot Kellogg Peak where elk, deer, mountain lions and eagles can be seen as well as panoramic views of parts of Idaho, Montana, Washington and Canada. The Mountain Haus also features a nature gallery. Mountain bicycling, horseback riding and hiking are available. An outdoor amphitheater adjacent to the Mountain Haus features musical performances in an alpine setting. Food is available at the Mountain Haus and the base village at Kellogg.

Allow 1 hour minimum. Daily 10-5:30, mid-June to mid-Sept.; Sat.-Sun. 10-6, Memorial Day to mid-June and mid-Sept. to mid-Oct. Fare $8.95; over 64, $7.95; ages 7-17, $6.95; family rate $20. AE, MC, VI. Phone (208) 783-1111.

THE STAFF HOUSE MUSEUM, 820 McKinley Ave., occupies a house built in 1906 as the home of the top executive of the Bunker Hill Mine. The home was later used as a guest house for dignitaries visiting the Bunker Hill complex. The museum includes an art gallery, a medical exhibit, a Boy Scout exhibit, a minerals display room, a replica of a primitive mining area complete with tools, a smelting display and an exhibit about the domestic life of a miner's family.

Visitors also can see an 1895 Nordberg compressor, once used to pump air underground into mines. Allow 30 minutes minimum. Daily 10-5, Memorial Day-last Sun. in Sept. Admission $3; over 55, $2; ages 6-18, 75c. Phone (208) 786-4141.

 RECREATIONAL ACTIVITIES

Skiing

- **Silver Mountain Ski Area**, off I-90 at Kellogg Peak, 610 Bunker Ave., Kellogg, ID 83837-2200. Other activities are offered. Daily late Nov.-early Apr. Phone (208) 783-1111.

KETCHUM (E-3) pop. 2,500, elev. 5,821'

In the late 19th century Ketchum sprang up almost overnight as a shipping and smelting center for the remote mountain mines surrounding the Wood River Valley. Ores and supplies were transported by the giant ore wagons of the Horace Lewis Fast Freight Line. These relics of the area's past are displayed in the Ore Wagon Museum on East Avenue next to City Hall. The Ketchum Cemetery includes the grave of Ernest Hemingway.

Such outdoor recreational activities as swimming, bicycling, hiking and camping, are foremost among Ketchum's attractions. As the gateway to the Sun Valley *(see place listing p. 61)* resort area and the Sawtooth National Recreation Area *(see place listing p. 59)*, the town offers an abundance of activities year-round. For the spectator Ketchum offers some 20 art galleries and the NexStage Theatre where the Sun Valley Repertory Theater performs year-round. For theater information phone (208) 726-3706.

Sun Valley-Ketchum Chamber of Commerce: 411 N. Main St., P.O. Box 2420, Sun Valley, ID 83353; phone (208) 726-3423 or (800) 634-3347. *See color ad p. 61.*

Shopping areas: Downtown Ketchum1360 offers some 60 shops and restaurants offering everything from antiques and bookstores to children's toys and specialty gifts.

 RECREATIONAL ACTIVITIES

Horseback Riding

- **Galena Stage Stop Corrals—Trail Rides,** 24 mi. n. on SR 75. Write HC 64, Box 9999, Stanley, ID 83278. Other activities are offered.

Daily 8:30-3, May 31-Labor Day. Phone (208) 726-4010.

KOOSKIA (C-2) pop. 700, elev. 1,261'

KOOSKIA NATIONAL FISH HATCHERY is 2 mi. s.e. along the Middle Fork River. Chinook salmon eggs are collected, incubated and hatched, and the young fish are reared. The best times to visit are in early March before the young chinook are set free or during June and July when the adults return to spawn. Daily 7:30-4. Free. Phone (208) 926-4272.

KOOTENAI NATIONAL FOREST—
see Montana p. 99.

LAPWAI (C-2) pop. 900, elev. 891'

NORTHERN IDAHO INDIAN AGENCY, near Fort Lapwai, is the Bureau of Indian Affairs headquarters of Idaho's Nez Perce, Coeur d'Alene and Kootenai Indians. This is one of the sites that composes Nez Perce National Historical Park *(see place listing p. 54)*. The agency was established in 1862 to prevent clashes between the pioneers and the American Indians on the Nez Perce Reservation.

The U.S. Army occupied the fort until 1884. Some of the old buildings are still in use. The Nez Perce Tribal Community Building and Bureau of Indian Affairs Office are a quarter-mile north of Old Fort Lapwai. The agency is open Mon.-Fri. 8-noon and 12:30-4:30; closed legal holidays. Phone (208) 843-2300.

LAVA HOT SPRINGS (F-5) pop. 400, elev. 5,151'

Lava Hot Springs was named for the mineral springs that boil out of lava rocks at the base of massive cliffs along the Portneuf River. Geologists believe that the pools have remained at the same temperature—110 degrees F—for 50 million years. Lava Hot Springs is a popular health and pleasure resort offering hiking, bicycling, tubing and swimming.

For centuries the Shoshone and Bannock Indians regarded the springs as a neutral site. But the tribes' camp was disrupted during the 19th century when the springs were discovered by Oregon-bound travelers and Utah pioneers who founded a settlement called Dempsey. By 1902 the American Indians had ceded their rights to the springs, granting the land to the U.S. government, which in turn gave the area to the state.

Greater Pocatello Chamber of Commerce: P.O. Box 626, Pocatello, ID 83204; phone (208) 233-1525.

IDAHO WORLD FAMOUS HOT POOLS AND OLYMPIC SWIMMING COMPLEX, a resort on US 30E, consists of hot mineral pools on the eastern edge of the village and outdoor Olympic-size swimming pools on the western edge. The Sunken Gardens bloom on terraces that cling to the walls of an extinct volcano. Snowmobiling and skiing, subject to local weather conditions, are available on the surrounding mountains.

Mineral baths open daily 8 a.m.-11 p.m., Apr.-Sept.; 9 a.m.-10 p.m., rest of year. Closed Thanksgiving and Dec. 25. Pool open Memorial Day weekend-Labor Day. All-day pass allows visitors to exit and re-enter. Mineral baths $4.50

(all-day pass $6); over 61 and ages 4-11, $4 (all-day pass $5). Combination pass for baths and pool (available Memorial Day weekend-Labor Day) $8, 1-day family pass $11 (Mon.-Thurs. only). Family passes are not valid during holidays and do not allow readmission. Phone (208) 776-5221 or (800) 423-8597.

SOUTH BANNOCK COUNTY HISTORICAL CENTER AND MUSEUM, off US 30 on 110 E. Main St., contains a collection of American Indian and pioneer artifacts and a permanent exhibit showing the effects of transportation on the area and the six communities of south Bannock County. Daily noon-5; closed major holidays. Donations. Phone (208) 776-5254.

LEWISTON (C-1) pop. 28,100, elev. 738'

At the confluence of the Clearwater and Snake rivers, Lewiston is on a site where Meriwether Lewis and William Clark camped in 1805 and again in 1806. Following the discovery of gold nearby, the settlement became a supply point for mining camps and, subsequently, the territorial capital.

Lewiston is an inland seaport, where ships travel 465 miles down the Snake and Columbia rivers to the Pacific. US 95 leads north to the top of Lewiston Hill, where a viewpoint overlooks the valley. Lewiston lies on an especially scenic

section of US 95 that extends north to Plummer and south to Banks.

Lewiston Chamber of Commerce: 2207 E. Main, Lewiston, ID 83501; phone (208) 743-3531 or (800) 473-3543. *See color ad.*

BOAT TRIPS UP HELLS CANYON OF THE SNAKE RIVER are spectacular journeys into the main part of Hells Canyon, the deepest river gorge in North America. Most trips return the same day, but others require an overnight stop; all include one or more meals and offer refreshments. Inquire about age restrictions, refund and weather policies. Three- and 5-day float trips depart by aluminum jet boat, usually in the early morning. Rates vary. For information phone the chamber of commerce (208) 743-3531.

LUNA HOUSE MUSEUM, 3rd and C sts., is named after the original building on this site, the Luna House Hotel. Built in the 1930's, the current art deco-style building features displays of American Indian and pioneer artifacts and other relics. Tues.-Sat. 9-5; closed major holidays and Dec. 19-Jan. 1. Donations. Phone (208) 743-2535.

McCALL (D-2) pop. 2,000, elev. 5,025'

At the southern end of beautiful Payette Lake, McCall is a year-round recreational resort. Fishing, boating, water skiing, horseback riding, white-water rafting, golf, camping and hunting are available. Skiing and snowmobiling are popular winter sports.

Firefighting facilities at the Forest Service's Smokejumper Headquarters feature smokejumping equipment, a fire retardant mixing plant and communications services. Tours are offered; phone (208) 634-0390.

McCall lies on an especially scenic section of SR 55, also called the Payette River Scenic Route. The highway heads north, merges with US 95 and continues toward Coeur d'Alene. The southern terminus of the route is Boise.

McCall Area Chamber of Commerce: 1001 State St., P.O. Box D, McCall, ID 83638; phone (208) 634-7631 or (800) 260-5130.

MONTPELIER (F-5) pop. 2,700, elev. 5,934'

Montpelier, one of the state's oldest towns, is at the junction of US 89 and US 30N, the historic Old Oregon Trail. Brigham Young established a Mormon community and named the town for the capital of his home state, Vermont. In 1896 Butch Cassidy relieved the Bank of Montpelier of $7,000. Some of the largest known phosphate deposits are found in this area. Bear Lake resort is about 17 miles south on US 89.

Greater Bear Lake Convention and Visitors Bureau: P.O. Box 26, Fish Haven, ID 83287; phone (800) 448-2327.

MINNETONKA CAVE is s.w. via US 89 to St. Charles, then 10 mi. w. The cave, 7,700 feet above sea level, contains limestone cave formations and fossils of tropical plants and marine life. The temperature is a constant 40 degrees F. Guided tours daily 10-5:30, mid-June through Labor Day. Admission $4; ages 6-15, $3; family rate available. Phone (208) 945-2407.

MOSCOW (C-2) pop. 18,500, elev. 2,574′

Moscow (Mos-co) is the commercial center of the fertile Palouse country where black volcanic ash soil, ample rainfall and warm autumn temperatures combine to produce lentils, dry peas, wheat and barley. The agricultural yields of the Palouse are processed in Moscow and distributed throughout the country.

The town was once a favorite summer haven for the Nez Perce Indians as well as a base camp in the gold rush of the 1860s. Moscow was a preferred trapping ground of the French Canadians in the early 1800s and is known as the home of the Appaloosa horse. The town lies on an especially scenic section of US 95, which heads north toward Coeur d'Alene and south to Banks.

The University of Idaho was established in 1889, a year before statehood was gained. The 450-acre campus displays a variety of architecture, ranging from Gothic dormitories to the contemporary ASUI-Kibbie Dome Athletic Center.

Exhibits of rocks and minerals in the Life Science and College of Mines buildings at the university are open to visitors, as is the USDA Intermountain Forest and Range Experiment Station, a joint effort of the university and the U.S. Forest Service that conducts research to prevent disease in and insect damage to white pines.

Moscow Chamber of Commerce: 411 S. Main St., P.O. Box 8936, Moscow, ID 83843; phone (208) 882-1800 or (800) 380-1801.

APPALOOSA MUSEUM, w. on SR 8 in the Appaloosa Horse Club building, contains Nez Perce regalia and artifacts, cowboy tack, photographs and artwork illustrating Appaloosa history. Live horses can be viewed during summer. Allow 1 hour minimum. Mon.-Fri. 8-5, Sat. 9-3, July-Aug.; Mon.-Fri. 8-5, rest of year. Closed holidays. Donations. Phone (208) 882-5578, ext. 279.

McCONNELL MANSION, 110 S. Adams St., was built in the late 19th century by Gov. William J. McConnell. Now home of the Latah County Historical Society, the mansion displays relics and Victorian-style furniture from the late 1800s. Allow 1 hour minimum. Tues.-Sat. 1-4; closed holidays. Donations. Phone (208) 882-1004.

NAMPA (E-2) pop. 28,400, elev. 2,492′

Col. W.H. Dewey moved his fortune during the 1890s to Nampa, an agricultural hamlet just north of the Great Basin Desert. Dewey brought prosperity to Nampa by attracting several railway branches and constructing the Dewey Palace hotel, which was a town landmark for several decades until it was damaged by fire and torn down. Nampa's name comes from Nampuh, or "Bigfoot," a Shoshone chief who was so large that his feet were supposedly 17 inches long.

Exhibits depicting the region's history can be seen at the Canyon County Historical Museum, which occupies the restored 1906 Union Pacific Railroad depot at 1224 Front St.

Nampa is a central location from which to explore southwestern Idaho's natural wonders and historical sites. Givens' Hot Springs is 17 miles south on SR 45, then 8 miles west on SR 78 on the south side of the Snake River. There are steam baths, an indoor natural hot-water pool and a picnic area.

Celebration Park, with several fine groups of American Indian rock art, is off I-84, 9 miles south on SR 45, east on Butte, then south on Can-Ada Road to the end of Victory Lane. Among the petroglyphs is Map Rock, on which is a detailed carving thought to be a map of the Snake River, Jackson Lake in Wyoming and adjacent areas.

Silver City and DeLamar, high in the Owyhee Mountains, can be reached by taking SR 45 south to Walter's Ferry, then turning east on SR 78 4.5 miles past Murphy. The towns, at one time thriving mining communities in one of the greatest silver-producing areas in the nation, are on a rough gravel and earth road (see Silver City p. 59). DeLamar has been abandoned.

Nampa Chamber of Commerce: 1305 3rd. St. S., Nampa, ID 83651; phone (208) 466-4641.

DEER FLAT NATIONAL WILDLIFE REFUGE, 4 mi. s.w., consists of two sections: Lake Lowell, an irrigation reservoir, and 107 islands in the Snake River, from Walter's Ferry downstream to Farewell Bend in Oregon. The islands are accessible only by boat.

The refuge harbors migrant and resident waterfowls as well as other birds and mammals. In winter bald eagles move into the Lake Lowell area to feed on weak and injured birds. In spring and summer nesting marsh and water birds include western grebes, great blue herons and black-crowned night herons.

Shorebirds are plentiful on the mudflats of Lake Lowell in late summer and early fall. In November and December 60,000 mallards can be seen on the lake. Canada geese, gulls and wading birds nest on the islands, while mallards and goldeneyes winter on the river. Other birds commonly seen on the islands include American avocets, marbled godwits, spotted sandpipers, California quails and ring-necked pheasants.

Lake Lowell (see Recreation Chart) is one of the Boise-Nampa-Caldwell area's most popular recreation spots. Beaches, docks and boat ramps are provided at three developments; no lifeguards are on duty. Motorboats and sailboats are allowed during daylight hours, mid-April through September. Fishing and hunting are permitted in season in specified portions of the refuge. Daily dawn-dusk. Free. Phone (208) 467-9278.

NEZ PERCE NATIONAL FOREST

Elevations in the forest range from 1,350 ft. in Hells Canyon to 9,393 ft. at Devil's Peak. Refer to AAA maps for additional elevation information.

Nez Perce National Forest was named for the Nez Perce Indians, whose ancestral lands once included this rugged area of 2,223,594 acres. The forest contains the Gospel-Hump Wilderness and portions of the Selway-Bitterroot Wilderness, Frank Church-River of No Return Wilderness, Hells Canyon Wilderness and Hells Canyon National Recreation Area *(see place listing p. 46)*.

More than 150 miles of the Rapid, Salmon and Selway rivers and the Middle Fork of the Clearwater River are classified as wild and scenic rivers. Elk, moose, deer, cougars, mountain goats, bighorn sheep and bears inhabit the forest, while steelhead trout, white sturgeon and small-mouth bass can be found in the rivers and streams.

Portions of the forest are close to parts of Nez Perce National Historical Park *(see place listing p. 54)*. See Recreation Chart and the AAA Northwestern CampBook.

Magruder Corridor Road is open to forest visitors July through September. The road, rough but passable to two-wheel-drive vehicles, begins at the Red River Ranger Station and ends in Darby, Mont. For road information phone the Red River Ranger District at (208) 842-2255, or the supervisor's office in Grangeville at (208) 983-1950, or the West Fork Ranger District at (406) 821-3269.

NEZ PERCE NATIONAL HISTORICAL PARK (C-1)

Nez Perce National Historical Park encompasses 28 sites scattered across 12,000 square miles of north-central Idaho as well as 10 sites in Oregon, Washington and Montana. Each reflects part of the history and culture of the Nez Perce Indians and their relationships with white explorers, missionaries, miners, settlers and soldiers.

Some sites are scenic views, some are geologic formations and others contain historic places and buildings. They include the Lolo Trail, American Indian battlefields and former campsites of Meriwether Lewis and William Clark.

For thousands of years the Nez Perce lived in the valleys of the Clearwater and Snake rivers and their tributaries. Their first documented meeting with white settlers in Nez Perce territory took place in September 1805, when the Lewis and Clark expedition encountered them, and the American Indians gave supplies and assistance. In 1855 the Nez Perce reluctantly signed a treaty setting aside their ancestral home as a reservation.

A new treaty was negotiated in 1863 with some of the Nez Perce bands after gold was discovered within the reservation; this treaty reduced the reservation to one-tenth of its original size.

The first major battle of the Nez Perce War was on June 17, 1877, near White Bird. The U.S. Army pursued the bands of Nez Perce who had not signed the 1863 treaty across the Nez Perce Trail to Montana. After many battles the Nez Perce surrendered only 40 miles from the Canadian border. They were exiled for 8 years to Oklahoma Territory; the survivors eventually returned to the Pacific Northwest. Today the Nez Perce National Historic Trail parallels much of the original 1877 route.

The Weippe (WEE-eye-p) Prairie, 18 miles east of US 12 on SR 11, is part of Nez Perce National Historical Park. The Idaho section of the Nez Perce Trail and Pass climbs through 150 miles of rough terrain east of Weippe as it ascends the 5,187-foot Lolo Pass through the Bitterroot Mountains.

The park's headquarters and visitor center are in Spalding *(see place listing p. 60)*. A brochure for a self-guiding driving tour of White Bird Battlefield is available here and at the Forest Service office in Grangeville. The battlefield, 16 miles south of Grangeville on US 95, was the site of the first confrontation of the Nez Perce War. The American Indians won the 1877 battle. Also see Cottonwood, Grangeville, Kamiah, Lapwai, Nez Perce National Forest and Orofino.

Park open daily 8-6, Memorial Day weekend-Labor Day; 8-4:30, rest of year. Closed Jan. 1, Thanksgiving and Dec. 25. Big Hole Battlefield site $4 per private vehicle, $2 per bicycle. All other sites are free. Phone (208) 843-2261.

OROFINO (C-2) pop. 2,900, elev. 1,027'

In 1805 members of the Lewis and Clark expedition passed near the present site of Orofino on their way west. The first gold miners swarmed into the area 60 years later from California, and soon Idaho's first permanent settlements began to take shape. Orofino is on the Nez Perce Indian Reservation, and the Clearwater River runs through the town's boundaries. The Clearwater National Forest *(see place listing p.*

43) and Nez Perce National Forest *(see place listing p. 54)* are nearby.

Orofino's economy relies on lumbering, farming and government employment. A long growing season, ample precipitation and fertile soil contribute to the prosperity of this agricultural community. Northwest of Orofino, near Ahsahka *(see place listing p. 35)*, is the Dworshak National Fish Hatchery and Dworshak Dam and Reservoir.

Orofino Chamber of Commerce: 217 1st St., P.O. Box 2221, Orofino, ID 83544; phone (208) 476-4335.

LEWIS AND CLARK CANOE CAMP, 5 mi. w. on US 12, is part of the Nez Perce National Historical Park *(see place listing p. 54)*. After crossing the Bitterroot Mountains on horseback, Meriwether Lewis and William Clark camped and built dugout canoes for the remainder of their journey to the Pacific Ocean. Daily dawn-dusk. Free. Phone (208) 843-2261 or 843-7131.

PAYETTE NATIONAL FOREST

Elevations in the forest range from 1,464 ft. in Hells Canyon to 9,545 ft. at Mormon Mountain. Refer to AAA maps for additional elevation information.

Bounded by Boise National Forest, the Snake and Salmon rivers and the Middle Fork of the Salmon River, the Payette National Forest contains 2,307,897 acres that range in elevation from 1,600 to 9,000 feet above sea level. More than 2,000 miles of hiking trails include Lava Ridge National Recreation Trail and Sheep Rock Nature Trail. The forest's many rivers, streams and lakes provide good fishing.

Winter sports include alpine skiing at Brundage Mountain and the Payette Lakes Ski Hill as well as cross-country skiing and snowmobiling in many other areas. Major fires in 1994 burned several trails. Phone for trail conditions and availability of picnic areas.

A small portion of the Hells Canyon Wilderness and Hells Canyon National Recreation Area *(see place listing p. 46)* and a large portion of the Frank Church-River of No Return Wilderness lie within the forest. These mountainous areas overlap several national forests and contain extensive trail networks. For more information write Payette National Forest, P.O. Box 1026, McCall, ID 83638; phone (208) 634-0700. *See Recreation Chart and the AAA Northwestern CampBook.*

POCATELLO (F-5) pop. 46,100, elev. 4,365'

Originally part of the Fort Hall Indian Reservation, Pocatello is named for a 19th-century Bannock chief who granted the Utah & Northern a right-of-way for a Salt Lake City-to-Butte railroad line. The subsequent arrival in 1882 of the Union Pacific Railway, which linked the Midwest and Pacific Northwest, spawned a makeshift community—a congregation of tents at the meeting of the two lines—that was first called Pocatello Junction.

Pocatello maintains its position as one of the region's leading industrial, distribution and transportation centers. Education also is a principal concern; Idaho State University is one of the state's leading 4-year institutions. The town is the northern terminus of an especially scenic section of I-15, which heads south into Utah.

Just off Main Street visitors can see the Oregon Short Line Depot, a three-story passenger station designed in the late 1800s. Train passengers of the era stayed overnight across the street at the historic Yellowstone Hotel. Local entertainment includes pari-mutuel horse racing in the fall at Bannock County Fairgrounds, off I-15 exit 71; phone (208) 237-1340.

Note: Policies concerning admittance of children to pari-mutuel betting facilities vary. Phone for information.

Greater Pocatello Chamber of Commerce: 343 W. Center St., P.O. Box 626, Pocatello, ID 83204; phone (208) 233-1525.

BANNOCK COUNTY HISTORICAL MUSEUM is off I-15 exit 67, then 1 mi. n. on US 30/91 in Upper Ross Park. The museum contains American Indian and railroad displays, a restored stagecoach, a 1915 La France firetruck and a mural history/donor wall. Other displays include a 1900s parlor, a country kitchen, women's clothing, a dental office and a 1947 Linotype press.

Allow 1 hour minimum. Daily 10-6, Memorial Day weekend-Labor Day; Tues.-Sat. 10-2, rest of year. Closed Memorial Day, July 4, Thanksgiving and Dec. 25. Admission Memorial Day weekend-Labor Day $2.50; ages 12-18, $1.75; ages 6-11, $1 (includes Fort Hall Replica). Admission rest of year by donations. Phone (208) 233-0434.

FORT HALL REPLICA, off I-15 exit 67, then 1 mi. n. on US 30/91 in Upper Ross Park, re-creates the fur-trading post that operated nearby 1834-60. Original Hudson Bay Co. plans were used to create the full-scale replica. Buffaloes, elk, deer and pronghorn antelopes are kept in a field next to the fort. Allow 1 hour minimum. Daily 9-7, Apr.-Sept. Admission (includes Bannock County Historical Museum) $2.50; ages 12-18, $1.75; ages 6-11, $1. Phone (208) 234-1795 or 234-6232.

IDAHO MUSEUM OF NATURAL HISTORY, on the main floor of the museum building at the corner of 5th and Dillon sts., is on the Idaho State University campus. Collections include dinosaur bones, other fossils and mounted animals native to Idaho as well as Shoshone-Bannock basketry. The Discovery Room allows children hands-on encounters with fossils and computers. Allow 30 minutes minimum. Mon.-Sat. 10-5; closed holidays. Free. Fee charged for special events. Phone (208) 236-3168.

POST FALLS (B-2) pop. 7,300, elev. 2,169'

On the Spokane River at the Washington-Idaho stateline, Post Falls was founded in the late 1800s by Frederick Post when he harnessed the falls to generate power for his sawmill.

State Line Stadium Speedway features stock car racing; phone (208) 773-5019.

Post Falls Tourism: P.O. Box 908, Post Falls, ID 83854; phone (208) 773-4080 or (800) 292-2553. *See color ad.*

Shopping areas: The Factory Outlets Mall, off I-90 exit 2, contains some 60 outlet stores offering discounted name-brand merchandise 7 days a week.

FALLS PARK, off I-90 Spokane St. exit, 2 blks. s. on Spokane St., then 1.5 blks. w. to 305 W. 4th St., offers visitors a view of Post Falls and gorge as well as trails leading to nearby Treaty Rock *(see attraction listing)* which marks the site of Post Falls' founding. Picnicking is permitted. Daily dawn-dusk (weather permitting). Free. Phone (208) 773-0539 or 773-8147.

Q'EMILN TRAIL SYSTEM, I-90 exit 5, .9 mi. s. on Spokane St., then .2 mi. w. on Park Ave., includes 12 connected trails winding along the south bank of the Spokane River. Trails lead to historic sites, abandoned homesteads, mining camps, logging areas and scenic spots above and below Post Falls Dam. Picnicking is permitted. Allow 1 hour minimum. Daily dawn-dusk. Trails

are free. Parking $3, Memorial Day weekend-Labor Day weekend. Phone (208) 773-0539 or 773-8147.

TREATY ROCK HISTORIC SITE, at the jct. of 7th and Compton sts., commemorates the spot where Coeur d'Alene Indian Chief Andrew Seltice transferred land to Frederick Post, the founder of Post Falls. A marked trail features American Indian petroglyphs and paintings. Picnicking is permitted. Allow 30 minutes minimum. Daily dawn-dusk. Free. Phone (208) 773-0539 or 773-8147.

PRIEST LAKE—
see Coolin p. 44.

PRIEST RIVER (A-1) pop. 1,600, elev. 2,082'

Priest River, at the junction of the Pend Oreille and Priest rivers and 30 miles south of Priest Lake via SR 57, is the gateway to the Idaho Panhandle National Forests *(see place listing p. 49).*

ALBENI FALLS DAM, 3.5 mi. w. on US 2 on the Pend Oreille River, offers a scenic viewpoint, visitor center and picnic grounds. One-hour guided tours of the powerhouse are available daily at 10, 11, 2, 3 and 4, Memorial Day weekend-Labor Day. Free. Phone (208) 437-3133.

REXBURG (E-5) pop. 14,300, elev. 4,861'

In the late 1870s many miners heading into Montana in search of gold stopped along the west side of the Snake River and claimed land under the Homestead Act of 1862. Many of these first homesteaders were Mormons. In 1883 another influx of settlers drove their sleighs to the banks of the Snake River and established the present townsite of Rexburg.

In June 1976 the nearby Teton Dam collapsed and sent 8 billion gallons of flood water into the

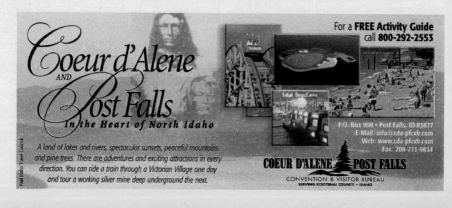

valley below. To see the site, travel 20 miles northeast on SR 33. Rexburg plays host to the Idaho International Folk Dance Festival in August. The Centennial Carousel, which took 5 years to restore, is in Porter Park.

Rexburg Chamber of Commerce: 420 W. 4th St. S., Rexburg, ID 83440; phone (208) 356-5700.

TETON FLOOD MUSEUM, 51 N. Center, offers shows and picture displays about the 1976 break in the Teton Dam and the subsequent flooding. Films about the Yellowstone Park fires of 1988 also are available. Other displays include a variety of quilts and more than 300 salt and pepper shakers. Mon.-Sat. 10-5, May-Sept.; Mon.-Fri. 11-4, rest of year. Donations. Phone (208) 356-9101.

RIGGINS (D-2) pop. 400, elev. 1,800′

Riggins, where the Little Salmon pours into the main Salmon River, is a starting point for a drive north along US 95 through the scenic gorge of the Salmon River. The town is considered the area's white-water capital for float trips; for information phone the chamber of commerce.

East of town lies the wilderness of the Payette National Forest *(see place listing p. 55).* To the west rise the 9,000-foot Seven Devils Mountains, which form a semicircle above the Snake River's chasm, Hells Canyon; some 30 alpine lakes are clustered around the peaks. To the south is the Rapid River Fish Hatchery, one of the Northwest's most successful Chinook salmon-breeding operations.

Salmon River Chamber of Commerce: P.O. Box 289, Riggins, ID 83549; phone (208) 628-3778.

☀❄ RECREATIONAL ACTIVITIES
White-water Rafting

- **Epley's Whitewater Adventures**, on US 95 at the n. end of town, P.O. Box 987, McCall, ID 83638. Trips depart daily at 9:15, May 15-Sept. 15. Phone (208) 634-5173 or (800) 233-1813.

- **Northwest Voyageurs** offers trips on the Salmon, Owyhee and Snake rivers. Write P.O. Box 373, Lucile, ID 83542. Other activities are offered. Departures daily Mar.-Nov. Phone (208) 628-3022 or (800) 727-9977. *See color ad p. 39.*

- **Salmon River Challenge**, on US 95 between mileposts 195 and 196, P.O. Box 1299, Riggins, ID 83549. Other activities are offered. Half-day trips depart daily at 12:30, May 1-late Sept. Full- and 2-day trips depart daily at 9, May 1-late Sept. Three- and 5-day trips depart every 8 days, late June-late Sept. Phone (208) 628-3264 or (800) 732-8574.

RUPERT (F-3) pop. 5,500, elev. 4,158′

Rupert was platted by the Bureau of Reclamation, which accounts for its business district being built around a square that is now a public park. Irrigation from dam projects on the Snake River has transformed the surrounding area from semiarid land to one of Idaho's principal agricultural areas. Potatoes and sugar beets are important crops.

Mini-Cassia Chamber of Commerce: 1177 7th St., P.O. Box 640, Heyburn, ID 83336; phone (208) 436-4793 or (800) 333-3408.

MINIDOKA NATIONAL WILDLIFE REFUGE extends 20 mi. up the Snake River from Minidoka Dam and includes Lake Walcott; refuge headquarters is 12 mi. n.e. via SR 24 and CR 400N. As many as 100,000 waterfowls stop at the refuge during their migrations along the Pacific flyway. Some 200 species of birds as well as mule deer, pronghorn antelopes and various predators inhabit the 20,721-acre refuge.

Fishing, boating and picnicking are permitted on the western end of Lake Walcott; there are no tour routes or developed hiking trails, and roads are primitive. Daily dawn-dusk; office closed Sat.-Sun. and holidays. Phone (208) 436-3589 or (800) 333-3408.

SALMON (D-3) pop. 2,900, elev. 4,040′

Once the winter campsite of fur trappers, including Jim Bridger and Kit Carson, Salmon is at the fork of the Salmon and Lemhi rivers near the edge of the Salmon Valley, a prosperous livestock and mining area. The town is a favorite starting point for pack trips into the Frank Church-River of No Return Wilderness and for float trips down the Salmon River and its wildest branch, the Middle Fork. Permanent settlement of this region began with the discovery of gold in 1866.

Salmon lies on a scenic section of US 93, which heads north to the Montana border and southwest toward Sawtooth National Forest *(see place listing p. 59).*

Salmon Valley Chamber of Commerce: 200 Main St., Suite #1, Salmon, ID 83467; phone (208) 756-2100 or (800) 727-2540.

LEMHI COUNTY HISTORICAL MUSEUM, 210 Main St., displays tools, domestic items and American Indian artifacts dating back to pioneer times. A collection of antiques from China, Japan and Tibet also is exhibited. Mon.-Sat. 10-5, July-Aug.; 1-5, Apr.-June and Sept.-Oct. Donations. Phone (208) 756-3342.

☀❄ RECREATIONAL ACTIVITIES
White-water Rafting

- **Barker-Ewing River Trips**, on the main channel of the Salmon River with ground transportation options from Idaho Falls and Salmon.

Write P.O. Box 450, Jackson, WY 83001. Departures Apr.-Sept. Phone (307) 733-1000 or (800) 448-4202.

- **SAVE Idaho Adventures**, on the Salmon River, P.O. Box 834-AA, Salmon, ID 83467. Float trips offered Apr.-Sept. Phone (208) 756-2986 or (800) 789-9283.

- **SAVE Kookaburra Scenic Whitewater**, on the Salmon River, P.O. Box 20, Carmen, ID 83462. Trips run daily in summer. Phone (208) 756-4386.

- **North Fork Guides**, at the North Fork Store, Motel and Campground, P.O. Box 808, North Fork, ID 83466. Trips run mid-Apr. to mid-Nov. Phone (208) 865-2412 or (800) 259-6866.

- **Rawhide Outfitters**, 204 Larson St., Salmon, ID 83467. Trips depart Sun.-Fri. 9-5, May-Oct. Phone (208) 756-4276.

SALMON-CHALLIS NATIONAL FOREST

Elevations in the forest range from 2,200 ft. in the lower canyon of the Salmon River to 12,662 ft. at Borah Peak. Refer to AAA maps for additional elevation information.

From the headwaters of the Salmon River, down the Lost River, Pahsimeroi and Lemhi Mountain Ranges, to the western slope of the Continental Divide, the Salmon-Challis National Forest covers 4.3 million acres. Over 130,000 acres are in the Frank Church-River of No Return Wilderness *(see Payette National Forest p. 55)*.

The historic Lewis and Clark Trail passes through part of the forest, where several monuments to the explorers have been erected. The Custer Motorway Loop and adjacent Salmon River Road provide glimpses of historic mining towns and native wildlife.

Because of swift currents the Salmon River west of Salmon is known as the "River of No Return." Now, however, it is possible to navigate this river upstream via jet boats. Boat trips down the river can be arranged in Salmon *(see place listing p. 57)*.

More than 2,800 miles of trail stripe the forest floor. Hiking season is generally between April and October; hunting, fishing, camping and wildlife viewing also are excellent.

The section of the river between Corn Creek and Riggins can be traveled by kayaks, jet boats or rubber rafts. Skiing is available nearby on the Idaho-Montana border at Lost Trail Pass. For more information write the Salmon-Challis National Forest Headquarters, R.R. 2, Box 600, Salmon, ID 83467; phone (208) 756-5100. *See Recreation Chart and the AAA Northwestern CampBook.*

SANDPOINT (A-2) pop. 5,200, elev. 2,086'

Sandpoint, at the north end of Pend Oreille Lake, is a year-round resort town and artists' community that offers a wide variety of land- and water-based recreational opportunities.

The city is the starting point for single- and multi-day train tours through the Montana Rockies to Glacier, Grand Teton and Yellowstone national parks. Guides on board Montana Rockies Rail Tours provide historic narration and tales of folklore as the *Montana Daylight* follows the original route of the Northern Pacific Railroad; phone (800) 519-7245 for information.

Greater Sandpoint Chamber of Commerce: US 95N, P.O. Box 928, Sandpoint, ID 83864; phone (208) 263-2161 or (800) 800-2106.

Shopping areas: One of downtown Sandpoint's focal points is the Cedar Street Bridge Public Market, home to Coldwater Creek Nature and Clothing Store. Formerly a city bridge over Sand Creek, this renovated two-level structure is patterned after the famed Ponte Vecchio bridge shops in Florence, Italy, and contains two long streets of restaurants and shops.

BONNER COUNTY HISTORICAL MUSEUM, 609 S. Ella Ave., uses pioneer relics and other exhibits to chronicle the history of the county, with emphasis on the Kootenai Indians and the local timber industry. Allow 30 minutes minimum. Tues.-Sat. 10-4, Apr. 1-Nov. 1; Thurs. 10-4, rest of year. Closed holidays. Admission $2; ages 6-18, $1. Phone (208) 263-2344.

PEND OREILLE LAKE (pon-duh-RAY), formed by glaciers and encircled by lofty mountain peaks, is one of the largest freshwater lakes in the Pacific Northwest. Early French trappers named the area after an Indian tribe they called Pend Oreilles because they wore pendant ornaments in their ear lobes. Noted for its scenic coves and 1,150-foot depth, the lake is stocked with Kamloop rainbow trout; a special fishing season runs from early May to late November.

Swimming, boating, picnicking and tennis are popular, as is the 2-hour guided boat tour; facilities for other types of recreation are found at Trestle Creek, Hope, Clark Fork *(see place listing p. 43)*, Garfield Bay, Bottle Bay, Bayview and Farragut State Park. Allow a full day minimum. *See Recreation Chart.*

SAWTOOTH NATIONAL FOREST

Elevations in the forest range
from 4,514 ft. at Rock Creek Drain
to 12,009 ft. at Hyndman Peak.
Refer to AAA maps for additional
elevation information.

The Sawtooth National Forest of south-central Idaho embraces approximately 2.1 million acres. Offering a wide range of recreational opportunities and spectacular scenery, the forest consists of a northern division containing the Sawtooth National Recreation Area and a southern division along the Nevada and Utah borders.

Adjacent to Sun Valley *(see place listing p. 61)*, the northern division is bisected by the Sawtooth Scenic Route (SR 75 or Sawtooth National Forest Scenic Byway) and provides hundreds of miles of hiking and horseback-riding trails in the Smoky, Pioneer, Sawtooth, Boulder and White Cloud mountains. The Baumgartner Nature Trail, near Baumgartner Campground in the Fairfield District, is a popular hiking area.

The southern division contains the Rock Creek Canyon, Howell Canyon, Black Pine, Raft River and Sublett areas. Alpine and cross-country skiing as well as snowmobiling are available in areas near Twin Falls *(see place listing p. 62)*, Burley *(see place listing p. 42)*, Fairfield and Sun Valley *(see place listing p. 61)*.

Information about campgrounds and recreational opportunities is available at the forest headquarters in Twin Falls and the district ranger stations. For further information write Sawtooth National Forest, 2647 Kimberly Rd. E., Twin Falls, ID 83301; phone (208) 737-3200, or TDD (208) 737-3235. *See Recreation Chart and the AAA Northwestern CampBook.*

SAWTOOTH NATIONAL RECREATION AREA (D-3)

Comprising 756,000 acres of the northern division of the Sawtooth National Forest, the Sawtooth National Recreation Area features three mountain ranges of peaks exceeding 10,000 feet, deep forests and high mountain lakes. The recreation area includes the Sawtooth Wilderness, the White Cloud-Boulder Mountains, the Salmon River and five major lakes. The backcountry has 750 miles of hiking trails and more than 300 lakes.

Nature trails in the forest include the Fishhook Creek Nature Trail, adjacent to Redfish Lake Visitor Center, and the Wood River Adventure Trail, bordering the Wood River Campground.

A free tape tour explaining the area's history and features can be borrowed at the Sawtooth National Recreation Area headquarters, Stanley Ranger Station or the Ketchum Ranger District. For more information write Sawtooth National Recreation Headquarters, Star Route, Ketchum, ID 83340; phone (208) 727-5013 or (800) 260-5970. *See Recreation Chart and the AAA Northwestern CampBook.*

SHOSHONE (F-3) pop. 1,200, elev. 3,968'

Shoshone, in an irrigated farming belt and sheep-raising area, was settled in 1882. Many buildings, including the Community Methodist Church at Apple and C streets, are made from local dark, porous lava rock.

Shoshone Chamber of Commerce: P.O. Box 575, Shoshone, ID 83352; phone (208) 886-2030.

SHOSHONE INDIAN ICE CAVES, 17 mi. n. on SR 75, are caves of ice that maintain a temperature of 18 to 28 degrees F, while a few feet away on the surface the thermometer might register more than 100. Wear sturdy shoes and a coat. Guided tours are given every 30 minutes. The .75-mile tour includes 100 feet of stairs. A museum features collections of gems, minerals and rocks.

Allow 1 hour minimum. Museum and caves open daily 8-7, May-Sept. Admission $5; over 64, $4.50; ages 6-17, $3.75. DS, MC, VI. Phone (208) 886-2058.

SILVER CITY (F-1) elev. 6,179'

Silver City, high in the Owyhee Mountains of southwestern Idaho, became an important gold and silver mining center after prospectors struck it rich near the headwaters of Jordan Creek in 1862. A 500-pound solid silver crystal from the nearby Poorman mine on War Eagle Mountain won a prize at the 1866 exposition in Paris.

Mining remained a force until 1912, then continued sporadically through the 1930s. In its heyday Silver City boasted a courthouse, hotels, Idaho's first daily newspaper and a population of 3,000. By 1920 its population had fallen to 100.

A walk down Silver City's unpaved streets is a living-history tour. Some 75 buildings remain of this once boisterous mining town. The 1892 schoolhouse and drugstore are now museums. On the knoll near the school is the 1898 Our Lady of Tears Catholic Church. The 20-bedroom Idaho Hotel, which is also a museum, dominates Main Street and was once the finest in the territory. Several historic cemeteries are in the community.

Note: The 23-mile gravel and dirt road leading to Silver City from SR 78 south of Murphy has many rough, winding sections and is not recommended for trailers or oversize vehicles. The road is not maintained in winter and is normally closed Nov. 1 to late May. Phone (208) 583-4104 or write P.O. Box 75, Murphy, ID 83650-0075 for weather and road conditions.

The first 8 miles of the 25-mile road leading west from Silver City to Jordan Valley, Ore., are rough, winding and narrow. There are no automobile service facilities in the vicinity.

SODA SPRINGS (F-5) pop. 3,100, elev. 5,777'

Since pioneer days Soda Springs has been known for its 30 mineral salt springs. Early trappers called Hooper Spring, a mile north of town, "Beer Spring" because of its natural soda water, which visitors can sample today.

Nearby Captive Geyser is a carbon dioxide geyser controlled to erupt hourly, winds permitting. Foot-deep wagon ruts from the Old Oregon Trail that date from the mid-1800s provide an unusual hazard on the local golf course. The Pioneer Museum downtown displays mementos reflecting area history.

Soda Springs Chamber of Commerce: 9 W. 2nd S., P.O. Box 687, Soda Springs, ID 83276; phone (208) 547-2600 or (888) 399-0888.

SPALDING (C-2) elev. 840'

Catholic, Protestant and Mormon missionaries occupied much of central Idaho during the early and mid-1800s in an attempt to convert the American Indians. Spalding, now within the boundaries of the Nez Perce National Historical Park *(see place listing p. 54)*, is named for Rev. Henry H. Spalding, who built a mission near the present town of Lapwai *(see place listing p. 51)* in 1836.

Two years later he moved the mission 2 miles north to the Clearwater River, where the headquarters of the Nez Perce National Historical Park is today.

Several geologic formations near Spalding have significance in Nez Perce tradition. Coyote's Fishnet, about 4 miles west, is a formation on the bluffs of the Clearwater River's south shore. A talus slope known as The Bear is high on the north side of the river. Ant and Yellowjacket is a rock arch 1.5 miles west off US 12 just before its junction with US 95.

Idaho's first homestead, the Craig Donation Land Claim, is about 8 miles south along US 95. In 1840 mountain man William Craig settled on 630 acres given to him by the Nez Perce. He is buried in the nearby town of Jacques. St. Joseph's Mission, 4 miles south of Jacques in the village of Slickpoo, was dedicated in 1874 and was the first Catholic church in Nez Perce country.

NEZ PERCE NATIONAL HISTORICAL PARK, on US 95, contains exhibits of Nez Perce culture. Audiovisual programs highlight Nez Perce culture and area history. A park folder is available for a self-guiding driving tour of the 38 sites included in the park. Allow 30 minutes minimum. Daily 8-5:30, Memorial Day weekend-Labor Day; 8-4:30, rest of year. Closed Jan. 1, Thanksgiving and Dec. 25. Donations. Phone (208) 843-2261.

SPALDING SITE, .25 mi. e., is the location of the second mission built by Rev. Henry H. Spalding and his wife Eliza in 1838. The Presbyterian mission included the Idaho Territory's first printing press, sawmill and gristmill. The site was later used as Indian Agency headquarters. The Spaldings and many Nez Perce are buried here in the Spalding Mission Cemetery. A self-guiding tour is available. Allow 30 minutes minimum.

The Spaldings' first homesite, 2 miles south at Thunder Hill, was built in 1836, the year they arrived in the Northwest.

STANLEY (D-3) pop. 100, elev. 6,260'

On the Salmon River (the "River of No Return"), Stanley is at the center of the Sawtooth National Recreation Area *(see place listing p. 59)*, Sawtooth Valley and the spectacular Sawtooth Basin. Most float trips on the Middle Fork of the Salmon River are outfitted at this site. The town lies on two exceptionally scenic highways, SRs 21 and 75.

The Ponderosa Pine Scenic Byway (SR 21) passes through part of the Sawtooth National Forest *(see place listing p. 59)* and ends in Boise; motorists should check for possible temporary closures due to snow. The northeastern segment of SR 75, the Salmon River Scenic Byway, passes through the Sawtooth National Recreation Area and then merges with US 93. The southeastern segment of SR 75, the Sawtooth Scenic Byway, heads south toward Twin Falls and Sun Valley.

Stanley-Sawtooth Chamber of Commerce: P.O. Box 8, Stanley, ID 83278; phone (208) 774-3411 or (800) 878-7950.

SAWTOOTH FISH HATCHERY, 5 mi. s. on SR 75, is used for trapping and holding spring Chinook salmon and steelhead trout. The hatchery produces Chinook and collects steelhead eggs for later transport to the Hagerman and Magic Valley hatcheries. An observation deck is on the premises. Visitor center daily 8-5. Guided tours are available at 1:30 and 3, Memorial Day weekend-Labor Day. Free. Phone (208) 774-3684.

RECREATIONAL ACTIVITIES
Horseback Riding

- **Redfish Lake Corrals—Trail Rides,** Red Fish Lake, Stanley, ID 83278. Departures daily 9-3, Memorial Day-Labor Day. Phone (208) 774-3591 or (888) 722-5432.

- **Sawtooth Wilderness Pack Trips,** on SR 75 in the Sawtooth National Recreation Area. Write Mystic Saddle Ranch, Stanley, ID

83278. Trips depart daily May 15-Nov. 15. Phone (208) 774-3591 or (888) 722-5432.

White-water Rafting

- **Middle Fork River Expeditions**, on the Middle Fork River, P.O. Box 199, Stanley, ID 83278. Departures June-Sept. Phone (800) 801-5146. *See ad.*

- **The River Company**, .7 mi. w. on SR 21, P.O. Box 250, Stanley, ID 83278. Departures daily May-Oct. Phone (208) 788-5775 or (800) 398-0346.

- **Rocky Mountain River Tours**, on the Middle Fork of the Salmon River, P.O. Box 8596, Boise, ID 83707. Four- to 6-day trips depart June-Sept. Phone (208) 345-2400, or (208) 756-4808 in summer.

SUN VALLEY (E-3) pop. 900, elev. 5,926'

Sun Valley got its start in 1935 when Union Pacific Railroad Chairman Averell Harriman hired Austrian Count Felix Shaffgotsch to find the most scenic snow spot in the country for a huge ski resort. Passing up places that would become Aspen, Jackson Hole and Mount Hood, Shaffgotsch chose Sun Valley and soon stars from all across the country came to ski down Baldy Mountain and hobnob in the huge wooden lodge Harriman built. Gary Cooper and Clark Gable frequented; novelist Ernest Hemingway spent his last years in the area and a memorial to him stands alongside Trail Creek.

Today Sun Valley, along with the neighboring town of Ketchum *(see place listing p. 50),* offer heated outdoor pools, saunas and indoor and outdoor ice skating rinks. The list of local summer activities includes golf, tennis, swimming, white-water rafting, camping, bicycling, hiking, horseback riding, skeet shooting, trapshooting, fishing, mountaineering and kayaking.

Winter brings sleigh rides, snowmobiling and ice skating as well as downhill, cross-country and helicopter skiing. Saturday nights are reserved for hockey games in winter and professional ice shows in summer. Skiing begins on Thanksgiving.

Sun Valley-Ketchum Chamber of Commerce: 411 N. Main St., P.O. Box 2420, Sun Valley, ID 83353; phone (208) 726-3423 or (800) 634-3347. *See color ad.*

 RECREATIONAL ACTIVITIES

Skiing

- **Bald Mountain**, SR 75 to Third Ave., P.O. Box 10, Sun Valley Resort, Sun Valley, ID 83353. Daily 9-4, late Nov.-May 1. Phone (208) 622-2231 or (800) 635-4150.

- **Dollar Mountain**, adjacent to Sun Valley, P.O. Box 10, Sun Valley Resort, Sun Valley, ID

8335. Daily 9-4, late Nov.-May 1. Phone (208) 622-2231.

TARGHEE NATIONAL FOREST

Elevations in the forest range from 5,300 ft. at Warm River to 12,197 ft. at Diamond Peak. Refer to AAA maps for additional elevation information.

Targhee National Forest, in the Teton, Centennial, Palisades and Caribou ranges, was named for Tygee, a Bannock Indian Chief. The forest lies partially in Wyoming, but the majority of its 1.8 million acres is in Idaho; it extends in a semicircle around the headwaters of Henry's Fork of the Snake River. The Continental Divide forms most of the northern boundary; Yellowstone and Grand Teton national parks make up most of the eastern border. Canyons, high peaks and desert add to the picturesque scenery.

Water is abundant throughout the forest. Big Springs, one of the largest springs in the United States, is reached by SR 59 from US 20 at Macks Inn. It issues from the base of a high plateau at a constant 52 degrees F and is the headwaters of Henry's Fork.

A 3- to 5-hour canoe/float trip can be taken along a 5-mile national recreation water trail just below Big Springs. Moose, trumpeter swans, ospreys and bald eagles can often be seen. Further down Henry's Fork, boaters must portage around several sections of dangerous water between Macks Inn and Ashton.

Upper and Lower Mesa falls are east of US 20 and north of Ashton on Mesa Falls Scenic Byway. The Upper Mesa Falls is 114 feet high; the Lower Mesa Falls is 65 to 70 feet high.

Trout fishing is excellent throughout the forest: Palisades Reservoir, Henry's Lake, Island Park Reservoir, Henry's Fork and South Fork of the Snake River are noted spots. Winter sports areas near Ashton, Heise, Island Park and Driggs have snowmobiling, downhill and cross-country skiing. More than 1,100 miles of trails provide back-country experiences.

For more information contact the Forest Supervisor's Office, Targhee National Forest, 420 N. Bridge St., P.O. Box 208, St. Anthony, ID 83445-0208; phone (208) 624-3151. *See Recreation Chart and the AAA Northwestern CampBook.*

TWIN FALLS (F-3) pop. 27,600, elev. 3,745'

Twin Falls is in the center of 500,000 acres of prime farmland irrigated by the waters of the Snake River. Since the turn of the 20th century, the "Magic Valley" area has been known as one of the nation's more prolific crop producing regions. Twin Falls also is on the edge of the Snake River Canyon, which was gouged out some 30,000 years ago by the Great Bonneville Flood.

Five miles northeast, the white waters of the Snake River plunge more than 212 feet at Shoshone Falls, known as the "Niagara of the West." The best time to view the falls is late April through early June, since irrigation waters are retained upstream during the summer months.

Twin Falls Area Chamber of Commerce: 858 Blue Lakes Blvd. N., Twin Falls, ID 83301; phone (208) 733-3974 or (800) 255-8946.

⟨SAVE⟩ **THE HERRETT CENTER FOR ARTS & SCIENCE,** at 315 Falls Ave. on the College of Southern Idaho campus, contains pre-Columbian and other artifacts from Indian civilizations of the Western Hemisphere. Arranged in various themes, exhibits interpret Indian life and cultures. An art gallery and planetarium offer changing contemporary exhibits and shows.

Allow 30 minutes minimum. Museum open Tues. and Fri. 9 a.m.-9:30 p.m., Wed.-Thurs. 9:30-4:30, Sat. 1-9. Planetarium shows Tues. and Fri. at 7 p.m., Sat. at 2, 3:30 and 7. Hours may vary; phone ahead. Museum admission free.

Planetarium $5; over 60, $4; students with ID $3. Under 4 are not permitted in planetarium. MC, VI. Phone (208) 733-9554, ext. 2655.

PERRINE MEMORIAL BRIDGE, on the northern edge of town, spans the spectacular Snake River Gorge. This four-lane arch-span bridge is 1,500 feet long and rises 486 feet above the water. Pedestrian walkways along the bridge allow views of sheer cliffs, the Blue Lakes, waterfalls, a park and two golf courses along the river. A road descends to these areas from the bridge.

A mile east of the bridge is where daredevil Evel Knievel attempted to leap across the Snake River Canyon in 1974. The dirt ramp used to launch his rocket-powered vehicle remains. The Buzz Langdon Visitor Center next to the bridge provides information April through October. Bridge open year-round.

WALLACE (B-2) pop. 1,000, elev. 2,744'

The center of a great lead- and silver-mining region, Wallace is at the junction of four major canyons, three of which lead to important active mining districts. This region claims several of the world's largest and deepest silver mines; some of the mines founded in the late 1800s have 200 miles of tunnels.

Among the historic buildings still standing in town are the railroad depot with its original Chinese bricks; the Smokehouse Building, which was once the courthouse; and the Rossi Building with its Queen Anne-style turret.

Wallace Chamber of Commerce Visitor Center: P.O. Box 1167, Wallace, ID 83873; phone (208) 753-7151.

Self-guiding tours: Brochures describing driving and walking tours of the mining and historic districts are available at the Wallace District Mining Museum *(see attraction listing).*

NORTHERN PACIFIC DEPOT RAILROAD MUSEUM, at 219 Sixth St., occupies a restored station that was built in 1901 and operated until 1980. Exhibits include a re-creation of an early 1900s railroad depot and photographs and railway relics that focus on the railroading history of the Coeur d'Alene mining district.

Allow 30 minutes minimum. Daily 9-7, May-Sept.; Mon.- Fri. 9-5, in Apr. and Oct. (Pacific time); Oct.-Nov. hours vary; phone ahead Admission $2; over 60, $1.50; ages 6-16, $1; family rate $6. Phone (208) 752-0111.

SAVE **SIXTH STREET MELODRAMA** is at 212 Sixth St. in the 1899 Lux Building. Audience participation is encouraged each summer during a family-style melodrama that reflects the area's mining background. The play is followed by the Kelly's Alley Revue, during which visitors can enjoy old-fashioned music and humor. Plays and

musicals are also produced in February, April and November; call for schedule and rates.

Allow 2 hours minimum. Summer performances Tues.-Sat. at 8 p.m., early July-late Aug. (Pacific time). Admission $8; over 55, students and children $6; family rate $25. Phone (208) 752-8871, 786-8611, or 752-3081.

WALLACE DISTRICT MINING MUSEUM, 509 Bank St., displays local mining equipment, photographs and a model of a working mine. A 20-minute videotape depicts the life of early miners and the development of one of the richest silver mining districts in the world. Allow 1 hour minimum. Daily 8-8, June-Aug.; Mon.-Sat. 8-6, in May and Sept. Admission $1.50; over 54, $1. DS, MC, VI. Phone (208) 556-1592.

[SAVE] **Sierra Silver Mine Tour,** 420 Fifth St., allows visitors to witness mining in the silver-laden veins of the Coeur d'Alene district. Visitors are guided through a tunnel where they can view exhibits, equipment in operation and techniques used to mine silver ore. The 1.25-hour guided tours leave every 30 minutes aboard a San Francisco-style trolley to the mine entrance.

Allow 1 hour, 30 minutes minimum. Daily 9-6, July-Aug.; 9-4, May-June and Sept.-Oct.

(Pacific time). Fee $7.50; senior citizens and ages 4-16, $6.50; family rate $28. Under 4 are not permitted. MC, VI. Phone (208) 752-5151.

WEISER (E-2) pop. 4,600, elev. 2,114'

Named for Sgt. Peter Weiser (WEE-zer) of the Lewis and Clark expedition, Weiser is on the Idaho-Oregon border at the confluence of the Weiser and Snake rivers.

Scenic views of Hells Canyon are afforded from viewpoints north of Weiser; open only in summer, the viewpoints can be reached via US 95 and SR 71. Closer looks at the canyon are made possible by the float trips and jet boat tours that are available from Hells Canyon Dam. The minimum age for most float trips is 6 years; inquire about refund and weather policies.

Greater Weiser Chamber of Commerce: 8 E. Idaho St., Weiser, ID 83672; phone (208) 549-0452 or (800) 437-1280.

★YELLOWSTONE NATIONAL PARK—
see Wyoming p. 163.

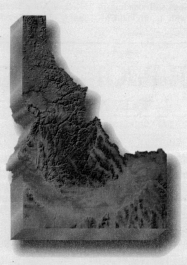

Montana

Big Sky Country

Vast plains of prairie grass merge with endless skies

Cowboys and Indians

Bucking horses and ceremonial dances are the focus at numerous rodeos and pow-wows

The Treasure State

Rugged mountains yield a wealth of gold and silver

Going-to-the-Sun Road

Stretching across the Continental Divide in Glacier National Park, this engineering marvel climbs 6,680 feet

Rocky Mountain High

Grassy-floored valleys give way to mountains flourishing with towering evergreens

picture this

Take a journey through Montana. Bring a camera, preferably with a wide lens, and lots of film.

Snapping here, there and everywhere, you'll have a choice of views that extend as far as your eye (or lens) can see. Copper-colored wheat fields dance with the wind, spotlighted by the sun; jagged peaks loom in the distance, bathed in evergreen; mesas serve as steps to heaven amid grassy prairies. And a royal blue sky has its own formations: clouds are stretched, feathered and puffed.

You can get a little closer, too. Zoom in on what remains of ghost towns and abandoned homesteads. Catch a candid shot of a tribe member in native dress, celebrating his heritage at a powwow. Use high-speed film to capture an actual cattle drive.

Focus on wildlife doing what they do best: living peacefully in an unspoiled habitat. More prevalent than people, grizzly bears, thousands of migrating elk, bighorn sheep, mountain goats, moose and bald eagles call Montana home.

The rolling hills, river valleys, deserts, peaks and plains in this state often sit for portraits. "A River Runs Through It," "The Horse Whisperer," "Far and Away" and "The River Wild" are just a sampling of the movies that have relied upon Montana for a backdrop.

Take home the beauty of Montana. You're sure to be back in a flash.

Sent by President Thomas Jefferson to look for a Northwest Passage joining the Mississippi and the Pacific, Meriwether Lewis and William Clark arrived in Montana in 1805. Through their struggles to reach their destination Lewis and Clark were able to study the terrain and its inhabitants as well as map the uncharted Western frontier. After a second harsh winter the expedition was divided into two groups with Clark heading down the Yellowstone River and Lewis sailing down the Missouri River.

The success of the Lewis and Clark expedition in exploring the territory between the Mississippi River and the Pacific Ocean brought an increased interest in fur trade to the region. The fur trade continued as the area's main draw until the discovery of gold. The gold rush that ensued with the strike at Gold Creek in 1858 sparked the interest of others hoping to prosper from the land.

Along with this prosperity came increased hostilities with the American Indians. In 1876, Lt. Col. George Armstrong Custer and his 7th Cavalry were annihilated by the Sioux and Cheyenne near the Little Bighorn River in Custer's Last Stand. Further aggressions occurred in 1877, when the U.S. government attacked the fleeing Nez Perce led by Chief Joseph as they fled to Canada in search of freedom. Although both sides experienced great losses, the 2-day battle at Big Hole culminated in a Nez Perce victory. Despite their triumph, the Nez Perce eventually were forced to surrender some 40 miles from the Canadian border.

Granted statehood in 1889, the Treasure State continued with its mining booms, first gold and then copper. Agriculture and ranching soon became part of the state's big picture with the arrival of the railroad in the late 1880s, bringing homesteaders ready to raise wheat and cattle. However, World War I, drought and local factors such as a weak banking structure destroyed those dreams for many. The homestead boom soon came to a crashing halt.

The 1920s gave way to new opportunities. Petroleum production and the inception of the automobile brought a new focus to Montanans. Bootlegging was another booming industry during this time. These new industries, combined with improved harvests and the rise in metal prices, brought new optimism to the region.

Meriwether Lewis and William Clark arrive in what is now the state of Montana.
1805

Lt. Col. George Armstrong Custer and troops are defeated by the Dakota and Cheyenne at the Battle of Little Big Horn
1876

Miners strike gold at Grasshopper Creek near Bannack followed by strikes at Diamond City and Virginia City.
1862

Montana Republican Jeanne Rankin becomes the first U.S. congresswoman and the only representative to vote against both world wars. **1916**

1864
Montana, part of the Idaho Territory, is granted territorial status with Bannack as the capital; it becomes the 41st state in 1889.

1880s
Copper magnate Marcus Daly purchases a depleted silver mine for its rich copper reserve; with the invention of the telephone, copper is in high demand and Daly becomes wealthy.

Historical Timeline

Times changed for Montanans with the implementation of a new constitution in 1972 that stressed environmental consciousness. Although the traditional industries—farming, mining and lumbering—suffered set-backs in the 1980s, the state is expanding its tourism industry and is focusing on technology. What the future holds for Montana's resilient natural beauty is unclear but as the people of this state have proven in the past, they certainly will rise to the challenge that awaits them.

Geography

Montana embraces two of the more dramatic natural features in the nation: the northern portion of the Rocky Mountains and the Great Plains. Grasslands cover the eastern three-fifths of Montana, part of the larger and semiarid Great Plains. Except for isolated mountain ranges and river banks, Montana's prairie rolls uninterrupted to the Rockies on the western horizon. Dramatic weather changes are common.

The great rock slabs of the northern Rockies' eastern slope run along a line stretching from Browning in the north, to the west of Great Falls, and to Montana's southern border near Livingston, Red Lodge and West Yellowstone. Areas left undisturbed by mountain building became high flat valleys that separate the ranges. Montana's dramatic mountain ranges are apparent especially in Glacier National Park and the northern section of Montana's Rockies.

Of the many rivers fed by the mountain snowpack, the Missouri and the Yellowstone are Montana's most important. Originating in Wyoming, the Yellowstone carves its way north through the southern mountains of Montana. As it passes east of Billings, it becomes a prairie river. The Missouri River originates in Three Forks, west of its junction with the Yellowstone. Unlike the Yellowstone, which remains much as Lewis and Clark first found it, the Missouri has been dammed in a number of places.

Montana's natural heritage still can be explored in the state's 10 national forests and 13 wilderness areas. Two national parks, Glacier National Park and portions of Yellowstone National Park, also are in Montana. Particularly special are Montana's rivers, which include designated Wild and Scenic Rivers like the Flathead, portions of the Missouri and the longest free-flowing river left in the lower 48 states, the Yellowstone.

Numerous forest fires sweep through drought-stricken Montana for nearly 3 months, wiping out trees and wildlife in Yellowstone National Park. **1988**

Leaders of the anti-government Montana Freeman are convicted on various charges by federal jurors as a result of their 81-day armed stand-off with FBI agents in 1996. **1998**

Launched in 1967, the Libby Dam hydroelectric project is finally completed. **1984**

1955 The Anaconda Aluminum Co. opens a $65 million plant in northwestern Montana.

1996 Suspected Unabomber Theodore Kaczynski, accused of constructing a series of mail bombs that killed three people, is arrested at his cabin near Lincoln; he is sentenced to life in prison in 1998.

1987 Originally started in Montana in 1956, the final sections of the nation's first interstate highway system are completed.

FAST FACTS

POPULATION: 878,800.

AREA: 147,138 square miles; ranks 4th.

CAPITAL: Helena.

HIGHEST POINT: 12,799 ft., Granite Peak.

LOWEST POINT: 1,862 ft., Kootenai River.

TIME ZONE: Mountain. DST.

MINIMUM AGE FOR DRIVERS: 16; with driver's training, 15.

SEAT BELT/CHILD RESTRAINT LAWS: Seat belts required for driver and all passengers; child restraints required for under 4 or under 40 pounds.

HELMETS FOR MOTORCYCLISTS: Required for under 18.

RADAR DETECTORS: Permitted.

FIREARMS LAWS: Vary by state and/or county. Contact the Montana Department of Justice, 301 S. Park, Drawer 10081, Helena, MT 59626; phone (406) 444-3625.

HOLIDAYS: Jan. 1; Martin Luther King Jr. Birthday (3rd Mon. in Jan.); Lincoln's Birthday, Feb. 12; Washington's Birthday, Feb. (3rd Mon.); Memorial Day, May (last Mon.); July 4; Labor Day, Sept. (1st Mon.); Columbus Day, Oct. (2nd Mon.); Veterans Day, Nov. 11; Election Day; Thanksgiving; Dec. 25.

TAXES: Montana does not have a statewide sales tax. Designated resort communities may enact a resort tax of up to 3 percent for goods and services. There is a 4 percent statewide Lodging Tax.

STATE INFORMATION CENTERS are on US 2 1 mile east of Culbertson; off I-94 in Wibaux; on I-90 southbound .5 miles east of Hardin; jct. US 191 and US 20N in West Yellowstone; and off I-15 southbound in Dillon. Travel information is available from Travel Montana at 1424 Ninth Ave. in Helena; phone (406) 444-2654, or (800) 847-4868 out of Mont. The Highway Building in Helena shares information about highway conditions and construction; phone (406) 444-6200.

Economy

That which can be mined, harvested or cut remains at the core of Montana's economy, a pattern that has endured since the first trappers and gold barons. Oil and gas fields are found in the Williston Basin and around Shelby and Sunburst. Enormous coal reserves lie roughly between the Bighorn and Powder rivers. Gold, copper and other minerals still are being mined and processed in western and southern Montana.

Despite its mineral wealth, Montana remains an agricultural state, second only to Texas in cultivated farmland. Cattle and sheep have supplanted the millions of buffalo that once thrived on the prairies, and although the prairies seem endless, forests carpet one fourth of Montana and support the state's lumber and wood products industry.

Such resources are only a part of Montana's economy; the second largest basic industry employer and fourth major source of income in the state is tourism, fostered by the beauty and legend of this wide, wide land.

Recreation

Its spacious beauty makes Montana a favorite vacation state. A major focus of activity is the region around Glacier National Park, Flathead Lake and Hungry Horse Reservoir. **Hiking** trails cover hundreds of miles throughout the park's magnificent alpine scenery; Flathead and Hungry Horse lakes offer **fishing, boating** and **swimming**.

Columbia Falls, Kalispell, Polson and Whitefish provide access to the park and lakes. A second recreational nucleus centers on West Yellowstone, Gardiner, Bozeman and Livingston, the major gateways to Yellowstone National Park. South of Billings and Hardin, Bighorn Canyon National Recreation Area surrounds the impoundment that reaches 70 miles from Yellowtail Dam into northern Wyoming.

Ten national forests cover a total of more than 16 million acres in Montana and abutting portions of Idaho. **Hunting,** fishing **camping** and **picnicking** are possible at many developed recreation sites within their boundaries. Also within the forests are more than 2 million acres of designated wilderness areas. **Backpacking,** hunting **trail riding, mountain climbing** and **rafting** are available but accessible only afoot on horseback or by aircraft.

The largest regions are the Anaconda-Pintler Wilderness, which includes part of Beaverhead-Deerlodge National Forest Area; the Bob Marshall Wilderness in the Flathead and Lewis and Clark national forests; and the Absaroka-Beartooth Wilderness in the Gallatin and Custer National Forests.

Backpacking and hiking trails that connect with alpine meadows and lakes are found in the Mission Mountain Wilderness south of Glacier National Park and the Jewel Basin Hiking Area between Kalispell and Hungry Horse Reservoir. Water sports, including fishing and guided white-water trips, abound on the Flathead Wild and Scenic Rivers—part of the nation's preserved river system. The Middle Fork and upper South Fork above Hungry Horse Dam are suited only to the experienced rafter.

Montana is one of the nation's great wildlife reserves. Bears, elk, deer, moose, bighorn sheep and mountain goats roam the mountains; deer and pronghorn antelopes inhabit the plains. Ruffed, blue, sharptailed and sage grouse are common gamebirds; ducks and geese breed near the thousands of lakes, ponds, rivers and marshes. Trout, bass and other species abound in the clear, cold streams and many lakes.

Winter sports of all types are available; good snow conditions usually prevail from mid-November to mid-April. A few better known areas for **snow skiing** are Big Sky, Big Mountain near Whitefish, Bridger Bowl at Bozeman, Red Lodge Mountain near Red Lodge and Snow Bowl near Missoula.

The units of the state park system encompass scenic and historical points as well as recreational facilities. There are overnight and day-use fees for most state parks and state recreation areas. Montana also has an extensive system of more than 300 fishing access sites, which also offer hiking, swimming and primitive camping. For more complete information about camping areas *see the AAA Northwestern CampBook.*

Throughout the TourBook, you may notice a Recreational Activities heading with bulleted listings of recreation-oriented establishments listed underneath. Since normal AAA inspection criteria cannot be applied, these establishments are presented only for information. Age, height and weight restrictions may apply. Reservations often are recommended and sometimes are required. Visitors should phone or write the attraction for additional information, and the address; phone numbers are provided for this purpose.

FOR YOUR INFORMATION

FURTHER INFORMATION FOR VISITORS:
Montana Travel Promotion Division
Department of Commerce
1424 9th Ave.
Helena, MT 59620
(406) 444-2654
(800) 847-4868 out of Mont.

FISHING AND HUNTING REGULATIONS:
Montana Dept. of Fish, Wildlife & Parks
1420 E. 6th Ave.
Helena, MT 59620
(406) 444-2535, or (406) 444-1200 (TDD)

NATIONAL FOREST INFORMATION:
U.S. Forest Service
Northern Region
Federal Bldg.
Missoula, MT 59801
(406) 329-3511
(800) 280-2267 (reservations)

DID YOU KNOW?

Montana is home to 11 American Indian tribes housed on 11 reservations.

"A River Runs Through It," "The Horse Whisperer" and "The River Wild" were filmed in Montana.

Montana borders the most Canadian provinces of all the 50 states—British Columbia, Alberta and Saskatchewan.

Three of Yellowstone National Park's five entrances are in Montana.

More gem sapphires are found in Montana than in any other state.

Glacier National Park is home to more than 50 glaciers.

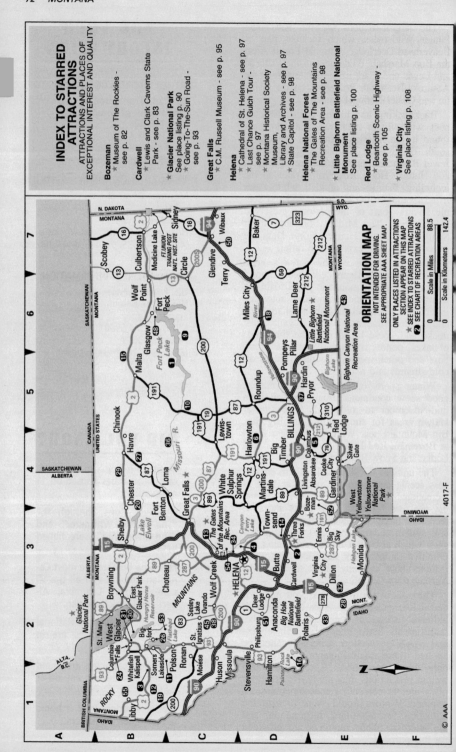

INDEX TO STARRED ATTRACTIONS

ATTRACTIONS AND PLACES OF EXCEPTIONAL INTEREST AND QUALITY

Bozeman
★ Museum of The Rockies - see p. 82

Cardwell
★ Lewis and Clark Caverns State Park - see p. 83

Glacier National Park
★ See place listing p. 90
★ Going-To-The-Sun Road - see p. 93

Great Falls
★ C.M. Russell Museum - see p. 95

Helena
★ Cathedral of St. Helena - see p. 97
★ Last Chance Gulch Tour - see p. 97
★ Montana Historical Society Museum, Library and Archives - see p. 97
★ State Capitol - see p. 98

Helena National Forest
★ The Gates of The Mountains Recreation Area - see p. 98

Little Bighorn Battlefield National Monument
See place listing p. 100

Red Lodge
★ Beartooth Scenic Highway - see p. 105

Virginia City
★ See place listing p. 108

ORIENTATION MAP

NOT INTENDED FOR DRIVING.
SEE APPROPRIATE AAA SHEET MAP.

ONLY PLACES LISTED IN ATTRACTIONS SECTION APPEAR ON THIS MAP
★ SEE INDEX TO STARRED ATTRACTIONS
② SEE CHART OF RECREATION AREAS

Scale in Miles   88.5

Scale in Kilometers   142.4

4017-F

© AAA

RECREATION AREAS	MAP LOCATION	CAMPING	PICNICKING	HIKING TRAILS	BOATING	BOAT RAMP	BOAT RENTAL	FISHING	SWIMMING	PETS ON LEASH	BICYCLE TRAILS	WINTER SPORTS	VISITOR CENTER	LODGE/CABINS	FOOD SERVICE
NATIONAL PARK *(See place listing p. 91)*															
Glacier (A-2) 1,000,000 acres. Horse rental.		•	•	•	•	•	•	•	•	•		•	•	•	•
NATIONAL RECREATION AREA *(See place listing p. 79)*															
Bighorn Canyon (E-5) 120,000 acres.		•	•	•	•	•		•	•	•			•		•
NATIONAL FORESTS *(See place listings)*															
Beaverhead-Deerlodge National Forest Area 3,392,930 acres. Southwestern Montana. Horse rental.		•	•	•	•	•		•	•	•		•		•	
Bitterroot 1,577,883 acres. Western Montana.		•	•	•	•			•	•	•		•	•	•	
Custer 1,112,382 acres. Southeastern Montana.		•	•	•	•	•		•	•	•		•			
Flathead 2,330,029 acres. Northwestern Montana. Horse rental.		•	•	•	•	•		•	•	•		•		•	
Gallatin 1,735,239 acres. South-central Montana. Horse rental.		•	•	•	•	•		•	•	•		•		•	
Helena 976,000 acres. West-central Montana.		•	•	•	•			•	•	•		•		•	
Kootenai 2,245,000 acres. Northwestern Montana. Horse rental.		•	•	•	•	•	•	•	•	•		•		•	
Lewis and Clark 1,843,397 acres. Central Montana.		•	•	•	•			•	•	•		•			
Lolo 2,100,000 acres. Western Montana. Horse rental.		•	•	•	•	•		•	•	•		•	•	•	•
ARMY CORPS OF ENGINEERS															
Fort Peck Lake (B-6) off SR 24 in Fort Peck. *(See Fort Peck p. 89)*	48														
Downstream 347 acres 1 mi. e. of Fort Peck off SR 117. Museum, playground.		•	•	•	•	•		•		•					
Dredge Cuts 650 acres .5 mi. n. of Fort Peck off SR 117. Playground.			•		•	•		•	•	•					
Nelson Creek 468 acres 45 mi. s. of Fort Peck off SR 24.		•	•		•	•		•		•					
The Pines 927 acres 4.5 mi. n.w. of Fort Peck on SR 24, 14 mi. s.w. via a gravel road, then 12 mi. s.e. via a gravel road. Playground.		•	•		•	•		•		•					
Rock Creek 345 acres 32 mi. s.e. of Fort Peck off SR 24.		•	•		•	•		•		•					
Fourchette Bay (C-5) 80 acres 60 mi. s. of Malta off SR 191.	1	•	•		•	•		•		•					
Libby Dam (Lake Koocanusa) (B-1) 46,000 acres 17 mi. n.e. of Libby on SR 37. *(See Libby p. 101)*	55	•	•	•	•	•		•	•	•			•	•	•
STATE															
Bannack (E-2) 196 acres 21 mi. w. of Dillon on SR 278, then 3 mi. s. Historic. *(See Dillon p. 87)*	33	•	•					•		•			•		
Beartooth (C-3) 27,000 acres 10 mi. s.e. of Wolf Creek via a gravel road.	13	•	•		•	•		•	•	•					
Black Sandy (C-3) 55 acres 14 mi. n.e. of Helena via I-15 and CR 415.	34	•			•	•		•	•	•				•	
Canyon Ferry Lake (D-3) e. of Helena.	4														
Canyon Ferry 5,000 acres s.e. of Helena off US 287 on Canyon Ferry Lake. Hunting.			•	•	•	•	•	•	•	•					•
Cave Bay 19 mi. e. of Helena via US 287 and CR 284.			•		•	•		•	•	•					•
Chinaman 19 mi. e. of Helena via US 287 and CR 284.		•	•		•	•		•	•	•					
Court Sheriff 18 mi. e. of Helena via US 287 and CR 284.		•	•		•			•	•	•					
Hellgate 27 mi. e. of Helena via US 287 and CR 284.		•	•		•	•		•	•	•					
Indian Road 1 mi. n. of Townsend on US 287.		•	•		•	•		•		•					
Ponderosa 18 mi. e. of Helena via US 287 and CR 284.		•	•		•			•	•	•					
Riverside 18 mi. e. of Helena via US 287 and CR 284.		•	•		•	•		•		•					
Silos 8 mi. n.w. of Townsend off US 287.		•	•		•	•		•		•					
White Earth 5 mi. e. of Winston.		•	•		•	•		•		•					
Cooney (E-4) 304 acres 5 mi. w. of Boyd via a gravel road.	5	•	•		•	•		•	•	•					•
Deadman's Basin (D-4) 500 acres 29 mi. e. of Harlowton off US 12.	6	•	•		•	•		•	•	•					
Flathead Lake (B-2) n. of Polson on SR 93. *(See Polson p. 105)*	26														

RECREATION AREAS

RECREATION AREAS	MAP LOCATION	CAMPING	PICNICKING	HIKING TRAILS	BOATING	BOAT RAMP	BOAT RENTAL	FISHING	SWIMMING	PETS ON LEASH	BICYCLE TRAILS	WINTER SPORTS	VISITOR CENTER	LODGE/CABINS	FOOD SERVICE
Big Arm 55 acres 15 mi. n. of Polson on US 93.		•	•		•	•	•	•	•	•					
Elmo 40 acres 19 mi. n. of Polson on US 93.		•	•		•	•	•	•	•	•					
Finley Point 24 acres about 12 mi. n.e. of Polson off SR 35.		•	•		•	•		•	•	•					
Wayfarers 68 acres 1 mi. s. of Bigfork off SR 35.		•	•		•	•		•	•	•					
West Shore 146 acres about 20 mi. s. of Kalispell on US 93.		•	•		•	•		•	•	•					
Yellow Bay 10 acres 20 mi. n.e. of Polson off SR 35.			•		•	•		•	•	•					
Hell Creek (C-6) 172 acres 26 mi. n. of Jordan via a gravel road on Fort Peck Reservoir.	9	•	•		•	•		•						•	•
Holter Lake (C-3) 22 acres 2 mi. e. of Wolf Creek on Missouri River Rd., then 3 mi. s. via a gravel road.	54	•	•		•	•		•	•	•				•	•
Lake Mary Ronan (B-2) 76 acres 7 mi. n.w. of Dayton off US 93.	11	•	•		•	•		•	•	•					
Lewis and Clark Caverns (D-3) 2,735 acres 7.3 mi. e. of Cardwell on I-90. *(See Cardwell p. 84)*	2	•	•	•				•		•			•		•
Logan (B-1) 18 acres 45 mi. w. of Kalispell off US 2.	12	•	•		•	•		•	•	•					
Makoshika (C-7) 8,123 acres 1 mi. s. of Glendive at 1301 Snyder Ave. *(See Glendive p. 95)*	50	•	•	•					•	•			•		
Missouri Headwaters (D-3) 527 acres 3 mi. e. of Three Forks, then 3 mi. n. of US 10. *(See Three Forks p. 109)*	14	•	•	•	•	•		•		•					
Painted Rocks (D-2) 263 acres 20 mi. s.w. of Conner off SR 473.	16	•	•		•	•		•							
Placid Lake (C-2) 32 acres 6 mi. s.w. of Seeley Lake via CR 83.	45	•	•		•	•		•	•	•					
Rosebud (D-6) 32 acres e. of Forsyth off I-94.	18	•	•					•	•						
Salmon (C-2) 42 acres 5 mi. s. of Seeley Lake on SR 83.	38	•	•	•	•	•		•	•						
Thompson Falls (B-1) 36 acres 3 mi. w. of Thompson Falls off SR 200.	19	•	•		•	•		•							
Tongue River Reservoir (E-6) 640 acres 6 mi. n. of Decker on CR 314, then 1 mi. e.	43	•	•		•	•		•	•	•					•
Whitefish Lake (B-1) 10 acres 5 mi. w. of Whitefish on US 93.	24	•	•		•	•		•	•	•					

OTHER

OTHER	MAP LOCATION	CAMPING	PICNICKING	HIKING TRAILS	BOATING	BOAT RAMP	BOAT RENTAL	FISHING	SWIMMING	PETS ON LEASH	BICYCLE TRAILS	WINTER SPORTS	VISITOR CENTER	LODGE/CABINS	FOOD SERVICE
Barretts Park (E-2) 38 acres 8 mi. s.w. of Dillon off I-15.	32	•	•		•			•	•	•					
Beaver Creek (B-4) 10,000 acres 11 mi. s. of Havre on SR 234. Birdwatching.	27	•	•	•				•	•	•		•			
Bitterroot Lake (B-1) 36 acres 5 mi. n. of US 2 at Marion.	3	•	•		•	•		•	•				•		
Clark Canyon Reservoir (E-2) 4,131 acres 20 mi. s.w. of Dillon on I-15. Hunting.	28	•	•		•	•	•	•	•	•					
Fresno Reservoir (B-4) 25,668 acres n.w. of Havre. Hunting, water skiing.	29		•		•	•		•							
Georgetown Lake (D-2) 2,850 acres 15 mi. w. of Anaconda on US 10A. Water skiing; playground. *(See Beavertown-Deerlodge National Forest p. 78)*	51	•	•		•	•	•	•	•	•				•	•
Hungry Horse Reservoir (B-2) 6,836 acres 10 mi. e. of Columbia Falls on SR 40, then s. 5 mi. via a gravel road. Hunting. *(See Flathead National Forest p. 88)*	30	•	•	•	•	•		•				•	•	•	
Hyalite Canyon (E-4) 35,000 acres 14 mi. s. of Bozeman on SR 85.	52	•	•	•	•	•		•		•		•	•		
James Kipp (C-5) 465 acres 65 mi. n.e. of Lewistown off US 191.	10	•	•		•	•		•							
Judith Landing (C-4) 44 mi. s.e. of Big Sandy on CR 236.	36	•			•	•		•							
Lake Blaine (B-2) 13 acres 7 mi. e. of Kalispell.	31	•		•	•	•		•	•	•				•	•
Lake Elwell (B-4) 6,197 acres 18 mi. s.w. of Chester.	20	•	•		•	•		•							•
Nelson Reservoir (B-5) 7,702 acres 18 mi. n.e. of Malta off US 2.	15	•	•		•	•		•							
Riverfront Park (D-5) 1 mi. s. of Billings on CR 416.	37		•	•	•			•					•	•	
Swan Lake (B-2) 10 acres 14 mi. s.e. of Bigfork on SR 83. Water skiing.	53	•	•		•	•		•	•	•					

STARRED ATTRACTIONS

Beartooth Scenic Highway—A series of scenic overlooks can be found along this 64-mile road that begins in Yellowstone National Park at 5,650 feet and rises to almost 11,000 feet at the Beartooth Plateau. See Red Lodge p. 106.

Cathedral of St. Helena—This neo-Gothic church is modeled after the Votive Church in Vienna, Austria. See Helena p. 98.

C.M. Russell Museum—Works of the cowboy artist are displayed here. See Great Falls p. 96.

The Gates of the Mountain Recreation Area—The Missouri River pushes through this area where 1,200-foot granite walls line the canyon. See Helena National Forest p. 99.

Glacier National Park—Some 1 million acres of woods, lakes, glaciers and mountains offer refuge to nearly every large mammal found within the country. See place listing p. 91.

Going-to-the-Sun Road—Crossing the Continental Divide, this road is one of the most scenic in the country. See Glacier National Park p. 93.

Last Chance Gulch Tour—A 1-hour automobile tour highlights Helena's past. See Helena p. 98.

Lewis and Clark Caverns State Park—This 3,005-acre park contains a limestone cavern featuring various rock formations. See Cardwell p. 84.

Little Bighorn Battlefield National Monument—This 1.2-square-acre monument commemorates the American Indian wars and features a national cemetery, visitor center, monuments, memorials and a museum. See place listing p. 101.

Montana Historical Society Museum, Library and Archives—This museum captures the essence of Montana with exhibits pertaining to area history. See Helena p. 98.

continued on p. 77

Points of Interest

ABSAROKEE (E-4) pop. 1,100, elev. 4,039'

RECREATIONAL ACTIVITIES
White-water Rafting

- **Absaroka River Adventures,** on SR 78. Write P.O. Box 328, Absarokee, MT 59001. Daily 7 a.m.-10 p.m., mid-May to late Aug. Other activities are offered. Phone (406) 328-4608 or (800) 334-7238.

- **Beartooth Whitewater** meets passengers off SR 78 s. at the south end of town. Write P.O. Box 781, Red Lodge, MT 59068. Daily May-Sept. Other activities are offered. Phone (406) 446-3142 or (800) 799-3142.

ANACONDA (D-2) pop. 10,300, elev. 5,288'

Because it had ample water and was surrounded by one of the world's richest copper deposits, Anaconda was chosen for the site of a copper smelter by the originator of Montana's copper industry, Marcus Daly. Daly, an Irish immigrant who was a manager of a mine in Utah, bought the mine when it was worthless after the silver lode ran out. However, Daly saw the mine's potential in its copper reserves—with the invention of the telephone and telegraph, copper wire was in high demand. By the time Daly died in 1900, he was one of the world's richest men. Today all that is left of Daly's smelter is the 585-foot smokestack. Daly also founded the nearby town of Hamilton *(see place listing p. 97)*, where he spent summers with his family.

A number of buildings from the 1800s remain, including the Montana Hotel, Park and Main streets, which was supposed to house the state legislators; Deer Lodge County Courthouse, 800 S. Main St.; City Hall Center at 401 E. Commercial St.; Hearst Library at Fourth and Main streets; and St. Mark's Episcopal Church, corner of Fifth and Main streets. Anaconda's architecture spans Romanesque to Victorian styles. At 305 Main St. is the art deco, neoclassical 1936 Washoe Theatre. The theater's interior is among stops of a 90-minute bus tour of the historic business district.

A popular scenic highway, SR 1, begins in Anaconda and heads west over Flint Creek Pass.

Anaconda Visitor's Center: 306 E. Park St., Anaconda, MT 59711; phone (406) 563-2400.

Self-guiding tours: The visitor's center offers a $2 walking-tour map of the historic district.

BAKER (D-7) pop. 1,800

Named for the superintendent of construction of the Milwaukee Road, Baker is near the middle of vast oil and gas fields. Until 1915 Baker was solely a grazing and farming town. Then a driller in search of water struck a natural-gas pocket, setting fire to his well, which burned as a natural torch for 6 years. Baker is now a center for both the local petroleum and agricultural interests.

Baker Chamber of Commerce: P.O. Box 849, Baker, MT 59313; phone (406) 778-3344.

MEDICINE ROCKS STATE PARK, 320 acres 24 mi. s. on SR 7, contains huge sandstone formations once used by American Indians for ceremonies. Free.

BEAVERHEAD-DEERLODGE NATIONAL FOREST

Elevations in the forest range from 4,075 ft. in the valleys to 11,361 ft. on Hilgard Peak. Refer to AAA maps for additional elevation information.

Beaverhead-Deerlodge National Forest is part of the huge complex of national forests occupying most of western Montana. In 1996, Deerlodge National Forest's 1,194,124 acres (nearly 100 square miles) were combined with Beaverhead National Forest to form a 3.3-million-acre outdoor recreation area.

Glaciated peaks rise from broad valleys in the area to form some of Montana's most majestic ranges—the Anaconda, Bitterroot, Beaverhead, Flint Creek, Gravelly, Highland, Madison, Tobacco Root and Sapphire. Mountains in these ranges are among the loftiest in the state; more than 40 surpass 10,000 feet. Mount Evans rises to 10,604 feet, and several more, including Hilgard Peak, exceed 11,000 feet.

From the snowpack of these ranges spring the Big Hole, Beaverhead and Ruby rivers, which form three major tributaries of the Missouri River. The high country also supplies some of the tributaries of the Madison River.

Through this maze of mountains and river valleys Sacajawea led Meriwether Lewis and William Clark in their search for a passage to the Pacific. This was the land of Sacajawea's people, the Shoshones, who reprovisioned and led the expedition over Lemhi Pass in 1805 and north to a final passage to the West. Despite the inroads of progress—lumbering, mining and ranching—

STARRED ATTRACTIONS

Museum of the Rockies—Dinosaurs and geology exhibits help explain Montana's past. See Bozeman p. 82.

State Capitol—Charles M. Russell's "Lewis and Clark Meeting Indians at Ross' Hole," is on display in this 1899 building made of Montana granite, copper and sandstone. See Helena p. 98.

Virginia City—This former mining town now features some 20 restored buildings as well as opportunities for fishing, hunting and gold panning. See place listing p. 109.

Yellowstone National Park—The more than 3,400 acres of America's first national park are home to buffaloes, bighorn sheep, elk, moose and pronghorn antelopes as well as thousands of thermal pools and springs. See place listing in Wyoming p. 163.

DID YOU KNOW?

Chocolate-covered huckleberries are a delicacy in Montana.

One of the richest deposits of gold was found Alder Gulch, now Virginia City, in 1863.

Gideon Bibles were first placed in hotel rooms in 1908 in the Superior Hotel in Superior.

The nation's largest intercontinental ballistic missile complex is headquartered in Great Falls.

much of the forest's lands have changed little since Lewis and Clark's visit.

The area's largest roadless tracts are portions of the Anaconda-Pintler, Lee Metcalf, Sapphire, Flint Range-Dolus Lakes and Middle Mountain-Tobacco Root wilderness areas. Typical features of the roadless areas are glacial lakes, trout streams and rugged mountain vistas.

The Anaconda-Pintler area straddles 30 miles of the Anaconda Range and the Continental Divide. The land gradually rises from dense stands of lodgepole pine to open parks dotted with lakes, culminating in jagged peaks in the heart of the range. Anglers prize the clear mountain streams and alpine lakes for their abundance and variety of trout.

Another major area is the Taylor-Hilgard portion of the Lee Metcalf Wilderness. This unit is one of the four portions of wilderness along the spine of the Madison Range, which lies just northwest of Yellowstone National Park. Soaring peaks, knife-edged ridges and alpine lakes are characteristics of this popular area. Birdwatchers will find more than 260 species frequenting a variety of habitats in the forest. The region provides winter range for bighorn sheep and mountain goats and a home to grizzly and black bears, mule deer, mountain lions, elk and moose.

Many endangered species reside in Beaverhead-Deerlodge National Forest. The bald eagle nests in the southeastern Gravelly Range and winters along the Red Rock, Ruby, Jefferson, Madison, Big Hole and Beaverhead rivers. Most migration and wintering activities occur in the large river valleys adjoining the forest. The endangered gray wolf is an occasional visitor to parts of the Continental Divide southwest of Dillon. Threatened grizzly bears occupy portions of the Madison Range within the Lee Metcalf Wilderness and are occasional visitors to the Tobacco Root Mountains and the Gravelly Range.

The forest offers fishing streams, hiking trails, groomed snowmobile trails, developed campgrounds and sites for motorized boating. Visitors can explore many old mines near Deer Lodge, plus the ghost town of Elkhorn, an 1880s mining town with a few corporeal residents. Fourteen miles west of Anaconda on SR 1 is Georgetown Lake, one of the area's busiest recreation sites and an area favored for its excellent fishing. Snowmobiling and cross-country and downhill skiing are available at Discovery Basin, north of Georgetown Lake.

The forest's most unusual feature is Sheepshead Recreation Area, a site designed for the physically impaired. In addition to meadows, forests and a 15-acre lake, the setting offers paved trails, a campground and a fishing pier.

Detailed information about campgrounds and recreational opportunities is available at the district ranger stations in Dillon, Ennis, Sheridan, Wisdom and Wise River. For further information contact the Beaverhead-Deerlodge National Forest Supervisor's Office, USDA Service Center, 420 Barrett St., Dillon, MT 59725; phone (406) 683-3900. *See Recreation Chart and the AAA Northwestern CampBook.*

BIGFORK (B-2) pop. 1,000, elev. 2,968'

On the bay formed by the Swan River on the northeastern shore of Flathead Lake, Bigfork once was a small fishing village and trade center for nearby orchards and farms. Its reputation as an artists' and writers' colony now make it a popular cultural retreat. Among recreational pursuits are snowmobiling and skiing in winter and a host of water sports in summer.

Glacially formed Flathead Lake is the largest natural body of fresh water west of the Mississippi River; at points along its 38-mile length the lake stretches 15 miles wide. Jewel Basin, one of the country's most popular hiking areas with 35 miles of trails, is 11 miles north. A Flathead National Forest *(see place listing p. 88)* ranger station provides information about recreational opportunities in the nearby mountains.

Cultural highlights in Bigfork include the Riverbend Concert Series which stages Sunday performances throughout the summer. From late June through Labor Day, Bigfork Summer Playhouse presents a regular repertory of Broadway musicals; phone (406) 837-4846 for ticket information.

Flathead Convention & Visitors Bureau: 15 Depot Park, Kalispell, MT 59911; phone (406) 756-9091 or (800) 543-3501

SAVE *QUESTA* SAIL BOAT, a 51-foot racing sloop on Flathead Lake, offers 2-hour tours. Tours depart daily at 10, 1, 4 and 7, mid-June to mid-Sept. Day fare $20; over 64 and under 12, $16. Sunset fare $27. A sister ship is available in case the *Questa* is filled. MC, VI. Phone (406) 837-5569.

BIG HOLE NATIONAL BATTLEFIELD (D-2)

Ten miles west of Wisdom on SR 43, Big Hole National Battlefield covers 655 acres of Nez Perce National Historical Park *(see place listing in Idaho p. 54).* It commemorates the battle fought Aug. 9-10, 1877, when U.S. troops aided by civilian volunteers staged a surprise attack against several bands of Nez Perce Indians. The Nez Perce were attempting to escape confinement to a reservation by fleeing to Canada from a conflict begun in Idaho. After eluding Gen. Oliver O. Howard for 2 months, the Nez Perce and their leader, Chief Joseph, camped in the Big Hole Valley where they were attacked while they slept.

Although victorious at Big Hole, the Nez Perce sustained severe losses during the less than 36-hour battle; between 60 and 90 men, woman and children were killed. These loses forced their surrender 2 months later on Oct. 5, 1877, in the Bear Paw Mountains. Some 150 Nez Perce escaped to Canada.

The battlefield became a military reserve in 1883 and a national battlefield in 1963. The visitor center displays American Indian and military items and presents an audiovisual program about the battle. An interpretive trail traverses the battlefield and passes the area where the Nez Perce camped.

Allow 30 minutes minimum for the visitor center and 1 hour, 30 minutes for the battlefield. Park open daily 8-6, late May-Labor Day; 9-5, rest of year. Closed Jan. 1, Thanksgiving and Dec. 25. Admission $2 per person, $4 per family, Memorial Day-Labor Day; free rest of year. Phone (406) 689-3155.

BIGHORN CANYON NATIONAL RECREATION AREA (E-5)

Covering about 120,000 acres in Montana and northern Wyoming, Bighorn Canyon National Recreation Area centers on a 71-mile-long lake bounded by steep canyon walls. Facilities for boat launching, picnicking and camping are available at Ok-A-Beh Marina at the northern end of the area, 42 miles southwest of Hardin via SR 313.

Horseshoe Bend in Wyoming, 17 miles north of Lovell, Wyo., via SR 37, and Barry's Landing in Montana, 32 miles south of Yellowtail Dam by boat or north of Lovell, Wyo., via SR 37, have areas for swimming, camping, picnicking and boat launching. Hunting and fishing also are available.

Campfire programs are given at Afterbay and Horseshoe Bend campgrounds on Friday and Saturday from Memorial Day through Labor Day. Guided nature and history walks also are conducted in summer.

Yellowtail Visitor Center in Fort Smith offers an orientation film about the area and exhibits about wildlife, Yellowtail Dam and American Indian culture; phone (406) 666-3234. The center is open daily 8-5, Apr.-Sept. The solar-energized Bighorn Canyon Visitor Center, at the junction of US 310 and US 14A in Lovell, Wyo., is open daily 8:15-5.

For further information, contact Bighorn Canyon National Recreation Area, P.O. Box 7458, Fort Smith, MT 59035; to verify schedule phone (406) 666-2412. *See Recreation Chart and the AAA Northwestern CampBook.*

YELLOWTAIL DAM, near Fort Smith, is said to be the highest dam in the Missouri River Basin. Yellowtail Dam Visitor Center has historical displays and information about the dam's construction. Guided tours are available. Allow 1 hour minimum. Daily 10-4, mid-May to mid-Sept. Free. Phone (406) 666-2443.

BIG SKY (E-3)

Surrounded by the mountain meadows and forested slopes of Gallatin National Forest *(see place listing p. 90)* and the Spanish Peaks Wilderness, Big Sky is an all-year resort community. Lone Mountain serves as the centerpiece for this village conceived and developed by newsman Chet Huntley.

Skiing and snowmobiling are popular in winter, while summer activity revolves around hiking, horseback riding and mountain biking.

MOUNTAIN TAXI TOURS picks up passengers in the Bozeman, Big Sky and West Yellowstone areas. Narrated van and bus tours of Yellowstone National Park are offered. The Lower Loop Tour includes the Fountain Paintpots, Midway Geyser Basin, Old Faithful, Yellowstone Lake and Mud Volcano. The Upper Loop Tour visits the northern portion of the park and includes Norris Geyser Basin, Mammoth Hot Springs and waterfalls of the Grand Canyon of the Yellowstone.

Tour pickups occur daily 6:35 a.m.-9:15 a.m., with returns 5:30-7:30, June 1-Labor Day. Lower Loop Tours are given Sun.-Mon., Wed. and Fri.; Upper Loop Tours are given Tues., Thurs. and Sat. Fare (depending on pickup point) $48-$68; over 59 and under 12, $40-$60. Tours require at least four or five passengers. Inquire about refund policies. AE, DS, MC, VI. Phone (406) 995-4895 or (800) 423-4742.

 RECREATIONAL ACTIVITIES

Skiing

- **Big Sky Ski and Summer Resort**, at Lone Mountain. Write P.O. Box 160001, Big Sky, MT 59716. Other activities are offered. Daily mid-June to mid-Sept. and mid-Nov. to late Apr. Phone (406) 995-5000.

White-water Rafting

- **Geyser Whitewater Expeditions**, 1 mi. s. on US 191. Write 47200 Gallatin Rd., Gallatin Gateway, MT 59730. Daily May 1 to mid-Sept. Phone (406) 995-4989 or (800) 914-9031.

- **Yellowstone Raft Co./Mountain Whitewater**, 7 mi. n. on US 191. Write P.O. Box 160262, Big Sky, MT 59716. Daily Memorial Day weekend-Labor Day. Phone (406) 995-4613 or (800) 348-4376.

BIG TIMBER (D-4) pop. 1,600, elev. 4,075'

BIG TIMBER WATERSLIDE, 9 mi. e. off I-90 exit 377, has seven large waterslides, an Olympic-size pool, wading pools and a moat featuring a lazy river ride. Picnic facilities and food are available. Daily 10-7, early June-Labor Day.

Admission $12.95; ages 3-6, $8.50. Phone (406) 932-6570.

BILLINGS (D-5) pop. 81,200, elev. 3,124′

In 1823 at Alkali Creek, the site of present-day Billings, 29 trappers of the American Fur Co. were attacked by 400 Blackfeet. Some pelts taken by the Blackfeet were traded to Hudson's Bay Co. and later appeared on the London market. An American recognized the stolen pelts, touching off an international incident.

The Northern Pacific Railroad arrived in 1882, literally putting Billings on the map. Refusing to pay the exorbitant prices the landowners in Coulson were demanding, Northern Pacific Railroad laid out a new city 2 miles upriver and named it in honor of its president, Frederick Billings. In 5 months the town grew from a single building to 250 buildings and 2,000 citizens.

The Rimrocks, Billings' most striking natural feature, rise 400 feet above the Yellowstone Valley, running the length of the city and beyond. Legend has it that Crow warriors once rode over Sacrifice Cliff to appease their gods and to halt the spread of smallpox among their people. At the top of the Rimrocks on Black Otter Trail is Boothill Cemetery. The only vestige of the town of Coulson, the cemetery is the final resting place of two dozen individuals, including peace officers, massacre victims and Muggins Taylor, the scout who brought the world the news of Lt. Col. George Custer's last stand.

Pictograph Cave State Park, 7 miles southeast at the I-90 Lockwood exit, features caverns that have sheltered people of many American Indian cultures. Pictorial records adorn the walls of one cave.

Billings Area Chamber of Commerce and Visitor Center: 815 S. 27th St., P.O. Box 31177, Billings, MT 59107-1177; phone (406) 252-4016 or (800) 735-2635.

Self-guiding tours: A map of historic sites can be obtained at the chamber of commerce.

Shopping areas: Rimrock Mall, at the junction of Central Avenue and 24th Street West, includes Hennessy's and JCPenney among its 95 stores.

CHIEF BLACK OTTER TRAIL is a scenic drive that follows the edge of the Rimrocks north of the city. Chief Black Otter was a Crow war chief who was killed in a battle with the Sioux. His grave and that of Yellowstone Kelly, renowned American Indian scout, trapper and governor of the Philippines, are two points of interest along the drive.

Range Rider of the Yellowstone stands on the Rimrocks off the Chief Black Otter Trail. Cowboy motion picture star William S. Hart posed for the bronze statue of a cowboy and his horse, which commands an impressive view of the city.

MOSS MANSION, 914 Division St., is an Old World house designed by architect H.J. Harden-bergh. The massive red sandstone mansion, completed in 1903, has ornate ceilings, woodwork molding and other architectural details. The Moss family, which occupied the house until 1984, left the interior intact, including the original furniture, carpet, wallpaper and light fixtures. Thus the three-story mansion is an unusually complete example of early 20th-century decorative arts.

Guided tours are given on the hour Mon.-Sat. 10-4, Sun. 1-3, June 1-Labor Day; Mon.-Fri. 1-3, Sat. 10-4, Sun. 1-4, fourth week in Nov.-Dec. 30 daily 1-3, rest of year. Last tour at closing. Closed Jan. 1, third week in Nov., Thanksgiving and Dec. 25. Fee $6; over 61, $5; ages 6-12, $3. Phone (406) 256-5100 to confirm schedule.

PETER YEGEN JR. YELLOWSTONE COUNTY MUSEUM, 1950 Terminal Circle across from Billings Logan International Airport, depicts frontier life through dioramas and American Indian, pioneer and cowboy items. Exhibits include a chuck wagon, dinosaur bones, Western military weaponry, jewelry, clothing, a steam locomotive, American Indian artifacts, art works, a sheep wagon and a reconstructed cabin. Allow 30 minutes minimum. Mon.-Fri. 10:30-5, Sat. 10:30-3, closed holidays. Donations. Phone (406) 256-6811.

WESTERN HERITAGE CENTER, 2822 Montana Ave., is housed in the original 1901 Parmly Billings Library. The center features changing exhibits about the history and culture of the Yellowstone River region. Audiovisual programs are presented regularly. Allow 1 hour minimum. Tues.-Sat. 10-6, Sun. 1-5, June-Aug.; Tues.-Sat. 10-6, rest of year. Closed holidays. Donations. Phone (406) 256-6809.

YELLOWSTONE ART MUSEUM, 401 N. 27th St. is housed in the original Yellowstone County jail. The museum features changing exhibitions of historic and contemporary art. A permanent exhibit features contemporary Western art. Historic works by cowboy illustrator Will James also are presented. Guided tours are available. Allow 30 minutes minimum. Tues.-Sat. 10-5 (also Thurs. 5-8), Sun. noon-5. Admission $3; senior citizens and students with ID $2; ages 6-18, $1. Phone (406) 256-6804.

ZOOMONTANA, I-90 exit King Ave. W., 3 mi. w., then 1.5 mi. s. to 2100 S. Shiloh Rd., is a 72-acre home to northern latitude temperate animals. Highlights include river otters, Sika deer, Siberian tigers, grey wolves, bighorn sheep, black-footed ferrets and bald eagles. Also featured are a sensory garden, a Native American encampment, education center with exhibits and an amphitheater. A picnic area, food and a playground are available. Allow 2 hours minimum. Daily 10-5, Apr. 15-Oct. 15; 10-4, rest of year. Closed Dec. 25. Admission $5; over 64, $3; ages 3-15, $2. AE, MC, VI. Phone (406) 652-8100.

BITTERROOT NATIONAL FOREST

Elevations in the forest range
from 3,500 ft. at the Kootenai
Creek Trail to 10,175 ft. on Trapper
Peak. Refer to AAA maps for
additional elevation information.

Covering some 1.6 million acres in Montana and Idaho, Bitterroot National Forest has its headquarters in Hamilton. The Montana section curves around the headwaters of the Bitterroot River, reaching into the Sapphire and Bitterroot ranges. This is a region of strong contrasts, with rolling subalpine woodland, open parks and lakes and jagged, glaciated peaks and canyons.

The national forest takes its name from the bitterroot plant, whose pink flowers carpet the valleys and foothills from late April to July. Meriwether Lewis, on his journey through the region, added the bitterroot flower to his botanical collection and sampled the meal that the American Indians ground from its root. A British botanist later honored Lewis' contribution by using his name as the basis of the flower's Latin name, *Lewisia rediviva*.

As one of the first forest reserves, Bitterroot National Forest also is the site of the first Forest Service ranger station, at Alta. The forest's Idaho portion encompasses the headwaters of the Selway River and a stretch of the Salmon River. Both rivers are components of the National Wild and Scenic River system. Wilderness areas, which occupy about half of the forest's acreage, include portions of the Frank Church River of No Return, the Selway-Bitterroot and the Anaconda-Pintler.

For further information contact the Forest Supervisor, Bitterroot National Forest, 1801 N. 1st St., Hamilton, MT 59840; phone (406) 363-7161. *See Recreation Chart and the AAA Northwestern CampBook.*

BOZEMAN (D-4) pop. 22,700, elev. 4,755'

Bozeman was named for John Bozeman, who brought the first wagon train of pioneers to settle the Gallatin Valley. The trail he blazed became not only a highway for settlers and miners but also a flashpoint between the American Indians and the settlers. Three years after bringing settlers to the valley, Bozeman was killed by the Sioux, and his trail remained unused for 9 years because of repeated attacks upon wayfarers.

The valley that Bozeman helped settle once was a neutral and sacred hunting ground known to the American Indians as the "Valley of the

Flowers." The area has blossomed into one of the state's more agriculturally productive regions.

The city is a gateway to the nearby mountains in the national forests that flank the city and to Yellowstone National Park to the southeast.

One of the city's chief cultural resources is Montana State University, the largest unit of the state university system.

Bozeman Area Chamber of Commerce: 1205 E. Main, Box B, Bozeman, MT 59715; phone (406) 586-5421 or (800) 228-4224.

Self-guiding tours: Maps and brochures of the South Willson Historic District are available from Museum of the Rockies *(see attraction listing).*

AMERICAN COMPUTER MUSEUM, 234 E. Babcock St., chronicles the evolution of the computer from abacus to microchips. Guided tours are available. Allow 30 minutes minimum. Daily 10-4, June-Aug.; Tues.-Wed. and Fri.-Sat. noon-4, rest of year. Closed holidays. Admission $3; ages 6-12, $2. Phone (406) 587-7545. *See color ad p. 81.*

GALLATIN COUNTY PIONEER MUSEUM, 317 W. Main St. in a 1911 county jail, contains exhibits of early settlement and 20th-century history, old photographs and American Indian artifacts. Mon.-Fri. 10-4:30, Sat. 1-4, June-Sept.; Tues.-Fri. 11-4, rest of year. Free. Phone (406) 582-3195.

[SAVE] ★ **MUSEUM OF THE ROCKIES** is s. of the Montana State University campus at S. 7th Ave. and Kagy Blvd., opposite the football stadium. The museum interprets the history of the northern Rockies through dinosaur exhibits and displays pertaining to American Indians and pioneers, as well as traveling exhibits. Other exhibits put time into context, explain geological concepts and detail the evolution of humans.

Montana's past is outlined in Paugh History Hall, which includes a furnished 1930s house and gas station. Varied means of transportation, including a stagecoach, sleigh, fire wagon and vintage automobiles, are displayed. Two galleries house changing exhibitions.

A 40-foot domed planetarium uses computer graphics in its changing programs. A mural on the planetarium's curved walls represents the evolution of the universe. Laser shows are offered during the school year.

Food is available. Daily 8-8, Memorial Day weekend-Labor Day; Mon.-Sat. 9-5, Sun. 12:30-5, rest of year. Planetarium shows are given daily at 11, 1, 2, 3, 4 and 7 (also Fri.-Sat. at 8), Memorial Day weekend-Labor Day; Mon.-Fri. at 1 and 3 (also Fri. at 7 and 8), Sat.-Sun. on the hour 1-4 (also Sat. at 11), rest of year. Closed Jan. 1, Thanksgiving and Dec. 25. Museum $6; ages 5-18, $4. Laser show $4. Planetarium $2.50. Phone (406) 994-3466 or 994-2251.

RECREATIONAL ACTIVITIES

White-water Rafting

• **Montana Whitewater Inc.** departs from offices 2 mi. n. of Gallatin Gateway. Write P.O. Box 1552, Bozeman, MT 59771. Daily Memorial Day weekend-Labor Day. Phone (406) 763-4465 or (800) 799-4465. *See color ad.*

BROWNING (B-2) pop. 1,200, elev. 4,366'

Founded in 1895, Browning is the hub of the Blackfeet Nation and a center for reservation activities. It also is the site of the Blackfeet Tribal Headquarters, which includes a nine-member business council, the governing board of the Blackfeet Tribe. Fifteen miles east on the reservation, a monument marks the northernmost point reached by the Lewis and Clark expedition on July 23, 1806. About 10,000 American Indians live on the Blackfeet Indian Reservation, which covers 1.5 million acres.

MUSEUM OF THE PLAINS INDIAN, jct. US 2 and US 89, exhibits murals, dioramas, historical and contemporary American Indian arts as well as artifacts of the Northern Plains region. An audiovisual presentation and changing exhibits

e offered. Allow 1 hour minimum. Daily 9-5,
ine-Sept.; Mon.-Fri. 10-4:30, rest of year.
losed Jan. 1, Thanksgiving and Dec. 25. Ad-
ission June-Sept. $4; ages 6-12, $1. Phone
·06) 338-2230.

**CRIVER'S MUSEUM OF MONTANA WILDLIFE
ND HALL OF BRONZE,** jct. US 2 and US 89,
isplays dioramas, models and mounted animals
itive to the region. The museum also has an art
allery, studio, foundry and workshop. Allow 30
inutes minimum. Daily 8-5, June 1 until first
iowfall. Admission $5; ages 13-18, $2.50; un-
er 13, $1. Phone (406) 338-5425.

BUTTE (D-3) pop. 33,300, elev. 5,716'

Silver Bow Creek's gold and silver first
rought the mineral wealth of remote Butte to
ie attention of the world. But it was copper that
iade Butte's reputation as "the richest hill on
arth," producing almost 11 billion pounds of
ie metal. Copper kings fought for control of
utte's wealth. Marcus Daly's Anaconda Co.
ventually gained ownership of every mine in
iutte and became the dominant power in
Iontana.

By 1955 the high-grade copper ore was almost
layed out, and excavation began on Berkeley
)pen Pit Mine to extract low-grade ore. The
iine was one of the larger truck-operated pit
iines in the world. The Berkeley Pit Viewing
tand, open daily dawn to dusk, March to mid-
Jovember, is free and provides an excellent view
f the old open mine. As a transportation hub,
ie city has become one of the nation's larger in-
ind ports, with containerized cargo from the
)rient being cleared and routed to points
iroughout the Midwest.

The Anselmo Mine Yard, uptown at Caledonia
ind Excelsior streets, is a fine example of sur-
ace support facilities that once served the min-
rs. An interpretive center and tours are offered
uring the summer. The Granite Mountain Mine
Memorial, 1308 N. Main St., is dedicated to the
68 men who died in a 1917 mine disaster.

Butte is surrounded by Beaverhead-Deerlodge
Jational Forest *(see place listing p. 77),* which
·ffers varied recreational opportunities. Sheeps-
.ead Recreation Area, about 10 miles north via
-15, was designed for the physically impaired.
/isitors can experience the beauty of the nearby
ugged mountains, verdant forests and meadows
y driving either north to Helena or south to
Ionida on I-15.

**Butte-Silver Bow Chamber of Commerce and
Visitor Center:** 1000 George St., Butte, MT
9701; phone (406) 723-3177 or (800) 735-6814.

Self-guiding tours: Brochures detailing two
valking tours of the historic district are available
t the chamber of commerce.

ARTS CHATEAU, 321 W. Broadway, was
uilt as a home by Charles W. Clark in 1898.

Modeled after a French chateau, the building
shows the works of Montana artists in exhibits
that change monthly. Allow 1 hour minimum.
Tues.-Sat. 10-5, Sun. noon-5, Memorial Day-
Labor Day; hours vary rest of year. Admission
$3.75; over 49, $3; under 16, $1.25. Phone (406)
723-7600.

COPPER KING MANSION, 219 W. Granite St.,
was the residence of W.A. Clark, a U.S. senator
and "copper king." The 32-room Victorian
house, now a national historic landmark and bed
and breakfast, was built 1884-88 and has been
restored and furnished in period. The mansion is
a showcase for numerous collections. Allow 1
hour minimum. Guided tours are given daily 9-4,
May-Sept.; Sat.-Sun. 9-4 in Apr. and Oct.; by appointment rest of year. Last tour is given at closing. Admission $5; under 15, $3.50. Phone (406)
782-7580.

MINERAL MUSEUM, 1 mi. w. of Montana St. on
Park St., is in the Museum Building of Montana
Tech. The museum exhibits more than 1,500
specimens, including fluorescent minerals, a gold
nugget considered to be the largest in Montana
and a 400-pound quartz crystal found near Butte.
Other features are a geological relief map and an
earthquake studies laboratory. Daily 8-5, Memorial Day-Labor Day; Mon.-Fri. 8-5, Sun. 1-5, rest
of year. Free. Phone (406) 496-4414.

OLD NO. 1 departs from the chamber of commerce; take I-90 exit 126 to 1000 George St.
This replica of an early open streetcar carries
passengers on a 90-minute tour of the city. Sights
include the historic district, Victorian neighbor-
hoods and Berkeley Pit. Tours depart daily
(weather permitting) at 10:30, 1:30, 3:30 and 7,
June-Aug.; at 10:30-1:30 in Sept. Fare $5; ages
4-12, $2.50. Reservations are required. Phone
(406) 723-3177 or (800) 735-6814.

OUR LADY OF THE ROCKIES is e. atop the
Continental Divide; tours to the site depart from
Plaza Mall, 3100 Harrison Ave. The 90-foot-high
statue of the Virgin Mary—a nondenominational
tribute to motherhood—took 6 years to build and
was airlifted into place in 1985. Visitors may
step inside the metal structure. The road to the
statue is not open to public traffic. An observatory is available. Two-hour bus tours depart
Mon.-Sat. 10-2, Sun. 11-2, June-Sept. Fare $10;
over 54 and ages 13-17, $9; ages 5-12, $5. DS,
MC, VI. Phone (406) 782-1221 or (800)
800-5239.

**WORLD MUSEUM OF MINING & 1899 MINING
CAMP** is on Park St. at the site of the original
Orphan Girl mine, .2 mi. w. of Montana Tech.
The Garrett-Pegasus Gold Mineral Exhibit features a black-light room. The hoist house contains mining memorabilia and photographs.
Structure in the mining camp house old dental
tools, vintage gowns and a marble ice cream
counter. A walk-through mining display details

the processes and equipment involved in underground mining.

Allow 2 hours minimum. Daily 9-6, Apr.-Oct.; otherwise varies. Admission $4, under 12 free. Phone (406) 723-7211. *See color ad.*

CARDWELL (D-3) elev. 4,271'

★ LEWIS AND CLARK CAVERNS STATE PARK, 7.3 mi. e. on I-90, affords fine views. The 3,005-acre park includes a limestone cavern of vaulted chambers, intricate passageways and delicate, varicolored formations that make this one of the most beautiful caverns in the country. Camping facilities are available.

Cavern daily 9-6:30, June 15-Labor Day; 9-4:30, May 1-June 14 and day after Labor Day-Sept. 30. Park open daily dawn-dusk, May-Sept. Two-hour guided cavern tour $7; ages 6-11, $3. Park fee $3 per private motorized vehicle or 50c per person arriving by bicycle, bus or on foot; camping fee $6. Rubber-soled shoes are advised. Because the cavern temperature remains around 50 degrees, a jacket is recommended. Phone (406) 287-3541. *See Recreation Chart and the AAA Northwestern CampBook.*

CHESTER (B-4) pop. 900

LIBERTY COUNTY MUSEUM, 210 2nd St. E. in a former Methodist church, contains artifacts,

photographs and other items depicting the homestead days on the High Plains. Allow 30 minut minimum. Daily 2-5 and 7-9, Memorial Day mid-Sept. Free. Phone (406) 759-5256.

CHINOOK (B-5) pop. 1,500, elev. 2,405'

Chinook was named after the American Indi word for the winds that often whip through th area during January and February, causing t temperature to rise as much as 70 degrees in few hours. Melting the snow and exposing t grass, chinooks have saved many cattle her from disaster. Charles Russell captured the si nificance of these winds to the range cattlem in his picture of a starving cow titled "Waiti for a Chinook."

Chinook Chamber of Commerce: P.O. B 744, Chinook, MT 59523; phone (40 357-2100.

BEAR PAW BATTLEFIELD-NEZ PERCE N. TIONAL HISTORICAL PARK, 16 mi. s. off US is the site where Chief Joseph, leader of the N Perce Indians, surrendered to Col. Nelson Miles on Oct. 5, 1877. Picnic facilities and a 1. mile walking trail are at the site. Blaine Coun Museum *(see attraction listing),* 16 miles nor in Chinook, serves as a visitor center. Daily 2 hours, May-Sept. Free. Phone (406) 357-3130, 357-2590 for the museum.

BLAINE COUNTY MUSEUM, 4 blks. s. of US at 501 Indiana St., contains fossil exhibi American Indian and pioneer artifacts and r creations of an early dentist's office, a schoo room, a church altar and a doctor's office. Th museum also offers an audiovisual recount of t Battle of Bear Paw as well as information ar presentations about Bear Paw Battlefield-N Perce National Historical Park *(see attractic listing).* Allow 1 hour minimum. Mon.-Sa 8-noon and 1-5, Sun. noon-5, Memorial Da weekend-Labor Day weekend; Mon.-Fri. 1-5, re of year. Free. Phone (406) 357-2590.

CHOTEAU (B-3) pop. 1,700, elev. 4,000'

Choteau (SHO-toe) was named after Frenc fur trader Pierre Chouteau; the name is spelle with one "u" to distinguish it from the adjoinin county, also named after the Frenchman.

Choteau Chamber of Commerce: P.O. Bc 897, Choteau, MT 59422; phone (406) 466-53 or (800) 823-3866.

OLD TRAIL MUSEUM, 823 N. Main Ave., is local history and paleontology museum set in Western village. Exhibits chronicle the history the Rocky Mountain Front beginning with the d nosaur era. Hands-on paleontology classes f families and dinosaur enthusiasts are available. Daily 9-6, mid-May to mid-Sept.; Tues.-Sat. 10-3, rest of year. Admission $2; under 18, 50c. Reservations are required for classes. Phone (406) 466-5332.

CIRCLE (C-7) pop. 800, elev. 2,424'

Circle takes its name from a cattle ranch that once stood on this site. In the late 19th century the area around Circle was booming cattle country, but the devastation caused by the winter of 1886-87 put many ranchers out of business. Circle remains an agricultural community and the seat of McCone County.

Circle Chamber of Commerce: P.O. Box 321, Circle, MT 59215; phone (406) 485-2414.

McCONE COUNTY MUSEUM, 801 SR 200 S., contains a large collection of mounted birds and animals as well as artifacts, farm machinery, tools and guns from the homestead era. Allow 1 hour minimum. Mon.-Fri. 8-5, Sat.-Sun. only by appointment, May-Sept. Admission $2, under 12 free. Phone (406) 485-2414.

COLUMBIA FALLS (B-2) pop. 2,900, elev. 3,098'

The union of the North and Middle forks of the Flathead River has carved out Bad Rock Canyon, at the entrance of which lies Columbia Falls. The abundance of water and timber in the area supports Columbia Falls Aluminum Co. and Plum Creek Timber Co., the town's major industries. Glacier National Park's western entrance, Hungry Horse Dam *(see Hungry Horse p. 99)* and the Great Bear and Bob Marshall wilderness areas also are nearby.

Flathead Convention & Visitor Bureau: 15 Depot Park, Kalispell, MT 59911; phone (406) 756-9091 or (800) 543-3105.

BIG SKY WATERSLIDE, 2 blks. w. of jct. US 2 and SR 206, has a game arcade, miniature golf course, water-wars game, tube and other waterslides and picnic and recreational facilities. Allow 2 hours minimum. Daily 10-8, Memorial Day weekend-Labor Day weekend. Admission, including waterslides, $11.95; over 59 and ages 4-11, $9.95. After 4 p.m., including waterslides, $8; over 59 and ages 4-11, $6.50. Miniature golf $4.75; over 59 and ages 4-11, $3.75. Admission (only park) $5; over 59, $4. After 4 p.m. (only park) $4. Phone (406) 892-2139.

COLUMBUS (D-4) pop. 1,600, elev. 3,600'

In 1875 travelers stopped at Countryman stage station on the north bank of the Yellowstone River. The hardy travelers referred to the settlement as Eagle's Nest, or as Sheep Dip, because of its vile whiskey. With the coming of the Northern Pacific Railroad in 1882 the town became a livestock and agricultural center. Initially called Stillwater by the railroad because it lay at the confluence of the Stillwater and Yellowstone rivers, it was renamed Columbus in 1893 to avoid confusion with Stillwater, Minn.

Today the town's economy still rests upon cattle, sheep and small grains but also incorporates Montana's largest platinum mine as well as manufacturers of laminated structural wood, Western-style jewelry and saddle trim.

MUSEUM OF THE BEARTOOTHS is off I-90 exit 408, w. on 4th Ave., then n. on 5th St. to the corner of 5th Ave. and 5th St. Displays illustrate the history of Stillwater County. Items include a caboose, spring wagons and halters, vintage pharmaceuticals and washing machines. The museum also pays tribute to a local Congressional Medal of Honor winner, Donald J. Ruhl, in whose name SR 78 was designated a Memorial Highway. An additional building on the grounds displays outdoor machinery. Allow 30 minutes minimum. Tues.-Sun. 1-5, June-Sept. Donations. Phone (406) 322-4588.

COOKE CITY (E-4) elev. 7,675'

Gold miners settled Cooke City in the early 1870s, and by 1880 the town numbered 7,000 fortune-seeking souls. Gold mining continued until the late 1950s when commercial mining finally ceased. Gold-panning in area streams remains popular.

Cooke City is 4 miles from Yellowstone National Park's northeast gate. Beartooth Scenic Highway *(see Red Lodge p. 106)*, the town's eastern access, usually is open May through September. Cooke City can be reached all year via the road from Gardiner through Yellowstone.

Cooke City Area Chamber of Commerce: P.O. Box 1071, Cooke City, MT 59020; phone (406) 838-2495.

YELLOWSTONE WILDLIFE MUSEUM, on US 212, is 3.5 mi. e. of the entrance to Yellowstone National Park. More than 100 mounted animals and birds native to the area are displayed in scenes depicting their natural habitats. Allow 30 minutes minimum. Daily 9-7, mid-May to mid-Oct. Admission $2, under 12 free. Phone (406) 838-2265.

CULBERTSON (B-7) pop. 800, elev. 1,919'

About 20 miles upriver from the site of Fort Union, Culbertson takes its name from the second agent of that fur-trading fort, Maj. Alexander Culbertson. Culbertson's son built a ranch nearby in 1879, and about 10 years later a community was established. Culbertson became a center for the local ranches and farms, a role it continues.

Culbertson Chamber of Commerce: P.O. Box 639, Culbertson, MT 59218; phone (406) 787-5821.

CUSTER NATIONAL FOREST

Elevations in the forest range from 4,000 ft. near the town of Ashland to 12,799 ft. on Granite Peak. Refer to AAA maps for additional elevation information.

The mountainous section of Custer National Forest—the Beartooth District—includes a portion of the Absaroka-Beartooth Wilderness and Granite Peak, the highest point in Montana. The eastern portions range from the pine-clad hills and rough break country of southeastern Montana to the rolling grassland of northwestern South Dakota and the badlands of western North Dakota. In all, forest and grassland encompass approximately 2.5 million acres.

Beartooth Scenic Highway (see Red Lodge p. 106), usually open May through September, traverses the mountain country. Other good routes provide access to campgrounds and trailheads. Guide and pack services are available in nearby towns.

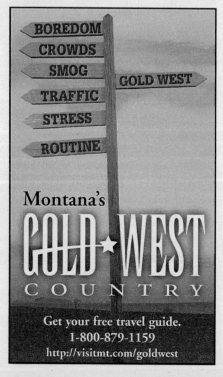

Montana's

GOLD★WEST

C O U N T R Y

Get your free travel guide.
1-800-879-1159
http://visitmt.com/goldwest

Trail information, which can be obtained from Forest Service offices, should be checked and updated at Red Lodge Ranger Station before trip into Absaroka-Beartooth Wilderness is attempted. The ranger station, south of Red Lodge on US 212, is open daily 8-5, June 16-Aug. 31 Mon.-Fri. 8-noon and 1-5, rest of year.

For further information contact the Forest Supervisor, Custer National Forest, 1310 Main St P.O. Box 50760, Billings, MT 59105; phone (406) 248-9885. See Recreation Chart and the AAA Northwestern CampBook.

DEER LODGE (D-2) pop. 3,400, elev. 4,519′

The second oldest city in Montana, Deer Lodge is on the Clark Fork River midway between Yellowstone and Glacier national parks The city was established in 1862 as the result of a nearby gold discovery. With fresh food and a blacksmith as drawing cards, Deer Lodge was a welcome stop for the many settlers and miners who passed through the area.

Gold West Country: 1155 Main St., Deer Lodge, MT 59722; phone (406) 846-1943. See ad.

Self-guiding tours: Brochures for the Hike 'n Bike Tour and an automobile tour of the surrounding area are available from Powell Chamber of Commerce at 1711 Main St.; phone (406) 846-2094.

GRANT-KOHRS RANCH NATIONAL HISTORIC SITE, exit 184 or 187 on I-90 Bus. Rte., was established in the early 1860s. The ranch had grown to 27,000 acres by the early 1900s, and the owners controlled more than a million acres of public range in four states and Canada Though much reduced, the 1,500-acre ranch still has livestock and more than 80 buildings, from bunkhouse row to the 23-room ranch house.

Daily 8-5:30, May 1 to mid-Sept.; 9-4, rest of year. Closed Jan. 1, Thanksgiving and Dec. 25 Guided tours are given daily on the hour 9-4, May 1 to mid-Sept.; 10-3, rest of year. May 1 to mid-Sept. admission $4 per private vehicle or $2 per person over age 16; free rest of year. Hours and admission may vary; phone ahead. Phone (406) 846-3388.

OLD MONTANA PRISON, off I-90 exit 184 or 187 to 1106 Main St., functioned as a prison 1871-1979. Self-guiding tours of the cellhouse, maximum-security areas and walled prison grounds provide a view of early prison life and area history.

Allow 30 minutes minimum. Daily 8-8, June-Aug.; 8:30-5:30, Apr.-May and Sept.-Oct.; otherwise varies. Guided tours are available June-Aug. Closed Jan. 1, Thanksgiving and Dec. 25. Admission (includes Frontier Montana Museum, Towe Ford Museum and Yesterday's Playthings oll & Toy Museum) $7.95; over 61, $7; ages 0-15, $4; ages 7-9, $1. Phone (406) 846-3111 or 46-3114. *See ad.*

Frontier Montana Museum features among s exhibits two extensive private collections of Western memorabilia from the 1800s, Civil War ems, a gun collection containing 250 weapons, American Indian artifacts, a saloon diorama, a arge bourbon-bottle collection and a display of gambler's essentials." Guided tours are available June through August. Daily 9-5, May 15-ept. 30. Phone (406) 846-0026. *See ad.*

Montana Auto Museum contains more than 00 vintage Fords and Lincolns, making this one f the most complete Ford collections in the vorld. The museum houses a representative collection from 1903 through the 1960s. An original fordson tractor and 20 Lincolns are highlights. aily 8 a.m.-9 p.m., June-Aug.; 8:30-5:30, Apr.-May and Sept.-Oct.; otherwise varies. Closed an. 1, Thanksgiving and Dec. 25. Phone (406) 46-3111. *See ad.*

Montana Law Enforcement Museum features Montana law enforcement memorabilia, including weapons and uniforms. A memorial is dedicated to Montana officers who died in the line of uty. Allow 1 hour minimum. Wed.-Sun. 9-5, May 15-Oct. 31. Donations. Phone (406) 46-3777.

Powell County Museum, 1193 Main St., contains permanent and changing exhibits that depict he history of Powell County and Deer Lodge Valley. Displays include mining and ranching quipment and household and school items. A allery features historic photographs as well as un, jukebox and slot machine collections. Daily oon-5, June 1-Labor Day. Free. Phone (406) 46-3111.

Yesterday's Playthings Doll & Toy Museum chronicles the history of children's toys rom the 19th century to the present. The museum's extensive collection includes dolls that are more than 100 years old, dolls from different ultures and dolls made from materials ranging rom papier-mâché to china. A working model rain also is displayed. Allow 30 minutes minimum. Daily 9:30-5, mid-May through Sept. 30. Phone (406) 846-1480. *See ad.*

DILLON (E-3) pop. 4,000, elev. 5,102'

Named for the president of Union Pacific Railroad, Dillon is a focal point for five rich stockaising valleys, including the Big Hole, Grasshopper and Beaverhead valleys. Beaverhead County is among the top cattle- and hay-roducing regions in the state. The town was stablished in 1880 by a group of businessmen who bought out a rancher who refused to give up is land to the railroad.

In 1863 Sidney Edgerton, a lawyer from Ohio, arrived in the area and stayed throughout the

winter season. When he visited Washington, D.C., in the spring, he advocated the creation of a new territory; President Abraham Lincoln named Edgerton governor, and Bannack the temporary capital. The following year the territory's seat was moved to the active mining town of Virginia City.

Fishing is a popular recreational pursuit. Some of Montana's higher mountains can be seen from scenic I-15, which follows the Beaverhead and Red Rock rivers to the Idaho border.

Dillon Visitor Information Center: 125 S. Montana St., P.O. Box 425, Dillon, MT 59725; phone (406) 683-5511.

Self-guiding tours: A brochure outlining a walking tour of historic Dillon is available at the visitor center or Beaverhead County Museum *(see attraction listing).*

BANNACK STATE HISTORIC PARK, 21 mi. w. on SR 278, then 3 mi. s., following signs, was Montana's first territorial capital and one of the original gold-rush towns of this area. The park includes weathered remains of the first capitol, jail, hotel and log cabins. The visitor center offers 19th-century photographs of the region and a videotape about mining. Picnic and primitive camping facilities are available.

Allow 1 hour minimum. Park open daily 7 a.m.-9 p.m. Visitor center open daily 10-6, Memorial Day weekend-Labor Day. Fee $4 per private vehicle or 50¢ per person arriving by bicycle, bus or on foot. Phone (406) 834-3413. *See Recreation Chart and the AAA Northwestern CampBook.*

BEAVERHEAD COUNTY MUSEUM, 15 S. Montana St. next to the depot, displays items pertaining to American Indian and pioneer life in Beaverhead County. An outdoor interpretive area features a 1,300-foot boardwalk and an 1885 homesteader's cabin and sheep wagon. Mon.-Fri. 10-8, Sat.-Sun. 1-5, Memorial Day weekend-Aug. 31; Mon.-Fri. 10-5, Mar. 1-day before Memorial Day weekend and Sept.-Nov. Donations. Phone (406) 683-5027.

WESTERN MONTANA COLLEGE GALLERY/ MUSEUM, 710 S. Atlantic, features student art, rotating exhibits and a permanent collection that focuses on Western art. A collection of Asian, African and North American wildlife also is displayed. Mon.-Thurs. 10-3 (also Tues. and Thurs. 7-9 p.m.). Closed mid-Dec. to mid-Jan. and school holidays. Free. Phone (406) 683-7126 to confirm schedule.

EAST GLACIER PARK (B-2) pop. 300, elev. 4,795'

In the Two Medicine Valley, East Glacier Park is the recreational center and eastern gateway to Glacier National Park *(see place listing p. 90).* The community maintains an Old West appearance.

ENNIS (E-3) pop. 800, elev. 4,939'

Ennis is in the broad, rolling Madison Valley, flanked on both sides by mountain ranges. Built along the Madison River, the town is convenient to the historic gold-mining towns of Virginia City and Nevada City as well as the trout-filled lakes and streams of the Gallatin and Beaverhead-Deerlodge National Forests *(see place listings p. 90 and 77).*

Ennis Chamber of Commerce: P.O. Box 291, Ennis, MT 59729; phone (406) 682-4388.

FLATHEAD LAKE (B-2)

A recreational mecca, Flathead Lake appeals to those who enjoy a wide array of activities ranging from water skiing and fishing to sailing and sightseeing. The 28-mile-long, 15-mile-wide lake boasts several islands; sheep, deer, bears, eagles and ospreys inhabit Wild Horse. Nearby communities include Bigfork, Kalispell, Lakeside, Polson and Somers *(see place listings).*

DRIVE DEFENSIVELY!

FLATHEAD NATIONAL FOREST

Elevations in the forest range from 3,500 ft. at the valley floor to 9,289 ft. on Swan Peak in the Swan Valley. Refer to AAA maps for additional elevation information.

Stretching along the spine of the Rocky Mountains, Flathead National Forest's 2.3 million acres extend south from the Canadian border for more than 130 miles. With parts of its eastern and northern boundaries bordering Glacier National Park *(see place listing p. 90),* Flathead National Forest shares much of the park's spectacular scenery of high ridges and mountains. The forest's principal rivers are the Swan, Stillwater and the three forks of the Flathead—the North Fork, Middle Fork and South Fork that are all in the National Wild and Scenic River system. This is augmented by 3,400 miles of streams and many small lakes.

Almost half the national forest's acreage lies within the Bob Marshall Wilderness complex, which includes the Bob Marshall, Great Bear and Scapegoat wilderness areas. The combined wilderness region comprises 1.5 million acres and attracts those who seek out a challenging recreation experience in a natural setting, where mechanized travel and equipment is prohibited.

Popularly known as the "Bob," the Bob Marshall Wilderness straddles the Continental Divide. There are many rugged peaks, alpine lakes, mountain valleys with meandering streams in wildflower-strewn meadows, waterfalls and towering trees. Sunsets often are highlighted by long streamers of wave-shaped clouds, a phenomenon created partly by strong winds blowing perpendicular to a mountain range.

For those seeking utter solitude, winter use of the "Bob" is almost nil. This vast reserve, appropriately named for the man who helped preserve millions of acres of the wilderness system, shelters one of the country's largest wildlife populations, including elk, bighorn sheep, black bears and several hundred grizzly bears. About 50 outfitting and guiding businesses serve the area.

Other areas of interest in the forest are Mission Mountain Wilderness and Hungry Horse Reservoir, along the shores of which are almost half of the forest's camping and picnic areas. The 15,000-acre Jewel Basin Hiking Area, reached by forest roads from SRs 83 or 35, is a scenic area of rushing waterways, open meadows and subalpine forests; mechanized vehicles and pack animals are not permitted. Hiking, fishing and floating the three forks of the Flathead River are popular activities.

Information about the forest's 34 campgrounds and recreational opportunities is available at the forest headquarters in Kalispell and the district ranger stations. For further information contact the Forest Supervisor, Flathead National Forest, 1935 3rd Ave. E., Kalispell, MT 59901; phone (406) 758-5204. *See Recreation Chart and the AAA Northwestern CampBook.*

FORT BENTON (B-4) pop. 1,700, elev. 2,632'

At the head of navigation on the Missouri River, Fort Benton is one of Montana's oldest communities and was the link between east and west. Thousands of immigrants and miners marked this landing as the beginning of the way west along Mullan Road or north along WhoopUp Trail. Fort Benton also was their chief means of supply, as all goods were brought by steamboat from St. Louis. In 1868, 39 steamboats unloaded 8,000 tons of freight and 10,000 passengers; one steamboat returned to St. Louis with $1.5 million in gold.

The Lewis and Clark Memorial overlooks the Missouri River from the Levee not far from the old fort; the memorial stands as a reminder of the explorers' stay in the area and the role they and Fort Benton played in opening the West. A statue of Lt. John Mullan, the first white man to pave the way across the west from Fort Benton to Walla Walla, WA, and for whom the Mullan Trail is named, also stands on the Levee.

Fort Benton Chamber of Commerce: P.O. Box 879, Fort Benton, MT 59442; phone (406) 622-3864.

Self-guiding tours: A brochure outlining a walking and driving tour of Fort Benton is available at the Museum of the Upper Missouri River *(see attraction listing)* and at Fort Benton Visitor Information Center, on Front Street.

MUSEUM OF THE UPPER MISSOURI RIVER, in Old Fort Park, features dioramas and exhibits about early trading and river steamers. The Agriculture, Northern Great Plains and Homestead Days Museum also is included. The mounted remains of the Hornaday bull, the bovine model for the buffalo nickel, can be viewed. Daily 10-5, mid-May through Sept. 30; by appointment rest of year. Admission $4; ages 6-12, $1. Phone (406) 622-5494, 622-5133 or 622-5316.

UPPER MISSOURI WILD & SCENIC RIVER VISITOR CENTER, 1718 Front St., offers a slide presentation about Lewis and Clark's expedition on the 149-mile Upper Missouri River and displays about the area's natural and cultural resources. The center also provides assistance in preparing self-guided river trips. Allow 30 minutes minimum. Daily 8-6, late May-early Sept. Free. Phone (406) 622-5185.

FORT PECK (B-6) pop. 300, elev. 2,100'

The federal government developed Fort Peck in the early 1930s as a support community for the construction of Fort Peck Dam. Built by the U.S. Army Corps of Engineers, the dam harnesses the Missouri River to provide electric power, irrigation and flood control. The town was named after Col. Campbell K. Peck, who established a trading post in the area after the Civil War.

Fort Peck Summer Theatre, west on SR 24, presents contemporary productions from late June to late August; phone Fort Peck Fine Arts Council at (406) 228-9219 or 228-2222.

FORT PECK DAM, on SR 24, is one of the larger hydraulic earth-filled dams in the world; its construction created Fort Peck Lake *(see Recreation Chart and the AAA Northwestern CampBook),* which offers excellent fishing and camping along its 130-mile length. A hard-surfaced highway follows the crest of the dam, 250 feet above the tunnel outlets, onto the spillway. Illustrated talks and information about the project are available. Phone (406) 526-3411.

Fort Peck Museum, at Powerhouse 1, outlines the geology, paleontology and history of the area. Nearly 300 specimens of dinosaur bones and other fossils are displayed. Daily 9-5:30. Free.

Powerhouse Tour describes how the power plants at Fort Peck Dam transform water into electricity. Also displayed are generators, surge tanks and turbines. Allow 1 hour minimum. Daily 9-5, Memorial Day-Labor Day. Free.

FORT UNION TRADING POST NATIONAL HISTORIC SITE (B-7)

Fort Union Trading Post National Historic Site is reached via US 2 and SR 1804, 24 miles southwest of Williston, N.D. At its founding in 1828, the fort was 1,776 miles by river from St. Louis, the nearest supply point.

Although the buildings and walls disappeared long ago, the stone foundations of the bourgeois house, palisades, Indian trade house, icehouse and other structures have been excavated. The trade house and several other buildings have been rebuilt and furnished as they might have been in the early 1850s. The fort's walls and bastions also have been reconstructed. The 1850s Bourgeois House visitor center features photographs, paintings, a videotape about fort history, artifacts and furs.

Allow 30 minutes minimum. Daily 8-8, Memorial Day weekend-Labor Day; 9-5:30, rest of year. Closed Jan. 1, Thanksgiving and Dec. 25. Donations. Phone (701) 572-9083.

GALLATIN NATIONAL FOREST

Elevations in the forest range
from 4,300 ft. at Derby Gulch to
12,799 ft. on Granite Peak. Refer to
AAA maps for additional elevation
information.

The mountains within Gallatin National Forest's 1,735,239 acres in south-central Montana are among the most rugged in Montana. On the western side of the forest are the Madison and Gallatin ranges; to the east, the Absaroka and Beartooth; and to the north, the Bridger and the isolated block encompassing the Crazy Mountains.

To some, such as the Crow Indians who sought their visions in the Crazies, these mountains inspire a mystical reverence; to others, such as the mountain men who thought the Beartooth Range resembled the teeth of a familiar predator, they inspire a sense of awe. Much of this region remains unchanged, protected in the forest's two wilderness units, the Lee Metcalf and the Absaroka-Beartooth.

Absaroka-Beartooth Wilderness is named for its two very different mountain ranges. Rugged mountains, broad forested valleys and a variety of plant life characterize the Absaroka Range, which receives precipitation that is unusually abundant for this region. In contrast, the Beartooths present a jagged silhouette of monumental walls and spires soaring to heights of more than 12,000 feet. Forming the roof of these massive peaks are broad plateaus of alpine tundra carpeted with summer wildflowers and hundreds of lakes. The ranges are an integral part of the Yellowstone ecosystem, offering shelter to grizzlies, moose, deer, eagles and turkeys.

The Yellowstone, Gallatin, Madison and Boulder, which are the principal rivers, are renowned for excellent fishing. Natural Bridge State Monument, 28 miles south of Big Timber via SR 289, features a 100-foot waterfall at the mouth of the Boulder River Canyon. Several short trails lead from the parking area to observation sites of the falls.

Hikers favor Lee Metcalf Wilderness *(see Beaverhead-Deerlodge National Forest p. 77)* and the Hyalite area of the Gallatin Range. Also scenic are the ridge trails in the Bridger Mountains near Bozeman. To experience the region's beauty by car travel Beartooth Scenic Highway *(see Red Lodge p. 106);* US 91 from West Yellowstone to Gallatin Gateway; or the self-guiding tour in the Madison River Earthquake Area.

Information about the forest's 26 campgrounds and recreational opportunities is available at district ranger stations. For further information write the Forest Supervisor, Gallatin National Forest, P.O. Box 130, Federal Building, Bozeman, MT 59771; phone (406) 587-6701. *See Recreation Chart and the AAA Northwestern CampBook.*

MADISON RIVER CANYON EARTHQUAKE AREA—
see West Yellowstone p. 110.

GARDINER (E-4) elev. 5,267'

The northern entrance to Yellowstone National Park, Gardiner is the only approach open all year. The Devil's Slide, an unusual rock formation 5 miles northwest on US 89, is visible from the highway. A mile north of town by gravel road is a travertine rock quarry. Theodore Roosevelt dedicated Roosevelt Arch in 1872.

Gardiner Chamber of Commerce: 233 Main, Suite A, P.O. Box 81, Gardiner, MT 59030; phone (406) 848-7971.

 RECREATIONAL ACTIVITIES
White-water Rafting

- **Montana Whitewater,** departs from the office 7 mi. n on SR 89. Write P.O. Box 1552, Bozeman, MT 59771. Daily Memorial Day weekend-Labor Day. Phone (406) 763-4465 or (800) 799-4465.

- **Yellowstone Raft Co.,** on US 89 at the north entrance to Yellowstone National Park. Write P.O. Box 46AA, Gardiner, MT 59030. Daily Memorial Day weekend to mid-Sept. Phone (406) 848-7777 or (800) 858-7781.

★ GLACIER NATIONAL PARK (A-2)

See map page 92.

Elevations in the park range from a low of 3,200ft. in the West Glacier Area to 10,448 ft. on Mt. Cleveland. Refer to AAA maps for additional elevation information.

Glacier National Park, in northwestern Montana, contains a million acres of the finest mountain scenery in America. Geologic processes have formed and sculpted the peaks and left about 50 glaciers and 200 lakes. The mountains to the east are a result of an overthrust of the Earth's crust. Rock layers about a billion years old lie above layers millions of years younger.

The U-shaped valleys, as well as most of the lakes, are the legacy of the last ice age. Most glaciers are accessible only by trail; a few can be viewed from the road. Glacier National Park and Waterton Lakes National Park, in Alberta, together form Waterton-Glacier International Peace Park although each is administered separately. Scenic Going-to-the-Sun Road *(see attraction listing)* connects the east and west sections of Glacier National Park.

Though Glacier is a refuge for nearly every large mammal species native to the United States, most of the animals seek the undisturbed areas, and few are seen along the roads during the travel season. The park also is a haven for 235 species of birds.

The brilliance and diversity of its floral life is one of Glacier's outstanding features; July marks the height of bloom for the 1,000-odd species of flowering plants. In the valleys on the east side are dense stands of Engelmann spruce, subalpine fir and lodgepole pine. The western valleys present a different picture with their many dense stands of western red-cedars and other conifers.

General Information and Activities

The park's travel season is roughly from mid-June to mid-October. Bus service is maintained for guests between all hotels, and visitors can use these tour buses for one-way or round-trip travel to various park locations from mid-June to early September; phone (406) 226-9311. Canoe and motor boat rentals are available at Apgar dock.

Note: Vehicles and vehicle combinations longer than 21 feet or wider than 8 feet (including mirrors) are prohibited from traveling Going-to-the-Sun Road between the Avalanche picnic area and Sun Point parking areas, where they may park. A paid shuttle service with stops along Going-to-the-Sun Road and in West Glacier and St. Mary is available; phone (406) 881-4311 May-September, or 863-1200 rest of year.

About 700 miles of horseback and foot trails penetrate the park, and many points of interest are within easy walking distance of the hotels and chalets. Mule Shoe Outfitter offers guided horseback rides through the park. Tours depart from Lake McDonald Corral near Lake McDonald Lodge and Many Glacier Corral; phone (406) 888-5121 or 732-4203. There are more than 60 campsites for backpackers; back-country camping permits are required ($4) and can be obtained at Apgar, St. Mary and Two Medicine visitor centers or the Many Glacier ranger station. Topographic maps can be purchased at the park visitor centers or ordered by mail from Glacier Natural History Association, West Glacier, MT 59936.

Mountain whitefish and cutthroat trout are the most common fish. Lake trout are taken from the larger lakes, principally Lake McDonald and St. Mary and Waterton lakes. Grayling thrive in Elizabeth Lake. No fishing license is required; regulations are available at the visitor centers.

Several concessioners within the park provide tours. Glacier Park Inc. offers trips by bus (*see color ad p. xxx*). Glacier Wilderness Guides arranges guided backpacking trips. Glacier Park Boat Co. operates guided lake cruises on McDonald, St. Mary, Two Medicine, Swiftcurrent and Josephine lakes. Boats and canoes can be rented at Two Medicine, Swiftcurrent and McDonald lakes (shuttle service transportation only).

Trail rides ranging from 1 hour to all day depart from Lake McDonald Lodge and Many Glacier Hotel. Daily schedules of naturalist-guided hikes, boat trips and campfire programs are printed as a supplement to the *Waterton-Glacier Guide*, the park's newspaper, which is handed out at entrance stations and visitor centers. *See Recreation Chart and the AAA Northwestern CampBook.*

Note: Although the animals in the park might appear tame, they are wild and potentially dangerous. Do not approach, feed, molest or tease them in any manner. Bears and mountain lions especially should be avoided; if one approaches, stay in your closed vehicle.

ADMISSION to the park is by 7-day ($10 per private vehicle, $5 per person arriving by bicycle, bus, motorcycle or on foot) permit.

PETS are permitted in the park only if they are leashed, crated or otherwise physically restrained at all times. They are not allowed on park trails.

ADDRESS inquiries to the Superintendent, Glacier National Park, West Glacier, MT 59936; phone (406) 888-7800.

CCINC. AUTO TAPE TOURS are available at West Glacier Gift Shop in West Glacier, St. Mary's Lodge in St. Mary, or by contacting CCInc., P.O. Box 227, Allendale, NJ 07401. The tapes describe the history, geology, flora and

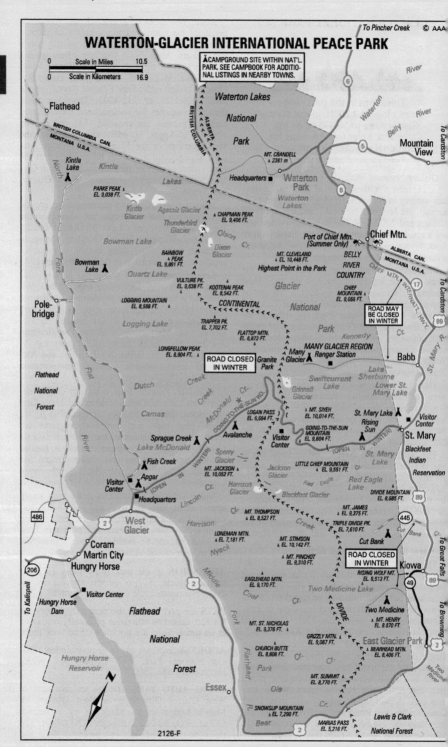

WATERTON-GLACIER INTERNATIONAL PEACE PARK

To Pincher Creek © AAA

Scale in Miles 0 — 10.5

Scale in Kilometers 0 — 16.9

▲ CAMPGROUND SITE WITHIN NAT'L. PARK. SEE CAMPBOOK FOR ADDITIONAL LISTINGS IN NEARBY TOWNS.

2126-F

fauna and points of interest in the park. A detailed map is included. The 90-minute tapes cost $12.95 (plus $2 postage and handling if ordered by mail). Phone (201) 236-1666.

Points of Interest

AVALANCHE CREEK, on Going-to-the-Sun Rd., has cut a deep, narrow gorge through brilliant red mudstone. It is filled with potholes scoured out by stones swirled in the foaming torrent. From the gorge a 2-mile trail travels to Avalanche Basin and Lake, a semicircular amphitheater with walls more than 2,000 feet high, over which plunge a half-dozen waterfalls. A nature trail with a boardwalk for physically impaired visitors leads to the gorge. Allow 30 minutes minimum.

BELLY RIVER COUNTRY is accessible by trail from Many Glacier through Ptarmigan Tunnel, from Waterton Lake over Stoney Indian Pass, or from Chief Mountain customs station on Chief Mountain International Road. In addition to the trails, spurs are available to Helen, Cosley, Glenns, Mokowanis and Elizabeth lakes and Gros Ventre and Dawn Mist falls. The region is wild and heavily forested in some places. A 33-mile drive through the Chief Mountain area to Waterton Lakes National Park in Canada offers scenic views. A launch operates on Waterton Lake mid-June to early September.

Allow 2 hours minimum. Round-trip launch fare (in Canadian dollars) $14; under 12, $7. One-way $8; under 12, $4.

CUT BANK is a primitive, densely wooded valley. At the head of the valley is 8,011-foot Triple Divide Peak.

★ **GOING-TO-THE-SUN ROAD,** acclaimed as one of the outstanding scenic roadways of the world, traverses the width of the park, crossing the Continental Divide through Logan Pass at an elevation of 6,680 feet. Joining US 89 at St. Mary and US 2 at West Glacier, the 52-mile route affords magnificent views of some of Glacier National Park's loveliest scenery. Coming from the east, one has exceptionally grand views of the mountains and St. Mary's Lake from high, level roads hacked out of the mountainside. Once over Logan Pass a continuous descent begins to the floor of the valley.

The National Park Services closes the Logan Pass section of the road for the season no later than the Monday morning following the third Sunday in October. The road re-opens in mid-June (weather permitting). For vehicle restrictions, *see General Information and Activities.* A hiker's shuttle stops at several trails along Going-to-the-Sun Road; one-way fare $8.

GRANITE PARK is reached from Waterton by the northern portion of the Highline Trail, from Logan Pass along the Highline Trail and from

Many Glacier over Swiftcurrent Pass Trail. Exposed is a great mass of lava that once spread over the region. Trails radiate into the surrounding mountains. Granite Park Chalet is open from early July to mid-Sept.; reservations are required. Write to Glacier Wilderness Guides, P.O. Box 535, West Glacier, MT 59936; phone (800) 521-7238.

LAKE McDONALD, 10 miles long and 1 mile wide, is the largest lake in the park. Its shores are heavily forested, and impressive rocky summits rise 6,000 feet above. Going-to-the-Sun Road runs along the eastern shore. Lake McDonald Lodge, near the upper end of the lake, is the focal point for trails to Sperry Chalet, Gunsight Pass, Sperry Glacier, Upper McDonald Valley and the summit of Mount Brown. A cruise boat operates from the lodge mid-June to early September. Boats, horses and naturalist programs are available at the lodge and at Apgar.

LOGAN PASS lies between the headwaters of Logan and Reynolds creeks. At an elevation of 6,680 feet, it straddles the Continental Divide and carries Going-to-the-Sun Road from St. Mary to West Glacier. Though there are no overnight stopping places, easy access by automobile makes it a favorite starting point for several walks, including the trail to Hidden Lake Overlook. Naturalist-led day trips are conducted along the Garden Wall in summer, and orientation talks are given at the visitor center.

MANY GLACIER REGION, in the n.e. sector of the park, encompasses Swiftcurrent Lake, from which branch many deep, glaciated valleys. The area is 13 miles by road from US 89 at Babb or by trail from Sun Point, Granite Park, Belly River and Waterton Lake. Other trails lead around Swiftcurrent and Josephine lakes and to Morning Eagle Falls, Grinnell Glacier, Ptarmigan Lake and Tunnel and Cracker, Grinnell and Iceberg lakes.

Launch trips on Swiftcurrent and Josephine lakes depart daily at 9, 11, 2 and 4 (also at 3, July-Aug.), mid-June to early Sept. Allow 2 hours minimum. Naturalists conduct daily field walks and nightly programs at the campground and hotel.

RED EAGLE LAKE in Red Eagle Valley is reached by trail from the St. Mary park entrance, from Sun Point via Red Eagle Trail and from Cut Bank over Triple Divide Pass.

ST. MARY LAKE lies at the foot of the Lewis Range, a front barrier of the Rockies. Peaks soar a mile above its waters. Trails radiate from Sun Point; one of the shortest and best is the trail to Baring Falls. Red Eagle Trail along the south shore leads to Red Eagle Lake. Programs are presented nightly in summer at the visitor center and at Rising Sun campground. Launch trips and motorboats are available at the boat landing at Rising Sun from mid-June to early September.

SCENICRUISE BOAT TOURS departs from the docks at Lake McDonald Lodge, Many Glacier and Two Medicine and St. Mary lakes and offer narrated boat tours of wilderness scenes, glacier formations, waterfalls and rugged cliffs. Some tours dock for hiking and picnicking.

Allow 1 hour, 30 minutes minimum. Tours depart from Lake McDonald Lodge daily at 10, 1:30, 3:30 and 7 (also at 5:30 July-Aug.), early June-late Sept.; from Many Glacier at 9, 11, 2 and 4 (also at 3, July-Aug.); from Two Medicine Lake at 10:30, 1, 2:30, 3:45 and 6:45; and from St. Mary Lake at 9, 11, 2, 4 and 6:30. Hours may vary; phone ahead. Fare $8-$10; ages 4-12, $4-$5. Departures require a minimum of six adults. Phone (406) 257-2426 year-round, (406) 888-5727 for Lake McDonald Lodge and Two Medicine, (406) 732-4480 for Many Glacier, or (406) 732-4430 for St. Mary Lake.

SPERRY CHALET, in a high steep hollow at the upper end of a mountain valley, is hemmed in on three sides by precipitous peaks. The chalet can be reached only by foot or horseback from Lake McDonald and by foot from Sun Point via Gunsight and Lincoln passes. Hiking and exploring the Sperry Glacier and fishing in nearby Lake Ellen Wilson are the chief diversions. Mountain goats frequently are seen on the cirque walls,

usually during the late afternoon. For further information write to Glacier Wilderness Guides, P.O. Box 535, West Glacier, MT 59936; phone (800) 521-7238.

TWO MEDICINE VALLEY, 11 mi. from East Glacier and 7 mi. off SR 49, features a lake surrounded by majestic peaks separated by deep, glaciated valleys. Trails for hikers and saddle horse parties radiate to adjacent points of interest; one short trail leads through dense evergreen forest to the foot of Twin Falls. Launch trips across Two Medicine Lake depart daily, mid-June to early Sept.

A readily accessible scenic trail is at Running Eagle Falls, 2 miles below the lake near the road bridge across Two Medicine Creek. A portion of the falls' waters flows from a cave beneath the brink of the main falls. Early in the year it appears to be an ordinary waterfall, but late in the season water issues from the cave alone, and the waterfall above it is dry.

GLASGOW (B-6) pop. 3,600, elev. 2,090'

In the midst of the Milk and Missouri River valleys, Glasgow began as a railroad station. It is now an agricultural and commercial trade center for northeastern Montana, and the surrounding area is known as a good fossil-hunting locale.

Glasgow Area Chamber of Commerce and Agriculture: 740 US 2E, P.O. Box 832, Glasgow, MT 59230; phone (406) 228-2222 or (800) 228-2223.

PIONEER MUSEUM, .5 mi. w. on US 2, displays 19th-century American Indian and pioneer artifacts, photographs and agricultural tools. Mounted wildlife and historic barroom exhibits also are shown. Allow 1 hour minimum. Mon.-Sat. 10-7, Sun. 1-5, Memorial Day-Labor Day; by appointment rest of year. Closed July 4. Free. Phone (406) 228-8692.

GLENDIVE (C-7) pop. 4,800, elev. 2,070'

Once a center for cattle ranches, Glendive is now a distribution point for diverse agricultural products. The surrounding area is rich in petroleum, natural gas and coal. Another natural resource, the boneless paddlefish, roams the bottom of the Yellowstone River in such numbers that Glendive has assumed the title of "Paddlefish Capital." Paddlefish season is mid-May to late June. Besides anglers, Glendive attracts rockhounds in search of moss agates and fossils, which are plentiful in the area.

Glendive Area Chamber of Commerce and Agriculture: 313 S. Merrill, Glendive, MT 59330; phone (406) 365-5601 or (800) 859-0824.

Self-guiding tours: Brochures of a walking tour of the downtown historic district are available from the chamber of commerce.

FRONTIER GATEWAY MUSEUM is 1 mi. e. off I-94 exit 215 on Belle Prairie Rd. This museum contains dinosaur fossils, American Indian artifacts, farm machinery and other items depicting eastern Montana from prehistoric times to the present. Among buildings on the grounds are a rural schoolhouse, log cabin and smithy. Mon.-Sat. 9-noon and 1-5, Sun. and holidays 1-5, June-Aug.; daily 1-5, mid-May through May 31 and Sept. 1 to mid-Sept. Donations. Phone (406) 365-8168.

MAKOSHIKA STATE PARK is 1 mi. s. at 1301 Snyder Ave. Makoshika comes from the Sioux word meaning "bad earth" or "badlands." The area encompasses 8,123 acres of eroded and vividly colored buttes and gullies, which can be viewed along the Kinney Coulee, Cap Rock and Diane Gabriel nature trails; explanatory brochures are available at trail heads. Within the park and its vicinity are fossils and moss agates. Visitors can ride snowmobiles or cross-country ski in the badlands. A visitor center displays fossils and a triceratops skull.

Allow 4 hours minimum. Park open daily 24 hours (weather permitting). Admission $4 per private motorized vehicle or $1 per person arriving by bicycle, bus or on foot. Camping fee $7. Phone (406) 365-6256. *See Recreation Chart and the AAA Northwestern CampBook.*

GREAT FALLS (C-4) pop. 55,100, elev. 3,312'

The Great Falls of the Missouri River first was seen by Capt. Meriwether Lewis in 1805. Capt. William Clark mapped the area while the others portaged around the rapids. The party returned to this site on its trip from the Pacific coast a year later. In 1882 Paris Gibson visited the site; he returned in the spring of 1883 with a surveyor and an attorney, and a townsite soon was platted and named Great Falls. Important contributors to the economy are Malmstrom Air Force Base and agriculture.

Rivers Edge Trail, which begins north of US 89 on River Drive and stretches 5 miles along the Missouri River, is popular with pedestrians and bicyclists.

A large American flag marks the visitor center on the Broadwater Overlook; follow directional signs on the approach and throughout the city. The center can provide information about guided tours; phone (406) 771-0885.

Great Falls Historic Trolley offers 2-hour guided tours of the city. Highlights include the Historic Home District, the Historic Railroad Area and Historic Downtown. Tour de Great Falls features a 21-passenger bus offering guided tours. For reservations and times phone (406) 771-1100.

Great Falls Area Chamber of Commerce: 815 2nd St. S., Great Falls, MT 59405; phone (406) 761-4434.

Shopping areas: Holiday Village Mall, 2.5 miles east of US 15 at 1200 10th Ave. S., houses 95 stores including Herberger's, JCPenney and Sears.

CASCADE COUNTY HISTORICAL MUSEUM AND ARCHIVES, 1400 1st Ave. N. at Paris Gibson Sq., offers exhibits about the pioneer and mining eras as well as the county's commercial history. Allow 1 hour minimum. Mon.-Fri. 10-5, Sat.-Sun. noon-5, Memorial Day-Labor Day. Archives closed Sat.-Sun. Museum and archives closed holidays. Donations. Phone (406) 452-3462.

★ **C.M. RUSSELL MUSEUM,** in the n.e. section at 400 13th St. N., displays watercolors, sculptures, oil paintings and illustrated cards and letters of the cowboy artist Charles M. Russell. Allow 2 hours minimum. Mon.-Sat. 9-6, Sun. 1-5, May-Sept.; Tues.-Sat. 10-5, Sun. 1-5, rest of year. Closed Jan. 1, Easter, Thanksgiving and Dec. 25. Admission $4; over 59, $3; students with ID $2; under 5 free. AE, MC, VI. Phone (406) 727-8787.

C.M. Russell Home, next to the studio, was the Russells' permanent residence and is furnished in period. Mon.-Sat. 9-5, Sun. 1-5, May-Sept.

Log Cabin Studio of Charles M. Russell, adjacent to the museum, was built in 1903 and contains Russell's pallet and brushes, American Indian artifacts he used as models, and cowboy memorabilia. Mon.-Sat. 9-6, Sun. 1-5, May-Sept.; Tues.-Sat. 10-5, Sun. 1-5, rest of year. Closed Jan. 1, Easter, Thanksgiving and Dec. 25.

CHARLES M. BAIR FAMILY MUSEUM is 1 mi. s. of Martinsdale turnoff on US 12 between White Sulphur Springs and Harlowton, following signs. This former home of wealthy sheep owner Charles M. Bair is a repository of antiques dating from the 18th century; paintings by Ralston, Russell and Sharp; and rare American Indian artifacts.

Especially notable are the American Indian beadwork, Meissen porcelain, Duncan Phyfe dining table, Paul Storr silver, European crystal chandeliers and memorabilia from around the world. Guided tours are available. Allow 1 hour minimum. Wed.-Sun. 10-5, May-Sept. Admission $3; under 17, $1.50. Phone (406) 727-8787.

GIANT SPRINGS FISH, WILDLIFE AND PARKS VISITOR CENTER AND FISH HATCHERY, 2.5 mi. n.e. off US 87 on River Dr., has wildlife displays, photographs about park history and film presentations in the regional headquarters visitor center. Across the street is the hatchery for rainbow trout and salmon; the hatchery visitor center explains fish raising. The park preserves one of the largest freshwater springs in the world. Scenic overlooks are available from two dams within 2 miles of the site.

Allow 1 hour minimum. Park open daily dawn-dusk. Fish, Wildlife and Parks visitor center open Mon.-Fri. 8-7, Sat.-Sun. 10-7, second weekend in May to mid-Sept.; Mon.-Fri. 8-5, rest of year. Hatchery visitor center open daily 8-4:30. Park admission $4 per private vehicle or $1 per person arriving by bicycle, bus or on foot. Visitor centers free. Phone the regional headquarters visitor center at (406) 454-5840, or the hatchery at 452-5734.

LEWIS AND CLARK AUDIO TOUR, available at Cascade County Historical Museum and Archives *(see attraction listing)*, recounts the adventures of the Lewis and Clark expedition as listeners follow their path to the Great Falls, Black Eagle Falls, Giant Springs and Rainbow Falls. A map with detailed directions guides travelers along the 34-mile route. The tour takes about 90 minutes. The tape is $11. Phone (406) 452-3462.

LEWIS AND CLARK NATIONAL HISTORIC TRAIL INTERPRETIVE CENTER is in Giant Springs Heritage State Park, across the 15th St. Bridge, then 1.7 mi. e. on River Dr. to 4201 Giant Springs Rd. Exhibits detail the 1804-06 Lewis and Clark expedition, particularly the portion that took place in what is now Montana. Highlights include a look at the Indian tribes of the Plains and Pacific Northwest who helped Lewis and Clark along the way. Costumed interpreters conduct demonstrations of events from the journey. A half-hour introductory film is offered on the hour.

Allow 2 hours minimum. Daily 9-8, Memorial Day-Labor Day; Tues.-Sat. 9-5, rest of year. Closed major holidays. Admission $5; over 61, $4; ages 6-17, $2. Phone (406) 727-8733.

MALMSTROM AIR FORCE BASE MUSEUM AND AIR PARK is on Malmstrom Air Force Base, just inside the main gate at the east end of 2nd Ave. N. The museum displays uniforms, equipment and photographs relating to base history. The outdoor air park contains aircraft and missiles that date from the mid-20th century. Allow 1 hour minimum. The museum is closed for renovations; phone for details of the reopening. Free. Phone (406) 731-4044.

MEHMKE STEAM MUSEUM, 10 mi. e. on US 87/89, displays operable antique steam engines and gas tractors along with other farming artifacts. Allow 1 hour minimum. Daily dawn-dusk. Donations. Phone (406) 452-6571.

PARIS GIBSON SQUARE MUSEUM OF ARTS, corner of 14th St. and 1st Ave. N. in Norman Architectural Building, contains contemporary art exhibits. Allow 1 hour, 30 minutes minimum. Mon.-Fri. 10-5 (also Tues. 7-9 p.m.), Memorial Day-Labor Day; Tues.-Fri. 10-5, Sat.-Sun. noon-5, rest of year. Closed holidays. Donations. Phone (406) 727-8255.

HAMILTON (D-1) pop. 2,700, elev. 3,572'

The seat of Ravalli County and headquarters of Bitterroot National Forest, Hamilton was founded by 19th-century copper magnate Marcus Daly.

Bitterroot Valley Chamber of Commerce: 105 E. Main St., Hamilton, MT 59840; phone (406) 363-2400.

SAVE **DALY MANSION,** 251 Eastside Hwy. (CR 269), was the riverside estate of Montana's copper baron, Marcus Daly. Containing its original furniture and Italian marble fireplaces, the Georgian Revival house is surrounded by a 22,000-acre stock farm where Daly raised Thoroughbred racehorses. Allow 1 hour minimum. Guided tours are given daily 11-4, Apr. 15-Oct. 15; by appointment rest of year. Fee $5; ages 5-14, $3. Only grounds $1. Phone (406) 363-6004.

RAVALLI COUNTY MUSEUM, 205 Bedford St., is in the original Ravalli County courthouse and contains various exhibitions, including an American Indian artifacts collection, a laboratory display about Rocky Mountain tick fever, period rooms, a veterans exhibit and historical photographs and newspapers. A program of cultural or historical significance is presented Sundays at 2. Allow 1 hour minimum. Thurs.-Mon. 10-4, Sun. 1-4; closed holidays. Donations. Phone (406) 363-3338.

HARDIN (D-5) pop. 2,900, elev. 2,902'

Hardin borders Crow Indian Reservation and serves as a trading center for its people. The town was named after Samuel Hardin, a rancher from Wyoming who leased land on the reservation. Nearby is the former site of Fort Custer, a military garrison said to have been one of the finest cavalry posts in the world. It was established in 1877, just after Lt. Col. George A. Custer's defeat.

The 4-day Little Big Horn Days celebration takes place the last weekend in June. Festivities include a grand ball with period music, costumes and dances; a re-enactment of Custer's Last Stand; a powwow; arts and crafts shows; and dancing.

Hardin Area Chamber of Commerce: 219 N. Center Ave., Hardin, MT 59034; phone (406) 665-1672.

BIG HORN COUNTY HISTORICAL MUSEUM AND STATE VISITOR CENTER is 1 mi. e. to I-90 exit 497, then 3 blks. s. on Third St. The museum features early Montana memorabilia and 14 historic buildings, including a 1911 farmhouse, American Indian log cabin, railroad depot, doctor's building and the Fort Custer stage station. A visitor information center and picnic facilities are on the grounds. A self-guiding audiotape tour of Little Bighorn Battlefield National Monument

(see place listing p. 101) can be purchased at the center. Picnicking is permitted.

Museum open daily 8-8, May-Sept.; Mon.-Sat. 9-5, rest of year. Free. Phone (406) 665-1671.

★**LITTLE BIGHORN BATTLEFIELD NATIONAL MONUMENT—**
see place listing p. 101.

HARLOWTON (D-4) pop. 1,000

UPPER MUSSELSHELL MUSEUM, 11 S. Central Ave., re-creates life in the early 1900s through replicas of a general store, schoolroom, kitchen and living room. Supplementing these exhibits are displays of period clothing, farm tools and other artifacts. Also displayed is a replica of an Avaceratops-Lammeri dinosaur, whose remains were found north of town, on Careless Creek. Allow 30 minutes minimum. Tues.-Sat. 10-5, Sun. 1-5, May-Oct.; by appointment rest of year. Donations. Phone (406) 632-5519.

HAVRE (B-4) pop. 10,200, elev. 2,493'

Havre was named by railroad officials after the French city Le Havre, but its citizens gave it a different pronunciation: HAV-ver.

Havre Area Chamber of Commerce: 1st St., P.O. Box 308, Havre, MT 59501; phone (406) 265-4383.

H. EARL & MARGARET TURNER CLACK MEMORIAL MUSEUM, 306 3rd Ave., chronicles local history through artifacts and dioramas and has exhibits about the geological and archeological features of the area. Guided tours of Fort Assinniboine, 8 miles southwest off US 87, are offered. A large section of the museum displays items from the nearby Wahkpa Chu'gn Bison Kill Archeology Site.

Allow 1 hour minimum. Museum open daily 8-8, mid-May to mid-Sept. Fort tours are given daily June 15-Sept. 30 (weather permitting). Donations. Fort tours $3, students with ID $1.50. Phone (406) 265-4000.

HAVRE BENEATH THE STREETS, 120 Third St., is a guided walking tour through the city's historical underground. Built in 1904, many of the original buildings are now beneath the city streets. Highlights along the tour include 17 exhibits, including a Chinese laundry, post office, bordello, meat market, bakery, opium den, barber shop and saloon. Allow 1 hour minimum. Daily 9-5, May-Sept.; Mon.-Sat. 9-5, rest of year. Closed holidays. Admission $6; over 54, $5; ages 6-12, $4. Phone (406) 265-8888.

ROCKY BOY INDIAN RESERVATION is 15 mi. s. of US 87 in the Bear Paw Mountains. Established in 1916, the reservation is named for a Chippewa leader whose Indian name, meaning "Stone Child," later was changed to "Rocky Boy." Fishing is available in a number of well-stocked streams and ponds. A tribal license—$5 for 1 day or $10 for 3 days—is required. Bear Paw Ski Bowl is open mid-December to early April. Phone (406) 395-4282.

HELENA (C-3) pop. 24,600, elev. 4,047'

Helena succeeded the other gold camps of Bannack and Virginia City as the territorial capital in 1875. It became the state capital in 1889 after a hotly contested fight between W.A. Clark and Marcus Daly. The city owes its existence to "The Georgians," four weary and discouraged Southern prospectors, who in 1864 stumbled down a gulch and grimly dubbed it "Last Chance Gulch," only to find gold where the city's main street now runs.

Later a more suitable name, Helena (He-LAY-na), was put to a vote. But the miners and the bullwhackers did not like the name's feminine ring. Consequently the emphasis was shifted to the first syllable, with the second "e" almost silent, and HEL-e-na became the accepted pronunciation. The gold rush faded quickly, and Helena settled down to become a trade center for the surrounding goldfields.

Marysville, a ghost town, is 25 miles northwest off CR 279. During the 1880s and '90s the town reigned as Montana's leading gold producer. The remnants of its saloons, shops and sidewalks still can be seen.

Helena Area Chamber of Commerce: 225 Cruise Ave., Suite A, Helena, MT 59601; phone (406) 442-4120 or (800) 743-5362.

Shopping areas: Once the quarters of miners, muleskinners and Chinese laborers during the gold rush, the buildings along Reeder's Alley, 100 S. Park Ave., now contain specialty shops.

★ **CATHEDRAL OF ST. HELENA** (Roman Catholic), jct. of Lawrence and Warren sts., is a handsome neo-Gothic structure modeled after the Votive Church of Vienna, Austria. Interior furnishings are of Carrara marble, and the stained-glass windows were made in Munich, Germany. Allow 30 minutes minimum. Mon.-Fri. 10-4, Sat. 10-6:30, Sun. 7-noon. Phone (406) 442-5825.

★ **LAST CHANCE GULCH TOUR** departs from Montana Historical Society Museum *(see attraction listing).* This 1-hour jaunt makes a circuit through the present and past of Helena on "The Last Chancer," an automotive tour train. Tours depart daily on the hour 10-11, 1-4 and 6, July-Aug; at 10, 11, 1, 2 and 3, in June; at 11, 1, and 3, May 15-30 and in Sept. Fare $5; over 64, $4.50; under 12, $4. Phone (406) 442-1023.

Pioneer Cabin, 218 S. Park Ave., is on the tour route. This 1865 cabin is furnished with pioneer articles. Allow 30 minutes minimum. Mon.-Fri. 10:30-noon and 1-3, Memorial Day-Labor Day; by appointment rest of year (contact the caretaker in the adjacent cabin at 212 S. Park St.). Admission $1, children free. Phone (406) 443-7641.

★ **MONTANA HISTORICAL SOCIETY MUSEUM, LIBRARY AND ARCHIVES,** across from the State Capitol at 225 N. Roberts St., recounts the history of Montana and the Northwest. One of the larger collections of C.M. Russell's paintings and sculpture, and a gallery containing the work of noted photographer F. Jay Haynes, are of interest. The Montana Homeland exhibition uses more than 2,000 artifacts, photographs and documents to trace Montana history from the end of the last ice age through World War II.

Mon.-Fri. 8-6, Sat.-Sun. and holidays 9-5, Memorial Day-Labor Day; Mon.-Fri. 8-5, Sat. 9-5, rest of year. Closed holidays the day after Labor Day-day before Memorial Day. Donations. Phone (406) 444-2694.

ORIGINAL GOVERNOR'S MANSION is at 304 N. Ewing. Built in 1888, the mansion was the Victorian home of nine Montana governors 1913-59. The house is furnished in period. Allow 30 minutes minimum. Guided tours are given on the hour Tues.-Sun. noon-4, Memorial Day-Labor Day; Tues.-Sat. noon-4, Apr. 1-day before Memorial Day and day after Labor Day-Dec. 31; by appointment rest of year. Closed holidays. Free. Phone (406) 444-4789.

★ **STATE CAPITOL,** 6th and Montana sts., is faced with sandstone and Montana granite and topped with a dome of Montana copper. The cornerstone was laid July 4, 1899, and the building was dedicated July 4, 1902. Historical paintings and statues decorate the interior; prominent among these is Charles M. Russell's largest painting, the 12-by-25-foot "Lewis and Clark Meeting Indians at Ross' Hole," in the House of Representatives.

Allow 30 minutes minimum. Daily 8-5; closed holidays. Guided tours are given daily on the hour 9-4, early June to mid-Sept.; by appointment rest of year. Free. Phone (406) 444-4789.

HELENA NATIONAL FOREST

Elevations in the forest range from 3,600 ft. at the gates of the Missouri River to 9,411 ft. on Red Mountain in the Lincoln district. Refer to AAA maps for additional elevation information.

Helena National Forest, in west central Montana, encompasses 976,000 acres, straddles the Continental Divide and embraces the Big Belt and the Elkhorn mountains. The Missouri River passes through the Helena Valley near the center of the forest. Vegetation ranges from sagebrush and bunchgrass to Douglas fir, lodgepole pine and spruce.

There are more than 700 miles of trails and ,600 miles of forest roads. Continental Divide National Scenic Trail passes through the forest. Ten campgrounds, picnic grounds, good hunting and fishing, rockhounding, historic sites, wilderness areas and several ghost towns are among the forest's attractions. For further information contact the Forest Supervisor, Helena National Forest, 2880 Skyway Dr., Helena, MT 59601; phone (406) 449-5201. *See Recreation Chart and the AAA Northwestern CampBook.*

★ **THE GATES OF THE MOUNTAINS RECREATION AREA**, reached by boat or trails, is 20 mi. . of Helena via I-15 exit 209 to Gates of the Mountains Landing. Magnificent 1,200-foot limestone walls line the canyon, where the Missouri River pushes through the Big Belt Range. Foot trails lead to interesting rock formations and Gates of the Mountain Wilderness. Good fishing waters are nearby on the Missouri River.

Boat trips, with stopovers at Meriwether picnic area, depart every 2 hours Mon.-Fri. 11-3, Sat. 10-4, on the hour Sun. and holidays 10-5, July-Aug.; Mon.-Fri. at 11 and 2, every 2 hours Sat.-Sun. and holidays 10-4, in June; Mon.-Fri. at 11 and 2, every 2 hours Sat.-Sun. 11-3, in Sept. Fare $8.50; over 59, $7.50; ages 4-17, $5.50. Phone (406) 458-5241.

HUNGRY HORSE (B-1) pop. 900, elev. 3,100'

HUNGRY HORSE DAM is 15 mi. s.e. of Glacier National Park. One of the world's largest concrete dams, its 2,115-foot crest is crossed by a 10-foot-wide roadway. A visitor center 4 miles east of US 2 has interactive displays, a videotape and information about guided tours. Visitor center open daily 9:30-6, Memorial Day-Labor Day. Guided tours are given daily on the hour 10-5. Free. Phone (406) 387-5241, ext. 361.

HUSON (C-1) pop. 100, elev. 3,015'

THE NINEMILE REMOUNT DEPOT AND RANGER STATION, off I-90 to exit 82, then 4 mi. n. on Remount Rd., is a working ranger station on a 5,000-acre ranch featuring Cape Cod style buildings. A self-guiding tour through the historic site reveals the daily life of the firefighting rangers 1930-53; tour brochures are available at the visitor center. Grand Menard Discovery Trail, 1.5 miles north of the station, features two .7-mile self-guiding tours through a pine forest; trail brochures are available at the visitor center and the trailhead.

Allow 1 hour minimum. Site open daily dawn-dusk. Ranger station open daily 8-4:30. Visitor center open daily 9-5, Memorial Day-Labor Day. Donations. Phone (406) 626-5201.

KALISPELL (B-1) pop. 11,90 elev. 2,956'

Kalispell (KAL-is-pell) is in the Flathead Valley between Glacier National Park *(see place listing p. 91)* and Flathead Lake, a region noted for the production of sweet cherries. The area was known only to the Salish, who called it "the park between the mountains" until 1891 when the Great Northern Railroad laid track to this point. The nearby settlements of Demersville and Ashley were moved to create Kalispell.

Kalispell is circled by dense forests, lakes, rivers and mountains. To the east is the Swan Range of the Rocky Mountains, and to the west, the Kootenai Range. Flathead National Forest *(see place listing p. 88)* has its headquarters in the city.

Local parks include Woodland Park, with lagoons, formal gardens and picnicking. Three forks of the Flatbed river drain into Flatbed Lake, making the area an ideal place for fly fishing, as well as whitewater rafting, kayaking and sailing.

Flathead Convention and Visitors Bureau: 15 Depot Park, Kalispell, MT 59901-4008; phone (406) 756-9091 or (800) 543-3105.

Self-guiding tour: Information about walking tours of historic buildings is available from Kalispell Chamber of Commerce; phone (406) 758-2800. For information about the greater northwestern Montana area contact Glacier Country at (800) 338-5072.

Shopping areas: The Kalispell Farmer's Market, in the Kalispell Center Mall parking lot, offers more than 100 vendors selling homemade and home-grown products.

CONRAD MANSION NATIONAL HISTORIC SITE MUSEUM, 6 blks. e. of Main St. at 4th St. E., was built in 1895 for Kalispell's founder, Charles E. Conrad, who traded and freighted on the Missouri River. The 26-room mansion, restored to its Victorian splendor, contains original furnishings. Visitors can take guided tours of the mansion and self-guided tours of the gardens on the 3-acre site.

Allow 1 hour minimum. Guided tours are given daily 9-8, mid-June to mid-Sept.; 10-5:30, mid-May to mid-June and mid-Sept. to mid-Oct. Last tour 1 hour before closing. Fee $7; senior citizens $6; under 12, $1. MC, VI. Phone (406) 755-2166.

A Starred Attraction

When you see a ★ before an attraction, it's a ***must*** see!

KOOTENAI NATIONAL FOREST

Elevations in the forest range
from 1,862 ft. where the Kootenai
River crosses into Idaho to 8,736 ft.
on Snowshoe Peak. Refer to AAA
maps for additional elevation
information.

In the northwest corner of Montana and a
small section of Idaho, Kootenai National Forest
covers 2,245,000 acres. High, craggy peaks characterize the region; portions of the Cabinet,
Whitefish and Purcell mountains are the main
ranges, attaining elevations as high as 8,700 feet.

The area's climate is modified Pacific Mari-
time, and as a result Kootenai has an abundance
of plant species more common to the Pacific
Coast than to other parts of Montana. Since most
of the forest produces commercial timber, there
is an extensive network of roads.

The Clark Fork elk herd is well known to
hunters. The forest also is home to many non-
game species. Throughout the year bald eagles
can be seen along the Kootenai River north of
Libby; 191 species of birds have been recorded
in the forest. Cabinet Mountains Wilderness has
141 lakes, many that are scenic, stocked with
fish and easily reached by trail. Skiing facilities
are available northwest of Libby. The area has 40
campgrounds and 1,440 miles of hiking trails.

Ross Creek Cedars Scenic Area, off SR 56
southwest of Libby, and Ten Lakes Scenic Area,
on the Canadian border northeast of Eureka, are
reached by local and forest roads. Lake Koocanusa also is a popular recreational spot *(see
Libby p. 100).*

For further information, write the Forest Su-
pervisor, Kootenai National Forest, 506 US 2W,
Libby, MT 59923; phone (406) 293-6211. *See
Recreation Chart and the AAA Northwestern
CampBook.*

LAKESIDE (B-2) pop. 600, elev. 2,900′

On Flathead Lake's west shore, Lakeside offers summer and winter recreation, including
boating, fishing, swimming, cross-country skiing,
snowmobiling and ice fishing.

**West Shore Flathead Lake Chamber of Com-
merce:** P.O. Box 177, Lakeside, MT 59932;
phone (406) 844-3715.

LAME DEER (D-6) pop. 1,900, elev. 3,380′

Lame Deer is the headquarters for the Northern Cheyenne Indian Reservation. Activities on
the reservation include the Sun Dance (dates

vary) and a powwow in July. Cheyenne crafts ar
available at the chamber of commerce, across th
street from the police station.

Lame Deer Chamber of Commerce: P.O. Bo
991, Lame Deer, MT 59043; phone (406
477-8844.

LEWIS AND CLARK NATIONAL FOREST

Elevations in the forest range
from 4,000 ft. in the valley bottoms
to 9,204 ft. on Scapegoat
Mountain. Refer to AAA maps for
additional elevation information.

Lewis and Clark National Forest consists c
1,843,397 acres in west-central Montana. Th
Rocky Mountain Division, which embraces abou
half of the forest, lies along the eastern slope c
the Continental Divide south of Glacier Nationa
Park. It includes part of Bob Marshall Wilder
ness *(see Flathead National Forest p. 88)* and
portion of Scapegoat Wilderness.

The Rocky Mountain Division rises sharpl
from grasslands to peaks between 7,000 an
8,000 feet in elevation. Access to the area is by
number of gravel roads off US 89 that conne
with forest roads and trailheads and serve severa
campgrounds.

Southeast of Great Falls is the Jefferson Div
sion, scattered inland mountain ranges dottin
the prairie, including the Little Belt, Castle
Highwoods, Big Snowy and Little Snowy moun
tain ranges and the north end of the Craz
Mountains. The Jefferson Division has shor
domelike mountains rather than jagged peaks.

The mountains are forest-covered and hav
moderate slopes that present less demanding hik
ing and riding trails than those found in th
Rocky Mountain Division. There are man
streams but no large rivers or lakes.

Winter sports are available near Kings Hi
Summit, some 40 miles north of White Sulphu
Springs, Choteau *(see place listings p. 111 an
84),* and Neihart. For further information conta
the Forest Supervisor, Lewis and Clark Nationa
Forest, 1101 15th St. N., P.O. Box 869, Gre
Falls, MT 59403; phone (406) 791-7700. *Se
Recreation Chart and the AAA Northweste
CampBook.*

LEWISTOWN (C-4) pop. 6,100, elev. 3,963′

Lewistown originally was a trading post on th
Carroll Trail between Helena and Carroll. Fir
called Reed's Fort, it later was renamed Lewi
town after the military officer who established

ort nearby in 1876. Trading, only on a larger scale, continues to support the town, which is a market for the large cattle ranches and wheat arms of central Montana.

Lewistown Area Chamber of Commerce: 408 N.E. Main St., P.O. Box 818, Lewistown, MT 9457; phone (406) 538-5436.

CENTRAL MONTANA MUSEUM, 408 N.E. Main St., documents area history through collections of minerals, guns and American Indian and Western artifacts. Allow 30 minutes minimum. Mon.-Fri. 8-5 (also Sat.-Sun. 10-4, Memorial Day-Labor Day); closed Jan. 1, July 4, Thanksgiving nd Dec. 25. Donations. Phone (406) 538-5436.

LIBBY (B-1) pop. 2,500, elev. 2,086′

Natural resources have been the mainstay of Libby's economy since its settlement in the 860s. Drawn by stories of gold in the north, prospectors first gathered in this region and named the town after the daughter of one of the men who discovered gold in a nearby creek. Logging and lumbering are the town's leading businesses.

Libby's environs contribute to the town's popularity as a recreational center. The nearby Kootenai National Forest *(see place listing p. 00)* provides extensive lands for public use, and anglers enjoy fishing in the Kootenai River and its tributaries. About 17 miles north, Libby Dam *(see Recreation Chart and the AAA Northwestern CampBook)* impounds the Kootenai River, creating 90-mile-long Lake Koocanusa, an excellent area for boating, fishing and swimming.

Libby Area Chamber of Commerce: 905 W. 9th St., P.O. Box 704, Libby, MT 59923; phone 406) 293-4167.

HERITAGE MUSEUM, .5 mi. e. at 1367 US 2S, is in a 12-sided log building. It contains an exhibit about Kootenai Indians and artifacts of such early inhabitants as American Indians, trappers, miners and lumbermen. Art, wildlife and agricultural and machinery exhibits also are presented both inside and outside. Mon.-Sat. 10-5, Sun. -5, June-Aug. Donations. Phone (406) 293-7521 or 293-4733.

★ LITTLE BIGHORN BATTLEFIELD NATIONAL MONUMENT (E-6)

Covering 1.2 square miles, Little Bighorn Battlefield National Monument commemorates the dramatic climax of the Indian Wars by preserving the site of this American Indian victory. In the Valley of the Little Bighorn River in June 876, Lt. Col. George A. Custer and the 210 men of the 7th Cavalry Regiment under his command made their last stand against several thousand Lakota, Arapaho and Northern Cheyenne, many of whom were fleeing the restrictions of the reservation.

The monument embraces a national cemetery established in 1879, various monuments and memorials and a historical museum with maps, photographs and dioramas depicting the battle. The main entrance is 15 miles southeast of Hardin via exit 510 off I-90, then a half-mile east via US 212. Just inside the entrance is a visitor center where park rangers provide tour information and self-guiding tour brochures. Summer bus tours also are available; allow 1 hour minimum.

Monument and visitor center open daily 8-8, Memorial Day-Labor Day; 8-6, Apr. 1-day before Memorial Day and day after Labor Day-Sept. 30; 8-4:30, rest of year. Closed Jan. 1, Thanksgiving and Dec. 25. Admission mid-Apr. to mid-Nov. $6 per private vehicle, $3 per person arriving by bicycle, bus, motorcycle or on foot; free to all rest of year. Phone (406) 638-2621.

LITTLE BIGHORN BATTLEFIELD AUTO TOUR tapes are available at the Little Bighorn Battlefield visitor center and Big Horn County Historical Museum and Visitor Center *(see Hardin p. 97)* as well as other local outlets. The self-guiding audiotape tour of Little Bighorn Battlefield guides motorists along 5-mile Battlefield Road to the Reno-Benteen Entrenchment Defense Site and back to the area of Custer's last stand. Two color maps are included. Including the Reno-Benteen Entrenchment Trail Walk, the tour takes about 2 hours; it takes 80 minutes without the walk.

Also available is an audiotape called "Custer's Last Battle." The automobile-tour tape is $9.95 and the Custer tape is $12.95. For information or to order tapes phone (406) 638-2465.

LIVINGSTON (D-4) pop. 6,700, elev. 4,489′

The lush grasses of Paradise Valley were ideal for raising cattle, and the valley's warm chinook winds protected the area from bitter Montana winters. When the Northern Pacific Railroad laid tracks in 1882, both the cattle industry and Livingston flourished. Among the town's more memorable residents was Calamity Jane, but after she was jailed following a disturbance, her fondness for Livingston faded and she left town.

Livingston is at the head of Paradise Valley, through which flows the Yellowstone River and around which rise the Crazy Mountains and the Absaroka and Gallatin ranges of the Rockies. The area offers opportunities for wildlife viewing, hunting, fishing, rafting, backpacking, camping, skiing and snowmobiling. A scenic drive, US 89, connects Livingston to Gardiner and the northern entrance to Yellowstone National Park. Livingston was the original entrance to Yellowstone.

Livingston Area Chamber of Commerce: 208 W. Park St., Livingston, MT 59047; phone (406) 222-0850.

Self-guiding tours: A brochure outlining a walking tour of the historic business district is available at Park County Museum *(see attraction listing)* and the chamber of commerce.

DEPOT CENTER MUSEUM, 200 W. Park St., features the exhibit "Rails Across the Rockies: A Century of People and Places." Built in 1902, the restored Northern Pacific Railroad station depot is in the Italian Renaissance style. It was designed by the same architectural firm that designed New York's Grand Central Station. Events are scheduled throughout the year. Picnicking is permitted. Mon.-Sat. 9-5, Sun. 1-5, mid-May to Sept. 30. Admission $3; over 61 and ages 6-16, $2; family rate $8. Phone (406) 222-2300.

INTERNATIONAL FLY FISHING CENTER is off I-90 exit 333, 1.3 mi. n.e. on US 89, then s.e. on B Street to 215 E. Lewis. Displays include a large collection of fly-fishing and fishing art, and rooms are devoted to aquariums of cold- and warm-water fish. Other rooms feature fly-fishing memorabilia from antique to present-day equipment, hundreds of flies and a hands-on display for fly-tiers. Allow 1 hour, 30 minutes minimum. Mon.-Sat. 10-6, June 15-Sept. 15; by appointment rest of year. Admission $3; ages 7-14, $1. Phone (406) 222-9369.

PARK COUNTY MUSEUM is off I-90 exit 333, then 10 blks. n to 118 W. Chinook St. The museum chronicles Northern Pacific Railroad history, native cultures, natural resources and pioneer lifestyles in Montana. Other displays include a Yellowstone Park stagecoach and a Northern Pacific caboose. Allow 30 minutes minimum. Daily 9-5, June 1-Labor Day; by appointment rest of year. Admission $3; over 59 and ages 12-18, $2; ages 6-11, $1. Phone (406) 222-4184.

LOLO NATIONAL FOREST

With Missoula as its headquarters, Lolo National Forest embraces about 2,100,000 acres in western Montana from the Swan Range in the northeast to the Idaho border, an area 120 miles long and 40 to 80 miles wide. Although the Lolo is an important timber producer, many of its south-facing slopes are open and grassy. It also is one of the principal elk areas in western Montana. The 60,000-acre Rattlesnake National Recreation Area and Wilderness is within the forest.

Recreational opportunities abound on 3,500 miles of streams, including Rock Creek, a haven for trout-fishing enthusiasts. The forest has numerous camping and/or picnic sites and 1,780 miles of hiking trails; winter activities include downhill and cross-country skiing, snowmobiling along 360 miles of designated trails and ice fishing. Some recreation facilities are designed for handicapped access; inquire at a ranger station.

Approximately 485 species of fish and wildlife inhabit the forest.

The forest has four visitor center Smokejumpers Visitor Center; The Ninemile Re mount Depot and Ranger Station *(see Huson 99)*; Missoula Area Visitor Information at Fo Missoula; and the Northern Region Office in th federal building at the junction of Pine and Pa tee sts. in Missoula.

For further information, write the Forest S pervisor, Lolo National Forest, Building 24 Fort Missoula, Missoula, MT 59804; phone (40 329-3814. *See Recreation Chart and the AA Northwestern CampBook.*

LOMA (B-4) pop. 100, elev. 2,574′

At the convergence of the Missouri and Ma ias rivers, Lomas was the site of an importa decision in June 1805. When the snowme swelled both rivers to the point that Lewis ar Clark had trouble determining which was th Missouri, they fortunately made the correct ca and continued westward.

Lewis named the other river Maria's after h cousin and sweetheart Maria Wood, to whom h later proposed. Eventually the apostrophe w dropped, as was Lewis by his beloved.

RECREATIONAL ACTIVITIES
Canoeing
• **Virgelle Mercantile & Missouri River Cano Co.,** 12 mi. n. on US 87 then 7.5 mi. e. on gravel road. Write HC 67, Box 50, Virgell MT 59460. Other activities are offered. Dai mid-May to mid-Sept. Phone (406) 378-3110.

MALTA (B-5) pop. 2,300, elev. 2,248′

Named for the island in the Mediterranea Malta was the center of a cattle empire th reached from Glasgow to Havre and from th Missouri River to Canada during the late 19 century. Wheat and alfalfa have joined cattle a the area's leading products.

A large boulder east at the intersection of U 2 and Sleeping Buffalo Resort looks like a slee ing buffalo. The Assiniboine Indians revered and the markings on it had a part in their trib rituals.

The Little Rocky Mountains, called "islan mountains" by early American Indians, are 4 miles southwest on US 191. Gold was discov ered in the mountains in 1884, and the histori remains set the scene for the mountain commun ties of Zortman and Landusky. Legend has it tha Butch Cassidy and Kid Curry hid out in th area.

Malta Area Chamber of Commerce: 10½ 4th St. E., Drawer GG, P.O. Box 1420, Malt MT 59538; phone (406) 654-1776 or (80 704-1776.

BOWDOIN NATIONAL WILDLIFE REFUGE, mi. e. on CR2 following signs, is a 15,500-ac

eeding and feeding area for migratory water-
wl, shorebirds and other wildlife, including
er. It is one of the few northwestern nesting ar-
s of the white pelican. The refuge can be seen
a a 15-mile self-guiding automobile tour
eather permitting); ideal viewing times are
rly fall and late spring. Allow 1 hour mini-
um. Refuge open daily dawn-dusk. Headquar-
s open Mon.-Fri. 7-3:30. Visitor center open
ily 24 hours. Free. Phone (406) 654-2863.

ILLIPS COUNTY MUSEUM, 431 US 2E, con-
ns exhibits relating to the county's pioneer
ys, agriculture and mining. Featured are a
ge collection of American Indian buckskins
d beadwork and a dinosaur exhibit, which in-
ides fossils, a complete tyrannosaur skull, a
e-size albertosaurus skeleton cast and photo-
aphs of the dig. Allow 1 hour minimum. Daily
-6, mid-May to mid-Sept. Admission $3, under
free. Phone (406) 654-1037.

MEDICINE LAKE (B-7) pop. 400, elev. 1,951'

EDICINE LAKE NATIONAL WILDLIFE REF-
GE, 31,458 acres 24 mi. n. on SR 16, is a nest-
g place for waterfowl and shorebirds. The
fuge houses about 230 species of birds at vari-
s times of the year. Fishing and hunting for
aterfowl, upland game birds and deer are per-
tted in season; obtain maps and information at
fuge headquarters, 1 mile south and 2 miles
st of Medicine Lake. An 18-mile self-guiding
tomobile tour route and picnic facilities are
ailable. Refuge open daily dawn-dusk, May-
pt. Refuge headquarters open Mon.-Fri.
3:30. Free.

MILES CITY (D-6) pop. 8,500, elev. 2,364'

Miles City, once the hunting and camping land
the Crow Nation, developed on the bottom-
nd at the confluence of the Tongue and Yellow-
ne rivers. Gen. Nelson A. Miles arrived at the
outh of the Tongue River in August 1876 to
rce the Cheyenne and Sioux to return to the
servations. Miles built Fort Keogh at the site in
77 and used it as a base for controlling the lo-
l tribes.

Main Street in times past was a block of sa-
ons, gambling dens and brothels on the south,
d banks, businesses and pawn shops on the
rth. Miles City has become a growing retail
d service hub for eastern Montana and a center
r cattle, sheep and crop farms.

iles City Area Chamber of Commerce: 901
ain St., Miles City, MT 59301; phone (406)
2-2890.

JSTER COUNTY ART CENTER is on Water
ant Rd. in the park overlooking the Yellow-
ne River. Housed in a 1910 former water-

treatment plant, the center's two galleries feature
changing exhibits of Western, historical and contemporary art. Tues.-Sun. 1-5; closed holidays.
Free. Phone (406) 232-0635.

**RANGE RIDERS MUSEUM AND BERT CLARK
GUN COLLECTION** is 1 mi. w. on US 10/I-94
Bus. Loop. This nine-building complex features
antiques and artifacts, archeological and geological specimens, and one of the Fort Keogh officer's quarters. A detailed miniature replica of Fort
Keogh is in the coach house. The Bert Clark gun
collection comprises more than 400 pieces, including an elephant gun and a set of Belgian du-
eling pistols. Allow 1 hour minimum. Daily 8-8,
Apr.-Oct. Admission $3.50; over 64, $3; ages
13-22, $1; ages 6-12, 50c. Phone (406)
232-6146.

MISSOULA (C-2) pop. 42,900, elev. 3,223'

Missoula, at the mouth of Hell Gate Canyon,
straddles the route the Salish Indians traveled to
reach the Great Plains to hunt buffalo. Meriwether Lewis and William Clark later followed
the same route through the canyon and camped
west of its entrance on the site of present-day
Missoula. Many American Indians died in the
canyon, as the Blackfoot regularly ambushed the
Salish, which prompted French-Canadian trappers to christen the site Porte de L'Enfer, "Gate
of Hell."

One of the first lumber mills in the region began in Missoula. Lumber remains not only a major industry but also a major concern. The U.S.
Forest Service maintains in Missoula its Region
No. 1 headquarters; a research station devoted to
forest fire research; and the smokejumpers' training center. The University of Montana supports
these studies with a 22,000-acre experimental
forest in addition to conservation and wildlife research stations.

A short drive in any direction will lead into a
national forest or a wilderness area. The Rattlesnake Creek Watershed, 6 miles north of downtown, has many small lakes, streams and trails.

A Carousel for Missoula is a hand-carved
1918 merry-go-round created by volunteers. Located in Caras Park, rides are offered year-round;
phone (406) 549-8382.

Missoula Convention & Visitors Bureau: 825
E. Front St., P.O. Box 7577, Missoula, MT
59807; phone (406) 543-6623 or (800) 526-3465.

Self-guiding tours: Brochures outlining a driving tour of historic sites and a walking tour
along the Clark Fork River through downtown,
are available from the convention and visitors
bureau.

Shopping areas: Southgate Mall, US 93 and
South Avenue, counts Hennessy's, JCPenney and
Sears among its 105 stores. The restored historic

downtown, with a lighted riverfront nearby, also offers distinctive shopping opportunities.

ART MUSEUM OF MISSOULA, 335 N. Pattee St., contains art of the Western states. Monthly changing exhibits feature works by national and international artists. Guided tours are available. Tues. noon-8, Wed.-Sat. noon-6. Admission $2, under 18 free; free to all Tues. Reservations for tours are recommended. Phone (406) 728-0447.

HISTORICAL MUSEUM AT FORT MISSOULA is s. on Reserve St. to South Ave., then 1 mi. w. following signs. The museum is at the center of what was Fort Missoula, established in 1877 at the height of the conflict with the Nez Perce under Chief Joseph. Galleries and exhibits depict the roles of the timber industry, forest management and early settlement in Missoula County history. Of the 13 structures and original fort buildings that remain, five have been renovated. Guided tours are available. Festivals are held in May and on July 4.

Allow 1 hour minimum. Mon.-Sat. 10-5, Sun. noon-5, Memorial Day weekend-Labor Day; Tues.-Sun. noon-5, rest of year. Closed holidays, except Memorial Day, July 4 and Labor Day. Donations. Reservations are required for tours. Phone (406) 728-3476.

SAVE **MONTANA HOSPITALITY TOURS** departs from several area hotels and offers guided tours to Glacier National Park. The narrated tours journey past St. Ignatius Mission, Port Polson, Flathead Lake, Lake McDonald, Going-to-the-Sun Road and Logan Pass. A continental breakfast, picnic lunch and dinner are provided. Other excursions include American Indian, historic, wildlife, working-ranch and city tours. Allow a full day. Tours depart Mon.-Fri. at 7:30 a.m., June 15-Sept. 15. Fare $150. Reservations are required. AE, MC, VI. Phone (406) 883-1055.

ROCKY MOUNTAIN ELK FOUNDATION/WILDLIFE VISITOR CENTER, 2291 W. Broadway, contains a wildlife art gallery, a collection of world-record elk displays and many life-size mounts, including grizzly bear, mountain goats and bighorn sheep. Wildlife films are shown continuously. Daily 8-6, Memorial Day-Labor Day; Mon.-Fri. 8:30-5, Sat.-Sun. 10-5, rest of year. Closed Jan. 1, Easter, Thanksgiving and Dec. 25. Donations. Phone (406) 523-4545.

ST. FRANCIS XAVIER CHURCH, 420 W. Pine St., was built in 1889 and is noted for its 144-foot steeple, stained-glass windows and paintings by Brother Joseph Carignano. Visitors may watch a 5-minute videotape explaining the paintings. Allow 30 minutes minimum. Mon.-Sat. 8:30-6. Free. Phone (406) 542-0321.

SMOKEJUMPERS BASE AERIAL FIRE DEPOT, 7 mi. w. on W. Broadway, is next to Johnson-Bell Airport. Displays include dioramas, historical photographs, and artifacts relating to the history of firefighting in the Forest Service. Forest Service smokejumpers give guided tours of the ba and offer firsthand accounts of firefighting a smokejumping. Tours are given daily on the h 10-11 and 2-4, Memorial Day-Labor Day. De open daily 8:30-5, Memorial Day-Labor Day; appointment rest of year. Donations. Phone (4(329-4934 or 329-4900.

 RECREATIONAL ACTIVITIES

Skiing

- **Snowbowl Ski Area,** 12 mi. n.w. Write 17 Snowbowl Rd., Missoula, MT 59802. Ot activities are offered. Wed.-Mon. late Nov. mid-Apr. Phone (406) 549-9777.

White-water Rafting

- **Pangaea Expeditions** departs from Albert Gorge. Write P.O. Box 5753, Missoula, M 59806. Daily May 15-Sept. 1. Phone (4(721-7719 or (888) 721-7719.

MOIESE (C-2) elev. 2,600'

NATIONAL BISON RANGE, s.w. via SR 2: contains from 375 to 500 buffaloes as well herds of elk, pronghorn antelopes, deer a mountain sheep on its 18,540 acres. From m May to mid-October the range can be explo via a 19-mile self-guiding driving tour, whi takes about 2 hours; during the rest of the ye only portions of the site are open. Range op daily dawn-dusk. Visitor center open daily 8 mid-May to mid-Oct.; Mon.-Fri. 8-4:30, rest year. Closed holidays during the off season.

Admission $4 per private vehicle. Tw wheeled vehicles are not allowed on any bisc range tours. Trailers and motorhomes permitted only in portions of the range; check the visitor center. The gravel and dirt roa present some long climbs and steep downgrad Visitors must keep their vehicles on the t road, and *must* remain in or near them. Ph (406) 644-2211.

MONIDA (E-3)

Monida is a former railroad town at the f of Monida Pass and the Continental Divide. S nic highway I-15 passes near town, offeri views of the Centennial Mountains to the e and the Italian Peaks to the west. The na Monida is derived from the combination of Mc tana and Idaho.

RED ROCKS LAKES NATIONAL WILDLI REFUGE, I-15 exit 0, then 28 mi. e. on a gra road, was established as a refuge for trumpe swans in 1935. The lakes, marshes, creeks a the isolation of the Centennial Valley have ma this sanctuary one of North America's more i portant nesting areas for the swans. The pri ewing season is June through September. Camping and primitive camping facilities are vailable. No fuel available after exiting the interstate. Mon.-Fri. 7:30-4. Office hours Mon.-Fri. :30-4. Inquire locally about road conditions. ree. Phone (406) 276-3536.

NEVADA CITY—
see Virginia City p. 109.

OVANDO (C-2) elev. 4,100'

 RECREATIONAL ACTIVITIES

Hunting

WTR Outfitters, n. on SR 200 to 520 Cooper Lake Rd., Ovando, MT 59854. Other activities are offered. Mid-Sept. through Nov. 30 Phone (406) 793-5666 or (800) 987-5666.

PHILIPSBURG (D-2) pop. 1,000, elev. 5,270'

GRANITE COUNTY MUSEUM & CULTURAL CENTER, downtown at 135 Sansome St., offers a ook at a miner's life beginning with a mural depicting above-ground activities, an assay office nd a reconstructed cabin. Visitors can then view what a real vein would have looked like as well s tools, an ore car and other mining memorabilia. Daily 10-4, Apr. 15-Dec. 15. Admission $3, nder 12 free. Phone (406) 859-3020.

POLARIS (E-2) elev. 6,355'

Polaris is the beginning point of the Pioneer scenic Byway, which stretches for 32 miles to he Wise River and affords glimpses of Montana's wildlife including antelope, deer and awks. En route lies Crystal Park, a natural crystal mountain where visitors can dig for various rystals. Another stop along the drive is Elkhorn Hot Springs, a hot springs pool. This picturesque oad is open until the first snowfall.

POLSON (C-2) pop. 3,300, elev. 2,931'

Polson is in a natural amphitheater at the foot of Flathead Lake. During May and June water ours through the 200- to 500-foot perpendicular valls of the Flathead River Gorge at the rate of 00,000 gallons per second. Legend has it that 'aul Bunyan dug the channel connecting the iver and the lake.

Polson Area Chamber of Commerce: P.O. Box 67, Polson, MT 59860; phone (406) 883-5969.

FLATHEAD LAKE STATE PARK, just n., contains he largest natural freshwater lake west of the Mississippi. Points of interest include Big Arm,

Elmo, Finley Point, Wayfarers, West Shore and Yellow Bay state parks *(see Recreation Chart and the AAA Northwestern CampBook);* Somers Fish Hatchery; Montana University Biological Station; and Station Creek Fish Hatchery. Kerr Dam, one of the larger privately owned hydroelectric developments in Montana, is south of the lake on the Flathead River. Admission $3 per private vehicle or 50c per person arriving by bicycle, bus, motorcycle or on foot. Phone (406) 837-4196 for Big Arm, (406) 887-2715 for Finley Point, or (406) 982-3291 for Yellow Bay.

KWA TAQ NUK PRINCESS, on US 93, offers narrated tours of scenic Flathead Lake. A 3-hour tour departs daily at 1:30 and a 90-minute tour at 10:30 a.m. and 7:30 p.m., June 1-early Sept. Evening departure time varies; phone ahead. Three-hour tour $16; over 64, $14; ages 6-12, $8; family rate $40. Ninety-minute tour $10; over 64, $9; ages 6-12, $5; family rate $25. Reservations are suggested. MC, VI. Phone (406) 883-2448.

MIRACLE OF AMERICA MUSEUM, 2 mi. s. on US 93, contains a potpourri of American military collectibles, logging and pioneer artifacts, antique musical instruments, motorized and horse-drawn vehicles, and dolls and toys. A pioneer village of 20 walk-in buildings, the Montana Fiddlers Hall of Fame and Paul Bunyan's 65-foot logging boat also are displayed. Picnic facilities are available. Daily 8 a.m.-dusk, June 2-Aug. 31; 8-5, rest of year. Closed Jan. 1, Thanksgiving and Dec. 25. Admission $2.50; ages 3-12, $1. Phone (406) 883-6804.

POLSON-FLATHEAD HISTORICAL MUSEUM, 802 Main St., exhibits items commemorating the pioneer heritage of the surrounding area. Included are a wildlife display, farm machinery and American Indian artifacts. Mon.-Sat. 9-6, Sun. noon-6, Memorial Day-Labor Day. Donations. Phone (406) 883-3049.

 RECREATIONAL ACTIVITIES

White-water Rafting

• Flathead Raft Co., on US 93. Write Box 946-A, Polson, MT 59860. Daily early June-early Sept. Phone (406) 883-5838 or (800) 654-4359.

POMPEYS PILLAR (D-5) elev. 2,880'

Pompeys Pillar acquired its name from the nearby national landmark. Capt. William Clark named the rock after guides Charbonneau and Sacajawea's son, Baptiste, whom he nicknamed Pomp.

POMPEYS PILLAR NATIONAL HISTORIC LANDMARK, 1 mi. n. off I-94, is the huge sandstone formation where Capt. William Clark carved his name in 1806. This inscription is the only physical evidence of the Lewis and Clark expedition. The pillar also bears the names of early trappers, soldiers and settlers who made their way into the area as well as American Indian pictographs. Interpretive tours are available upon request at the visitor center.

Daily 8-8, Memorial Day-Labor Day; 9-5, day after Labor Day-Sept. 30. The site is accessible the rest of the year only by a half-mile walk from a parking area. Admission $3 per private vehicle. Phone (406) 875-2233 for the visitor center, or (406) 657-6262 for the Bureau of Land Management.

PRYOR (E-5) pop. 700, elev. 4,065'

CHIEF PLENTY COUPS STATE PARK, 1 mi. w. off SR 416 following signs, has a museum featuring relics of Chief Plenty Coups, last traditional chief of the Crow Indians. Interpretive displays about Crow Indian culture also are shown. The chief is buried nearby at Medicine Spring. Picnic facilities and fishing opportunities are available. Allow 1 hour minimum. Park open daily 8-8, May-Sept. Visitor Center open daily 10-5, May-Sept.; by appointment rest of year. Admission $3 per private vehicle or 50c per person arriving by bicycle, bus, motorcycle or on foot. Phone (406) 252-1289.

RED LODGE (E-5) pop. 2,000, elev. 5,548'

At the base of the Beartooth Mountains, Red Lodge is an all-year resort town. Winter sports include downhill and cross-country skiing, while summer pursuits range from trout fishing and boating to water skiing on Cooney Reservoir *(see Recreation Chart).*

Local legend attributes the town's name to a tribe of Crow Indians called the Red Lodge Clan, who covered their tepees with the local red clay. Coal-mining operations later drew many Europeans to the area.

Red Lodge Area Chamber of Commerce: 601 N. Broadway, P.O. Box 988, Red Lodge, MT 59068; phone (406) 446-1718.

Self-guiding tour: A visitor guide distributed by the chamber of commerce includes information about a walking tour.

★**BEARTOOTH SCENIC HIGHWAY,** US 212, leads from Red Lodge to the northeastern entrance of Yellowstone National Park via Cooke City. The American Indians called the original Beartooth Pass the "trail above the eagles." This 64-mile road begins at 5,650 feet and rises to the Beartooth Plateau via a series of switchbacks.

After cresting the plateau at an elevation of almost 11,000 feet, where an unobstructed view of more than 75 miles is possible, the road winds past snowfields, small lakes and fields of flow-

ers. Finally it descends into a dense pine fores passing tumbling waterfalls and streams inte spersed with occasional jagged peaks.

Many scenic overlooks have been constructe Even in mid-summer, cool temperatures can t expected at higher elevations; a jacket or sweat is recommended. Allow 3 hours minimum. Th two-lane highway is usually open May throug September.

CARBON COUNTY HISTORICAL SOCIET, 1011 S. Broadway, chronicles local history. E hibits include American Indian, Western, rode and coal-mining items. Allow 1 hour minimun Daily 10-6. Donations. Phone (406) 446-3667.

 RECREATIONAL ACTIVITIES

Skiing

- **Red Lodge Mountain Resort,** 6 mi. w. to 10 Ski Run Rd., P.O. Box 750, Red Lodge, M 59068. Daily 9-4, early Nov. to mid-Ap Phone (406) 446-2610.

White-water Rafting

- 〔SAVE〕 **Adventure Whitewater Inc.** meets passe gers on SR 78 at the Paintbrush Adventur red barn 1 mi. n. of Absarokee. Write P.O. Bo 636, Red Lodge, MT 59068. Other activitie are offered. Daily Memorial Day weeken Labor Day. Phone (406) 446-3061 or (80(897-3061.

RONAN (C-2) pop. 1,500

NINEPIPE AND PABLO NATIONAL WILDLIF REFUGES are 5 mi. s. off US 93, and 7 mi. off US 93, then 3 mi. w. on Reservoir Rd., r spectively. Each refuge covers more than 2,00 acres. Primarily of interest to birdwatchers, thes areas are inhabited by thousands of ducks, gees and other water birds. Surrounding the refuge are 2,700 acres of state wildlife-management a eas open for hunting. Fishing opportunities ar available at certain times (a joint tribal/state pe mit is required).

A cooperative state, federal and tribal wildlif viewing area is available at Ninepipe Nation Wildlife Refuge. Refuge open daily dawn-dusl closed during hunting season, approximately la Sept.-Dec. 31. Some portions are closed durin nesting season, Mar. 1-July 15. The south an west sides of Pablo National Wildlife Refuge a closed to the public. Free. Phone (406) 644-221

ROUNDUP (D-5) pop. 1,800, elev. 3,226'

Renowned for the natural geographical desig that made it ideal for herding livestock, Roundu features mountainous scenery and tree-line streets.

MUSSELSHELL VALLEY HISTORICAL MU SEUM, 524 1st St. W., contains fossils, America Indian artifacts, paintings and exhibits detailin

oundup's history. Changing exhibits are fea-
ured in summer. On the grounds are a smithy,
rint shop and the 1884 NF Ranch home. Daily
-5, late Apr.-late Sept. Donations. Phone (406)
23-1403.

ST. IGNATIUS (C-2) pop. 800, elev. 2,940'

**OUG ALLARD'S FLATHEAD INDIAN MU-
EUM**, on US 93, displays mounted coyotes,
awks, bears and prairie animals as well as pho-
ographs of area residents of the past and present.
xhibits also include clothing, jewelry, pottery
nd tools dating to the 1800s. Allow 30 minutes
iinimum. Daily 9-9, May-Sept.; 9-5:30, rest of
ear. Closed Thanksgiving and Dec. 25. Free.
hone (406) 745-2951.

T. IGNATIUS MISSION, .2 mi. s. on US 93 to
ign, then .2 mi. e., was established by Jesuit
iissionaries in 1854. The mission consists of
wo original residences, the rectory and the brick
hurch built in 1891. The church is decorated
vith 58 dry-fresco paintings executed about 1900
y Brother Joseph Carignano, the mission cook.
museum displays American Indian and reli-
ious items. Mission open daily 9-7, June-Aug.;
-dusk, rest of year. Museum schedule varies;
hone ahead. Donations. Phone (406) 745-2768.

ST. MARY (B-2) elev. 4,550'

OVERED WAGON TOURS, 6 mi. s. on US 89,
ffer a 2-hour narrated tour aboard a horse-
rawn wagon. The guide relates the natural and
ultural history of the timber area. A Western-
tyle meal and entertainment after the ride are
vailable by reservation. Allow 2 hours mini-
ium. Daily 10-6, early June-Sun. after Labor
)ay. Tour $20; ages 7-16, $10. Tour, meal and
ntertainment $35; ages 7-16, $15. Phone (406)
61-5025.

SCOBEY (B-7) pop. 1,200, elev. 2,507'

**ANIELS COUNTY MUSEUM AND PIONEER
OWN**, 7 County Rd., is a restored pioneer town
vith some 40 buildings portraying early 20th-
entury homestead life. A collection of period
ntiques includes vintage vehicles. Guided tours
re available. Allow 1 hour, 30 minutes mini-
ium. Daily 12:30-4:30, Memorial Day-Labor
)ay. Admission $5; ages 6-11, $2.50. Phone
406) 487-5965.

SEELEY LAKE (C-2) pop. 900, elev. 4,028'

Seeley Lake is a year-round recreation area
ucked between the Mission Mountains and
wan Range on scenic route SR 83. In the sum-
ier visitors can indulge in fishing, swimming,
oating, backpacking and horseback riding.
ewer than 10 miles from town are Placid Lake

and Salmon Lake state parks *(see Recreation
Chart)*; Seeley Lake itself has three Forest Service campgrounds, and at the north end of the
lake is the 3.5-mile long Clearwater Canoe Trail.
Northeast of Seeley Lake is the 2.5-mile long
Morrell Falls National Recreation Trail, rated as
"easy." Just east of the Morrell Falls trailhead
access road is the Pyramid Pass Trail into Bob
Marshall Wilderness Area.

In the winter the average snow on the ground
is about 3 feet, and 350 miles of groomed snowmobile trails, primarily in Lolo National Forest,
attract enthusiasts. For information about possible logging activities on the trails contact the
Seeley Lake Ranger District office at (406)
677-2233. Three miles north of town on SR 83,
the ranger station's visitor center provides maps
and brochures about the area. Other local winter-
time diversions include cross-country skiing, ice
fishing and dog sledding.

Seeley Lake Area Chamber of Commerce:
P.O. Box 516, Seeley Lake, MT 59868; phone
(406) 677-2880.

SHELBY (B-3) pop. 2,800, elev. 3,276'

Shelby was one of the towns that the Great
Northern Railroad left in its path as it pushed
across the prairie. In its heyday, the town was
paradise to cowboys after months on the range. A
Saturday night might include carousing, horse
racing, or—as once happened—holding up a
passing opera troupe and making the train con-
ductor do a clog dance to the rhythm of bullets.

Shelby remained a cowboy town until the discovery of oil at the nearby Kevin-Sunburst fields
in 1922. Since then Shelby has settled down as a
commercial center and one of the larger grain-
storage centers in the region. It also is an inland
port for shipping by rail through the Northwest
Express Transportation Authority.

Shelby Area Chamber of Commerce: 187
Main St., P.O. Box 865, Shelby, MT 59474;
phone (406) 434-7184.

MARIAS MUSEUM OF HISTORY AND ART, 4
blks. s. of US 2 at 206 12th Ave., depicts the history of Toole County. This museum presents exhibits about the oil industry, homesteading, the
1923 Dempsey-Gibbons prize fight, barbed wire,
and dinosaur and other fossil bones. Allow 1
hour minimum. Mon.-Fri. 1-5 and 7-9, Sat. 1-4,
Memorial Day-Labor Day; Tues. 1-5, rest of
year; other times by appointment. Closed holidays. Free. Phone (406) 434-2551.

SIDNEY (C-7) pop. 5,200, elev. 1,950'

Sidney is a marketing center for sugar beets
and wheat and serves an active oil drilling and
coal mining region. Tours can be arranged at the
Northern Plains Soil and Water Research Center
on North Central Avenue. One of the larger auction houses in Montana, the Sidney Livestock

Market Center on East Main Street conducts auctions every Wednesday. Local attractions include Fort Union, a late 1800s trapping and trading post, and horseback and wagon train rides.

Sidney Chamber of Commerce: 909 S. Central Ave., Sidney, MT 59270; phone (406) 482-1916.

MON-DAK HERITAGE CENTER, 120 Third Ave. S.E., contains a 17-unit street scene typical of pioneer Montana. Other exhibits include an art gallery, a gun collection, photographs and dinosaur bones and fossils. Allow 2 hours minimum. Daily 10-noon and 1-5, June 1-Labor Day; Tues.-Sun. 1-5, rest of year. Closed Easter and Dec. 25. Admission $2.50; ages 6-18, $1.50. Phone (406) 482-3500.

SILVER GATE (E-4) pop. 100, elev. 7,389′

Silver Gate is at the northeast entrance to Yellowstone National Park. Resembling an alpine village, the town is said to be the only municipality in the nation whose building codes mandate that all structures be made of logs and other materials native to the area.

Silver Gate is an outfitting center for both cross-country skiing and snowmobiling. Fly fishing is excellent in the nearby lakes and streams.

Cooke City Area Chamber of Commerce: US 212, P.O. Box 1071, Cooke City, MT 59020; phone (406) 838-2495.

★ **BEARTOOTH SCENIC HIGHWAY—** *see Red Lodge p. 106.*

SNOWBOWL SKI AREA—
see Missoula p. 104.

SOMERS (B-2) pop. 800, elev. 2,910′

SAVE *FAR WEST* CRUISE SHIP, 8 mi. s. on US 93 at Somers dock, provides 90-minute scenic cruises on Flathead Lake. Brunch and sunset cruises also are offered. Cruises depart daily at 2, mid-June to mid-Sept. Sunset cruise departs Sun.-Tues. at 7. Fare $8; over 64, $7; under 12, $5. Reservations are required. MC, VI. Phone (406) 857-3203 or 837-5569.

STEVENSVILLE (D-2) pop. 1,200, elev. 3,524′

ST. MARY'S MISSION, w. end of Fourth St., was established in 1841 by Father Pierre DeSmet. The present mission complex includes the 1880s-style restored chapel and Father Anthony Ravalli's log house, which contains a pharmacy with a "ride-up" window. A cemetery is on the grounds. Chief Victor's cabin is a small museum that displays American Indian artifacts, original furnishings and items created and used by the early missionaries.

Picnic facilities are available. Allow 30 mi utes minimum. Guided tours are given daily 1 4:15, Apr. 15-Oct. 15. Admission $3, studen with ID $1. Phone (406) 777-5734.

TERRY (C-7) pop. 700, elev. 2,253′

In the heart of agate country, Terry is t home of acclaimed photographer Evelyn Car eron. Many of the pictures she took 1894-192 to chronicle the lives of Terry's early settle were compiled in a book more than 50 yea later.

PRAIRIE COUNTY MUSEUM, Logan and Lau dre sts., housed in the Old State Bank of Ter building, displays local memorabilia. A dentist office, barber shop, library and butcher shop a among features. Area fossils also are displaye Mon. and Wed.-Fri. 9-3, Sat.-Sun. 1-5, Memori Day weekend-Labor Day. Donations. Phor (406) 635-4040.

THREE FORKS (D-3) pop. 1,200, elev. 4,061′

Three Forks was a favorite American Indi hunting ground near the headwaters of the Mi souri River. In 1805 Meriwether Lewis and Wi liam Clark documented their discovery of t beginning of the world's longest river syster Sacajawea, the wife of one of their guides, live in this area with the Shoshone until she was ki napped and raised by the Minnetaree. A plaqu in Sacajawea Park downtown commemorates h contribution to the success of the Lewis ar Clark expedition.

The region supported several trading posts f trappers during the early 1800s; however, due skirmishes with the Indians, their existence w short-lived. The first permanent non-native settl ment was established nearby in 1864. As rai roads and highways provided access to the are settlers arrived, and Three Forks was founded 1908. Excellent hunting and fishing opportuniti attract visitors.

Three Forks Chamber of Commerce: P.O. B 1103, Three Forks, MT 59752; phone (40 285-4556.

HEADWATERS HERITAGE MUSEUM, Cedar ar Main sts., depicts life in an early 1900s villa through replicas of rooms from a settler's hous blacksmith shop, railroad dispatcher's offic schoolroom and millinery shop. Daily 9-5, Jun Sept.; by appointment rest of year. Closed July Free. Phone (406) 285-4778.

★ **LEWIS AND CLARK CAVERNS STAT PARK—** *see Cardwell p. 84.*

MADISON BUFFALO JUMP STATE HISTORI SITE is 5 mi. e. on I-90, then 7 mi. s. on Buffa Jump Rd. As long as 2,000 years ago, America

Indians hunted by driving buffaloes off a cliff on this 618-acre site. Picnic facilities are available. Allow 30 minutes minimum. Park open daily dawn-dusk. Admission $3 per private motorized vehicle. Trailers are not allowed; the approach road is gravel. Phone (406) 285-4556.

MISSOURI HEADWATERS STATE PARK, 527 acres, is 3 mi. e., then 3 mi. n. of US 10 at Trident Junction. Discovered July 27, 1805, by the Lewis and Clark expedition, the headwaters are formed by the joining of the Madison, Gallatin and Jefferson rivers. A scenic overlook building and a campground are nearby.

Park open daily dawn-dusk, May-Sept. Admission $3 per private vehicle or 50c per person arriving by bicycle, bus, motorcycle or on foot; camping fee $8. Phone (406) 285-3198. *See Recreation Chart and the AAA Northwestern CampBook.*

TOWNSEND (D-3) pop. 1,600, elev. 3,813'

BROADWATER COUNTY MUSEUM, 133 N. Walnut St., contains pioneer artifacts that chronicle local history. Allow 30 minutes minimum. Daily 1-5, mid-May to mid-Sept. Donations. Phone (406) 266-5252.

★ VIRGINIA CITY (E-3) pop. 100, elev. 5,822'

After fruitless panning along the Yellowstone River, six prospectors stumbled onto Alder Creek in May 1863, and their discovery of gold led to the establishment of a town. The settlement attracted thousands of miners and a band of renegades said to have committed more than 190 murders in 6 months. The miners formed a secret group called The Vigilantes, who captured and hanged 21 of the criminals, including the outlaws' leader, the sheriff.

One of the older cities in the state, Virginia City served as territorial capital 1865-76. More than 20 early buildings have been reconstructed; others have been reconstructed and can be visited. Among these are the state's first newspaper office, an equipped pharmacy of the period, the Wells Fargo Express Office, the Bale of Hay Saloon and the general stores, which carry 1860-80 merchandise.

Gold panning, hunting and fishing opportunities are available. A 1935 gold dredge can be seen at the Alder Gulch River of Gold Mining Museum. All facilities are open mid-June through Labor Day.

Virginia City Chamber of Commerce: P.O. Box 122, Virginia City, MT 59755; phone (800) 829-2969.

GILBERT BREWERY, corner of Hamilton and Cover sts., features "The Brewery Follies," a va-

riety show by the Virginia City Players. Performances are given Sat. at 6 and 9 p.m., Wed.-Fri. and Sun.-Mon. at 8:30 p.m., the first Sat. in June-Labor Day. Admission $12. Reservations are suggested. Phone (406) 843-5377 or (800) 648-7588.

J. SPENCER WATKINS MEMORIAL MUSEUM (Madison County Museum), 219 W. Wallace St., displays items that chronicle the history of pioneer miners, ranchers and farmers. Daily 9-6, mid-June to mid-Sept. Donations. Phone (406) 843-5321.

NEVADA CITY, 1.5 mi. w. on SR 287, sprang up with the discovery of gold in 1863. Some of Montana Territory's original buildings have been moved to this site and restored to form the Nevada City Museum. The Music Hall contains a collection of mechanical musical machines. Allow 1 hour minimum. Daily 10-7 mid-May to mid-Sept. Museum $5; senior citizens $4; ages 4-12, $3. Museum and a round-trip ride on the Alder Gulch Work Train $7; ages 6-12, $5. Phone (406) 843-5377.

Alder Gulch Work Train makes regular trips between Virginia City and Nevada City on a narrow-gauge line. Allow 1 hour minimum. Daily 10:30-5, Memorial Day-Labor Day. Round-trip fare (includes a museum housed in restored railroad cars) $4; senior citizens $3; ages 6-12, $2.50.

THOMPSON-HICKMAN MEMORIAL MUSEUM, downtown at 218 E. Wallace St., contains state and local memorabilia interpreting the history, geology and culture of 19th-century Virginia City. Allow 30 minutes minimum. Daily 10-5, mid-May to mid-Sept. Donations. Phone (406) 843-5346.

VIRGINIA CITY OPERA HOUSE, 340 W. Wallace St., presents mysteries, comedies and melodramas performed in the style of the 19th-century touring companies that regularly stopped in this town. For reservations write Fairweather Inn, P.O. Box 314, Virginia City, MT 59755. Shows Tues.-Fri. at 8 p.m., Sat. at 4 and 8 p.m., Sun. at 4, mid-June to early Sept. Admission $12; under 12, $7. Phone (406) 843-5377 or (800) 648-7588.

WEST GLACIER (B-2) pop. 300, elev. 3,215'

West Glacier is the western rail and highway entrance to Glacier National Park (*see place listing p. 91*). Golf and fishing are popular in the area. One golf course has rules that include: "do not throw clubs or balls at tame deer" and "players may move balls without penalty to avoid elk tracks."

RECREATIONAL ACTIVITIES
Backpacking
• **Glacier Wilderness Guides**, 1.5 mi. w. on US 2. Write P.O. Box 535-J, West Glacier, MT

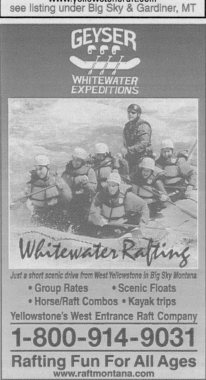

59936. Other activities are offered. Daily May-Sept. Phone (406) 387-5555 or (800) 521-7238.

White-water Rafting

- **Glacier Raft Co.**, on Going-to-the-Sun Rd. at the west entrance to Glacier National Park. Write P.O. Box 218T, West Glacier, MT 59936. Other activities are offered. Daily May-Sept. Phone (406) 888-5454 or (800) 235-6781. *See colr ad p. 94.*

- **Great Northern Whitewater Float Trips**, 1 mi. w. on US 2. Write P.O. Box 278, West Glacier, MT 59936. Other activities are available. Daily May 1 to mid-Sept. Phone (406) 387-5340 or (800) 735-7897. *See color ad p. 93.*

- **Montana Raft Co.**, 1.5 mi. w. on US 2. Write P.O. Box 535-J, West Glacier, MT 59936. Other activities are offered. Daily May-Sept. Phone (406) 387-5555 or (800) 521-7238.

- SAVE **Wild River Adventures**, 1 mi. w. on US 2. Write P.O. Box 272, West Glacier, MT 59936. Other activities are available. Daily May 15-Sept. 15. Phone (406) 387-9453 or (800) 700-7056. *See color ad p. 93.*

WEST YELLOWSTONE (E-4) pop. 900, elev. 6,667'

As its name suggests, West Yellowstone is at the west entrance to Yellowstone National Park. Due to this strategic location, the town's major industry is tourism. Numerous outfitters and rental operations supply visitors with various sports equipment, particularly snowmobiles and cross-country skis, for use in the park and in bordering national forest areas. Fly-fishing, hiking and horseback riding can be enjoyed during summer.

Two miles north of West Yellowstone on US 287, the Interagency Aerial Fire Control Center provides summer tours that explain firefighting techniques; reservations are required and may be made by phoning (406) 646-7691. For evening entertainment the Playmill Theatre at 29 Madison presents 2-hour musical comedy and melodrama performances; reservations are suggested. For information and schedules contact the theater; phone (406) 646-7757.

West Yellowstone Chamber of Commerce: 30 Yellowstone Ave., P.O. Box 458, W. Yellowstone, MT 59758; phone (406) 646-7701.

GRIZZLY DISCOVERY CENTER, 5 blks. s. of the Yellowstone National Park west entrance at 201 S. Canyon St. in Grizzly Park, offers views of grizzly bears and a gray wolf pack in naturalistic habitats. Educational exhibits illustrate the biology, behavior, history and population decline of the grizzlies and wolves. The center also offers films and presentations. Allow 1 hour minimum. Daily 8:30-8:30. Admission $7.50; over 61,

$6.50; ages 5-15, $3. AE, DS, MC, VI. Phone (406) 646-7001 or (800) 257-2570.

MADISON RIVER CANYON EARTHQUAKE AREA is on US 287, 17 mi. n.w. of jct. US 191, in the Hebgen Lake Area. This is a 37,800-acre tract that embraces Hebgen and Earthquake lakes. Traces remain of the 1959 earthquake, which blocked a river, moved huge boulders and silted a lakebed. An observation room with recorded talks depicts the damage and tells the story of the devastating quake.

The visitor center contains photographs of the earthquakes in Charleston in 1886, San Francisco in 1906, Anchorage, Alaska, in 1964 and Madison River Canyon in 1959, as well as an exhibit about threatened and endangered wildlife. Allow 30 minutes minimum. Visitor center open daily 8:30-6, Memorial Day to mid-Sept. Admission $3 per vehicle, $1 per motorcycle or bicycle. Phone (406) 646-7369.

SAVE **MUSEUM OF THE YELLOWSTONE**, 124 Yellowstone Ave., is in a Union Pacific Railroad depot. The museum displays area wildlife and artifacts of the mountain men, U.S. cavalry, cowboys and Plains Indians. Videotape programs about grizzly bears and Yellowstone National Park are shown regularly. Exhibits about trains and Yellowstone National Park also are offered. Daily 8 a.m.-10 p.m., mid-May to mid-Oct. Admission $5.95; over 59 and students with ID, $4.95; under 5 free; family rate $17.95. Phone (406) 646-7814.

NATIONAL GEOGRAPHIC THEATER is at 101 S. Canyon St., adjacent to Yellowstone National Park's west entrance. A 35-minute IMAX® film that interprets the history, wildlife, geothermal activity and grandeur of America's first national park is shown on a six-story screen with stereo surround sound. Food is available. Shows daily on the hour 9-9, May 1-Oct. 15; 1-8, rest of year. Hours may vary; phone ahead. Admission $7.50; ages 3-11, $4.50. Phone (406) 646-4100.

WHITEFISH (B-1) pop. 4,400, elev. 3,033'

Whitefish Lake borders Whitefish and extends 7 miles north. The area offers scenic vistas, fishing, swimming, boating and beach activities.

Restored to its 1927 chaletlike appearance, the Great Northern Railway Depot now houses railroad artifacts and area memorabilia. On the grounds is the Great Northern Locomotive #181, one of only seven ever built.

Offering spectacular views of the Flathead Valley and Glacier National Park, the Big Mountain Chairlift carries passengers to the 7,000-foot summit; phone (406) 862-1900.

Flathead Convention & Visitors Bureau: 15 Depot Park, Kalispell, MT 59911; phone (406) 756-9091 or (800) 543-3105.

Self-guiding tours: Brochures outlining self-guiding tours of the historic area are available

from the Whitefish Visitor Information Center in the Mountain Mall.

DIAMOND K CHUCKWAGON, at Big Mountain Ski & Summer Resort, offers a Western-style barbecue dinner followed by an evening of Western songs, poems and tall tales with a cowboy band. Long wooden tables with bench seating, tin cups and plates, and a barn stage set add to the rustic atmosphere. Allow 2 hours minimum. Wed.-Sun. and holidays at 6:15, May 22-30 and mid-June through Labor Day; Fri.-Sun. at 6:15, June 1 to mid-June. Admission $18.95; ages 13-16, $13.95; ages 4-12, $8.95; under 4 free when sharing parent's plate. MC, VI. Phone (406) 862-8828.

 RECREATIONAL ACTIVITIES

Skiing

- **Big Mountain Ski & Summer Resort**, 8 mi. n. Write P.O. Box 1400, Whitefish, MT 59937. Other activities are offered. Daily Thanksgiving to mid-Apr. Phone (406) 862-1900 or (800) 858-4157.

WHITE SULPHUR SPRINGS (D-4) pop. 1,000, elev. 5,100'

CASTLE MUSEUM CARRIAGE HOUSE is 4 blks. n.e. off US 12/89 via 2nd Ave. at E. Baker St. The museum is entered from the carriage house behind the castle. This museum is a restored Victorian house built in 1892 by B.R. Sherman, a cattleman and mine owner. The gray stone chateau-type structure is on a hilltop overlooking the town, and is furnished in period. Allow 30 minutes minimum. Daily 10-6, mid-May to mid-Sept. Admission $3; over 64 and under 13, $2. Phone (406) 547-2324.

WIBAUX (C-7) pop. 600, elev. 2,634'

A statue of Frenchman Pierre Wibaux (WEE-bo), for whom the town is named, stands on the western edge of town.

Wibaux County Chamber of Commerce: P.O. Box 159, Wibaux, MT 59353.

Self-guiding tours: Brochures of a walking tour are available at the information center in Wibaux Historical Museum.

THE PIERRE WIBAUX MUSEUM COMPLEX, downtown on E. Orgain Ave., features the Pierre Wibaux house, built in 1892. The house and an adjoining barbershop are restored and contain antique furnishings. Displays include dinosaur fossils and homestead artifacts. Daily 9-5, May-Sept. Donations. Phone (406) 796-9969.

WOLF CREEK (C-3) elev. 3,560'

Wolf Creek is a popular point for sports enthusiasts bound for Holter Lake *(see Recreation*

Chart and the AAA Northwestern CampBook), 6 miles southeast of town. The result of one of a series of dams on the upper Missouri River, the lake is bordered by the Sleeping Giant, Beartooth Wildlife Management Area and Helena National Forest *(see place listing p. 98)*.

Almost all of the lake's recreational facilities are on its eastern shore. A particularly scenic drive begins at the junction of US 287 and SR 200 north of Wolf Creek, proceeds south on US 287 to the junction with I-15 and then on to Helena, Butte and the Idaho border, passing some of Montana's most impressive mountains.

WOLF POINT (B-7) pop. 2,900, elev. 2,001'

While sustained mostly by agriculture, Wolf Point's economy also benefits from small manufacturing firms and Honeyland Inc., which maintains more than 4,000 bee colonies and produces about a half-million pounds of honey annually. Wolf Point also is the home of many Sioux and Assiniboine, who perform dances and observe celebrations June through August. The Wild Horse Stampede, said to be the state's oldest rodeo, takes place the second week in July.

Wolf Point Chamber of Commerce & Agriculture: 201 4th Ave. S., P.O. Box 237, Wolf Point MT 59201; phone (406) 653-2012.

WOLF POINT AREA HISTORICAL SOCIETY MUSEUM is in the lower level of the public library at 220 2nd Ave. S., 1 blk. w. of the Sherman Motor Inn. The museum exhibits artifacts of the area's American Indians and early settlers, including clothing and arrowheads, as well as Marlin and Winchester rifle collections. A small gallery displays works by local artists. Mon.-Fri 10-5, June-Aug.; closed holidays. Donations Phone (406) 653-1912.

★YELLOWSTONE NATIONAL PARK—

see Wyoming p. 163.

Wyoming

Spectacular Springs

Burgeoning trees, snowmelt swollen streams and verdant valleys

Summer Storms

Leave behind green skies of dazzling clarity

The Land Developers Forgot

Nearly every road is scenic when you're roaming Wyoming

Yellowstone

A "pleasuring ground... [of] natural curiosities... [and] wonders..."

However You See Wyoming

Driving, riding, hiking, biking, rafting or dog sledding, it's forever in your mind's eye

her best face forward

D eep gorges snaking between high rock walls. Impenetrable stands of ponderosa pines. Intricate systems of limestone caves.

These are but three of the spectacular natural features for which the outdoor wonderland of Wyoming is known.

Some thermal basins in Yellowstone National Park spit bursts of scalding water; others bubble unassumingly. Not far from this heated activity, steam vents utter strange sounds. Bison and bears wander through the back country and along the park's roadways.

Devils Tower National Monument, which resembles a gargantuan stone tree stump, challenges climbers to take on its imposing face.

Shared by Bridger-Teton and Shoshone national forests, 13,804-foot

Gannett Peak is impressive as the state's highest mountain.

Lakes, glaciers, snowfields and forests unite amid the mountains and valleys of Grand Teton National Park. The Jackson Hole valley—a recreational hub—beckons to the adventurous. Hiking, skiing and snowmobiling provide exhilarating thrills; float trips leave you agape at the spectacular scenery along the Snake River.

Wyoming's stunningly diverse landscape is nature's masterpiece.

A land of beauty. A land of serenity. A land of awe.

Possibly the first European to venture into the region was Pierre Verendrye, who explored the Big Horn Mountains in 1743. Although the Lewis and Clark Expedition of 1805-06 did not enter the state, one of its members, John Colter, did in 1807. After Colter came a stream of trappers, explorers and traders. South Pass, discovered in 1824, was the scene of several of the great fur rendezvous, during which hundreds of trappers, fur company agents and Indians convened to trade and socialize.

The call of the Oregon country supplanted the lure of furs during the 1840s, when increasing numbers of pioneer wagon trains began rolling over the Oregon and Mormon trails, etching ruts so deep that they are still visible. But real development rode in on the Union Pacific Railroad, which was pushed across southern Wyoming 1867-68 on its way to meet the Central Pacific line.

Indian hostility grew in proportion to settlement. The worst years, 1866-67, were marked by such incidents as the Fetterman Massacre near Sheridan. Red Cloud and his Sioux nation finally agreed to an uneasy accord in 1868, and Wyoming began to grow in earnest. It became a territory in 1869.

News spread quickly of the region's valuable grazing lands, and once the danger of Indian trouble abated the great cattle drives began. Along with the cowboy and his mystique, huge herds of longhorns arrived from the overstocked ranges of Texas. However, the cattle multiplied so rapidly that within a decade Wyoming was overstocked. Market prices fell and fortunes collapsed; then the terrible winter of 1886-87 destroyed one-sixth of the herds.

These disasters coincided with an influx of farmers into northern Wyoming, an area targeted by the territorial governor to be converted from open range into small farms. Spurred by an epidemic of rustling the stockmen's intense antipathy toward the "nesters" erupted into the Johnson County War in 1892. It took the U.S. Army to quell the disturbance.

With the control of rustling relegated to the proper authorities, the cattlemen and sheepmen reverted to warring with each other. Murder, arson and livestock slaughter were common through the first decade of

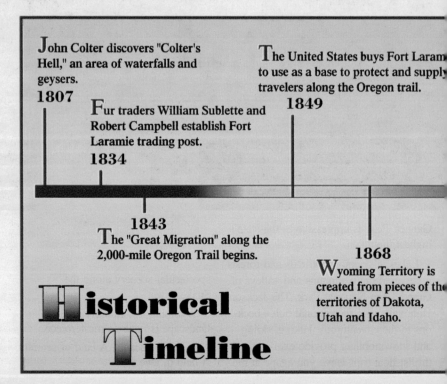

John Colter discovers "Colter's Hell," an area of waterfalls and geysers.
1807

Fur traders William Sublette and Robert Campbell establish Fort Laramie trading post.
1834

The United States buys Fort Laramie to use as a base to protect and supply travelers along the Oregon trail.
1849

1843
The "Great Migration" along the 2,000-mile Oregon Trail begins.

1868
Wyoming Territory is created from pieces of the territories of Dakota, Utah and Idaho.

Historical Timeline

the 20th century. Yet amid all this Wild West activity, Wyoming found time to become a state. Despite its small population, it was admitted into the Union in 1890.

Preoccupation with cattle and sheep during the late 1800s did little to slow Wyoming's political and cultural strides. Otherwise known as the Equality State, the territory approved the country's first women's suffrage legislation in 1869, an act that also was incorporated into the new state's constitution in 1890. Wyoming was first to have a woman justice of the peace and first to select women jurors.

The country's earliest successful county library system was established in the state, and in 1887 the territory founded a university at Laramie. Nellie Tayloe Ross, governor of Wyoming 1925-27, was the first woman governor in the United States; in 1933, she became the first woman director of the U.S. Mint.

With the quieting of the rangeland conflicts by 1910, Wyoming's attentions turned to the lucrative pursuit of oil, coal and other natural reserves. Teapot Dome near Midwest/Edgerton—one of the first oil fields discovered in the state—became the

object of a national scandal in 1922, when the U.S. Supreme Court sent Secretary of the Interior Albert Fall to jail for secretly leasing the oil field without taking competitive bids.

The state still relies heavily on its oil industry. Since the energy shortages of the 1970s, Wyoming's vast oil reserves have gained increasing national attention.

Geography

Wyoming's "firsts" echo the breadth and beauty of its landscape. Yellowstone, with its thermal phenomena, became the first national park. Devils Tower National Monument, the first area to be so designated, preserves the most conspicuous landmark in the northeastern part of the state. The Shoshone National Forest in northwestern Wyoming was the first timberland to be designated as a reserve and later became the National Forest System in the United States.

In addition to these renowned protected areas, there are spectacular Grand Teton National Park, Fossil Butte National Monument, Fort Laramie National Historic Site and two national recreation areas—Flaming Gorge and Bighorn Canyon, the former

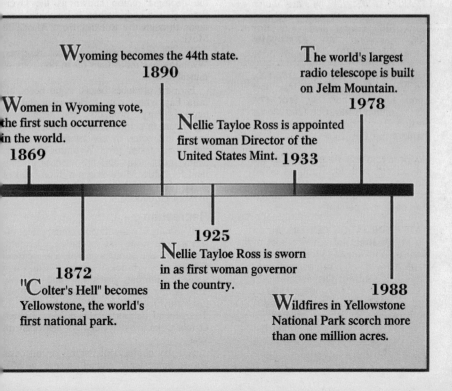

Wyoming becomes the 44th state.
1890

The world's largest radio telescope is built on Jelm Mountain.
1978

Women in Wyoming vote, the first such occurrence in the world.
1869

Nellie Tayloe Ross is appointed first woman Director of the United States Mint. **1933**

1925
Nellie Tayloe Ross is sworn in as first woman governor in the country.

1872
"Colter's Hell" becomes Yellowstone, the world's first national park.

1988
Wildfires in Yellowstone National Park scorch more than one million acres.

FAST FACTS

POPULATION: 479,700.

AREA: 97,914 square miles; ranks 9th.

CAPITAL: Cheyenne.

HIGHEST POINT: 13,804 ft., Gannett Peak.

LOWEST POINT: 3,100 ft., Belle Fourche River Valley.

TIME ZONE: Mountain. DST.

MINIMUM AGE FOR DRIVERS: 16; under 18 need consent of parent or guardian.

SEAT BELT/CHILD RESTRAINT LAWS: Seat belts required for driver and front-seat passengers; child restraints required for under 4 or under 40 pounds.

HELMETS FOR MOTORCYCLISTS: Required for driver under 19.

RADAR DETECTORS: Permitted.

FIREARMS LAWS: Vary by state and/or county. Contact the Wyoming Highway Patrol, 5300 Bishop Blvd., P.O. Box 1708, Cheyenne, WY 82002-9019; phone (307) 777-4301.

HOLIDAYS: Jan. 1; Presidents Day, Feb. (3rd Mon.); Memorial Day, May (last Mon.); July 4; Labor Day, Sept. (1st Mon.); Columbus Day, Oct. (2nd Mon.); Election Day; Veterans Day, Nov. 11; Thanksgiving; Dec. 25.

TAXES: Wyoming's statewide sales tax is 4 percent, with local options or an additional increment up to 2 percent. Localities may also impose lodgings taxes of up to 4 percent.

STATE INFORMATION CENTERS are on I-90 at 5th Street interchange east of Sheridan; on I-90 exit 187 at Sundance; on US 26/89/187 on north edge of Jackson; 1 mile south of Cheyenne on I-25 at College Drive interchange; on I-80 on east edge of Evanston; on I-80 exit 401 south of Pine Bluffs; and on I-80, 10 miles east of Laramie at Sherman Hill exit. Daily 8-6, Memorial Day-Labor Day; 8-5, rest of year.

shared with Utah and the latter shared with Montana. Seven national forests wholly or partially within the state and a national grassland now encompass approximately 15 percent of Wyoming's land area.

The National Elk Refuge, the winter home to one of the largest elk herds in North America, is near Jackson. Twelve state parks complete the list of public areas set aside to preserve their scenic, historical or recreational value.

These features are superimposed on a land that averages more than 6,000 feet in elevation. From the highest point, 13,804-foot Gannett Peak in the Wind River Range, the altitude drops to a low of 3,100 feet in the northeastern corner of the state.

Economy

Petroleum and minerals, tourism and agriculture—all resulting directly from some aspect of the land—are the state's chief industries. The largest single contributor to the economy is oil. More than 50 percent of the Rocky Mountain region's crude oil spouts from the fields of Wyoming.

The former railroad town of Evanston is now the center of drilling operations that are drawing crude oil and natural gas from the geologic region known as the Overthrust Belt, a hydrocarbon-rich area that extends through the Rockies from Alaska to Mexico.

Second in the nation in coal reserves, Wyoming has more than 65 billion tons of mineable coal.

Farming produces beans, sugar beets, alfalfa, hay, wheat, oats, barley, corn and potatoes. Dairy products and eggs are significant in certain areas. Lodgepole pine, spruce and some fir constitute the bulk of the timber taken from Wyoming's forests. Many forest areas also are used as grazing land for cattle. More than a million head of sheep place the state second in the country in wool production.

Recreation

Wyoming's magnificent countryside offers a wide variety of recreation. The cold, clear lakes and streams provide unsurpassed **fishing** for brook, brown, California golden, cutthroat, mackinaw and rainbow trout, along with bass, black crappie, bluegill, grayling, perch, pike and whitefish. The general fishing season is May through October, but most waterways are open all year.

A 1-day nonresident fishing permit costs $6. A nonresident annual license is $65, plus $5 for a conservation stamp; for ages 14-18, the cost is $15, plus $5 for a conservation stamp. Contact the Wyoming Game and Fish Department for more information; phone (307) 777-4601.

Those interested in **hunting** will find pronghorns and mule deer the most widely distributed big game animals. The high country around Jackson offers four species of trophy game: elk, moose, bears and mountain sheep. Bears can be hunted in all areas open to the hunting of deer and elk. Nonresident hunters must be accompanied by a licensed guide for any big game hunting in the state's wilderness areas.

Although most of the high-altitude lakes are too chilly for swimming, several large reservoirs offer opportunities for **boating, water skiing** and **windsurfing.** South of Rock Springs lies Flaming Gorge National Recreation Area, which outlines the reservoir that twists southward into Utah.

Jenny and Jackson lakes in Grand Teton National Park and Yellowstone Lake in Yellowstone National Park are popular for boating and fishing. Reservoirs in Boysen, Buffalo Bill, Curt Gowdy, Glendo, Guernsey, Keyhole and Seminoe state parks, as well as Pathfinder Reservoir, south of Alcova, are easily accessible.

Many dude ranches and professional outfitters offer **horseback riding** and **pack trips** through some of the most scenic sections of the state during the summer. The national parks and the Big Horn Mountains are popular. Long, snowy winters turn trails into runs for **cross-country skiing** and **snowmobiling,** and there are developed **downhill skiing** areas near Casper, Cody, Evanston, Jackson, Laramie and Ten Sleep.

In addition to the national parks and forests, the state parks have facilities for boating, fishing, **swimming, picnicking** and **camping**. For listings of recreational vehicle and tent camping areas, both public and private, *consult the AAA Northwestern CampBook.*

Throughout the TourBook, you may notice a Recreational Activities heading with bulleted listings of recreation-oriented establishments listed underneath. Since normal AAA inspection criteria cannot be applied, these establishments are presented for information only. Age, height and weight restrictions may apply. Reservations are often recommended and sometimes required. Visitors should phone or write the attraction for additional information, and the address and phone number are provided for this purpose.

FOR YOUR INFORMATION

FURTHER INFORMATION FOR VISITORS:
Wyoming Division of Tourism and State Marketing
I-25 at College Dr.
Cheyenne, WY 82002
(307) 777-7777 or (800) 225-5996

RECREATION INFORMATION:
Wyoming Department of Commerce
Public Information Office
6101 Yellowstone Rd.
Cheyenne, WY 82002
(307) 777-7519

FISHING AND HUNTING REGULATIONS:
State of Wyoming
Game and Fish Commission
5400 Bishop Blvd.
Cheyenne, WY 82002
(307) 777-4600

STATE PARK INFORMATION:
Division of State Parks and Historic Sites
6101 Yellowstone Rd.
Cheyenne, WY 82002
(307) 777-6323

NATIONAL FOREST INFORMATION:
Federal Center
Building 85
Denver, CO 80225
(303) 236-9431
Federal Center
324 25th St.
Ogden, UT 84401
(801) 625-5306
(800) 280-2267 (reservations)

DID YOU KNOW?

Near Guernsey you can see the ruts worn into a layer of soft sandstone by thousands of wagon wheels traveling the Oregon Trail during the mid-1800s.

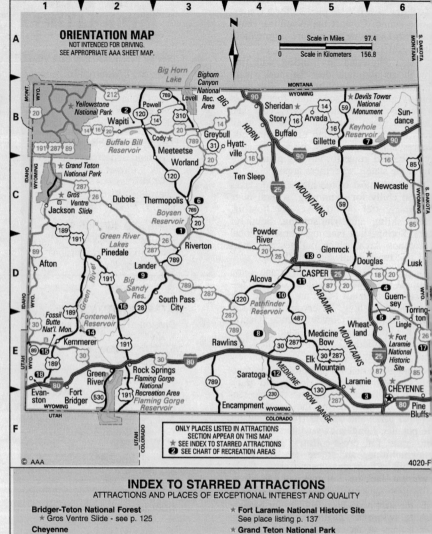

ORIENTATION MAP
NOT INTENDED FOR DRIVING.
SEE APPROPRIATE AAA SHEET MAP.

Scale in Miles   97.4
Scale in Kilometers   156.8

ONLY PLACES LISTED IN ATTRACTIONS
SECTION APPEAR ON THIS MAP
★ SEE INDEX TO STARRED ATTRACTIONS
❷ SEE CHART OF RECREATION AREAS

© AAA

4020-F

INDEX TO STARRED ATTRACTIONS
ATTRACTIONS AND PLACES OF EXCEPTIONAL INTEREST AND QUALITY

Bridger-Teton National Forest
★ Gros Ventre Slide - see p. 125

Cheyenne
★ Cheyenne Frontier Days Old West Museum - see p. 129

Cody
★ Buffalo Bill Historical Center - see p. 133
★ Trail Town - see p. 134

★ **Devils Tower National Monument**
See place listing p. 134

Douglas
★ Wyoming Pioneer Memorial Museum - see p. 135

★ **Fort Laramie National Historic Site**
See place listing p. 137

★ **Grand Teton National Park**
See place listing p. 139
★ Float Trips - see p. 143

Laramie
★ Wyoming Territorial Prison and Old West Park - see p. 153

Sheridan
★ Bradford Brinton Memorial—Historic Ranch and Western Art Collection - see p. 158

★ **Yellowstone National Park**
See place listing p. 163

Travel With Someone You Trust.®

RECREATION AREAS

	MAP LOCATION	CAMPING	PICNICKING	HIKING TRAILS	BOATING	BOAT RAMP	BOAT RENTAL	FISHING	SWIMMING	PETS ON LEASH	BICYCLE TRAILS	WINTER SPORTS	VISITOR CENTER	LODGE/CABINS	FOOD SERVICE
NATIONAL PARKS															
Grand Teton (C-1) 485 square miles. Horse rental. *(See place listing p. 139.)*		•	•	•	•	•	•	•	•	•	•	•	•	•	•
Yellowstone (B-2) 3,472 square miles. Horse rental. *(See place listing p. 163.)*		•	•	•	•	•	•	•			•		•	•	•
NATIONAL MONUMENTS															
Devils Tower (B-6) 1,347 acres. *(See place listing p. 134.)*		•	•	•				•	•	•			•	•	
Fossil Butte (E-1) 8,198 acres. *(See place listing p. 137.)*			•	•						•					
NATIONAL RECREATION AREAS															
Bighorn Canyon (B-3) 120,000 acres. *(See place listing p. 123.)*		•	•	•	•	•	•	•	•	•			•		•
Flaming Gorge (E-2) 91 miles long. *(See place listing p. 136.)*		•	•	•	•	•	•	•	•	•			•	•	•
NATIONAL FORESTS															
Bighorn 1,115,171 acres. North-central Wyoming. Horse rental. *(See place listing p. 124.)*		•	•	•		•		•		•		•		•	•
Black Hills 175,000 acres. Northeast Wyoming. *(See place listing p. 124.)*		•	•	•				•	•	•					
Bridger-Teton 3,439,809 acres. Western Wyoming. Horse rental. *(See place listing p. 125.)*		•	•	•		•		•		•		•	•	•	
Medicine Bow 1,093,618 acres. Eastern Wyoming. Horse rental. *(See place listing p. 154.)*		•	•	•		•		•		•		•		•	
Shoshone 2,466,586 acres. Northwestern Wyoming. *(See place listing p. 159.)*		•	•	•		•		•	•	•		•	•	•	•
STATE															
Bear River (E-1) 280 acres on I-80 near Evanston.	18		•	•				•		•					
Big Sandy (D-2) 6,190 acres 6 mi. n. of Farson on US 191.	16	•	•		•	•		•							
Boysen (C-3) 39,545 acres 14 mi. n.w. of Shoshone off US 20.	1	•	•		•	•	•	•	•	•					•
Buffalo Bill (B-2) 12,000 acres 9 mi. w. of Cody on US 14/16/20.	2	•	•		•	•		•		•			•		
Curt Gowdy (F-6) 1,960 acres 26 mi. w. of Cheyenne off I-80.	3	•	•		•	•		•		•			•		
Edness Kimball Wilkins (D-5) 315 acres 6 mi. e. of Casper off I-25.	13		•					•	•	•					
Glendo (D-6) 22,430 acres 4 mi. e. of Glendo off US 87.	4	•	•	•	•	•	•	•	•	•			•		•
Guernsey (E-6) 8,638 acres 3 mi. w. of Guernsey off US 26.	5	•	•		•	•		•	•	•			•		
Hawk Springs (E-6) 2,000 acres 39 mi. s. of Torrington off US 85.	17	•	•		•	•		•		•					
Hot Springs (C-3) 1,034 acres in n.e. Thermopolis on SR 789 and US 20. *(See Thermopolis p. 161.)*	6		•						•	•			•	•	•
Keyhole (B-6) 15,674 acres 7 mi. n. of I-90 between Moorcroft and Sundance.	7	•	•		•	•	•	•	•	•			•	•	•
Seminoe (E-4) 10,381 acres 35 mi. n. of Sinclair off I-80.	8	•	•		•	•		•		•					•
Sinks Canyon (D-2) 600 acres 9 mi. s.w. of Lander on SR 131.	9	•	•	•				•		•		•	•		
OTHER															
Alcova Reservoir (D-4) 3,400 acres 4 mi. s. of Alcova off SR 220. Horse rental.	10	•	•	•	•	•		•	•	•					
Casper Mountain Park (D-5) 3,315 acres 7 mi. s. of Casper on SR 251. Cross-country and downhill skiing, snowmobiling; archery range, braille nature trail, bridle trails, horse rental.	11	•	•							•		•			
Fontenelle Reservoir (E-2) 8,000 acres 35 mi. n. of Kemmerer via US 189.	14	•	•		•	•		•		•					
Lake Viva Naughton (E-1) 1,375 acres 12 mi. n. of Kemmerer via SR 233.	15	•													
Saratoga Lake (E-4) 270-acre lake 1.5 mi. n. of Saratoga off SR 130.	12	•	•	•	•	•		•	•	•	•	•			

STARRED ATTRACTIONS

Bradford Brinton Memorial—Historic Ranch and Western Art Collection—This 20-room ranch house preserves the lifestyle of a prosperous early rancher. See Sheridan p. 158.

Buffalo Bill Historical Center—Because of the variety of its collections, this museum complex has been called "The Smithsonian of the Old West." See Cody p. 133.

Cheyenne Frontier Days Old West Museum—Learn about the rodeo and cowboy life or sit in a bronc riding saddle. See Cheyenne p. 129.

Devils Tower National Monument—Visitors are permitted to climb the 1,267-foot-high monolith at this site which is considered a sacred site of worship by many American Indians. See place listing p. 134.

Float Trips—Admire mountain scenery and wildlife from the sinuous curves of the Snake River. See Grand Teton National Park p. 143.

Fort Laramie National Historic Site—To travelers along the Oregon and Mormon trails and to Pony Express riders, this command post, staging area, and communications and transportation depot was a welcome site. See place listing p. 137.

Grand Teton National Park—The recreational possibilities in this magnificent park are endless. See place listing p. 139.

Gros Ventre Slide—Nature's fury was unleashed here June 23, 1925. See Bridger-Teton National Forest p. 125.

Trail Town—If raindrops keep fallin' on your head, you might want to nip inside Butch Cassidy and the Sundance Kid's Hole-in-the-Wall cabin. See Cody p. 134.

continued on p. 123.

Points of Interest

AFTON (D-1) pop. 1,400, elev. 6,267'

Mormon emigrants surveyed the already settled site of Afton in 1896, using a carpenter square, a rope and an almanac and taking the bearings from the North Star and the sun. An official survey made years later found the plot on about 5 feet off.

In addition to the arch of 3,011 elk antlers that spans Washington Street at the center of town, Afton is noted for Periodic Spring, a natural cold-water geyser. The spring is 5 miles east i Bridger-Teton National Forest *(see place listing p. 125.)*

Afton lies in Star Valley along the scenic portion of US 89, which runs 255 miles between Mammoth Hot Springs in Yellowstone National Park *(see place listing p. 170)* and Geneva on the Idaho border.

Star Valley Chamber of Commerce: P.O. Box 1097, Afton, WY 83110; phone (800) 426-883

LINCOLN COUNTY DAUGHTERS OF UTAH PIONEER MUSEUM, .5 blk. e. off US 89 at 46 E. 5th, displays artifacts chronicling Mormon history in southwestern Wyoming. Mon.-Fri. 1-5 June-Aug. Free. Phone (307) 886-3856 886-5489.

ALCOVA (D-4) elev. 5,364'

Alcova lies in a small valley rimmed by rock hills. In 1891 a group of Easterners bought nearby site where hot springs flowed from the walls of a canyon. An analysis of the water showed a high concentration of minerals, but the $250,000 the syndicate planned to spend on improvements never materialized.

The water that finally proved important to the town is that impounded by Alcova Dam, 4 miles south of town off SR 220. The dam stretches 700 feet in length and rises 800 feet from the canyon riverbed. Reservoirs created by Alcova and nearby Pathfinder dams provide popular recreation sites for residents of Casper and other communities. *See Recreation Chart and the AA. Northwestern CampBook.*

One of the more colorful local legends involves Ella "Cattle Kate" Watson, unpopular with townsfolk because of her free-wheeling life style and skill at raising cattle. She secretly married rancher Jim Averill so they could double their herd while she retained her homestead in her own name. Other ranchers demanded that both leave town, but before they could make their getaway the two were hanged unceremoniously from a scrub pine. Cattle Kate's 188

ynching made her the only woman to suffer this
ate in Wyoming.

NDEPENDENCE ROCK STATE HISTORIC SITE,
5 mi. w. on SR 220, is a well-known landmark
n the Sweetwater River. Called "The Great
Register of the Desert," it is a 193-foot-high
ranite boulder with a base that covers more than
7 acres.

Members of an expedition led by Robert Stu-
rt, credited with the discovery of the Oregon
Trail, first visited the rock in 1812. Since then
nore than 5,000 explorers, adventurers, mission-
ries and soldiers have carved their names on it.
ndependence Rock was named during a celebra-
ion held July 4, 1830, by a party of fur trappers
ed by William Sublette. Daily dawn-dusk.

ARVADA (B-5) pop. 50, elev. 3,649'

POWDER RIVER EXPERIENCE, 3 mi. s. on CR
73, offers recreation on a 25,000-acre working
anch. Activities, which vary by month, range
rom working with cattle during branding, calv-
ng and weaning to participating in a cattle drive.
Camping, fishing and wildlife watching also are
vailable. Daily dawn-dusk. Day adventure $120;
nder 12, $60. Reservations are suggested. Phone
307) 736-2402 or (888) 736-2402.

BIGHORN CANYON NATIONAL RECREATION AREA (B-3)

Covering about 120,000 acres in Montana and
northern Wyoming, Bighorn Canyon National
Recreation Area centers on a 71-mile-long lake
bounded by steep canyon walls. Facilities for
boat launching, picnicking and camping are
vailable at OK-A-BEH Marina at the northern
end of the area, 42 miles southwest of Hardin,
Mont., via SR 313.

Horseshoe Bend, 14 miles north of Lovell via
SR 37, and Barry's Landing in Montana, 32
miles south of Yellowtail Dam by boat or north
of Lovell via SR 37, have areas for boat launch-
ng, camping, picnicking and swimming. Hunting
nd fishing also are available.

Marinas in OK-A-BEH and Horseshoe Bend
rovide rental boats and gas Memorial Day
hrough Sept. 15.

Campfire programs are given at Afterbay and
Horseshoe Bend campgrounds; schedules are
vailable at visitor centers. Guided nature and
istory walks also are conducted in summer.

The Yellowtail Visitor Center in Fort Smith,
Mont., offers an orientation film about the area
nd exhibits about Yellowtail Dam and American
ndian culture. The center is open daily 9-5, Memorial Day-Labor Day; schedule varies Apr.
-day before Memorial Day and day after Labor
Day-Sept. 30. Phone (406) 666-3234. The Big-
orn Canyon Visitor Center, at the junction of
JS 310 and US 14A in Lovell, is open daily

STARRED ATTRACTIONS

Wyoming Pioneer Memorial Museum—
The collections here will give you an
understanding of the privations the
pioneers endured. See Douglas p. 135.

**Wyoming Territorial Prison and Old
West Park—**Belly-up to the bar, meet
Calamity Jane and see the only prison
cell ever to hold Butch Cassidy, all in
this frontier town. See Laramie p. 153.

Yellowstone National Park—Yellowstone certainly is the first national park
ever created and undoubtedly one of
the most spectacular. See place listing
p. 163.

DID YOU KNOW?

Wyoming has a designated
State Dinosaur, the Triceratops.

"Wyoming" comes from two
Delaware Indian words,
mecheweami ing meaning "at
the big plains," or "on the
great plain."

The average size of a farm or
ranch in Wyoming is 3,742
acres.

Only 42 percent of the land in
Wyoming is privately owned.
The federal government owns
48 percent, the state 6 percent,
and 4 percent is in American
Indian trust.

The three most important seg-
ments of the Wyoming economy are mining, tourism and
agriculture.

Wyoming is the ninth largest
state and the second highest;
its mean elevation is 6,700
feet.

Devils Tower, dedicated in
1906, was the nation's first national monument.

8:15-5; closed Jan. 1, Thanksgiving and Dec. 25. Phone (307) 548-2251.

For further information contact the Superintendent, Bighorn Canyon National Recreation Area, P.O. Box 7458, Fort Smith, MT 59035; phone (406) 666-2412. *See Recreation Chart and the AAA Northwestern CampBook.*

BIGHORN NATIONAL FOREST

Elevations in the forest range from 4,600 ft. in the northern section to 13,165 ft. at Cloud Peak. Refer to AAA maps for additional elevation information.

The Bighorn National Forest encompasses 1,115,171 acres in the Big Horn Mountains of north-central Wyoming. It is traversed by US 14 (Big Horn Scenic Byway), which crosses 8,950-foot Granite Pass and winds through scenic Shell Falls and Canyon; US 14A (Medicine Wheel Passage), which passes by Medicine Mountain near the enigmatic medicine wheel; and US 16 (Cloud Peak Skyway), which crosses 9,677-foot Powder River Pass and threads through beautiful Ten Sleep Canyon.

Cloud Peak is the highest peak within the forest. Motorists pulling trailers should use caution on US 14 and US 14A.

Backpacking and saddle and pack trips can be taken into 189,039-acre Cloud Peak Wilderness; horse and foot trails begin at trail heads accessible via gravel roads off US 14 and US 16. This scenic area has miles of streams and more than 200 lakes containing brook, cutthroat, California golden and rainbow trout. Hunters come in search of pronghorns, deer and elk.

Throughout the forest are 47 campgrounds, picnic areas and a good trail network, including the Bucking Mule Falls National Recreation Trail. Downhill skiing is available east of Worland and Greybull (west of Buffalo and west of Sheridan); cross-country skiing can be pursued in all sections of the forest. Mountain climbing and snowmobiling also are popular.

Maps of the forest are available for $4 at the District Ranger's office in Sheridan at 1969 S. Sheridan Ave., (307) 672-0751; in Worland at 2009 Big Horn, (307) 347-8291; in Lovell at 604

E. Main, (307) 548-6541; in Greybull at 1220 N 8th, (307) 765-4435; or in Buffalo at 300 Spruc (307) 684-7981.

Two visitor centers offer nature trails, exhibi maps and other information about the forest, re reational activities and nearby communities dai 9-5 Memorial Day weekend through Labor Da Burgess Junction Visitor Center is on US 14 half-mile east of Burgess Junction; Shell Fal Interpretive Center also is on US 14, but 5 mil west of Burgess Junction.

For additional information contact the Fore Supervisor's Office, 1969 S. Sheridan Ave Sheridan, WY 82801; phone (307) 672-0751. *Se Recreation Chart and the AAA Northwester CampBook.*

MEDICINE WHEEL is off US 14A on Medicin Mountain, about 27 mi. e. of Lovell. The prehi toric structure, a circular arrangement of stone 245 feet in circumference with 28 spokes extend ing from a central cairn, is believed to have bee used for religious ceremonies or celesti observations.

Note: The road to Medicine Wheel is close to vehicular traffic. Visitors are required to wal 1.5 miles to the site. Exceptions can be made f elderly or physically impaired visitors.

SHELL CANYON AND FALLS, 30 mi. e. of Grey bull on US 14, can be seen from the Shell Fall overlook on US 14. An interpretive trail provide views of the imposing limestone cliffs and dee granite gorge cut by Shell Creek.

BLACK HILLS NATIONAL FOREST

The Black Hills National Forest, most c which is in South Dakota, includes 175,000 acre of Wyoming's northeast corner. The area typi cally displays a mixture of Eastern hardwood with Western coniferous forests. Ponderosa pin white spruce, burr-oak, birch and quaking aspe provide habitats for a variety of wildlife includ ing turkeys, elk and white-tailed and mule dee Fire lookout towers at Cement Ridge, Elk Moun tain and Warren Peak offer expansive views c the Black Hills and surrounding plains.

Maps and information are available at the Dis trict Rangers' offices in Newcastle and Sundance Maps, which cost $4 each, show roads, streams recreation areas and public attractions throughou the Black Hills. Most of the forest's develope recreational facilities are in South Dakota, bu the Wyoming segment does have four camp grounds with 76 sites. *See Recreation Chart an the AAA Northwestern and North Centra CampBooks.*

For additional information contact the Fores Supervisor's Office, R.R. 2, Box 200, Custer, S 57730; phone (605) 673-2251. *See Recreatio Chart and the AAA Northwestern and Nort Central CampBooks.*

BRIDGER-TETON NATIONAL FOREST

Elevations in the forest range from 5,660 ft. near Alpine to 13,804 ft. at Gannett Peak. Refer to AAA maps for additional elevation information.

Bordering Grand Teton (see place listing p. 39) and Yellowstone national parks (see place listing p. 163), Bridger-Teton National Forest covers 3,439,809 acres in the Gros Ventre, Salt River, Teton, Wind River and Wyoming ranges. Within the forest are several live glaciers, an outstanding example of a geologic landslide and the state's highest mountain, Gannett Peak, shared by Shoshone National Forest (see place listing p. 59). Fishing, hunting, white-water rafting and winter sports attract visitors to the area.

The forest has three wilderness areas, all accessible only on foot or horseback. The Bridger Wilderness, 428,169 acres of scenic mountain country, lies on the west slope of the Continental Divide in the Wind River Range. More than 1,300 lakes, Gannett Peak and many glaciers highlight this rugged landscape, which is traversed by more than 500 miles of hiking trails.

The Green River, beginning at the base of Gannett Peak, races through the Wind River Mountains before turning southward to join the Colorado River. The Teton Wilderness preserves 585,468 acres in the northern section of the forest. Snow sometimes stays on the ground until early July in this barren alpine country of steep canyons, broad meadows, lakes, streams and waterfalls.

At Two Ocean Pass, Two Ocean Creek divides and sends one stream to the Pacific Ocean and another to the Atlantic; this geographic phenomenon supposedly exists nowhere else on the continent. The 287,000-acre Gros Ventre Wilderness, immediately east of Jackson, also is rugged, mountainous country ideally suited to backpacking, fishing and hunting.

Scenic drives include Centennial National Scenic Byway from Dubois to Pinedale, the Green River Road from Pinedale north to the Green River Lakes, and the Skyline Drive from Pinedale northeast to Elkhart Park. Greys River Road leaves US 89 near Alpine and follows the river on its southward run; from its headwaters roads lead to US 89 near Geneva and to US 189 at Big Piney or Fontenelle reservoirs.

Pinedale (see place listing p. 155) and the resort town of Jackson (see place listing p. 146) are recreational activity centers. Near these two towns are the forest's three ski areas; trails for cross-country skiing also are available. Nearby hot springs include Astoria Mineral Hot Springs, 17 miles south of Jackson on US 26/89, and Granite Hot Springs, 28 miles southeast of Jackson on US 189, then 9 miles north. The Jackson Visitor Center is open Mon.-Sat. 8:30-5:30, June-Aug.; Mon.-Fri. 8:30-4:30, rest of year.

For additional information contact the Forest Supervisor's Office, P.O. Box 1888, Jackson, WY; phone (307) 739-5500. See Recreation Chart and the AAA Northwestern CampBook.

★GROS VENTRE SLIDE is 5 mi. e. of Kelly on Gros Ventre Rd. When the landslide occurred on the morning of June 23, 1925, this large earth movement dammed up the Gros Ventre (Big Belly) River. In a matter of minutes, trees and land fell from an elevation of 9,000 feet. Two years later part of the slide gave way, and the resulting wall of water, mud and rock destroyed the town of Kelly. A self-guiding tour traverses the area.

PERIODIC SPRING is about 5 mi. e. of Afton on FR 10211 (Swift Creek Rd.). In late summer the spring ceases to flow every 18 minutes, then gradually builds to a thundering, ice-cold torrent. This cycle occurs regularly for 9 months and fluctuates during the period of highest snow melt, from about mid-May to mid-August. A narrow dirt road leads to within half a mile of the spring; the last 200 yards of the hike are very steep. The road, not recommended for trailers, is closed during winter.

BUFFALO (B-4) pop. 3,300, elev. 4,645'

Retaining the atmosphere and hospitality of the Old West, Buffalo is a ranching town on the eastern slope of the Big Horn Mountains. Many Indian battles took place in this area 1866-77, triggered by the presence of the Bozeman Trail and the forts built to protect it.

After the area was opened to settlement, Buffalo was founded in 1879. Buffalo became known as the "Rustlers' Capital," and by 1892 the tensions between the region's big cattlemen and farmers, or "nesters," had erupted into the Johnson County War. It took the U.S. Army to restore order.

The growth of sheep ranching in the late 1890s brought Basque herders, who were drawn to Buffalo because of the Big Horn Mountains' resemblance to their homeland in the Pyrenees. Basque descendants continue to practice their time-honored traditions.

Guided saddle trips and jeep tours of nearby scenic and historical attractions can be arranged through local operators. Sightseeing is most rewarding along the Cloud Peak Scenic Byway portion of US 16 that runs between Buffalo and Ten Sleep.

Hunters can visit the Hunters Information Station at 55 N. Main St.; phone (307) 684-5544 or (800) 227-5122.

Buffalo Chamber of Commerce: 55 N. Main St., Buffalo, WY 82834; phone (307) 684-5544 or (800) 227-5122. *See color ad.*

Self-guiding tours: Information about walking and driving tours is available from the chamber of commerce.

CAROUSEL PARK, 655 E. Hart St. at jct. I-25 and US 16 exit 299, features a renovated 1925 Spillman carrousel with reproductions of bucking horses. Cloud Peak Ferris Wheel, built during the 1930s, faces the Big Horn Mountains and the Cloud Peak Wilderness Area. Visitors also can enjoy miniature golf. Food is available. Allow 1 hour minimum. Daily 11-10, Memorial Day weekend-Labor Day. Carrousel $1, Ferris wheel $1. Phone (307) 684-7033. *See color ad p. 267.*

JIM GATCHELL MEMORIAL MUSEUM is at 100 Fort St. The museum, which honors a frontier pharmacist known for his friendship with and knowledge of the Plains Indians, houses more than 15,000 artifacts. Included in the displays are a variety of pioneer items, Indian artifacts, firearms and historical photographs depicting the early days of the West. Daily 8-8, May-Oct.; closed July 4. Admission $2, under 14 free. Phone (307) 684-9331.

OCCIDENTAL HOTEL is at 10 N. Main St. Throughout its history, the 1880 building was the center of community activity and served as town

hall, polling place, hospital and headquarters f county government. Mon.-Sat. 10:30-4:30 a 6-8, June 1-Labor Day. Donations. Phone (30 684-7451.

CARIBOU NATIONAL FOREST—
see place listing in Idaho p. 42.

CASPER (D-5) pop. 46,700, elev. 5,123'

Casper's roots are buried in commerce. Th town began as a ferry site on the Oregon Trail 1847, when a group of Mormon immigrants wh were camping realized that there was money be made by boating travelers across the Nor Platte River. The idea caught on, and in the ear 1850s a toll bridge was built; soon a milita post was established to protect the span and i traffic.

The town's real asset, however, was not di covered until 1889, when the first well in th Salt Creek oil field was tapped; by 1915 th town was in an oil boom that matched the frenz of the California, Montana and Colorado go rushes.

The boom brought not only prosperity but als a national scandal over the nearby Teapot Don oil field. In 1927 the U.S. Supreme Court hande down verdicts in the case, which included se tencing Secretary of the Interior Albert Fall

prison for secretly leasing the rich field to Mammoth Crude Oil Co. without taking competitive bids.

Casper is a major service and supply center for mineral, oil, natural gas, uranium and coal industries, as well as a center for many medical and financial services.

Stargazers can view astronomy-related programs at Casper Planetarium, a half-mile north of I-25 exit 220 at 904 N. Poplar, June through August; phone (307) 577-0310.

Pathfinder Dam Museum, southwest on SR 220, features displays relating to the construction of the dam; phone (307) 261-5628. Along SRs 20/26 and 220, markers identify the Oregon, Mormon, California and Pony Express trails. Wagon rides are available during the summer.

Casper Area Convention and Visitors Bureau: 500 N. Center, P.O. Box 399, Casper, WY 82602; phone (800) 852-1889. *See color ad and p. 270.*

DAN SPEAS FISH REARING STATION, 10 mi. w. on SR 220, then 4.5 mi. on CR 308 following signs, is one of Wyoming's most productive fish hatcheries. Its use of a nearby spring, which promotes rapid fish growth, enables it to produce a 4-inch fish in 120 days. About 1 million fish are stocked annually. Daily 8-5. Free. Phone (307) 473-8890.

FORT CASPAR MUSEUM is .5 mi. n. of SR 220 off Wyoming Blvd. at 4001 Fort Caspar Rd. The site has a reconstruction of Fort Caspar, named in honor of Caspar Collins, a lieutenant killed while trying to reach an army supply train under Indian attack in 1865. An interpretive center has exhibits of Indian and pioneer artifacts.

Interpretive center open Mon.-Sat. 8-7, Sun. noon-7, mid-May to mid-Sept.; Mon.-Fri. 8-6, Sun. 1-4, rest of year. Fort buildings open Mon.-Sat. 9-6:30, Sun. noon-6:30, mid-May to mid-Sept. Free. Phone (307) 235-8462.

HELL'S HALF ACRE—
see Powder River p. 155.

HISTORIC TRAILS EXPEDITIONS, departing from Fort Caspar, features a wagon train that travels along the actual ruts of the California, Oregon and Mormon trails. Visitors also can take an excursion where they ride horses as Indian warriors did on the old trails. Historical accounts are given. Other types of expeditions also are available. Daily 10-4, May-Oct. (weather permitting). Fare $25-$95. Reservations are recommended. DS, MC, VI. Phone (307) 266-4868.

INDEPENDENCE ROCK STATE HISTORIC SITE—*see Alcova p. 123.*

NICOLAYSEN ART MUSEUM AND DISCOVERY CENTER, 400 E. Collins St., presents changing exhibits by national and regional artists. The Discovery Center offers informal hands-on and supervised programs, including a painting center, an image-rubbing table, a library and an art gallery. Tues.-Sat. 10-5 (also Thurs. 5-8), Sun. noon-4; closed federal holidays. Admission $2; ages 2-12, $1; free to all Thurs. 5-8. Phone (307) 235-5247.

TATE GEOLOGICAL MUSEUM is on the Casper College campus at 125 College Dr.; take Wolcott St./Casper Mountain Rd. s. Displays include fossils, minerals, meteorites and jade as well as traveling exhibits. Highlights include dinosaur, fish, bird, mammal and reptile bones and fossils that are more than 50 million years old. Also present is a fossil preparation lab. Allow 1 hour minimum. Mon.-Fri. 9-4, Sat. 10-3. Free. Phone (307) 268-2447.

WERNER WILDLIFE MUSEUM, s. via Wolcott St. to 405 E. 15th St., houses an antelope diorama, a collection of Western birds and mounted specimens of wildlife native to Wyoming and other parts of North America. The Werner Trophy Room exhibits specimens from around the world. Mon.-Sat. noon-5, early June-Labor Day; Mon.-Fri. 2-5, rest of year. Free. Phone (307) 235-2108.

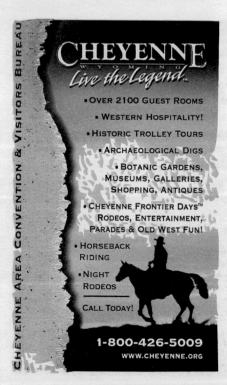
CHEYENNE (E-6) pop. 50,000, elev. 6,060′

Cheyenne was named for the tribe of Plains Indians that once roamed southeastern Wyoming. In 1867 Union Pacific Railroad chief engineer Maj. Gen. Grenville M. Dodge built a depot on the site, which was situated at the junction of several roads leading to military camps.

Before the track even reached town, it was overrun by gamblers, cowboys, speculators, shopkeepers and real estate salesmen, thus earning Cheyenne the nickname "Hell on Wheels." The town's reputation was so widespread that in 1868 a resident received a letter from Pennsylvania addressed simply "Cheyenne."

By 1869 Cheyenne had outgrown some of its cowtown adolescence to assume the more mature stature of territorial capital, an honor it retained when Wyoming became the 44th state in 1890.

Noted town residents include Nellie Tayloe Ross, the first woman governor in the United States; and Esther Morris, a pioneer for women's suffrage in Wyoming and former justice of the peace of South Pass City *(see place listing p. 160).* A statue honoring Morris is on Capitol Avenue.

Since it was established in 1867 as a headquarters for the cavalry troops protecting pioneers and railroad construction workers, F.E. Warren Air Force Base has served various branches of the military, including the nation's first intercontinental ballistic missile group. Guided tours of the base museum are available; phone (307) 775-3381.

The renovated, Romanesque-style Union Pacific Railroad Depot downtown now houses a museum. "Big Boy," one of the world's largest steam locomotives, is on permanent display in Holliday Park.

At Wyoming Hereford Ranch, summer visitors can see a Western cattle operation at work. Buffalos and elk reside at the miniature zoo in Lions Park.

Happy Jack Road (SR 210) is a 38-mile scenic byway to Laramie that runs from rolling grasslands to the rocky foothills of the Pole Mountain Division of Medicine Bow National Forest. Equally interesting is a trip to Snowy Range, a region of fishing streams and mountain lakes.

Cheyenne Area Convention and Visitors Bureau: 309 W. Lincolnway, Cheyenne, WY 82001; phone (307) 778-3133 or (800) 426-5009. *See ad.*

Shopping areas: Frontier Mall, 1400 Dell Range Blvd., has more than 75 stores including Dillard's, JCPenney, Joslins, and Sears.

Self-guiding tours: A pamphlet describing a self-guiding walking tour of Cheyenne's historic downtown area is available at the convention and visitors bureau.

★ **CHEYENNE FRONTIER DAYS OLD WEST MUSEUM**, next to Frontier Park on N. Carey Ave., includes among its exhibits a horse-drawn vehicle collection and classic Western art. A bronc riding saddle lets aspiring cowboys learn the rigors of the rodeo. An interactive electronic program lets visitors navigate through frontier history. Children can explore hands-on exhibits in the "Hole in the Wall" room.

Mon.-Fri. 9-5, Sat.-Sun. 10-5, with extended hours during Frontier Days; closed holidays. Admission $4, under 12 free with adult. Phone (307) 778-7290.

CHEYENNE STREET RAILWAY TROLLEY departs from the intersection of Lincolnway and Capitol. Highlights of the 2-hour sightseeing tours include historic downtown and F.E. Warren Air Force Base. Tickets can be purchased at the convention and visitors bureau. Tours Mon.-Sat. at 10 and 1:30, Sun. at 1:30, mid-May to mid-Sept. (extra tours in July). Ghost tours Thurs.-Fri. at 7:30 p.m. Fare $8; ages 2-12, $4. Phone (307) 778-3133 or (800) 426-5009.

HISTORIC GOVERNORS' MANSION STATE HISTORIC SITE, 300 E. 21st St., was the home of Wyoming's chief executives 1905-76. A videotape provides a historical background of Wyoming's first families and describes the interior design of the 1904 Colonial-style mansion. Allow 1 hour minimum. Tues.-Sat. 9-5, June-Aug.; Tues.-Fri. 9-noon and 1-5, Sat. 9-5, rest of year. Closed Saturdays preceding 3-day holidays. Free. Phone (307) 777-7878 or 777-7014.

STATE CAPITOL is on Capitol Ave. between 24th and 25th. This neoclassic sandstone building, with a golden dome 50 feet in diameter, is architecturally uncommon for the region. Within the building are murals, woodwork, marble floors and displays of native wildlife. Mon.-Fri. 8-4:30; closed holidays. Free. Phone (307) 777-7220.

TERRY BISON RANCH, off I-25 exit 2, then s. on Terry Ranch Rd. to ranch entrance, is an historic working bison ranch with more than 2,500 bison. Features include wagon tours through a herd of buffaloes. Chuckwagon dinners with entertainment, a rodeo, horseback rides and fishing also are offered.

Horseback and wagon tours daily, phone for times; rodeo at 7. Chuckwagon dinners Fri.-Sat. at 6:30 p.m., Memorial Day-Labor Day. Horseback rides $17. Wagon rides $12.50. Chuckwagon dinner $14; ages 6-12, $7. Rodeo $8; under 13, $4. Under 9 are not permitted on horseback rides, but pony rides are available. DS, MC, VI. Phone (307) 634-4171 or (800) 319-4171. *See color ad.*

WILDLIFE VISITOR CENTER, 5400 Bishop Blvd. (I-25 Central Ave. exit), is administered by the Wyoming Game & Fish Department. The center has photographic displays spotlighting some of the 600-plus species of free-ranging mammals, birds, reptiles and fish that inhabit the state. Also included are several bird and big game mounts. Allow 30 minutes minimum. Mon.-Fri. 8-5, Sat.-Sun. 9-5, Memorial Day-Labor Day; Mon.-Fri. 8-5, rest of year. Free. Phone (307) 777-4541.

CODY (B-2) pop. 7,900, elev. 5,095' 60

Founded by Col. William "Buffalo Bill" F. Cody in 1896, Cody is near the east and northeast entrances to Yellowstone National Park (*see place listing p. 163*). Some of the state's most scenic areas, including Shoshone National Forest (*see place listing p. 159*), Sunlight Basin, the Absaroka and Beartooth mountains and the Bighorn Canyon National Recreation Area (*see place listing p. 123*), are nearby.

US 14/16/20, alternately known as the Buffalo Bill Cody Scenic Byway, was designated the "most scenic 52 miles in America" by President Theodore Roosevelt; of note along the route are the many unusual rock formations. The highway runs 182 miles between Ranchester and Yellowstone National Park. Cody also is the northern terminus of the scenic section of SR 120 that travels 83 miles southeast to Thermopolis (*see*.

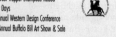

place listing p. 161). Scenic US 14A heads 107 miles northeast to Burgess Junction.

Outfitters offer horseback riding, fishing, pack and hunting trips, hayrides and river float trips. Scenic flights over the Big Horn Mountains and Grand Teton and Yellowstone national parks can be arranged through Spirit Mountain Aviation; phone (307) 587-6732.

Of interest downtown are historic buildings dating from the beginning of the 20th century. Irma Hotel, 12th Street and Sheridan Avenue, has been a meeting place for local cattlemen, oilmen and sheepherders since the early 1900s. Its $100,000 bar was a gift from Queen Victoria to Buffalo Bill in appreciation of his Wild West Show. Pahaska Tepee, Buffalo Bill's first hunting lodge, is at the east entrance to Yellowstone National Park.

Cody Chamber of Commerce: 836 Sheridan Ave., P.O. Box 2777, Cody, WY 82414; phone (307) 587-2297. *See color ads p. 130 & 131.*

BUFFALO BILL DAM VISITOR CENTER is 7 mi. w. on US 14/16/20. In addition to a dam overlook, the visitor center has a natural history museum, views of Shoshone Canyon, area wildlife displays and dinosaur and fossil exhibits. Allow 30 minutes minimum. Daily 8-8, June 1-Labor

Day; 8-6 in May and day after Labor Day-Sept. 30. Free. Phone (307) 527-6076. *See color ads p. 130 & 131.*

★ BUFFALO BILL HISTORICAL CENTER is at jct. US 14/16/20 and 720 Sheridan Ave. The four museums that comprise the center have more than 237,000 square feet of exhibit space dedicated to the art, artifacts, crafts, cultures, traditions and history of the American West. In addition, a research library contains book and manuscript collections, historic photographs and an archive of Western songs and ballads. Food is available.

Allow 4 hours minimum. Daily 7 a.m.-8 p.m., June-Sept.; daily 8-8 in May; daily 8-5 in Oct.; daily 10-5 in Apr.; Thurs.-Mon. 10-2, rest of year. Admission (valid for 2 consecutive days for all four museums) $8; over 64, $6.50; ages 13-21, $4; ages 6-12, $2. AE, DS, MC, VI. Phone (307) 587-4771. *See color ads p. 130 & 131.*

Buffalo Bill Museum displays belongings of the showman, scout and Pony Express rider, along with possessions of Annie Oakley and artifacts of the early West. Exhibits provide insight into the history of the American cowboy, conservation and dude ranching. *See color ads p. 130 & 131.*

The Cody Firearms Museum is noted for its exhibits of American firearms, including the Winchester collection. The museum, featuring more than 5,000 items, traces the development of firearms from the early 16th century. Examples range from centuries-old projectile arms to flintlocks and Gatling guns to modern sport rifles. *See color ads p. 130 & 131.*

The Plains Indian Museum has an extensive collection of art, artifacts, ceremonial items and beadwork as well as dress and weaponry of the Arapaho, Blackfeet, Cheyenne, Crow, Shoshone and Sioux tribes. Exhibits depict the everyday existence of these Plains tribes. *See color ads p. 130 & 131.*

Whitney Gallery of Western Art houses a comprehensive collection of paintings, sculpture and prints depicting the West. Artists represented include Albert Bierstadt, George Catlin, Thomas Moran, Frederic Remington, Charles M. Russell and Dallas Sharp. Reconstructed studios enable visitors to view artists' work areas. *See color ads p. 130 & 131.*

BUFFALO BILL STATUE, at the w. end of Sheridan Ave., represents young William Cody as a mounted Army scout signaling the discovery of enemy tracks.

CODY CHAPEL MURALS INFORMATION CENTER, in Cody Chapel at Wyoming Ave. and 18th St., displays exhibits, artifacts, murals, paintings and sculpture relating to the Mormon colonization of the Big Horn Basin. Film presentations and guided tours are given. Open Mon.-Sat. 8-8, Sun. 3-8, June 1-Sept. 15; by appointment rest of year. Closed Jan. 1, Thanksgiving and Dec. 25. Free. Phone (307) 587-3290. *See color ads p. 130 & 131.*

CODY NITE RODEO, 2 mi. w. on US 14/16/20, features nightly rodeo performances. Daily at 8:30 p.m., first Sat. in June-last Sat. in Aug. Special performances are held July 1-4 during Stampede Days. Grandstand seats $9; under 12, $4. Buzzards Roost seats $11; under 12, $6. Phone (307) 587-5155. *See color ads p. 130 & 131.*

TECUMSEH'S OLD WEST MINIATURE VILLAGE AND MUSEUM, 2.5 mi. w. on US 14/16/20, features American Indian artifacts, paintings, arrowheads, spears, knives and other items. The history of Wyoming is characterized in miniature in a 66-scene display with moving trains and audio narratives. Allow 1 hour minimum. Daily 8 a.m.-9 p.m., June-Aug.; 9-6 in May and Sept.; by appointment rest of year. Admission $2; ages 6-12, $1. AE, DS, MC, VI. Phone (307) 587-5362.

★ **TRAIL TOWN**, 3 mi. w. on US 14/16/20, is a group of historic buildings with indoor exhibits reassembled on the first site of the frontier town of Old Cody. Included are the grave of John "Jeremiah" Johnson and a log cabin used as a hideout by Butch Cassidy, the Sundance Kid and other members of the Wild Bunch.

The Museum of the Old West houses guns, carriages, clothing and many prehistoric and historic Plains Indian relics. Daily 8-7, May 20-Sept. 15. Admission $3, under 12 free with adult. Phone (307) 587-5302.

 RECREATIONAL ACTIVITIES

White-water Rafting

• **Red Canyon River Trips**, 1220 Sheridan Ave., Cody, WY 82414. Trips depart daily 8:30-8, May 1 through mid-Sept. Phone (307) 587-6988 or 587-9476. *See color ads p. 130 & 131.*

• **River Runners**, 1491 Sheridan Ave., Cody, WY 82414. Trips run May 20-Sept. 15. Phone (307) 527-7238 or (800) 535-7238. *See color ads p. 130 & 131.*

• **Wyoming River Trips** depart the Holiday Inn/ Buffalo Bill Village Complex at jct. SR 120 and US 14/16/20. Write P.O. Box 1541-A, Cody, WY 82414. Trips offered several times daily, May-Sept. Phone (307) 587-6661 or (800) 586-6661.

★ **DEVILS TOWER NATIONAL MONUMENT** (B-6)

Devils Tower National Monument, which occupies 1,347 acres in the area between Sundance and Hulett, contains Devils Tower, the most conspicuous landmark in northeastern Wyoming.

The monument is accessible from SR 24, north off I-90 via US 14 or west from Belle Fourche, S.D.; from Alzada, Mont., SR 112 runs southwest off US 212.

The tower, a huge monolith resembling a colossal stone tree stump, rises 867 feet from its base and 1,267 feet above the Belle Fourche River. The 1.5-acre top has a growth of sagebrush and grass, and the almost perpendicular sides are fluted columns. The tower was formed when numerous sedimentary layers eroded from around a volcanic intrusion that had cooled in a teardrop formation.

About a half-mile from the entrance is a prairie dog colony. Near the monument's campground is an outdoor amphitheater. Ranger-naturalists conduct summer interpretive walks, climbing demonstrations and nightly campfire programs.

The Tower Trail, marked to identify plants and rocks, encircles Devils Tower. Climbing on the tower is permitted, but climbers must sign in before and after expeditions. Fishing, swimming and tubing are permitted on the Belle Fourche River. A visitor center about 3 miles from the park entrance contains geological specimens, artifacts and exhibits. Trailers are prohibited at the monument and must be dropped at the base parking lot. Dogs, which must be leashed, are not permitted on the trails.

Allow 2 hours, 30 minutes minimum. The monument is open daily 24 hours. The visitor center and campground are open daily 8-7:30, June-Aug.; 8:30-5, Apr.-May and Sept.-Oct. Admission $8 per private vehicle or $3 per person arriving by bicycle, motorcycle, horseback or on foot; U.S. citizens over 62 or under 17 free. Phone (307) 467-5283 Mon.-Fri. 8-4:30. *See Recreation Chart and the AAA Northwestern CampBook.*

DOUGLAS (D-6) pop. 5,100, elev. 4,815'

Known as Tent Town at its founding in 1886, Douglas served as a supply post for cattlemen and a distribution point for railroad consignments. The town's history is typical of the colorful, brawling days when cavalrymen, cowboys and railroad crews were opening the West, but in contrast to many other towns, few killings were recorded.

One of the town's rowdiest characters was George Pike, a cowhand whose rustling habits were so well-known that the cattle companies decided to hire him so he would at least benefit his current employer. One company thought so highly of Pike that at his death it erected an expensive tombstone with the following inscription:

Underneath this stone in eternal rest, Sleeps the wildest one of the wayward west. He was a gambler and sport and cowboy, too, And he led the pace in an outlaw crew. He was sure on the trigger and staid to the end, But was never known to quit on a friend. In the relations of death all mankind's alike, But in life there was only one George Pike.

Douglas also is said to be the original home of the "jackalope," a fanciful creation of Wyoming's taxidermists. Doubters are confronted with dozens of convincing mounted specimens of this animal—best described as a jackrabbit sporting antlers—on display throughout the state. A 10-foot replica of the "hybrid" stands downtown in Centennial Jackalope Square at 3rd and Center streets.

Scenic River Path, running along the bank of the North Platte River in downtown, offers 2.5 miles of trails for walking, biking and observing nature.

Douglas Area Chamber of Commerce: 121 Brownfield Rd., Douglas, WY 82633; phone (307) 358-2950.

AYRES NATURAL BRIDGE, in Ayres Park, is 12 mi. w. on I-25, then 5 mi. s. on Natural Bridge Rd. La Prele Creek has worn a passageway through thick stone, leaving an arch 30 feet high and 50 feet wide. Camping and picnic facilities are available. Daily 8-8, Apr.-Oct. Free.

FORT FETTERMAN STATE HISTORIC SITE, 11 mi. n.w. via SR 93 off the North Douglas exit of I-25, preserves the fort's restored officers' quarters and an ordnance warehouse. Built in 1867, the fort was once a major Army supply post. A museum contains exhibits depicting the history of the military and Fetterman City. Period rooms, weapons, artifacts and clothing are on display. A living-history program is offered during Fort Fetterman Days the second week of June.

Allow 2 hours minimum. Daily 9-5, Memorial Day weekend-Labor Day. Free. Phone (307) 358-2864, 777-7014 or 684-7629.

★ **WYOMING PIONEER MEMORIAL MUSEUM,** on the state fairgrounds, has an extensive collection of Wyoming pioneer items, American Indian artifacts, maps, charts, newspapers and photographs from the late 1800s. An addition to the museum contains clothing worn during Wyoming's territorial period, an art display with changing exhibits and a research library about Wyoming history.

Mon.-Fri. 8-5 (also Sat. 1-5, June-Sept.) Free. Phone (307) 358-9288.

DUBOIS (C-2) pop. 900, elev. 6,917'

Dubois grew from a rendezvous point for French, American and Indian trappers at the head of the Wind River Valley into a headquarters for cattle outfits, tie hack crews and river tie drives. From 1914 to 1946, stacked decks of railroad ties were floated down the Wind River from tie camps west of town to the railhead at Riverton. Dubois is now bordered by extensive cattle and dude ranching operations.

Northwest of Dubois is Union Pass, said to be the only place in the United States from which three rivers flow in different directions: Fish Creek is the source of the Columbia River, Jakeys Fork flows to the Mississippi, and Roaring Fork is part of the Colorado River drainage system.

Pack trips leave Dubois for Gannett Peak, Wyoming's highest peak, and the Fitzpatrick Wilderness, where there are 44 active glaciers.

Snowmobiling, dog sledding and cross-country skiing are popular at Union Pass and Togwotee Pass; both cross the Continental Divide west of Dubois.

Dubois Chamber of Commerce: 616 W. Ramshorn St., P.O. Box 632, Dubois, WY 82513; phone (307) 455-2556.

DUBOIS FISH HATCHERY is 3 mi. e. on US 26/287, then 1.5 mi. s. at 411 Fish Hatchery Rd. Fed by two springs and the Jakey's Fork, the station incubates and ships to other hatcheries nationwide up to 7 million eggs; it also rears nearly a half million fish yearly for stocking. Varieties include cutthroat, rainbow, Snake River and Bear River trout. Daily 8-5. Free. Phone (307) 455-2431.

DUBOIS MUSEUM, 909 W. Ramshorn St., contains local artifacts depicting the industry, history, cultures and geology of Dubois and the region between the Wind River and the Absaroka Mountains. Log buildings include a schoolhouse, gas station and bunkhouse. Daily 9-7, July-Aug.; Mon.-Fri. 10-5 in June and Sept. Admission $1; under 12, 50c. Phone (307) 455-2284.

NATIONAL BIGHORN SHEEP INTERPRETIVE CENTER is at 907 W. Ramshorn. Through the use of dioramas, mounted animals, hands-on exhibits and videotapes visitors can learn about the history and biology of the bighorn sheep. "Sheep Mountain" replicates the bighorn's natural habitat. It focuses on predator-prey relationships, seasonal changes in habitat conditions, and plant and animal life with which bighorns interact.

Allow 1 hour minimum. Daily 9-8, day after Memorial Day-day before Labor Day; 9-5, May 1-Memorial Day and Labor Day-Nov. 15. Admission $2; under 13, 75c; family rate $5. MC, VI. Phone (307) 455-3429 or (888) 209-2795. *See color ad p. 167.*

ELK MOUNTAIN (E-5) pop. 200, elev. 7,240'

Elk Mountain, originally known as "The Crossing" by pioneers who traversed the Overland Trail, is noted for the wild game that take shelter on the nearby refuge in the shadow of 11,156-foot Elk Mountain. Both Elk Mountain Hotel and Garden Spot Pavillion Dance Hall, next to the hotel, are on the National Register of Historic Places.

ENCAMPMENT (F-4) pop. 500, elev. 7,323'

Encampment takes its name from an Indian camp where tribes gathered to hunt big game between the Medicine Bow and Sierra Madre ranges. It was a copper mining town from 1897 until the vein was exhausted in 1908; a gold strike was reported as late as 1937. Stock raising and lumbering are now the principal industries.

Legend has it that Thomas Edison conceived of the light bulb filament while looking at a frayed line during a fishing trip near Encampment.

GRAND ENCAMPMENT MUSEUM, 3 blks. s. of the post office, houses memorabilia recalling the area's American Indian encampment and copper mining days. The museum complex also encompasses a pioneer village whose 14 buildings include a two-story outhouse and a forest service lookout tower. A park next to the museum has picnic facilities.

Allow 2 hours minimum. Mon.-Sat. 10-5, Sun. 1-5, Memorial Day-Labor Day; daily 1-5, day after Labor Day-Oct. 31; by appointment rest of year. Tours are given daily at 1. Donations. Phone (307) 327-5308 or 327-5329.

SEAT BELTS ARE A MUST.

EVANSTON (E-1) pop. 10,900, elev. 6,743'

Designated the seat of Uinta County in 1870 Evanston lies in the center of the energy-rich Overthrust Belt. It also is a departure point for trips into the Uinta Mountains to the south. Depot Square Park is the center of such summer activities as band concerts and barbecues. Other recreational opportunities include water sports at Woodruff Narrows Reservoir, north via US 89 and cross-country skiing at Bear River State Park. *See Recreation Chart and the AAA North western CampBook.*

Thoroughbred and quarter horses run every weekend from Memorial Day through the first weekend in August at Wyoming Downs, a pari mutuel track; phone (800) 842-8722.

Note: Policies vary concerning admittance of children to pari-mutuel betting facilities. Phone for information.

Bear River Information Center: 601 Bear River Dr., Evanston, WY 82930; phone (307) 789-6540.

UINTA COUNTY HISTORICAL MUSEUM, 3 10th St., preserves the artifacts and photograph of the area's first pioneers. Displayed are item used on a 19th-century Uinta County ranch gambling and bootleg whiskey paraphernalia clothing from the era and objects used by the Indian and Chinese people who emigrated to the region. Mon.-Fri. 9-5, Sat.-Sun. 10-4, Memorial Day-Labor Day; Mon.-Fri. 9-5, rest of year Closed Jan. 1, Thanksgiving and Dec. 25. Free Phone (307) 789-2757.

FLAMING GORGE NATIONAL RECREATION AREA (E-2)

Flaming Gorge National Recreation Area straddles the border between Wyoming and Utah and is reached by SR 530 or US 191 from I-80 in Wyoming or US 191 from Utah. The area includes a 91-mile-long reservoir and the Flaming Gorge and Red canyons, which were carved through the Uinta Mountains by the Green River.

Lake Flaming Gorge is bounded primarily by Red Canyon to the south and by rolling hills and occasional abrupt cliffs and promontories to the north. Of geological interest are the exposed strata in Firehole Canyon and the Sheep Creek Geological Loop.

Once belonging to Mexico, the Flaming Gorge region was annexed to the United States after the Mexican War. John Wesley Powell, a one-armed Army major and professor, mapped the area on his way down the Green River in the late 1860s and early 1870s and named Flaming Gorge and many other prominent landmarks.

I-80 is connected to SR 530 and US 191. In Utah, US 191 joins with SRs 43 and 44, which then link with SR 530 again, to form a complete

60-mile loop around the recreation area. Along the route are Flaming Gorge Dam and Visitor Center, Red Canyon Visitor Center, the Sheep Creek Geological Loop and Flaming Gorge.

Known for its bountiful fishing waters, Lake Flaming Gorge also is a popular setting for swimming, boating and water skiing. Large boat ramps are found near campgrounds at convenient access points along the western and eastern sides of the lake.

The western shore, accessible from Buckboard and Lucerne Valley, has campsites and two marinas that provide boat rentals and supplies. Cedar Springs to the southeast is similarly equipped. Other campgrounds are scattered throughout the Utah and Wyoming sections.

Red Canyon Visitor Center and Overlook, off SR 44, offers a spectacular view from 1,400 feet above Red Canyon and Flaming Gorge Reservoir. The Red Canyon Visitor Center is open daily 10-5, Memorial Day-Labor Day; phone (801) 889-3713 or 784-3445. The Flaming Gorge Dam Visitor Center, off US 191 adjacent to the Bureau of Reclamation offices, is open daily 8-6, Memorial Day-Labor Day; 9-5 in spring and fall; 10-4, rest of year. Phone (801) 885-3135 or 784-3445.

The recreation area is open all year, but most facilities are closed during the winter. Seasonal hunting is permitted except near public-use facilities. The reservoir contains a broad sampling of fish, including German brown, lake, rainbow and cutthroat trout; small-mouth bass; and kokanee salmon. Fishing is permitted all year. A license from either Utah or Wyoming is required.

Cross-country skiing, snowmobiling and ice fishing are popular winter activities. For further information contact the Flaming Gorge Ranger District, Flaming Gorge National Recreation Area, P.O. Box 279, Manila, UT 84046; phone (801) 784-3445. *See Recreation Chart and the AAA Northwestern CampBook.*

FLAMING GORGE DAM, near Dutch John, Utah, is a concrete arch structure rising 502 feet above bedrock. Self-guiding tours are available daily 9-4:30, Mar.-Nov. Guided tours are offered daily 9-5, Memorial Day-Labor Day; otherwise varies. Free. Phone (801) 784-3445.

FORT BRIDGER (F-1)

One of Fort Bridger's early residents was the renowned mountain man and scout Jim Bridger. Bridger, who hired himself out as a wilderness guide, was known for telling tall tales. According to popular lore, one of Bridger's most repeated stories was the one in which he tried to jump across a gorge in a petrified forest. The gorge turned out to be wider than he expected, but Bridger managed to escape death by remaining aloft on the gorge's petrified air.

Self-guiding tours: A driving tour atop an original hand-built roadbed of the Union Pacific begins 9 miles west of Fort Bridger at Leroy. The tour continues past the abandoned town of Piedmont, several beehive-shaped charcoal kilns and the Uinta Mountains before entering Evanston *(see place listing p. 136).*

FORT BRIDGER STATE HISTORIC SITE is 3 mi. s. of I-80 exit 34. The fort was established in 1843 by Jim Bridger and Louis Vasquez. Some buildings constructed during Army occupation 1858-90 are in ruins, but many still stand. Recent excavations have revealed the site of the original trading post, which has been reconstructed nearby. A museum offers living-history interpretations throughout the summer. Picnicking is permitted.

Allow 2 hours minimum. Grounds open daily 9-dusk. Museum open daily 9-4:30, May-Sept.; Sat.-Sun. 9-4:30, in Apr. and Oct. Admission $1, under 18 free. Phone (307) 782-3842 or 777-7014.

★ FORT LARAMIE NATIONAL HISTORIC SITE (E-6)

Fort Laramie National Historic Site covers 832 acres off US 26, 3 miles southwest of the town of Fort Laramie, near the confluence of the Laramie and North Platte rivers. From its founding as Fort William in 1834 and until 1849, the fort was an important fur-trading post. Purchased by the U.S. government in 1849 and renamed Fort Laramie, the fort served to aid in the migrations to Oregon and California. By 1890 the fort had outlived its usefulness and was abandoned, its land and buildings sold at public auction.

Eleven structures, including the 1874 cavalry barracks, have been restored and refurnished to recall the flavor of daily life at this post. A visitor center museum displays artifacts relating to civilian, military and Indian history on the northern Plains. From June to mid-August, staff members in period clothing demonstrate aspects of both military and civilian life in the 1870s. A vehicle for the physically impaired is available when the number of staff permits. An 1875 iron Army bridge that spans the North Platte River is 2 miles above the fort.

Grounds open daily 8-dusk. Visitor center open daily 8-7, June 1-Labor Day; 8-4:30, rest of year. Closed Jan. 1, Thanksgiving and Dec. 25. Admission $2, under 17 free; free to all July 4 and Aug. 25. Phone (307) 837-2221.

FOSSIL BUTTE NATIONAL MONUMENT (E-1)

Fossil Butte National Monument, 14 miles west of Kemmerer on US 30, rises nearly 1,000 feet above the Twin Creek Valley. The buff-to-white beds of the Green River formation contain one of the world's largest deposits of the fossils of freshwater fish that lived 50 million years ago. Fossils of mammals, plants and fish can be seen

at the visitor center; a video presentation also i
available.

A self-guiding hiking trail, 2.5 miles long
leads to the site of an historic fossil quarry, and a
1.5-mile trail takes visitors through an aspen tree
grove. Ranger-guided hikes around the monu
ment are offered Sat.-Sun. at 10:30 and 1 or by
appointment, Memorial Day-Labor Day.

Allow 2 hours, 30 minutes minimum. Ground
open all year but may be snow covered Oct.-Apr
Visitor center open daily 8-7, June-Aug.; 8-4:30
rest of year. Free. Phone (307) 877-4455. See
Recreation Chart.

GILLETTE (B-5) pop. 17,600, elev. 4,538′

Gillette lies on a high plateau between the
Black Hills and the Big Horn Mountains. The
town's livestock industry dates from the early
1800s. Mule deer, pronghorns and buffaloes
graze on unspoiled land nearby.

Named for railroad surveyor Edward Gillette
the town was developed as a ranching area and
became a hub for transporting livestock to mar
ket. Now coal and oil industries fuel Gillette's
economy. During summer, free coal mine tours
can be arranged through the convention and visi
tors bureau. The bureau also offers an assistance
program for hunters interested in the mule deer
antelope and elk populations in the area.

**Campbell County Convention and Visitors
Bureau:** 1810 S. Douglas Hwy., Suite A
Gillette, WY 82718; phone (307) 686-0040. See
ad.

ROCKPILE MUSEUM, 1 mi. from I-90 exit 124
on Second St. (US 14/16E), takes its name from
a nearby rock formation. Local history is de
picted through extensive displays that include
firearms, pioneer and Indian artifacts, an early
horse-drawn hearse and a restored sheep wagon
Next to the museum is a furnished rural school
house that could hold only 12 students. Mon.-
Sat. 9-8, Sun. 12:30-6:30, May-Sept.; Mon.-Sat
9-5, rest of year. Free. Phone (307) 682-5723
See ad.

GLENROCK (D-5) pop. 2,200

Glenrock, once called Deer Creek Station, be
gan as a mail and stage station on the Oregon
Trail and served as a vital supply station for emi
grants traveling westward. More than 350,000
pioneers passed through the valley where Glen
rock is located and stopped at the rock in the
glen east of town, giving the town its present
name. Ruts made by the pioneers' wagon wheels
still can be seen. The discovery of gas and oil in
1912 contributed to the area's economy. Several
buildings from the late 1880s can be seen
downtown.

★ GRAND TETON NATIONAL PARK
(C-1)

See map page 140.

Elevations in the park range
from 6,800 ft. at the valley floor to
13,770 ft. at Grand Teton Peak.
Refer to AAA maps for additional
elevation information.

Grand Teton National Park's 485 square miles
include the major portion of Wyoming's Teton
Range and the valley of Jackson Hole. Together
the mountain range and valley frame a majestic
landscape of eight large lakes and many smaller
ones, glaciers, numerous snowfields and extensive pine, fir and spruce forests.

The park's southern entrance is north of Jack-
son on US 26/89/191; an eastern entrance is at
Moran Junction on US 26/287. From this point
US 89/191/287 heads north through the park into
Yellowstone National Park *(see place listing p. 163).*

The Tetons are among the youngest mountains
on the continent. The elevations established by
the U.S. Geological Survey for the major peaks
are Grand Teton, 13,770 feet; Mount Owen,
12,928 feet; Middle Teton, 12,804 feet; Mount
Moran, 12,605 feet; South Teton, 12,514 feet;
Teewinot Mountain, 12,325 feet; Thor Peak,
12,028 feet; Buck Mountain, 11,938 feet; Nez
Perce Peak, 11,901 feet; Mount Wister, 11,490
feet; and Mount St. John, 11,430 feet.

Few mountain ranges have a greater variety of
glaciated canyons than the Tetons. The block-
faulted mountains of this alpine park are rare in
this country. Part of the park area lies above the
tree line, which is at about 10,000 feet.

The Tetons were first photographed by William H. Jackson, a member of the Hayden Expedition sent by the government to survey the area
in 1872.

General Information

The park is open all year, although most park
facilities operate only from mid-May to mid-
October. General information as well as information about weather and road conditions is
available daily 24 hours; phone (307) 739-3600.

Visitor information is available at the Colter
Bay, Flagg Ranch, Jenny Lake and Moose visitor
centers. Free ranger-led activities in summer include hikes and campfire programs. Entrance stations and visitor centers distribute a schedule of
activities, which also is in the park newspaper.

ADMISSION to the park is by private vehicle
permit ($20), valid in both Grand Teton and Yel-
lowstone national parks for 7 days; by annual
area permit ($40/both parks) or annual permit
($50/entrance to all national parks); by single en-
try via motorcycle or horseback ($15), or by bi-
cycle or foot ($10). A Golden Age Passport for
U.S. citizens over 61 is $10; a Golden Access
Passport (for the physically impaired) provides
free admission for U.S. citizens.

PETS are permitted in the park only if they are
on a leash or otherwise physically restricted at
all times. They are not permitted on trails, in the
back country or in any public building.

ADDRESS inquiries to the Superintendent,
Grand Teton National Park, P.O. Drawer 170,
Moose, WY 83012; phone (307) 739-3600.

COLTER BAY VISITOR CENTER, near Jackson
Lake, exhibits examples of Indian art and culture, with emphasis on the Plains tribes. Slides
and movies are shown regularly. Daily 8-8, early
June-Labor Day; 8-5, early to mid-May and day
after Labor Day-late Sept.; 8-7 late May-early
June. Free. Phone (307) 739-3594.

FLAGG RANCH INFORMATION STATION, at
Flagg Ranch, 15 mi. n. of Colter Bay on US 89/
191/287, provides information about John D.
Rockefeller and the Yellowstone area. Daily 9-6,
early June-early Sept. Free.

JENNY LAKE VISITOR CENTER, 8 mi. n. of
Moose Junction on Teton Park Rd., has an exhibit about geology. Daily 8-7, early June-early
Sept. Free. Phone (307) 739-3392. *See color ad
p. 142.*

MOOSE VISITOR CENTER, at the park headquarters in Moose, has natural history and geology
exhibits and provides permits and park information. Daily 8-7, early June-Labor Day; 8-5, rest
of year. Closed Dec. 25. Free. Phone (307)
739-3399.

Activities

More than 200 miles of trails afford short
walks, strenuous hikes and overnight back-
country trips. Trail booklets can be found at
some trail heads and at the visitor centers. Campsites along back-country trails require a camping
permit, available at the visitor centers.

Game fish include brook, brown, cutthroat,
mackinaw, and rainbow trout, as well as whitefish. Fish can be taken with artificial flies during
most of the summer and autumn, but the mackinaw trout in Jackson and Jenny lakes are best
caught by trolling with heavy tackle.

A Wyoming fishing license is required; a nonresident 1- or 5-day license or season permit is
available for a fee. Special fishing regulations
apply in the park, and changes are made annually
regarding limits and waters open to fishing;
check the current regulations.

Mountain climbing is a popular summer pas-
time. Authorized guide services are available, and

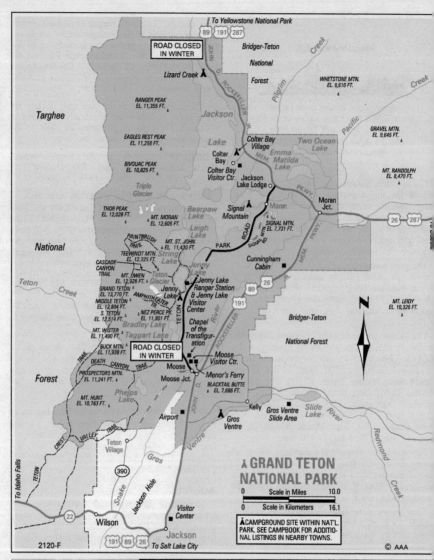

To Yellowstone National Park

ROAD CLOSED IN WINTER

Bridger-Teton

National

Forest

Lizard Creek ⚑

Targhee

RANGER PEAK
EL. 11,355 FT. ▲

Jackson

WHETSTONE MTN.
EL. 9,610 FT. ▲

Colter Bay Village

Colter Bay

Colter Bay Visitor Ctr.

Lake

EAGLES REST PEAK
EL. 11,258 FT. ▲

GRAVEL MTN.
EL. 9,645 FT. ▲

BIVOUAC PEAK
EL. 10,825 FT. ▲

Triple Glacier

Two Ocean Lake

Emma Matilda Lake

MT. RANDOLPH
EL. 8,470 FT. ▲

Jackson Lake Lodge

Moran

Moran Jct.

26   287

THOR PEAK
EL. 12,028 FT. ▲

MT. MORAN
EL. 12,605 FT. ▲

Bearpaw Lake

Signal Mountain ⚑

SIGNAL MTN.
EL. 7,731 FT. ▲

Leigh Lake

National

PAINTBRUSH TRAIL

MT. ST. JOHN
EL. 11,430 FT. ▲

String Lake

PARK

Cunningham Cabin

TEEWINOT MTN.
EL. 12,325 FT. ▲

CASCADE CANYON TRAIL

MT. OWEN
EL. 12,928 FT. ▲

Teton Glacier

Jenny Lake

Jenny Lake Ranger Station & Jenny Lake Visitor Center

89   26

191

GRAND TETON
EL. 13,770 FT. ▲

AMPHITHEATER TR

Jenny Lake

Bridger-Teton

MIDDLE TETON
EL. 12,804 FT. ▲

S. TETON
EL. 12,514 FT. ▲

NEZ PERCE PK.
EL. 11,901 FT. ▲

Chapel of the Transfiguration

National Forest

MT. WISTER
EL. 11,490 FT. ▲

Bradley Lake

Taggart Lake

ROAD CLOSED IN WINTER

BUCK MTN.
EL. 11,938 FT. ▲

DEATH CANYON TRAIL

Moose Visitor Ctr.

PROSPECTORS MTN.
EL. 11,241 FT. ▲

Moose

Moose Jct.

Menor's Ferry

BLACKTAIL BUTTE
EL. 7,686 FT. ▲

Forest

MT. HUNT
EL. 10,783 FT. ▲

Phelps Lake

Kelly

Gros Ventre Slide Area

Slide Lake

Airport ◼

Gros Ventre ⚑

Redmond Creek

MT. LEIDY
EL. 10,326 FT. ▲

N

Teton Village

390

Jackson Hole

Visitor Center

Gros

Ventre

▲ **GRAND TETON NATIONAL PARK**

0	Scale in Miles	10.0
0	Scale in Kilometers	16.1

22

Wilson

191   89   26

Jackson

To Salt Lake City

2120-F

▲ CAMPGROUND SITE WITHIN NAT'L. PARK. SEE CAMPBOOK FOR ADDITIONAL LISTINGS IN NEARBY TOWNS.

© AAA

To Idaho Falls

because of the difficulty of the Teton peaks, climbers are urged to use them. Prospective climbers should consult rangers for information about routes and appropriate equipment. The Jenny Lake Ranger Station is the park's climbing information center.

The usual alpine equipment is essential: ice axes, ropes and rubber-soled boots or climbing shoes. Two park-approved mountaineering schools offer lessons and guide service.

The climbing season in Grand Teton National Park ordinarily spans mid-June to mid-September, but conditions are best from July to early September. In most cases it is advisable to allow 2 days for an ascent of Grand Teto Mount Owen or Mount Moran and 1 or 2 da for all the other peaks, depending upon yo experience.

Riding on horses trained for mountain trails another popular way to explore the park. Fro corrals at Colter Bay Village and Jackson Lal Lodge (see color ad p. 142), the Grand Tet Lodge Co. conducts daily guided 2- and 3-ho rides, half-day trail rides and wagon rides; pho (307) 543-2811.

Morning and evening horse or wagon rid with breakfast or dinner also are available f $30-$35. Guide fees vary according to trail, b

all rates are regulated by the park and range from $18 to $42. Restrictions apply to horseback riding.

Boat and canoe rentals, guided fishing trips and scenic boat trips can be arranged at the Colter Bay Marina at Colter Bay Village and at the booking office at Jackson Lake Lodge. Jackson Lake boat cruises lasting 1 hour, 30 minutes leave the Colter Bay Marina several times daily. Daily trout breakfast cruises to Elk Island as well as Monday, Wednesday and Sunday evening dinner cruises also are offered.

Cruise rates range from $10 to $35; $7 to $23 for children under 12. Contact the Grand Teton Lodge Co. for schedules and exact fares; phone (307) 543-3100.

Teton Boating Co. offers scenic cruises and shuttle service to the west shore of Jenny Lake. Round-trip shuttle service $4; ages 7-12, $2.25. One-way shuttle service $3.25; ages 7-12, $2. The booking office is at the south end of Jenny Lake near the ranger station; phone (307) 733-2703.

Motorboats can be operated on Jackson, Jenny and Phelps lakes, but motors more than 7.5 horsepower cannot be used on Jenny and Phelps lakes. Hand-propelled craft are permitted on Bearpaw, Bradley, Emma Matilda, Jackson, Jenny, Leigh, Phelps, String, Taggart and Two Ocean lakes and on the Snake River. Water skiing, jet skiing and windsurfing are permitted only on Jackson Lake.

Mandatory boating permits, which are good for the season in both Grand Teton and Yellowstone national parks, cost $5 for nonmotorized craft and $10 for motorized craft. Permits can be purchased at the visitor centers.

Winter activities include snowmobiling, cross-country skiing, snowshoe hikes and ice fishing. All vehicles traveling over snow are subject to special regulations, including a $5 registration permit; contact the Moose Visitor Center for details.

Concessioner-guided snowmobile trips are available, as are snowcoach tours into Yellow-stone National Park from Flagg Ranch daily between Dec. 25 and mid-March; phone (307) 543-2861. Marked trails for cross-country skiing also are provided.

Five campgrounds, Colter Bay, Gros Ventre, Jenny Lake, Lizard Creek and Signal Mountain, are open on a first-come-first-served basis. Opening dates vary from late April to early June; closing dates are from early September to mid-October. Reservations are not accepted. *See Recreation Chart and the AAA Northwestern CampBook.*

★**FLOAT TRIPS** are conducted by experienced guides who thread rubber rafts down the Snake River through Grand Teton National Park. These trips, which offer spectacular mountain scenery and opportunities to view native wildlife, are carefully supervised by the National Park Service. Reservations are recommended for all trips. **Note:** A minimum weight of 35-40 pounds is required for most float trips.

Barker-Ewing Scenic Float Trips departs from the float trip parking lot at the Moose Visitor Center. Scenic 10-mile trips on the Snake River are offered. Transportation from the meeting place to the launch area is provided. For information write P.O. Box 100-A, Moose, WY 83012. Trips several times daily, May 15-Sept. 30, water conditions permitting. Fare $40; under 13, $25. Under 4 are not permitted. Reservations are required. DS, MC, VI. Phone (307) 733-1800 or (800) 365-1800. *See color ad p. 140.*

Fort Jackson Scenic Snake River Float Trips, which provides round-trip transportation from a central location in the town of Jackson, offers 14-mile scenic float trips which provide good opportunities for wildlife and mountain viewing and photography. The trips last 3.5 to 4 hours. For information write P.O. Box 1176, Jackson Hole, WY 83001. A 14-mile trip departs several times daily, mid-May through late Sept., weather and water conditions permitting. Float trips $32.50; ages 4-13, $22.50. Reservations are required. MC, VI. Phone (307) 733-2583 or (800) 735-8430. *See color ad.*

THE OREGON TRAIL

Zebulon Pike proclaimed the first westbound trail through the Rockies as "unfit for any but a nomad population." But this warning did not deter the more than 300,000 emigrants who used the trail. The lure of the Oregon country unleashed one of the greatest peacetime migrations in the history of the world.

These early pioneers, with their possessions and dreams for a new beginning, were ill-prepared for the trail's dangers: drought, blizzards, disease, wild animals and hostile Indians. However, as the number of settlements increased, conditions and the nature of the journey improved.

The gateway to the northwest was actually several major emigrant trails starting at the Missouri River and ending in Oregon City, Ore. In all, the trail extended 2,000 miles and stretched across six states. Traffic along this highway was so relentless, swelled by lengthy wagon trains, that ruts 5-6 feet deep scarred the fragile prairie. Many of the ruts are still visible.

On rock faces of landmark buttes the emigrants chiseled names and dates, poignant testimony to a journey that is now gauged along blacktop highways in hours instead of days.

DID YOU KNOW?

Near Guernsey you can see the ruts worn into a layer of soft sandstone by thousands of wagon wheels traveling the Oregon Trail during the mid-1800s.

The first book printed in Wyoming was the "Dictionary of the Sioux Language" in 1866.

Women have been able to vote in Wyoming since Dec. 10, 1869.

Grand Teton Lodge Co. Float Trips, 5 mi. n.w. of Moran Junction on US 89/191/287, offers short float trips. Transportation to and from the river is provided. For information write Grand Teton Lodge Co., P.O. Box 240, Moran, WY 83013.

Daily trips from Colter Bay Village run May 22-Sept. 27; from Jackson Lake Lodge, May 17-Sept. 30. Luncheon trips, which depart only from Jackson Lake Lodge, are offered May 24-Sept. 25. Dinner trips, departing from Jackson Lake Lodge, also are available. Short float trip $35; ages 6-11, $17. Lunch trip $40; ages 6-11, $26. Dinner trip $46; ages 6-11, $34. Under 6 are not permitted. MC, VI. Phone (307) 543-3100.

National Park Float Trips, which offers free transportation for large parties from Jackson and the float trip parking lot in Moose Village, offers 10-mile scenic float rides down the Snake River in Grand Teton National Park. Trips depart several times daily, May-Sept. Fare $35; under 18, $25. MC, VI. Phone (307) 733-5500 or 733-6445.

Osprey Snake River Float Trips, which departs near the visitor center at Moose Junction, offers 5-mile, 1- to 1.5-hour scenic trips down the Snake River. Trips leave several times daily, early June-late Aug. Fare $21; under 18, $16. Transportation is included. MC, VI. Phone (307) 733-5500 or 733-6445.

Solitude Float Trips depart the float-trip parking lot near the Moose Visitor Center. Five and 10-mile, 2.5 to 3-hour scenic trips are available. Trips offered several times daily, May-Sept., water and weather conditions permitting. Fare $18-$35; under 12, $25. Reservations are recommended. MC, VI. Phone (307) 733-2871 or (888) 704-2800. *See color ad p. 141.*

Triangle X Ranch Float Trips begins at the Triangle X Guest Ranch, 11 mi. n. of Moose and 6 mi. s. of Moran Junction on US 26/89. Five- and 10-mile float trips, an evening supper trip and sunrise and evening wildlife trips are available. For information write Triangle X Float Trips, Grand Teton National Park, Moose, WY 83012. Several trips are offered daily, May-Sept. Fare $32-$42. Reservations are required. MC, VI. Phone (307) 733-5500 or 733-6445. *See color ad p. 141.*

TAPE TOURS, available at gift shops, RV campgrounds, Colter Bay Village, Moose Village Store, Jackson Lake Lodge and Jenny Lake Store, allows drivers to set their own pace while a cassette narrative describes the park's attractions and history. The 90-minute tapes can be ordered from CCInc., P.O. Box 227, Allendale, NJ 07401. The cost is $12.95, plus $2 postage and handling. Phone (201) 236-1666.

Points of Interest
AMPHITHEATER LAKE TRAIL extends up the eastern slope of Disappointment Peak to two alpine lakes, Surprise and Amphitheater, both at altitudes of more than 9,000 feet. Amphitheater

Lake occupies a protected glacial cirque, or steep hollow. An overlook, reached by several trails climbing 3,000 feet above the valley floor, offers a sweeping panorama of Jackson Hole and a view extending eastward 80 miles to the Wind River Mountains. A branch from the trail leads into Garnet Canyon. Trail conditions are available at the visitor centers. Allow 6 hours minimum.

CASCADE CANYON TRAIL explores the deepest recesses of the Tetons, passing through a broad, glacier-carved canyon with walls that rise thousands of feet on either side. Lake Solitude, near the head of the canyon at the tree line, is a pristine example of an alpine lake. Allow 7 hours minimum.

CHAPEL OF THE TRANSFIGURATION is near Moose. Above the altar of the 1925 log chapel is a large window framing a view of the Teton Range. Episcopal services are held during the summer; schedules are posted on a board outside the chapel. Allow 30 minutes minimum.

CUNNINGHAM CABIN, 6 mi. s. of Moran Junction on US 26/89/191, was the base of Pierce Cunningham's Bar Flying U Ranch. A booklet outlining a self-guiding trail through the area also describes the life of the homesteader in Jackson Hole. Allow 30 minutes minimum.

DEATH CANYON TRAIL traverses the length of a canyon of profound depth and grandeur to broad meadows. No canyon better illustrates the contrasts of the Teton area. Allow 6 hours minimum.

★ **GROS VENTRE SLIDE—**
see Bridger-Teton National Forest p. 125.

HIDDEN FALLS AND INSPIRATION POINT TRAILS lead from the southern shore of Jenny Lake off Teton Park Rd. A boat ride to the trail head is available in the summer. Ranger-guided tours to Hidden Falls and Inspiration Point depart the trail head daily at 8:30 in season; departure time may vary. Allow 2 hours minimum.

JACKSON HOLE, a high mountain valley about 50 miles long and 6 to 12 miles wide, is completely surrounded by mountains and bisected by the Snake River. The wilderness enveloping this valley provides a habitat for many large mammals. The rare trumpeter swan is among the birds inhabiting the area. Streams and lakes abound with fish and waterfowls, and summer wildflowers dot alpine meadows bordered by rugged peaks.

Teton Park Road leads to Jenny Lake Lodge, campgrounds, fishing sites and most of the trails. East of Snake River, Jackson Hole Highway (US 26/89/191) runs parallel to Teton Park Road between Moran and Moose and affords superb views of the Teton Range.

MENOR'S FERRY, near park headquarters in Moose, is a reconstruction of the craft that was once the only means of crossing the Snake River in central Jackson Hole country. The original home of Bill Menor, one of the area's first settlers, is in the area; it contains historical objects and exhibits. Allow 30 minutes minimum. Daily in summer.

PAINTBRUSH TRAIL starts near the outlet of Leigh Lake, follows the bottom of Paintbrush Canyon, crosses Paintbrush Divide and joins the Cascade Canyon Trail at Lake Solitude. The many wildflowers along this trail give the canyon its name. Wildlife, especially moose, can be seen near lakes and marshes. This trail affords several good views of Jackson and Leigh lakes. Since dangerous snow and ice remain on the divide until late in the year, check conditions at the visitor centers. Horses cannot be taken over the divide to Lake Solitude until late August.

SIGNAL MOUNTAIN, 2 mi. s. of Jackson Lake Junction on Teton Park Rd., affords a panorama of the valley, Jackson Lake, a portion of southern Yellowstone and the Teton, Gros Ventre and Hoback mountain ranges. A narrow paved road 5 miles long leads to the summit. Trailers are not allowed on this road. Allow 1 hour minimum.

TETON CREST TRAIL traverses the Tetons from Teton Pass to Cascade Canyon. This high alpine country can be explored by foot or horseback.

VALLEY TRAIL, which runs parallel to the mountains from the eastern shore of Leigh Lake s. to Teton Village, is the point of origin of all trails into the Teton range. From this point, trails run westward into Cascade, Death, Granite, Open and Paintbrush canyons; others encircle String Lake and Jenny Lake. A popular hike follows the south shore of Jenny Lake to Hidden Falls.

GREEN RIVER (E-2) pop. 12,700, elev. 6,082'

The northern gateway to the Flaming Gorge National Recreation Area *(see place listing p. 136)*, Green River developed as a stop along the Overland Trail in the mid-1800s. One prominent traveler was Maj. John Wesley Powell, who began his explorations of the Green and Colorado rivers in 1869. The town is a railroad center and the seat of Sweetwater County.

Green River Chamber of Commerce: 1450 Uinta Dr., Green River, WY 82935; phone (307) 875-5711 or (800) 354-6743.

SWEETWATER COUNTY HISTORICAL MUSEUM, 80 W. Flaming Gorge Way, contains permanent and temporary exhibits, including a large collection of historical photographs of southwestern Wyoming. Allow 30 minutes minimum. Mon.-Fri. 9-5, Sat. 1-5, July-Aug.; Mon.-Fri. 9-5, rest of year. Free. Phone (307) 872-6435.

GREYBULL (B-3) pop. 1,800, elev. 3,788'

Greybull derives its name from a local Indian legend that claimed a great albino buffalo once roamed the area. The Indians revered the bull, considering it a sign from their Great Spirit. Indian arrowheads, fossils and semiprecious stones can be found around town. The site of widespread oil and mineral activity, Greybull recently has focused its attention on bentonite mining.

Scenic attractions in the vicinity include Shell Canyon Falls *(see Bighorn National Forest p. 124)*, 24 miles east of US 14, and the drive over the Big Horn Mountains via scenic US 14 to Sheridan. Devil's Kitchen, a few miles northeast, and Sheep Mountain to the north are interesting geological formations.

Stone Schoolhouse Gallery & Bookstore, 6 miles east on US 14, is an example of the one-room schoolhouse common to 19th-century America. Area homesteaders quarried sandstone to construct the building in 1903.

Greybull Chamber of Commerce: 333 Greybull Ave., Greybull, WY 82426; phone (307) 765-2100. *See color ad p. 133.*

GREYBULL MUSEUM, .25 mi. e. on US 14 at 325 Greybull Ave., houses fossils, minerals, Indian artifacts and early Western memorabilia. Of interest are large ammonite fossils, which date from the Mesozoic era when the Greybull area was part of a large inland sea. Daily 10-8, June 1-Labor Day; Mon.-Fri. noon-6, day after Labor Day-Oct. 31; Mon.- Fri. noon-5, Apr.-May; Mon., Wed. and Fri. noon-4, rest of year. Free. Phone (307) 765-2444.

GREYBULL WILDLIFE MUSEUM, 420 Greybull Ave., features wildlife taxidermy specimens in natural settings. Mon.-Fri. 9-4, May 1-Dec. 15; closed holidays. Free. Phone (307) 765-2002.

 RECREATIONAL ACTIVITIES

Horseback Riding

- **The Hideout,** 3208 Beaver Creek Rd., Greybull, WY 82426. Trips offered Apr.-Oct. Phone (307) 765-2080 or (800) 354-8637.

GUERNSEY (D-6) pop. 1,200, elev. 4,361'

Just below the mouth of Platte River Canyon, Guernsey is in an area known for its limestone beds and a profusion of such artifacts as agricultural and war implements. Indians driven from their homes east of the Mississippi River and pioneers headed westward followed the river through this area.

During one of his expeditions in 1842, John C. Fremont camped near what is now the Oregon Trail Ruts State Historic Site *(see attraction listing).* The small prairie next to the river (the present town site) impressed him as a good spot

for a military installation because of its cottonwood trees, pines and abundant rock for building.

Prospectors discovered early that the rock formations around Guernsey were good for more than just building. Moss agate stone, unearthed from what is believed to be the first commercially developed deposit of moss agate in the nation, was found in the Guernsey-Hartville region and exported to Germany in the late 1800s. The additional discovery of copper led to the founding of nearby communities Hartville and Sunrise.

Guernsey Visitors Center: 91 S. Wyoming, P.O. Box 667, Guernsey, WY 82214; phone (307) 836-2715.

GUERNSEY STATE PARK MUSEUM is 1.25 mi. w. on US 26, then 2.75 mi. n. on SR 317 in Guernsey State Park *(see Recreation Chart and the AAA Northwestern CampBook).* Exhibits depict the natural and human history of the region. Allow 30 minutes minimum. Daily 10-6, May-Oct. Park admission $2 per in-state private vehicle, $3 per out-of-state private vehicle. Museum free. Phone (307) 836-2900.

OREGON TRAIL RUTS STATE HISTORIC SITE, 1 mi. s. on S. Wyoming Ave. from jct. US 26, presents well-preserved examples of mid-19th-century pioneer trails. Some of the ruts are 5 to 6 feet deep. Next to the ruts are footpaths used by muleteers and others who walked beside the wagons. Self-guiding trails provide an explanation of the site. Allow 30 minutes minimum. No facilities are available.

REGISTER CLIFF STATE HISTORIC SITE, 3 mi. s. on S. Wyoming Ave. from jct. US 26, contains a 100-foot cliff with the carved names of thousands of pioneers who journeyed past this point. Many of the inscriptions were made 1840-60. A walkway and an explanatory sign are at the base of the cliff.

HYATTVILLE (B-4) elev. 4,447'

Hyattville, which began as an isolated frontier cow town, is at the confluence of Medicine Lodge and Paintrock creeks in a region that mixes rolling foothills with rugged canyons to create a series of caves, ledges and grassy knolls. The protective nature of this area is what lured its first inhabitants in prehistoric times.

Artifacts of early paleo-Indian family groups were preserved in the layers of sediment beneath a sandstone cliff containing myriad petroglyphs and pictographs. Some of these can be seen at Medicine Lodge State Archeological Site, 6 miles northeast of town off SR 31 on Cold Springs Road (an oiled road); phone (307) 469-2234.

JACKSON (C-1) pop. 4,500, elev. 6,123'

The southern entrance to Grand Teton National Park *(see place listing p. 139),* Jackson is the supply point and center of activity for ranchers and vacationers in Jackson Hole country. Recreation in the mountain-rimmed valley includes boating, fishing, hiking, horseback riding, mountain climbing, downhill and cross-country skiing, snowmobiling, whitewater rafting and windsurfing on Jackson Lake.

Jackson is on a scenic portion of US 89 that extends south 255 miles from Mammoth Hot Springs to Geneva, Idaho.

Live musical comedies are presented in summer at Jackson Hole Playhouse and Grand Teton Main Stage. The J.H. Rodeo also operates in the summer; phone (307) 733-2805.

Jackson Hole Chamber of Commerce: 532 N. Cache St., P.O. Box E, Jackson, WY 83001; phone (307) 733-3316.

BAR J CHUCKWAGON, 6 mi. w. on Teton Village Rd., presents a traditional Western meal followed by an evening of family entertainment. Cowboys sing and play guitars, yodel and offer ranch-style humor. Daily 5:30-9:30, June-Sept. Admission $14-$18; ages 4-8, $5. Reservations are suggested. DS, MC, VI. Phone (307) 733-3370 or (800) 905-2275.

JACKSON HOLE HISTORICAL SOCIETY, jct. N. Glenwood St. and Mercill Ave., is a historical research facility displaying artifacts from American Indians and early pioneers. An extensive collection of Old West photographs also is available. Mon.-Fri. 8-5; closed holidays. Free. Phone (307) 733-9605.

JACKSON HOLE IDITAROD SLED DOG TOURS, 20 mi. s. on SR 191/189 at 11 Granite Creek, offers sled dog trips in Bridger-Teton National Forest. Warm clothing is advisable. Transportation from lodging is provided. For information write P.O. Box 1940, Jackson, WY 83001. Full- and half-day trips are scheduled mid-Nov. to mid-Apr. Full-day trip $225, half-day trip $135 (meals included). Reservations are required. MC, VI. Phone (307) 733-7388 or (800) 554-7388.

JACKSON HOLE MUSEUM, jct. N. Glenwood and Deloney, features exhibits about archeology, fur-trade and early settler history. Artifacts include firearms, tools and historic photographs.

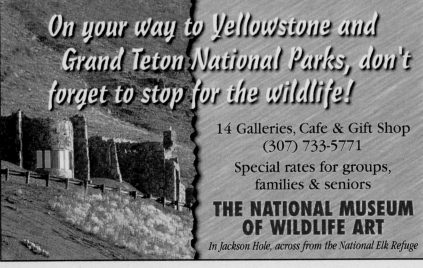

Guided walking tours of Jackson's historic downtown area are conducted three times a week; a fee is charged. Museum open Mon.-Sat. 9:30-6, Sun. 10-5, Memorial Day weekend-early Oct. Admission $3; over 64, $2; students under 18, $1; family rate $6. Phone (307) 733-2414.

JACKSON NATIONAL FISH HATCHERY, 4 mi. n. on US 26/89/191 at 1500 Fish Hatchery Rd., raises predominantly cutthroat trout. Allow 30 minutes minimum. Daily 8-4. Free. Phone (307) 733-2510.

NATIONAL ELK REFUGE, 1 mi. e. on Broadway to Elk Refuge Rd., is the winter home of between 7,500 and 10,000 elk, one of the largest herds in North America. Elk can be seen at the 24,700-acre refuge November through April; during the summer they migrate to various mountain meadows in Grand Teton and Yellowstone national parks and Bridger-Teton National Forest. The habitat also attracts other wildlife, including trumpeter swans. The visitor center at 532 N. Cache St. offers exhibits and wildlife videotapes. Refuge open daily 24 hours; closed Dec. 25. Visitor center open daily; hours vary. Phone (307) 733-9212.

Sleigh Rides, offered through National Museum of Wildlife Art (*see attraction listing*), provide up-close elk viewing. Warm clothing is recommended on the 45-minute trips. Daily 10-4, mid-Dec. through Mar. 31; closed Dec. 25. Fare $10; ages 6-12, $6. Phone (307) 733-9212.

NATIONAL MUSEUM OF WILDLIFE ART is on Rungius Rd. across from the National Elk Refuge. The museum is in a stone building wedged into a Wyoming hillside so that it appears part of its surroundings. Displays include more than 2,500 paintings and sculptures of North American wildlife by such artists as George Catlin,

John Clymer, C.M. Russell, Conrad Schwiering and Carl Rungius. Of note are the JKM Collection of big game animals and the American Bison exhibit. Educational programs and changing exhibits occur year-round. Food is available.

Daily 9-5, early Dec.-early Apr. and Memorial Day-Labor Day; Mon.-Sat. 9-5, Sun. 1-5, rest of year. Closed Dec. 25. Admission $6, senior citizens and students with ID $5, under 6 free, family rate $14. Phone (307) 733-5771. *See color ad p. 147.*

RIPLEY'S BELIEVE IT OR NOT! MUSEUM is n. of jct. U.S. 26/89/189/191 at 140 N. Cache St. The oddities of this collection include such weird wonders as a shrunken head, a jeweled horse, Annie Oakley's pistol, a huge cigar and art created by using lint from the dryer. Allow 1 hour minimum. Daily 9 a.m.-10 p.m., May-Sept.; 10-8, rest of year. Closed Jan. 1, Thanksgiving and Dec. 25. Admission $6.95; ages 6-12, $4.50. DS, MC, VI. Phone (307) 734-0000.

TETON COUNTRY WAGON TRAIN offers a 4-day, 3-night guided wagon train trip along back roads between Grand Teton and Yellowstone national parks, with a stop at a different camp each night. The excursions also include horseback trips from camp, evening entertainment and canoeing. Under 4 are not permitted. For reservations write Bar-T-Five Outfitters, P.O. Box 2140, Jackson, WY 83001.

Departures Mon. mornings, last week in June-last week in Aug. Fare $695; ages 9-14, $645; ages 4-8, $545. Fare includes all transfers, 3 nights' camping and all chuckwagon meals. Sleeping bags and camping gear are provided.

Reservations are required. AE, DS, MC, VI. Phone (307) 734-6101 or 888 734-6101.

WAGONS WEST traverses the foothills of the Tetons in Jackson Hole. Two-, 4- and 6-day wagon treks, as well as hourly, day-long and multiday horse pack rides, are available. Marshaled by a wagon master, a covered-wagon train carries passengers along scenic wilderness trails. Gentle riding horses, chuckwagon meals and campfire entertainment are provided. Write Wagons West, P.O. Box 1156, Afton, WY 83110.

Trips depart June-Aug. Two-day trip $300; under 14, $260. Four-day trip $575; under 14, $485. Six-day trip $775; under 14, $675. Horse pack rates $28-$95. Reservations are required. Phone (800) 447-4711.

 RECREATIONAL ACTIVITIES

Alpine Slide
- **Snow King Alpine Slide** is 8 blks. s.e. of Jackson Town Square at 400 E. Snow King

Ave., Jackson, WY 83001. Daily Memorial Day weekend and early June-Labor Day; Sat.-Sun. day after Labor Day to mid-Sept. Phone (307) 733-7680. *See color ad.*

Mountain Biking
- **Teton Mountain Bike Tours** arranges for riders to be picked up at local lodgings. Write P.O. Box 7027, Jackson, WY 83002. Tours daily mid-May to mid-Oct. Phone (307) 733-0712 or (800) 733-0788.

Skiing
- **Jackson Hole Mountain Resort**, 12 mi. w. via SRs 22 and 390. Write P.O. Box 290, Teton Village, WY 83025. Other activities are offered. Daily 9-4, first Sat. in Dec.-first Sun. in Apr. Phone (307) 733-2292 or (800) 443-6931.

- **Snow King Resort**, 400 E. Snow King Ave. Write P.O. Box SKI, Jackson, WY 83001.

Other activities are offered. Daily late Nov.-late Mar. Phone (307) 733-5200 or (800) 522-5464. *See color ad p. 149.*

White-water Rafting

- **Barker-Ewing Whitewater River Trips** begins in Jackson at 45 W. Broadway for both Snake and Salmon rivers. Write P.O. Box 450, Jackson, WY 83001. Half-day trips depart daily, mid-May to late Sept. Other types of trips also are available. Phone (307) 733-1000 or (800) 448-4202. *See color ad p. 141.*

- **Charles Sands' Wild Water River Trips**, 110 W. Broadway. Write P.O. Box 10489, Jackson, WY 83002. Daily trips available May 15-Sept. 30. Phone (307) 733-4410 or (800) 358-8184. *See color ad p. 148.*

- **Dave Hansen River Trips** operates from Wagon Wheel Village at 515 N. Cache St., across from Wyoming Information Center. Write P.O. Box 328-A, Jackson, WY 83001. Half-day trips depart three times daily, full-day trips depart daily in the morning, May 25-Sept. 30. Phone (307) 733-6295 or (800) 732-6295.

- **Jackson Hole Whitewater**, 650 W. Broadway. Write P.O. Box 125, Jackson, WY 83001. Trips daily May 15-Sept. 30. Phone (307) 733-1007, or (888) 700-7238 out of Wyo. *See color ad p. 149.*

- SAVE **Lewis & Clark River Expeditions**, 33. N. Cache Dr. Write P.O. Box 720, Jackson WY 83001. Trips depart several times daily mid-May to mid-Sept. Phone (307) 733-4022 or (800) 824-5375.

- **Lone Eagle Whitewater** is 13 mi. s.e. on US 26/89/189/191 to Hoback jct., then 4 mi. e. on US 189/191 at Lone Eagle Resort. Write Star Route 45C, Jackson, WY 83001. Snake River trips depart seven times daily, May 15-Sept 15. Phone (307) 733-1090, or (800) 321-3800 out of Wyo. *See color ad p. 147.*

- **Mad River Boat Trips Inc.**, with offices at Whitewater Warehouse at 1255 S. US 89 and at Chets Way on Jackson Town Square. Write P.O. Box 10940, Jackson, WY 83002. Trips depart daily, May 15-Sept. 30. Phone (307) 733-6203 or (800) 458-7238. *See color ad.*

- **Snake River Park Whitewater**, 12 mi. s. on US 89. Write 9705 S. US 89, Jackson, WY 83001. Trips depart four to five times daily, May 15-Sept. 5 (weather permitting). Phone (307) 733-7078 or (800) 562-1878.

- **Teton Expeditions**, 650 W. Broadway. Write P.O. Box 125, Jackson, WY 83001. Trips depart daily May-Sept. Phone (307) 733-1007.

JACKSON HOLE—
see Grand Teton National Park p. 145.

KEMMERER (E-1) pop. 3,000, elev. 6,908′

One feature of the boom that followed the discovery of coal near Kemmerer in 1897 was the saloon of "Preaching Lime" Huggins, who maintained that he never sold a drink to a man already under the influence. Over the bar mirror hung such mottos as "Don't buy a drink before seeing that your baby has shoes." One of his patrons liked the establishment because he could do his repenting during his sinning and "get the whole thing over at once."

A nationwide retail chain originated in Kemmerer when J.C. Penney opened his first store, the Golden Rule, in 1902 with an initial investment of $500. The original home of the founder is now a museum at 107 JC Penney Ave.

Native fossils and historical artifacts are displayed at Kemmerer City Visitor Center in Triangle Park.

Kemmerer/Diamondville Area Chamber of Commerce: 800 Pine Ave., Kemmerer, WY 83101; phone (307) 877-9761 or (888) 300-3413.

FOSSIL COUNTRY MUSEUM is at 400 Pine Ave. Permanent exhibits in this museum include a replica of an underground coal mine and a moonshine still, mountain man artifacts, Union Pacific

Look For The Lodging Signs Backed By A 100% Satisfaction Guarantee

HOW TO RUN A HOTEL.℠

Free local calls and in-room coffee makes Quality the perfect place for today's traveler. For over 50 years, Quality has been making everything just right.

It's more than a room. It's Comfort.℠

You always enjoy extra amenities when you stay at Comfort Inn & Comfort Suites. Like our Free Breakfast to help you start the day off right.

Upgrade your room, not your rate.℠

At Clarion, you'll find everything you expect at an upscale hotel. Well, everything except the high rates. And AAA members save 20% at most Clarions.

In a class by itself.℠

With low rates and state-of-the-art rooms, it's no wonder Sleep Inn is rated among the best hotels for satisfaction, service and value.

Stay longer for less.℠

The reasonably-priced option for travelers who are looking for a comfortable extended-stay hotel. A great place for visits that last a night, a week, or more.

For Reservations Call
1-800-228-1AAA
Or Contact Your Local AAA Club.

 TourBookMark
Lodging Listing Symbols

Member Values

SAVE	Official Appointment lodging providing minimum 10% discount
SAVE	SYC&S chain partners offering member benefits
AAA	Official Appointment
ASK	May offer discounts to members upon request
S/D	Senior Discount

Member Services

	Transportation to Airport
	Pets Allowed
	Cocktail Lounge
	Restaurant on Premises
	Restaurant off Premises (walking distance)
	24 Hour Room Service
	Night Club
	Entertainment

Room Amenities

	Coffee Maker in Room
	Honor Bar
	Data Port/Modem Line
	No Cable TV
	Movies
VCR	VCR
	Radio
	Non-Smoking Rooms
	Microwaves
	Refrigerator
	No Air Conditoner
	No Telephones

Safety Features

	Safe

Special Features

	Child Care
	Business Services
	Laundry Service
	Fully Accessible
	Semi-Accessible
	Roll-in Showers
	Hearing Impaired
	Valet Parking

Sports/Recreation

	Pool
	Fitness Center
	Recreation Facilities

Call property for detailed information about fees & restrictions relating to the lodging listing symbols.

CHOICE HOTELS
INTERNATIONAL

HOW TO RUN A HOTEL.℠

Inns·Hotels·Suites

Inns·Suites

It's more than a room. It's Comfort.℠

Inns·Hotels·Resorts

Upgrade your room, not your rate.℠

In a class by itself.℠

Stay longer for less.℠

Show Your Card & Save

For Reservations Call
1-800-228-1AAA
Or Contact Your Local AAA Club.

(king of the road)

Don't hit the road without
enrolling in the **AT&T One
Rate® Calling Card Plan.**
Unlike some other calling card
plans that have a hidden service
charge for every call, this plan
has just a flat $1 monthly fee.
Plus a low per minute rate for
domestic AT&T Calling Card calls.
Just call **1 800 378-8562
x62549** for this outstanding
travel value.

AT&T
It's all within your reach.

Railroad and World Wars I and II memorabilia, vintage clothing, fossils and a dinosaur footprint from a local coal mine. Allow 30 minutes minimum. Mon.-Sat. 10-4, Labor Day-Memorial Day; Mon.-Fri. 9-5, rest of year. Closed Jan. 1, July 4, Thanksgiving and Dec. 25. Free. Phone (307) 877-6551.

LANDER (D-2) pop. 7,000, elev. 5,372'

Lander began around 1869 when Camp Augur was built to protect the settlers and Shoshone Indians. In 1884 Lander became the seat of newly created Fremont County, which is as large as some Eastern states. The county covers 5,861,120 acres and is an important wildlife habitat for moose, elk, bighorn sheep, deer and antelopes.

North of Lander is the vast Wind River Mountain Range. Part of this range is now the Wind River Indian Reservation. Further northwest near Dubois is an area that was the site of a horse ranch operated by George Parker, alias Butch Cassidy. Cassidy frequently sold his stock in Lander, whose citizens maintained that he always had more to sell than he had raised.

SR 131 follows the middle fork of the Popo Agie River southwest of Lander to Sinks Canyon State Park *(see attraction listing)* and Shoshone National Forest *(see place listing p. 159)*. Lander is the trailhead for the Continental Divide Snowmobile Trail.

Lander Area Chamber of Commerce: 160 N. 1st St., Lander, WY 82520; phone (307) 332-3892, or (800) 433-0662.

FREMONT COUNTY PIONEER MUSEUM, 1 blk. n. of Main St. at 630 Lincoln St., contains exhibits about the history of Fremont County. Mon.-Fri. 9-5; closed holidays. Donations. Phone (307) 332-4137.

SINKS CANYON STATE PARK is 7.5 mi. s.w. on SR 131. Moose, bighorn sheep and other wild game often can be sighted. The Popo Agie River disappears into the sinks of the Madison Limestone and reappears in a rise one-quarter of a mile down the canyon in a large trout pool.

The Sinks Canyon State Park Visitor Center provides information about natural features and recreational opportunities. Visitor center daily 9-7, Memorial Day-Labor Day. Phone (307) 332-3077. *See Recreation Chart and the AAA Northwestern CampBook.*

WIND RIVER INDIAN RESERVATION is about 15 mi. n.w. on US 287. Of different linguistic stock and cultural background, the Shoshone and Arapaho tribes occupy different sections of the 2.5 million-acre reservation. The graves of Chief Washakie and Sacajawea, as well as the Shoshone Cultural Center, which offers displays and tours, are in Fort Washakie. Arapaho artifacts are in a museum at St. Michael's Mission in Ethete.

Sun Dances are performed near Fort Washakie and Ethete for 3 days in July. Photography is prohibited. Powwows and rodeos are held throughout the summer. Christmas dances are performed Dec. 24 through Jan. 1. For further information write P.O. Box 217, Fort Washakie, WY 82514. The tribal information office is at the joint tribal administrative complex, 16 miles north on US 287. Office open Mon.-Fri. 8-4:45. Phone (307) 332-3040 or 332-9106.

LARAMIE (E-5) pop. 26,700, elev. 7,171'

Although Indians roamed the Laramie Plains as early as 8000 B.C., Laramie's recorded history began in the early 19th century with the arrival of the area's first white man, Jacques LaRamie, a trapper for American Fur Co. In his steps followed mountain men, trappers, emigrants, soldiers and explorers, many tracing the old Cherokee Trail.

Fort Sanders, a short distance south, provided protection for the Overland Stage Line and for the Union Pacific. The railroad brought the bulk of Laramie's citizenry—including a sizable population of lawless riffraff who finally left town at the prompting of self-appointed vigilance committees.

The first women jurors served in Laramie in March 1870. In the fall "Grandma" Eliza A. Swain became the first woman to vote in a general election.

Recreational opportunities abound nearby. Cross-country skiing is available east of Laramie, and downhill skiing and snowmobiling can be found in the Snowy Range of the Medicine Bow Mountains, west of the city on SR 130. Both regions are equally attractive to vacationers during the summer, with many camping and picnic areas.

Of geological interest is Sand Creek, a 6,000-acre natural landmark about 20 miles southwest of Laramie. Some of North America's finest examples of cross-bedded sandstone and "topple blocks" can be seen.

Laramie serves as the eastern end of a scenic portion of I-80, which runs 99 miles northwest to Walcott. Snowy Range Scenic Byway (SR 130), off the I-80 Snowy Range exit, offers a view of mountains, lakes and forests. At the summit, the Libby Flats Observatory and a viewing platform offer a panorama of the area.

Albany County Tourism Board: 800 S. Third St., Laramie, WY 82070; phone (307) 745-4195 or (800) 445-5303. *See color ad p. 152.*

Self-guiding tours: Brochures describing downtown and architectural highlights walking tours are available at the Laramie Chamber of Commerce, 800 S. Third St., Laramie, WY 82070; phone (307) 745-7339.

ABRAHAM LINCOLN MEMORIAL MONUMENT is 10 mi. s.e. on I-80, exit 323, at the edge of a rest area. The 48.5-foot-tall monument stands at an 8,640-foot summit off I-80 near Sherman Hill; the monument marks the highest point on this transcontinental route. I-80 follows the path of the first transcontinental railroad line.

AMES MONUMENT, 17 mi. s.e. on I-80, then 2 mi. s. on Ames Rd., is a 60-foot granite pyramid honoring Oliver and Oakes Ames, the two promoters of the transcontinental railroad. Built 1881-82, the monument marks the site of Sherman, a train inspection point before it became a ghost town with the relocation of the Union Pacific tracks. A plaque relates local history.

SAVE **LARAMIE PLAINS MUSEUM,** 1 blk. n. of I-80 and US 30 Business Loop at 603 Ivinson Ave., is the restored 1892 Victorian mansion of Edward Ivinson, one of the city's original settlers. Period furnishings and thousands of artifacts are on display. The grounds include a carriage house and a one-room log schoolhouse. Guided tours are given Mon.-Sat. 9-6, Sun. 1-4, June-Aug.; Mon.-Sat. 1-3, rest of year. Admission $4, ages 6-18 and students with ID $2; family rate $12. Phone (307) 742-4448.

UNIVERSITY OF WYOMING, 9 blks. n. at Ivinson and 9th sts., opened its doors in 1887. The 785-acre campus contains buildings of native sandstone. Cultural and fine arts programs and concerts are held year-round. The visitors center is at 1408 Ivinson St. Phone (307) 766-4075.

American Heritage Center, at 22nd St. and Willett Dr. in the Centennial Complex, has more than 7,000 historical manuscripts plus photographs, maps and art about Wyoming and Western American history. The center features changing displays from its collections including the art of Alfred Jacob Miller, Henry Farny and Frederic Remington. Mon.-Fri. 8-5, Sat. 11-5,

Sept.-May; Mon.-Fri. 7:30-4:30, Sat. 11-5, rest of year. Closed major holidays. Free. Phone (307) 766-2570.

Anthropology Museum, in the Anthropology (Old Law) Building at 14th and Ivinson sts., chronicles Wyoming's cultural history, Northwest Plains Indians and other North American Indians. Collections include archeological and ethnological materials. Mon.-Fri. 8-5, Sept.-May; Mon.-Fri. 7:30-4:30, rest of year. Closed holidays. Free. Phone (307) 766-5136.

Art Museum, at 22nd St. and Willett Dr. in the Centennial Complex, contains more than 7,000 sculptures, prints, paintings and artifacts from many cultures and periods. The permanent collection focuses on American art and art from other countries that has influenced American artists. Works by established artists as well as traveling exhibitions are displayed.

Tues.-Fri. 9:30-7, Sat. 10-5, Sun. noon-4:30, June-Aug.; Tues.-Sat. 10-5, Sun. 10-3, rest of year. Closed holidays. Free. Phone (307) 766-6622.

Geological Museum, in the e. wing of the S.H. Knight Building, interprets the physical and historical geology of Wyoming through displays of rocks, minerals and fossils. Of interest is a mounted skeleton of a brontosaurus, purported to be one of only five exhibited in the world. Other dinosaur displays include an allosaurus, tyrannosaurus and triceratops. Mon.-Fri. 8-5, Sat.-Sun. 10-3; closed holidays. Free. Phone (307) 766-4218.

VEDAUWOO, 17 mi. s.e. via I-80, is a recreation area that takes its name from the Arapaho Indian word meaning "earth born spirits." The picnic

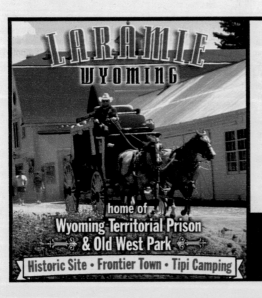

and camping areas are marked by rock formations developed during the ice age and rounded by weathering. Both expert and novice rock climbers practice their skills on the rocks. Daily 24 hours, May-Oct. (weather permitting). Free. Parking $3. Phone (307) 745-2300. *See the AAA Northwestern CampBook.*

★WYOMING TERRITORIAL PRISON AND OLD WEST PARK, 975 Snowy Range Rd. at jct. I-80, features a restored 19th-century prison, the National U.S. Marshals Museum, a re-created frontier town with living-history characters, special events and a dinner theater.

The Wyoming Territorial Prison, built in 1872, is believed to be the only prison where outlaw Butch Cassidy was incarcerated. Until 1903 it housed some of the most notorious criminals in the West. The history of the U.S. Marshals Service is chronicled through exhibits in the museum. A highlight is the collection of Western film clips that portrays Hollywood's view of gunfighters. The Horse Barn Dinner Theatre features live Western music and a dinner.

Sites at Frontier Town include a mercantile, saloon, livery stable, smithy, marshal's office and jail; activities include gunfights, stagecoach and train rides, a prison-break posse, puppet theater and ropemaking. A petting corral is featured. Throughout the park visitors will encounter Old-West characters like Calamity Jane, saloon hall girls and deputy U.S. marshals. Events are scheduled every weekend in the summer. Guided and self-guiding museum and prison tours are available. Food is available.

Allow 4 hours minimum. Daily 9-5, May-Sept. (Frontier Town open only Memorial Day-Labor Day). Theater performances Thurs.-Sat. at 6. Park admission $2. Museum/prison admission $5.50; ages 6-12, $3.25; family rate $18. Dinner theater $23.95; ages 3-12, $16.95. Reservations are required for the theater. DS, MC, VI. Phone (307) 745-6161 or (800) 845-2287. *See color ad p. 152.*

LINGLE (E-6) pop. 500, elev. 4,171'

WESTERN HISTORY CENTER, 1 mi. w. on US 26, has displays about archeological excavations and the physical evidence left behind by the area's earliest citizens. In addition to a working lab, visitors can see fossils, mammoth bones and arrowheads—items found in local digs that enable researchers to understand the lives of early residents of the Western plains. Allow 1 hour minimum. Mon.-Sat. 10-6, Sun. 1-6. Admission $1.50, under 12 free. Phone (307) 837-3052.

LOVELL (B-3) pop. 2,000, elev. 3,837'

Lovell, founded by Mormons in 1900, serves as an outfitting center at the southern entrance to Bighorn Canyon National Recreation Area *(see place listing p. 123).* A recreation area visitor center offering interpretive displays, movies and campfire programs is at the junction of US 310 and scenic US 14A.

Next to Bighorn Canyon is Pryor Mountain Wild Horse Range, a 32,000-acre area being developed as a refuge for wild horses, elk, bears and bighorn sheep.

Lovell Area Chamber of Commerce: 287 E. Main St., P.O. Box 295, Lovell, WY 82431; phone (307) 548-7552.

LUSK (D-6) pop. 1,500, elev. 5,014'

Named for an early settler, Lusk is a trading center for a ranching and dry-farming district that also is involved in some oil production. To the west are red-colored cliffs from which Indians obtained material for paint. Through this area ran the Cheyenne and Black Hills Stage Line, whose route is marked by two rows of white posts. Three miles east on US 20, a marker indicates the location of a segment of the Texas Trail. The trail was used to herd cattle from Texas to the open ranges of Wyoming, Montana and the Dakotas.

Niobrara Chamber of Commerce: 322 S. Main, P.O. Box 457, Lusk, WY 82225; phone (307) 334-2950 or (800) 223-5875. *See color ad.*

STAGECOACH MUSEUM, 322 S. Main St., displays many relics of pioneer and Indian days, including an original Concord stagecoach. The coach's Cheyenne-Deadwood running mate is in the Smithsonian Institution in Washington, D.C. Mon.-Fri. 10-4. Admission $2, under 12 free. Phone (307) 334-3444. *See color ad p. 153.*

MEDICINE BOW (E-5) pop. 400, elev. 6,564'

Faced with no available lodgings when he arrived in Medicine Bow in 1885, American author Owen Wister was forced to spend his first night at the counter of the town's general store. Had he visited 26 years later, he could have slept at the Virginian Hotel, named after his well-known novel "The Virginian." Published in 1902, Wister's book became the inspiration for two stage plays, two silent films, a "talking" film and a television series in the 1960s.

Although Wister first described the modest town of Medicine Bow as a "wretched husk of squalor," he later wrote: "I don't wonder a man never comes back [East] after he has once been here a few years." Medicine Bow's general store and still-operating Virginian Hotel now stand as town landmarks. A landmark of a different sort is the giant wind turbine 5 miles south of town.

MEDICINE BOW MUSEUM, on US 30 across from the Virginian Hotel, is housed in a 1913 railroad depot. Local and traveling historical exhibits depict the history of Medicine Bow and the West. Among the displays are such Western items as cowboys' chaps and branding irons. A picnic area, restored caboose and Owen Wister's cabin are on the grounds. Allow 30 minutes minimum. Mon.-Sat. 10-5, Sun. noon-5, Memorial Day-Labor Day. Donations. Phone (307) 379-2383.

MEDICINE BOW NATIONAL FOREST

Elevations in the forest range from 5,000 ft. north of the Laramie River to 12,013 ft. at Medicine Bow Peak. Refer to AAA maps for additional elevation information.

Medicine Bow-Routt National Forest consists of three separate districts that together cover 1,093,618 acres in southeastern Wyoming. Scenic SR 130 (closed in winter) crosses the Laramie and Brush Creek/Hayden districts, which extend northward from Colorado along the Snowy Range.

The Brush Creek/Hayden District spans the Continental Divide in the Sierra Madre Mountains west of Encampment. Douglas District, the northernmost section, is high in the rugged Laramie Mountains south of Douglas. Between Cheyenne and Laramie I-80 crosses the Pole Mountain Unit, noted for its unusual rock formations.

The Thunder Basin National Grassland *(see place listing p. 162)* lies in the energy-rich Powder River Basin north of Douglas. There also are four wilderness areas with 79,135 acres of forested land west of Laramie.

Opportunities for such winter sports as cross-country skiing and snowmobiling abound in the area; Snowy Range Ski Area west of Centennial provides downhill skiing. Camping, fishing, hiking and hunting also are available. For additional information contact the Forest Supervisor, 2468 Jackson St., Laramie, WY 82070. Phone (307) 745-2300. *See Recreation Chart and the AAA Northwestern CampBook.*

MEETEETSE (B-3) pop. 400, elev. 5,798'

Meeteetse lies along the scenic portion of SR 120, which runs 83 miles between Cody and Thermopolis.

MEETEETSE BANK ARCHIVES, 1033 Park Ave., occupies a former 1901 bank building. Artifacts and records document local and regional history. Tues.-Sat. 9-5. Donations. Phone (307) 868-2423. *See color ad p. 131.*

MEETEETSE HALL MUSEUM, 942 Mondell, displays local artifacts in an early 1900s Masonic hall. Mon.-Sat. 10-4, Sun. 1-4, Memorial Day-Sept. 30. Donations. Phone (307) 868-2423. *See color ad p. 131.*

NEWCASTLE (C-6) pop. 3,000, elev. 4,321'

Founded in 1889 when coal was discovered in the area, Newcastle was named after its sister community in England, Newcastle-Upon-Tyne. Mining is a continuing industry, along with ranching, lumbering and petroleum exploration. The yield of Newcastle's oil field is processed by its own refinery.

Newcastle Area Chamber of Commerce: 1334 Washington, P.O. Box 68, Newcastle, WY 82701; phone (307) 746-2739.

Self-guiding tours: Brochures about driving tours are available from the visitor center at the junction of US 85 and US 16.

ANNA MILLER MUSEUM, 1 mi. e. on US 16 at Delaware St. in East Newcastle, displays wildlife, antique firefighting apparatus, pioneer articles, fossils, minerals and Indian artifacts housed in a historic National Guard cavalry stable.

Also at the site is the Jenny Stockade, built in 1857 by the expedition sent into the Black Hills area by the U.S. government to investigate reports of gold. Though it served several functions

hroughout its career, the structure is best known
s a way station on the Cheyenne-Deadwood
tage line, which began in 1876 and operated for
bout 10 years. Mon.-Fri. 9-5 (also Sat. 9-noon,
une-Aug.); closed holidays. Free. Phone (307)
'46-4188.

PINE BLUFFS (F-6) pop. 1,100, elev. 5,047'

Pine Bluffs, named for the stunted pine trees
on the bluffs overlooking the area, was once an
mportant watering place along the Texas Cattle
Trail. In 1871 more than 600,000 head of cattle
vere herded through the Pine Bluffs Crossroads,
naking it the largest cattle-shipping point in the
vorld.

Texas Trail Museum preserves historic trea-
ures of the area; phone (307) 245-3713. The
Jniversity of Wyoming Archaeological Dig pre-
ents a look into civilization 10,000 years ago
hrough extracted nomadic Indian artifacts dis-
olayed at the University of Wyoming Archaeo-
ogical Educational Center, Second and Elm
treets.

Pine Bluffs Area Chamber of Commerce: P.O.
Box 486, Pine Bluffs, WY 82082; phone (307)
245-3695. An information center is at the I-80
est area.

PINEDALE (D-2) pop. 1,200, elev. 7,176'

Pinedale serves as an outfitting point for recreation in the Bridger-Teton National Forest (see
place listing p. 125). Outdoor activities in the
area include trout fishing and various water
sports on nearby Fremont Lake, the second largest natural lake in Wyoming. Fishing float trips
originate on the Green River, while camping,
climbing, backpacking and cross-country skiing
also are available.

Ten miles west of town, Father DeSmet
Monument designates the site where the first
Catholic Mass in Wyoming was held in 1840.

Upper Green River Rendezvous National His-
oric Landmark is 6 miles west of Pinedale on
JS 191. Indians from throughout the West and
uch legendary mountain men as Jim Bridger and
William Sublette gathered each year throughout
he 1830s to meet the supply caravans from St.
Louis and barter, trade for furs and cavort.

Pinedale Area Chamber of Commerce: 32 E.
Pine, P.O. Box 176, Pinedale, WY 82941; phone
307) 367-2242.

Self-guiding tours: Brochures detailing a tour of
he historic district as well as day trips in the
area are available at the chamber of commerce.

MUSEUM OF THE MOUNTAIN MAN, Fremont
Lake Rd., contains exhibits relating to these rug-
ged individuals who opened the West to settlers.
Displays focus on the fur trade, exploration,

Plains Indians and early settlement. Allow 30
minutes minimum. Daily 10-6, May 1-Oct. 1; by
appointment rest of year. Admission $4; over 54,
$3; ages 6-11, $2. Phone (307) 367-4101.

POWDER RIVER (D-4) elev. 5,694'

HELL'S HALF ACRE, 5 mi. w. on US 20/26, is
an outstanding example of nature at its most
freakish. This 320-acre curiosity, sometimes
called the "Baby Grand Canyon," is a depres-
sion with brightly colored and grotesque rock
figures. The canyon is filled with the fantastic
shapes of great towers and spires caused by ero-
sion. Delicate pastel coloring augments the eerie
effects of the formations. Many fossils and Indian artifacts have been found in the region.
Sheepherders Fair is held in mid-July. An observation point is open May-Nov. Free.

POWELL (B-3) pop. 5,300, elev. 4,365'

American Indians from the Crow, Blackfoot
and Shoshone tribes inhabited the area exclusively until explorer John Colter arrived in 1807.
Following his arrival came a stream of explorers,
trappers and miners. Powell was named after
Mayor John Wesley Powell, an early-day
explorer.

A memorial and honor-roll marker are at the
site 10 miles west on US 14A where people of
Japanese descent were imprisoned during World
War II.

A variety of wildlife inhabits the area, and recreational activities are readily available. Historic
walking tours of the city are available.

Powell Valley Chamber of Commerce: 111 S.
Day, P.O. Box 814, Powell, WY 82435; phone
(307) 754-3494 or (800) 325-4278.

HOMESTEADERS MUSEUM, 133 S. Clark St.,
features exhibits about Powell's early settlers as
well as displays of old farm machinery and
implements. Tues.-Fri. 1-5, May-Sept.; Fri.-Sat.
10-noon and 1-5, rest of year. Free. Phone (307)
754-9481.

RAWLINS (E-4) pop. 9,400, elev. 6,758'

In traditionally wool- and hay-producing Carbon County, Rawlins was a departure point for
the Union Pacific Railroad and for miners bound
for the gold-rich Black Hills. Nearby mines produced the "Rawlins Red" pigment that was used
on the Brooklyn Bridge in 1874. The ruins of
Fort Fred Steele, built in 1868 to protect early
railroads and settlers, are 15 miles east of town
off I-80.

Throughout the 1870s Rawlins was a wild
town with more than its share of outlaw activity.
However, it came to an abrupt halt by the end of
the decade when exasperated citizens employed
vigilante tactics against one of the region's most

notorious outlaws. After the lynching of "Big Nose" George Parrot, warnings were sent out to 24 other known outlaws, who left town the next morning.

On the southern edge of the Sweetwater jade fields and the eastern edge of the gem-riddled Red Desert, Rawlins is noteworthy for its geological features.

Rawlins-Carbon County Chamber of Commerce: 519 W. Cedar, P.O. Box 1331, Rawlins, WY 82301; phone (307) 324-4111 or (800) 228-3547. *See color ad.*

CARBON COUNTY MUSEUM, 9th and Walnut, has displays of Western artifacts, including a sheep wagon, large stained-glass windows and a 1919 hook-and-ladder firetruck. Mon.-Fri. 10-noon and 1-5, May-Sept.; Mon., Wed. and Sat. 1-5, rest of year. Donations. Phone (307) 328-2740.

WYOMING FRONTIER PRISON, 5th and Walnut, replaced the territorial prison in Laramie in 1901 and operated until 1981. A 1-hour guided tour includes the cell blocks, infirmary, visiting rooms and death house. The reception area contains a museum with photographs and prison artifacts. Tours daily 8:30-5:30 (also Fri.-Sat. at 9:30 p.m. by appointment), May-Sept.; by appointment rest of year. Admission $4.25; over 55 and ages 6-12, $3.75; family rate $15. Night tours $5. Phone (307) 324-4422.

RIVERTON (D-3) pop. 9,200, elev. 4,956'

Once part of Wind River Indian Reservation (*see Lander p. 151*), the lower Wind River Basin now supports 130,000 acres of farmland surrounding Riverton. Castle Gardens, a state historical monument 40 miles east, is a formation knobs, pinnacles and spires rising abruptly 10 100 feet above the prairie. Petroglyphs depictin warriors, hunters and animals decorate the so sandstone formations.

Riverton Area Chamber of Commerce: Fir and Main, Depot Bldg., Riverton, WY 8250 phone (307) 856-4801.

RIVERTON MUSEUM, 700 E. Park Ave., inte prets the story of 20th-century homesteaders wh brought the town to life in 1906. Displays in clude fixtures and merchandise from an earl 20th-century general store, drugstore, schoo beauty salon, dentist's office, church and post o fice. An outdoor display features early 20th century farm machinery. Northern Arapaho an Shoshone Indian artifacts also are exhibited. A low 1 hour, 30 minutes minimum. Tues.-Sa 10-4; closed holidays. Free. Phone (307 856-2665.

ROCK SPRINGS (E-2) pop. 19,100, elev. 6,261'

Rock Springs began in 1862 as a way statio along the Overland Stage route. The Union Pa cific also chose this route because of the area' rich coal deposits that fueled the railroad's loc motives. Mining and refining are still major in dustries, with resources expanding to includ trona and natural gas. Some of the world's larg est deposits of trona, used in the manufacture c glass, phosphates, silicates and soaps, lie 3 miles west of the city.

To the north and stretching more than 10 miles between the town of Eden and the Semi noe Mountains is the Red Desert, an area c moving sand dunes second in size only to th

ahara Desert. Of archeological and geological
nterest, the Sands, as the region is known, has
roduced evidence of human habitation as far
ack as 5000 B.C.

Petroglyphs and pictographs adorn the walls of
ock outcrops in Cedar, Pine and Killpecker can-
ons and White Mountain. Visitors also can see
vidence of prehistoric Wyoming at Western
Vyoming Community College, which maintains
collection of fossils.

Boars Tusk, a volcanic monolith, rises 400 feet
bove Killpecker Valley at the edge of the Sands.
he rock tower, 28 miles north of Rock Springs,
s visible from US 191.

The Red Desert is home to one of the nation's
argest herds of wild horses. To control the size
f the herds, the Bureau of Land Management
BLM) conducts roundups several months of the
ear. Mustangs captured by the BLM are kept at
ock Springs' Wild Horse Holding Facility,
vhich conducts an Adopt-a-Horse program;
hone (307) 382-5350. The BLM roundups do
ot allow spectators, who might disrupt the deli-
ate operation.

ock Springs Chamber of Commerce: 1897
)ewar Dr., P.O. Box 398, Rock Springs, WY
2902; phone (307) 362-3771 or (800) 463-8637.

elf-guiding tours: A self-guiding walking tour
f downtown Rock Springs covers sites related
) the community's coal mining history. Bro-
hures are available at the chamber of commerce.

OMMUNITY FINE ARTS CENTER, 400 C St.,
ontains a collection of more than 450 works by
Vyoming and other Western artists as well as na-
ionally and internationally known artists such as
Iorman Rockwell, Grandma Moses and Loren
IcGiver. Mon.-Sat. 10-noon and 1-5 (also Mon.
nd Wed.-Thurs. 6-9 p.m.). Free. Phone (307)
62-6212.

OCK SPRINGS HISTORIC MUSEUM is at 201
St. This museum depicts local coal mining his-
ory and the diverse nationalities that settled
ock Springs. The building, constructed in 1894
nd restored in 1992, is a fine example of
omanesque-style architecture. Tues.-Fri. 11-5,
at. noon-4, Memorial Day-Labor Day; Wed.-
at. noon-5, rest of year. Allow 1 hour minimum.
ree. Phone (307) 362-3138.

**VESTERN WYOMING COMMUNITY COLLEGE
ATURAL HISTORY MUSEUM** exit 103 off I-80,
hen 1 mi. s. to 2500 College Dr., contains life-
ize replicas of dinosaurs, prehistoric fossil
pecimens and artifacts gathered from various
ormations around southwestern Wyoming. Ex-
ibits, which are scattered throughout the student
enter, include reproductions of cave art from the
Jpper Paleolithic era and a nine-ton replica of an
:aster Island statue. Maps are available at the
ntrance. Allow 30 minutes minimum. Daily 9-9.
ree. Phone (307) 382-1666 or 382-1600.

SARATOGA (E-4) pop. 2,000, elev. 6,791'

Saratoga, named for Saratoga Springs, N.Y., is
a supply center and access point for recreation
on the North Platte River and in Medicine Bow
National Forest *(see place listing p. 154).* The 64
miles of the North Platte River between the
Colorado border and Saratoga are a nationally
designated blue-ribbon trout fishery and include
a stretch of white water rated as high as 10 on
the U.S. Forest Service scale.

Saratoga Hot Springs offers a natural hot
springs pool open free to the public. Fishing areas are available on the Platte and golf facilities
are nearby.

**Saratoga-Platte Valley Chamber of Com-
merce:** 115 W. Bridge, P.O. Box 1095, Saratoga,
WY 82331; phone (307) 326-8855.

SARATOGA MUSEUM, 104 Constitution, in the
1917 Union Pacific Railroad depot on SR 130,
contains historical and archeological artifacts depicting the settlement and growth of the Platte
Valley. Geological displays and a sheep wagon
also are included. Allow 1 hour minimum. Daily
1-5, Memorial Day weekend-Labor Day; by appointment rest of year. Admission $2; ages 6-17,
$1; over 70 free; family rate $5; free to all Mon.
Phone (307) 326-5511.

SARATOGA NATIONAL FISH HATCHERY is 2.5
mi. n. on SR 130, then 1.5 mi. e. on a dirt road,
following signs. Constructed in 1915, the hatchery produces lake and brown trout eggs for ex-
port. Allow 1 hour minimum. Daily 8-4. Free.
Phone (307) 326-5662.

  RECREATIONAL ACTIVITIES

Fishing

- **Great Rocky Mountain Outfitters Inc.,** 216
  E. Walnut St., Box 1636, Saratoga, WY 82331.
  Daily 7-7, May-Oct.; Mon.-Sat. 9-5, rest of
  year. Phone (307) 326-8750.

SHERIDAN (B-4)pop. 13,900, elev. 3,724'

Sheridan is located half-way between the
Black Hills and Yellowstone National Park. Access through the Bighorn Mountains via US 14
(Bighorn Scenic Byway) or US 14A (Medicine
Wheel Passage)1280 offers spectacular sightseeing opportunities. The majestic Bighorn Mountains rise to the west, rolling plains slope to the
east, and Sheridan lies in the valley of the Little
and Big Goose.

Sheridan is rich in Western history. In 1866
the area was part of unreserved Indian territory
that was home for the Sioux, Cheyenne and
Arapaho. Indian chiefs such as Dull Knife, Red
Cloud and Crazy Horse fought battles to keep
the white man from their precious hunting
grounds.

The Bozeman Trail, a shortcut scouted by John Bozeman through eastern Wyoming, cut across Indian hunting grounds to the rich gold fields of Montana. The trail, which ran south of Sheridan along part of what is now US 87, was the scene of so many battles that it became known as the Bloody Bozeman. The U.S. Cavalry forbade trains of fewer than 100 wagons to take this trail.

The discovery of gold in the Black Hills brought a new influx of fortune seekers and further confrontations, culminating in the Battle of Little Big Horn just north of Sheridan in southern Montana (see Little Bighorn Battlefield National Monument in Mont. p. 101).

Many battle sites are in the area, including those of the Wagon Box Fight and the Fetterman Massacre, near Fort Phil Kearny (see attraction listing p. 160); Dull Knife Battle, south of town; the Sawyer Fight, 20 miles north near Dayton; Rosebud Battle, north in Montana; and the Conner Battlefield in Ranchester, 15 miles north of Sheridan.

After the wars ended, Sheridan was incorporated and built up by the profitable businesses of cattle ranching, farming and coal mining. For today's outdoor enthusiast, recreational activities are nearly unlimited in the nearby Bighorn National Forest and include wildlife viewing, hiking, fishing, hunting, snowmobiling and cross-country and downhill skiing (see place listing 123.).

City of Sheridan Convention & Visitors B reau: P.O. Box 7155, Sheridan, WY 828(phone (307) 672-2485 or (800) 453-3650. S color ad.

Self-guiding tours: A walking tour of the cit historic Main Street District covers many ori nal buildings from the late 1800s and ea 1990s. A map is available from the conventi and visitors bureau.

★BRADFORD BRINTON MEMORIAL—H TORIC RANCH AND WESTERN ART COLLE TION is reached from the s. by the Meade Cre exit off I-90, then US 87N to SR 335; from n. by I-90 exit 25, then US 87S to Big Hc turnoff. The facility re-creates the atmosphere Western ranch life. A large collection of Weste art includes paintings, sculpture and etchings Edward Borein, Frank Tenney Johnson, Frede Remington and Charles M. Russell.

Extensive collections of equipment, Plains I dian crafts, rare books and documents, and ite pertaining to the history of the ranch are d played in a reception gallery, the 20-room m house and other buildings.

Allow 1 hour minimum. Daily 9:30-5, m May through Labor Day. Donations. Phone (3C 672-3173.

FETTERMAN MONUMENT stands 20 mi. s. on
US 87. On this site in 1866 Col. William J. Fetterman disobeyed orders to stay off the Bozeman
Trail and took to the trail with only 81 men under his command. Crazy Horse and 2,000 warriors ambushed and killed the entire force. The
site is near Fort Phil Kearny.

FORT PHIL KEARNY STATE HISTORIC SITE—
ee Story p. 160.

HISTORIC SHERIDAN INN, Fifth and Broadway
ts., opened June 22, 1893. The inn was the first
building in town to have electricity, steam heat, a
telephone and running water. Exhibits highlight
the history of the inn and Sheridan. Noted guests
include "Calamity Jane" Canary, "Buffalo Bill"
Cody, Ernest Hemingway, Presidents Herbert
Hoover, Theodore Roosevelt and William Taft,
and Will Rogers. Food is available.

Allow 1 hour minimum. Mon.-Sat. 9-5, Memorial Day-Labor Day; otherwise varies. Closed
Jan. 1 and Dec. 25. Guided tour $3; over 55 and
ages 12-18, $2; family rate $10. Self-guiding
tour $1. MC, VI. Phone (307) 674-5440 to verify
schedule.

TRAIL END STATE HISTORIC SITE, 400 Claren-
don Ave., is the former home of Sen. John B.
Kendrick, the "Cowboy Senator." Set on 3.5
acres, the fully furnished Flemish-style mansion
has elaborate woodwork, stained-glass windows,
chandeliers and hand-painted walls and ceilings.
Guided tours are available by appointment. Allow 1 hour minimum. Daily 9-6, June-Aug.; 1-4,
Apr.-May and Sept. 1-Dec. 14. Donations. Phone
307) 674-4589.

WYO THEATER, 42 N. Main St., is an art deco
structure built in 1923 and renovated in 1989. It
is said to be the oldest operating vaudeville theater in the state. Musical entertainment, ballets
and stage presentations are featured year-round.
Admission varies depending on event. Phone
307) 672-9084.

SHOSHONE NATIONAL FOREST

Elevations in the forest range
from 4,600 ft. at Clarks Fork
Canyon to 13,804 ft. at Gannett
Peak. Refer to AAA maps for
additional elevation information.

Established by presidential proclamation in
1891 as the nation's first forest reserve, the Shoshone National Forest occupies nearly 2.5 million acres in northwestern Wyoming. Its

HIGH-ALTITUDE HEALTH

Temples throbbing, gasping for breath and nauseated, you barely notice the sparkling snow, the scudding clouds or the spectacular view below.

You might be suffering from Acute Mountain Sickness (AMS). Usually striking at around 8,000 feet (2,500 meters) in altitude, AMS is your body's way of coping with the reduced oxygen and low humidity of high altitudes. Among the symptoms are headaches, shortness of breath, loss of appetite, insomnia and lethargy. Some people complain of temporary weight gain or swelling in the face, hands and feet.

If your AMS is severe, you should stop ascending; you will recover in a few days. On the other hand, a quick descent will end the suffering immediately.

You can reduce the impact of high altitude by being in top condition. If you smoke or suffer from heart or lung ailments, consult your physician. Alcohol and certain drugs will intensify AMS symptoms.

A gradual ascent with a couple days of acclimatization is the best bet if you have time. On the way up, eat light, nutritious meals and drink water copiously. A spicy, high-carbohydrate diet may mitigate the effects of low oxygen and encourage you to drink more. But beware of those crystal-clear mountain streams where parasites might lurk. Boil such water at least 10 minutes.

Other high-altitude health problems include sunburn and hypothermia. Dress in layers to protect yourself from the intense sun and wide fluctuations in temperature.

Finally, after you unwind in the sauna or whirlpool bath at your lodgings, remember to stand up carefully, for the heat will relax your blood vessels and lower your blood pressure.

boundaries extend south from Montana and include parts of the Beartooth, Absaroka and Wind River mountains. The forest includes the state's highest mountain, Gannett Peak.

Forest watersheds and glacial runoff feed several rivers of the Missouri River Basin and serve as a major water source for many communities and ranches within or near the forest.

Scenic drives include Buffalo Bill Cody Scenic Byway (US 14/16/20) through the North Fork of the Shoshone River canyon en route to the east entrance of Yellowstone National Park *(see place listing p. 163)*; the Wyoming Centennial Scenic Byway over Togwotee Pass on US 287/26 between Dubois and Moran Junction; the Beartooth Highway Scenic Byway (US 212) over the Beartooth Plateau; and the Chief Joseph Scenic Highway (SR 296) from its junction with SR 120 to the junction of US 212. SRs 296, 291 and 131 also travel past spectacular mountain scenery.

Back-country hiking, trail riding, fishing and primitive camping are available in the Fitzpatrick Wilderness Area, which has two of Wyoming's highest peaks and some of the nation's largest glaciers; the Washakie Wilderness Area, remarkable for its abundance of petrified wood; the Popo Agie Wilderness Area, dotted by more than 200 lakes; the Absaroka-Beartooth Wilderness Area, containing many lakes and granite peaks; and the North Absaroka Wilderness Area, scored by steep canyons. Skiing also is available.

Information and maps can be obtained by writing the Forest Supervisor, 808 Meadow Ln., Cody, WY 82414-4516. Phone (307) 527-6241. *See Recreation Chart and the AAA Northwestern CampBook.*

SOUTH PASS CITY (D-3) elev. 7,805'

When early travelers traversed South Pass, the gradual incline often left them unaware that they were crossing the Continental Divide. From 1840 to 1860 an estimated 300,000 settlers traveled through the gap.

Gold was discovered at a site about 12 miles north of the pass in 1842, but takings were not impressive at first. In 1867 the Carissa, a hardrock lode, was found and a boom began. By 1871 South Pass City boasted 2,000 inhabitants and was the seat of Carter County, which encompassed a third of Wyoming.

William H. Bright, a South Pass City saloon keeper and Wyoming senator, introduced a bill granting women the right to vote, hold office and own property. With passage in 1869, Wyoming women became the first in the nation to participate in government and Wyoming became nicknamed the "Equality State." One town citizen was Esther Hobart Morris, who in 1870 became the city's justice of the peace, the first woman in the country to hold any political office.

Despite its successes, South Pass City was n∈ to escape the usual fate of boom towns: By 187 the city was nearly deserted. The death of th mines did not, however, mean the end of Sou Pass City. In the 1950s a new boom came—on that involved not gold but iron ore. While th iron mines are now closed, the gold mines per odically operate, helping the town's econom Tourism also has enabled the town to capitali on its rambunctious past.

SOUTH PASS CITY STATE HISTORIC SITE e∖ compasses the entire town; turn off SR 28 Milepost 43 and follow signs. This ghostly r∈ minder of South Pass City's mining era is bein restored. Twenty-five log, frame and stone stru∈ tures remain on 39 acres of land, includin Carissa Saloon, South Pass Hotel, a jail, liver stable and butcher shop. A visitor center contair interpretive displays and a movie describing th town's past. Living-history programs also are o fered. The site has a historic nature trail and pi∈ nic facilities.

Allow 2 hours minimum. Buildings open dai 9-6, May 15-Sept. 30. Admission $1, under 1 free. Phone (307) 332-3684 or 777-7695.

TRAILS WEST, departing from 5 mi. s. at 23 Three Forks Atlantic City Rd., offers covere wagon excursions and overnight trail rides. Th 3-day trip departs Tues. at noon and return Thurs. at noon, July-Aug. Sat. night trail ride depart Sat. at noon and return Sun. at noon, July Aug. Three-day trip $400; ages 6-12, $300; ur der 6, $75. Trail rides $125. Reservations a∖ required. Phone (307) 332-7801, or (80C 327-4052 out of Wyo.

STORY (B-4)

Story took its name from Charles P. Story, a early mayor of nearby Sheridan who was relate to Nelson Story, one of the first to drive Texa cattle over the Bozeman Trail into Montana i 1866. His northbound trip was the only signif cant use of the trail. Because the costs of mair taining the forts along the trail were immense i terms of both money and lives lost, the U.S. go ernment eventually abandoned them and close the Bozeman Trail.

Nestled at the base of the Big Horn Mountair in thick stands of Ponderosa pine and aspen Story offers abundant recreational activitie Camping, hiking, fishing, hunting and horsebac riding are readily available.

FORT PHIL KEARNY STATE HISTORIC SITI reached by following signs from I-90 exit 44W preserves the remains of Fort Phil Kearny. Of th three forts built along the Bozeman Trail, Fo Phil Kearny suffered the worst. A visitor cente houses displays and photographs. A self-guidin tour is available. Markers identify the sites of th Fetterman interpretive trail and Wagon Bo fights.

Allow 2 hours minimum. Visitor center open daily 8-6, May 15-Sept. 30; Wed.-Sun. noon-4, Apr. 1-May 14 and Oct.-Nov. Admission $1, under 18 free. Phone (307) 684-7629 or 777-7014.

THE STORY FISH HATCHERY, 2 mi. w. to end of SR 194, was built 1907-08 and is the oldest operating fish hatchery in the state. The hatchery raises lake, rainbow and splake trout. Besides incubating and hatching fish eggs, the hatchery serves as a holding facility for fish and eggs destined for other stations throughout Wyoming. It includes an indoor hatchery and outdoor raceways and ponds. Daily 8-5. Free. Phone (307) 883-2234.

SUNDANCE (B-6) pop. 1,100, elev. 4,750'

Sundance lies at the foot of Sundance Mountain, so named because the Sioux Indians held their councils and religious ceremonies at a place called Wi Wacippi Paha, or Temple of the Sioux. It is believed that Harry Longabaugh, better known as "The Sundance Kid," assumed his nickname in Sundance during his 18-month sentence in the Crook County jail for horse stealing.

Sundance is a convenient departure point for trips to nearby Devils Tower National Monument (see place listing p. 134) and Black Hills National Forest (see place listing p. 124). An 82-mile circle tour via US 14, SRs 24 and 111 and I-90 rings a portion of the national forest and offers opportunities to see the volcanic core of Devils Tower as well as pronghorns, wild turkeys and white-tailed deer.

Sundance Area Chamber of Commerce: P.O. Box 1004, Sundance, WY 82729; phone (307) 283-1000.

CROOK COUNTY MUSEUM AND ART GALLERY, on the lower level of the courthouse at 309 Cleveland St., contains more than 20,000 items from the Old West, including a re-creation of the original county courtroom. Photographs and legal papers of the Sundance Kid, who was incarcerated in the county jail for 18 months, also are on display. Works by local artists are exhibited. Mon.-Fri. 8-8, June-Aug.; 8-5, rest of year. Free. Phone (307) 283-3666.

TARGHEE NATIONAL FOREST—
see place listing in Idaho p. 62.

TEN SLEEP (C-4) pop. 300, elev. 4,513'

Because Indians who traversed the Big Horn Basin of Wyoming reckoned time and distance in "sleeps," this midway point became known as Ten Sleep.

Range wars between cattle and sheep ranchers—quite common in the West during the 1890s and early 1900s—reached a climax with the Ten Sleep-Spring Creek Raid in 1909. This attack on the camp of an ex-cattleman who had brought a large herd of sheep into Big Horn Basin resulted in an investigation that eventually led to the peaceful arbitration of disputes.

Nearby Ten Sleep Canyon, on the western side of the Big Horn Mountains, is an outstanding feature of Bighorn National Forest (see place listing p. 124). Near the mouth of the canyon are a trout hatchery and a fish-rearing station; visitors are welcome at both stations. A scenic section of US 16 runs between Ten Sleep and Buffalo (see place listing p. 133).

THERMOPOLIS (C-3) pop. 3,200, elev. 4,326'

A treaty between the Shoshone and Arapaho nations and the United States specified that the waters of the hot mineral springs at Thermopolis would be available to everyone free of charge. The agreement continues to be honored at Hot Springs State Park. Petroglyphs, 21 miles north of Thermopolis on SR 120, are etched on a south-facing cliff at Legend Rock State Petroglyph Site.

Thermopolis is a favorite destination for hunters in search of pronghorns, game birds, elk and deer. South of Thermopolis on US 20 is Boysen Reservoir, with developed recreational facilities at Boysen State Park (see Recreation Chart).

Thermopolis provides access to two scenic highways—US 20 along Wind River Canyon and SR 120 traveling north to Cody.

Thermopolis-Hot Springs Chamber of Commerce: 700 Broadway, P.O. Box 768, Thermopolis, WY 82443; phone (307) 864-3192 or (800) 786-6772. See color ad p. 132.

HOT SPRINGS HISTORICAL MUSEUM, 700 Broadway, is a two-story museum containing period rooms, a cherrywood bar said to be visited by the Hole in the Wall gang, American Indian artifacts, a restored country school, wildlife and mining exhibits, arts and crafts, and geological, agricultural and oil industry displays. Mon.-Sat. 8-5; closed major holidays. Admission $2; over 55, $1.50; ages 10-17, $1; family rate $5. Phone (307) 864-5183.

HOT SPRINGS STATE PARK, n.e. edge of town on US 20 and SR 789, contains mineral baths, pools, hot mineral springs, terraces and hot waterfalls, and is home to the state's bison herd. Of particular interest is Bighorn Hot Spring, which releases 2.8 million gallons daily and is one of the largest hot mineral springs in the world. Black Sulphur Springs, White Sulphur Springs and Ponce de Leon Springs are other springs within the park. Daily 6 a.m.-10 p.m. Free. Phone (307) 864-2176. See Recreation Chart.

WIND RIVER CANYON, 5 mi. s. via US 20, is a channel carved more than 2,000 feet deep by the rushing waters of the Wind River. US 20 was blasted from the rock and tunneled through solid granite in three places. Remarkable rock formations highlight the canyon walls, which are identified in terms of geological era and formation by strategically placed highway signs. One of the canyon's most prominent landmarks is Chimney Rock, about 10 miles south of Thermopolis. At the south end of the canyon is Boysen Dam.

WIND RIVER CANYON WHITEWATER, 210 US 20S, Suite 5, operates scenic float trips as well as white-water, dinner and fishing trips. Daily 8-5, Memorial Day-Labor Day. Scenic trip fare $25. Under 6 are not permitted (age may vary depending on river conditions). Reservations and deposit are required for overnight, dinner or fishing trips. DS, MC, VI. Phone (307) 864-9343 in season or (307) 486-2253 rest of year. *See color ad p. 132.*

THE WYOMING DINOSAUR CENTER is at 110 Carter Ranch Rd. on the e. side of town (follow the green dinosaur footprints on the street from the stoplight). The center houses a recent extensive find of well-preserved dinosaur remains from the nearby Morrison Formation. Visitors may tour the preparation lab, where bones are recovered and prepared, and the paleontological site to see discoveries being made.

Daily 8-8, May-Sept.; 10-5, rest of year. Museum admission $6; over 60, veterans, students with ID and ages 5-18, $3.50. Dig site admission $10; over 60, veterans, students with ID and ages 5-18, $7. Combination museum and dig site admission $12; over 60, veterans, students with ID and ages 5-18, $8. Full-day dig $100; family rate $250. MC, VI. Phone (307) 864-2997. *See color ad p. 132.*

THUNDER BASIN NATIONAL GRASSLAND

Covering 1,800,339 acres in Campbell, Converse, Crook, Niobrara and Weston counties, Thunder Basin National Grassland was once a dust bowl. Settlers from the East, familiar only with the homesteading methods for a humid climate, met with disaster when they tried to establish farms in Wyoming's semiarid plains. Poor soil and recurrent droughts foiled attempts to cultivate the land, which soon deteriorated into dust bowls.

The grassland serves as an example of the regenerative use of land deemed unsuitable for cultivation. Sheep and cattle graze on the grassland's vast acreage, which also supports one of the world's largest herds of pronghorns. The Bozeman and Texas trails traverse a portion of the grassland.

Use Your Safety Belts!

The grassland lies within the Powder Ri[ver] Basin and contains a wealth of natural resourc[es] for energy development, including oil, gas a[nd] coal. The Black Thunder Mine, 9 miles from [SR] 59 on east SR 450, is one of the largest c[oal] mines in the country. It operates on the grassla[nd] under a special state permit with forest servi[ce] consent and produces more than 30 million to[ns] of coal per year. For further information pho[ne] (307) 939-1300.

TORRINGTON (D-6) pop. 5,700, elev. 4,098′

Traversed by the Oregon, Mormon and Ca[li-]fornia trails, the Overland Stage, Pony Expre[ss] and overland telegraph lines, Torrington serv[ed] as a Western gateway for pioneers. Named af[ter] settler William Curtis' hometown in Connectic[ut,] Torrington is primarily a livestock exchange ce[n-]ter, with cattle raising and agriculture its m[ain] economic contributors.

Goshen County Chamber of Commerce: 3[50] W. 21st Ave., Torrington, WY 82240; pho[ne] (307) 532-3879.

HOMESTEADERS MUSEUM is s. on US 85 [at] 495 Main. The museum is in the former Uni[ted] Pacific depot and contains artifacts that dep[ict] the homestead period, which occurred from [the] 1880s to 1929. Mon.-Sat. 10-4, Sun. 1-4, Mem[o-]rial Day-Fri. before Labor Day weekend; Mo[n.-] Fri. 10-4, rest of year. Free. Phone (30[7] 532-5612.

WAPITI (B-2) pop. 100, elev. 5,641′

The Wapiti Valley was popularized by Willia[m] F. "Buffalo Bill" Cody. He brought guests to [the] area to enjoy the beauty of the valley and Y[el-]lowstone National Park. Wapiti Valley provides [a] scenic byway into or out of Yellowstone Natio[nal] Park *(see place listing p. 163)*. Among wildli[fe] inhabiting the valley are elk, deer, buffalo[,] moose, bighorn sheep, bears, coyotes, bald a[nd] golden eagles, and even mountain lions.

Characterized by historic resorts, the vall[ey] also offers abundant recreational activities, i[n-]cluding hiking, horseback riding, fishing, win[d] surfing, snowmobiling and skiing.

Wapiti Valley Association: P.O. Box 21-AA[,] Wapiti, WY 82450; phone (307) 587-9595. S[ee] *color ad p. 164.*

WHEATLAND (E-6) pop. 3,300, elev. 4,738′

Attracted by the cheap land and irrigation w[a-]ter that were made available by the Carey Act [in] 1894, settlers streamed into Platte County a[nd] transformed its dry landscape into producti[ve] farmland, dotted with such aptly named towns [as] Wheatland.

Wheat continues to be the region's princip[al] crop, sustained in part by the Wheatland Irriga[-]tion Project, one of the largest privately own[ed] terprises of its type in the country. Wheatland so is the home of a white marble quarrying usiness and Laramie River Power Station, hich supplies electric power to Wyoming and k neighboring states.

Recreational opportunities include camping nd winter sports in nearby Medicine Bow National Forest *(see place listing p. 154)*. Grayrocks eservoir, 16 miles northeast, is stocked with ame fish and offers boating.

latte County Chamber of Commerce: 65 16th t., P.O. Box 427, Wheatland, WY 82201; phone 07) 322-2322.

ARAMIE PEAK MUSEUM, 2 mi. n. on 16th St. om exit 78 off I-25, displays items relating to e early settlers of Platte County, the Oregon rail and the cattle baron era. Some artifacts date om the late 1800s. Allow 30 minutes minimum. ues. and Thurs.-Fri. 1-8, June-Aug.; Tues.-Sat. -5, last 2 weeks in May and first 2 weeks in ept.; by appointment rest of year. Closed holiays. Free. Phone (307) 322-2052.

WORLAND (C-3) pop. 5,700, elev. 4,061'

Worland is in a rich farming and stock-feeding rea in the center of Wyoming's Big Horn Basin. ugar beets, beans, malt barley and hay are harested on irrigated lands; local industries prouce aluminum cans, soft drinks, beet sugar and at litter.

On the grounds of the county courthouse is a 50-year-old Douglas fir that has been carved to a monument honoring American Indians, art of sculptor Peter Toth's "Trail of the Whisering Giants." Among the city's nine parks is ioneer Square, which has statues honoring the rea's early settlers. A nearby drinking fountain ffers artesian mineral water from the Big Horn Iountains.

Washakie County Museum and Cultural Center exhibits mammoth bones and archeological nds discovered in Big Horn Basin.

The Big Horn Mountains are popular with ampers, hikers, hunters, skiers and snowmobilrs. Passing through the city is Big Horn River, ffering abundant fishing opportunities.

Vestiges of a far earlier time are the Gooseerry Formations and Painted Desert west on SR 31. In this area of dramatically eroded formaons were found the remains of eohippus (dawn orse), the earliest known equine. Wild horses till can be viewed north of town.

Vorland Area Chamber of Commerce: 120 N. 0th St., Worland, WY 82401; phone (307) 47-3226.

★ YELLOWSTONE NATIONAL PARK (B-2)

See map page 165.

Elevations in the park range from 5,314 ft. at the northern entrance in Gardiner, Mont., to 11,358 ft. at Eagle Peak in the southeastern side of the park. Refer to AAA maps for additional elevation information.

Yellowstone National Park was established in 1872 as the world's first national park. The park, named from the Minnetaree Indian phrase *mi tsi a-da-zi* (Yellow Rock River), is accessible by several scenic approaches to its five entrances: Gardiner, Mont. (north); West Yellowstone, Mont. (west); Jackson, via Grand Teton National Park (about 60 miles south); Cody (about 53 miles east); and Cooke City, Mont. (northeast).

The approach to Cooke City from Red Lodge, Mont., via the Beartooth Scenic Highway (US 212), negotiates Beartooth Pass at an elevation of almost 11,000 feet. From Cody the approach to Sylvan Pass follows US 14/16/20 through the carved red walls of Wapiti Valley.

The road between Canyon and Tower-Roosevelt is particularly scenic. This drive runs along Mount Washburn and passes Tower Fall, where the spectacles of the gorge, the falls on Tower Creek and the palisades of rock high above the Yellowstone River have few equals.

Although most of the park's 3,472 square miles lie in northwestern Wyoming, they also extend into Montana and Idaho. The central portion of the park is essentially a broad, elevated volcanic plateau that lies between 6,500 and 8,500 feet above sea level. On the south, east, north and northwest are mountain ranges with peaks and ridges rising between 2,000 and 4,000 feet above the enclosed tableland.

The most outstanding of Yellowstone's natural phenomena are the thousands of displays that compose the world's largest thermal basins. Bursts of scalding water spurt high into the air from some of these, while others bubble and spit in murky depths.

Multihued pools born from steaming springs tint the land's surface. Algae and bacteria color the formations in areas of thermal activity, while not far away vigorous steam vents emit uncanny sounds.

Note: Visitors should keep a close watch over children while in this area of the park, and be sure to stay on established boardwalks in all thermal areas.

Yellowstone National Park is one of the most successful wildlife sanctuaries in the world. Grizzly and black bears can be seen occasionally in the back country and sometimes from park roadways. The park also has several thousand elk; many mule deer, pronghorns and moose; bands of bighorn sheep; and about 4,000 bison. These animals are visible along park roadways and trails in the more remote areas.

General Information

The park roads are open to auto travel from May through October (weather permitting). The 60 miles of road between Gardiner and Cooke City, Mont., is open all year. During the o season this road is accessible only from northern entrance near Gardiner, Mont.; northeastern entrance near Cooke City is op only about May 30 to Oct. 15.

Most park facilities are open May 30 to C 15, but food and lodging facilities are limited ter Sept. 1. During the off-season gas is availa only at Gardiner and Cooke City, Mont. Inter park roads are open to snowmobiles from m December to mid-March. During the summ rental cars are available at Cody and Jackson well as at Billings, Bozeman and West Yello stone, Mont.

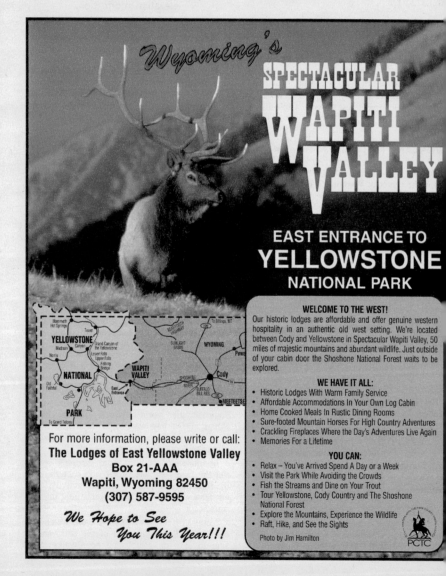

⛰ YELLOWSTONE NATIONAL PARK

© AAA

⛰ CAMPGROUND SITE WITHIN NAT'L. PARK. SEE CAMPBOOK FOR ADDITIONAL LISTINGS IN NEARBY TOWNS.

| 0 | Scale in Miles | 13.9 |
| 0 | Scale in Kilometers | 22.4 |

To Livingston
Corwin Springs
Gallatin
National
Forest
BIG HORN PEAK EL. 9,930 FT.
Specimen Cr.
NORTH ENTRANCE EL. 5,314 FT.
Gardiner
ELECTRIC PEAK EL. 10,992 FT.
MONT.
WYO.
Mammoth
Mammoth Hot Springs EL. 6,239 FT.
Visitor Center (Park Hdqrs.)
GRAY PEAK EL. 10,292 FT.
Indian Creek
ANTLER PEAK EL. 10,023 FT.
MT. HOLMES EL. 10,336 FT.
Obsidian Cliff
OBSERVATION PEAK EL. 9,397 FT.
Norris
Norris Visitor Center
Norris Geyser Basin
EL. 7,484 FT.

ROAD CLOSED IN WINTER

West Yellowstone
WEST ENTRANCE EL. 6,667 FT.
Madison
Madison EL. 6,806 FT.
NATIONAL PARK MTN. EL. 7,500 FT.
Gibbon Falls
Mary Lake
Nez Perce Creek
LOWER GEYSER BASIN
Fountain Paintpots
MIDWAY GEYSER BASIN
UPPER GEYSER BASIN
Beach Lake
Old Faithful Geyser
Visitor Center
Old Faithful EL. 7,367 FT.
CRAIG PASS EL. 8,262 FT.
SHOSHONE GEYSER BASIN
CONTINENTAL

Slough Creek
Tower Jct. EL. 6,264 FT.
Petrified Tree
Tower Fall
FOLSOM PEAK EL. 9,326 FT.
Grand Canyon of the Yellowstone
DUNRAVEN PASS EL. 8,859 FT.
MT. WASHBURN EL. 10,243 FT.
Canyon
Canyon Visitor Center
Inspiration Point
Artist Point
Canyon EL. 7,734 FT.
Lower Falls
Upper Falls
Wapiti Lake
White Lake
Mud Volcano
Lake Village EL. 7,792 FT.
Fishing Bridge
Fishing Bridge Visitor Center
Bridge Bay
Fishing Bridge
Lake Village
Yellowstone Lake EL. 7,733 FT.
West Thumb
WEST THUMB GEYSER BASIN
West Thumb EL. 7,784 FT.
Grant Village
Grant Village Visitor Center

NORTHEAST ENTRANCE EL. 7,365 FT.
Silver Gate
Cooke City
MONTANA
BARRONETTE PEAK EL. 10,404 FT.
COLTER PASS EL. 8,066 FT.
WYOMING
Pebble Creek
ABIATHAR PEAK EL. 10,928 FT.
Gallatin
CACHE MTN. EL. 9,596 FT.
National
MT. NORRIS EL. 9,936 FT.
Forest
PARKER PEAK EL. 10,203 FT.
SADDLE MTN. EL. 10,670 FT.
PELICAN CONE EL. 9,643 FT.
POLLUX PEAK EL. 11,067 FT.
CATHEDRAL PEAK EL. 10,760 FT.
PYRAMID PEAK EL. 10,497 FT.
Shoshone National Forest
MT. CHITTENDEN EL. 10,181 FT.
Turbid Lake
LAKE BUTTE EL. 8,348 FT.
CODY PEAK EL. 10,267 FT.
Pahaska Tepee
EAST ENTRANCE EL. 6,951 FT.
SYLVAN PASS EL. 8,530 FT.
RESERVATION PEAK EL. 10,629 FT.
MT. DOANE EL. 10,656 FT.
ATKINS PEAK EL. 11,043 FT.
PLENTYCOUPS PEAK EL. 10,937 FT.
MT. SCHURZ EL. 11,139 FT.
Shoshone National Forest

ROAD CLOSED IN WINTER

MONTANA
IDAHO
WYOMING
Targhee
National
Forest
Bechler Ranger Station

ROAD CLOSED IN WINTER

Shoshone Lake
Lewis Lake
Lewis Lake
MT. SHERIDAN EL. 10,308 FT.
Heart Lake
DIVIDE
South Arm
Southeast Arm
OVERLOOK MTN. EL. 9,321 FT.
EAGLE PEAK EL. 11,358 FT.
Bridger-Teton
National
Forest

SOUTH ENTRANCE EL. 6,886 FT.
MT. HANCOCK EL. 10,214 FT.
Snake R.
To Grand Teton National Park

To Red Lodge & Billings
To Cody & Buffalo

2121-F

The roads through the park make many of the most prominent attractions readily accessible. During the summer travel season visitors may encounter slow traffic. Be especially alert for others stopped in the road to watch wildlife; if you must stop, pull well off the highway onto a marked wayside.

Note: According to National Park Service figures, about 80 percent of the park roads are "in a structurally deficient state...[including] narrow shoulders [and] rough surfaces." The roads are being gradually repaired under a 20-year program. For up-to-date road information, phone (307) 344-7381.

The park headquarters is at Mammoth Hot Springs, 5 miles from the north entrance. The main post office is at Mammoth; ranger stations are at Old Faithful, Grant Village, Tower-Roosevelt, Mammoth Hot Springs, Lake, Madison, South Entrance and Canyon. The Mammoth and Tower-Roosevelt ranger stations, which are open all year, are accessible by car in winter via the north entrance.

Park information can be received by tuning radios to 1610 AM. Low-powered transmitters broadcast from entrance stations and campgrounds.

From mid-June through Labor Day ranger-naturalists conduct geyser walks, natural and living-history talks, photographic workshops and

children's programs at Mammoth Hot Sprin; Norris Geyser Basin, Old Faithful, West Thun Geyser Basin, Fishing Bridge Lake and Bri Bay, Tower-Roosevelt, Grant Village and C yon. Free evening programs are given at m park campgrounds during the summer seas Some programs are available on a limited sch ule after August.

The park's visitor centers offer a variety of terpretive exhibits and information. The Albri; Visitor Center at Mammoth Hot Springs conce trates on a general survey of the natural and h man history of the park; the Madison Museu 14 miles east of the west entrance, is the ho of the Caldera Art Center, which features litera visual and performing art. The Old Faithful Vi tor Center is devoted largely to geyser activ and its effects.

The Museum of the National Park Rang Norris, at Norris Geyser Basin, traces the dev opment of the park ranger profession. The Fi; ing Bridge Visitor Center/Museum de primarily with the biological life in the park a the history and geology of Yellowstone Lal The Grant Village Visitor Center houses an e hibit about "Fire and Yellowstone."

The Canyon Visitor Center displays art exh its, designed by students, that treat the natu and historical aspects of Yellowstone Natior Park. A field exhibit near Obsidian Cliff explai the mountain, which was created from a la flow containing obsidian, a glassy rock.

Tape tours offered by CCInc. Auto Tape Tou allow drivers to set their own pace; each tape 90 minutes long. The entire park is covered two tapes, available in either a clockwise counterclockwise driving direction, beginning the north and south entrances. The park's histo geology, flora and fauna are described throu, narration, music and sound effects. The tap which cost $12.95 each, can be ordered fr CCInc., P.O. Box 227, Allendale, NJ 0740 phone (201) 236-1666. They also can be p chased at stores and gift shops throughout t park, and in Gardiner and West Yellowstor Mont.

The TourGuide System consists of a C Player with an accompanying disc available f half- and full-day rental from mid-May throu; October. It features stories about the folklo history, wildlife, geology and ecology of t park. Visitors can select information about pa attractions at their convenience. The unit plu into the vehicle's cigarette lighter. The Tou Guide can be rented at nine in-park hotel loc tions. Rental vouchers may be purchased advance; phone (800) 247-1213 or (80 549-3883. Rates are $24.95 for a full day a $15.95 for a half-day.

ADMISSION to the park is by private vehic permit ($20), valid in both Yellowstone a Grand Teton national parks for 7 days; by annu ea permit ($40/both parks) or annual permit 50/entrance to all national parks); by single en- y via motorcycle or snowmobile ($15 per ma- ine); or by bicycle, foot or horseback ($10 per rson). A Golden Age Passport for U.S. citizens ver 61 is $10; a Golden Access Passport (for e physically impaired) provides free admission r U.S. citizens.

ETS are permitted in the park only if they are n a leash, crated or otherwise physically re- ricted at all times. They are not permitted more an 25 feet from the roads, and are not permit- d in the back country or on the board walk- ays or around the hot springs; it is illegal to ave pets unattended.

ADDRESS inquiries to the Superintendent, Yellowstone National Park, P.O. Box 168, Yellowstone National Park, WY 82190; phone (307) 344-7381. For lodging and guest service information write the Travel Director, TW Recreational Services Inc., P.O. Box 165, Yellowstone National Park, WY 82190; phone (307) 344-7311.

Activities

Not all of Yellowstone's grandeur can be seen from the boardwalks. More than 1,200 miles of back-country trails lead to many of the park's less accessible attractions. A free back-country use permit, obtainable from any area ranger station, is required for those who wish to camp in

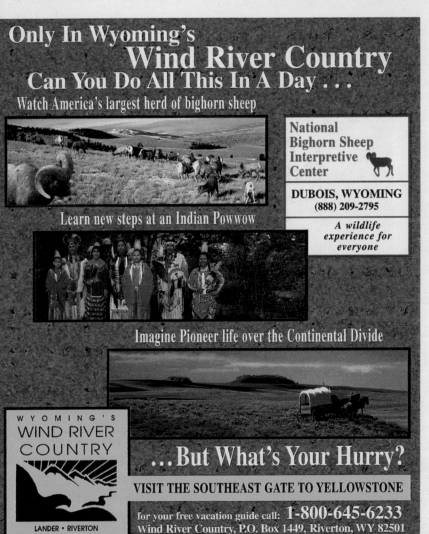

It's a land of wonder.
Visit and you'll wonder why you
didn't think of this sooner.

You've done the beach, the amusement parks, the pamper-yourself resorts. Now it's time for one of those vacations you've always heard about. The unforgettable. A trip to Yellowstone National Park promises that and more with steaming hot springs, breathtaking sunsets, Old Faithful Geyser, wild moose, bald eagles and tranquilizing waterfalls. No matter what season you visit, you'll find yourself wondering just why you waited.

For accommodations, campgrounds and activities please call 307-344-7311.

YELLOWSTONE
NATIONAL PARK LODGES
Operated By **AmFac** *Parks & Resorts*
Let the memories begin.
www.amfac.com

e back country. The permit can be obtained in person and no more than 48 hours in advance; r a $15 fee, the permit can be obtained by ail.

There is no better way to explore the park than n horseback over the trails. Private stock can be dden, or horses can be rented at Mammoth Hot prings, Tower-Roosevelt and Canyon from TW ecreational Services Inc. Horses cannot be nted without a guide.

Motorboats and rowboats can be rented from W Recreational Services Inc. at the Bridge Bay larina. Guided fishing trips also are available. rivately owned boats are permitted on Yellow-

stone and Lewis lakes, but operators must obtain a $5 permit for nonmotorized craft or a $10 permit for motorized craft. The permits are good for 7 days in both Yellowstone and Grand Teton national parks.

Guided snowcoach tours by TW Recreational Services Inc. to the interior of the park are available mid-December through early March from Mammoth Hot Springs, at the north entrance; West Yellowstone, Mont., at the west entrance; and at Old Faithful and Flagg Ranch, at the south entrance. They also rent snowmobiles and offer guided cross-country ski trips.

Most of the streams and lakes below the timberline contain one or more species of trout. Roadside streams and Yellowstone Lake offer some of the best fishing in the park. Fishing tackle is sold by Hamilton Stores at the general stores.

Persons over age 15 are required to purchase a fishing permit. A 10-day permit costs $10. A free fishing permit is required for ages 12-15. For further information write the Chief Rangers Office, P.O. Box 168, Yellowstone National Park, WY 82190. Fishing regulations and permits can be obtained at any ranger station, entrance station, visitor center or local store. The opening of the season varies from the Saturday of Memorial Day weekend to July 15 for different lakes and streams; it closes the first Sunday in November.

Check at park headquarters or ranger stations for season variations and legal limits. *See Recreation Chart and the AAA Northwestern CampBook.*

Note: It is not only contrary to park regulations but also dangerous to feed, touch or tease any wildlife. Animals in the park are wild and should be viewed only from a safe distance. Because the presence of food in a tent or camp may attract bears and other unwanted guests, it must be kept in locked hardtopped cars or in locked metal boxes or containers. All leftovers should be disposed of in bear-proof garbage cans provided for that purpose.

Points of Interest

GRAND CANYON OF THE YELLOWSTONE, a section along the Yellowstone River between Canyon and Tower-Roosevelt, is noted for its spectacular coloring. Vista points offer superb views; among the best are Artist's Point on the south rim and Inspiration Point on the north rim. Lookout Point provides the best view of the Lower Falls. Uncle Tom's Trail descends about

halfway to the canyon floor and ends at the ba of the Lower Falls on the south side. The Upp Falls are visible from several trails and lookou Allow 1 hour minimum.

MAMMOTH HOT SPRINGS are near the pa headquarters at the n. entrance. The springs a characterized by terrace-like formations create by limestone deposits. Well-marked trails allc the safe viewing of the formations at close rang however, visitors must stay on the trails at a times, since in many places the thin crust is da gerous. Allow 1 hour minimum.

OLD FAITHFUL AND THE GEYSERS exhib character and action. Many, like Old Faithful a Riverside, spout at predictable intervals; othe are irregular. Some burst upward with powe others shoot at angles or bubble. Most of the a proximately 10,000 thermal features (geysers, f maroles, hot springs and mud pots) are in th principal geyser basins—Norris, Lower, Midwa Upper, West Thumb, Heart Lake and Sh shone—in the western and south-central section Mud volcanoes also are interesting. Two sho one-way roads, Firehole Canyon Drive and Fir hole Lake Drive, should be included in any vis Allow 2 hours minimum.

THE PAINTPOTS are large springs filled with h clay ranging in color from white to shades pink and black. Fountain Paintpot, one of th most famous in the park, is in the Lower Geys Basin. Allow 30 minutes minimum.

YELLOWSTONE LAKE, 7,733 feet above s level, is e. and s. of the park road between We Thumb and Fishing Bridge. With a shoreline 110 miles, the lake is the largest body of wat in North America at so high an altitude. The ar is a haven for several rare bird species. Allow hour minimum.

Idaho

ASHTON—1,100

LODGING

SUPER 8 ◆◆ Motel

Rates Subject to Change

6/16-9/30		1P: $39	2P/1B: $41		2P/2B: $43	XP: $5	F12
4/1-6/15		1P: $37	2P/1B: $39		2P/2B: $40	XP: $5	F12
3/1-3/31 & 10/1-2/29		1P: $35	2P/1B: $37		2P/2B: $39	XP: $5	F12

Phone: 208/652-7885

Location: Just off US 20 on Pineview Dr. 164 Pineview Dr 83420. Fax: 208/652-7721. **Terms:** Reserv deposit. **Facility:** 38 rooms. New property on major scenic route to Yellowstone Park & Jackson Hole. 2 stories; interior corridors; designated smoking area; mountain view. **Cards:** AE, DS, MC, VI.

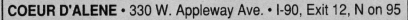

◆   **Diamonds are a guest's best friend.**   ◆

BLACKFOOT—9,600

LODGING

BEST WESTERN BLACKFOOT INN   Phone: (208)785-4144
5/15-9/15 [CP]   1P: $50- 84   2P/1B: $50- 84   2P/2B: $50- 84
3/1-5/14 & 9/16-2/29 [CP]   1P: $40- 74   2P/1B: $40- 74   2P/2B: $40- 74
Location: I-15, exit 93; just e on Bergener, 0.4 mi n on Parkway. 750 Jensen Grove Dr 83221.
Motel   Fax: 208/785-4304. **Terms:** Pets. **Facility:** 60 rooms. 2 stories; interior corridors; designated smoking area;
heated indoor pool, whirlpool. **Services:** winter plug-ins. **Recreation:** video movie rentals. **Cards:** AE, CB,
DI, DS, MC, VI. **Special Amenities:** Free breakfast and free local telephone calls.

BLISS—200

LODGING

AMBER INN   Phone: (208)352-4441
All Year   1P: $33   2P/1B: $39   2P/2B: $39   XP: $4
Location: Just s of I-84, exit 141. 17286 US Hwy 30 83314. Fax: 208/352-1115. **Terms:** Pets, $4.28 extra
charge. **Facility:** 30 rooms. Easy freeway access. Standard rooms in rural location; large parking area. 1 two-
Motel   bedroom unit. 2 stories; interior corridors. **Cards:** AE, DS, MC, VI.

BOISE—125,600

OA	✈ Airport Accommodations			
	BOISE AIR TERMINAL	Rating	Rate	Listing Page
ⒶⒶⒶ	**Best Western Airport Motor Inn, adjacent to airport entrance**	◆◆◆	$55-69 SAVE	174
ⒶⒶⒶ	**Best Western Vista Inn, adjacent to airport entrance**	◆◆◆	$65-79 SAVE	
	Boise Super 8 Lodge, 0.5 mi n of airport	◆◆	$63-66	174
ⒶⒶⒶ	**Comfort Inn, adjacent to airport entrance**	◆◆◆	$57-64 SAVE	175
	Fairfield Inn by Marriott, 0.5 mi n of airport	◆◆◆	$62-67	175
	Hampton Inn, 0.5 mi n of airport	◆◆◆	$69-79	176
ⒶⒶⒶ	**Holiday Inn, 0.5 mi n of airport**	◆◆◆	$79 SAVE	177
	Holiday Inn Express, 1 mi n of airport	◆◆◆	$69-79	177
ⒶⒶⒶ	**Inn America-A Budget Motel, adjacent to airport**	◆◆◆	$39-59 SAVE	177
ⒶⒶⒶ	**Quality Inn Airport Suites, 1 mi n of airport**	◆◆◆	$57-64 SAVE	177
ⒶⒶⒶ	**Sleep Inn, adjacent to airport**	◆◆	$55-69 SAVE	178

LODGINGS

AMERITEL INN   Rates Subject to Change   **Phone:** 208-378-7000
All Year [CP]   1P: $90- 130   2P/1B: $90- 130   2P/2B: $90- 130   XP: $8   F12
Motel   **Location:** I-84, exit 49 (Franklin St), just w on Franklin St & just n on Milwaukee. 7965 W Emerald St 83704.
Fax: 208/378-7040. **Terms:** Weekend rates avail. **Facility:** 124 rooms. Stylish rooms, many with mountain
view. Close to shopping mall. 4 stories; interior corridors; heated indoor pool. **All Rooms:** combo or shower baths.
Some Rooms: 3 efficiencies, 12 kitchens. **Cards:** AE, DI, DS, MC, VI. *(See color ad p 172)*

BESTREST INN

◆◆
Motel

		1P:		2P/1B:		2P/2B:		XP:		
6/1-8/31 [CP]		1P:	$50	2P/1B:	$50	2P/2B:	$50	XP:	$5	F18
3/1-5/31 & 9/1-2/29 [CP]		1P:	$46	2P/1B:	$46	2P/2B:	$46	XP:	$5	F18

Rates Subject to Change

Phone: 208/322-4404

Location: Just sw of I-84; exit 50A eastbound, exit 50A westbound; just s on Cole, just w. 8002 Overland Rd 83709. Fax: 208/322-7487. **Facility:** 87 rooms. Small to average size rooms; 24 hour video rental; coin laundry & shopping adjacent. 2 stories; exterior corridors; small heated pool. **Cards:** AE, CB, DI, DS, MC, VI. *(See color ad p 173)*

🛇 🐕 [↑↑] 🐾 [VCR] ✕

BEST WESTERN AIRPORT MOTOR INN

(AAA) [SAVE]
◆◆◆
Motel

Phone: (208)384-5000

All Year [CP]　　1P: $49- 65　2P/1B:　$55- 69　2P/2B:　$55- 69　XP: $5　F18
Location: Just s of I-84, exit 53. 2660 Airport Way 83705. Fax: 208/384-5566. **Facility:** 50 rooms. Many rooms with mountain view. 2 stories; exterior corridors; designated smoking area; small solar-heated pool. **Dining:** Restaurant nearby. **Cards:** AE, CB, DI, DS, MC, VI. **Special Amenities:** Free breakfast and free local telephone calls.

🛇 🐕 [↑↑] ✛ 🛆 🐾 🖭 🖳 🖬 ✕

BEST WESTERN SAFARI MOTOR INN

(AAA) [SAVE]
◆◆◆
Motel

Phone: (208)344-6556

		1P:		2P/1B:		2P/2B:		XP:		
6/1-2/29 [CP]		1P:	$60	2P/1B:	$66	2P/2B:	$75	XP:	$6	F18
3/1-5/31 [CP]		1P:	$55	2P/1B:	$60	2P/2B:	$70	XP:	$5	F18

Location: City center; at 11th & Grove sts. 1070 Grove St 83702. Fax: 208/344-7240. **Terms:** Weekly rates. **Facility:** 103 rooms. Varied accommodations; close to shopping & civic buildings. 5 suites, $69-$125; 3 stories; interior corridors; sauna, whirlpool, small seasonal heated pool. **Dining:** Restaurant nearby. **Some Rooms:** whirlpools. **Cards:** AE, DI, DS, MC, VI. **Special Amenities:** Free breakfast and free local telephone calls.

🛇 🐕 [3⋆] 🐦 [↑↑] ✛ 🛆 🐾 🖭 🖳 🖬 ✕ 🗐

BEST WESTERN VISTA INN

(AAA) [SAVE]
◆◆◆
Motel

Phone: (208)336-8100

All Year [CP]　　1P: $59- 75　2P/1B:　$65- 79　2P/2B:　$65- 79　XP: $5　F18
Location: Just s of I-84, exit 53. 2645 Airport Way 83705. Fax: 208/342-3060. **Facility:** 87 rooms. Some rooms with mountain view. 2 stories; interior/exterior corridors; heated indoor pool, whirlpool. **Dining:** Restaurant nearby. **All Rooms:** combo or shower baths. **Some Rooms:** color TV. **Cards:** AE, CB, DI, DS, MC, VI. **Special Amenities:** Free breakfast and free local telephone calls.

🛇 🐕 [3⋆] 🐦 [↑↑] ✛ 🛆 🐾 🖭 🖳 🖬 🖨 ✕ 🗐

BOISE RIVER INN

(AAA) [SAVE]
◆◆
Motel

Phone: (208)344-9988

All Year　　1P: $45- 55　2P/1B:　$45- 55　2P/2B:　$50- 60　XP: $5　F16
Location: 2.3 mi n of I-84, exit 54; just e on Beacon. 1140 Colorado Ave 83706. Fax: 208/336-9471. **Terms:** Weekly/monthly rates. **Facility:** 87 rooms. Quiet residential area; adjacent to creek & Boise Greenbelt; close to Boise State University. 2 stories; interior/exterior corridors; small heated pool. **Recreation:** jogging. **All Rooms:** kitchens. **Cards:** AE, CB, DI, DS, MC, VI. **Special Amenities:** Free breakfast and free local telephone calls.

🐕 🐦 🛆 ✕ 🐾 🖳 🖬 ✕

BOISE SUPER 8 LODGE

◆◆
Motel

		1P:		2P/1B:		2P/2B:		XP:		
5/1-10/7		1P:	$53- 56	2P/1B:	$59- 62	2P/2B:	$63- 66	XP:	$5	F12
4/1-4/30		1P:	$50- 53	2P/1B:	$56- 63	2P/2B:	$60- 63	XP:	$5	F12
3/1-3/31 & 10/8-2/29		1P:	$47- 50	2P/1B:	$53- 56	2P/2B:	$57- 60	XP:	$5	F12

Rates Subject to Change

Phone: (208)344-8871

Location: Just n of I-84, exit 53. 2773 Elder St 83705. Fax: 208/344-8871. **Facility:** 110 rooms. Rooms vary in size, some with mountain view. 3 stories; interior corridors; designated smoking area; small heated indoor pool. **Cards:** AE, CB, DI, DS, MC, VI.

🛇 🐕 🐦 [↑↑] ✛ 🛆 🐾 [VCR] ✕

CAVANAUGHS PARKCENTER SUITE

◆◆◆
Suite Motel

		1P:		2P/1B:		2P/2B:		XP:		
Mon-Thurs [CP]		1P:	$125	2P/1B:	$125	2P/2B:	$125	XP:	$10	F12
Fri-Sun [CP]		1P:	$69	2P/1B:	$69	2P/2B:	$69	XP:	$10	F12

Rates Subject to Change

Phone: 208/342-1044

Location: 2.3 mi n of I-84, exit 54; 1 mi e on Beacon & Park Center Blvd. 424 E Park Center Blvd 83706. Fax: 208/342-2763. **Facility:** 238 rooms. Located in Park Center Business Park; close to greenbelt river path & Boise State University. 3 stories; interior corridors; heated pool. **Services:** area transportation. **All Rooms:** combo or shower baths. **Cards:** AE, DI, DS, MC, VI.

🐕 [3⋆] 🐦 [↑↑] ✛ 🛆 🐾 🖭 [↑] 🖳 🖬 🖨 🗐 ✕ 🗐

THE CLUB HOTEL BY DOUBLETREE

(AAA)
◆◆◆
Motor Inn

Phone: (208)345-2002

All Year　　1P: $59- 140　2P/1B:　$59- 140　2P/2B:　$59- 140　XP: $5-10　F18
Location: I-84, exit 54 (Broadway), 2.3 mi n on Broadway, 0.3 mi e on Beacon & Park Center Blvd. 475 W Park Center Blvd 83706. Fax: 208/345-8354. **Facility:** 158 rooms. In Park Center Office Development near the Boise River greenbelt pathways; close to Boise State University. 6 stories; interior corridors; small heated pool, whirlpool. **Dining:** Coffee shop; cocktails. **Services:** area transportation, to shopping & attractions. **Cards:** AE, CB, DI, DS, JC, MC, VI. *(See ad below)*

[ASK] 🛇 🐕 [3⋆] 🐦 [↑↑] 🍴 ✛ 🛆 🐾 🖭 🖳 🖨 ✕

COMFORT INN Phone: (208)336-0077
AAA SAVE All Year [CP] 1P: $47- 54 2P/1B: $52- 58 2P/2B: $57- 64 XP: $7 F18
◆◆◆ **Location:** Just s of I-84, exit 53. 2526 Airport Way 83705. Fax: 208/342-6592. **Terms:** Reserv deposit.
Motel **Facility:** 61 rooms. Some rooms with mountain view. Pleasant contemporary decor. No discount on family room; 2 stories; interior/exterior corridors; small heated indoor pool, whirlpool. **Dining:** Restaurant nearby. **Recreation:** Fee: video movie rentals. **Some Rooms:** whirlpools. **Cards:** AE, CB, DI, DS, JC, MC, VI.
Special Amenities: Early check-in/late check-out and free local telephone calls.

COURTYARD BY MARRIOTT Phone: (208)331-2700
AAA SAVE All Year 1P: $95- 105 2P/1B: $105- 115 2P/2B: $105- 115 XP: $10 F18
◆◆◆ **Location:** 3 mi n of I-84, exit 54. 222 S Broadway Ave 83702. Fax: 208/331-3296. **Terms:** Monthly rates.
Motor Inn **Facility:** 162 rooms. All rooms with 2 phones, 2 lines, iron, ironing board & voice mail. 4 stories; interior corridors; designated smoking area; heated indoor pool, whirlpool. **Dining:** Restaurant; 6:30 am-10 & 5-9 pm, Sat & Sun 7 am-11 & 5-9 pm; cocktails. **Cards:** AE, CB, DI, DS, MC, VI. **Special Amenities:** Early check-in/late check-out and preferred room (subject to availability with advanced reservations).
(See color ad below)

DOUBLETREE HOTEL BOISE DOWNTOWN Rates Subject to Change Phone: 208/344-7691
◆◆◆ All Year 1P: $109 2P/1B: $109 2P/2B: $109 XP: $15 F18
Motor Inn **Location:** 1 mi n of I-184, Fairview Ave exit. 1800 Fairview Ave 83702. Fax: 208/336-3652. **Facility:** 182 rooms. 2 phones, iron & ironing board in all rooms. 3-7 stories; interior corridors; mountain view; small heated pool. **Services:** area transportation. **All Rooms:** combo or shower baths. **Cards:** AE, CB, DI, DS, JC, MC, VI.
(See ad p 176)

DOUBLETREE HOTEL RIVERSIDE Rates Subject to Change Phone: (208)343-1871
◆◆◆ Sun-Thurs 1P: $98- 108 2P/1B: $98- 108 2P/2B: $98- 108 XP: $15 F18
Motor Inn Fri & Sat 1P: $80- 90 2P/1B: $80- 90 2P/2B: $80- 90 XP: $15 F18
Location: Just n of I-84, Fairview Ave exit; just w on Garden. 2900 Chinden Blvd 83714. Fax: 208/344-1079. **Terms:** Check-in 4 pm. **Facility:** 304 rooms. Spacious landscaped grounds adjacent to Boise River & Greenbelt. Close to downtown & mall. 2 two-bedroom units. 2 stories; interior corridors; designated smoking area; heated pool. **Services:** giftshop; area transportation. **Recreation:** jogging. **All Rooms:** combo or shower baths. **Cards:** AE, CB, DI, DS, JC, MC, VI. *(See ad p 176)*

ECONO LODGE BOISE Phone: (208)344-4030
AAA SAVE All Year 1P: $40- 42 2P/1B: $42- 45 2P/2B: $48- 55 XP: $6 F16
◆◆ **Location:** Just n of I-184, Fairview Ave exit. 4060 Fairview Ave 83706. Fax: 208/342-1635. **Terms:** Reserv deposit; weekly rates, 10/1-2/28; pets. **Facility:** 52 rooms. 3 stories; interior corridors. **Dining:** Restaurant nearby. **Cards:** AE, CB, DI, DS, JC, MC, VI. **Special Amenities:** Early check-in/late check-out and free breakfast.
Motel

EXTENDED STAY AMERICA Rates Subject to Change Phone: 208/363-9040
◆◆ All Year 1P: $44- 54 2P/1B: $49- 59 2P/2B: $49- 59
Extended Stay **Location:** I-84, exit 53 (Vista Ave), 0.3 mi n. 2500 S Vista Ave 83705. Fax: 208/363-9039. **Terms:** Reserv deposit. **Facility:** 107 rooms. Modern, comfortably furnished units well equipped for extended stays or overnight accommodation. 2 person max occupancy. 2 stories; interior corridors. **All Rooms:** efficiencies.
Motel
Cards: AE, CB, DI, DS, MC, VI.

FAIRFIELD INN BY MARRIOTT Rates Subject to Change Phone: (208)331-5656
◆◆◆ 5/1-2/29 [CP] 1P: $62- 67 2P/1B: $62- 67 2P/2B: $62 XP: $5 F18
Motel 3/1-4/30 [CP] 1P: $59- 64 2P/1B: $59- 64 2P/2B: $59 XP: $5 F18
Location: Just n of I-84, exit 53. 3300 S Shoshone St 83705. Fax: 208/424-3169. **Facility:** 63 rooms. Spacious rooms; some with mountain view. 3 stories; interior corridors; heated indoor pool. **All Rooms:** combo or shower baths. **Cards:** AE, CB, DI, DS, JC, MC, VI.

THE GROVE HOTEL-A WEST COAST GRAND HOTEL   **Phone:** (208)333-8000
Ⓐ SAVE   All Year   1P: $129- 139   2P/1B: $149- 159   2P/2B: $149- 159   XP: $15   F12
FYI   Too new to rate. **Location:** City center; at Capital Blvd & Front St. 245 S Capitol Blvd 83702.
    Fax: 208/333-8800. **Terms:** Check-in 4 pm. **Facility:** 250 rooms. 20 two-bedroom units. 17 stories; interior cor-
Hotel   ridors; heated indoor pool, sauna, steamroom, whirlpool. Fee: parking. **Dining:** Dining room, restaurant; 6
am-11 pm; piano bar; cocktails. **Services:** giftshop; area transportation, city center.
Some Rooms: whirlpools. **Cards:** AE, CB, DI, DS, MC, VI. **Special Amenities:** Early check-in/late
check-out and free newspaper. *(See color ad below)*

HAMPTON INN   Rates Subject to Change   **Phone:** (208)331-5600
◆◆◆   All Year [CP]   1P: $64- 74   2P/1B: $69- 79   2P/2B: $69- 79
Motel   **Location:** Just n of I-84, exit 53. 3270 S Shoshone St 83705. Fax: 208/389-1220. **Facility:** 64 rooms. Spacious & well lighted rooms, some with mountain view. 3 stories; interior corridors; designated smoking area;
heated indoor pool. **All Rooms:** combo or shower baths. **Cards:** AE, DI, DS, MC, VI.

HOLIDAY INN

AAA **SAVE**
◆◆◆
Motor Inn

5/1-8/31	1P:	$79	2P/1B:	$79	2P/2B:	$79	XP: $10	F
3/1-4/30 & 9/1-2/29	1P:	$69	2P/1B:	$69	2P/2B:	$69	XP: $10	F

Phone: (208)344-8365

Location: Just n of I-84, exit 53. 3300 Vista Ave 83705. Fax: 208/343-9635. **Terms:** Package plans; small pets only. **Facility:** 265 rooms. Holidome features children's recreational area. 2 two-bedroom units. 2 stories; interior corridors; heated indoor pool, wading pool, saunas, whirlpool; playground. **Dining:** Restaurant; 6 am-2 & 5-11 pm; $8-$16; cocktails. **All Rooms:** combo or shower baths. **Cards:** AE, DI, DS, JC, MC, VI. **Special Amenities:** Early check-in/late check-out and free room upgrade (subject to availability with advanced reservations). *(See color ad below & opposite title page)*

HOLIDAY INN EXPRESS

◆◆◆
Motel

All Year [CP]
Rates Subject to Change
1P: $69- 79 2P/1B: $69- 79 2P/2B: $69- 79
Phone: 208/388-0800

Location: 0.5 mi n of I-84, exit 53. 2613 S Vista Ave 83705. Fax: 208/388-0846. **Facility:** 63 rooms. Convenient access to airport & interstate. Well lighted rooms. 3 stories; interior corridors; designated smoking area; small heated indoor pool. **Cards:** AE, CB, DI, DS, JC, MC, VI.

IDAHO HERITAGE INN BED & BREAKFAST

◆◆◆
Historic Bed
& Breakfast

All Year [BP]
Rates Subject to Change
1P: $60- 95 2P/1B: $60- 105 2P/2B: $90- 105
Phone: (208)342-8066

Location: I-84, exit 54 3 mi n on Broadway, just w. 109 W Idaho St 83702. Fax: 208/343-2325. **Terms:** Age restrictions may apply. **Facility:** 6 rooms. Former home of Idaho Governor Chase Clark; National Historic Register; close to downtown & medical complex. 3 stories, no elevator; interior/exterior corridors; smoke free premises. **Recreation:** Fee: bicycles. **All Rooms:** comb, shower or tub baths. **Some Rooms:** efficiency, color TV. **Cards:** AE, DS, MC, VI.

INN AMERICA-A BUDGET MOTEL

AAA **SAVE**
◆◆◆
Motel

All Year
1P: $35- 49 2P/1B: $39- 59 2P/2B: $39- 59 XP: $5 F18
Phone: (208)389-9800

Location: 0.3 mi se of I-84, exit 53. 2275 Airport Way 83705. Fax: 208/338-1303. **Facility:** 73 rooms. Oversize vehicle parking avail, some rooms with mountain views. 2 two-bedroom units. 3 stories; interior corridors; designated smoking area; small heated indoor pool. **All Rooms:** combo or shower baths. **Cards:** AE, CB, DI, DS, MC, VI. **Special Amenities:** Free local telephone calls.

JJ SHAW HOUSE BED & BREAKFAST INN

◆◆◆
Historic Bed
& Breakfast

All Year [BP]
Rates Subject to Change
1P: $79- 109 2P/1B: $79- 109 2P/2B: $79- 109 XP: $20
Phone: 208/344-8899

Location: I-184, 13th St exit; 0.6 mi n on 13th St & just w. 1411 W Franklin St 83702. Fax: 208/344-6677. **Terms:** Age restrictions may apply. **Facility:** 5 rooms. Complete restored distinctive Queen Anne Victorian 1907 home with gracious well appointed rooms in quiet residential neighborhood near City Center. 10 am check out Sun. 3 stories, no elevator; interior corridors; smoke free premises; street parking only. **All Rooms:** comb, shower or tub baths. **Cards:** AE, DS, MC, VI.

OWYHEE PLAZA HOTEL

◆◆◆
Historic Motor
Inn

All Year
Rates Subject to Change
1P: $68- 124 2P/1B: $78- 134 2P/2B: $78- 134 XP: $10 F18
Phone: (208)343-4611

Location: City center; at 11th & Main sts. 1109 Main St 83702. Fax: 208/336-3860. **Terms:** Reserv deposit. **Facility:** 100 rooms. Historic 1910 restored hotel; close to shopping, convention center/sports arena; varied room styles; some poolside rooms & parking at room. 3 stories; interior/exterior corridors; designated smoking area; heated pool. **All Rooms:** combo or shower baths. **Cards:** AE, MC, VI.

THE PLAZA SUITE HOTEL

◆◆◆
Motel

All Year [CP]
Rates Subject to Change
1P: $72- 150 2P/1B: $72- 200 2P/2B: $72- 150 XP: $9-27 F5
Phone: 208/375-7666

Location: 0.5 mi n of I-84, exit 50A. 409 S Cole 83709. Fax: 208/376-3608. **Facility:** 38 rooms. Spacious rooms. Atrium houses pool & breakfast area. 4 stories; interior corridors; designated smoking area; small heated indoor pool. **Services:** area transportation. **All Rooms:** combo or shower baths. **Cards:** AE, DI, DS, MC, VI.

QUALITY INN AIRPORT SUITES

AAA **SAVE**
◆◆◆
Motel

All Year [CP]
1P: $50- 57 2P/1B: $57- 64 2P/2B: $57- 64 XP: $7 F18
Phone: (208)343-7505

Location: 0.5 mi n of I-84, exit 53. 2717 Vista Ave 83705. Fax: 208/342-4319. **Terms:** Reserv deposit; weekly rates; pets, $10 extra charge. **Facility:** 79 rooms. Oversize rooms with kitchen or wetbar. 2 stories; exterior corridors; small heated pool. **Services:** complimentary evening beverages, except Sun. **Recreation:** movie video rentals. **Some Rooms:** 20 kitchens, no utensils. **Cards:** AE, CB, DI, DS, JC, MC, VI. **Special Amenities:** Free local telephone calls and free newspaper.

RODEWAY INN OF BOISE
Phone: (208)376-2700

AAA [SAVE]

1/1-2/29 [BP]	1P:	$76-	90	2P/1B:	$86- 102	2P/2B:	$86- 102	XP: $10-12	F17
5/1-12/31 [BP]	1P:	$74-	88	2P/1B:	$84- 100	2P/2B:	$84- 100	XP: $10-12	F17
3/1-4/30 [BP]	1P:	$72-	87	2P/1B:	$82- 99	2P/2B:	$82- 99	XP: $10-12	F17

Motor Inn   **Location:** Just sw of I-184, Curtis Rd exit. 1115 N Curtis Rd 83706. Fax: 208/377-0324. **Terms:** Weekly rates; small pets only, $25 dep req. **Facility:** 98 rooms. Contemporary style rooms. 2 stories; interior/exterior corridors; putting green; small heated indoor/outdoor pool, sauna, whirlpool. **Dining:** Restaurant; 6:30 am-10 pm, Sun from 7 am; $6-$20; cocktails. **Services:** area transportation, to mall. **Recreation:** shuffleboard & tetherball. **Cards:** AE, CB, DI, DS, JC, MC, VI.

SHILO INN-BOISE AIRPORT
Rates Subject to Change   **Phone: (208)343-7662**

◆◆◆   All Year [CP]   1P: $65- 115   2P/1B: $65- 115   2P/2B: $65- 115   XP: $10   F13
Motel   **Location:** Just sw of I-84, exit 54. 4111 Broadway Ave 83705-5302. Fax: 208/344-0318. **Facility:** 125 rooms. Large to spacious rooms & many with mountain views. 4 stories; interior corridors; heated pool
All Rooms: combo or shower baths. **Cards:** AE, CB, DI, DS, JC, MC, VI. *(See ad below)*

SHILO INN-BOISE RIVERSIDE
Rates Subject to Change   **Phone: (208)344-3521**

◆◆   All Year [CP]   1P: $65- 99   2P/1B: $65- 99   2P/2B: $65- 99   XP: $10   F12
Motel   **Location:** I-184, Fairview Ave exit; 0.5 mi n, just w on S 30th St. 3031 Main St 83702-2048. Fax: 208/384-1217. **Facility:** 112 rooms. Adjacent to Boise River & greenbelt; hair dryers avail. 3 stories; interior corridors; designated smoking area; heated indoor pool. **Recreation:** jogging. **Cards:** AE, CB, DI, DS, JC, MC, VI. *(See ad p 201, p 187 & below)*

SLEEP INN
Phone: (208)336-7377

AAA [SAVE]

◆◆   All Year [CP]   1P: $49- 65   2P/1B: $55- 69   2P/2B: $55- 69   XP: $5   F18
Motel   **Location:** Just s of I-84, exit 53. 2799 Airport Way 83705. Fax: 208/336-2035. **Facility:** 69 rooms. Some rooms with mountain view. 2 stories; interior corridors; designated smoking area. **All Rooms:** combo or shower baths. **Cards:** AE, CB, DI, DS, JC, MC, VI. **Special Amenities:** Free local telephone calls and free newspaper.

STATEHOUSE INN
Rates Subject to Change   **Phone: (208)342-4622**

◆◆◆   Sun-Thurs   1P: $89- 99   2P/1B: $99- 109   2P/2B: $99- 109   XP: $10   F18
Motor Inn   Fri & Sat   1P: $69- 79   2P/1B: $69- 79   2P/2B: $69- 79   XP: $10   F18
Location: City center; at 10th & Grove sts. 981 Grove St 83702. Fax: 208/344-5751. **Facility:** 88 rooms. Covered parking. 5 stories; interior corridors; designated smoking area. **All Rooms:** combo or shower baths. **Cards:** AE, CB, DI, DS, MC, VI.

UNIVERSITY INN
Phone: (208)345-7170

AAA [SAVE]

All Year   1P: $36- 100   2P/1B: $41- 110   2P/2B: $42- 110   XP: $5-7
Motor Inn   **Location:** 2.5 mi n of I-84, exit 53. 2360 University Dr 83706. Fax: 208/345-5118. **Terms:** BP avail. **Facility:** 82 rooms. Varied room styles; adjacent to Boise State University. 1-2 stories; exterior corridors; heated pool, whirlpool. **Dining:** Coffee shop; 6 am-2 pm, Sun 7 am-3 pm; cocktails. **All Rooms:** combo or shower baths. **Cards:** AE, CB, DI, DS, MC, VI. **Special Amenities:** Free breakfast and free local telephone calls.

RESTAURANTS

BOISE RIVER RAM & BIG HORN BREWING CO
Lunch: $5-$14   **Dinner:** $5-$14   **Phone:** 208/345-2929

◆◆   **Location:** 2.8 mi n of I-84, exit 54. 709 E Park Blvd 83712. **Hours:** 11 am-2 am, Sun-midnight. Closed:
American   12/25. **Features:** casual dress; children's menu; carryout; cocktails; a la carte. Sports oriented & featuring a variety of burgers, sandwiches, pizza, salad, steak & seafood. Close to Boise State University. **Cards:** AE, CB, DI, DS, MC, VI.

EL CAZADOR MEXICAN GRILL
Lunch: $4-$7   **Dinner:** $8-$12   **Phone:** 208/323-1801

◆   **Location:** I-184, Curtis Rd exit; just n & w. 5900 Fairview Ave 83704. **Hours:** 11 am-10 pm, Fri & Sat-11 pm,
Mexican   Sun noon-10 pm. Closed: 11/25 & 12/25. **Reservations:** accepted. **Features:** casual dress; children's menu; carryout; cocktail lounge; beer & wine only; a la carte. Festive & family owned featuring traditional & unique Mexican selections. **Cards:** AE, DS, MC, VI.

GAMEKEEPER RESTAURANT
Lunch: $6-$10   **Dinner:** $15-$30   **Phone:** 208/343-4611

◆◆◆   **Location:** City center; at 11th & Main sts; in Owyhee Plaza Hotel. 1109 Main St 83702. **Hours:** 11:30 am-2
Continental   & 5:30-10 pm, Sat from 5:30 pm. Closed: 1/1, 7/4 & 12/25. **Reservations:** suggested. **Features:** cocktails & lounge; entertainment; area transportation; a la carte. Comfortable decor & formal service. Expansive selection of Continental & American entrees with tableside flambe. Piano bar. **Cards:** AE, MC, VI.

JJ NORTH'S GRAND BUFFET　　　**Lunch:** $6　　　**Dinner:** $8　　　**Phone:** 208/375-7161
◆
American
Location: Just n of I-184, Curtis Rd exit; 0.5 mi w. 6681 Fairview Ave 83704. **Hours:** 8 am-8:30 pm, Sat-9 pm, Sun-8 pm. **Features:** casual dress; senior's menu; carryout; salad bar; buffet. Family atmosphere; breakfast buffet on weekends. Smoke free premises. **Cards:** DS, MC, VI.

MONGOLIAN BBQ　　　**Lunch:** $4-$7　　　**Dinner:** $5-$9　　　**Phone:** 208/387-0393
◆
Ethnic
Location: I-84, exit 54; 1.7 mi n. 1808 Broadway Ave 83706. **Hours:** 10:45 am-9 pm, Fri & Sat-10 pm. Closed: 1/1, 11/25, 12/25 & Sun. **Features:** casual dress; children's menu; health conscious menu items; carryout; buffet. Unique dining experience featuring Mongolian stirfry cooking. **Cards:** DS, MC, VI.

MOON'S KITCHEN CAFE　　　**Lunch:** $3-$7　　　　　　　　　　　**Phone:** 208/385-0472
◆
American
Location: City center; between 8th & 9th sts. 815 W Bannock 83702. **Hours:** 7 am-3 pm, Sat from 8 am. Closed major holidays & Sun. **Features:** No A/C; casual dress; carryout; street parking. Old time traditional soda fountain & sandwich shop. Specializing in shakes, malts, sirloin burgers, chicken & sandwiches. Big homestyle breakfast. **Cards:** AE, DS, MC, VI.

MURPHY'S SEAFOOD CHOPHOUSE　　　**Lunch:** $7-$14　　　**Dinner:** $10-$30　　　**Phone:** 208/344-3691
◆◆◆
Steak and
Seafood
Location: 2 mi n of I-84, exit 54 (Broadway Ave). 1555 Broadway Ave 83705. **Hours:** 11 am-10 pm, Fri & Sat-11 pm, Sun 10 am-10 pm. **Reservations:** suggested. **Features:** casual dress; Sunday brunch; children's menu; carryout; cocktails & lounge. Featuring seafood, steak & prime rib in addition to sandwiches, salad & soup. Close to Boise State University & Park Center business area. **Cards:** AE, DI, DS, MC, VI.

NOODLES　　　**Lunch:** $5-$7　　　**Dinner:** $7-$12　　　**Phone:** 208/342-9300
◆◆
Italian
Location: City center; at 8th & Idaho sts. 800 W Idaho St 83702. **Hours:** 11:30 am-9 pm, Fri & Sat-10 pm, Sun 11:30 am-8 pm. Closed: 1/1, 11/25, 12/25 & Super Bowl Sun. **Reservations:** suggested; 8 or more. **Features:** casual dress; children's menu; senior's menu; health conscious menu; carryout; cocktails & lounge; street parking; a la carte. Bustling European style eatery specializing in homemade traditional Italian cuisine. Large wine selection; parking validation. **Cards:** AE, MC, VI.

PEG LEG ANNIE'S　　　**Lunch:** $6-$9　　　**Dinner:** $9-$25　　　**Phone:** 208/375-3050
◆◆
American
Location: 3 mi n of I-84, exit 50 (Cole Rd). 3019 N Cole Rd 83704. **Hours:** 11:30 am-9:30 pm, Fri-10 pm, Sat noon-10 pm, Sun 4 pm-8 pm. Closed major holidays & Sun. **Reservations:** accepted. **Features:** casual dress; children's menu; health conscious menu; carryout; cocktails & lounge; entertainment. Karaoke in lounge. Interesting collectables, greenhouse room & patio dining. Selection of steak, seafood, prime rib & barbecue baby back ribs. **Cards:** AE, DI, DS, MC, VI.

PIPER PUB & GRILL　　　**Lunch:** $6-$13　　　**Dinner:** $6-$13　　　**Phone:** 208/343-2444
◆◆
American
Location: City center; at 8th & Main sts. 150 N 8th St, Suite 200 83702. **Hours:** 10 am-midnight, Sun 9 am-2 pm. Closed: 1/1, 11/25 & 12/25. **Features:** casual dress; carryout; cocktails & lounge; street parking. Large selection of appetizers, sandwiches & salad. **Cards:** AE, DI, DS, MC, VI.

RENAISSANCE RISTORANTE ITALIANO　　　　　　**Dinner:** $9-$21　　　**Phone:** 208/344-6776
◆◆◆
Northern
Italian
Location: City center; at 5th & Main sts. 110 S 5th St 83702. **Hours:** 5:30 pm-10 pm. Closed major holidays & Sun. **Reservations:** required. **Features:** casual dress; health conscious menu items; beer & wine only; street parking; a la carte. Innovative Italian cuisine served in a romantic lower level setting. Smoke free premises. **Cards:** AE, DI, DS, MC, VI.

THE SANDPIPER RESTAURANT　　　**Lunch:** $7-$10　　　**Dinner:** $13-$25　　　**Phone:** 208/344-8911
◆◆
American
Location: City center; at 11th St & Jefferson. 1100 W Jefferson 83702. **Hours:** 11:30 am-2 & 5:30-10 pm, Sun 5 pm-9 pm. Closed major holidays. **Reservations:** suggested. **Features:** casual dress; children's menu; health conscious menu; carryout; cocktails & lounge. Steak & seafood selections with prime rib as house specialty. **Cards:** AE, DI, DS, MC, VI.

BONNERS FERRY—2,200

LODGINGS

BEST WESTERN KOOTENAI RIVER INN　　　　　　　　　　　**Phone:** (208)267-8511

		1P:		2P/1B:		2P/2B:	
6/1-9/30		1P: $90- 100	2P/1B: $90- 100	2P/2B: $95- 105			
5/1-5/31		1P: $80- 90	2P/1B: $80- 90	2P/2B: $85- 95			
3/1-4/30 & 10/1-2/29		1P: $70- 80	2P/1B: $70- 80	2P/2B: $75- 85			

◆◆◆
Motor Inn
Location: City center; on US 95. 7160 Plaza St 83805. Fax: 208/267-3744. **Terms:** Pets. **Facility:** 47 rooms. All rooms & restaurant/lounge view Kootenai River. Bingo & video pultab machine gaming avail. Suite with whirlpool, $225; 2 stories; interior corridors; mountain view; heated indoor pool, sauna, whirlpool. **Dining:** Restaurant; 6 am-9 pm; Fri & Sat-10 pm; Sun brunch; $6-$15; cocktails. **Services:** winter plug-ins. **All Rooms:** extended cable TV. **Cards:** AE, CB, DI, DS, JC, MC, VI. **Special Amenities:** Free local telephone calls.

BONNERS FERRY LOG INN　　　　　　　　　　　　　　**Phone:** 208/267-3986

		1P:		2P/1B:		2P/2B:		XP:		
6/1-9/30 [CP]		1P: $50		2P/1B: $64		2P/2B: $69		XP: $8		F8
3/1-5/31 & 10/1-2/29 [CP]		1P: $47		2P/1B: $55		2P/2B: $61		XP: $8		F8

◆◆◆
Motel
Location: 2.5 mi n on Hwy 95. HCR 85, Box 6 83805. Fax: 208/267-5150. **Facility:** 22 rooms. Modern log building offers homey accommodations with unique hand crafted log furniture. 1 story; exterior corridors; designated smoking area; mountain view; whirlpool. **Services:** giftshop; winter plug-ins. **All Rooms:** shower baths. **Cards:** AE, DS, MC, VI.

BURLEY—8,700

LODGINGS

BEST WESTERN BURLEY INN & CONVENTION CENTER　　　　　**Phone:** (208)678-3501

		1P:		2P/1B:		2P/2B:		XP:		
All Year		1P: $50- 64		2P/1B: $56- 70		2P/2B: $62- 76		XP: $6		F17

◆◆◆
Motor Inn
Location: Just s of I-84, exit 208. 800 N Overland Ave 83318. Fax: 208/678-9532. **Terms:** Pets. **Facility:** 126 rooms. Family oriented shaded courtyard, many poolside rooms. Oversized paved parking area, park at some rooms. 2 stories; interior/exterior corridors; designated smoking area; heated pool, wading pool; outdoor sports court; playground. **Dining:** Restaurant; 6 am-2 am, Sun-midnight; $6-$15; cocktails. **Recreation:** volleyball. **Some Rooms:** whirlpools. **Cards:** AE, CB, DI, DS, MC, VI. **Special Amenities:** Free local telephone calls and free newspaper.

BUDGET MOTEL OF BURLEY   Rates Subject to Change   **Phone:** (208)678-2200
◆◆   All Year   1P: $38- 48   2P/1B: $42- 52   2P/2B: $48- 58   XP: $6   F17
Motel   **Location:** Just s of I-84, exit 208. 900 N Overland Ave 83318. Fax: 208/677-2576. **Facility:** 139 rooms. Attractive exterior & appealing rooms; park at some rooms. Oversize paved parking area. 2 stories; exterior corridors; small pool. **Services:** winter plug-ins. **Cards:** AE, CB, DI, DS, MC, VI.

GREENWELL MOTEL   Rates Subject to Change   **Phone:** 208/678-5576
◆   All Year   1P: $32- 40   2P/1B: $36- 48   2P/2B: $40- 52   XP: $6
Motel   **Location:** I-84, exit 208; 2 mi s, 0.5 mi e. 904 E Main St 83318. Fax: 208/678-7002. **Facility:** 30 rooms. Park at rooms; varied room sizes. 2 two-bedroom units. 4 housekeeping apartments $6 extra, no utensils; 1 story; exterior corridors. **Cards:** AE, CB, DI, DS, MC, VI. IMA.

CALDWELL—18,400

LODGINGS

BEST WESTERN CALDWELL INN & SUITES   Rates Subject to Change   **Phone:** (208)454-7225
◆◆◆   5/1-2/29 [CP]   1P: $62   2P/1B: $67   2P/2B: $76   XP: $5   F12
Motel   3/1-4/30 [CP]   1P: $53   2P/1B: $58   2P/2B: $62   XP: $5   F12
   Location: Just s of I-84 exit 29. 908 Specht Ave 83605. Fax: 208/454-3522. **Facility:** 69 rooms. 3 stories; interior corridors; heated indoor pool. **All Rooms:** combo or shower baths. **Cards:** AE, CB, DI, DS, JC, MC, VI.

COMFORT INN   **Phone:** (208)454-2222
AAA SAVE   6/1-10/15 [CP]   1P: $51   2P/1B: $62   2P/2B: $79   XP: $8   F18
   3/1-5/31 & 10/16-2/29 [CP]   1P: $50   2P/1B: $56   2P/2B: $67   XP: $8   F18
◆◆◆ Motel   **Location:** Just s of I-84, exit 29. 901 Specht 83605. Fax: 208/454-9334. **Terms:** Pets, $10 dep req. **Facility:** 65 rooms. Coffee & cookies in the evening; 24 hr recreation facility. Suites avail, $84-$120; 2 stories; interior corridors; designated smoking area; heated indoor pool, wading pool, sauna, whirlpool. **Dining:** Restaurant nearby. **Services:** giftshop. **Recreation:** sports court, video movie rental. **All Rooms:** combo or shower baths. **Some Rooms:** 3 kitchens, whirlpools. **Cards:** AE, CB, DI, DS, JC, MC, VI. **Special Amenities:** Early check-in/late check-out and free breakfast. *(See color ad below)*

CHUBBUCK—7,800

RESTAURANT

JJ NORTH'S GRAND BUFFET   **Lunch:** $6   **Dinner:** $8   **Phone:** 208/237-6235
◆   **Location:** I-86, exit 61; 0.5 mi s on Yellowstone Rd; at Pine Ridge Mall. 850 W Quinn Rd 83202. **Hours:** 11 am-8:30 pm, Fri-9 pm, Sat 8:30 am-9 pm, Sun 8 am-8 pm. **Features:** casual dress; children's menu; senior's menu; carryout. Homestyle family buffet. Breakfast buffet only Sat & Sun 8:30-11:30 am. Smoke free premises. **Cards:** DS, MC, VI.
American

COEUR D'ALENE—24,600

LODGINGS

AMERITEL INN   Rates Subject to Change   **Phone:** (208)665-9000
◆◆◆   6/1-9/1   1P: $90- 100   2P/1B: $90- 100   2P/2B: $90- 100
Motel   5/1-5/31 & 9/2-9/30   1P: $70- 80   2P/1B: $70- 80   2P/2B: $70- 80
   3/1-4/30   1P: $60- 70   2P/1B: $60- 70   2P/2B: $60- 70
   10/1-2/29   1P: $69   2P/1B: $69   2P/2B: $69
Location: Just s of I-90, exit 12. 333 Ironwood 83814. Fax: 208/665-9900. **Facility:** 118 rooms. 4 stories; interior corridors; heated indoor pool. **All Rooms:** combo or shower baths. **Some Rooms:** 12 kitchens. **Cards:** AE, DI, DS, MC, VI.
(See color ad p 172)

BUDGET HOST PLEASANT INN Phone: (208)765-3011

	6/1-9/6 [CP]	1P:	$55	2P/1B:	$67	2P/2B:	$67	XP: $7	F17
	9/7-10/1 [CP]	1P:	$49	2P/1B:	$59	2P/2B:	$64		
◆	4/1-5/31 [CP]	1P:	$45	2P/1B:	$52	2P/2B:	$57	XP: $7	F17
Motel	3/1-3/31 & 10/2-2/29 [CP]	1P:	$39	2P/1B:	$49	2P/2B:	$54	XP: $7	F17

Location: Just ne of I-90, exit 12. 330 W Appleway 83814. Fax: 208/664-2096. **Terms:** Weekly/monthly rates, 10/1-5/1. **Facility:** 60 rooms. 3 stories, no elevator; interior corridors. **Dining:** Restaurant nearby. **Cards:** AE, DI, DS, MC, VI. *(See color ad p 172)*

COEUR D'ALENE INN & CONFERENCE CENTER Phone: (208)765-3200

	6/1-9/15	1P: $109- 139	2P/1B: $109- 139	2P/2B: $109- 139	XP: $10	F17
	3/1-5/31 & 9/16-10/31	1P: $79- 99	2P/1B: $79- 99	2P/2B: $79- 99	XP: $10	F17
◆◆◆	11/1-2/29	1P: $59- 69	2P/1B: $59- 69	2P/2B: $59- 69	XP: $10	F17

Motor Inn **Location:** Just n of I-90, exit 12. W 414 Appleway 83814. Fax: 208/664-1962. **Terms:** Package plans; pets. **Facility:** 122 rooms. Voice mail system & hairdryer in all rooms. 1 whirlpool suite, $200-$275; courtyard suite, $175-$250; 2 stories; interior corridors; designated smoking area; heated indoor/outdoor pool, indoor whirlpool. **Dining:** Restaurant; 6 am-11 pm; $8-$16; cocktails. **Services:** giftshop; area transportation, Hagadone Facilities; winter plug-ins. **Recreation:** pass for Coeur D'Alene Resort recreational facilities. **Cards:** AE, CB, DI, DS, JC, MC, VI. **Special Amenities:** Free local telephone calls and free newspaper. *(See color ad below)*

THE COEUR D'ALENE RESORT Rates Subject to Change Phone: 208/765-4000

◆◆◆◆	5/17-9/30	1P: $139- 399	2P/1B: $139- 399	2P/2B: $139- 399	XP: $10	F17
	4/1-5/16 & 10/1-10/31	1P: $99- 350	2P/1B: $99- 350	2P/2B: $99- 350	XP: $10	F17
Resort	3/1-3/31 & 11/1-2/29	1P: $69- 250	2P/1B: $69- 250	2P/2B: $69- 250	XP: $10	F17

Location: 2 mi s of I-90, exit 11. 115 S 2nd Ave 83816-1941 (PO Box 7200, 83816). Fax: 208/664-7220. **Terms:** Check-in 4 pm; reserv deposit, 7 day notice; handling fee imposed. **Facility:** 338 rooms. Resort lakefront hotel with accommodations ranging from standards to suites. Enjoyable floating boardwalk around marina & 30 store shopping plaza. Famous golf course with floating green. Executive suites from $600; 1-17 stories; interior/exterior corridors; designated smoking area; heated indoor pool; boat dock, boat ramp, marina. Fee: parking; racquetball court, 4 lighted tennis courts. **Services:** giftshop. Fee: massage, area transportation. **Recreation:** swimming, charter fishing, fishing. Rental: boats; bicycles. **All Rooms:** combo or shower baths. **Cards:** AE, CB, DI, DS, MC, VI.

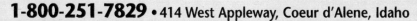

Checkout time is noted in the listing if the required time is before 10 a.m.

COMFORT INN
Phone: (208)765-5500

(AAA) (SAVE)

5/1-9/15 [CP] | 1P: $89- 119 | 2P/1B: $89- 119 | 2P/2B: $89- 119 | XP: $10 | F18
3/1-4/30 & 9/16-2/29 [CP] | 1P: $49- 99 | 2P/1B: $49- 99 | 2P/2B: $49- 99 | XP: $10 | F18

◆◆◆ **Location:** Just ne of I-90, exit 12. 280 W Appleway 83814. Fax: 208/664-0433. **Terms:** Pets. **Facility:** 51
Motel rooms. Good freeway access. Some theme rooms. 7 whirlpool & exec theme suites, $99-$169; 3 stories, no
elevator; interior corridors; heated indoor pool, sauna, whirlpool; playground. **Dining:** Complimentary evening
snacks; restaurant nearby. **Services:** giftshop; winter plug-ins. **All Rooms:** combo or shower baths. **Some Rooms:** 21
efficiencies, kitchen. **Cards:** AE, CB, DI, DS, JC, MC, VI. **Special Amenities: Free local telephone calls and free room
upgrade (subject to availability with advanced reservations).** *(See color ad p 181)*

🔟 📠 🏠 📞 💺 🍴 🛗 🍽 🐾 🦌 💻 🖥 🖨 📇 🚪 ✕

DAYS INN-COEUR D'ALENE Rates Subject to Change
Phone: 208/667-8668

◆◆

5/15-9/30 [CP] | 1P: $75 | 2P/1B: $80 | 2P/2B: $80 | XP: $5 | F18
Motel 10/1-12/31 [CP] | 1P: $55 | 2P/1B: $60 | 2P/2B: $60 | XP: $5 | F18
3/1-5/14 & 1/1-2/29 [CP] | 1P: $45 | 2P/1B: $55 | 2P/2B: $55 | XP: $5 | F18

Location: Just se of I-90, exit 11. 2200 NW Blvd 83814. Fax: 208/765-0933. **Facility:** 61 rooms. Business park location; easy
freeway access. 2 stories; interior corridors; smoke free premises. **All Rooms:** combo or shower baths. **Cards:** AE, CB, DI,
DS, JC, MC, VI.

(SAVE) 📠 🏠 📞 (VCR) 💻 🖨 📇 🚪 🍴 🐾 ✕ 🔟

FAIRFIELD INN Rates Subject to Change
Phone: 208/664-1649

◆◆◆

6/12-10/1 [CP] | 1P: $61 | 2P/1B: $68 | 2P/2B: $68 | XP: $7 | F18
Motel 4/1-6/11 [CP] | 1P: $50 | 2P/1B: $50 | 2P/2B: $50 | XP: $7 | F18
3/1-3/31 & 10/2-2/29 [CP] | 1P: $46 | 2P/1B: $46 | 2P/2B: $46 | XP: $7 | F18

Location: Just n of I-90, exit 13. 2303 N 4th 83814. Fax: 208/664-1649. **Terms:** Check-in 4 pm. **Facility:** 69 rooms. Easy
freeway access. Close to shopping & restaurants. 3 stories; interior corridors; small heated indoor pool. **All Rooms:** combo
or shower baths. **Cards:** AE, CB, DI, DS, JC, MC, VI.

🔢 💺 🍴 🏠 🛗 🍽 🖥 🖨 📇 ✕

FLAMINGO MOTEL
Phone: (208)664-2159

(AAA) (SAVE)

5/25-9/16 | 1P: $69- 76 | 2P/1B: $72- 76 | 2P/2B: $78- 95 | XP: $5 | F5
4/1-5/24 & 9/17-10/15 | 1P: $59- 66 | 2P/1B: $62- 66 | 2P/2B: $68- 80 | XP: $5 | F5
3/1-3/31 & 10/16-2/29 | 1P: $42- 47 | 2P/1B: $45- 47 | 2P/2B: $49- 65 | XP: $5 | F5

◆ **Location:** 1.1 mi s of I-90, exit 15 (Sherman Ave). 718 Sherman Ave 83814. **Terms:** Reserv deposit, 3 day
Motel notice; small pets only, $10 extra charge, $25 dep req, no cats. **Facility:** 13 rooms. Theme rooms; park at
room; close to downtown & lake. 2 two-bedroom units. Kitchen unit, $56.50-$125.50; efficiency unit, $49.50-$82.50; 1 story;
exterior corridors; smoke free premises; heated pool, whirlpool. **Dining:** Restaurant nearby. **Services:** winter plug-ins.
Recreation: adjacent to city park with basketball courts, playground & tennis courts. **Cards:** AE, CB, DI, DS, MC, VI.
Special Amenities: Free local telephone calls.

🔟 📠 🏠 💺 🍴 🍽 🦌 💻 🖥 ✕

GREGORY'S MCFARLAND HOUSE BED & BREAKFAST Guaranteed Rates
Phone: 208/667-1232

◆◆◆

5/1-10/14 & 11/15-1/3 [BP] | 1P: $110- 135 | 2P/1B: $110- 135 | 2P/2B: $110- 135 | XP: $25-35
Historic Bed 3/1-4/30, 10/15-11/14 &
& Breakfast 1/4-2/29 [BP] | 1P: $90- 125 | 2P/1B: $90- 125 | 2P/2B: $90- 125 | XP: $25-35

Location: I-90, exit 13; 1.3 mi s on 3rd St, just e. 601 Foster Ave 83814. **Terms:** Age restrictions may apply;
reserv deposit, 14 day notice; handling fee imposed; 2 night min stay, in season & weekends. **Facility:** 5 rooms. Charming
turn-of-the-century mansion located in quiet, tree-lined residential neighborhood. 2 stories; interior corridors; smoke free premises; street parking only. **Cards:** DS, MC, VI. *(See ad below)*

(PYI) (Z) 🖨

HOLIDAY INN EXPRESS
Phone: (208)667-6777

(AAA) (SAVE)

6/16-10/15 [CP] | 1P: $99- 109 | 2P/1B: $99- 109 | 2P/2B: $99- 119 | XP: $10 | F19
5/1-6/15 [CP] | 1P: $70- 90 | 2P/1B: $70- 90 | 2P/2B: $70- 100 | XP: $10 | F19
◆◆◆ 3/1-4/30 & 10/16-2/29 [CP] | 1P: $59- 70 | 2P/1B: $59- 70 | 2P/2B: $59- 80 | XP: $10 | F19

Motel **Location:** Just s of I-90, exit 15. 2209 E Sherman Ave 83814. Fax: 208/769-7332. **Terms:** Package plans;
small pets only. **Facility:** 62 rooms. Easy freeway access. Homemade cookies in evening. Spa suites, $159;
kitchen suites, $75-$109; 3 stories, no elevator; interior corridors; heated indoor pool, sauna, whirlpool. **Dining:** Cafeteria
nearby. **Services:** giftshop. **All Rooms:** combo or shower baths. **Some Rooms:** 9 efficiencies, 3 kitchens, whirlpools.
Cards: AE, DI, DS, MC, VI. **Special Amenities: Free breakfast and free local telephone calls.** *(See color ad p 183)*

📠 💺 🔢 🏠 🍴 🍽 🦌 (VCR) 💻 🖥 🖨 📇 🍴 🐾 ✕

Gregory's McFarland House
The Ultimate Award Winning
BED & BREAKFAST

"English charm, old-fashioned warmth
& quiet ambience of another era."

Acclaimed by the L.A. Times, Country Inns, Honeymoon Magazine, Doris Kennedy's
Recommended Country Inns. Chosen as the 1989 recipient of the Special Heritage
Preservation Award by Cranbrook Archives, Museum and Landmark Foundation
for preservation and restoration of this Circa 1905 Historic home.

Private Baths • Air Conditioning
For Reservations Only 1-800-335-1232, ext. 5

RODEWAY INN PINES RESORT MOTEL
Phone: (208)664-8244
AAA **SAVE** 6/15-9/14 [CP]   1P: $53- 79   2P/1B: $59- 89 2P/2B: $79- 89 XP: $6   F16
◆◆   3/1-6/14 & 9/15-10/31 [CP] 1P: $49- 69   2P/1B: $52- 69 2P/2B: $69- 79 XP: $6   F16
Motor Inn   11/1-2/29 [CP]   1P: $39- 65   2P/1B: $42- 65 2P/2B: $51- 62 XP: $6   F16
Location: 0.8 mi s of I-90, exit 11. 1422 North West Blvd 83814. Fax: 208/664-5547. **Terms:** Reserv deposit; BP, CP avail; small pets only, in smoking rooms only. **Facility:** 65 rooms. Set on 5 acres with huge pine trees. Varied room styles & sizes; Most rooms with balcony & parking at door. Boat parking & bicycle storage avail. Breakfast coupon for adults. 7 two-bedroom units. 1 whirlpool suite, $149. Refrigerator avail upon request; 2 stories; exterior corridors; heated indoor pool, whirlpool. **Dining:** Coffee shop nearby. **Services:** winter plug-ins. **Cards:** AE, CB, DI, DS, JC, MC, VI. **Special Amenities: Free local telephone calls and free room upgrade (subject to availability with advanced reservations).**

SHILO INN
Rates Subject to Change   Phone: (208)664-2300
◆◆◆   All Year [CP]   1P: $79- 159 2P/1B: $79- 159 2P/2B: $79- 159 XP: $12   F12
Motel   **Location:** Just n of I-90 exit 12, just w. 702 W Appleway 83814-9338. Fax: 208/667-2863. **Terms:** Check-in 4 pm. **Facility:** 139 rooms. 24 hr recreational facilities. 4 efficiency units, $109-$145; 4 stories; interior corridors; heated indoor pool. **All Rooms:** combo or shower baths. **Some Rooms:** kitchen. **Cards:** AE, CB, DI, DS, JC, MC, VI.
(See ad below)

SILVER LAKE MOTEL
Rates Subject to Change   Phone: (208)772-8595
◆◆   7/1-8/31 [CP]   1P: $79- 89   2P/1B: $79- 89 2P/2B: $79- 89 XP: $5   F12
Motel   5/1-6/30 & 9/1-9/30 [CP] 1P: $59- 79   2P/1B: $59- 79 2P/2B: $79- 89 XP: $5   F12
          3/1-4/30, 5/1-5/31 &
          10/1-2/29 [CP]   1P: $46- 53   2P/1B: $49- 57 2P/2B: $49- 57 XP: $5   F12
Location: 2.2 mi n of I-90, exit 12. 6160 Sunshine St 83815. Fax: 208/772-2368. **Terms:** Check-in 4 pm. **Facility:** 49 rooms. Parking at many doors, many large rooms; close to shopping. Whirlpool suites, $95-$150; 2 stories; exterior corridors; heated pool. **Services:** winter plug-ins. **All Rooms:** combo or shower baths. **Some Rooms:** 12 kitchens. **Cards:** AE, DI, DS, MC, VI.

SUPER 8 MOTEL
Rates Subject to Change   Phone: 208/765-8880
◆◆   5/22-9/30   1P: $56   2P/1B: $70   2P/2B: $76   XP: $5   F12
Motel   4/1-5/21   1P: $45   2P/1B: $53   2P/2B: $58   XP: $5   F12
          3/1-3/31 & 10/1-2/29 1P: $36   2P/1B: $43   2P/2B: $47   XP: $5   F12
Location: Just n of I-90, exit 12. 505 W Appleway 83814. Fax: 208/765-8880. **Terms:** Weekend rates avail. **Facility:** 95 rooms. Easy access to freeway; close to shopping & restaurants. 3 stories, no elevator; interior corridors. **Services:** winter plug-ins. **Cards:** AE, CB, DI, DS, MC, VI.

RESTAURANTS

BEACHOUSE　　　　　**Lunch:** $5-$9　　　　　　**Dinner:** $11-$24　　　　　　**Phone:** 208/644-6464
◆◆
American
Location: I-90, exit 15; just s, then 1.1 mi e. 3204 E Coeur D'Alene Lake Dr 83814. **Hours:** 5 pm-10 pm, Fri & Sat 11:30 am-3 & 5-11 pm, Sun 11:30 am-3 & 5-10 pm; Wed & Thurs 5 pm-9 pm, Fri & Sat 5 pm-10 pm, 11/1-3/31. Closed: 1/1, 12/24 & 12/25. **Reservations:** suggested. **Features:** casual dress; children's menu; cocktails & lounge. Overlooking marina & lake featuring seafood, steak & barbecue. **Cards:** AE, CB, DI, DS, MC, VI.　☒

BEVERLY'S　　　　　**Lunch:** $8-$13　　　　　　**Dinner:** $15-$27　　　　　　**Phone:** 208/765-4000
◆◆◆◆
Continental
Location: 2 mi s of I-90, exit 11; in The Coeur d'Alene Resort. 115 S 2nd St 83816-1941. **Hours:** 11 am-2:30 & 5-10 pm. **Reservations:** accepted. **Features:** casual dress; health conscious menu items; cocktails & lounge; entertainment; valet parking; a la carte. Casully elegant dining with panoramic view of lake from the 7th floor. Menu changes seasonally; featuring wild game, beef, veal, chicken & seafood. Exceptional award winning wine cellar. Appropriate attire. **Cards:** AE, CB, DI, DS, MC, VI.　☒

CAPERS MEDITERANEAN MARKET & BISTRO　　　**Lunch:** $5-$8　　　　**Dinner:** $9-$15　　　**Phone:** 208/664-9036
◆◆
Continental
Location: I-90, exit 13; 0.7 mi s on 3rd St. 315 Walnut 83814. **Hours:** 11 am-9 pm, Sun brunch 9 am-2 pm. Closed: 11/25, 12/25 & Mon. **Reservations:** suggested; evenings. **Features:** casual dress; Sunday brunch; children's menu; beer & wine only. A close intimate dining experience with seasonal dishes from the Mediterranean regions of the world having mix & match salad selections. Smoke free premises. **Cards:** MC, VI.　☒

CEDARS FLOATING RESTAURANT　　　　　　　　**Dinner:** $15-$23　　　　　　**Phone:** 208/664-2922
◆◆
American
MC, VI.
Location: I-90, exit 12; 1.5 mi s on US 95. No 1 Marina Dr 83814. **Hours:** 5:30 pm-10 pm, Sun 5 pm-9 pm. Closed: 11/25, 12/24 & 12/25. **Reservations:** required. **Features:** casual dress; carryout; salad bar; cocktails & lounge. Floating restaurant on Lake Coeur D'Alene featuring steak & fresh seafood. **Cards:** AE, DI, DS, 　☒

3RD STREET CANTINA　　　　　**Lunch:** $4-$8　　　　　　**Dinner:** $5-$12　　　　　　**Phone:** 208/664-0581
◆◆
Mexican
Location: 2 mi s of I-90, exit 11; just e on Lakeside. 201 N 3rd 83814. **Hours:** 11 am-9 pm. Closed: 11/25 & 12/25. **Features:** casual dress; children's menu; cocktails & lounge; a la carte. Festive atmosphere with creative menu featuring traditional & unique Mexican dishes. **Cards:** AE, DI, DS, MC, VI.　☒

TOMATO STREET　　　　　**Lunch:** $5-$7　　　　　　**Dinner:** $8-$12　　　　　　**Phone:** 208/667-5000
◆◆
Italian
Location: I-90, exit 13; then just n & w. W 221 Appleway 83814. **Hours:** 11:30 am-11 pm; Sun-Thurs to 10 pm. Closed: 11/25 & 12/25. **Features:** casual dress; children's menu; health conscious menu items; carryout; beer & wine only; a la carte. Family oriented Italian market style eatery featuring brick oven pizza, calzone, salad, sandwiches & traditional items. Smoke free premises. **Cards:** AE, MC, VI.　☒

COOLIN—200

LODGING

OLD NORTHERN INN　　　　　　　　　　　　　　　　　　　　　　　**Phone:** (208)443-2426
ⒶⒶⒶ Ⓢ̲Ⓐ̲Ⓥ̲Ⓔ̲
◆◆◆
Historic Bed
& Breakfast
　　　5/25-10/15　　　　　　1P: $80- 130　2P/1B:　$80- 130　　　　　　XP: $20
Location: Downtown. Sherwood Beach Rd 83821 (PO Box 177). Fax: 208/443-3856. **Terms:** Open 5/25-10/15; age restrictions may apply; reserv deposit, 7 day notice. **Facility:** 6 rooms. Warmth & nostalgic charm in this 1890 lakeside retreat built by the Great Northern Railway with a large deck overlooking Priest Lake & surrounding forests. 2 stories; interior corridors; smoke free premises; mountain view; marina. **Dining:** Restaurant nearby. **Services:** complimentary evening beverages, appetizers. **Recreation:** swimming, fishing. **All Rooms:** combo or shower baths. **Cards:** MC, VI. **Special Amenities:** Early check-in/late check-out and free local telephone calls.　⧉ ☒ 🄿🄿 🅉 🄺 ☒

DRIGGS—800—See also GRAND TETON NATIONAL PARK.

LODGINGS

BEST WESTERN TETON WEST MOTEL　　　　Rates Subject to Change　　　　**Phone:** (208)354-2363
ⒶⒶⒶ
◆◆
Motel
　　　All Year [CP]　　　　1P: $46　　2P/1B:　$60　　2P/2B:　$65　　XP:　$6　　F12
Location: 0.7 mi n on SR 33. 476 S Main St 83422 (PO Box 780). Fax: 208/354-2962. **Terms:** Small pets only, $25 dep req. **Facility:** 40 rooms. Quiet location with spectacular view of Teton Mountains with varied room sizes. 2 kitchen units, $100; 2 stories; interior corridors; designated smoking area; small heated indoor pool, whirlpool. **Services:** winter plug-ins. **Some Rooms:** whirlpools. **Cards:** AE, CB, DI, DS, MC, VI.
🛏 🐾 🚤 🔌 🄐 🄹 ▣ ⬜ 🄱 🄳 ☒

INTERMOUNTAIN LODGE　　　　　　　　　　　　　　　　　　　　**Phone:** (208)354-8153
ⒶⒶⒶ Ⓢ̲Ⓐ̲Ⓥ̲Ⓔ̲
◆◆
Cottage
　　　3/1-4/15, 6/15-9/15 &
　　　11/15-2/29　　　　　1P: $59　　2P/1B:　$59　　2P/2B:　$59　　XP:　$5
　　　4/16-6/14 & 9/16-11/14　1P: $49　　2P/1B:　$49　　2P/2B:　$49　　XP:　$5
Location: 0.8 mi e on on Little Ave from SR 33 E. 34 Ski Hill Rd 83422 (PO Box 468). **Terms:** Reserv deposit. **Facility:** 14 rooms. Quaint, attractive cabins hidden in trees, some with bunk beds. 1 story; exterior corridors; designated smoking area; whirlpool. **Services:** winter plug-ins. **All Rooms:** efficiencies, utensils extra charge, shower baths. **Cards:** AE, DS, MC, VI. **Special Amenities:** Free local telephone calls.　🄐 🄿🄿 Ⓥ̲Ⓒ̲Ⓡ̲ 🄺 🄱 ☒

SUPER 8 TETON WEST　　　　　　　　　　　　　　　　　　　　**Phone:** (208)354-8888
ⒶⒶⒶ Ⓢ̲Ⓐ̲Ⓥ̲Ⓔ̲
◆◆
Motel
　　　7/1-9/8 & 12/19-1/5 [CP]　1P: $70　　2P/1B:　$70　　2P/2B:　$70　　XP:　$8
　　　3/1-6/30, 9/9-12/18 &
　　　1/6-2/29 [CP]　　　　1P: $42　　2P/1B:　$50　　2P/2B:　$50　　XP:　$8
Location: 1.3 mi n. 133 N SR 33 83422 (PO Box 780). Fax: 208/354-2962. **Terms:** Handling fee imposed. **Facility:** 22 rooms. Quiet location with magnificent view of Teton Mountains. Large rooms & good decor. 2 stories; interior corridors; designated smoking area; whirlpool. **Services:** winter plug-ins. **Cards:** AE, CB, DI, DS, MC, VI. **Special Amenities:** Free breakfast and free local telephone calls.　🔌 🄐 🄿🄿 🎿 Ⓥ̲Ⓒ̲Ⓡ̲ ⬜ 🄱 ☒

GRANGEVILLE—3,200

LODGINGS

DOWN TOWNER INN   Guaranteed Rates   **Phone:** 208/983-1110
All Year   1P: $32- 36 2P/1B: $36- 40 2P/2B: $39- 42 XP: $2-5   F12
Location: 0.8 mi e on SR 13 from jct at US 95, just n on Hall St. 113 E North St 83530. **Facility:** 16 rooms. Large contemporary rooms. 1 story; exterior corridors; designated smoking area. **Dining:** Restaurant nearby.
Services: winter plug-ins. **Cards:** AE, DS, MC, VI.

MONTY'S MOTEL   Rates Subject to Change   **Phone:** 208/983-2500
All Year   1P: $35- 40 2P/1B: $39- 42 2P/2B: $44- 50 XP: $5
Location: Jct SR 13 & US 95. W 700 Main 83530. Fax: 208/983-1458. **Facility:** 24 rooms. 2 stories; exterior corridors; designated smoking area; small heated pool. **All Rooms:** combo or shower baths. **Cards:** AE, CB, DI, DS, MC, VI.

HAGERMAN—600

LODGING

HAGERMAN VALLEY INN   **Phone:** (208)837-6196
All Year   1P: $38- 43 2P/1B: $38- 43 2P/2B: $38- 43 XP: $5   F
Location: S end of town on US 30. 661 Frog's Landing 83332 (PO Box 480). **Terms:** Reserv deposit; pets, $5 extra charge. **Facility:** 16 rooms. 2 stories; interior/exterior corridors. **Dining:** Restaurant nearby. **Cards:** MC, VI. **Special Amenities:** Early check-in/late check-out and free local telephone calls.

HAILEY—3,700

LODGING

AIRPORT INN   Rates Subject to Change   **Phone:** (208)788-2477
All Year   1P: $60- 75 2P/1B: $68- 75 2P/2B: $68- 75 XP: $8   F12
Location: Just n of Hwy 75 at 4th Ave, near airport. 820 4th Ave S 83333 (PO Box 984). Fax: 208/788-3195. **Terms:** Pets, $5 extra charge, in smoking rooms only. **Facility:** 29 rooms. Adjacent to Wood River Trail System. Suite, $75 for up to 2 persons; 1-2 stories; exterior corridors; designated smoking area; whirlpool. **Services:** winter plug-ins. **Some Rooms:** 4 efficiencies. **Cards:** AE, CB, DI, DS, MC, VI.

IDAHO CITY—300

LODGING

A ONE STEP AWAY B&B LODGING   Rates Subject to Change   **Phone:** 208/392-4938
All Year [BP]   1P: $55   2P/1B: $75
Location: Center, just w of SR 21. 112 Cottonwood St 83631 (PO Box 55). Fax: 208/392-4938. **Terms:** Age restrictions may apply; reserv deposit, 30 day notice. **Facility:** 4 rooms. Converted 102 year old Idaho Canadian Dredging Company "line shack & barn" located in small mountain community with cozy rooms & private baths; antique shop. 1-2 stories; exterior corridors; smoke free premises. **Recreation:** fishing; cross country skiing, snowmobiling; hiking trails, jogging. **All Rooms:** combo or shower baths. **Cards:** DI, MC, VI.

IDAHO FALLS—43,900

LODGINGS

AMERITEL INN   Rates Subject to Change   **Phone:** (208)523-1400
6/1-9/15 [CP]   1P: $120   2P/1B: $120   2P/2B: $120   XP: $8   F12
3/1-5/31 & 9/16-2/29 [CP]   1P: $110   2P/1B: $110   2P/2B: $110   XP: $8   F12
Location: I-15, exit 118; 0.4 mi e on Broadway, just n on Lindsay Blvd; from I-15 exit 119, 0.4 mi se. 645 Lindsay Blvd 83402. Fax: 208/523-0004. **Facility:** 126 rooms. Oversize rooms complimented with 3 phones & 25 inch TV; across street from greenbelt walkway along Snake River. 2 rooms with double whirlpool & fireplace. 4 stories; interior corridors; designated smoking area; heated indoor pool. **All Rooms:** combo or shower baths. **Some Rooms:** 14 kitchens. **Cards:** AE, DI, DS, JC, MC, VI. *(See color ad p 172)*

BEST WESTERN COTTONTREE INN   **Phone:** (208)523-6000
6/1-9/30 [CP]   1P: $86- 106 2P/1B: $86- 106 2P/2B: $86- 106 XP: $8   F12
3/1-5/31 & 1/1-2/29 [CP]   1P: $78- 98 2P/1B: $78- 98 2P/2B: $78- 98 XP: $8   F12
10/1-12/31 [CP]   1P: $78- 98 2P/1B: $78- 98 2P/2B: $78- 98 XP: $8   F12
Location: I-15, exit 119; just e. 900 Lindsay Blvd 83402. Fax: 208/523-0000. **Terms:** Pets, $30 dep req. **Facility:** 94 rooms. 3 stories; interior corridors; designated smoking area; heated indoor pool, whirlpool. **Dining:** Restaurant nearby. **Services:** winter plug-ins. **Some Rooms:** 6 kitchens, whirlpools. **Cards:** AE, CB, DI, DS, MC, VI. **Special Amenities:** Free breakfast and free local telephone calls.

BEST WESTERN DRIFTWOOD MOTEL   **Phone:** (208)523-2242
6/1-8/31   1P: $55- 85 2P/1B: $59- 89 2P/2B: $59- 95 XP: $8
9/1-9/30   1P: $49- 69 2P/1B: $49- 75 2P/2B: $49- 79 XP: $8
3/1-5/31 & 10/1-2/29   1P: $49- 65 2P/1B: $49- 65 2P/2B: $49- 65 XP: $8
Location: I-15, exit 118; 0.5 mi e on Broadway, 0.3 mi n. 575 River Pkwy 83402. Fax: 208/523-0316. **Terms:** Weekly/monthly rates; small pets only, $3-$10, extra charge. **Facility:** 74 rooms. Some rooms overlooking Snake River & falls. 11 kitchen units, $10-$20 extra charge; 2 stories; exterior corridors; designated smoking area; small heated pool. **Dining:** Restaurant nearby. **Recreation:** bicycles. **All Rooms:** combo or shower baths. **Some Rooms:** whirlpools. **Cards:** AE, CB, DI, DS, MC, VI. **Special Amenities:** Free local telephone calls and free room upgrade (subject to availability with advanced reservations). *(See color ad p 186)*

BEST WESTERN STARDUST

Phone: (208)522-2910

7/1-8/31 [BP]	1P:	$65-	85	2P/1B:	$65-	85	2P/2B:	$85-	95	XP: $10	F1*
5/1-6/30 [BP]	1P:	$55-	75	2P/1B:	$55-	75	2P/2B:	$65-	85	XP: $10	F1*
3/1-4/30 & 9/1-2/29 [BP]	1P:	$47-	57	2P/1B:	$47-	57	2P/2B:	$47-	57	XP: $10	F1*

Motor Inn

Location: I-15, exit 119 (Broadway); just e. 700 Lindsay Blvd 83402 (PO Box 51420). Fax: 208/529-8361. **Terms:** Weekly/monthly rates; pets. **Facility:** 248 rooms. Some rooms overlook Snake River. 2 stories; interior/exterior corridors; designated smoking area; small heated pool, sauna, whirlpool. **Dining:** Dining room, coffee shop 6:30 am-10 pm; $7-$15; cocktails. **Services:** winter plug-ins. **Cards:** AE, CB, DI, DS, MC, VI. **Special Amenities:** Free breakfast and free newspaper. *(See color ad below)*

CAVANAUGHS ON THE FALLS
◆◆◆ All Year
Motor Inn
Rates Subject to Change
Location: I-15, exit 118; 0.5 mi e on Broadway, then just n. 475 River Pkwy 83402. Fax: 208/529-9610.
Facility: 142 rooms. Adjacent to Snake River with some rooms with view of falls. 2-8 stories; interior/exterior corridors; designated smoking area; heated pool. **Cards:** AE, CB, DI, DS, JC, MC, VI.
1P: $85- 105 2P/1B: $85- 105 2P/2B: $85- 105 XP: $6
Phone: 208/523-8000

HAMPTON INN
◆◆◆ All Year [CP]
Motel
Rates Subject to Change
Location: I-15, exit 118; 0.9 mi e on Broadway, 0.5 mi s on Yellowstone, 2.7 mi e on 17th, just s. 2500 Channing Way 83404. Fax: 208/529-9455. **Facility:** 63 rooms. Adjacent to Grand Teton Mall & close to hospital. 3 stories; interior corridors; designated smoking area; small heated indoor pool. **Cards:** AE, CB, DI, DS, JC, MC, VI.
1P: $64- 95 2P/1B: $69- 99 2P/2B: $69- 99
Phone: (208)529-9800

SHILO CONFERENCE HOTEL
◆◆◆ All Year [BP]
Motor Inn
Rates Subject to Change
Location: I-15, exit 119; just se. 780 Lindsay Blvd 83402-1822. Fax: 208/522-7420. **Facility:** 161 rooms. Many rooms overlooking scenic Snake River; all rooms with hairdryer. 4 stories; interior corridors; designated smoking area; heated indoor pool. **Cards:** AE, CB, DI, DS, JC, MC, VI. *(See ad p 201, below & p 178)*
1P: $79- 129 2P/1B: $79- 129 2P/2B: $79- 129 XP: $10 F12
Phone: (208)523-0088

TOWNE LODGE
AAA SAVE 5/15-9/10
3/1-5/14 & 9/11-2/29
◆ Location: I-15, exit 118; 0.6 mi e on Broadway, just n on Memorial, just e. 255 E St 83402.
Motel Fax: 208/523-2960. **Terms:** Weekly rates. **Facility:** 40 rooms. 2 stories; interior/exterior corridors; designated smoking area. **Services:** winter plug-ins. **All Rooms:** combo or shower baths. **Cards:** AE, DS, MC, VI.
Special Amenities: Early check-in/late check-out and free local telephone calls.
1P: $40- 44 2P/1B: $47- 52 2P/2B: $49- 59 XP: $4
1P: $31- 36 2P/1B: $38- 44 2P/2B: $42- 47 XP: $4
Phone: (208)523-2960

RESTAURANTS

BROWNSTONE RESTAURANT **Lunch:** $8-$18 **Dinner:** $8-$18 **Phone:** 208/535-0310
◆◆ Location: I-15, exit 118 (Broadway); 0.5 mi e to River Pkwy, then just n. 455 River Pkwy 83402. **Hours:** 11
American am-10:30 pm. Closed: Sun. **Features:** No A/C; casual dress; cocktails & lounge; a la carte. Attractive setting overlooking falls. Friendly informal service. Polished steel & copper brewing tanks part of the decor. Brewery tours avail. Smoke free premises. **Cards:** AE, DI, DS, MC, VI.

JJ NORTH'S GRAND BUFFET **Lunch:** $6 **Dinner:** $8 **Phone:** 208/529-0181
◆ Location: I-15, exit 118; 0.9 mi e on Broadway, 0.5 mi s on Yellowstone, 3 mi e on 17th; ne corner of Grand
American Teton Mall parking lot. 2450 E 17th St 83404. **Hours:** 11 am-8:30 pm, Fri-9 pm, Sat 8:30 am-9 pm, Sun 8:30 am-8 pm. **Features:** casual dress; children's menu; senior's menu; salad bar. Family style all American buffet. Smoke free premises. **Cards:** DS, MC, VI.

MELINA'S MEXICAN RESTAURANT **Lunch:** $4-$9 **Dinner:** $4-$9 **Phone:** 208/524-5430
◆ Location: I-15, exit 118; 0.8 mi e on Yellowstone, 0.5 mi n on Memorial, just e. 187 E First St 83401.
Mexican **Hours:** 11 am-9 pm, Fri & Sat-10 pm, Sun 11 am-8 pm. Closed major holidays. **Features:** casual dress; children's menu; carryout; beer & wine only. Traditional Mexican food served in a festive family atmosphere. Smoke free premises. **Cards:** AE, DI, MC, VI.

THE SANDPIPER **Lunch:** $7-$10 **Dinner:** $11-$23 **Phone:** 208/524-3344
◆◆ Location: Just e of I-15, exit 119. 750 Lindsay Blvd 83402. **Hours:** 11 am-2 & 5-10 pm, Sun 4 pm-9 pm.
Steak and Closed: 11/25 & 12/25. **Reservations:** accepted. **Features:** casual dress; children's menu; cocktails & Seafood lounge; a la carte. Adjacent to Snake River with seasonal patio dining. **Cards:** AE, DI, DS, MC, VI.

SNAKE BITE RESTAURANT **Lunch:** $5-$9 **Dinner:** $5-$16 **Phone:** 208/525-2522
◆◆ Location: I-15, exit 118 (Broadway); 0.5 mi e to River Pkwy, just n. 425 River Pkwy 83402. **Hours:** winter,
American 11 am-9 pm; summer, 11 am-10 pm, Sat 11:30 am-10 pm, Mon 11 am-2 pm. Closed: Sun & Mon for dinner. **Features:** casual dress; carryout; beer & wine only; a la carte. Contemporary decor. Large selection of sandwiches soups & some entrees. Friendly service. Counter service avail. Very good ingredients; not "Fast Food". Smoke free premises. **Cards:** DS, MC, VI.

JEROME—6,500

LODGINGS

BEST WESTERN SAWTOOTH INN AND SUITES   Phone: (208)324-9200
(AAA) (SAVE)   6/1-10/31   1P: $59- 89   2P/1B: $59- 89 2P/2B: $59- 89
             3/1-5/31 & 11/1-2/29   1P: $54- 79   2P/1B: $54- 79 2P/2B: $54- 79
◆◆◆   **Location:** I-84 exit 168 just n on SR 79. 3057 S Lincoln 83338. Fax: 208/324-9292. **Terms:** Pets. **Facility:** 57
Motel   rooms. 2 stories; interior corridors; heated indoor pool, whirlpool. **Dining:** Restaurant nearby
        Some Rooms: whirlpools. **Cards:** AE, CB, DI, DS, JC, MC, VI. **Special Amenities:** Free breakfast and
free newspaper.

SLEEP INN   Rates Subject to Change   Phone: (208)324-6400
◆◆   All Year [CP]   1P: $49- 90   2P/1B: $54- 95 2P/2B: $54- 95 XP: $5   F18
Motel   **Location:** I-84 exit 173, just n on US 93. 1200 Centennial Spur 83338. Fax: 208/324-6400. **Facility:** 74 rooms.
        3 stories; interior corridors. **All Rooms:** combo or shower baths. **Cards:** AE, DI, DS, MC, VI.

KAMIAH—1,200

LODGING

LEWIS CLARK RESORT & MOTEL   Rates Subject to Change   Phone: (208)935-2556
◆◆   All Year [CP]   1P: $32   2P/1B: $37   2P/2B: $41   XP: $5   F3
Motor Inn   **Location:** 1.5 mi e on US 12. 83536 (Rt 1, Box 17). Fax: 208/935-0366. **Terms:** Reserv deposit. **Facility:** 21
        rooms. Log motel with large modern rooms; coupon given out that can be applied on breakfast of choice. 2
stories; exterior corridors; designated smoking area; small heated pool. **Services:** giftshop. **All Rooms:** combo or shower
baths. **Cards:** AE, DS, MC, VI.

KELLOGG—2,600

LODGINGS

SILVERHORN MOTOR INN   Rates Subject to Change   Phone: (208)783-1151
(AAA)   All Year   1P: $51   2P/1B: $56   2P/2B: $61   XP: $4   F12
        Location: Just ne of I-90, exit 49. 699 W Cameron Ave 83837. Fax: 208/784-5081. **Terms:** Reserv deposit
◆◆   pets. **Facility:** 40 rooms. Easy freeway access. 2 stories; interior corridors; mountain view; whirlpool.
Motor Inn   **Dining:** Restaurant; 6 am-9:30 pm; $6-$14; wine/beer only. **Services:** giftshop; winter plug-ins. **Cards:** AE
        CB, DI, DS, MC, VI.

SUPER 8 MOTEL-KELLOGG   Phone: (208)783-1234
(AAA) (SAVE)   3/1-3/31, 6/11-9/18 &
             12/17-2/29 [CP]   1P: $50- 58   2P/1B: $57- 63 2P/2B: $63- 80 XP: $5   F12
◆◆   4/1-6/10 & 9/19-12/16 [CP]   1P: $43- 48   2P/1B: $48- 53 2P/2B: $53- 73 XP: $5   F12
Motel   **Location:** 0.5 mi s of I-90, exit 49. 601 Bunker Ave 83837. Fax: 208/784-0461. **Terms:** Monthly rates; pets,
        $20 dep req. **Facility:** 61 rooms. Adjacent to Silver Mountain Ski. 2 stories; interior corridors; designated
smoking area; heated pool, small heated indoor pool, whirlpool. **Dining:** Restaurant nearby. **Services:** winter plug-ins.
Recreation: ski storage room. **Some Rooms:** kitchen. **Cards:** AE, CB, DI, DS, JC, MC, VI. **Special Amenities:** Free
breakfast and free local telephone calls.

KETCHUM—2,500

LODGINGS

BEST WESTERN KENTWOOD LODGE   Phone: (208)726-4114
(AAA) (SAVE)   3/1-3/28, 6/4-9/26 &
             12/17-2/29   1P: $109- 149 2P/1B: $109- 149 2P/2B: $109- 149 XP: $10   F12
◆◆◆   3/29-6/3 & 9/27-12/16   1P: $79- 119   2P/1B: $79- 119 2P/2B: $79- 119 XP: $10   F12
Motor Inn   **Location:** S end of downtown on SR 75. 180 S Main St 83340 (Box 2172). Fax: 208/726-2417.
        Terms: Reserv deposit, 7 day notice. **Facility:** 57 rooms. Good use of custom log furniture; ski lockers; some
covered parking & many rooms with fireplace. Hair dryer in all rooms. Covered parking avail. 3 stories; interior corridors; smoke
free premises; heated indoor pool, whirlpool. **Dining:** Coffee shop; 7:30 am-2 pm; $7-$15; wine/beer only. **Services:** winter
plug-ins. **Some Rooms:** 5 efficiencies, whirlpools. **Cards:** AE, CB, DI, DS, MC, VI. **Special Amenities:** Early check-in/late
check-out and free local telephone calls. (See ad below)

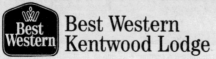 

BEST WESTERN TYROLEAN LODGE
Phone: (208)726-5336

(AAA) (SAVE)
◆◆◆
Motel

	3/1-4/15, 6/15-9/12 &						
	12/1-2/29 [CP]	1P: $80- 95	2P/1B:	$90- 115	2P/2B:	$95- 150	XP: $8
	4/16-6/14 & 9/13-11/30 [CP]	1P: $70- 85	2P/1B:	$80- 95	2P/2B:	$85- 115	XP: $8

Location: S end of town, just w of SR 75 on Rivers St, just s on 3rd Ave. 260 Cottonwood 83340 (PO Box 802). Fax: 208/726-2081. **Terms:** Pets, in smoking rooms, $5 extra charge. **Facility:** 56 rooms. Decorated in classic Austrian style & many rooms with balcony. 3 stories, no elevator; interior corridors; designated smoking area; mountain view; heated pool, sauna, whirlpools. **Services:** winter plug-ins. **Recreation:** game room. Fee: bicycles. **All Rooms:** combo or shower baths. **Some Rooms:** whirlpools. **Cards:** AE, DI, DS, MC, VI. **Special Amenities: Free breakfast and preferred room (subject to availability with advanced reservations).**

CHRISTIANIA MOTOR LODGE
Phone: (208)726-3351

(AAA) (SAVE)
◆◆
Motel

	3/1-3/31, 6/21-9/15 &						
	12/21-2/29	1P: $75- 119	2P/1B:	$75- 119	2P/2B:	$85- 129	XP: $10	F14
	4/1-6/20 & 9/16-12/20	1P: $65- 99	2P/1B:	$65- 99	2P/2B:	$75- 109	XP: $10	F14

Location: Just ne on Sun Valley Rd from jct of SR 75. 651 Sun Valley Rd 83340 (PO Box 2196). Fax: 208/726-3055. **Terms:** Reserv deposit, 7 day notice, in winter; handling fee imposed; pets, by reservation only. **Facility:** 38 rooms. Some units with view of Mt. Baldy; some with fireplace. 2 stories; exterior corridors; designated smoking area; heated pool, whirlpool. **Dining:** Restaurant nearby. **Services:** winter plug-ins. **Some Rooms:** 8 efficiencies. **Cards:** AE, CB, DI, DS, MC, VI. **Special Amenities: Free local telephone calls.**

CHRISTOPHE CONDO HOTEL
Rates Subject to Change **Phone: (208)726-5601**

◆◆◆
Condominium

	12/18-1/3				2P/2B: $340	XP: $10	F5
	3/1-3/13 & 2/12-2/29	1P: $90- 120	2P/1B:	$90- 120	2P/2B:	$90- 120	
	3/14-4/3, 6/19-9/11 &						
	1/4-2/11	1P: $90- 95	2P/1B:	$80- 95	2P/2B:	$80- 95	
	4/4-6/18 & 9/12-12/17	1P: $70- 80	2P/1B:	$70- 80	2P/2B:	$70- 80	

Location: S end of town, just w of SR 75 on Rivers St, just s. 351 2nd Ave S 83340 (PO Box 21). Fax: 208/726-5617. **Terms:** Check-in 4 pm; reserv deposit. **Facility:** 40 rooms. One room units often avail as well as condo units & property has some underground parking. Registration: 9 am-5 pm at 200 W Rivers St in Camas Bldg. 20 two-bedroom units. 1- & 2-bedroom condos, $90-$290; 3 stories; exterior corridors; smoke free premises; mountain view; heated pool. **All Rooms:** combo or shower baths. **Some Rooms:** 20 kitchens. **Cards:** AE, MC, VI.

CLARION INN OF SUN VALLEY
Phone: (208)726-5900

(AAA) (SAVE)
◆◆
Motel

	3/1-4/15, 7/1-9/20 &						
	12/20-2/29 [CP]	1P: $89- 112	2P/1B:	$89- 112	2P/2B:	$89- 112	XP: $5-25	F18
	9/21-12/19 [CP]	1P: $69- 104	2P/1B:	$69- 104	2P/2B:	$69- 104	XP: $5-25	F18
	4/16-6/30 [CP]	1P: $69- 89	2P/1B:	$69- 89	2P/2B:	$69- 89	XP: $5-25	F18

Location: N end of downtown on SR 75 (Main St), corner of 6th & Main sts. 600 N Main St 83340 (PO Box 160, SUN VALLEY, 83353). Fax: 208/726-3761. **Terms:** Pets, $50 dep req. **Facility:** 57 rooms. Some rooms with fireplace, ski lockers, balcony. 3 stories; interior/exterior corridors; designated smoking area; heated pool, whirlpool. **Some Rooms:** whirlpools. **Cards:** AE, CB, DI, DS, JC, MC, VI. **Special Amenities: Early check-in/late check-out and free breakfast.**

HEIDELBERG INN
Phone: (208)726-5361

(AAA) (SAVE)
◆◆
Motel

	6/14-10/20 & 2/2-2/29 [CP]	1P: $80- 95	2P/1B:	$95- 105	2P/2B:	$95- 120	XP: $8	F13
	12/21-1/2 [CP]	1P: $85- 100	2P/1B:	$95- 110	2P/2B:	$100- 115	XP: $8	F13
	3/1-6/13, 10/21-12/20 &						
	1/3-2/1 [CP]	1P: $60- 75	2P/1B:	$65- 105	2P/2B:	$70- 90	XP: $8	F13

Location: 1.3 mi w on Warm Springs Rd from jct of SR 75 (Main St). 1908 Warm Springs Rd 83340 (PO Box 5704). Fax: 208/726-2084. **Terms:** Pets, $5 extra charge. **Facility:** 30 rooms. Spacious rooms, some with fireplace. 30 day cancellation notice 12/23-1/1; 2 stories; exterior corridors; designated smoking area; mountain view; small heated pool, sauna, whirlpool. **Dining:** Continental breakfast delivered to rooms; restaurant nearby. **Services:** winter plug-ins. **Recreation:** video movie rental. Fee: bicycles. **All Rooms:** combo or shower baths. **Some Rooms:** 14 efficiencies. **Cards:** AE, CB, DI, DS, MC, VI.

TAMARACK LODGE
Rates Subject to Change **Phone: (208)726-3344**

◆◆
Motel

	All Year	1P: $102- 124	2P/1B:	$102- 124	2P/2B:	$102- 134	XP: $10	F12

Location: Downtown; just ne on Sun Valley Rd from jct of SR 75. 291 Walnut Ave 83340 (PO Box 2000, SUN VALLEY, 83353). Fax: 208/726-3347. **Terms:** Reserv deposit, 7 day notice; handling fee imposed. **Facility:** 26 rooms. All rooms with hairdryer; some with fireplace. 1 two-bedroom unit. 2 stories; interior/exterior corridors; small heated pool. **Cards:** AE, DI, DS, MC, VI.

RESTAURANTS

THE KNEADERY
Lunch: $5-$8 **Phone: 208/726-9462**

(AAA)
◆◆
American

Location: SR 75 (Main St), e on Sun Valley Rd, just s. 260 Leadville 83340. **Hours:** 7:30 am-2 pm. Closed: 12/25. **Features:** No A/C; casual dress; children's menu; carryout; beer & wine only; street parking. Rustic setting featuring creative breakfast selections; sandwiches, salad, soup; seasonal deck dining. Smoke free premises. **Cards:** AE, DS, MC, VI.

MICHEL'S CHRISTIANIA RESTAURANT & OLYMPIC BAR
Dinner: $17-$27 **Phone: 208/726-3388**

◆◆◆
French

Location: Just n of SR 75 (Main St) on Sun Valley Rd. 303 Walnut Ave 83340. **Hours:** 6:30 pm-10 pm, in winter from 6 pm. Closed: 5/1-5/31 & 11/1-11/30. **Reservations:** suggested. **Features:** casual dress; cocktails & lounge; street parking; a la carte. Seasonal patio dining. **Cards:** AE, DS, MC, VI.

SAWTOOTH CLUB
Dinner: $11-$22 **Phone: 208/726-5233**

◆◆
American
VI.

Location: Corner of Second in downtown Ketchum. 231 N Main St 83340. **Hours:** 5:30 pm-10:30 pm, to 10 pm in summer. Closed: 11/25. **Features:** casual dress; carryout; cocktails & lounge; street parking; a la carte. Natural mesquite wood cooking. Relaxed atmosphere. Very popular bar & restaurant. **Cards:** AE, MC,

LEWISTON—28,100

LODGINGS

COMFORT INN ◆◆◆ Motel
Rates Subject to Change **Phone:** (208)798-8090
All Year [CP] 1P: $55- 62 2P/1B: $62- 64 2P/2B: $64 XP: $7 F18
Location: 1.2 mi s on US 12 from jct US 95, just s on 21st. 2128 8th Ave 83501. Fax: 208/798-8988
Facility: 52 rooms. Expanded continental breakfast served in breakfast room. 6 whirlpool rms, $82.99-$125.99
2 stories; interior corridors; designated smoking area; heated indoor pool. **All Rooms:** combo or shower baths. **Cards:** AE
CB, DI, DS, MC, VI.

HOWARD JOHNSON (AAA) (SAVE) ◆◆ Motel
Phone: (208)743-9526
All Year [CP] 1P: $58- 66 2P/1B: $62- 71 2P/2B: $66- 71 XP: $5 F17
Location: 1.6 mi s on US 12 from jct US 95. 1716 Main St 83501. Fax: 208/746-6212. **Terms:** Small pets
only, $20 dep req. **Facility:** 66 rooms. Close to downtown & Levee pathways; executive rooms avail. 4 efficien
cies, 2-bedroom units, $67.50-$72.50; 1-2 stories; exterior corridors; designated smoking area; small heated
pool, whirlpool. **Dining:** Restaurant nearby. **Cards:** AE, DI, DS, MC, VI. **Special Amenities:** Free breakfast
and free local telephone calls.

INN AMERICA ◆◆◆ Motel
Rates Subject to Change **Phone:** (208)746-4600
All Year 1P: $42- 52 2P/1B: $52- 62 2P/2B: $52- 62 XP: $5-10 F17
Location: 1.2 mi s on US 12 from jct US 95, just s. 702 21st St 83501. Fax: 208/746-7756. **Facility:** 61 rooms
Scenic hilltop location with easy highway access, many of the large rooms have view of Snake River. 4 two-
bedroom units. 3 stories; interior corridors; small heated pool. **Services:** winter plug-ins. **All Rooms:** combo or shower
baths. **Cards:** AE, CB, DI, DS, JC, MC, VI.

RED LION HOTEL ◆◆ Motor Inn
Rates Subject to Change **Phone:** 208/799-1000
4/1-9/30 [CP] 1P: $77- 89 2P/1B: $87- 99 2P/2B: $87- 99 XP: $10 F18
3/1-3/31, 10/1-11/19 &
2/16-2/29 [BP] 1P: $67- 71 2P/1B: $77- 81 2P/2B: $77- 81 XP: $10 F18
11/20-2/15 [BP] 1P: $60- 64 2P/1B: $69- 71 2P/2B: $69- 71 XP: $10 F18
Location: 1.2 mi s on US 12 from jct US 95, just s. 621 21st St 83501. Fax: 208/799-1000. **Facility:** 134 rooms. Some spacious rooms; adjacent to greenbelt along river. 3 deluxe whirlpool suite from $195. 1 whirlpool suite, $400. Mini suites from
$89; 2-4 stories; interior corridors; heated pool. **All Rooms:** combo or shower baths. **Some Rooms:** efficiency. **Cards:** AE
CB, DI, DS, JC, MC, VI.

SACAJAWEA SELECT INN (AAA) (SAVE) ◆◆ Motor Inn
Phone: (208)746-1393
All Year [CP] 1P: $46- 52 2P/1B: $52- 58 2P/2B: $52- 58 XP: $3 F13
Location: 1.5 mi s on US 12 from jct US 95. 1824 Main St 83501. Fax: 208/743-3620. **Terms:** Pets, $2
extra charge, in designated rooms. **Facility:** 90 rooms. Varied room accommodations; park at many rooms. 7
two-bedroom units. 2 whirlpool rms with microwave from $58; 4 whirlpool rms from $43; 1-2 stories
interior/exterior corridors; heated pool, whirlpool. **Dining:** Restaurant; 6 am-10 pm, Sun-9 pm; $8-$19
cocktails. **All Rooms:** combo or shower baths. **Cards:** AE, CB, DI, DS, MC, VI. **Special Amenities:** Free breakfast and
free local telephone calls.

SUPER 8 MOTEL ◆◆ Motel
Rates Subject to Change **Phone:** (208)743-8808
All Year 1P: $40 2P/1B: $44 2P/2B: $44 XP: $5 F12
Location: Just e on US 12 from jct US 95. 3120 North & South Hwy 83501. Fax: 208/743-8808. **Facility:** 62
rooms. Located in busy commercial area. 2 stories; interior corridors. **Services:** winter plug-ins. **Cards:** AE
CB, DI, DS, JC, MC, VI.

RESTAURANTS

PANHANDLER PIE RESTAURANT & BAKERY ◆◆ American
Lunch: $5-$7 **Dinner:** $8-$13 **Phone:** 208/746-0016
Location: 1.9 mi s on US 12 from jct US 95. 1407 Main St 83501. **Hours:** 6 am-10 pm. Closed: 11/25 &
12/25. **Features:** casual dress; children's menu. Family dining, good food fast. Smoke free premises
Cards: CB, DI, MC, VI.

ZANY'S ◆◆ American
Lunch: $5-$7 **Dinner:** $5-$19 **Phone:** 208/746-8131
Location: 1.2 mi s on US 12 from jct US 95; 1 mi s on 21st St. 2006 19th St 83501. **Hours:** 10:30 am-9:30
pm. Closed major holidays. **Features:** casual dress; children's menu; senior's menu; health conscious men
items; beer & wine only; a la carte. Casual family dining in a 50's theme setting featuring burgers
sandwiches, salads, steaks. Seasonal patio dining. **Cards:** AE, DS, MC, VI.

MACKAY—600

LODGING

WAGON WHEEL MOTEL (AAA) (SAVE) ◆ Motel
Phone: (208)588-3331
All Year 1P: $28- 50 2P/1B: $35- 80 2P/2B: $38- 80 XP: $5
Location: 0.3 mi n on Hwy 93. 809 W Custer 83251 (PO Box 22). Fax: 208/588-3334. **Terms:** Reser
deposit; handling fee imposed; weekly/monthly rates; pets, $5 extra charge. **Facility:** 16 rooms. Beautiful view
of Lost River Mountain Range. 3 two-bedroom units. 1 two-bedroom cottage & 1 rm with fireplace; 1 story; ex
terior corridors; designated smoking area; playground. **Services:** winter plug-ins. **Recreation:** sand box fo
children; single basketball court, volleyball. **All Rooms:** combo or shower baths. **Some Rooms:** efficiency, 3 kitchens
Cards: AE, DS, MC, VI. **Special Amenities:** Free local telephone calls.

MARSING—800

RESTAURANT

SANDBAR RIVER HOUSE ◆◆ Steak and Seafood
Lunch: $5-$8 **Dinner:** $5-$18 **Phone:** 208/896-412
Location: SR 55, just w of bridge, then n. 18 E 1st Ave 83639. **Hours:** 7 am-8 pm, Fri & Sat-9:30 pm, Su
4 pm-8 pm. Closed: 7/4, 11/25, 12/24, 12/25 & Mon. **Reservations:** suggested. **Features:** casual dress
children's menu; carryout; beer & wine only. Overlooking Snake River in southwest Idaho's wine country
Outside deck dining avail. Features Idaho & Northwestern wines. **Cards:** DS, MC, VI.

MCCALL—2,000

LODGINGS

AR CREEK LODGE
Phone: (208)634-3551
All Year [BP]   1P: $125- 200   2P/1B: $125- 200   2P/2B: $125- 200   XP: $25   F12
Location: 4 mi n on SR 55 at MM 149. 3492 SR 55, MM 149 83638 (PO Box 8, NEW MEADOWS, 83654).
Fax: 208/634-7699. **Terms:** Reserv deposit, 30 day notice; handling fee imposed; weekly rates; package
plans. **Facility:** 13 rooms. Nestled on 65 acres in wilderness mountain setting adjacent to Bear Creek; close
to Brundage ski area. TV & VCR's avail on request. Cabins, $150-$175; 1 story; exterior corridors; smoke free
mises; whirlpool. **Dining:** Dining room, see separate listing. **Services:** area transportation, Brundage ski area; winter
g-ins. **Recreation:** fishing; snowshoes,; mountain bike & riding trails. Fee: horse boarding. **Some Rooms:** whirlpools.
ds: AE, DS, MC, VI. **Special Amenities:** Early check-in/late check-out and free local telephone calls.

ST WESTERN MCCALL
Phone: (208)634-6300
6/15-9/14 [CP]   1P: $64- 80   2P/1B: $69- 85   2P/2B: $73- 85
3/1-6/14 & 9/15-2/29 [CP]   1P: $60- 75   2P/1B: $64- 80   2P/2B: $69- 80
Location: SR 55, just s of jct of Lake St & SR 55. 415 3rd St 83638. Fax: 208/634-2967. **Terms:** Pets.
Facility: 79 rooms. Close to downtown & Payette Lake; ski lockers; some mini-suites & spa rooms. 2 stories;
interior/exterior corridors; designated smoking area; heated indoor pool, whirlpool. **Dining:** Restaurant
arby. **Services:** winter plug-ins. **Some Rooms:** whirlpools. **Cards:** AE, DI, DS, JC,
, VI. **Special Amenities:** Early check-in/late check-out and free local telephone calls.

TEL MCCALL
Phone: (208)634-8105
All Year   1P: $50- 195   2P/1B: $50- 195   2P/2B: $50- 195   XP: $10   F10
Under major renovation. **Location:** City Center; SR 55 at jct of Lake St. 1101 N Third St 83638 (PO Box
1778). Fax: 208/634-8755. **Terms:** Reserv deposit; package plans. **Facility:** 22 rooms. Restored 1904 railroad
storic inn adjacent to Payette Lake with varied room styles & mountain inn breakfast. Scheduled for completion July,
untry Inn 1999; 2 stories, no elevator; interior corridors; smoke free premises; mountain view. **Dining:** Dining room; 5
pm-10 pm; $14-$19; wine only. **Services:** complimentary evening beverages, snacks. **Recreation:** fishing;
d free newspaper. bicycles. **Some Rooms:** kitchen. **Cards:** AE, DS, MC, VI. **Special Amenities:** Free local telephone calls

CCALL SUPER 8 LODGE
Phone: 208/634-4637
6/1-9/7 & 12/18-1/3   1P: $56- 108   2P/1B: $61- 108   2P/2B: $63- 108   XP: $5   F17
3/1-3/31, 9/8-10/15 &
1/4-2/29   1P: $52- 98   2P/1B: $56- 98   2P/2B: $58- 98   XP: $5   F17
4/1-5/31 & 10/16-12/17   1P: $46- 98   2P/1B: $50- 98   2P/2B: $56- 98   XP: $5   F17
Location: S end of town on SR 55. 303 S 3rd 83638. Fax: 208/634-4637. **Terms:** Reserv deposit; pets, by
ervation only. **Facility:** 60 rooms. Lodge style lobby & breakfast room. 2 stories; interior corridors; designated smoking area;
untain view; whirlpools. **Services:** winter plug-ins. **Recreation:** video game room. **All Rooms:** combo or shower baths.
me Rooms: whirlpools. **Cards:** AE, DS, MC, VI.

RTHWEST PASSAGE BED & BREAKFAST   Guaranteed Rates   **Phone: 208/634-5349**
All Year [BP]   1P: $55- 60   2P/1B: $65- 85   XP: $15   D
Location: 1.4 mi n on SR 55 from jct of Lake St, 0.7 mi w on Boydston St, just s. 201 Rio Vista Blvd 83638
d & (PO Box 4208). Fax: 208/634-4977. **Terms:** Age restrictions may apply; check-in 4 pm; reserv deposit, 14
eakfast day notice; handling fee imposed. **Facility:** 6 rooms. Secluded in ponderosa pines & built in 1938 by MGM to
use Spencer Tracy & film crew during filming of "Northwest Passage.". 3 stories, no elevator; interior corridors; designated
oking areas. **Services:** area transportation. **Recreation:** cross country skiing; snowmobiling; hiking trails.
me Rooms: color TV. **Cards:** AE, MC, VI.

ANDIA INN MOTEL   Rates Subject to Change   **Phone: 208/634-7394**
6/15-9/15   1P: $46   2P/1B: $50   2P/2B: $54
3/1-6/14 & 9/16-2/29   1P: $40   2P/1B: $46   2P/2B: $50
Location: SR 55, just s of jct of Lake St & SR 55. 401 N 3rd St 83638 (PO Box 1436). **Terms:** Reserv
osit, 7 day notice on cabin. **Facility:** 17 rooms. Quiet location not visible from highway; very clean rooms. 1 three-bedroom
t. 1 three-bedroom cabin with washer/dryer, $150 for up to 10 persons; 1 story; exterior corridors; designated smoking area.
me Rooms: kitchen. **Cards:** AE, DI, DS, MC, VI.

RESTAURANTS

AR CREEK LODGE RESTAURANT   **Dinner: $15-$21**   **Phone: 208/634-3551**
Location: 4 mi n on US 55 at MM 149; in Bear Creek Lodge. 3492 Hwy 55, MM 149 83638. **Hours:** 5
ntinental pm-10 pm. Closed: 6/20-9/5 Mon; 1/1-6/19 & 9/6-12/31 Mon-Tues. **Reservations:** suggested.
Features: casual dress; Sunday brunch; children's menu; health conscious menu items; cocktail lounge;
er & wine only. a la carte. Northwestern cuisine featuring fresh seafood & game with different offerings presented nightly.
oke free premises. **Cards:** AE, DS, MC, VI.

MANO'S RISTORANTE   **Dinner: $8-$17**   **Phone: 208/634-4396**
Location: SR 55 from jct of Lake St. 203 E Lake St 83638. **Hours:** 5:30 pm-10 pm; 9 pm in winter. Closed:
ian 11/25, 12/25 & Sun in winter. **Reservations:** accepted; 6 or more. **Features:** No A/C; casual dress;
children's menu; health conscious menu items; cocktails; street parking; a la carte. Located on ground floor
Yacht Club with seasonal patio dining overlooking Payette Lake. **Cards:** AE, MC, VI.

MERIDIAN—9,600

LODGING

ST WESTERN RAMA INN
Phone: (208)887-7888
3/1-9/30 [CP]   1P: $60- 83   2P/1B: $65- 88   2P/2B: $70- 93   XP: $5   F12
10/1-2/29 [CP]   1P: $55- 78   2P/1B: $60- 83   2P/2B: $65- 88   XP: $5   F12
Location: Just ne of I-84, exit 44. 1019 S Progress Ave 83642. Fax: 208/887-7600. **Facility:** 61 rooms. Easy
tel freeway access. 8 whirlpool suites, $125; 2 stories; interior corridors; mountain view; heated indoor pool,
sauna, whirlpool. **Dining:** Restaurant nearby. **Recreation:** video movie rentals. **All Rooms:** combo or
wer baths. **Cards:** AE, CB, DI, DS, JC, MC, VI. **Special Amenities:** Free breakfast and free local telephone calls.

MONTPELIER—2,700

LODGINGS

BEST WESTERN CLOVER CREEK INN   Phone: (208)847-17
(AAA) (SAVE)   5/1-9/30 [CP]   1P: $53- 68   2P/1B: $55- 73 2P/2B: $60- 75 XP: $6
◆◆◆   3/1-4/30 & 10/1-2/29 [CP] 1P: $43- 53   2P/1B: $48- 58 2P/2B: $48- 58 XP: $6
Motel   **Location:** Just n on US 30 from jct of US 89S. 243 N 4th St 83254. Fax: 208/847-3519. **Terms:** Small p
only. **Facility:** 65 rooms. Remodeled property in 1997. 2 two-bedroom units. 2-room units with 3 queen be
$80-$92; 2 stories; exterior corridors; whirlpool. **Dining:** Restaurant nearby. **Services:** winter plug-
Recreation: video rentals. **Some Rooms:** efficiency. **Cards:** AE, CB, DI, DS, MC, VI. **Special Amenities:** Free break
and free local telephone calls.

THE FISHER INN   Phone: (208)847-17
(AAA) (SAVE)   6/1-9/15   1P: $33- 43   2P/1B: $35- 43 2P/2B: $43- 50 XP: $5
◆◆   3/1-5/31 & 9/16-2/29 1P: $26- 36   2P/1B: $30- 36 2P/2B: $36- 40 XP: $5
Motel   **Location:** 0.8 mi n on US 30 jct of US 89S. 601 N 4th 83254. **Terms:** Small pets only. **Facility:** 10 roo
Convenient hwy location on major scenic route to Yellowstone National Park; large grassy picnic area; park
at door. 1 story; exterior corridors; designated smoking area; small heated seasonal. **Services:** win
plug-ins. **All Rooms:** extended cable TV. **Cards:** AE, DS, MC, VI. **Special Amenities:** Free local telephone calls.

SUPER 8 MOTEL MONTPELIER   Rates Subject to Change   Phone: 208/847-88
◆◆   4/1-9/30 [CP]   1P: $49- 51   2P/1B: $53- 54 2P/2B: $58- 59 XP: $5
Motel   3/1-3/31 & 10/1-2/29 [CP] 1P: $35   2P/1B: $35   2P/2B: $39   XP: $5
Location: Just n on US 30 from jct US 89 S. 276 N 4th (US 30) St 83254. Fax: 208/847-3888. **Facility:**
rooms. 2 stories; interior corridors. **Cards:** AE, DI, DS, MC, VI.

RESTAURANT

BUTCH CASSIDY'S   **Lunch:** $4-$9   **Dinner:** $11-$27   Phone: 208/847-35
◆   **Location:** Jct US 89 & 30N. 230 N 4th St 83254. **Hours:** 6 am-10 pm. Closed: 12/25. **Features:** cas
American   dress; children's menu; carryout; salad bar; cocktail lounge. **Cards:** AE, DI, DS, MC, VI.

MOSCOW—18,500

LODGINGS

BEST WESTERN UNIVERSITY INN   Phone: (208)882-05
(AAA) (SAVE)   All Year   1P: $63   2P/1B: $63- 98 2P/2B: $63- 98 XP: $10
◆◆◆   **Location:** 1 mi w on SR 8 from jct of US 95. 1516 Pullman Rd 83843. Fax: 208/883-3056. **Terms:** Chec
Motor Inn   4 pm; pets, $10 extra charge. **Facility:** 173 rooms. Adjacent to University of Idaho, mall & movie theaters
two-bedroom units. 2 stories; interior corridors; designated smoking area; heated indoor pool, wading p
sauna, whirlpool. **Dining:** Dining room, coffee shop; 11:30 am-2 pm, Sat 5:30 pm-10 pm, Sun 9 am-2
coffee shop open 24 hrs; $10-$18. **Services:** giftshop; area transportation, to university. **All Rooms:** combo or sho
baths. **Some Rooms:** whirlpools. **Cards:** AE, CB, MC, VI. **Special Amenities:** Free local telephone calls and f
newspaper. *(See color ad below)*

MARK IV MOTOR INN   Phone: (208)882-75
(AAA) (SAVE)   All Year   1P: $32- 41   2P/1B: $37- 46 2P/2B: $45- 51 XP: $5
◆◆   **Location:** 0.4 mi n on US 95 from jct of SR 8. 414 N Main St 83843. Fax: 208/883-0648. **Terms:** Res
Motor Inn   deposit, 3 day notice; weekly rates; pets, $5 extra charge, in designated rooms. **Facility:** 86 rooms. 2 stor
interior/exterior corridors; designated smoking area; heated indoor pool, whirlpool. **Dining:** Restaurant
am-9 pm, Fri & Sat-10 pm; $8-$13; cocktails. **Services:** area transportation, university; winter plug-
All Rooms: combo or shower baths. **Cards:** AE, DI, DS, MC, VI. **Special Amenities:** Free local telephone calls a
preferred room (subject to availability with advanced reservations).

MOUNTAIN HOME—7,900

LODGINGS

BEST WESTERN FOOTHILLS MOTOR INN   Phone: (208)587-8477
Motel
All Year [CP]   1P: $60- 65 2P/1B: $65- 70 2P/2B: $70- 80 XP: $5   F
Location: Just n of I-84, exit 95. 1080 Hwy 20 83647. **Fax:** 208/587-5774. **Terms:** Pets, $50 dep req. **Facility:** 76 rooms. Parking at most rooms; close to Oregon Trail Historical site; Oversize vehicle parking area. 2 stories; exterior corridors; heated indoor pool, sauna, whirlpool. **Dining:** Restaurant nearby. **Services:** giftshop; winter plug-ins. **All Rooms:** combo or shower baths. **Some Rooms:** kitchen, whirlpools. **Cards:** AE, CB, DI, DS, JC, MC, VI. **Special Amenities:** Free breakfast and free newspaper.

HILANDER MOTEL & STEAK HOUSE   Rates Subject to Change   Phone: 208/587-3311
Motor Inn
All Year   1P: $35   2P/1B: $39   2P/2B: $43   XP: $4
Location: I-84, exit 90; 4 mi s on Business Loop 84. 615 S 3rd W 83647. **Facility:** 34 rooms. Varied room styles. 7 two-bedroom units. 4 efficiencies, $45-$65; 2 stories; exterior corridors; small heated pool. **All Rooms:** combo or shower baths. **Cards:** AE, CB, DI, DS, MC, VI.

MOTEL THUNDERBIRD   Rates Subject to Change   Phone: 208/587-7927
Motel
5/1-10/31   1P: $26   2P/1B: $32   2P/2B: $36   XP: $3   F6
3/1-4/30 & 11/1-2/29   1P: $24   2P/1B: $28   2P/2B: $32   XP: $3   F6
Location: I-84, exit 90, 3.3 mi s on Sunset Strip. 910 Sunset Strip 83647. **Terms:** Reserv deposit. **Facility:** 27 rooms. 2 stories; exterior corridors; designated smoking area; small pool. **All Rooms:** combo or shower baths. **Some Rooms:** 2 kitchens. **Cards:** MC, VI.

SLEEP INN   Rates Subject to Change   Phone: 208/587-9743
Motel
All Year [CP]   1P: $54   2P/1B: $59   XP: $5   F18
Location: I-84, exit 95 just n on US 20. 1180 Hwy 20 83647. **Fax:** 208/587-7382. **Facility:** 60 rooms. 2 stories; interior corridors. **All Rooms:** combo or shower baths. **Cards:** AE, CB, DI, DS, JC, MC, VI.

RESTAURANT

CARLOS' MEXICAN STYLE FAMILY DINING   **Lunch:** $5-$8   **Dinner:** $5-$8   **Phone:** 208/587-2966
Mexican
Location: 1 mi sw of I-84, exit 95. 1525 American Legion Blvd 83647. **Hours:** 11 am-9 pm. Closed major holidays & Sun. **Features:** casual dress; children's menu; senior's menu; carryout; beer & wine only; a la carte. Casual, friendly family style dining. **Cards:** AE, DS, MC, VI.

NAMPA—28,400

LODGINGS

INN AMERICA   Rates Subject to Change   Phone: 208/442-0800
Motel
All Year   1P: $43- 50 2P/1B: $49- 56 2P/2B: $49- 56 XP: $5-10   F18
Location: Just s of I-84, exit 35. 130 Shannon Dr 83687. **Fax:** 208/442-0229. **Facility:** 61 rooms. 4 two-bedroom units. 3 stories; interior corridors; designated smoking area; small heated pool. **Cards:** AE, CB, DI, DS, MC, VI.

SHILO INN-NAMPA BOULEVARD   Rates Subject to Change   Phone: (208)466-8993
Motel
All Year [CP]   1P: $55- 75 2P/1B: $55- 75 2P/2B: $55- 75 XP: $7   F12
Location: Just sw of I-84, exit 35. 617 Nampa Blvd 83687-3065. **Fax:** 208/465-3239. **Facility:** 61 rooms. Easy access to freeway. Hair dryers avail. 2 stories; interior corridors; designated smoking area. **Cards:** AE, CB, DI, DS, JC, MC, VI. *(See ad p 178)*

SHILO INN NAMPA SUITES   Rates Subject to Change   Phone: (208)465-3250
Motor Inn
All Year   1P: $79- 109 2P/1B: $79- 109 2P/2B: $79- 109 XP: $10   F12
Location: I-84, exit 36; just nw. 1401 Shilo Dr 83687-3065. **Fax:** 208/465-5929. **Facility:** 83 rooms. All rooms equipped with wet bar, hair dryer & 3 phones. 4 stories; interior corridors; small heated indoor pool. **Some Rooms:** 8 efficiencies. **Cards:** AE, CB, DI, DS, JC, MC, VI. *(See ad p 178)*

SLEEP INN-NAMPA   Guaranteed Rates   Phone: (208)463-6300
Motel
All Year [CP]   1P: $45- 95 2P/1B: $49- 105 2P/2B: $49- 105 XP: $8   F18
Location: Just s of I-84, exit 36. 1315 Industrial Rd 83687. **Fax:** 208/463-6300. **Facility:** 81 rooms. 3 stories; interior corridors; designated smoking area; small heated indoor pool. **All Rooms:** combo or shower baths. **Cards:** AE, DI, DS, JC, MC, VI.

RESTAURANT

NOODLES   **Lunch:** $4-$8   **Dinner:** $6-$12   **Phone:** 208/466-4400
Italian
Location: I-84, exit 36; just n. 1802 Franklin Blvd 83687. **Hours:** 11 am-9:30 pm, Fri-10:30 pm, Sat noon-10:30 pm, Sun noon-9 pm. **Closed:** 11/25, 12/25 & Super Bowl Sun. **Reservations:** accepted. **Features:** casual dress; children's menu; early bird specials; health conscious menu; carryout; cocktails & lounge; a la carte. Traditional homemade Italian cuisine; informal atmosphere & service. **Cards:** AE, MC, VI.

NEW MEADOWS—500

LODGING

HARTLAND INN & MOTEL   Phone: (208)347-2114
Motel
All Year   1P: $42- 102 2P/1B: $42- 102 2P/2B: $42- 102 XP: $7   F12
Location: US 95, just n of jct of SR 55. 211 Norris St 83654 (PO Box 215). **Fax:** 208/347-2535. **Terms:** Reserv deposit; daily rates; pets, in motel units only. **Facility:** 14 rooms. 11 unit motel, plus a historic bed & breakfast home with 3 charming rooms, $78-$102. Designated smoking area for bed & breakfast. 1-3 stories; interior/exterior corridors; mountain view; whirlpool. **Dining:** Restaurant nearby. **All Rooms:** combo or shower baths. **Some Rooms:** 2 kitchens. **Cards:** AE, DS, MC, VI. **Special Amenities:** Free local telephone calls.

OROFINO—2,900

LODGING

KONKOLVILLE MOTEL
AAA
◆◆
Motel
　All Year　　　　Rates Subject to Change　　　　　　Phone: (208)476-558
　　　　1P: $33- 37　2P/1B: $37- 41　2P/2B: $38- 42　XP: $2-4　F1
Location: 2.7 mi e on Michigan Ave from jct US 12 & SR 7 (Bridge). 2000 Konkolville Rd 8354
Fax: 208/476-3268. **Terms:** Weekly rates, off season; pets, designated rooms, $2 extra charge. **Facility:** 4
rooms. Adjacent to creek & sawmill; varied appealing room styles. Suite, $46; 2 stories; exterior corridors; des
ignated smoking area; heated pool, whirlpool. **Dining:** Restaurant nearby. **All Rooms:** extended cable TV
Cards: AE, DI, JC, MC.

POCATELLO—46,100

LODGINGS

AMERITEL INN
AAA
◆◆◆
Motel
　All Year [BP]　Rates Subject to Change　　　　　　Phone: (208)234-750
　　　　1P: $89- 150　2P/1B: $89- 150　2P/2B: $89- 150　XP: $10-30　F1
Location: Just e of I-15, exit 71. 1440 Bench Rd 83201. Fax: 208/234-0000. **Terms:** Reserv deposi
Facility: 148 rooms. Oversize rooms complimented with 3 phones & 25 inch TV. 3 two-bedroom units. 3 sto
ries; interior corridors; designated smoking area; heated indoor pool. **Some Rooms:** 10 kitchens. **Cards:** AE, DI, DS, MC
VI. *(See color ad p 172)*

BEST WESTERN COTTONTREE INN
AAA SAVE
◆◆◆
Motor Inn
　All Year　　　　　1P: $66- 81　2P/1B: $66- 81　2P/2B: $66- 81　　Phone: (208)237-765
Location: Just e of I-15, exit 71. 1415 Bench Rd 83201. Fax: 208/238-1355. **Terms:** Monthly rates; pets
$25 dep req. **Facility:** 149 rooms. All rooms with iron & ironing board. 2-3 stories; interior corridors; designate
smoking area; heated indoor pool, whirlpool, sun deck; racquetball courts. **Dining:** Restaurant; 6 am-10 pm
Fri & Sat-11 pm; $5-S11; cocktails. **Services:** winter plug-ins. **Recreation:** Fee: in room video game
Some Rooms: whirlpools. **Cards:** AE, CB, DI, DS, JC, MC, VI. **Special Amenities:** Free local telephone calls and fre
newspaper.

BEST WESTERN WESTON INN
◆◆◆
Motel
　All Year [CP]　　Rates Subject to Change　　　　　　Phone: 208/233-553
　　　　1P: $45- 55　2P/1B: $50- 55　2P/2B: $60　　XP: $4　F1
Location: 1.8 mi w of I-15, exit 67; across from Idaho State University. 745 S 5th Ave 8320
Fax: 208/233-7929. **Facility:** 60 rooms. 2 stories; interior/exterior corridors; designated smoking area; sma
heated indoor pool. **Cards:** AE, CB, DI, DS, MC, VI.

COMFORT INN
◆◆◆
Motel
　All Year [CP]　　Rates Subject to Change　　　　　　Phone: (208)237-815
　　　　1P: $48- 54　2P/1B: $54- 61　2P/2B: $55- 65　XP: $5-10　F1
Location: Just e of I-15, exit 71. 1333 Bench Rd 83201. Fax: 208/237-5695. **Facility:** 52 rooms. 2 stories; in
terior corridors; small heated indoor pool. **Services:** winter plug-ins. **Cards:** AE, CB, DI, DS, JC, MC, VI.

ECONOLODGE-UNIVERSITY
◆◆
Motor Inn
　All Year [CP]　　Rates Subject to Change　　　　　　Phone: (208)233-045
　　　　1P: $39- 49　2P/1B: $44- 54　2P/2B: $49- 54　XP: $5　F1
Location: 1.8 mi w of I-15, exit 67; across from Idaho State University. 835 S 5th Ave 8320
Fax: 208/233-5548. **Facility:** 53 rooms. 2 stories; interior corridors. **Services:** winter plug-ins. **Cards:** AE, D
JC, MC, VI.

HOLIDAY INN-POCATELLO
AAA SAVE
◆◆◆
Motor Inn
　　　　　　　　　　　　　　　　　　　　　　　　　Phone: (208)237-140
　6/1-9/30　　　1P: $65　　　2P/1B: $65　　2P/2B: $65
　10/1-12/31　　1P: $63　　　2P/1B: $63　　2P/2B: $63
　3/1-5/31 & 1/1-2/29　1P: $59　2P/1B: $59　2P/2B: $59
Location: Just e of I-15, exit 71. 1399 Bench Rd 83201. Fax: 208/238-0225. **Terms:** Pets, outside smokin
rooms. **Facility:** 185 rooms. Park at many room doors; some poolside rooms. 12 two-room suites, $110-$13
2 stories; interior/exterior corridors; putting green; heated indoor pool, sauna, whirlpool. **Dining:** Restaurant; 6 am-2 & 5-1
pm; $6-$15; cocktails. **Cards:** AE, CB, DI, DS, JC, MC, VI. **Special Amenities:** Free local telephone calls.
(See color ad opposite title page)

QUALITY INN POCATELLO
AAA SAVE
◆◆◆
Motor Inn
　All Year　　　　1P: $62- 79　2P/1B: $62- 79　2P/2B: $62　　Phone: (208)233-220
　　　　　　　　　　　　　　　　　　　　　　　　　　XP: $5　F1
Location: Just e of I-15, exit 71. 1555 Pocatello Creek Rd 83201. Fax: 208/234-452
Terms: Weekly/monthly rates; pets, $10 dep req. **Facility:** 152 rooms. Good size rooms. Spacious publi
areas. 2 stories; interior corridors; heated indoor pool, wading pool, sauna, whirlpool. **Dining:** Dining roor
coffee shop; 5:30 pm-10 pm, 24 hr coffee shop; $6-$18; cocktails. **Cards:** AE, DI, DS, MC, V
Special Amenities: Free local telephone calls.

SUPER 8 MOTEL
AAA SAVE
◆◆
Motel
　　　　　　　　　　　　　　　　　　　　　　　　　Phone: (208)234-088
　4/1-2/29 [CP]　　1P: $43　　2P/1B: $47　　2P/2B: $50　XP: $4　F1
　3/1-3/31 [CP]　　1P: $41　　2P/1B: $45　　2P/2B: $48　XP: $4　F1
Location: Just e of I-15, exit 71. 1330 Bench Rd 83201. Fax: 208/232-0347. **Terms:** Reserv deposit; sma
pets only, $2 extra charge. **Facility:** 80 rooms. 3 stories; interior corridors; designated smoking are
Dining: Restaurant nearby. **All Rooms:** combo or shower baths. **Some Rooms:** whirlpools. **Cards:** AE, C
DI, DS, MC, VI. **Special Amenities:** Free breakfast and free local telephone calls.

THUNDERBIRD MOTEL
◆
Motel
　All Year　　　　Rates Subject to Change　　　　　　Phone: (208)232-633
　　　　1P: $35- 40　2P/1B: $40- 45　2P/2B: $45- 50　XP: $3　F1
Location: I-15, exit 67; 1.3 mi n, just s of Idaho State University. 1415 S 5th Ave 83201. Fax: 208/232-633
Facility: 45 rooms. 1-2 stories; exterior corridors; heated pool. **Services:** winter plug-ins. **Cards:** AE, DI, DS
MC, VI.

RESTAURANTS

BUDDY'S   Lunch: $5-$11   Dinner: $5-$11   Phone: 208/233-1172
Location: I-15, exit 69; 1 mi w on Clark St, 2 blks s on 6th St. 626 E Lewis 83201. **Hours:** 11 am-12:45 am.
Closed major holidays, 12/24 & Sun. **Features:** casual dress; carryout; cocktails & lounge; a la carte.
Bustling local favorite; family owned for 30 years. **Cards:** MC, VI.

Italian

CONTINENTAL BISTRO   Lunch: $5-$7   Dinner: $9-$21   Phone: 208/233-4433
Location: City Center; on Main between Lewis & W Center. 140 S Main 83204. **Hours:** 11 am-10 pm.
Closed: 1/1, 12/25 & Sun. **Reservations:** suggested. **Features:** casual dress; health conscious menu items;
cocktail lounge; beer & wine only; street parking; a la carte. American Continental cuisine with Northern
Italian & French influences. Seasonal patio dining. Parking lot avail after 5 pm.

Continental

FRONTIER PIES RESTAURANT & BAKERY   Lunch: $6-$11   Dinner: $6-$11   Phone: 208/237-7159
Location: I-15, exit 71; 1 mi w, just n; 1.7 mi e of I-86, exit 71. 1205 Yellowstone Ave 83201. **Hours:** 7
am-10 pm, Fri & Sat-11 pm. Closed: 12/25. **Features:** casual dress; children's menu; carryout; a la carte.
Relaxed family dining in an Old West atmosphere. Smoke free premises. **Cards:** DI, DS, MC, VI.

American

THE SANDPIPER   Lunch: $5-$8   Dinner: $10-$32   Phone: 208/233-1000
Location: I-15, exit 71; just e, just n. 1400 Bench Rd 83201. **Hours:** 11:30 am-2 & 5-10:30 pm, Fri & Sat
5-10:30 pm, Sun 4:30 pm-9 pm. Closed: 11/25 & 12/25. **Reservations:** suggested; weekends.
Features: cocktails & lounge. Informal bustling atmosphere. Deck dining in season. **Cards:** AE, DS, MC, VI.

Steakhouse

POST FALLS—7,300

LODGINGS

BEST WESTERN CAVANAUGH TEMPLIN'S RESORT   Phone: (208)773-1611

	1P:	2P/1B:	2P/2B:	XP:	
6/15-9/15	1P: $86- 101	2P/1B: $96- 111	2P/2B: $96- 111	XP: $10	F18
3/1-6/14 & 9/16-2/29	1P: $71- 86	2P/1B: $81- 96	2P/2B: $81- 96	XP: $10	F18

Location: I-90; exit 5 eastbound, just s to First Ave; exit 6 westbound, 1 mi w on Seltice Way to Spokane St,
0.5 mi s. 414 E First Ave 83854. Fax: 208/773-4192. **Terms:** Monthly rates; pets, in designated areas.
Facility: 167 rooms. Relaxing, casual accommodations in suburban setting along the Spokane River. Some
rooms with balcony overlooking river. Official Idaho wildlife viewing site. Suites from $110; 2-3 stories; interior corridors; moun-
tain view; beach, heated indoor pool, sauna, whirlpool; 2 tennis courts; boat dock, boat ramp, marina. **Dining:** Cocktails;
Marina Grill, seasonal; also, Mallards, see separate listing. **Services:** giftshop; winter plug-ins. Fee: area transportation, to
area attractions. **Recreation:** swimming, fishing; guest moorage, pontoon boats, inner tubes. Fee: boating, canoeing.
All Rooms: combo or shower baths. **Some Rooms:** whirlpools. **Cards:** AE, DI, DS, JC, MC, VI. **Special Amenities: Free
newspaper and preferred room (subject to availability with advanced reservations).**

Motor Inn

HOWARD JOHNSON EXPRESS   Phone: (208)773-4541
All Year [CP]   1P: $49- 84   2P/1B: $49- 84   2P/2B: $49- 84   XP: $5   F18
Location: Just ne of I-90, exit 2. W 3705 5th Ave 83854. Fax: 208/773-0235. **Terms:** Weekly/monthly rates;
pets, $35 dep req. **Facility:** 100 rooms. Close to outlet. 2 spa suites, $115-$134; 2-4 stories; interior corridors;
heated indoor pool, whirlpool. **Dining:** Restaurant nearby. **Recreation:** video rental. **All Rooms:** combo or
shower baths. **Some Rooms:** whirlpools. **Cards:** AE, CB, DI, DS, JC, MC, VI. **Special Amenities: Free
breakfast.**

Motel

RIVERBEND INN   Rates Subject to Change   Phone: (208)773-3583
5/22-9/30 [CP]   1P: $50- 120   2P/1B: $70- 120   2P/2B: $70- 120   XP: $5   F11
3/1-5/21 & 10/1-2/29 [CP]   1P: $43- 90   2P/1B: $48- 90   2P/2B: $48- 90   XP: $5   F11
Location: Just s of I-90, exit 2. 4105 W Riverbend Ave 83854. Fax: 208/773-1306. **Facility:** 71 rooms. Adjacent to outlet mall & Centennial Trail. Efficiencies, $57-$80; 2 stories; interior corridors; heated pool. **Services:** winter
plug-ins. **All Rooms:** combo or shower baths. **Cards:** AE, DI, DS, MC, VI.

Motel

SLEEP INN   Rates Subject to Change   Phone: 208/777-9394
6/28-9/15 [CP]   1P: $70   2P/1B: $70   2P/2B: $75   XP: $5   F18
5/1-6/27 [CP]   1P: $50   2P/1B: $50   2P/2B: $60   XP: $5   F18
3/1-4/30 & 9/16-2/29 [CP]   1P: $45   2P/1B: $45   2P/2B: $55   XP: $5   F18
Location: Just s of I-90, exit 2. 100 N Pleasant View Rd 83854. Fax: 208/777-8994. **Terms:** Check-in 4 pm. **Facility:** 84
rooms. Adjacent to outlet malls & Centennial Trail. 2 stories; interior corridors; heated indoor pool. **Services:** winter plug-ins.
All Rooms: combo or shower baths. **Cards:** AE, CB, DI, DS, JC, MC, VI.

Motel

RESTAURANTS

CARNEGIE'S RESTAURANT & LOUNGE   Lunch: $6-$8   Dinner: $9-$23   Phone: 208/773-0066
Location: 1 mi n of I-90, exit 7; at Highlands Golf & Country Club. N 707 Inverness Dr 83854. **Hours:** 11
am-9 pm, Fri & Sat-10 pm. Closed: 11/25 & 12/25. **Reservations:** accepted. **Features:** casual dress; health
conscious menu items; salad bar; cocktails & lounge. Panoramic dining overlooking Spokane River Valley.
Cards: AE, DI, DS, MC, VI.

*Steak and
Seafood*

MALLARDS   Lunch: $5-$7   Dinner: $8-$15   Phone: 208/773-1611
Location: I-90; exit 5 eastbound, just s to First Ave; exit 6 westbound, 1 mi w on Seltice Way to Spokane St,
0.5 mi s; in Best Western Cavanaugh Templin's Resort. 414 E First Ave 83854. **Hours:** 6 am-10 pm.
Reservations: accepted. **Features:** casual dress; Sunday brunch; children's menu; early bird specials;
carryout; cocktails & lounge; buffet. Dining room and lounge overlooking Spokane River with surrounding view of Post Falls
mountains; featuring soup, salad, sandwiches, seafood, prime rib, pasta, steak & vegetarian. **Cards:** AE, CB, DI, DS, MC,
VI.

American

REXBURG—14,300

LODGINGS

BEST WESTERN COTTONTREE INN   **Phone:** (208)356-464▮

6/16-8/31	1P:	$69-	79	2P/1B:	$74-	84	2P/2B:	$74- 84	XP: $5	F▮
9/1-12/31	1P:	$62-	72	2P/1B:	$67-	77	2P/2B:	$67- 77	XP: $5	F▮
3/1-6/15 & 1/1-2/29	1P:	$59-	69	2P/1B:	$64-	74	2P/2B:	$64- 74	XP: $5	F▮

🔺🔺🔺 Motor Inn
Location: 1 mi e of US 20, S Rexburg exit. 450 W 4th S 83440. Fax: 208/356-7461. **Terms:** Small pets onl▮ **Facility:** 100 rooms. Some rooms with balcony. All rooms with iron & ironing board. 2 stories; interior corridor designated smoking area; heated indoor pool, whirlpool. **Dining:** Restaurant; 6:30 am-10 pm. **Services:** winter plug-in **Some Rooms:** whirlpools. **Cards:** AE, CB, DI, DS, MC, VI. **Special Amenities:** Free newspaper and free room upgrac (subject to availability with advanced reservations).

COMFORT INN   **Phone:** (208)359-131▮

5/15-9/15 [CP]	1P:	$50-	84	2P/1B:	$50-	84	2P/2B:	$50- 84
3/1-5/14 & 9/16-2/29 [CP]	1P:	$40-	74	2P/1B:	$40-	74	2P/2B:	$40- 74

🔺🔺🔺 Motel
Location: Just e of jct of US 20, Salmon/Rexburg exit & SR 33. 1565 W Main St 83440. Fax: 208/359-138▮ **Terms:** Pets. **Facility:** 52 rooms. 2 stories; interior corridors; designated smoking area; heated indoor poc whirlpool. **Services:** winter plug-ins. **Cards:** AE, CB, DI, DS, JC, MC, VI.

DAYS INN   **Phone:** (208)356-922▮

6/16-8/31 [CP]	1P:	$50-	55	2P/1B:	$55-	60	2P/2B:	$55- 60	XP: $5	F▮
3/1-6/15 & 9/1-2/29 [CP]	1P:	$45-	50	2P/1B:	$50-	55	2P/2B:	$50- 55	XP: $5	F▮

🔺🔺 Motel
Location: US 20, S Rexburg exit; 1.8 mi s, just n. 271 S 2nd W 83440. Fax: 208/356-9242. **Terms:** Sma pets only. **Facility:** 43 rooms. Adjacent to Ricks College. All rooms with iron & ironing board. 2 stories; exteri corridors; designated smoking area; small heated pool. **Services:** winter plug-ins. **Cards:** AE, CB, DI, D MC, VI. **Special Amenities:** Free breakfast and free local telephone calls.

PORTER HOUSE B&B   Guaranteed Rates   **Phone:** 208/356-663▮

3/15-9/15 [BP]	1P:	$50-	55	2P/1B:	$57- 62	XP: $5-10

🔺🔺🔺 Bed & Breakfast
Location: US 20, Salmon/Rexburg exit; 0.3 mi w on SR 33, 1 mi n on 2000 W & 2.2 mi w. 4232 W 100 North 83440. Fax: 208/529-3006. **Terms:** Open 3/15-9/15; check-in 4 pm; reserv deposit. **Facility:** 4 rooms Valley countryside location on 10 acres with family atmosphere. Family rate, $85-$100; 2 stories; interior co ridors; smoke free premises. **Some Rooms:** combo, shower or tub baths, shared bathrooms. **Cards:** DS, MC, VI.

RESTAURANTS

FRONTIER PIES RESTAURANT & BAKERY   **Lunch:** $5-$7   **Dinner:** $6-$12   **Phone:** 208/356-360▮

🔺🔺 American
Location: 1 mi se of US 20. 460 W 4th St S 83440. **Hours:** 6:30 am-10 pm, Fri & Sat-11 pm. Closed: 12/2▮ **Features:** casual dress; children's menu; a la carte. Rustic atmosphere. All food items made from scratc including a large variety of pie. Smoke free premises. **Cards:** DS, MC, VI.

ME-N-STANS RESTAURANT   **Lunch:** $4-$16   **Dinner:** $7-$16   **Phone:** 208/356-733▮

🔺🔺 American
Location: Center. 167 W Main St 83440. **Hours:** 6:30 am-9 pm, Fri & Sat-10 pm. Closed: 11/25 & 12/2▮ **Features:** casual dress; children's menu; senior's menu; carryout; salad bar. Simple pleasant decor. We prepared food. Cordial, efficient service. Smoke free premises. **Cards:** AE, DS, MC, VI.

RIGGINS—400

LODGING

PINEHURST RESORT COTTAGES   Rates Subject to Change   **Phone:** 208/628-332▮

3/1-11/30	1P:	$25-	35	2P/1B:	$35-	55	2P/2B:	$40- 55	XP: $5	D▮

🔺 Cottage
Location: 13 mi s on US 95. MM 182 on US 95 83549 (5604 Hwy 95, NEW MEADOWS, 83654 **Terms:** Open 3/1-11/30; reserv deposit, 7 day notice; weekly rates; pets; $3 extra charge. **Facility:** 6 room Peaceful area on banks of Little Salmon River, with very clean rooms. 2 two-bedroom units. 1 story; exteri corridors; designated smoking area. **Dining:** Restaurant nearby. **Recreation:** swimming, fishing; picn tables, volleyball, croquet, horseshoes. **All Rooms:** shower baths. **Some Rooms:** 2 efficiencies, 2 kitchens. **Cards:** MC, V▮

SAGLE—200

LODGING

BOTTLE BAY RESORT & MARINA   Rates Subject to Change   **Phone:** 208/263-591▮

6/15-9/4	1P:	$85	2P/1B:	$85	2P/2B:	$85	XP: $5	F▮
3/1-6/14 & 9/5-2/29	1P:	$60	2P/1B:	$60	2P/2B:	$60	XP: $5	F▮

🔺🔺 Cottage
Location: 8.3 mi e on Bottle Bay Rd from US 95. 115 Resort Rd 83860. Fax: 208/263-591▮ **Terms:** Check-in 4 pm; reserv deposit, 30 day notice, 14 day notice, 9/15-6/15; handling fee imposed. **Facility:** 7 rooms. Sma quiet lakeside retreat offers contemporary log cabins. 1 two-bedroom unit. 1-2 stories; exterior corridors; boat ramp, marin **Services:** winter plug-ins. **Recreation:** swimming, fishing, waterskiing. **Rental:** boats, canoes. **All Rooms:** kitchen **Cards:** DS, MC, VI. (See color ad p 198)

RESTAURANT

SWAN'S LANDING   **Lunch:** $5-$12   **Dinner:** $10-$20   **Phone:** 208/265-200▮

🔺🔺🔺 Steak and Seafood
Location: Just s of bridge at Lake Pend Oreille on US 95. 41 Lakeshore Dr 83860. **Hours:** 11 am-10 p▮ Closed: 1/1 & 12/25. **Reservations:** suggested. **Features:** children's menu; carryout; cocktails & loung▮ Casual elegant dining in mountain lodge with sweeping waterfront & mountain views from dining room seasonal patio; featuring fine Northwestern menu. Sun brunch 10 am. **Cards:** AE, DS, MC, VI. (See color ad p 198)

ST. ANTHONY—3,000

LODGING

WEST WESTERN WESTON INN Phone: (208)624-3711
All Year 1P: $45- 50 2P/1B: $50- 55 2P/2B: $52- 57 XP: $5 F12
Location: US 20, St Anthony exit; just n on US 30 business route. 115 S Bridge St 83445.
Fax: 208/624-3711. **Facility:** 30 rooms. Adjacent to Henry's Fork of Snake River. 2 stories; exterior corridors;
designated smoking area. **Dining:** Restaurant; 6:30 am-9 pm; $6-$13. **Services:** winter plug-ins. **Cards:** AE,
CB, DI, DS, MC, VI. **Special Amenities:** Early check-in/late check-out and free local telephone calls.
Motor Inn

SALMON—2,900

LODGINGS

GREYHOUSE INN BED & BREAKFAST Phone: (208)756-3968
5/15-9/15 [BP] 1P: $65- 80 2P/1B: $65- 80 2P/2B: $65- 80 XP: $10
3/1-5/14 & 9/16-2/29 [BP] 1P: $55 2P/1B: $55 2P/2B: $55 XP: $10
Location: 12 mi s on US 93 (milepost 293). HC 61, Box 16 83467. **Terms:** Reserv deposit, 5 day notice.
Facility: 4 rooms. Charming Victorian gingerbread house built in 1894 situated in scenic river valley. 2 stories;
interior corridors; designated smoking area. **Dining:** Dinner avail on request. Complimentary afternoon
beverages & snacks. **Recreation:** badminton, lawn darts, croquet, board games. **Some Rooms:** combo or
shower baths, shared bathrooms. **Cards:** DS, MC, VI. **Special Amenities:** Early check-in/late check-out and free local
telephone calls.
Bed & Breakfast

MOTEL DELUXE Rates Subject to Change Phone: 208/756-2231
5/15-10/31 1P: $35- 39 2P/1B: $39- 41 2P/2B: $45- 50 XP: $5 F12
3/1-5/14 & 11/1-2/29 1P: $31- 33 2P/1B: $35- 37 2P/2B: $41- 45 XP: $4 F12
Location: Downtown; just s of Main St. 112 S Church St 83467 (PO Box 863). **Terms:** Reserv deposit, 7
day notice. **Facility:** 24 rooms. 5 two-bedroom units. 1 story; exterior corridors; designated smoking area.
All Rooms: combo or shower baths. **Some Rooms:** 5 efficiencies. **Cards:** AE, CB, DI, DS, JC, MC, VI.
Motel

STAGECOACH INN Rates Subject to Change Phone: 208/756-2919
All Year [CP] 1P: $53- 63 2P/1B: $59- 69 2P/2B: $61- 72 XP: $6 F12
Location: Just n on US 93 from jct of SR 28. 201 Hwy 93N 83467. **Terms:** Reserv deposit, 7 day notice.
Facility: 100 rooms. Adjacent to Salmon River with view. Many rooms with balcony. 2 stories; interior corridors;
designated smoking area; heated pool. **Services:** winter plug-ins. **Cards:** AE, CB, DI, MC, VI.
Motel

TWIN PEAKS RANCH Rates Subject to Change Phone: 208/894-2290
5/15-12/15 Wkly [AP] 1P:$1300-1540
Location: 20 mi s on US 93, 2 mi w. Rattlesnake Creek, US 93 83467 (PO Box 774). Fax: 208/894-2429.
Terms: Open 5/15-12/15; check-in 4:30 pm; reserv deposit, 30 day notice. **Facility:** 23 rooms. A true western
ranch in secluded setting. 3 two-bedroom units. 1 story; exterior corridors; smoke free premises; mountain view; heated pool.
Recreation: boating, charter fishing, fishing; hiking trails, horseback riding. **All Rooms:** combo or shower baths. **Cards:** MC,
VI.
Ranch

RESTAURANT

SHADY NOOK RESTAURANT Dinner: $9-$17 Phone: 208/756-4182
Location: 0.8 mi n on US 93. 83467. **Hours:** 5 pm-10 pm. **Reservations:** suggested; in summer.
Features: casual dress; children's menu; carryout; cocktails & lounge. A relaxed atmosphere. Collection of
big game trophies on walls & western gallery. Call for hrs & days of operation in winter. Also pasta. Happy
hour 5:30 pm-6:30 pm Mon-Fri. Patio dining avail. **Cards:** MC, VI.
Steak and Seafood

SANDPOINT—5,200

LODGINGS

WEST WESTERN CONNIE'S MOTOR INN Phone: (208)263-9581
7/1-8/31 1P: $79- 89 2P/1B: $89- 99 2P/2B: $89- 99 XP: $8 F18
5/1-6/30, 6/1-6/30 & 9/1-9/30 1P: $69- 79 2P/1B: $79- 89 2P/2B: $79- 89 XP: $8 F18
3/1-5/31 & 10/1-2/29 1P: $59- 69 2P/1B: $69 2P/2B: $79 XP: $8 F18
Location: Downtown; US 95S at Fourth & Cedar sts. 323 Cedar St 83864 (PO Box 126).
Fax: 208/263-3395. **Terms:** Small pets only. **Facility:** 53 rooms. Downtown location. Express checkout & some
covered parking. 1 whirlpool/fireplace suite, $100-$250; 2 suites with spa, $95-$185; 2-3 stories; interior/exterior corridors;
heated pool, whirlpool. **Dining:** Restaurant; 6 am-11 pm, Fri & Sat-midnight; $5-$15; cocktails. **Services:** winter plug-ins.
All Rooms: combo or shower baths, extended cable TV. **Cards:** AE, CB, DI, DS, MC, VI. **Special Amenities:** Early
check-in/late check-out and free local telephone calls. *(See color ad p 198)*
Motor Inn

COIT HOUSE BED & BREAKFAST Rates Subject to Change Phone: 208/265-4035
6/1-9/15 & 12/20-1/2 [BP] 1P: $65- 75 2P/1B: $85
3/1-5/31, 9/16-12/19 &
1/3-2/29 [BP] 1P: $55 2P/1B: $65- 75
Location: Just ne of US 95 at Fourth & Alder sts. 502 N Fourth Ave 83864. Fax: 208/265-4035. **Terms:** Age
restrictions may apply; check-in 4 pm; reserv deposit, 3 day notice, summer. **Facility:** 4 rooms. Turn-of-the-century charm in
restored 1907 Victorian manor located in the downtown area. 2 stories; interior corridors; smoke free premises; street parking
only. **All Rooms:** combo or shower baths. **Cards:** MC, VI.
Historic Bed & Breakfast

LAKESIDE INN   Phone: (208)263-371

6/27-9/7 [CP]	1P:	$63-	72	2P/1B:	$68-	79	2P/2B:	$79-	99	XP:	$5	F♦
12/19-1/2 & 2/12-2/16 [CP]	1P:	$57-	68	2P/1B:	$63-	75	2P/2B:	$73-	90	XP:	$5	F♦
3/1-6/26, 9/8-12/18, 1/3-2/11										
& 2/17-2/29 [CP]	1P:	$42-	44	2P/1B:	$49-	55	2P/2B:	$50-	65	XP:	$5	F♦

Motel   **Location:** Downtown; just e of US 95N. 106 Bridge St 83864. Fax: 208/265-4781. **Terms:** Reserv deposi weekly rates; package plans; pets, in smoking rooms, $5 extra charge. **Facility:** 60 rooms. Downtown property with varie room offerings located on Lake Pend Oreille at Sand Creek. Boat slips, spa & family suites. 3 two-bedroom units. 2 storie exterior corridors; designated smoking area; sauna, whirlpools; boat dock. **Dining:** Restaurant nearby. **Recreation:** boatin canoeing, fishing, paddleboats, waterskiing, daily lake cruises. **All Rooms:** extended cable TV. **Some Rooms:** 9 efficiencie kitchen, whirlpools. **Cards:** AE, CB, DI, DS, MC, VI. **Special Amenities:** Free breakfast and free local telephone calls. *(See color ad below)*

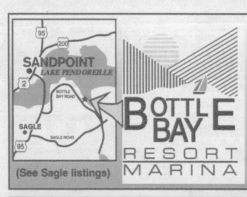

Double your pleasure with AAA Plus.

MONARCH WEST LODGE   Phone: (208)263-1222

6/15-9/30	1P: $45	2P/1B: $51	2P/2B: $60	XP: $5
3/1-6/14 & 10/1-2/29	1P: $39	2P/1B: $41	2P/2B: $43	XP: $5

◆ ◆
Motel
Location: 0.5 mi n on US 95N from jct SR 200. Bonner Mall, US 95N 83864 (PO Box 3171). **Fax:** 208/265-9472. **Terms:** Reserv deposit; handling fee imposed; pets. **Facility:** 49 rooms. Easy access off highway; adjacent to shopping mall. 2 stories; interior corridors; designated smoking area; sauna, whirlpools. **Dining:** Restaurant nearby. **Recreation:** garden area with grills. **All Rooms:** extended cable TV. **Cards:** AE, CB, DI, DS, JC, MC, VI. **Special Amenities:** Free breakfast and free local telephone calls.

QUALITY INN SANDPOINT   Phone: (208)263-2111

6/21-9/9	1P: $59- 89	2P/1B: $59- 89	2P/2B: $59- 89	XP: $6	F17
5/1-6/20 & 9/10-1/1	1P: $49- 79	2P/1B: $49- 79	2P/2B: $49- 79	XP: $6	F17
3/1-4/30 & 1/2-2/29	1P: $49- 69	2P/1B: $49- 69	2P/2B: $49- 69	XP: $6	F17

◆ ◆
Motor Inn
Location: US 2/95, just s of jct SR 200. 807 N 5th 83864 (PO Box 187). **Fax:** 208/263-3289. **Terms:** Pets, $5 extra charge. **Facility:** 62 rooms. Contemporary motor inn offers varied room selections. 1 two-bedroom unit. 2 stories; interior corridors; designated smoking area; heated indoor pool, whirlpool. **Dining:** Restaurant; 5 am-10 pm, Fri & Sat-11 pm; $7-$14; cocktails. **Services:** winter plug-ins. **Recreation:** video movie rental. **All Rooms:** combo or shower baths, extended cable TV. **Some Rooms:** efficiency, whirlpools. **Cards:** AE, CB, DI, DS, JC, MC, VI. **Special Amenities:** Free local telephone calls and free newspaper.

SANDPOINT MICROTEL INN   Rates Subject to Change   Phone: 208/263-5383

6/12-9/9	1P: $50- 70	2P/1B: $50- 70	2P/2B: $60- 80	XP: $5	F17
3/1-6/11 & 9/10-2/29	1P: $50- 70	2P/1B: $50- 70	2P/2B: $50- 70	XP: $5	F17

◆ ◆
Motel
Location: 477255 Hwy 95 N 83864. **Fax:** 208/263-0757. **Facility:** 70 rooms. 2 stories; interior corridors; designated smoking area. **Services:** winter plug-ins. **Cards:** AE, DI, DS, JC, MC, VI. *(See color ad below)*

SCHWEITZER MOUNTAIN BED & BREAKFAST   Rates Subject to Change   Phone: (208)265-8080

3/1-4/30 & 11/1-2/29 [BP]	1P: $75- 155	2P/1B: $85- 165	XP: $15
5/1-10/31 [BP]	1P: $58- 122	2P/1B: $68- 132	XP: $15

◆ ◆ ◆
Bed & Breakfast
Location: Schweitzer Mountain Village. 110 Crystal Ct 83864. **Fax:** 208/265-8781. **Terms:** Age restrictions may apply; reserv deposit, 30 day notice; handling fee imposed. **Facility:** 5 rooms. Mountain chalet retreat in alpine setting. 3 stories, no elevator; interior corridors; smoke free premises. **Services:** winter plug-ins. **Recreation:** hiking trails. **All Rooms:** shower baths.

SUPER 8 MOTEL   Rates Subject to Change   Phone: 208/263-2210

6/1-10/31	1P: $45- 56	2P/1B: $50- 60	2P/2B: $55- 65	XP: $5	F12
3/1-5/31 & 11/1-2/29	1P: $34- 38	2P/1B: $40- 44	2P/2B: $44- 48	XP: $5	F12

◆ ◆
Motel
Location: 0.7 mi n on US 95 from jct SR 200. 476841 Hwy 95N 83864. **Fax:** 208/263-2210. **Facility:** 61 rooms. Easy highway access; close to mall. Family rms, $55-$75; 2 stories; interior corridors; designated smoking area. **Cards:** AE, CB, DI, DS, MC, VI.

RESTAURANTS

CITY BEACH BISTRO   Lunch: $8-$10   Dinner: $15-$20   Phone: 208/255-1018

◆ ◆ ◆
Nouvelle Specialty
Location: Downtown. 204 N 1st Ave 83864. **Hours:** 11:30 am-1:30 & 5:30-8:30 pm, Fri-9 pm, Sat 5:30 pm-9 pm. Closed: 11/25 & 12/25. **Reservations:** accepted. **Features:** casual dress; health conscious menu items; beer & wine only; a la carte. Inventive, exciting, "world food" with frequently changing menu & interesting daily special dishes. Smoke free premises. **Cards:** DS, MC, VI.

HYDRA   Lunch: $6   Dinner: $7-$16   Phone: 208/263-7123

◆ ◆
Steak and Seafood
Location: City Center; just w of US 95 at 2nd & Lake sts. 115 Lake St 83864. **Hours:** 11:30 am-3 & 5-10 pm, Fri & Sat-10:30 pm, Sun 10 am-9 pm, buffet only. Closed: 11/25 & 12/25. **Reservations:** accepted; large parties. **Features:** casual dress; Sunday brunch; children's menu; salad bar; cocktails & lounge. Tues-Fri lunch buffet only. Dinners feature prime rib, steak & seafood specialties in a casual atmosphere; also creative pasta. **Cards:** AE, DI, DS, MC, VI.

IVANO'S   Dinner: $10-$18   Phone: 208/263-0211

◆ ◆
Regional Italian
Location: Downtown at corner of 2nd & Lake. 124 S Second 83864. **Hours:** 5 pm-9 pm, Fri & Sat-10 pm. Closed: 11/25 & 12/25. **Reservations:** accepted. **Features:** casual dress; carryout; cocktails. Traditional regional Italian cuisine in comfortable, casual surroundings. Smoke free premises. **Cards:** AE, DI, DS, MC, VI.

SODA SPRINGS—3,100

LODGING

J-R INN

(AAA) (SAVE)

◆

Motel

All Year   1P: $35   2P/1B: $35   2P/2B: $48

Phone: (208)547-3366

Location: US 30. 179 W 2nd S 83276. Fax: 208/547-3003. **Terms:** Pets. **Facility:** 44 rooms. 1 two-bedroom unit. 1 story; exterior corridors; designated smoking area. **Services:** winter plug-ins. **Cards:** AE, DI, DS, MC, VI. **Special Amenities:** Early check-in/late check-out and preferred room (subject to availability with advanced reservations).

STANLEY—100

LODGINGS

JERRY'S COUNTRY STORE & MOTEL   Rates Subject to Change   **Phone:** 208/774-3566

(AAA)

◆ ◆

Motel

6/1-9/30	1P: $55	2P/1B: $55	2P/2B: $65
10/1-2/29	1P: $48	2P/1B: $48	2P/2B: $58
3/1-5/31	1P: $45	2P/1B: $45	2P/2B: $55

Location: 1 mi n on SR 75 from jct of SR 21. 83278 (HC 67, Box 300). **Terms:** Reserv deposit, 5 day notice; pets, $5 extra charge. **Facility:** 9 rooms. On Salmon River; excellent view of Sawtooth Mountain range. 2 stories; exterior corridors; designated smoking area. **Services:** winter plug-ins. **Recreation:** video rental avail. **All Rooms:** efficiencies. **Cards:** AE, DS, MC, VI.

MOUNTAIN VILLAGE LODGE   Rates Subject to Change   **Phone:** 208/774-3661

◆ ◆

Motor Inn

5/22-9/30	1P: $74	2P/1B: $74	2P/2B: $74	XP: $5	F6
3/1-3/31 & 12/26-2/29	1P: $60	2P/1B: $60	2P/2B: $60	XP: $5	F6
4/1-5/21 & 10/1-12/25	1P: $50	2P/1B: $50	2P/2B: $50	XP: $5	F6

Location: Jct US 75 & SR 21. Corner US 75 & SR 21, #1 83278 (PO Box 150). Fax: 208/774-3761. **Terms:** Reserv deposit, 10 day notice. **Facility:** 63 rooms. Views of mountain ranges. 3 two-bedroom units. 2 stories; exterior corridors; designated smoking area. **Services:** winter plug-ins. **Some Rooms:** kitchen. **Cards:** DS, MC, VI.

STANLEY OUTPOST   Rates Subject to Change   **Phone:** (208)774-3646

(AAA)

◆ ◆

Motel

	1P:		2P/1B:		2P/2B:		XP:	
6/20-9/20	1P: $90- 95	2P/1B: $90- 95	2P/2B: $90- 95	XP: $5	F3
3/1-6/19 & 9/21-2/29	1P: $60- 70	2P/1B: $60- 70	2P/2B: $60- 70	XP: $5	F3

Location: 0.5 mi w on SR 21 from jct of SR 75. Hwy 21 83278 (PO Box 131). Fax: 208/774-3760. **Terms:** Reserv deposit, 14 day notice; pets, $5 extra charge. **Facility:** 6 rooms. Contemporary rooms with log exterior & log interior accents. 1 story; exterior corridors; designated smoking area. **Dining:** Cafeteria nearby. **All Rooms:** comb, shower or tub baths. **Some Rooms:** 5 kitchens. **Cards:** AE, DS, MC, VI.

RESTAURANT

MOUNTAIN VILLAGE RESTAURANT   **Lunch:** $5-$8   **Dinner:** $5-$16   **Phone:** 208/774-3317

◆

American

Location: Jct US 75 & SR 21; in Mountain Village Lodge. **Hours:** 7 am-10 pm; from 6 am in summer. **Features:** casual dress; children's menu; carryout; cocktails & lounge; a la carte. Relaxed family dining in log building at foot of scenic Sawtooth Mountains. **Cards:** AE, DS, MC, VI.

SUN VALLEY—900

LODGING

ELKHORN RESORT-SUN VALLEY   Rates Subject to Change   **Phone:** 208/622-4511

◆ ◆ ◆

Complex

	1P:		2P/1B:		2P/2B:		XP:	
3/1-3/31, 6/15-8/31 & 12/24-2/29	1P: $119- 139	2P/1B: $119- 139	2P/2B: $119- 139	XP: $10	F18
4/1-4/30 & 9/1-10/31	1P: $109- 129	2P/1B: $109- 129	2P/2B: $109- 129	XP: $10	F18
5/1-6/14 & 11/1-12/23	1P: $89- 109	2P/1B: $89- 109	2P/2B: $89- 109	XP: $10	F18

Location: 0.7 mi e on Dollar Rd, 1.7 mi s. 100 Elkhorn Rd 83354 (PO Box 6009). Fax: 208/622-3261. **Terms:** Check-in 4 pm; reserv deposit, 14 day notice; handling fee imposed. **Facility:** 132 rooms. Handsome setting. 4 stories; interior corridors; designated smoking area; heated pool; 18 tennis courts. Fee: 18 holes golf. **Services:** giftshop. **Recreation:** Fee: downhill & cross country skiing; horseback riding. Rental: bicycles. **Some Rooms:** 7 kitchens. **Cards:** AE, DI, DS, MC, VI. *(See ad below)*

RESTAURANT

SUN VALLEY LODGE DINING ROOM   **Dinner:** $18-$28   **Phone:** 208/622-2150
◆◆◆◆   **Location:** 1 Sun Valley Rd 83353. **Hours:** 6:30 pm-10 pm, Sun 9 am-2 pm. Closed: Sun & Mon in season,
Continental   Mon-Thurs off season. **Reservations:** suggested. **Features:** dressy casual; Sunday brunch; children's menu;
health conscious menu items; cocktails; entertainment; valet parking; a la carte, a la carte. Elegant dining in
relaxed atmosphere. Extensive wine list. **Cards:** AE, DI, DS, MC, VI.   ⊠

TENSED—100

LODGING

SEVEN SPRINGS FARM COUNTRY INN   Rates Subject to Change   **Phone:** (208)274-2470
◆◆   All Year [BP]   1P: $65- 75   2P/1B: $75   2P/2B: $75   XP: $20
Bed &   **Location:** 6 mi s on SR 95 to Sanders Rd, 2 mi e. HCR 1, Box 310 83870. **Terms:** Reserv deposit, 7 day
Breakfast   notice. **Facility:** 5 rooms. Unique new construction round house on working farm. 2 stories; interior corridors;
designated smoking area; mountain view. **Recreation:** bicycles, hiking trails. **Some Rooms:** combo or
shower baths, shared bathrooms, B/W TV. **Cards:** MC, VI.   ASK ⑤ 🍴 △ ⊠ 📺 📶 🐕 ⊠

TETONIA—100

LODGING

TETON MOUNTAIN VIEW LODGE   **Phone:** (208)456-2741
AAA SAVE   7/1-8/31 [CP]   1P: $60- 80   2P/1B: $70- 90   2P/2B: $70- 90   XP: $5   F17
   6/1-6/30 & 9/1-9/30 [CP]   1P: $40- 60   2P/1B: $50- 70   2P/2B: $50- 70   XP: $5   F17
◆◆   3/1-5/31 & 10/1-2/29 [CP]   1P: $35- 55   2P/1B: $45- 65   2P/2B: $45- 65   XP: $5   F17
Motel   **Location:** On Hwy 33. 510 Egbert Ave 83452 (PO Box 8). Fax: 208/456-2232. **Terms:** Reserv deposit;
handling fee imposed; pets. **Facility:** 27 rooms. Cozy, contemporary rustic rooms, some with fireplace. 1 two-
bedroom unit. 4 rms with fireplace; 2 stories; exterior corridors; whirlpool. **All Rooms:** combo or shower baths. **Cards:** AE,
DS, MC, VI. **Special Amenities:** Early check-in/late check-out and free local telephone calls.   🐕 📺 ⊠

TWIN FALLS—27,600

LODGINGS

AMERITEL INN   Rates Subject to Change   **Phone:** 208/736-8000
◆◆◆   5/1-9/30 [CP]   1P: $69- 75   2P/1B: $75- 85   2P/2B: $75- 85   XP: $5   F12
Motel   3/1-4/30 & 10/1-2/29 [CP]   1P: $65- 70   2P/1B: $69- 75   2P/2B: $69- 75   XP: $5   F12
  Location: I-84, exit 173; 3.9 mi s on US 93. 1377 Blue Lakes Blvd N 83301. Fax: 208/734-7777.
Facility: 118 rooms. Oversized rooms with 2 phones; close to Shoshone Falls & mall; expanded Continental breakfast. 7 whirlpool rms, extra charge; 3 stories; interior corridors; heated indoor pool. **Services:** winter plug-ins. **All Rooms:** combo or
shower baths. **Some Rooms:** 8 kitchens. **Cards:** AE, CB, DI, DS, MC, VI. *(See color ad p 172)*
🅿 🄪 🛥 🍴 ⊁ △ 📶 📺 📪 ⬛ 🖥 📞 ⊠ 📋

BEST WESTERN APOLLO MOTOR INN   **Phone:** (208)733-2010
AAA SAVE   5/17-10/15 [CP]   1P: $49- 63   2P/1B: $53- 66   2P/2B: $53- 66   XP: $4   F17
   3/1-5/16 & 10/16-2/29 [CP]   1P: $42- 54   2P/1B: $48- 58   2P/2B: $48- 58   XP: $4   F17
◆◆◆   **Location:** I-84, exit 173; 6.5 mi s on US 93, 1.2 mi w. 296 Addison Ave N 83301. Fax: 208/734-0748.
Motel   **Terms:** Small pets only, smoking rooms, 1 pet. **Facility:** 50 rooms. Park at rooms. 1 two-bedroom unit. 1 story;
exterior corridors; designated smoking area; heated pool, whirlpool. **Dining:** Restaurant nearby. **Cards:** AE,
DI, DS, MC, VI. **Special Amenities:** Free breakfast and free local telephone calls.   ⑤ 🐕 🛥 🍴 △ 📶 ⊠

BEST WESTERN SPRINGS PARK HOTEL   **Phone:** (208)734-5000
AAA SAVE   All Year   1P: $71- 73   2P/1B: $80- 82   2P/2B: $80- 82   XP: $10   F12
   Location: I-84, exit 173; 0.4 mi s on US 93. 1357 Blue Lakes Blvd N 83301. Fax: 208/734-5000.
◆◆◆   **Facility:** 112 rooms. Close to shopping; some rooms with balcony & pool view. 2 stories; interior corridors;
Motor Inn   sauna, whirlpool. **Dining:** Restaurant, deli; 6 am-10 pm; expresso shop 7 am-10 pm; $9-$17; cocktails.
Recreation: video movie rentals. **All Rooms:** combo or shower baths. **Cards:** AE, DS, MC, VI.
Special Amenities: Free local telephone calls and free newspaper.
🅿 🄪 🛥 🍴 🍽 ⊁ △ 📶 📶 VCR ⬛ ⊠ 📋

COMFORT INN

AAA SAVE
Motel

All Year   1P: $59- 75   2P/1B: $67- 91   2P/2B: $67- 109   XP: $7   F1   **Phone: (208)734-749***
Location: I-84, exit 173; 3.5 mi s on US 93. 1893 Canyon Springs Rd 83301. Fax: 208/734-749*
Terms: Reserv deposit, 7 day notice; pets. **Facility:** 52 rooms. Close to shopping malls. 2 stories; interior co
ridors; designated smoking area; small heated indoor pool, whirlpool. **Services:** winter plug-ins
Some Rooms: whirlpools. **Cards:** AE, CB, DI, DS, JC, MC, VI. **Special Amenities: Free breakfast an**
free newspaper.

MONTEREY MOTOR INN

Motel

Guaranteed Rates   **Phone: 208/733-515***
5/30-10/31   1P: $35   2P/1B: $39   2P/2B: $42   XP: $5   D1
3/1-5/29 & 11/1-2/29   1P: $28   2P/1B: $31   2P/2B: $35   XP: $5   D1
Location: I-84, exit 173; 6.5 mi s on US 93, 1.3 mi w. 433 Addison Ave W 83301. Fax: 208/734-509*
Facility: 28 rooms. Various room types; park at room. 2 two-bedroom units. Family lodge with kitchen, $75; 1 story; exterio
corridors; designated smoking area; heated pool. **Services:** winter plug-ins. **All Rooms:** combo or shower bath
Some Rooms: kitchen. **Cards:** AE, DI, JC, VI.

SHILO INN

Motel

Rates Subject to Change   **Phone: 208/733-754***
All Year [CP]   1P: $79- 119   2P/1B: $79- 119   2P/2B: $79- 119   XP: $10   F1
Location: I-84, exit 173; 3.7 mi s on US 93. 1586 Blue Lakes Blvd N 83301. Fax: 208/736-201*
Facility: 128 rooms. Overly spacious rooms; Most with 2 tv's; 4 phones with 2 lines; hairdryers; irons & boards
24 hr rec fac. 4 stories; interior corridors; designated smoking area; small heated indoor pool. **Some Rooms:** 5 kitchens
Cards: AE, CB, DI, DS, JC, MC, VI. *(See ad p 201, p 187 & p 178)*

TWIN FALLS SUPER 8 MOTEL

Motel

Guaranteed Rates   **Phone: 208/734-580***
All Year [CP]   1P: $45- 50   2P/1B: $50- 55   2P/2B: $55- 60   XP: $2-3   F1
Location: I-84, exit 173; 4.1 mi s on US 93. 1260 Blue Lakes Blvd N 83301. Fax: 208/734-7556. **Facility:** 9
rooms. Varied room styles including some oversize king rooms; oversize parking lot. 3 stories, no elevator; ir
terior corridors. **Services:** winter plug-ins. **Cards:** AE, CB, DI, DS, JC, MC, VI.

RESTAURANTS

A'ROMA ITALIAN CUISINE

Italian

Lunch: $5-$8   **Dinner:** $9-$19   **Phone:** 208/733-016*
Location: I-84, exit 73; 6.5 mi s on US 93, 0.6 mi sw. 147 Shoshone St N 83301. **Hours:** 11 am-2 & 5-9:3
pm, Mon 11 am-2 pm. Closed major holidays & Sun. **Reservations:** accepted. **Features:** casual dress
children's menu; beer & wine only. Fresh homemade pasta, fresh seafood, veal & steak dinner selection
accompanied by soup, salad & fresh bread in appealing country Italian atmosphere. Validated parking. **Cards:** DS, MC, VI.

CREEKSIDE STEAKHOUSE   Historical

American

Lunch: $6-$9   **Dinner:** $11-$29   **Phone:** 208/733-151*
Location: I-84, exit 173; 6.5 mi s on US 93, 1.5 mi sw on Shoshone St. 233 5th Ave S 83301. **Hours:**
pm-10 pm, Fri 11 am-2 & 5-10 pm, Sun 4 pm-8 pm. Closed: 7/4, 12/25 & Super Bowl Sun
Reservations: suggested. **Features:** casual dress; health conscious menu; beer & wine only; a la carte
Converted turn-of-the century warehouse, wood, brick, high ceilings. Well prepared steak, seafood & speciality items
Knowledgeable service. Smoke free premises. **Cards:** AE, DI, DS, MC, VI.

LA CASITA

Mexican

Lunch: $3-$9   **Dinner:** $3-$9   **Phone:** 208/734-797*
Location: I-84, exit 173; 6.5 mi s on US 93, then 1.3 mi sw on Shoshone St. 111 S Park Ave W 83301
Hours: 11 am-9 pm, Fri & Sat-10 pm. Closed major holidays & Sun. **Features:** casual dress; children'
menu; carryout; beer & wine only; a la carte. Casual eatery favored by the locals. Smoke free premises
Cards: MC, VI.

ROCK CREEK

AAA
**Steak and
Seafood**

Dinner: $9-$32   **Phone:** 208/734-415*
Location: I-84, exit 173; 6.5 mi s on US 93. 200 Addison Ave W 83301. **Hours:** 5:30 pm-10 pm, Fri
Sat-10:30 pm, Sun 5 pm-10 pm. Closed major holidays. **Reservations:** accepted. **Features:** casual dress
carryout; salad bar; cocktails & lounge. Casual dining in pleasant rustic atmosphere; specializing in prime ri
& fresh seasonal seafood. **Cards:** AE, DS, MC, VI.

THE SANDPIPER

**Steak and
Seafood**

Lunch: $6-$8   **Dinner:** $10-$22   **Phone:** 208/734-700*
Location: US 93, 3.5 mi s of jct I-84, exit 173. 1309 Blue Lakes Blvd N 83301. **Hours:** 11:30 am-2 & 5-1
pm, Sun 5 pm-9 pm. Closed: 11/25 & 12/25. **Reservations:** accepted. **Features:** casual dress; children
menu; cocktails & lounge. Established popular casual dining restaurant with outdoor deck area for summe
dining enjoyment; featuring prime rib & seafood selections, also pasta. **Cards:** AE, DS, MC, VI.

SODBUSTER PIES

AAA
American

Lunch: $4-$7   **Dinner:** $4-$12   **Phone:** 208/734-940*
Location: I-84, exit 173; 5 mi s on US 93. 598 Blue Lakes Blvd N 83301. **Hours:** 6 am-11 pm, Fri & Sat-midnigh
Closed: 11/25 & 12/25. **Features:** casual dress; children's menu; senior's menu; a la carte. Rust
atmosphere. Specializing in pie. **Cards:** DS, MC, VI.

UPTOWN BISTRO

Continental

Lunch: $5-$7   **Dinner:** $10-$20   **Phone:** 208/733-090*
Location: I-84, exit 173; 6.5 mi s on US 93, 0.8 mi sw on Shoshone St, just e. 117 Main Ave E 8330*
Hours: 11 am-3 & 5-9 pm, Mon & Tues 11 am-3 pm. Closed major holidays & Sun
Reservations: accepted. **Features:** casual dress; early bird specials; health conscious menu items
cocktails; street parking; a la carte. Eclectic atmosphere with friendly service, featuring lighter lunches & chicken, pasta o
seafood dinner entrees. Smoke free premises. **Cards:** AE, DS, MC, VI.

WALLACE—1,000

LODGING

EST WESTERN WALLACE INN   Phone: (208)752-1252
All Year   1P: $70- 72 2P/1B: $80- 82 2P/2B: $82- 84 XP: $8   F12
Location: Just s of I-90, exit 61. 100 Front St 83873 (PO Box 867). Fax: 208/753-0981. **Terms:** Check-in 4
pm; handling fee imposed; weekly/monthly rates; package plans; pets, $25 dep req. **Facility:** 63 rooms. Com-
plimentary paper & coffee in lobby. Adjacent to river, close to ATV trails & Silver Country 1000. 4 suites, 1 with
whirlpool, $220-$240; 2 stories; interior corridors; designated smoking area; mountain view; small heated in-
oor pool, sauna, steamroom, indoor whirlpool. **Dining:** Restaurant; 6:30 am-8:30 pm, Fri & Sat-9 pm; $8-$14; cocktails.
ervices: giftshop; area transportation; winter plug-ins. **All Rooms:** combo or shower baths. **Some Rooms:** whirlpools.
ards: AE, DS, MC, VI. **Special Amenities:** Early check-in/late check-out and free local telephone calls.

WEISER—4,600

LODGING

NDIANHEAD MOTEL   Rates Subject to Change   Phone: 208/549-0331
All Year   1P: $28   2P/1B: $38   2P/2B: $47
Location: 1 mi n on US 95. 747 US 95 83672. **Terms:** Reserv deposit, 7 day notice. **Facility:** 8 rooms. Easy
highway access; park at room. Attractive park setting with picnic area & grills. Close to public golf course. 1
two-bedroom unit. 1 story; exterior corridors; designated smoking area. **Dining:** Restaurant nearby.
Recreation: horseshoe pits. **All Rooms:** combo or shower baths. **Cards:** MC, VI.

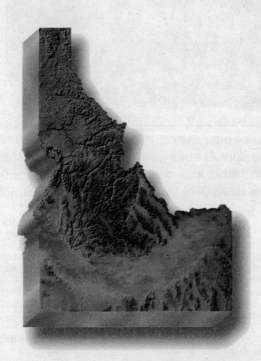

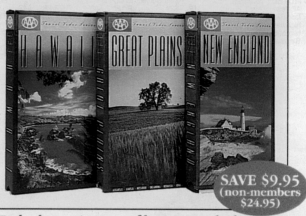

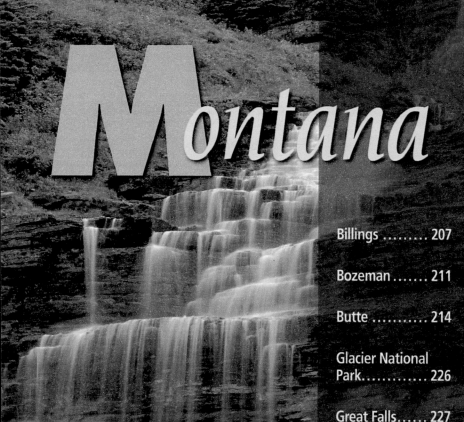

Montana

ANACONDA—10,300

RESTAURANT

BARCLAY II SUPPERCLUB & LOUNGE **Dinner:** $10-$26 **Phone:** 406/563-5541
◆◆
Steak and
Seafood
Location: I-90, Anaconda exit; sw on SR 1 7.5 mi. 1300 E Commercial 59711. **Hours:** 5 pm-10 pm, Sun 4 pm-9:30 pm. Closed major holidays & Mon. **Reservations:** suggested; weekends. **Features:** casual dress; cocktails & lounge; a la carte. Informal dining. Steak & seafood specialties. **Cards:** DS, MC, VI.

BELGRADE—3,400

LODGING

HOLIDAY INN EXPRESS **Phone:** (406)388-0800
AAA SAVE
◆◆◆
Motel

	1P:		2P/1B:		2P/2B:	
5/15-9/14 [CP]	$65-	75	$65-	75	$70-	80
3/1-5/14 & 9/15-2/29 [CP]	$65-	65	$55-	65	$65-	75

Location: I-90, exit 298; just s on SR 85. 6261 Jackrabbit Ln 59714. **Fax:** 406/388-0804. **Terms:** Weekly/monthly rates, in winter; pets. **Facility:** 67 rooms. Contemporary Southwestern appeal. 3 stories; interior corridors; smoke free premises; whirlpool. **Dining:** Restaurant; 6 am-10 pm, Fri & Sat-11 pm; $6-$8. **Services:** winter plug-ins. **All Rooms:** combo or shower baths, extended cable TV. **Cards:** AE, CB, DI, DS, JC, MC, VI. **Special Amenities:** Early check-in/late check-out and free local telephone calls.

BIGFORK—1,000

LODGINGS

BURGGRAF'S COUNTRY LANE BED N' BREAKFAST Rates Subject to Change **Phone:** (406)837-4608
◆◆
Bed &
Breakfast

	1P:	2P/1B:	2P/2B:	XP:	F12
5/15-9/15 [BP]	$85	$95- 115	$95- 110	$25	

Location: Jct of US 35, 3.3 mi e on SR 209 to fire station, 0.5 mi s on Ferndale Dr, 2 mi e on S Ferndale, 2 mi s. Rainbow Dr on Swan Lake 59911. **Fax:** 406/837-2468. **Terms:** Open 5/15-9/15; reserv deposit, 14 day notice; handling fee imposed. **Facility:** 5 rooms. On the shore of Swan Lake with beautiful lake & mountain views; recreational amenities & Internationally well traveled hostess. 2 stories; interior corridors; smoke free premises; off site parking only; boat dock, boat ramp. **Recreation:** swimming, canoeing, fishing. Rental: boats, paddleboats. **All Rooms:** shower baths. **Cards:** MC, VI.

O'DUACHAIN COUNTRY INN Rates Subject to Change **Phone:** 406/837-6851
◆◆◆
Bed &
Breakfast

	1P:	2P/1B:	2P/2B:	XP:
All Year [BP]	$95- 110	$95- 110	$95- 110	$20

Location: Jct of US 35, 3.3 mi e on SR 209 to fire station, 1.5 mi ne. 675 Ferndale Dr 59911. **Fax:** 406/837-0778. **Terms:** Reserv deposit, 30 day notice; handling fee imposed. **Facility:** 4 rooms. Log lodge nestled in wooded glen between the scenic Mission & Swan Mountains. 1 two-bedroom unit. Advance reservations preferred; 2 stories; interior corridors; designated smoking area. **Services:** winter plug-ins. **All Rooms:** combo or shower baths. **Cards:** AE, DS, MC, VI.

TIMBERS MOTEL Rates Subject to Change **Phone:** 406/837-6200
AAA
◆◆
Motel

	1P:		2P/1B:		2P/2B:		XP:	
6/12-9/6	$68-	71	$68-	71	$78-	81	$5	
5/15-6/11 & 9/7-10/3	$48-	50	$53-	55	$58-	60	$5	
3/1-5/14 & 10/4-2/29	$32-	33	$36-	37	$40-	42	$5	

Location: Just n on SR 35 from jct of SR 209. 8540 Hwy 35 59911 (PO Box 757). **Fax:** 406/837-6203. **Terms:** Pets, $5 extra charge, $50 dep req. **Facility:** 40 rooms. Contemporary room decor; adjacent coin laundry facility; park at some rooms. 2 stories; exterior corridors; designated smoking area; small heated pool, sauna, whirlpool. **Services:** winter plug-ins. **All Rooms:** combo or shower baths, extended cable TV. **Cards:** AE, DS, MC, VI.

RESTAURANT

SHOWTHYME **Lunch:** $7-$10 **Dinner:** $13-$22 **Phone:** 406/837-0707
◆◆◆
American
Location: Downtown. 548 Electric Ave 59911. **Hours:** 11:30 am-2:30 & 5-10 pm, Sat & Sun 5 pm-10 pm. Closed: 12/25 & Sun. **Reservations:** suggested. **Features:** casual dress; health conscious menu items; cocktails; street parking; a la carte. Casual atmosphere with summer deck dining. Seasonal menus feature creative entrees & dessert. Smoke free premises. **Cards:** AE, DS, MC, VI.

BIG SKY—500—*See also YELLOWSTONE NATIONAL PARK.*

LODGINGS

BEST WESTERN BUCK'S T-4 LODGE Phone: (406)995-4111
(AAA) (SAVE)

	1P:	2P/1B:	2P/2B:	XP:	
12/24-1/2 [CP]	$129- 144	$144- 159	$144- 159	$15-20	F12
3/1-4/11, 11/25-12/23 &					
1/3-2/29 [CP]	$104- 119	$119- 134	$119- 134	$15-20	F12
7/2-9/18 [CP]	$89- 99	$99- 109	$99- 109	$10-15	F12
5/21-7/1 & 9/19-11/24 [CP]	$69- 79	$79- 89	$79- 89	$10	F12

◆◆◆
Motor Inn

Location: US 191, 1 mi s of Big Sky entrance. 46625 Gallatin Rd 59716 (PO Box 160279). Fax: 406/995-2191. **Terms:** Open 3/1-4/11 & 5/21-2/29; BP avail, 11/25-4/11; package plans; small pets only, $5 extra charge. **Facility:** 74 rooms. Original rustic roadhouse with spacious contemporary rooms. Ski locker avail. 10 mi from ski resort. 2 two-bedroom units. Rental VCR's; 2 stories; interior corridors; whirlpools. **Dining:** Dining room, restaurant; 5 pm-10 pm; $7-$26. **Recreation:** fishing; cross country skiing, snowmobiling; rafting, hiking & horseback riding nearby. **Services:** winter plug-ins. **Some Rooms:** 2 efficiencies, whirlpools. **Cards:** AE, CB, DI, DS, JC, MC, VI. **All Rooms:** combo or shower baths. **Special Amenities: Free breakfast and free newspaper.** *(See color ad p 257)*

320 GUEST RANCH Phone: 406/995-4283
◆◆◆
Resort Ranch

	1P:	2P/1B:	2P/2B:	XP:	
7/2-9/1 [CP]	$152	$162	$162	$15	F12
3/1-4/15 & 12/25-2/29 [CP]	$128	$145	$145	$15	F12
6/1-7/1 & 9/2-10/1 [EP]	$124	$134	$134	$15	F12
4/16-5/31 & 10/2-12/24 [EP]	$106	$127	$127	$15	F12

Rates Subject to Change

Location: US 191, 11.8 mi s of Big Sky. 205 Buffalo Horn 59730. Fax: 406/995-4694. **Terms:** Reserv deposit, 31 day notice; handling fee imposed. **Facility:** 59 rooms. Deluxe log accomodations in the Gallatin National Forest, 5 mi from Yellowstone Park border; four rooms with fireplace. 13 two-bedroom units. 7 three-bedroom units. 7 three-bedroom houses, 3 night min stay; 1-2 stories; exterior corridors; designated smoking area; playground. **Recreation:** fishing; cross country skiing, snowmobiling; hiking trails. Fee: horseback riding. **Some Rooms:** 16 efficiencies, 7 kitchens. **Cards:** MC, VI.

BIG TIMBER—1,600

LODGINGS

BIG TIMBER SUPER 8 MOTEL Phone: 406/932-8888
◆◆◆
Motel

	1P:	2P/1B:	2P/2B:	XP:	
5/1-9/30 [CP]	$48	$53	$58	$5	F12
3/1-4/30 & 10/1-2/29 [CP]	$39	$43	$49	$5	F12

Rates Subject to Change

Location: I-90, exit 367. (PO Box 1441, 59011). **Facility:** 39 rooms. Convenient off interstate location. 2 stories; interior corridors; designated smoking area. **Services:** winter plug-ins. **Cards:** AE, CB, DI, DS, JC, MC, VI.

CM RUSSELL LODGE Phone: 406/932-5245
◆◆
Motor Inn

	1P:	2P/1B:	2P/2B:	XP:	
All Year	$39- 46	$45- 51	$51- 57	$6	F10

Rates Subject to Change

Location: I-90, exit 367; 0.3 mi n on US 10. (PO Box 670, 59011). Fax: 406/932-5243. **Facility:** 37 rooms. Spacious rooms. 2 stories; interior corridors; smoke free premises. **Services:** giftshop; winter plug-ins. **Cards:** DS, MC, VI.

RESTAURANT

THE 1890 GRAND HOTEL ROOM **Lunch:** $3-$6   **Dinner:** $17-$27   Phone: 406/932-4459
◆◆
American

Location: City Center. 139 McLeod 59011. **Hours:** 11 am-2 & 5-9 pm. Closed: 1/1, 12/24 & 12/25. **Features:** casual dress; health conscious menu; carryout; cocktails & lounge; street parking; a la carte. Romantic setting. Specialize in homemade, rich dessert. Seating also in lounge. **Cards:** DI, DS, MC, VI.

BILLINGS—81,200

LODGINGS

BEST WESTERN BILLINGS Phone: (406)248-9800
(AAA) (SAVE)
◆◆◆
Motel

	1P:	2P/1B:	2P/2B:	XP:	
6/1-9/15 [CP]	$61- 67	$69- 84	$69- 84	$5	F18
3/1-5/31 & 9/16-2/29 [CP]	$52- 58	$62- 72	$62- 72	$5	F18

Location: I-90, exit 446; just n. 5610 S Frontage Rd 59101. Fax: 406/248-2500. **Terms:** Small pets only. **Facility:** 80 rooms. Contemporary style rooms. Well-lighted rms. Close to water park. 8 whirlpool rms, extra charge; 3 stories; interior/exterior corridors; heated indoor pool, sauna, whirlpool. **Dining:** Restaurant nearby. **All Rooms:** combo or shower baths, extended cable TV. **Cards:** AE, CB, DI, DS, JC, MC, VI. **Services:** winter plug-ins. **Special Amenities: Free breakfast and preferred room (subject to availability with advanced reservations).**

BEST WESTERN PONDEROSA INN Phone: (406)259-5511
(AAA) (SAVE)
◆◆◆
Motel

	1P:	2P/1B:	2P/2B:	XP:	
All Year	$55- 65	$65- 75	$65- 75	$5	F12

Location: Downtown; I-90 Business Loop. 2511 1st Ave N 59101 (PO Box 1791, 59103). Fax: 406/245-8004. **Terms:** Small pets only. **Facility:** 130 rooms. Close to downtown shopping & businesses. Some covered parking. 1-3 stories; interior/exterior corridors; designated smoking area; heated pool, sauna. **Dining:** Restaurant; 24 hrs. **Services:** winter plug-ins. **Recreation:** exercise equipment. **All Rooms:** combo or shower baths. **Some Rooms:** whirlpools. **Cards:** AE, CB, DI, DS, JC, MC, VI. **Special Amenities: Early check-in/late check-out and free local telephone calls.**

BIG 5 MOTEL Phone: 406/245-6646
◆
Motel

	1P:	2P/1B:	2P/2B:	XP:	
All Year	$29	$32	$36	$5	F16

Rates Subject to Change

Location: I-90, exit 450; 1.6 mi n on 27th St, just e. 2601 4th Ave N 59101. Fax: 406/245-9358. **Facility:** 35 rooms. 3 mini-fridges avail; 2 stories; exterior corridors; designated smoking area. **Services:** winter plug-ins. **Cards:** AE, DS, MC, VI.

THE BILLINGS INN Phone: (406)252-680
(AAA) (SAVE) All Year [CP] 1P: $49- 59 2P/1B: $53- 59 2P/2B: $53- 59 XP: $5 F1
◆◆◆ **Location:** I-90, 27th St exit; 2 mi n on 27th St, just w on 9th Ave; across from Deaconess Hospital. 880
Motel 29th St 59101. Fax: 406/252-6800. **Terms:** Reserv deposit; pets, $5 extra charge. **Facility:** 60 rooms. Ve
good to excellent rooms. 6 mini-suites, $55 for up to 2 persons; 4 stories; interior corridors; designated smokir
area. **Dining:** Cafeteria nearby. **Services:** winter plug-ins. **All Rooms:** extended cable TV. **Cards:** AE, C
Special Amenities: Free breakfast and free local telephone calls. *(See ad below)*

🛏 🍴 📶 🛄 🖨 📠 🔒 ✕

BILLINGS SUPER 8 LODGE Rates Subject to Change Phone: (406)248-884
◆◆ 6/16-9/30 1P: $60- 65 2P/1B: $65- 70 2P/2B: $75- 85 XP: $5 F1
Motel 5/1-6/15 1P: $50- 60 2P/1B: $60- 65 2P/2B: $75- 85 XP: $5 F1
3/1-4/30 & 10/1-2/29 1P: $45- 55 2P/1B: $50- 65 2P/2B: $70- 80 XP: $5 F1
Location: I-90, exit 447; just n on S Billings Blvd, 0.8 mi w on King Ave, just s on Parkway Ln. 5400 Southgate Dr 5910
Fax: 406/248-8842. **Facility:** 115 rooms. 6 rooms with waterbed; 3 stories; interior corridors. **Services:** winter plug-in
Cards: AE, CB, DI, DS, MC, VI.

(ASK) 🛏 🍴 📺 (VCR) 🖨 🔒 ♿ ✕ 🐾

BILLINGS TRAVEL WEST INN Rates Subject to Change Phone: (406)245-634
(AAA) 5/1-9/30 1P: $48 2P/1B: $51 2P/2B: $54 XP: $3 F1
3/1-4/30 & 10/1-2/29 1P: $38 2P/1B: $42 2P/2B: $45 XP: $3 F1
◆◆ **Location:** Downtown. 3311 2nd Ave N 59101. Fax: 406/245-9882. **Terms:** Reserv deposit. **Facility:** 37 room
Motel Close to downtown shopping & businesses. 2 stories; interior/exterior corridors; designated smoking are
sauna. **Services:** winter plug-ins. **All Rooms:** combo or shower baths, extended cable TV. **Cards:** AE, D
DS, MC, VI.

📺 🖨 📠 🔒 ✕

CHERRY TREE INN Rates Subject to Change Phone: 406/252-560
(AAA) All Year [CP] 1P: $35- 37 2P/1B: $40- 42 2P/2B: $41- 43 XP: $3 F1
◆◆◆ **Location:** I-90, exit 450; 2 mi n on 27th St, just w on 9th Ave; opposite Deaconess Hospital. 823
Motel Broadway 59101. Fax: 406/254-0494. **Terms:** Weekly rates; pets. **Facility:** 65 rooms. Rooftop patio & su
deck. 2 stories; interior corridors. **Dining:** Cafeteria nearby. **Services:** winter plug-ins. **Some Rooms:**
kitchens. **Cards:** AE, CB, DI, DS, JC, MC, VI. *(See color ad below)*

🛏 🍴 🛄 📠 🖨 🔒 ✕

C'MON INN Rates Subject to Change Phone: 406/655-110
◆◆◆ 5/1-9/30 [CP] 1P: $59 2P/1B: $65 2P/2B: $74 XP: $6 F1
Motel 3/1-4/30 & 10/1-2/29 [CP] 1P: $50 2P/1B: $56 2P/2B: $65 XP: $6 F1
Location: I-90, exit 446; n on King Ave W, just s on Overland Ave, 1st stoplight. 2020 Overland Ave 5910
Fax: 406/652-7672. **Facility:** 80 rooms. Close to shopping. Most 2nd floor rms have balcony overlooking the tree lined atriu
with skylight. Well-lighted rooms. 8 whirlpool rms, extra charge; 2 stories; interior corridors; designated smoking area; heate
indoor pool. **Services:** winter plug-ins. **Cards:** AE, DS, MC, VI.

(ASK) 🛏 🍴 🐾 📺 🛄 🖨 📠 🔒 ✕

COMFORT INN OF BILLINGS

◆◆◆
Motel

Phone: (406)652-5200

6/1-8/31	1P:	$59- 72	2P/1B:	$65- 79	2P/2B:	$65- 79	XP: $5	F17
9/1-11/30	1P:	$54- 59	2P/1B:	$60- 74	2P/2B:	$60- 74	XP: $5	F17
3/1-5/31 & 12/1-2/29	1P:	$49- 59	2P/1B:	$55- 61	2P/2B:	$55- 61	XP: $5	F17

Rates Subject to Change

Location: I-90, exit 446; n on King Ave W, just s on Overland Ave, 1st stoplight. 2030 Overland Ave 59102. Fax: 406/652-5200. **Terms:** Reserv deposit. **Facility:** 60 rooms. Well-appointed spacious rooms. 2 stories; interior corridors; small heated indoor pool. **Services:** winter plug-ins. **Cards:** AE, CB, DI, DS, MC, VI.

DAYS INN

◆◆
Motel

Phone: 406/252-4007

6/1-9/30 [CP]	1P:	$51- 75	2P/1B:	$55- 95	2P/2B:	$62	XP: $5	F12
3/1-5/31 & 10/1-2/29 [CP]	1P:	$43- 75	2P/1B:	$55	2P/2B:	$47- 62	XP: $5	F12

Rates Subject to Change

Location: I-90, exit 447; just n on S Billings Blvd, 0.8 mi s on Parkway Ln, just s; I-90, exit 446; following signs eastbound. 843 Parkway Ln 59101. Fax: 406/896-1147. **Facility:** 63 rooms. 2 stories; interior corridors; designated smoking area. **Services:** winter plug-ins. **All Rooms:** combo or shower baths. **Cards:** AE, CB, DI, DS, JC, MC, VI.

FAIRFIELD INN BY MARRIOTT

◆◆◆
Motel

Phone: 406/652-5330

6/1-9/5 [CP]	1P:	$49- 65	2P/1B:	$59- 75	2P/2B:	$59- 75	XP: $6	F18
3/1-5/31 & 9/6-2/29 [CP]	1P:	$45- 55	2P/1B:	$55- 65	2P/2B:	$55- 65	XP: $6	F18

Rates Subject to Change

Location: I-90, exit 446; 0.5 mi n, just s. 2026 Overland Ave 59102. Fax: 406/652-5330. **Facility:** 63 rooms. Very clean rooms. 3 stories; interior corridors; small heated indoor pool. **Services:** winter plug-ins. **Cards:** AE, DI, DS, MC, VI.

HILLTOP INN

◉◉ [SAVE]
◆◆◆
Motel

Phone: (406)245-5000

All Year [CP]	1P:	$49- 59	2P/1B:	$53- 59	2P/2B:	$53- 59	XP: $5	F12

Location: I-90, 27th St exit; 2 mi n on 27th St, just w on 11th Ave, just n; adjacent to St Vincent Hospital. 1116 N 28th St 59101. Fax: 406/245-7851. **Terms:** Reserv deposit; pets, $5 extra charge. **Facility:** 45 rooms. Quiet contemporary rooms & attractive public areas. 2 mini-suites, $50 for up to 2 persons; 3 stories; interior corridors; designated smoking area. **Services:** winter plug-ins. **All Rooms:** extended cable TV. **Cards:** AE, DI, DS, MC, VI. **Special Amenities:** Free breakfast and free local telephone calls. (See color ad below)

HOWARD JOHNSON EXPRESS INN

◆◆◆
Motel

Phone: 406/248-4656

6/1-9/15 [CP]	1P:	$60	2P/1B:	$68	2P/2B:	$68
3/1-5/31 & 9/16-2/29 [CP]	1P:	$50	2P/1B:	$54	2P/2B:	$54

Rates Subject to Change

Location: I-90, exit 450; just n on SR 3 (S 27th St). 1001 S 27th St 59101. Fax: 406/248-7268. **Terms:** Reserv deposit, 7 day notice. **Facility:** 173 rooms. Contemporary room decor. Large breakfast room. 3 stories; interior corridors. **Services:** area transportation; winter plug-ins. **All Rooms:** combo or shower baths. **Cards:** AE, DI, DS, MC, VI.

KELLY INN

◉◉ [SAVE]
◆◆
Motel

Phone: (406)252-2700

6/1-9/15 [CP]	1P:	$44- 54	2P/1B:	$56- 66	2P/2B:	$64- 74	XP: $4	F12
3/1-5/31 & 9/16-2/29 [CP]	1P:	$36- 40	2P/1B:	$44- 52	2P/2B:	$52- 60	XP: $4	F12

Location: I-90, exit 446; 0.5 mi se. 5425 Midland Rd 59101. Fax: 406/252-1011. **Terms:** Pets. **Facility:** 89 rooms. Conveniently located to west end businesses & shopping. 2 stories; interior/exterior corridors; heated pool, sauna, whirlpool. **Dining:** Restaurant nearby. **Services:** winter plug-ins. **All Rooms:** combo or shower baths, extended cable TV. **Some Rooms:** kitchen. **Cards:** AE, CB, DI, DS, JC, MC, VI. IMA. (See color ad p 320 & p 281)

QUALITY INN HOMESTEAD

◆◆◆
Motel

Phone: (406)652-1320

5/1-9/15 [BP]	1P:	$53- 63	2P/1B:	$68- 78	2P/2B:	$70- 80	XP: $5	F18
9/16-12/31 [BP]	1P:	$50- 60	2P/1B:	$58- 66	2P/2B:	$58- 68	XP: $5	F18
3/1-4/30 & 1/1-2/29 [BP]	1P:	$48- 55	2P/1B:	$55- 66	2P/2B:	$58- 66	XP: $5	F18

Rates Subject to Change

Location: I-90, exit 446; n on King Ave W, 2 blks s, 1st stoplight. 2036 Overland Ave 59102. Fax: 406/652-1320. **Facility:** 119 rooms. Contemporary furnishings, large breakfast room. Close to movie theater & shopping. New pool room. 4 VCP's avail, extra charge; 2 stories; interior corridors; heated indoor pool. **Services:** winter plug-ins. **Cards:** AE, CB, DI, DS, JC, MC, VI.

RAMADA LIMITED

◆◆
Motel

Phone: 406/252-2584

All Year [CP]	1P:	$42- 67	2P/1B:	$60- 70	2P/2B:	$60- 70	XP: $5	F18

Rates Subject to Change

Location: I-90, exit 446; just s. 1345 Mullowney Ln 59101. Fax: 406/252-2584. **Facility:** 116 rooms. Expanded continental breakfast in fireplace room. Microwaves & mini-refrigerators avail, extra charge; 2 stories; interior corridors; designated smoking area; small heated pool. **Services:** winter plug-ins. **All Rooms:** combo or shower baths. **Cards:** AE, CB, DI, DS, MC, VI.

RIMVIEW INN
Phone: (406)248-2622
AAA SAVE
Motel
◆◆
| | | 2P/1B: | $44- | 48 | 2P/2B: | $48- | 55 |
5/1-9/30 [BP]
3/1-4/30 & 10/1-2/29 [BP] | | 2P/1B: | $37- | 42 | 2P/2B: | $40- | 45 | XP: | $3
Location: I-90, exit 450; 2 mi n. 1025 N 27th St 59101. Fax: 406/248-2622. **Terms:** Weekly rates; pets, $ extra charge. **Facility:** 54 rooms. Spacious rooms. Close to hospitals & downtown. 1,000 gallon fish tank in lobby. 2 whirlpool rms, extra charge; 3 stories, no elevator; interior/exterior corridors; designated smoking area whirlpool. **Services:** winter plug-ins. **All Rooms:** combo or shower baths, extended cable TV. **Some Rooms:** 20 efficiencies 7 kitchens. **Cards:** AE, CB, DI, DS, MC, VI. **Special Amenities:** Early check-in/late check-out and free breakfast. *(See color ad below)*

🛏 🕂 🕭 🎇 VCR ▢ 🖨 🖬 ✕

SHERATON BILLINGS HOTEL
◆◆◆
Hotel
Rates Subject to Change
Phone: 406/252-7400
| | 1P: | $89- | 99 | 2P/1B: | $89- | 99 | 2P/2B: | $89- | 99 | XP: | $10 |
All Year
Location: I-90 business loop & SR 3. 27 N 27th St 59101. Fax: 406/252-2401. **Facility:** 282 rooms. Close to businesses & shopping. All rooms with iron & ironing board. 23 stories; interior corridors; small heated pool **Services:** giftshop. **Cards:** AE, CB, DI, DS, MC, VI. *(See ad below)*

🛏 🕃 🈁 🏊 🍴 🍸 🕂 🕭 🕴 🎇 🖳 🖨 🖬 ✕

SLEEP INN
◆◆
Motel
Rates Subject to Change
Phone: (406)254-0013
| | 1P: | $55 | 2P/1B: | $63 | 2P/2B: | $63 | XP: | $5 | F18 |
5/1-2/29 [CP]
3/1-4/30 [CP] | | 1P: | $48 | 2P/1B: | $54 | 2P/2B: | $54 | XP: | $5 | F18 |
Location: I-90, exit 447; just w. 4904 Southgate Dr 59101. Fax: 406/254-9878. **Terms:** Reserv deposit. **Facility:** 75 rooms. 2 stories; interior corridors. **Services:** winter plug-ins. **All Rooms:** combo or shower baths. **Cards:** AE CB, DI, DS, JC, MC, VI.

SAVE 🖵 🈁 🎇 🕭 🕭 ✕

RESTAURANTS

BRUNOS PASTA & PIZZA
◆◆
Italian
Lunch: $5-$9
Dinner: $6-$11
Phone: 406/248-4146
Location: I-90, exit 452; 0.5 mi w on Business Loop 90; w on 1st Ave, just n. 1002 1st Ave N 59101 **Hours:** 11 am-9 pm, Fri-10 pm, Sat 5 pm-10 pm. Closed major holidays & Sun. **Features:** casual dress cocktails & lounge; a la carte. Traditional Italian favorites served in enjoyable relaxed dining atmosphere. **Cards:** AE, DS, MC, VI.

✕

C J'S RESTAURANT
◆◆
American
Lunch: $6-$12
Dinner: $10-$24
Phone: 406/656-1400
Location: I-90, exit 446; 1 mi w on King Ave, 1 mi n on 24th St, 0.3 mi w, s at light. 2456 Central Ave 59102. **Hours:** 11:30 am-3 & 5-10 pm, Fri & Sat 11:30 am-11 pm, Sun 11:30 am-9 pm. Closed: 1/1, 7/4, 11/25 & 12/25. **Reservations:** suggested. **Features:** casual dress; children's menu; carryout; salad bar; cocktails & lounge; a la carte. Relaxed atmosphere offering large selection of ribs, steak & seafood cooked over mesquite wood. Patio service weather permitting. **Cards:** AE, DI, DS, MC, VI.

✕

DOS MACHOS RESTAURANT   Lunch: $5-$18   Dinner: $5-$18   Phone: 406/652-2020
◆◆
Mexican   **Location:** I-90, exit 446 (W Billings); 1.3 mi nw on King Ave, w overpass to 24th St W, just n to Phyllis Ln; near Rimrock Mall. 300 S 24th St W 59102. **Hours:** 11 am-9 pm, Fri & Sat-10 pm, Sun 9 am-9 pm; to 10 pm, 5/2-10/31. Closed: 11/25 & 12/25. **Features:** casual dress; children's menu; carryout; cocktails; buffet. Old Mexico setting festively decorated. Large Mexican/American menu. Patio service weather permitting. Sun Champgne brunch. **Cards:** AE, DI, MC, VI.   ⊠

4 B'S RESTAURANT AND PRIME TIME CASINO   Lunch: $6-$9   Dinner: $6-$9   Phone: 406/652-4646
◆
American   **Location:** I-90, exit 446 (W Billings); 1.3 mi nw on King Ave, w overpass to 24th St W, then 2 mi n. 2349 Grand Ave 59102. **Hours:** 24 hrs. Closed: 11/25 & 12/25. **Features:** casual dress; children's menu; a la carte. Family restaurant. **Cards:** AE, DI, DS, MC, VI.   ⊠

GEORGE HENRY'S RESTAURANT   Historical   Lunch: $5-$8   Dinner: $8-$20   Phone: 406/245-4570
◆◆
American   **Location:** Downtown. 404 N 30th St 59101. **Hours:** 11 am-2 & 5:30-9 pm, Sat from 5:30 pm. Closed major holidays & Sun. **Reservations:** suggested. **Features:** casual dress; beer & wine only. Remodeled 1882 home with stained glass windows operated by the fourth generation offering traditional fare, seafood specialties & in season homemade dessert. Very popular. Smoke free premises. **Cards:** AE, DS, MC, VI.   ⊠

GOLDEN BELLE RESTAURANT   Lunch: $6-$11   Dinner: $14-$25   Phone: 406/245-2232
◆◆◆
Continental   **Location:** Downtown; in Radisson Northern Hotel. 19 N 28th St 59101. **Hours:** 6:30 am-2 & 5-10 pm, Sun 6:30 am-9 pm. **Reservations:** suggested. **Features:** casual dress; Sunday brunch; children's menu; cocktails & lounge. Contemporary western lobby decor. Wild game buffalo burgers, pasta & seafood served by attentive wait staff. **Cards:** AE, DI, DS, JC, MC, VI.   ⊠

JAKES OF BILLINGS   Lunch: $5-$10   Dinner: $12-$29   Phone: 406/259-9375
◆◆◆
American   **Location:** I-90 business loop & SR 3. 2701 1st Ave N 59101. **Hours:** 11:30 am-10 pm, Fri-10:30 pm, Sat 5:30 pm-10:30 pm. Closed: 11/25, 12/25 & Sun. **Reservations:** suggested; weekends. **Features:** casual dress; cocktail lounge; fee for parking. Informal dining in popular contemporary eatery. Smoke free premises. **Cards:** AE, DS, MC, VI.   ⊠

THE REX   Dinner: $6-$27   Phone: 406/245-7477
◆◆◆
American   **Location:** I-90, exit 450; 1.5 mi n on 27th St, just e. 2401 Montana Ave 59101. **Hours:** 5:30 pm-10:30 pm, Fri & Sat-11 pm. Closed: 11/25 & 12/25. **Reservations:** accepted. **Features:** casual dress; cocktails & lounge. Located in the historic Rex Hotel building. Fresh seafood, prime rib, steak specialities, game & pasta. Espresso. Smoke free premises. **Cards:** AE, DI, DS, MC, VI.   ⊠

BLACK EAGLE—900

RESTAURANTS

BORRIES   Dinner: $8-$20   Phone: 406/761-0300
◆◆
American   **Location:** 9th St & Smelter jct, 0.5 mi e. 1800 Smelter Ave 59414. **Hours:** 5 pm-10 pm, Fri & Sat-11 pm. Closed major holidays. **Reservations:** suggested; weekends. **Features:** casual dress; cocktails & lounge; cafeteria. Comfortable atmosphere. Steak a specialty. **Cards:** DS, MC, VI.

3D INTERNATIONAL   Lunch: $7   Dinner: $7-$19   Phone: 406/453-6561
◆◆
Chinese   **Location:** 9th St & Smelter jct, 0.5 mi e. 1825 Smelter Ave 59414. **Hours:** 11 am-2 & 5-10 pm, Fri & Sat 4:30 pm-10:30 pm, Sun 4 pm-10 pm. Closed: 4/4, 7/4, 11/25, 12/24 & 12/25. **Features:** casual dress; children's menu; carryout; cocktails & lounge; a la carte. Black tie service in casual, family dining setting. Popular Mongolian grill. Serve seafood, steak, Italian, Chinese & Thai menus. Live music Fri nights. **Cards:** DS, MC, VI.   ⊠

BOZEMAN—22,700

LODGINGS

BEST WESTERN GRANTREE INN   Phone: (406)587-5261

AAA SAVE	7/1-8/31	1P: $89	2P/1B: $89	2P/2B: $89	XP: $4	F18
	6/1-6/30 & 9/1-9/15	1P: $79	2P/1B: $79	2P/2B: $79	XP: $4	F18
◆◆◆	3/1-5/31 & 9/16-2/29	1P: $59	2P/1B: $69	2P/2B: $69	XP: $4	F18

Motor Inn   **Location:** I-90 business loop, just s of jct I-90, exit 306. 1325 N 7th Ave 59715. Fax: 406/587-9437. **Terms:** Check-in 4 pm; weekly rates. **Facility:** 103 rooms. Attractive public areas. Large, contemporary rooms. All rooms with iron & ironing board. 2 stories; interior corridors; heated indoor pool, whirlpool. **Dining:** Restaurant; 6 am-10 pm; casino; $6-$18. **Services:** winter plug-ins. **All Rooms:** extended cable TV. **Some Rooms:** whirlpools. **Cards:** AE, CB, DI, DS, JC, MC, VI. **Special Amenities:** Early check-in/late check-out and free local telephone calls.
🌐 📶 🈯 🏊 ❌ 🍽 🍸 🈂 🦽 🛋 💻 📠 ⊠

BOZEMAN DAYS INN AND CONFERENCE CENTER   Rates Subject to Change   Phone: (406)587-5251

◆◆	6/15-9/15 [BP]	1P: $58-	99	2P/1B: $79-	99	2P/2B: $88-	128	XP: $5	F17
Motel	3/1-6/14 & 9/16-2/29 [BP]	1P: $42-	69	2P/1B: $49-	79	2P/2B: $59-	99	XP: $5	F17

Location: I-90, exit 306; just s. 1321 N 7th 59715. Fax: 406/587-5351. **Facility:** 80 rooms. 1 two-bedroom unit. 2 stories; interior corridors; designated smoking area. **Services:** winter plug-ins. **All Rooms:** combo or shower baths. **Some Rooms:** kitchen. **Cards:** AE, CB, DI, DS, JC, MC, VI.
SAVE 🌐 🐾 🈂 💻 🛋 📠 🛢 ⊠

THE BOZEMAN INN   Phone: (406)587-3176

AAA SAVE	6/15-9/15 [CP]	1P: $50-	55	2P/1B: $63-	68	2P/2B: $73-	78	XP: $5	F18
	6/1-6/14 & 9/16-9/30 [CP]	1P: $45-	50	2P/1B: $58-	63	2P/2B: $65-	70	XP: $5	F18
◆◆	3/1-5/31 & 10/1-2/29 [EP]	1P: $35-	39	2P/1B: $40-	45	2P/2B: $50-	55	XP: $5	F18

Motel   **Location:** I-90, exit 306; just s. 1235 N 7th Ave 59715. Fax: 406/585-3591. **Terms:** Pets, $5 extra charge. **Facility:** 49 rooms. Just off interstate exit, very clean large rooms. 2 stories; exterior corridors; designated smoking area; heated pool, sauna, whirlpool. **Dining:** Restaurant nearby. **Services:** winter plug-ins. **All Rooms:** combo or shower baths, extended cable TV. **Some Rooms:** whirlpools. **Cards:** AE, CB, DI, DS, JC, MC, VI. **Special Amenities:** Early check-in/late check-out and free local telephone calls.
🌐 🐾 🈂 🍽 🛋 💻 📠 🛢 ⊠

BOZEMAN SUPER 8
◆◆ Motel

Rates Subject to Change
Phone: (406)586-152⌐

	1P:	2P/1B:	2P/2B:	XP:	
5/1-9/15	$61	$68	$72	$5	F1⌐
3/1-4/30 & 9/16-2/29	$45	$50	$56	$5	F1⌐

Location: I-90, exit 306; just n, just w. 800 Wheat Dr 59715. Fax: 406/586-1521. **Facility:** 108 rooms. 3 sto-ries, no elevator; interior corridors. **Services:** winter plug-ins. **Cards:** AE, CB, DI, DS, MC, VI.

(ASK) (S⌀) (🛏) (📺) (🎥) (VCR) (✕)

BOZEMAN'S WESTERN HERITAGE INN
AAA SAVE
◆◆◆ Motel

Phone: (406)586-853⌐

	1P:		2P/1B:		2P/2B:		XP:	
7/1-8/31 [CP]	$58-	68	$68-	78	$68-	78	$3	F1
6/1-6/30 & 9/1-9/15 [CP]	$49-	53	$53-	58	$58-	68	$3	F1
3/1-5/31 & 9/16-2/29 [CP]	$39-	49	$42-	49	$46-	49	$3	F1

Location: I-90 business loop, 0.5 mi w of jct I-90, exit 309. 1200 E Main St 59715. Fax: 406/587-8729. **Terms:** Weekly/monthly rates; small pets only, $7 extra charge. **Facility:** 38 rooms. Rustic lobby. Newly reno-vated, very clean rooms. 1 apartment from $85. Microwaves & refrigerators avial, exta charge; 3 stories, no elevator; interio corridors; designated smoking area; steamroom, whirlpool. **Dining:** Restaurant nearby. **Services:** winter plug-ins. **Recreation:** treadmill. Fee: tanning salon. **All Rooms:** extended cable TV. **Some Rooms:** efficiency, whirlpools. **Cards:** AE, CB, DI, DS, MC, VI. **Special Amenities: Early check-in/late check-out and preferred room (subject to availability with advanced reservations).** *(See color ad below)*

(🛏) (3⌐) (📺) (△) (✕) (VCR) (🔲) (✕)

BRIDGER MOUNTAINS HIGHLAND HOUSE
AAA
◆◆◆
Bed & Breakfast

Rates Subject to Change
Phone: 406/587-090⌐

	1P:	2P/1B:	XP:	
All Year [BP]	$82	$90	$10	F⌐

Location: I-90, exit 305, just n, just s on Springhill Rd, w on SR 205 0.9 mi, then n on Nelson Rd 1.5 m 1540 Nelson Rd 59718. Fax: 406/587-1813. **Terms:** Weekly rates; pets. **Facility:** 4 rooms. Rural, rustic el-egance. Located on the banks of the East Gallatin River with view of the Bridger Mountains. Owners rais Scotch Highland cattle. Public area fireplace & TV. Reading parlor. 2 stories; interior corridors; smoke fre premises; whirlpool. **Services:** winter plug-ins. **Recreation:** fishing. **Cards:** MC, VI.

(🛏) (✈) (✕) (CTV) (☑) (✕) (🔲) (✕)

ECONO LODGE
AAA SAVE
◆◆
Motel

Phone: (406)587-210⌐

	1P:	2P/1B:	2P/2B:	XP:	
6/16-9/30 [CP]	$54	$58	$62	$4	F1⌐
5/1-6/15 & 10/1-10/31 [CP]	$44	$48	$52	$4	F1⌐
3/1-4/30 & 11/1-2/29 [CP]	$34	$38	$42	$4	F1⌐

Location: I-90, exit 306; just n & just w. 805 Wheat Dr 59715. **Facility:** 42 rooms. Convenient interstate ac cess. 3 stories, no elevator; interior corridors; designated smoking area; sauna, whirlpool **Dining:** Restaurant nearby. **Services:** winter plug-ins. **All Rooms:** extended cable TV. **Cards:** AE, CB, DI, DS, JC, MC, V **Special Amenities: Free breakfast and free local telephone calls.**

(S⌀) (📺) (✕)

FAIRFIELD INN BY MARRIOTT
◆◆◆
Motel

Rates Subject to Change
Phone: (406)587-222⌐

	1P:		2P/1B:		2P/2B:		XP:	
6/1-9/30 [CP]	$79-	99	$79-	99	$79-	99	$5-10	F1⌐
3/1-5/31 & 10/1-2/29 [CP]	$44-	69	$44-	69	$44-	69	$5-10	F1⌐

Location: I-90, exit 306; just nw. 828 Wheat Dr 59715. Fax: 406/587-2222. **Facility:** 57 rooms. Convenient lo cation. Some rooms with data ports. 12 suites, $93-$98; 3 stories; interior corridors; designated smoking area; small heate indoor pool. **Services:** winter plug-ins. **Cards:** AE, CB, DI, DS, MC, VI.

(S⌀) (🔌) (📺) (🎥) (🔲) (🔲) (📞) (△) (✕)

HOLIDAY INN
AAA SAVE
◆◆◆
Motor Inn

Phone: (406)587-456⌐

	1P:		2P/1B:		2P/2B:	
6/1-9/30	$89-	94	$89-	94	$89-	94
3/1-5/31 & 10/1-2/29	$59-	69	$59-	69	$59-	69

Location: I-90 business loop; just s of jct I-90, exit 306. 5 Baxter Ln 59715. Fax: 406/587-4413. **Terms:** Small pets only. **Facility:** 179 rooms. Spacious rooms. 2 stories; interior corridors; heated indoor pool whirlpool. **Dining:** Dining room; 6 am-2 & 5-10 pm; $7-$17; cocktails. **Services:** winter plug-ins. Fee: massage. **Recreation:** pool table. **All Rooms:** combo or shower baths, extended cable TV. **Some Rooms:** whirlpools. **Cards:** AE, CB, DI, DS, JC, MC, VI. *(See color ad opposite title page)*

(🛏) (🔳) (3⌐) (△) (📺) (🍸) (✈) (△) (🐾) (🎥) (🔲) (🔲) (📞) (✕)

HOWLERS INN BED & BREAKFAST
◆◆◆
Bed & Breakfast

Rates Subject to Change
Phone: 406/586-030⌐

	1P:		2P/1B:		2P/2B:	XP:
All Year [BP]	$80-	100	$80-	100	$95	$15

Location: I-90, exit 319 (Jackson Creek Rd); 3.1 mi n, just e. 3185 Jackson Creek Rd 59715. **Terms:** Check-in 4 pm. **Facility:** 4 rooms. Contemporary rustic log home nestled in Bridger Canyon with view of two mountain ranges. Three acre wolf sanctuary on property. 1 two-bedroom unit. 2 bedroom guest house $145; rates for up to 4 persons; 2-3 stories, no elevator; interior/exterior corridors; smoke free premises; mountain view **Services:** winter plug-ins. **Some Rooms:** kitchen. **Cards:** MC, VI.

(3⌐) (✈) (🔳) (CTV) (VCR) (🔲) (✕) (🔲) (📞) (✕)

LINDLEY HOUSE   Guaranteed Rates   Phone: (406)587-8403
◆◆◆   5/1-10/15 [BP]   1P: $75- 250   2P/1B: $90- 250   2P/2B: $90- 250   XP: $20
Historic Bed   3/1-4/30 & 10/16-2/29 [BP]   1P: $65- 250   2P/1B: $85- 250   2P/2B: $95- 250   XP: $20
Breakfast   **Location:** I-90, exit 306; 1.3 mi s on 7th Ave, 0.9 mi e on Main St, just s on Bozeman St, then just e on
Olive St. 202 Lindley Pl 59715. Fax: 406/582-8112. **Terms:** Age restrictions may apply; reserv deposit, 7 day
notice. **Facility:** 5 rooms. Historic downtown home built in 1889. Elegant Victorian inn with French wallcoverings & antiques.
Full gourmet breakfast. 2 two-bedroom units. 1 kitchen unit with microwave & fridge avail 6/1-9/15, $225; 3 stories, no elevator;
interior corridors; smoke free premises. **Services:** winter plug-ins. **All Rooms:** combo or shower baths. **Some Rooms:** color
TV. **Cards:** DS, MC, VI.

RAINBOW MOTEL   Phone: (406)587-4201
AAA SAVE   All Year [CP]   1P: $45   2P/1B: $52   2P/2B: $55   XP: $5
Location: US 90 business loop, 0.8 mi s of jct I-90, exit 306. 510 N 7th Ave 59715. Fax: 406/587-9737.
Motel   **Terms:** Reserv deposit; weekly/monthly rates, in winter; small pets only, $10 extra charge, in smoking
rooms. **Facility:** 42 rooms. Commercial location. Kitchens, $8 extra charge; 1-2 stories; exterior corridors; des-
ignated smoking area; heated pool. **Services:** winter plug-ins. **All Rooms:** combo or shower baths, extended
cable TV. **Some Rooms:** 4 kitchens. **Cards:** AE, DI, DS, MC, VI. **Special Amenities:** Free breakfast and free local
telephone calls.

RAMADA LIMITED   Rates Subject to Change   Phone: (406)585-2626
◆◆   6/15-9/15 [CP]   1P: $79- 99   2P/1B: $89- 99   2P/2B: $89- 119   XP: $10   F
Motel   5/1-6/14 & 9/16-9/30 [CP]   1P: $49- 69   2P/1B: $49- 69   2P/2B: $59- 89   XP: $10   F
3/1-4/30 & 10/1-2/29 [CP]   1P: $39- 49   2P/1B: $49- 59   2P/2B: $59- 79   XP: $10   F
Location: I-90, exit 306; just n, just w. 2020 Wheat Dr 59715. Fax: 406/585-2727. **Facility:** 50 rooms. Convenient off interstate location. 2 stories; interior/exterior corridors; small heated indoor pool. **Services:** winter plug-ins. **Cards:** AE, CB, DI,
DS, MC, VI.

ROYAL "7" BUDGET INN   Guaranteed Rates   Phone: 406/587-3103
AAA   6/1-9/30   2P/1B: $40- 46   2P/2B: $43- 56   XP: $4
3/1-5/31 & 10/1-2/29   2P/1B: $37   2P/2B: $40- 47   XP: $4
◆◆   **Location:** I-90 business loop, 0.8 mi s of jct I-90, exit 306. 310 N 7th Ave 59715. Fax: 406/587-3103.
Motel   **Terms:** Weekly rates, in winter; pets. **Facility:** 47 rooms. Good size rooms. Very clean rooms. 1 two-bedroom
unit. 1 kitchen, $6 extra charge; 1 story; exterior corridors; designated smoking area; whirlpool; playground.
Dining: Restaurant nearby. **Services:** winter plug-ins. **All Rooms:** extended cable TV. **Cards:** AE, DI, DS, MC, VI.

TORCH & TOES BED & BREAKFAST   Guaranteed Rates   Phone: (406)586-7285
◆◆   All Year [BP]   1P: $70- 80   2P/1B: $80- 90   2P/2B: $80- 90   XP: $10   F5
Historic Bed   **Location:** I-90, exit 306; just w on Main to 8th, just s to Curtiss, then just e. 309 S 3rd Ave 59715.
Breakfast   Fax: 406/585-2749. **Terms:** Check-in 4 pm; reserv deposit, 14 day notice. **Facility:** 4 rooms. Circa 1906.
Eclectic collection of artwork & antiques. 1-2 stories; interior/exterior corridors; smoke free premises.
Services: winter plug-ins. **All Rooms:** combo or shower baths. **Cards:** AE, MC, VI.

WINGATE INN   Rates Subject to Change   Phone: (406)582-4995
Ⓦ   5/16-10/15 [CP]   1P: $79- 129   2P/1B: $79- 129   2P/2B: $79- 129   XP: $6   F
11/15-2/15 [CP]   1P: $69- 119   2P/1B: $69- 129   2P/2B: $69- 129   XP: $5   F
Motel   3/1-5/15 & 2/16-2/29 [CP]   1P: $59- 109   2P/1B: $59- 109   2P/2B: $59- 109   XP: $4   F
10/16-11/14 [CP]   1P: $55- 99   2P/1B: $55- 99   2P/2B: $55- 99   XP: $4   F
Too new to rate. **Location:** 2305 Catron 59718. Fax: 406/582-7488. **Facility:** 86 rooms. Scheduled to open March, 1999; 1
story. **Cards:** AE, CB, DI, DS, JC, MC, VI. *(See ad below)*

RESTAURANTS

THE BACCHUS PUB   Lunch: $7-$12   Dinner: $7-$12   Phone: (406)586-1314
◆◆   **Location:** Center. 105 W Main 59715. **Hours:** 7 am-9 pm, Fri-10 pm, Sat 8 am-10 pm, Sun 8 am-9 pm; 8
American   am-9 pm, 10/1-5/31. **Closed:** 11/25 & 12/25. **Features:** children's menu; carryout; cocktails; street parking.
Large variety of sandwiches, salad, soup & specialty dishes. **Cards:** AE, DS, MC, VI.

CASA SANCHEZ   Lunch: $6-$15   Dinner: $6-$15   Phone: (406)586-4516
◆◆   **Location:** 8 blks s of US 191 (W Main St) via 8th Ave; right on College to 9th Ave, just n. 719 S 9th Ave
Mexican   59715. **Hours:** 11 am-10 pm, Sat from noon, Sun 5 pm-9:30 pm. Closed major holidays.
Reservations: suggested. **Features:** casual dress; children's menu; carryout; beer & wine only; street
parking; a la carte. Informal dining in pleasant ambiance of old house. Homemade Mexican specialties. Adjacent to
university. Smoke free premises. **Cards:** DI, DS, MC, VI.

FERRARO'S ITALIAN RESTAURANT **Dinner:** $11-$21 Phone: 406/587-25!
◆◆ **Location:** I-90 exit 306, 0.6 mi s. 726 N 7th Ave 59715. **Hours:** 5 pm-10 pm, to 11 pm in summer. Close
Italian 9/6, 11/25, 12/24 & 12/25. **Features:** casual dress; carryout; cocktails & lounge. Authentic northern Itali
cuisine. All fresh ingredients, specializing in veal dishes & chicken marsala. Smoke free premise
Cards: MC, VI.

4 B'S BLACK ANGUS STEAK HOUSE **Dinner:** $9-$19 Phone: 406/587-06!
◆◆ **Location:** I-90 business loop, exit 306 or exit 309 off I-90. 520 W Mendenhall 59715. **Hours:** 5 pm-10 pm
Steakhouse Fri & Sat-11 pm, Sun-9 pm. **Closed:** 11/25, 12/24 & 12/25. **Features:** casual dress; children's menu; sal
bar; cocktails & lounge. Family restaurant. Pleasant, informal atmosphere. Lunch served in casin
Cards: AE, DI, DS, MC, VI.

4 B'S RESTAURANT **Lunch:** $6-$9 **Dinner:** $6-$9 Phone: 406/587-46!
◆ **Location:** I-90 business loop; exit 306 or 309, off I-90. 421 W Main St 59715. **Hours:** 24 hrs. **Closed:** 11/
American & 12/25. **Features:** casual dress; children's menu; senior's menu; buffet. Family dining. **Cards:** AE, DI, D
MC, VI.

FRONTIER PIES RESTAURANT & BAKERY **Lunch:** $6-$10 **Dinner:** $6-$10 Phone: 406/586-55!
◆◆ **Location:** I-90 business loop, I-90, exit 306; 1 mi s. 302 N 7th Ave 59715. **Hours:** 7 am-10 pm, Fri & Sat-
American pm; 6:30 am-11 pm in summer. **Features:** casual dress; children's menu; health conscious menu; carryout;
la carte. Old West decor. Homemade pie. Smoke free premises. **Cards:** AE, DI, DS, MC, VI.

JOHN BOZEMAN'S BISTRO **Lunch:** $8-$10 **Dinner:** $12-$19 Phone: 406/587-41(
◆◆ **Location:** Center. 242 E Main 59715. **Hours:** 11 am-3 & 5-9:30 pm, Sun 9 am-2 pm. **Closed:** Mc
American **Features:** casual dress; beer & wine only; street parking. Upbeat eatery in oldest building
Bozeman, circa 1872. Wide variety of international dishes & extensive beer menu. Smoke free premise
Cards: AE, DI, DS, MC, VI.

MACKENZIE RIVER PIZZA CO **Lunch:** $6-$18 **Dinner:** $6-$18 Phone: 406/587-00!
◆ **Location:** City Center. 232 E Main 59715. **Hours:** 11:30 am-9 pm, Fri & Sat-10 pm, Sun 2 pm-9 pm
Italian winter; 11:30 am-10 pm, Sun 2 pm-10 pm in summer. **Closed:** 1/1, 11/25, 12/24 & 12/25. **Features:** No A/
casual dress; street parking; a la carte. Lively, contemporary rustic eatery, specializing in gourmet pizz
Smoke free premises. **Cards:** AE, DS, MC, VI.

THE PASTA COMPANY **Dinner:** $12-$21 Phone: 406/586-131
◆◆ **Location:** Center. 105 W Main 59715. **Hours:** 5:30 pm-10 pm; in winter to 9 pm, Fri & Sat-10 pm. Close
Italian 11/25 & 12/25. **Features:** No A/C; casual dress; carryout; street parking. Northern & Southe
Italian & Continental specialties served in warm, comfortable atmosphere. Smoke free premises. **Cards:** A
DS, MC, VI.

SANTA FE RED'S **Lunch:** $6-$15 **Dinner:** $6-$15 Phone: 406/587-583
◆◆ **Location:** I-90, exit 306; just s. 1235 N 7th 59715. **Hours:** 11 am-11:30 pm & Sun-10 pm 5/1-9/30; 11 am-
Mexican pm, Fri & Sat-11:30 pm, Sun noon-9 pm 10/1-4/30. **Closed:** 12/25. **Features:** casual dress; children's men
carryout; cocktails & lounge; a la carte. Upbeat popular Mexican dining serving Southwestern US cuisin
Casino. **Cards:** AE, DS, MC, VI.

SPANISH PEAKS BREWING CO & ITALIAN CAFFE **Lunch:** $4-$10 **Dinner:** $7-$16 Phone: 406/585-229
◆◆ **Location:** I-90, exit 305; 2 mi s. 120 N 19th Ave 59715. **Hours:** 11:30 am-10 pm; Thurs-Sat to 10:30 p
Italian Sun noon-10 pm. **Closed:** 11/25 & 12/25. **Features:** casual dress. Unique ale house setting boas
Bozeman's only micro-brewery. Intimate cafe offers very good gourmet Italian pizza & pasta. Ri
homemade desserts. **Cards:** DS, MC, VI.

BROWNING—1,200

RESTAURANT

OLD NINE MILE INN **Lunch:** $5-$15 **Dinner:** $7-$15 Phone: 406/338-731
(AAA) **Location:** 10 mi w on US 89. US 89 59417. **Hours:** 8 am-8 pm. **Features:** No A/C; casual dress. Casu
dining in rustic atmosphere. Native American & American dishes. Homemade dessert. Outside dinir
◆◆ weather permitting. Smoke free premises. **Cards:** MC, VI.
American

BUTTE—33,300

LODGINGS

BEST WESTERN BUTTE PLAZA INN Phone: (406)494-350
(AAA) [SAVE] 6/1-9/15 [BP] 1P: $71- 80 2P/1B: $70- 89 2P/2B: $80- 89 XP: $9 F1
3/1-5/31 & 9/16-2/29 [BP] 1P: $62- 71 2P/1B: $71- 80 2P/2B: $71- 80 XP: $9 F1
◆◆◆ **Location:** I-90, exit 127 (Harrison Ave). 2900 Harrison Ave 59701. Fax: 406/494-761
Motor Inn **Terms:** Weekly/monthly rates; pets, $50 dep req. **Facility:** 134 rooms. Attractive public areas. Large breakfa
buffet. Phones with voice mail. Suites, $125-$175; 2 stories; interior corridors; designated smoking are
heated indoor pool, sauna, steamroom, whirlpool. **Dining:** Restaurant, 24 hrs; $5-$8. **Services:** area transportation; wint
plug-ins. **Some Rooms:** whirlpools. **Cards:** AE, CB, DI, DS, JC, MC, VI. **Special Amenities:** Free breakfast and free loc
telephone calls.

COMFORT INN OF BUTTE Phone: (406)494-885
(AAA) [SAVE] 5/1-10/31 [CP] 1P: $58- 85 2P/1B: $67- 94 2P/2B: $67- 94 XP: $5 F1
3/1-4/30 [CP] 1P: $54- 81 2P/1B: $63- 90 2P/2B: $63- 90 XP: $5 F1
◆◆◆ 11/1-2/29 [CP] 1P: $54- 81 2P/1B: $63- 90 2P/2B: $63- 90 XP: $5 F1
Motel **Location:** Just s off I-90 & I-15, exit 127. 2777 Harrison Ave 59701. Fax: 406/494-280
Terms: Weekly/monthly rates; pets, $5 extra charge. **Facility:** 150 rooms. Very clean rooms, convenient off i
terstate location. 4 whirlpool suites, $110-$125; executive suite, $100; 3 stories, no elevator; interior corridors; sauna, whi
pool. **Dining:** Restaurant nearby. **Services:** area transportation; winter plug-ins. **Recreation:** video rental
All Rooms: combo or shower baths, extended cable TV. **Some Rooms:** efficiency. **Cards:** AE, DI, DS, MC, V
Special Amenities: Free breakfast and free local telephone calls.

DAYS INN
◆◆◆
Motel
5/16-9/30 [CP]
3/1-5/15 & 10/1-2/29 [CP]

Rates Subject to Change
1P: $70- 85 2P/1B: $70- 85 2P/2B: $79- 95 XP: $8 F11
1P: $49- 65 2P/1B: $49- 68 2P/2B: $58- 80 XP: $8 F11

Phone: 406/494-7000

Location: I-15, exit 127; just n on Harrison Ave, e on Cornell St. 2700 Harrison Ave 59701. Fax: 406/494-7000. **Terms:** Reserv deposit. **Facility:** 74 rooms. Contemporary rustic styling; sporting good store off lobby. Convenient interstate access. 3 stories; interior corridors. **Services:** winter plug-ins. **All Rooms:** combo or shower baths. **Cards:** AE, CB, DI, DS, MC, VI.

FINLEN HOTEL
◆
Motel
All Year

Guaranteed Rates
1P: $32- 36 2P/1B: $36- 40 2P/2B: $40- 44

Phone: 406/723-5461

Location: I-15/90, exit 126; n on Montana St 1.4 mi, 0.3 mi e. 100 E Broadway 59701. Fax: 406/723-5461. **Facility:** 52 rooms. Close to uptown shopping & businesses. 3 two-bedroom units. 2-3 stories; interior/exterior corridors; designated smoking area. **All Rooms:** combo or shower baths. **Cards:** AE, DS, MC, VI.

HOLIDAY INN EXPRESS PARKSIDE
◆◆◆
Motel
6/15-9/15 [CP]
6/14 & 9/16-2/29 [CP]

Rates Subject to Change
1P: $62 2P/1B: $62 2P/2B: $62
1P: $53 2P/1B: $53 2P/2B: $53

Phone: 406/494-6999

Location: I-90, exit 127; just n to Cornell St, just e, following signs. 1 Holiday Park Dr 59701. Fax: 406/494-1300. **Facility:** 83 rooms. Opposite Father Shechan Park. Newer property. Very clean rooms. 17 suites; 5 stories; interior corridors; designated smoking area. **Services:** winter plug-ins. **All Rooms:** combo or shower baths. **Cards:** AE, CB, DI, DS, JC, MC, VI. (See color ad opposite title page)

RAMADA INN COPPER KING
AAA SAVE
◆◆◆
Motor Inn
6/16-9/15
3/1-6/15 & 9/16-2/29

1P: $72- 82 2P/1B: $82- 92 2P/2B: $82- 92 XP:$9-11 F18
1P: $63- 73 2P/1B: $73- 83 2P/2B: $73- 83 XP:$9-11 F18

Phone: 406/494-6666

Location: I-15 & I-90, exit 127A; 2 mi s on SR 2 (Harrison Ave). 4655 Harrison Ave S 59701. Fax: 406/494-3274. **Terms:** Weekly/monthly rates; pets, $8 extra charge. **Facility:** 150 rooms. Newly renovated rooms & public areas. 44 rooms with Grecian tubs, rental refrigerators & microwaves avail; 2 stories; interior corridors; designated smoking area; heated indoor pool, sauna, whirlpool; 3 tennis courts (3 indoor, 3 lighted). **Dining:** Dining room, coffee shop; 6 am-10 pm; $9-$19; cocktails. **Services:** area transportation; winter plug-ins. **All Rooms:** extended cable TV. **Some Rooms:** whirlpools. **Cards:** AE, CB, DI, DS, MC, VI. **Special Amenities:** Free local telephone calls and free room upgrade (subject to availability with advanced reservations). (See color ad below)

ROCKER INN
AAA
◆◆
Motel
6/1-9/30
3/1-5/31 & 10/1-2/29

Guaranteed Rates
1P: $42 2P/1B: $45 2P/2B: $48 XP: $4 F15
1P: $38 2P/1B: $42 2P/2B: $44 XP: $4 F15

Phone: (406)723-5464

Location: I-15 & I-90, exit 122 (Rocker). 122001 W Brown's Gulch Rd 59701. **Terms:** Pets. **Facility:** 49 rooms. Contemporary room decor. Very clean rooms. 2 stories; interior corridors. **Services:** winter plug-ins. **All Rooms:** combo or shower baths. **Cards:** AE, DS, MC, VI.

SUPER 8 MOTEL OF BUTTE | Rates Subject to Change | | **Phone:** (406)494-6000
◆◆
Motel

6/1-9/30 [CP]	1P:	$55	2P/1B:	$59	2P/2B:	$64	XP:	$5	F12
4/1-5/31 [CP]	1P:	$49	2P/1B:	$53	2P/2B:	$57	XP:	$5	F12
3/1-3/31 [CP]	1P:	$43- 46	2P/1B:	$51- 52	2P/2B:	$51- 52	XP:	$5	F12
10/1-2/29 [CP]	1P:	$47	2P/1B:	$51	2P/2B:	$52	XP:	$5	F12

Location: I-15 & I-90, exit 127; just s. 2929 Harrison Ave 59701. Fax: 406/494-6000. **Facility:** 104 rooms. Very clean rooms. 3 stories, no elevator; interior corridors. **Services:** winter plug-ins. **Cards:** AE, CB, DI, DS, MC, VI.

(ASK) (S◆) (🛏) (♨) (VCR) (🖨) (✕)

WAR BONNET INN | | | | **Phone:** (406)494-7800
(AAA) (SAVE)

6/1-9/30	1P:	$69- 75	2P/1B:	$75- 89	2P/2B:	$75- 89	XP:	$8	F18
3/1-5/31 & 10/1-2/29	1P:	$59- 69	2P/1B:	$59- 69	2P/2B:	$65- 75	XP:	$8	F18

◆◆◆
Motor Inn

Location: I-15 & I-90, exit 127B; just n on Harrison Ave, just e. 2100 Cornell Ave 59701. Fax: 406/494-2875. **Terms:** Weekly/monthly rates; small pets only, $10 extra charge, $50 dep req. **Facility:** 131 rooms. 2 stories; interior corridors; heated indoor pool, sauna, whirlpool. **Dining:** Restaurant; 6:30 am-10:30 pm; espresso bar; $7-$26; cocktails. **Services:** area transportation; winter plug-ins. **All Rooms:** extended cable TV. **Cards:** AE, DI, DS, MC, VI. **Special Amenities:** Free local telephone calls and preferred room (subject to availability with advanced reservations). (See color ad below)

(🛏) (🏃) (⊇) (♨) (🍴) (🛩) (💆) (🎿) (🔲) (🖨) (🔒) (✕) (🎯)

RESTAURANTS

4 B'S RESTAURANT | **Lunch:** $5-$8 | **Dinner:** $5-$8 | **Phone:** 406/494-1199
(AAA)

Location: I-90, exit 127A; s on Harrison Ave, just e. 1905 Dewey 59701. **Hours:** 44 hours. Closed: 11/25 & 12/25. **Features:** casual dress; children's menu; senior's menu; carryout; a la carte. Family restaurant. Casino/lounge next door. **Cards:** AE, DI, DS, MC, VI.

◆
American

(✕)

LYDIA'S SUPPER CLUB | **Dinner:** $11-$22 | | **Phone:** 406/494-2000
(AAA)

Location: 2.5 mi s on SR 2 from I-90, exit 127 (Harrison Ave). 4915 Harrison Ave 59701. **Hours:** 5:30 pm-10:30 pm. Closed: 5/31, 9/6, 11/25 & 12/25. **Reservations:** suggested. **Features:** casual dress; children's menu; carryout; cocktails & lounge; a la carte. Dinner served with antipasto & Italian accompaniment. Stained glass collection on walls. Espresso & cappuccino. Smoke free premises. **Cards:** AE, DS, MC, VI.

◆◆
Steakhouse

(✕)

UPTOWN CAFE | **Lunch:** $4-$7 | **Dinner:** $9-$22 | **Phone:** 406/723-4735
(AAA)

Location: I-15/90, exit 126; 1.5 mi n on Montana St, just e. 47 E Broadway 59701. **Hours:** 11 am-2 & 5-10 pm, Sat & Sun 5 pm-10 pm. Closed major holidays. **Reservations:** suggested; for dinner. **Features:** casual dress; early bird specials; carryout; cocktails; street parking. Informal setting with modern decor, art gallery. Dinners specializing in fresh seafood, steak, poultry & pasta. Convenient luncheon buffet. Smoke free premises. **Cards:** AE, DS, MC, VI.

◆◆◆
Continental

(✕)

CHINOOK—1,500

LODGING

CHINOOK MOTOR INN | | | | **Phone:** (406)357-2248
(AAA) (SAVE)

All Year	1P:	$44- 48	2P/1B:	$48- 52	2P/2B:	$52	XP:	$5	F12

◆
Motor Inn

Location: US 2. 100 Indiana St 59523 (PO Box 1418). Fax: 406/357-2261. **Terms:** Reserv deposit; pets, $5 extra charge. **Facility:** 38 rooms. Convenient highway location. 2 stories; interior corridors; designated smoking area. **Dining:** Restaurant; 7 am-9 pm; $4-$16; cocktails. **Services:** winter plug-ins. **All Rooms:** combo or shower baths, extended cable TV. **Cards:** AE, DS, MC, VI. **Special Amenities:** Free local telephone calls and preferred room (subject to availability with advanced reservations).

(S◆) (🛏) (🏃) (🍴) (💆) (🎿) (🖨) (✕)

Check out our **bold** listings!

CHOTEAU—1,700

LODGINGS

BEST WESTERN STAGE STOP INN   **Phone:** (406)466-5900
                    6/1-9/30 [CP]   1P: $70- 80 2P/1B: $75- 85 2P/2B: $75- 85 XP: $5   F12
AAA SAVE   3/1-5/31 & 10/1-2/29 [CP]   1P: $60- 70 2P/1B: $65- 75 2P/2B: $65- 75 XP: $5   F12
◆◆◆   **Location:** N on US 89. 1005 Main Ave N 59422 (PO BOX 1238). Fax: 406/466-5907. **Facility:** 43 rooms. New
Motel   property. High ceilings & contemporary rustic decor. 4 suites with wet bar, utensils included, $85-$105; 2 sto-
               ries; interior corridors; designated smoking area; small heated pool, whirlpool. **Services:** winter plug-ins.
All Rooms: combo or shower baths, extended cable TV. **Some Rooms:** whirlpools. **Cards:** AE, CB, DI, DS, JC, MC, VI.
Special Amenities: Free breakfast and free local telephone calls.

BIG SKY MOTEL   **Phone:** (406)466-5318
                    All Year   1P: $36- 45 2P/1B: $45- 55 2P/2B: $46- 65 XP: $5   F12
AAA SAVE   **Location:** US 89 from city center. 209 S Main 59422 (PO BOX 977). Fax: 406/466-5866. **Terms:** Handling
◆   fee imposed; weekly/monthly rates; pets, $5 extra charge. **Facility:** 13 rooms. Small cozy very clean rooms. 4
Motel   kitchens, $5-$10 extra charge; 1 story; exterior corridors; designated smoking area. **Dining:** Restaurant
               nearby. **Services:** winter plug-ins. **All Rooms:** shower baths, extended cable TV. **Cards:** AE, DS, MC, VI.
Special Amenities: Free local telephone calls and preferred room (subject to availability with advanced
reservations).

COUNTRY LANE BED & BREAKFAST   Rates Subject to Change   **Phone:** (406)466-2816
                    5/15-10/15 [BP]   1P: $50   2P/1B: $70   2P/2B: $80   XP: $15   D
Bed &   **Location:** US 89, 1.5 mi from n end of town, 0.8 mi w on private gravel lane. (Rt 2 Box 232, 59422).
Breakfast   Fax: 406/466-2816. **Terms:** Open 5/15-10/15; check-in 4 pm; reserv deposit, 14 day notice; handling fee
               imposed. **Facility:** 4 rooms. Contemporary split-level home located on Spring Creek Game Reserve. 2 stories;
interior/exterior corridors; smoke free premises; small heated indoor pool. **Services:** winter plug-ins. **Some Rooms:** color
TV. **Cards:** MC, VI.

CLINTON—200

RESTAURANT

EKSTROM'S STAGE STATION   Lunch: $6-$9   **Dinner:** $11-$14   **Phone:** 406/825-3183
AAA   **Location:** 4 mi e on I-90, exit 126 (Rock Creek Rd); then 0.5 mi s. 81 Rock Creek Rd 59825. **Hours:** Open
◆◆   4/1-10/10; 8 am-10 pm. **Features:** casual dress; children's menu; carryout; salad bar; beer & wine only.
American   Rustic decor in historic stage station log building; home baked goods & trout are specialties. Smoke free
               premises. **Cards:** MC, VI.

COLSTRIP—3,000

LODGING

SUPER 8 MOTEL OF COLSTRIP LLC   Rates Subject to Change   **Phone:** 406/748-3400
◆◆   All Year [CP]   1P: $43- 50 2P/1B: $45- 52 2P/2B: $50- 56
Motel   **Location:** SR 39. 6227 Main St 59323 (PO Box 1917). Fax: 406/748-3467. **Facility:** 40 rooms. Convenient lo-
               cation. Very clean rooms. Public area VCR; 2 stories; interior corridors; designated smoking area.
Services: winter plug-ins. **All Rooms:** combo or shower baths. **Cards:** AE, CB, DI, DS, MC, VI.

COLUMBIA FALLS—2,900—*See also GLACIER NATIONAL PARK.*

LODGINGS

BAD ROCK COUNTRY BED & BREAKFAST   Rates Subject to Change   **Phone:** (406)892-2829
                    3/1-3/31, 6/1-9/30 &
                    12/1-2/29 [BP]   1P: $105- 165 2P/1B: $115- 165   XP: $35   D16
Bed &   4/1-5/31 & 10/1-11/30 [BP] 1P: $93- 143 2P/1B: $103- 143   XP: $35   D16
Breakfast   **Location:** Jct US 2 & SR 206, 2.4 mi s on SR 206; 0.9 mi w. 480 Bad Rock Dr 59912. Fax: 406/892-2930.
Terms: Reserv deposit, 14 day notice; handling fee imposed. **Facility:** 7 rooms. Scenic mountain view from Flathead Valley
setting with antique filled spacious rooms in main house & adjacent log accommodations with private entrances & upscale log-
pole furnishings. Easy access to Glacier National Park. 1-2 stories; interior/exterior corridors; smoke free premises.
Services: area transportation; winter plug-ins. **All Rooms:** combo or shower baths. **Cards:** AE, CB, DI, DS, MC, VI.

GLACIER PARK SUPER 8   Rates Subject to Change   **Phone:** (406)892-0888
AAA   5/15-9/30 [EP]   1P: $62- 77 2P/1B: $67- 77 2P/2B: $77   XP: $5   F12
               3/1-5/14 & 10/1-2/29 [CP] 1P: $36- 43 2P/1B: $42   2P/2B: $43   XP: $5   F12
◆◆   **Location:** Just n on US 2 from jct of SR 40/206. 7336 US 2 E 59912. Fax: 406/892-8808. **Terms:** Reserv
Motel   deposit; weekly/monthly rates, off season; pets, $25 dep req. **Facility:** 32 rooms. Log structure with varied
               room styles. Suite with whirlpool & fireplace, $150; 2 stories; interior/exterior corridors; designated smoking
area; mountain view; whirlpool. **Dining:** Restaurant nearby. **Services:** winter plug-ins. **All Rooms:** combo or shower baths,
extended cable TV. **Some Rooms:** efficiency, whirlpools. **Cards:** AE, CB, DI, DS, MC, VI.

MEADOW LAKE RESORT

Phone: (406)892-7601

7/1-8/31 & 12/24-1/4	1P: $129- 179	2P/1B: $129- 179	2P/2B: $229- 259	XP: $15	F16
3/1-3/31, 5/1-6/30 & 9/1-10/9	1P: $109- 149	2P/1B: $109- 149	2P/2B: $189- 219	XP: $15	F16
4/1-4/30, 10/10-12/23 &					
1/5-2/29	1P: $79- 109	2P/1B: $79- 109	2P/2B: $139- 159	XP: $15	F16

Complex

Location: Jct US 2 & SR 40, 1.4 mi e on US 2, 1.1 mi n on Meadow Lake Blvd. 100 St Andrews Dr 59912. Fax: 406/892-0330. **Terms:** Check-in 4 pm; reserv deposit, 30 day notice; weekly/monthly rates; package plans; small pets only, $15 fee, some units. **Facility:** 122 rooms. Resort complex located on award winning golf course with motel rooms, condos, townhomes & villas. Many units with fireplace, gas grill; some with private recreational whirlpool & washer/dryer. 69 two-bedroom units, 9 three-bedroom units. 3-, 4- & 5-bedroom homes, $299-$439; 1-3 stories, no elevator; interior/exterior corridors; heated indoor pool, whirlpools; 1 tennis court. Fee: 18 holes golf. **Dining:** Dining room; 7 am-10 pm summer, 11 am-9 pm winter; seasonal patio dining.; $14-$21. **Services:** area transportation, Ski Area; winter plug-ins. **Recreation:** cross country skiing. **All Rooms:** extended cable TV. **Some Rooms:** 90 kitchens, whirlpools. **Cards:** AE, DI, DS, MC, VI. **Special Amenities:** Free local telephone calls. *(See color ad p 226)*

PLUM CREEK HOUSE-THE INN ON THE FLATHEAD RIVER

Phone: (406)892-1816

Guaranteed Rates

6/1-9/15 [BP]	1P: $95- 105	2P/1B: $105- 115	XP: $20	F8
3/1-5/31 & 9/16-2/29 [BP]	1P: $60	2P/1B: $75	XP: $20	F8

Bed & Breakfast

Location: Jct of US 2 & SR 486, 1.2 mi n on SR 486 (Nucleus Ave), stay to right; just s on 8th Ave E, n at Stop 'N Shop, just se at yield sign. 985 Vans Ave 59912. Fax: 406/892-1876. **Terms:** Age restrictions may apply; reserv deposit, 10 day notice; handling fee imposed. **Facility:** 5 rooms. Rooms with mountain/river or garden views; scenic views of mountains & Flathead River from pool, hottub & breakfast room. Full guest kitchen avail. 2 stories; interior/exterior corridors; designated smoking area; small heated pool. **Services:** area transportation; winter plug-ins. **Recreation:** fishing. **All Rooms:** combo or shower baths. **Cards:** AE, CB, DI, DS, MC, VI.

COLUMBUS—1,600

LODGINGS

RIVERSIDE GUEST CABINS

Rates Subject to Change

Phone: 406/322-5066

6/1-9/30 [CP]	1P: $30	2P/1B: $35	2P/2B: $35	XP: $5	F6
3/1-5/31 & 10/1-2/29 [EP]	1P: $25	2P/1B: $30	2P/2B: $30	XP: $5	F6

Cottage

Location: I-90, exit 408 (Ninth St); 0.8 mi s, 0.6 mi w. 44 W Pike Ave 59019 (Box 87). **Facility:** 7 rooms. Charming, well maintained cabins. Close to river. At door parking. Efficiencies with bunk beds; Continental breakfast 6/1-10/1; 1 story; exterior corridors; designated smoking area; playground. **All Rooms:** shower baths. **Some Rooms:** 2 efficiencies. **Cards:** MC, VI.

SUPER 8 OF COLUMBUS

Phone: (406)322-4101

6/1-9/30	1P: $45- 60	2P/1B: $50- 65	2P/2B: $56- 71	XP: $5	F12
3/1-5/31	1P: $41- 56	2P/1B: $47- 62	2P/2B: $52- 67	XP: $5	F12
10/1-2/29	1P: $40- 55	2P/1B: $46- 61	2P/2B: $51- 66	XP: $5	F12

Motel

Location: SR 78, just s jct I-90, exit 408. 602 8th Ave N 59019 (PO Box 88). Fax: 406/322-4636. **Terms:** Pets, $5 extra charge; 2 stories; interior corridors; sauna, whirlpool. **Dining:** Restaurant nearby. **Services:** winter plug-ins. **All Rooms:** combo or shower baths, extended cable TV. **Cards:** AE, DI, DS, MC, VI. **Special Amenities:** Free local telephone calls and free room upgrade (subject to availability with advanced reservations).

CONRAD—2,900

LODGING

SUPER 8 OF CONRAD

Phone: (406)278-7676

5/15-9/30	1P: $48- 63	2P/1B: $52- 67	2P/2B: $52- 67	XP: $5	F12
4/1-5/14	1P: $45- 60	2P/1B: $49- 64	2P/2B: $49- 64	XP: $5	F12
3/1-3/31 & 10/1-2/29	1P: $42- 57	2P/1B: $46- 61	2P/2B: $46- 61	XP: $5	F12

Motel

Location: I-15, exit 339; just w. 215 N Main 59425. **Terms:** Pets, $5 extra charge. **Facility:** 49 rooms. Very clean rooms. Executive rms avail; mini fridge avail, extra charge; 2 stories; interior corridors. **Dining:** Wine/beer only; mini-casino lounge; coffee shop nearby. **Services:** winter plug-ins. **All Rooms:** extended cable TV. **Cards:** AE, DI, DS, MC, VI. **Special Amenities:** Free local telephone calls and free room upgrade (subject to availability with advanced reservations).

COOKE CITY—100

LODGING

SODA BUTTE LODGE

Phone: (406)838-2251

All Year	1P: $65- 70	2P/1B: $65- 70	2P/2B: $70- 90	

Motor Inn

Location: Center; on US 212. 209 US 212 (PO Box 1119, 59020). Fax: 406/838-2253. **Terms:** Pets, $5 extra charge. **Facility:** 32 rooms. Contemporary rustic lobby. 2 two-bedroom units, $100 for up to 6 persons; 2 stories; interior corridors; small heated indoor pool, whirlpool. **Dining:** Dining room; $7-$23; cocktails. **Services:** winter plug-ins. **Recreation:** game room. Fee: snowmobiling. **Some Rooms:** whirlpools. **Cards:** AE, DI, DS, MC, VI.

RESTAURANT

JOAN & BILL'S RESTAURANT

Lunch: $4-$7   Dinner: $6-$15   Phone: 406/838-2280

American

Location: Center; on US 212. 214 Main 59020. **Hours:** 6 am-10 pm; 7 am-9 pm 12/27-4/15. **Features:** No A/C; casual dress; children's menu; beer & wine only. Relaxed family dining in a rustic atmosphere. Closed 4/16-5/25 & 9/26-12/26. **Cards:** DS, MC, VI.

CORAM—*See also GLACIER NATIONAL PARK.*

LODGING

A WILD ROSE BED & BREAKFAST Guaranteed Rates **Phone:** 406/387-4900
◆◆◆ All Year [BP] 1P: $100- 150 2P/1B: $100- 150 2P/2B: $100- 150 XP: $20
Bed & **Location:** Just n of town. 10280 US 2 E 59913 (PO Box 130396). Fax: 406/387-4900. **Terms:** Age
Breakfast restrictions may apply; check-in 4 pm; reserv deposit, 15 day notice, reservations suggested; handling fee
imposed. **Facility:** 4 rooms. Nestled in peaceful mountain valley with finely appointed rooms with Victorian flair
& each offering all natural linen, robe & hair dryer. 2 stories; interior/exterior corridors; smoke free premises; mountain view.
All Rooms: combo or shower baths. **Some Rooms:** color TV. **Cards:** DS, MC, VI. (CTV) (VCR) (☎) (☒) (🖨) (☒)

CORWIN SPRINGS—100

RESTAURANT

THE RANCH KITCHEN **Lunch:** $6-$8 **Dinner:** $6-$19 **Phone:** 406/848-7891
◆◆ **Location:** US 89 59030. **Hours:** noon-2 & 5-9:30 pm, Sat & Sun 8:30-11:30 am; call for winter hours.
American Closed: Tues. **Features:** casual dress; children's menu; health conscious menu; carryout. Home cooking
served in a cozy, rustic dining room. Smoke free premises. **Cards:** AE, DS, MC, VI. (☒)

CULBERTSON—800

LODGING

THE KINGS INN Rates Subject to Change **Phone:** 406/787-6277
◆◆ All Year 1P: $30- 35 2P/1B: $35- 40 2P/2B: $40- 50 XP: $5-10
Motel **Location:** US 2, just e of jct SR 16. 408 E 6th 59218 (PO Box 665). Fax: 406/787-6177. **Facility:** 20 rooms.
Well kept rooms. 1 story; interior corridors. **Services:** winter plug-ins. **Cards:** AE, DI, MC, VI. (🍴) (🅴) (🐾) (☒)

CUT BANK—3,300

LODGINGS

GLACIER GATEWAY INN **Phone:** (406)873-5544
(AAA) (SAVE) 7/1-8/31 1P: $44 2P/1B: $49 2P/2B: $54 XP: $5 D7
3/1-6/30 & 9/1-2/29 1P: $40 2P/1B: $45 2P/2B: $50 XP: $5 D7
Motel **Location:** US 2, just e from city center. 1121 E Railroad St 59427. Fax: m06/873-5546. **Terms:** Small pets
only, $2.50 extra charge. **Facility:** 18 rooms. Cozy, very clean rooms. 1 two-bedroom unit. 1 room with bed in
teepee, $65, 1 room with bed in jail, $59; mini refrigerators & microwaves avail, extra charge; 1 story; interior
corridors; whirlpool. **Dining:** Restaurant nearby. **Services:** giftshop; winter plug-ins. **Recreation:** exercise machines.
Some Rooms: whirlpools. **Cards:** AE, CB, DI, DS, MC, VI. **Special Amenities:** Free local telephone calls.
(🐾) (☎) (🍴) (VCR) (▭) (🖥) (☒)

NORTHERN MOTOR INN **Phone:** (406)873-5662
(AAA) (SAVE) All Year 1P: $46 2P/1B: $52 2P/2B: $56 XP: $6
◆◆ **Location:** 0.3 mi w on US 2. 609 W Main 59427. Fax: 406/873-3339. **Facility:** 61 rooms. Comfortable, clean
Motel rooms. 2 two-bedroom units. 3 stories, no elevator; interior corridors; heated indoor pool, whirlpool.
Dining: Restaurant nearby. **Services:** winter plug-ins. **Recreation:** exercise equipment. **Cards:** AE, CB, DI,
DS, MC, VI. **Special Amenities:** Free local telephone calls. (☎) (🏊) (🍴) (▭) (🖨) (🖥) (☒)

RESTAURANT

JR'S DINING & LOUNGE **Lunch:** $5-$8 **Dinner:** $5-$20 **Phone:** 406/873-4401
(AAA) **Location:** US 2, e end of town. 918 E Main St 59427. **Hours:** 11 am-9:30 pm, Fri & Sat-10:30 pm, Sun-9:30
◆◆ pm. Closed: 9/7. **Features:** casual dress; carryout; salad bar; cocktails & lounge. **Cards:** DS, MC, VI.
Steak and
Seafood

DEAN

RESTAURANT

MONTANA HANNA'S TROUT HOLE RESTAURANT **Lunch:** $5-$10 **Dinner:** $10-$19 **Phone:** 406/328-6780
◆ **Location:** SR 419. SR 419 59028. **Hours:** 11 am-9 pm, Fri-Sat to 10 pm; to 8 pm, Fri & Sat-9 pm , in
American winter. Closed: 11/25 & 12/25. **Reservations:** suggested; weekends. **Features:** No A/C; casual dress;
children's menu; carryout; cocktails & lounge; a la carte. Rustic quaint dining with view of mountains.
Specializing in fresh Montana fish & steak, ribs, chicken & shrimp. Smoke free premises. **Cards:** DS, MC, VI. (☒)

DEER LODGE—3,400

LODGINGS

SCHARF'S MOTOR INN **Phone:** (406)846-2810
(AAA) (SAVE) 5/1-9/30 1P: $35- 40 2P/1B: $40- 45 2P/2B: $45- 50 XP: $4 F11
3/1-4/30 & 10/1-2/29 1P: $30- 35 2P/1B: $35- 40 2P/2B: $40- 45 XP: $3 F11
◆◆ **Location:** Downtown; on I-90 business loop. 819 Main St 59722. Fax: 406/846-3412. **Terms:** Pets.
Motel **Facility:** 42 rooms. Located across from historic Territorial Prison. 1-2 stories; exterior corridors; playground.
Dining: Restaurant, see separate listing. **Services:** winter plug-ins. **All Rooms:** combo or shower baths.
Some Rooms: 3 kitchens, no utensils. **Cards:** AE, DI, DS, MC, VI. **Special Amenities:** Free local telephone calls and
preferred room (subject to availability with advanced reservations). (S₀) (🐾) (🍴) (△) (☒) (▭) (🖨) (☒)

SUPER 8 MOTEL
Phone: (406)846-2370

(AAA) (SAVE)
◆◆
Motel

6/1-9/30	1P:	$49	2P/1B:	$54	2P/2B:	$58	XP:	$4	F
4/1-5/31	1P:	$41	2P/1B:	$46	2P/2B:	$50	XP:	$4	F
10/1-2/29	1P:	$39	2P/1B:	$44	2P/2B:	$49	XP:	$3	F
3/1-3/31	1P:	$38	2P/1B:	$43	2P/2B:	$48	XP:	$3	F

Location: I-90, exit 184; 0.3 mi s. 1150 N Main St 59722. Fax: 406/846-2373. **Terms:** Small pets only, $5 extra charge. **Facility:** 54 rooms. Easy access. Very clean rooms. 2 stories; interior corridors; designated smoking area. **Dining:** Restaurant nearby. **Services:** winter plug-ins. **All Rooms:** extended cable TV. **Cards:** AE, CB, DI, DS, MC, VI. **Special Amenities:** Early check-in/late check-out and free local telephone calls.

RESTAURANTS

4 B'S RESTAURANT   **Lunch:** $6-$8   **Dinner:** $6-$8   Phone: 406/846-2620
◆
American
Location: I-90, exit 184; 0.3 mi s. 130 Sam Beck Rd 59722. **Hours:** 6 am-midnight, Fri & Sat 24 hrs. Closed: 11/25 & 12/25. **Features:** casual dress; children's menu; carryout. Informal, family atmosphere. **Cards:** AE, DI, DS, MC, VI.

SCHARF'S FAMILY RESTAURANT   **Lunch:** $4-$6   **Dinner:** $6-$10   Phone: 406/846-3300
(AAA)
◆
American
Location: Downtown; on I-90 business loop; adjacent to Scharf's Motor Inn. 819 Main St 59722. **Hours:** 6:30 am-9 pm; from 6 am, 4/1-10/1. Closed: 1/1, 11/25 & 12/25. **Features:** casual dress; children's menu; carryout; salad bar; beer & wine only; street parking; a la carte. Informal, family-style restaurant. **Cards:** AE, MC, VI.

DELL

LODGING

RED ROCK INN
Rates Subject to Change
Phone: 406/276-3501

◆◆
Historic
Country Inn

All Year [CP]	1P:	$47	2P/1B:	$52	2P/2B:	$57	XP:	$5-10	F14

Location: I-15, exit 23; just e to stop sign, 0.3 mi s, just e. 1 Main St 59724 (Box 23). **Terms:** Check-in 5 pm. **Facility:** 7 rooms. Cozy western theme decor. Originally built in 1895. 2 stories; interior corridors; designated smoking area. **Services:** winter plug-ins. **Cards:** MC, VI.

DILLON—4,000

LODGINGS

BEST WESTERN PARADISE INN
Phone: (406)683-4214

(AAA) (SAVE)
◆◆◆
Motor Inn

5/16-10/31	1P:	$52- 68	2P/1B:	$52- 68	2P/2B:	$52- 68	XP:	$2	F12
3/1-5/15 & 11/1-2/29	1P:	$44- 58	2P/1B:	$44- 58	2P/2B:	$44- 58	XP:	$2	F12

Location: I-15, exit 63; 0.3 mi s on SR 41. 650 N Montana St 59725. Fax: 406/683-4216. **Terms:** Small pets only. **Facility:** 65 rooms. Contemporay styled rooms. 1 two-bedroom unit. 2 rooms with large tubs; 2 stories; exterior corridors; designated smoking area; small heated indoor pool, whirlpool. **Dining:** Restaurant; 6 am-10 pm; to 11 pm, 5/16-10/31; $7-$13; cocktails. **Services:** winter plug-ins. **Cards:** AE, DI, DS, MC, VI. **Special Amenities:** Free local telephone calls and free newspaper.

COMFORT INN OF DILLON
Phone: (406)683-6831

(AAA) (SAVE)
◆◆◆
Motel

7/1-8/31 [CP]	1P:	$45- 63	2P/1B:	$50- 68	2P/2B:	$50- 68	XP:	$5	F18
5/1-6/30 [CP]	1P:	$43- 61	2P/1B:	$48- 66	2P/2B:	$48- 66	XP:	$5	F18
3/1-4/30 & 9/1-2/29 [CP]	1P:	$41- 59	2P/1B:	$46- 64	2P/2B:	$46- 64	XP:	$5	F18

Location: I-15, exit 63 (N Dillon). 450 N Interchange 59725. Fax: 406/683-2021. **Terms:** Pets, $3 extra charge. **Facility:** 48 rooms. Casino in lobby. Very clean rooms. 2 stories; interior corridors; small heated indoor pool. **Services:** winter plug-ins. **All Rooms:** extended cable TV. **Cards:** AE, DI, DS, MC, VI. **Special Amenities:** Free breakfast and free local telephone calls.

SUNDOWNER MOTEL
Phone: 406/683-2375

(AAA) (SAVE)
◆◆
Motel

6/1-11/1	1P:	$32- 34	2P/1B:	$35- 37	2P/2B:	$38- 40	XP:	$3
3/1-5/31 & 11/2-2/29	1P:	$29- 31	2P/1B:	$32- 34	2P/2B:	$35- 37	XP:	$3

Location: I-15, exit 63; just s. 500 N Montana St 59725. Fax: 406/683-2977. **Terms:** Pets. **Facility:** 32 rooms. Spacious rooms, commercial location. Mini-fridges, $3 extra charge; 2 stories; exterior corridors; playground. **Services:** winter plug-ins. **All Rooms:** extended cable TV. **Cards:** AE, CB, DI, DS, MC, VI.

SUPER 8 MOTEL
Rates Subject to Change
Phone: 406/683-4288

◆◆
Motel

6/1-9/30	1P:	$47- 51	2P/1B:	$54- 58	2P/2B:	$58- 62	XP:	$5	F12
3/1-5/31 & 10/1-2/29	1P:	$41- 45	2P/1B:	$49- 54	2P/2B:	$53- 57	XP:	$5	F12

Location: I-15, exit 63; just n on US 91. 550 N Montana St 59725. Fax: 406/683-4288. **Facility:** 48 rooms. Standard, very clean rooms. 3 stories, no elevator; interior corridors; designated smoking area. **Services:** winter plug-ins. **Cards:** AE, CB, DI, DS, JC, MC, VI.

EAST GLACIER PARK—300—See also GLACIER NATIONAL PARK.

LODGINGS

DANCING BEARS MOTEL
Phone: (406)226-4402

(AAA) (SAVE)
◆
Motel

6/15-9/15	1P:	$55	2P/1B:	$55	2P/2B:	$65	XP:	$4
3/1-6/14, 9/11-2/29 &						
9/16-2/29	1P:	$38	2P/1B:	$38	2P/2B:	$45	XP:	$4

Location: Center; just off US 2, following signs. 147 Montana St 59434 (PO Box 149). **Terms:** Reserv deposit, 4 day notice; handling fee imposed; pets. **Facility:** 14 rooms. Motel units, cabins & 1 two-bedroom house. 1 story; interior/exterior corridors. **Dining:** Restaurant nearby. **Services:** winter plug-ins. **All Rooms:** combo or shower baths. **Some Rooms:** 4 kitchens, whirlpools. **Cards:** AE, CB, DI, DS, MC, VI. **Special Amenities:** Free local telephone calls.

JACOBSON'S SCENIC VIEW COTTAGES

◆◆ Cottage

	Guaranteed Rates			Phone: 406/226-4422
6/11-9/14	1P: $49	2P/1B: $55	2P/2B: $59- 63	XP: $4 F6
5/1-6/10 & 9/15-10/1	1P: $39	2P/1B: $44	2P/2B: $48	XP: $4 F6

Location: 0.8 mi n on SR 49. (PO Box 216, 59434). **Terms:** Open 5/1-10/1; reserv deposit. **Facility:** 12 rooms. Tree shaded grounds. Contemporary styled, very clean rooms. 3 two-bedroom units. 1 kitchen, $7 extra charge. Portable refrigerator & microwave avail. Reservations 11/1-3/31: (406) 873-2154; 1 story; exterior corridors; designated smoking area; playground. **Cards:** AE, DS, MC, VI.

MOUNTAIN PINE MOTEL

◆◆ Motel

	Rates Subject to Change			Phone: 406/226-4403
6/15-9/15	1P: $50	2P/1B: $55	2P/2B: $60	XP: $3
5/1-6/14 & 9/16-10/1	1P: $44	2P/1B: $44	2P/2B: $48	XP: $3

Location: 0.5 mi n on SR 49. SR 49 N 59434 (PO Box 260). **Terms:** Open 5/1-10/1. **Facility:** 27 rooms. On quiet pine shaded grounds. Adjacent to scenic park trails. Very clean rooms. 1 two-bedroom unit. 1 three-bedroom unit. 1 three-bedroom house, $175, for up to 8 persons; 1 two-bedroom house, $60 for up to 2 persons. 2 two-bedroom units, $98-$110; 1-2 stories; exterior corridors; designated smoking area. **All Rooms:** combo or shower baths. **Some Rooms:** 2 kitchens. **Cards:** AE, DI, DS, MC, VI.

RESTAURANTS

GLACIER VILLAGE RESTAURANT

Ⓐ ◆◆ American

Lunch: $6-$13	Dinner: $6-$13	Phone: 406/226-4464

Location: US 2, at jct SR 49; opposite Glacier National Park gateway. 304-308 Hwy 2E 59434. **Hours:** Open 5/8-9/27; 6 am-10 pm. **Features:** casual dress; children's menu; health conscious menu; beer & wine only; street parking. Chef-owned. Popular family dining. Large selection of freshly baked pastry. Many microbrewed beer. Espresso bar. Community table. **Cards:** MC, VI.

SERRANO'S

◆ Mexican

Dinner: $9-$15	Phone: 406/226-9392

Location: Center. 29 Dawson Ave 59434. **Hours:** Open 5/1-10/1; 5 pm-10 pm. **Features:** No A/C; casual dress; carryout; cocktails; street parking; a la carte. In former Historic Dawson House. Traditional Mexican/Southwest cuisine. Smoke free premises. **Cards:** AE, DS, MC, VI.

EMIGRANT—100

LODGINGS

MOUNTAIN SKY GUEST RANCH

ⒶⒶ ◆◆◆◆ Ranch

	Rates Subject to Change			Phone: 406/587-1244
5/24-10/11 Wkly [AP]	1P:$2205-2345	2P/1B: $4200-4405	2P/2B:$4200-4410	

Location: US 89, 27 mi s of I-90; 6 mi s of Emigrant turn off, 4.5 mi w. Big Creek Rd 59027. **Fax:** 406/333-4911. **Terms:** Open 5/24-10/11; reserv deposit; handling fee imposed. **Facility:** 27 rooms. 1 to 3 room rustic & modern units in scenic mountain forest. 8 two-bedroom units, 2 three-bedroom units. Daily rates avail with 3 night min stay, 5/26-6/9 & 9/1-10/13; 1 story; exterior corridors; mountain view; heated pool, sauna, whirlpool; 2 tennis courts, tennis professional on staff. **Dining:** Dining room; guests only. **Services:** Fee: massage. **Recreation:** fishing; hiking trails, horseback riding. **Cards:** MC, VI.

PARADISE GATEWAY BED & BREAKFAST & GUEST CABINS

◆◆◆ Bed & Breakfast

	Rates Subject to Change			Phone: (406)333-4063
All Year [BP]	1P: $85- 150	2P/1B: $85- 150	2P/2B: $85- 150	XP: $20

Location: US 89, 4.5 mi s of Emigrant, e on gravel road 0.3 mi following signs. PO Box 84 59027. **Fax:** 406/333-4626. **Terms:** Age restrictions may apply; check-in 4 pm; reserv deposit, 14 day notice. **Facility:** 5 rooms. Country home nestled in Absaroka Mountains with Yellowstone River running right behind property. Charming, detailed guest rooms. 2 bedroom log cabin with full kitchen & CD player. 1 two-bedroom unit. Crib in guest log cabin only. Snack tray daily; 1-2 stories; interior/exterior corridors; smoke free premises. **Recreation:** fishing; hiking trails. **Some Rooms:** kitchen, color TV. **Cards:** MC, VI.

ENNIS—800

LODGINGS

EL WESTERN RESORT

ⒶⒶ SAVE ◆◆◆ Cottage

				Phone: 406/682-4217
6/15-9/15	1P: $65- 325	2P/1B: $65- 325	2P/2B: $65- 325	XP:$5-10 F11
5/1-6/14 & 9/16-10/15	1P: $55- 300	2P/1B: $55- 300	2P/2B: $55- 300	XP:$5-10 F14

Location: 0.8 mi s on US 287. US Hwy 287 S 59729 (PO Box 487). **Fax:** 406/682-5207. **Terms:** Open 5/1-10/15; reserv deposit, 3 day notice; handling fee imposed; weekly rates; pets. **Facility:** 29 rooms. Spacious grounds. Rustic log cabins. 1 to 4 bedroom units; some with fireplace. Walk to Madison River. 12 two-bedroom units, 2 three-bedroom units. 16 kitchens, $15-$60 extra charge; some with dishwasher & fireplace. Mostly duplex cottages; 1 story; exterior corridors; designated smoking area. **Recreation:** fishing, barbecue grills, croquet, horseshoes, horse corrals, volleyball. **Some Rooms:** whirlpools. **Cards:** AE, DS, MC, VI. *(See color ad p 222)*

FAN MOUNTAIN INN

ⒶⒶ ◆◆ Motel

	Rates Subject to Change			Phone: 406/682-5200
All Year	1P: $40- 55	2P/1B: $52- 80	2P/2B: $52- 60	XP:$5-10

Location: US 287, just nw of city center. 204 N Main 59729 (PO Box 1350). **Terms:** Pets. **Facility:** 28 rooms. Convenient location. Contemporary, very clean rooms. 2 stories; exterior corridors. **Dining:** Restaurant nearby. **Services:** winter plug-ins. **Cards:** AE, CB, DI, DS, MC, VI.

RAINBOW VALLEY MOTEL

ⒶⒶ SAVE ◆◆◆ Motel

				Phone: (406)682-4264
6/18-9/18	1P: $50- 65	2P/1B: $60- 75	2P/2B: $65- 75	XP:$5-10 F3
3/1-6/17 & 9/19-2/29	1P: $35- 45	2P/1B: $45- 55	2P/2B: $55- 65	XP:$5-10 F3

Location: 1 mi s on US 287. 59729 (PO Box 26). **Fax:** 406/682-5012. **Terms:** Reserv deposit, 14 day notice; handling fee imposed. **Facility:** 24 rooms. Back from highway; landscaped grounds. Log cabin decor. Adjacent to Bear Creek. Some rooms with mountain view. 6 horse corrals for boarding purposes. 8 two-bedroom units. 4 two-bedroom efficiencies, $10-$15 extra charge. 2 deluxe one-bedroom efficiencies, $20-$40 extra charge. 6 units with private patio; 1 story; exterior corridors; small heated pool. **Services:** winter plug-ins. **All Rooms:** extended cable TV. **Some Rooms:** 2 kitchens. **Cards:** AE, CB, DI, DS, MC, VI. IMA. *(See color ad p 320 & p 222)*

RIVERSIDE MOTEL

AAA [SAVE]

◆ Motel

Phone: (406)682-4240

		1P:	$42-	55	2P/1B:	$42-	55	2P/2B:	$55-	66	XP:	$5	F6
6/15-9/15													
5/1-6/14 & 9/16-11/30		1P:	$33-	38	2P/1B:	$35-	40	2P/2B:	$40-	50	XP:	$5	F6

Location: US 287, e of town. 346 Main St 59729 (Box 688). Fax: 406/682-7727. **Terms:** Open 5/1-11/30; reserv deposit, 14 day notice; handling fee imposed; pets, $3 extra charge. **Facility:** 12 rooms. Convenient location. Small cozy rooms. 7 two-bedroom units. 1 story; exterior corridors; designated smoking area. **Services:** winter plug-ins. **All Rooms:** combo or shower baths. **Some Rooms:** 2 efficiencies, 4 kitchens. **Cards:** DS, MC, VI. **Special Amenities:** Free local telephone calls and preferred room (subject to availability with advanced reservations). *(See color ad below)*

SPORTSMAN LODGE

AAA [SAVE]

◆ Motel

Phone: 406/682-4242

| 6/15-9/15 | | 1P: | $45- | 55 | 2P/1B: | $50- | 60 | 2P/2B: | $59- | 64 | XP: | $6 |
| 3/1-6/14 & 9/16-2/29 | | 1P: | $38- | 48 | 2P/1B: | $42- | 52 | 2P/2B: | $52- | 56 | XP: | $4 |

Location: US 287, just nw of city center. 310 US Hwy 287 N 59729 (PO Box 305). Fax: 406/682-7565. **Terms:** Reserv deposit, 10 day notice; handling fee imposed; weekly rates, 10/1-6/14 only; pets, $5 extra charge. **Facility:** 28 rooms. Motel units & rustic cabins. 4 two-bedroom units. Mini-fridges & microwaves avail; 1 story; exterior corridors. **Dining:** Restaurant; 9 am-9 pm; 7 am-10 pm, in summer; 4 am-9 pm hunting season; $9-$18. **Services:** winter plug-ins. **All Rooms:** combo or shower baths. **Cards:** DS, MC, VI.

ESSEX—100—*See also GLACIER NATIONAL PARK.*

LODGING

ZAAK WALTON INN   Rates Subject to Change   **Phone:** (406)888-5700
◆◆◆   All Year   1P: $98- 150   2P/1B: $98- 150 2P/2B: $98- 150   XP: $5
Historic   **Location:** US 2, just s. 123 Izaak Walton Inn Rd 59916 (PO Box 653). Fax: 406/888-5200. **Terms:** Reserv
Country Inn   deposit, 45 day notice; handling fee imposed. **Facility:** 33 rooms. Historic inn built in 1939 for service crews
of Great Northern Railway which preserves its railroad heritage while offering country charm in wooded setting
with appealing modern rooms/baths. Amtrak service. 4 detached authentic caboose efficiency units, 3-night min stay, $475-
$850 weekly for up to 4 persons; 3 stories, no elevator; interior corridors; designated smoking area. **Services:** giftshop;
winter plug-ins. **Fee:** area transportation. **Recreation:** cross country skiing, ice skating; hiking trails. **Fee:** bicycles.
All Rooms: combo or shower baths. **Some Rooms:** 4 efficiencies. **Cards:** MC, VI.

FORSYTH—2,200

LODGINGS

BEST WESTERN SUNDOWNER INN   **Phone:** (406)356-2115
🅐🅐🅐 SAVE   3/1-5/1   1P: $51- 53   2P/1B: $57- 65 2P/2B: $65- 75   XP: $5   F12
            5/2-9/15   1P: $51- 55   2P/1B: $65- 75 2P/2B: $70- 75   XP: $5   F12
◆ ◆   9/16-2/29   1P: $51- 55   2P/1B: $62- 70 2P/2B: $70- 72   XP: $5   F12
Motel   **Location:** I-94, exit 95; 0.5 mi nw on N Frontage Rd. 1018 Front St 59327 (PO Box 1080).
Fax: 406/356-2216. **Terms:** Small pets only, $3 extra charge. **Facility:** 40 rooms. Clean rooms. 2 stories; ex-
terior corridors. **Dining:** Restaurant nearby. **Services:** winter plug-ins. **All Rooms:** extended cable TV. **Cards:** AE, CB, DI,
DS, MC, VI. **Special Amenities:** Early check-in/late check-out and free local telephone calls.

RESTWEL MOTEL   **Phone:** (406)356-2771
🅐🅐🅐 SAVE   All Year [CP]   1P: $34   2P/1B: $38   2P/2B: $40   XP: $3   F10
            Location: I-94, exit 95; 0.8 mi nw on N Frontage Rd. 810 Front St 59327 (PO Box 287). **Terms:** Reserv
◆   deposit; weekly rates; small pets only. **Facility:** 18 rooms. Very clean, budgeted oriented rooms. 1 two-
Motel   bedroom unit. 1 story; exterior corridors; designated smoking area. **Services:** winter plug-ins.
        All Rooms: combo or shower baths, extended cable TV. **Cards:** AE, CB, DI, DS, MC, VI.
Special Amenities: Free local telephone calls and preferred room (subject to availability with advanced
reservations).**

WESTWIND MOTOR INN   **Phone:** (406)356-2038
🅐🅐🅐 SAVE   4/1-11/30 [CP]   1P: $39   2P/1B: $42   2P/2B: $47   XP: $5   F12
            3/1-3/31 & 12/1-2/29 [CP]   1P: $35   2P/1B: $38   2P/2B: $42   XP: $5   F12
◆   **Location:** 0.3 mi n of I-94, exit 93 (W Main St). 225 Westwind Lane 59327 (PO Box 5025). **Terms:** Check-in
Motel   6 pm; weekly/monthly rates; pets, $2 extra charge. **Facility:** 33 rooms. Very clean budget oriented rooms. 1
two-bedroom unit. 2 stories; interior corridors; designated smoking area. **Services:** winter plug-ins.
All Rooms: extended cable TV. **Cards:** AE, CB, DI, DS, MC, VI. **Special Amenities:** Free breakfast and free local
telephone calls.

GALLATIN GATEWAY—300

LODGINGS

GALLATIN GATEWAY INN   **Phone:** (406)763-4672
🅐🅐🅐 SAVE   7/1-9/7 [CP]   1P: $105- 160   2P/1B: $120- 160 2P/2B: $120- 175   XP: $15   F12
            6/1-6/30, 9/8-9/30 &
◆ ◆ ◆   12/24-12/31 [CP]   1P: $90- 140   2P/1B: $105- 140 2P/2B: $105- 155   XP: $15   F12
Historic   3/1-5/31, 10/1-12/23 &
Country Inn   1/1-2/29 [CP]   1P: $70- 115   2P/1B: $85- 115   2P/2B: $85- 130   XP: $15   F12
        Location: Just n on US 191 (Gallatin Rd). 76405 Gallatin Rd Hwy 191 59715 (PO Box 376, 59730).
Fax: 406/763-4672. **Terms:** Check-in 4 pm; reserv deposit. **Facility:** 35 rooms. Built in 1927 as a grand railroad hotel. Luxurious mahogany beamed grand room. Cozy guest rooms. 30 mi from ski resort. 1-2 stories; interior corridors; designated
smoking area; heated pool, whirlpool. **Dining:** Dining room, see separate listing. **Services:** winter plug-ins.
Recreation: casting pond. **Fee:** bicycles. **All Rooms:** extended cable TV. **Cards:** AE, DS, MC, VI. **Special Amenities:** Free
breakfast and free local telephone calls.

MILLERS OF MONTANA BED & BREAKFAST   Guaranteed Rates   **Phone:** (406)763-4102
            All Year [BP]   1P: $50- 75   2P/1B: $55- 75   2P/2B: $55   XP: $15   F5
Bed &   **Location:** 1.4 mi n on US 191, 0.7 mi e, veer just s, turn right, continue to end of drive. (1002 Zacharia Ln,
Breakfast   BOZEMAN, 59718). **Terms:** Check-in 4 pm; reserv deposit, 7 day notice; handling fee imposed. **Facility:** 4
rooms. On 20-acre ranch. Cozy guest rooms with view of surrounding mountains. Near ski resorts & rivers. 2
stories; interior corridors; smoke free premises. **Services:** winter plug-ins. **Recreation:** bicycles, jogging.
Some Rooms: combo or shower baths, shared bathrooms.

Hit the road with **AAA TourBooks,**
CampBooks and **TripTik** maps.

RESTAURANT

GALLATIN GATEWAY INN RESTAURANT **Dinner:** $15-$31 **Phone:** 406/763-467?
◆ ◆ ◆ **Location:** Just n on US 91(Gallatin Rd); in Gallatin Gateway Inn. 76405 Gallatin Rd Hwy 191 Rd 5973C
Continental **Hours:** 6 pm-9 pm, Fri & Sat-9:30 pm, Sun brunch 10 am-2 pm; 6 pm-9:30 pm in summe?
Reservations: suggested. **Features:** No A/C; casual dress; cocktails & lounge. Located in the historica
railway country inn. Intimate candlelit setting. Excellent entrees of steak, lamb & seafood. Cappuccino/espresso. Fin?
dessert. Smoke free premises. **Cards:** AE, DS, MC, VI.

GARDINER—700

LODGINGS

BEST WESTERN BY MAMMOTH HOT SPRINGS **Phone:** (406)848-731?

		1P:		2P/1B:		2P/2B:		XP:		F1?
6/8-9/22		$84-	94	$84-	94	$84-	94	$5		F1?
5/22-6/7 & 9/23-10/6		$63-	83	$63-	83	$63-	83	$5		F1?
3/1-5/21 & 10/7-2/29		$45-	57	$45-	57	$45-	57	$5		F1?

Motor Inn **Location:** 0.5 mi n on US 89. (PO Box 646, 59030). Fax: 406/848-7120. **Terms:** Check-in 4 pm; pets, $?
extra charge, in designated rooms. **Facility:** 85 rooms. Contemporary styled rooms. Some rooms overlookin?
river. 4 two-bedroom units. 2 stories, no elevator; interior/exterior corridors; designated smoking area; heated indoor poo?
saunas, whirlpool. **Dining:** Yellowstone Mine Restaurant, see separate listing. **Services:** winter plug-ins. **Recreation:** fishing?
All Rooms: combo or shower baths, extended cable TV. **Some Rooms:** 2 efficiencies, 2 kitchens, whirlpools. **Cards:** AE?
CB, DI, JC, MC, VI. **Special Amenities:** Early check-in/late check-out and free local telephone calls.

COMFORT INN YELLOWSTONE NORTH Rates Subject to Change **Phone:** (406)848-753?

		1P:		2P/1B:		2P/2B:		XP:		F1?
6/1-9/30 [CP]		$80-	165	$80-	165	$80-	165	$8		F1?
3/1-4/30 & 11/1-2/29 [CP]		$40-	70	$40-	70	$70	100	$8		F1?
5/1-5/31 & 10/1-10/31 [CP]		$50-	60	$50-	60	$55-	65	$8		F1?

Location: N entrance, just s on US 89. 107 Hellroaring 59030 (PO Box 268). Fax: 406/848-7536. **Terms:** Check-in 4 pm?
reserv deposit, 3 day notice; handling fee imposed. **Facility:** 80 rooms. Rustic lobby. Contemporary rustic rooms. Close to Ye?
lowstone Park entrance. 6 two-bedroom units. 3 stories; interior corridors. **Services:** winter plug-ins. **Cards:** AE, DS, MC, VI?
(See color ad below)

MAIDEN BASIN INN
Phone: 406/848-7080

AAA SAVE

6/15-8/14 [CP]	1P:	$85- 105	2P/1B:	$85- 105	2P/2B:	$85- 105	XP:	$10	F12
8/15-9/18 [CP]	1P:	$75- 95	2P/1B:	$75- 105	2P/2B:	$85- 95	XP:	$10	F12
6/1-6/14 & 9/19-10/18 [CP]	1P:	$65- 85	2P/1B:	$65- 100	2P/2B:	$65- 85	XP:	$10	F12
5/15-5/31 [CP]	1P:	$55- 75	2P/1B:	$55- 75	2P/2B:	$65- 75	XP:	$10	F12

♦♦♦
Motel

Location: 5 mi n on US 89, MM 5. 4 Maiden Basin Dr 59030. Fax: 406/848-7083. **Terms:** Open 5/15-10/18; check-in 4 pm; monthly rates. **Facility:** 8 rooms. Views of Electric Peak & Devils Slide. Adjacent Yellowstone River. Well appointed rooms. 1 two-bedroom unit. 2 rms with washer/dryer; 2 stories; exterior corridors; smoke free premises; whirlpool. **Some Rooms:** 2 efficiencies, 2 kitchens, whirlpools. **Cards:** AE, DS, MC, VI. *(See color ad p 224)*

MOTEL 6 - 4054
Phone: (406)848-7520

AAA

	Rates Subject to Change								
7/1-12/17	1P:	$34- 70	2P/1B:	$34- 70	2P/2B:	$34- 70	XP:	$6	F17
3/1-6/30	1P:	$30- 60	2P/1B:	$30- 60	2P/2B:	$30- 60	XP:	$6	F17
12/18-2/29	1P:	$30- 34	2P/1B:	$30- 34	2P/2B:	$30- 34	XP:	$6	F17

♦♦
Motel

Location: N entrance, just s on US 89; 0.5 mi n of Yellowstone n gate. 109 Hellroaring Rd 59030 (PO Box 48). Fax: 406/848-7555. **Terms:** Check-in 4 pm; reserv deposit, 3 day notice. **Facility:** 40 rooms. Brand new property. Small, comfortable, very clean rooms. 4 stories; exterior corridors; designated smoking area. **Services:** winter plug-ins. **All Rooms:** combo or shower baths. **Cards:** AE, DI, DS, MC, VI.

YELLOWSTONE RIVER MOTEL
Phone: (406)848-7303

AAA SAVE

6/15-9/30	1P:	$55- 77	2P/1B:	$55- 77	2P/2B:	$59- 77	XP:	$5	
5/1-6/14 & 10/1-10/30	1P:	$39- 59	2P/1B:	$39- 59	2P/2B:	$44- 59	XP:	$5	

♦
Motel

Location: Just e of US 89. 14 E Park St 59030 (PO Box 223). Fax: 406/848-7304. **Terms:** Open 5/1-10/30; reserv deposit; pets, $5 non-refunable fee. **Facility:** 38 rooms. Patio overlooking Yellowstone River. Some small rooms. 18 larger contemporary rooms. 2 two-bedroom units. 1 three-bedroom kitchen unit, extra charge. Some rms with ceiling fans; 1-2 stories; exterior corridors; designated smoking area. **Dining:** Restaurant nearby. **Recreation:** fishing. Fee: white water rafting; Yellowstone Park tours, horseback riding. **All Rooms:** combo or shower baths. **Cards:** AE, CB, DI, DS, MC, VI. **Special Amenities:** Free local telephone calls and preferred room (subject to availability with advanced reservations).

YELLOWSTONE SUPER 8-GARDINER
Phone: (406)848-7401

♦♦
Motel

	Rates Subject to Change								
9/14-9/30 [CP]	1P:	$65	2P/1B:	$65	2P/2B:	$65	XP:	$5	F12
4/1-5/24 [CP]	1P:	$45	2P/1B:	$45	2P/2B:	$45	XP:	$5	F12
3/1-3/31, 5/25-6/14 & 10/1-2/29 [CP]	1P:	$55	2P/1B:	$55			XP:	$5	F12
6/15-9/13 [CP]	1P:	$85	2P/1B:	$85			XP:	$5	F12

Location: On US Hwy 89 59030 (PO Box 739). Fax: 406/848-9410. **Terms:** Check-in 4 pm. **Facility:** 66 rooms. Conveniently located to entrance of Yellowstone National Park. 1 two-bedroom unit. 2-3 stories, no elevator; interior corridors; designated smoking area; small heated indoor pool. **Services:** winter plug-ins. **Some Rooms:** kitchen. **Cards:** AE, DI, DS, MC, VI.

YELLOWSTONE VILLAGE INN
Phone: (406)848-7417

AAA SAVE

6/15-9/1 [CP]	1P:	$50- 69	2P/1B:	$60- 69	2P/2B:	$69- 79	XP:	$5	F12
9/2-9/30 [CP]	1P:	$35- 54	2P/1B:	$40- 54	2P/2B:	$49- 59	XP:	$5	F12
5/21-6/14 [CP]	1P:	$30- 45	2P/1B:	$35- 45	2P/2B:	$35- 49	XP:	$5	F12
3/1-5/20 & 10/1-2/29 [CP]	1P:	$25- 35	2P/1B:	$30- 35	2P/2B:	$35- 39	XP:	$5	F12

♦♦
Motel

Location: 0.8 mi n on US 89. 1102 Scott St W 59030 (PO Box 297, 59030-0297). Fax: 406/848-7418. **Terms:** Check-in 3:30 pm; reserv deposit; handling fee imposed; monthly rates. **Facility:** 43 rooms. Rustic exterior cabin design. 0.3 mi from park entrance. 3 condo units, $95-$150 for up to 6 persons; 1-2 stories; interior/exterior corridors; heated indoor pool, sauna. **Services:** winter plug-ins. **Recreation:** basketball hoop. Fee: horseback riding, western dinner theater, white water rafting, Yellowstone Park tours. **All Rooms:** extended cable TV. **Some Rooms:** 3 kitchens. **Cards:** AE, CB, DI, DS, MC, VI. **Special Amenities:** Free breakfast and free local telephone calls. *(See color ad below)*

RESTAURANT

YELLOWSTONE MINE RESTAURANT
Dinner: $11-$20   **Phone:** 406/848-7336

AAA

Location: 0.5 mi n on US 89; at Best Western by Mammoth Hot Springs. Hwy 89 W 59030. **Hours:** 6 am-11 & 5-9 pm; to 9:30 pm, in summer. **Features:** casual dress; children's menu; cocktails & lounge; a la carte. Old west mine decor. Smoke free premises. **Cards:** AE, DI, DS, MC, VI.

♦♦
Steak and
Seafood

GLACIER NATIONAL PARK—*See also COLUMBIA FALLS, CORAM, EAST GLACIER PARK, ESSEX, HUNGRY HORSE, KALISPELL, WEST GLACIER & WHITEFISH.*

LODGING

APGAR VILLAGE LODGE
5/1-10/15

Guaranteed Rates
2P/1B: $57- 59 2P/2B: $74- 88 XP: $6

Phone: 406/888-5484

Location: 2 mi nw of West Glacier from jct of US 2; in Apgar Village. 200 Going to the Sun Rd 59936 (PO Box 398, WEST GLACIER). Fax: 406/888-5273. **Terms:** Open 5/1-10/15; check-in 4 pm; reserv deposit, 3 day notice; handling fee imposed. **Facility:** 48 rooms. In wooded setting adjacent to Lake McDonald & McDonald Creek with very clean & well maintained 1- to 3-bedroom cabins with modern baths & kitchens. Cabins, $86-$200 for up to 6 persons; 1 story; exterior corridors; designated smoking area; mountain view. **Dining:** Restaurants nearby. **Services:** Fee: area transportation, Park Shuttle. **Recreation:** swimming, fishing; hiking trails, jogging. **All Rooms:** shower baths. **Some Rooms:** 26 kitchens, color TV. **Cards:** AE, DS, MC, VI.

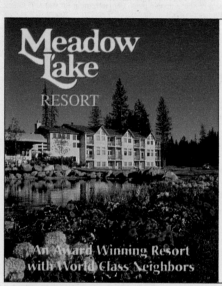
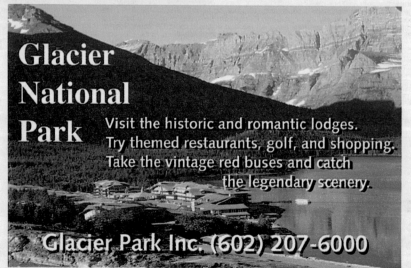
Choose an establishment with the ⦿ next to its listing!

RESTAURANT

EDDIE'S RESTAURANT   **Lunch:** $5-$15   **Dinner:** $9-$18   **Phone:** 406/888-5361
◆   **Location:** 2 mi nw of West Glacier from jct of US 2; in Apgar Village. 59936. **Hours:** Open 5/21-9/22; 7
American   am-9 pm. **Features:** casual dress; children's menu; beer & wine only; a la carte. Friendly staff in casual
family dining atmosphere serving sandwiches, salad, soup & featuring dinner entrees of Mt Whitefish &
Rocky Mountain Trout. Smoke free premises. **Cards:** DS, MC, VI.   ⊠

GLASGOW—3,600

LODGING

COTTONWOOD INN   Guaranteed Rates   **Phone:** (406)228-8213
◆◆◆   All Year   1P: $48- 52 2P/1B: $56- 62 2P/2B: $62- 68 XP: $5   F12
Motor Inn   **Location:** 0.5 mi e on US 2. 45 1st Ave NE 59230 (PO Box 1240). Fax: 406/228-8248. **Facility:** 92 rooms.
Contemporary styled rooms. 2 stories; interior corridors; heated indoor pool. **Services:** winter plug-ins.
All Rooms: combo or shower baths. **Cards:** AE, DI, DS, MC, VI.

(ASK) 🆂 ▦ 🏌 📶 ⊯ 🍴 🍸 ⊣ ⟨ ⚙ 🏦 ⊟ ⊠

GLENDIVE—4,800

LODGINGS

BEST WESTERN JORDAN INN   **Phone:** (406)365-5655
(AAA) (SAVE)   5/16-9/30   1P: $55- 60 2P/1B: $62- 67 2P/2B: $70- 75 XP: $5   F12
◆◆   3/1-5/15 & 10/1-2/29   1P: $48- 53 2P/1B: $55- 60 2P/2B: $63- 68 XP: $5   F12
Motor Inn   **Location:** Downtown; on I-94 business loop; from I-94, exit 215 (City Center). 222 N Kendrick Ave 59330
(PO Box 741). Fax: 406/365-6233. **Terms:** Small pets only, $5 extra charge. **Facility:** 93 rooms. Small to spa-
cious rooms. Casino. 2-3 stories; interior/exterior corridors; small heated indoor pool, sauna. **Dining:** Dining
room, coffee shop; 6 am-10 pm; to 9 pm, in winter; $4-$22. **Services:** giftshop; winter plug-ins. **All Rooms:** extended cable
TV. **Cards:** AE, DI, DS, MC, VI. **Special Amenities:** Early check-in/late check-out and free room upgrade (subject to
availability with advanced reservations).   🆂 ▦ 🏌 📶 ⊯ 🍴 🍸 ⊣ ⟨ ⚙ □ 🏦 ⊟ ⊠

BUDGET HOST RIVERSIDE INN   **Phone:** 406/377-2349
(AAA) (SAVE)   5/1-9/30 [CP]   1P: $35   2P/1B: $38   2P/2B: $42   XP: $4   D14
◆◆   3/1-4/30 & 10/1-2/29 [CP]   1P: $28   2P/1B: $34   2P/2B: $38   XP: $4   D14
Motel   **Location:** I-94, exit 213; just s. 44 Hwy 16 59330. Fax: 406/377-5564. **Terms:** Weekly/monthly rates; small
pets only, $10 dep req. **Facility:** 36 rooms. Convenient off interstate location. Coffee in lobby. 1 story; exterior
corridors; designated smoking area. **Services:** winter plug-ins. **Some Rooms:** 10 efficiencies, no utensils.
Cards: AE, DI, DS, MC, VI. *(See color ad p 206)*   ▦ ⚙ ⊟ ⊠

EL CENTRO MOTEL   Guaranteed Rates   **Phone:** (406)365-5211
(AAA)   All Year   1P: $24   2P/1B: $31   2P/2B: $35   XP: $3   F14
◆   **Location:** I-94, exit 215; 1.4 mi w on Merril Way, just n on Bell St, just w. 112 S Kendrick Ave 59330.
Motel   **Terms:** Small pets only. **Facility:** 25 rooms. Very clean economy style rooms. 6 efficiencies & 1 kitchen, $3
extra charge; 1 story; exterior corridors. **Services:** winter plug-ins. **All Rooms:** combo or shower baths.
Cards: CB, DI, DS, MC, VI.   (ASK) 🆂 ▦ □ ⊟ ⊠

GREAT FALLS—55,100

LODGINGS

BEST WESTERN HERITAGE INN   **Phone:** (406)761-1900
(AAA) (SAVE)   All Year   1P: $59- 69 2P/1B: $59- 69 2P/2B: $59- 69
◆◆◆   **Location:** Just s of I-15 business loop, US 89 & SR 200; 0.8 mi e of I-15, exit 278 (10th Ave S). 1700 Fox
Motor Inn   Farm Rd 59404. Fax: 406/761-0136. **Terms:** Monthly rates; small pets only. **Facility:** 239 rooms. Excellent indoor recreation facilities. 9 suites, $75-$104; 71 executive rooms with iron & ironing board, mini microwave &
mini fridge avail, extra charge. 2 rm suites avail; 2 stories; interior corridors; designated smoking area; small
heated indoor pool, saunas, whirlpools. **Dining:** Restaurant; 6 am-10 pm; $9-$16; cocktails. **Services:** giftshop; area
transportation; winter plug-ins. **All Rooms:** extended cable TV. **Cards:** AE, CB, DI, DS, JC, MC, VI. **Special Amenities:**
Early check-in/late check-out and free local telephone calls.

🆂 ▦ 🏌 📶 ⊯ 🍴 🍸 ⊣ ⟨ 🛏 ⚙ ▣ 🏦 ⊟ ⊠ ⟐

BEST WESTERN PONDEROSA INN

Phone: (406)761-3410

(AAA) (SAVE)

		1P:	$59	2P/1B:	$64	2P/2B:	$69	XP:	$5	F12
6/1-8/31 & 1/1-2/29										
3/1-5/31 & 9/1-12/31		1P:	$54	2P/1B:	$62	2P/2B:	$62	XP:	$5	F12

◆◆◆

Motor Inn

Location: Downtown. 220 Central Ave 59401. Fax: 406/761-3410. **Terms:** Weekly rates; small pets only, $5 extra charge. **Facility:** 105 rooms. Close to shopping & businesses. 4 stories; interior/exterior corridors; designated smoking area; heated pool, saunas. **Dining:** Restaurant; 6 am-10 pm, Fri & Sat-11 pm; $8-$13; cocktails. **Services:** winter plug-ins. **All Rooms:** extended cable TV. **Cards:** AE, DI, DS, JC, MC, VI. *(See color ad p 227)*

CENTRAL MOTEL

Phone: (406)453-0161

(AAA) (SAVE)

| All Year | 1P: | $35- 50 | 2P/1B: | $45- 60 | 2P/2B: | $50- 70 | XP: | $10 | D |

◆

Motel

Location: 1 mi e of I-15, exit 280 (Central Ave). 715 Central Ave W 59404. Fax: 406/453-7433. **Terms:** Reserv deposit, 14 day notice; handling fee imposed; small pets only. **Facility:** 28 rooms. Small contemporary-styled rooms. 2 two-bedroom units. 1 story; exterior corridors; designated smoking area; beachfront. **Dining:** Cafeteria nearby. **All Rooms:** extended cable TV. **Some Rooms:** 2 efficiencies, 8 kitchens. **Cards:** AE, DS, MC, VI. **Special Amenities:** Early check-in/late check-out and free local telephone calls.

COMFORT INN (GREAT FALLS)

Rates Subject to Change   **Phone:** (406)454-2727

◆◆◆

Motel

| 7/1-10/31 | 1P: | $70- 80 | 2P/1B: | $70- 90 | 2P/2B: | $70- 90 | XP: | $5 | F18 |
| 3/1-6/30 & 11/1-2/29 | 1P: | $55- 70 | 2P/1B: | $60- 80 | 2P/2B: | $60- 80 | XP: | $5 | F18 |

Location: I-15, exit 278; 3 mi on SR 200, just s on 9th St, 3.3 mi w on SR 200, just s. 1120 9th St S 59405. Fax: 406/454-2727. **Terms:** Reserv deposit. **Facility:** 64 rooms. 3 stories; interior corridors; designated smoking area; small heated indoor pool. **Services:** winter plug-ins. **Cards:** AE, CB, DI, DS, JC, MC, VI.

DAYS INN OF GREAT FALLS

Guaranteed Rates   **Phone:** (406)727-6565

◆◆

Motel

6/1-9/30 [CP]	1P:	$53- 60	2P/1B:	$59- 65	2P/2B:	$59- 65
10/1-2/29 [CP]	1P:	$44- 50	2P/1B:	$50- 56	2P/2B:	$50- 56
3/1-5/31 [CP]	1P:	$43- 50	2P/1B:	$49- 55	2P/2B:	$49- 55

Location: I-15, exit 280; 1.3 mi on Central Ave, 0.8 mi n 3rd St NW, just w. 101 14th Ave NW 59404. Fax: 406/727-6308. **Facility:** 62 rooms. Contemporary room decor. Running track & tennis courts avail at adjacent high school during summer months. Close to fairgrounds. 2 stories; interior corridors; designated smoking area. **Services:** winter plug-ins. **Cards:** AE, CB, DI, DS, JC, MC, VI.

FAIRFIELD INN BY MARRIOTT

Rates Subject to Change   **Phone:** 406/454-3000

◆◆◆

Motel

| 6/1-9/30 [CP] | 1P: | $49- 65 | 2P/1B: | $59- 79 | 2P/2B: | $59- 79 | XP: | $6 | F18 |
| 3/1-5/31 & 10/1-2/29 [CP] | 1P: | $46- 56 | 2P/1B: | $52- 62 | 2P/2B: | $52- 62 |

Location: I-15, exit 278; 3 mi e on SR 200, just n, 3.3 mi w on SR 200. 1000 9th Ave S 59405. Fax: 406/454-3000. **Facility:** 63 rooms. Comfortable modern decor; shopping mall adjacent. 3 stories; interior corridors; small heated indoor pool. **Services:** winter plug-ins. **Cards:** AE, DI, DS, MC, VI.

THE GREAT FALLS INN

Phone: (406)453-6000

(AAA) (SAVE)

| All Year [CP] | 1P: | $48- 55 | 2P/1B: | $49- 59 | 2P/2B: | $49- 59 | XP: | $5 | F12 |

◆◆◆

Motel

Location: US 87 & 89, to 26th St S, s 0.3 mi to 15th Ave S, just e. 1408 28th St S 59405. Fax: 406/453-6078. **Terms:** Reserv deposit; pets, $5 extra charge. **Facility:** 45 rooms. Adjacent to medical facilities. Stylish contemporary rooms. Spacious cozy lobby. 2 mini-suites, $63 for up to 2 persons; 4 stories; interior corridors. **Dining:** Restaurant nearby. **Services:** winter plug-ins. **All Rooms:** combo or shower baths, extended cable TV. **Cards:** AE, DI, DS, MC, VI. **Special Amenities:** Free breakfast and free local telephone calls. *(See ad below)*

HOLIDAY INN GREAT FALLS

Phone: (406)727-7200

(AAA) (SAVE)

| All Year | 1P: | $72- 78 | 2P/1B: | $72- 78 | 2P/2B: | $72- 78 |

◆◆◆

Motor Inn

Location: Just s of US 89 & SR 200; 2 mi e of I-15, exit 278 (10th Ave S). 400 10th Ave S 59405. Fax: 406/727-7200. **Terms:** AP avail; small pets only. **Facility:** 169 rooms. Spacious lobby. Casino. Modern decor in guest rooms. 1 whirlpool rm, extra charge; 7 stories; interior corridors; heated indoor pool, sauna, whirlpool. **Dining:** Dining room; 6 am-10 pm; $6-$16; cocktails. **Services:** winter plug-ins. **Recreation:** video games. **All Rooms:** extended cable TV. **Cards:** AE, CB, DI, DS, JC, MC, VI. **Special Amenities:** Free local telephone calls. *(See color ad opposite title page)*

O'HAIRE MOTOR INN

Phone: (406)454-2141

AAA SAVE
◆◆
Motor Inn

All Year   1P: $42- 55 2P/1B: $42- 55 2P/2B: $49- 75
Location: Center. 7th St & 1st Ave S 59403 (PO Box 1667). Fax: 406/454-0211. **Terms:** Reserv deposit. **Facility:** 69 rooms. Some covered parking. 3 two-bedroom units. 3 stories; interior/exterior corridors; designated smoking area; small heated indoor pool. **Dining:** Coffee shop; 6 am-8 pm, Sat from 7 am, Sun 7 am-3 pm; $7-$14. **Services:** winter plug-ins. **All Rooms:** extended cable TV. **Cards:** AE, DI, DS, MC, VI. **Special Amenities: Free local telephone calls and free room upgrade (subject to availability with advanced reservations).**

PLAZA INN

Phone: (406)452-9594

AAA SAVE
◆◆
Motel

3/1-10/31   1P: $36- 46 2P/1B: $45- 65 2P/2B: $50- 75 XP: $10
11/1-2/29   1P: $32- 42 2P/1B: $38- 58 2P/2B: $40- 60 XP: $10
Location: I-15 business loop, US 89 & SR 200. 1224 10th Ave S 59405. **Terms:** Reserv deposit; weekly rates; pets, $5 extra charge. **Facility:** 20 rooms. Newly renovated rooms. 1 story; designated smoking area. **Dining:** Restaurant nearby. **Services:** winter plug-ins. **All Rooms:** extended cable TV. **Cards:** AE, DS, MC, VI. **Special Amenities: Early check-in/late check-out and free local telephone calls.**

SKI'S WESTERN MOTEL

Phone: (406)453-3281

AAA SAVE
◆◆
Motel

All Year   1P: $35- 50 2P/1B: $45- 60 2P/2B: $50- 70 XP: $10
Location: 2 mi se on I-15 business loop, US 89 & SR 200. 2420 10th Ave S 59405. Fax: 406/453-3281. **Terms:** Reserv deposit, 14 day notice; handling fee imposed; weekly rates; pets, $6 extra charge. **Facility:** 25 rooms. Budget oriented rooms. 3 two-bedroom units. 1 story; exterior corridors; designated smoking area. **Dining:** Restaurant nearby. **Services:** winter plug-ins. **All Rooms:** combo or shower baths, extended cable TV. **Cards:** AE, DS, MC, VI. **Special Amenities: Early check-in/late check-out and free local telephone calls.**

TOWNHOUSE INN OF GREAT FALLS

Phone: (406)761-4600

AAA SAVE
◆◆◆
Motor Inn

7/1-8/31   1P: $63- 83 2P/1B: $68- 88 2P/2B: $69- 89 XP: $5   F12
3/1-6/30 & 9/1-2/29   1P: $60- 80 2P/1B: $65- 85 2P/2B: $66- 86 XP: $5   F12
Location: SR 200 & 15th St. 1411 10th Ave S 59405. Fax: 406/761-7603. **Terms:** Weekly/monthly rates; small pets only, $5 extra charge. **Facility:** 109 rooms. Updated guest rooms. Casino. 1 rm with in room treadmill; 2 stories; interior corridors; small heated pool, sauna, whirlpool. **Dining:** Dining room; 7 am-9 pm, Fri & Sat-10 pm; $10-$15; cocktails. **Services:** winter plug-ins. **All Rooms:** combo or shower baths, extended cable TV. **Some Rooms:** efficiency, whirlpools. **Cards:** AE, DI, DS, MC, VI. **Special Amenities: Free local telephone calls and free room upgrade (subject to availability with advanced reservations).**

RESTAURANTS

4 B'S RESTAURANT

Lunch: $6-$9   Dinner: $6-$9   Phone: 406-727-3366

◆
American

Location: 4 mi se on US 87 & 89. 4610 10th Ave S 59405. **Hours:** 6 am-11 pm, Sat & Sun-24 hrs. Closed: 11/25 & 12/25. **Features:** casual dress; children's menu; carryout; a la carte. Family restaurant. Informal atmosphere. **Cards:** AE, DI, DS, MC, VI.

PEKING GARDEN WEST

Lunch: $5-$5   Dinner: $7-$12   Phone: 406/727-3913

AAA
◆
Chinese

Location: US 87N, w on Black Eagle access road to Smelter Ave, 0.5 mi w. 801 Smelter Ave 59404. **Hours:** 11:30 am-10 pm, Fri-11 pm, Sat 4 pm-11 pm, Sun 3 pm-10 pm. Closed: 11/25 & 12/25. **Reservations:** suggested. **Features:** cocktail lounge; a la carte. Authentic entrees in casual family atmosphere. **Cards:** AE, MC, VI.

HAMILTON—2,700

LODGINGS

BEST WESTERN HAMILTON INN

Phone: (406)363-2142

AAA SAVE
◆◆◆
Motel

Thurs-Sat 5/1-9/30 [CP]   1P: $63- 94 2P/1B: $66- 94 2P/2B: $69- 94 XP: $5-8 F12
Sun-Wed 5/1-9/30 [CP]   1P: $53- 85 2P/1B: $58- 85 2P/2B: $63- 85 XP: $5-8 F12
3/1-4/30 & 10/1-2/29 [CP] 1P: $49- 85 2P/1B: $53- 85 2P/2B: $56- 85 XP: $5-8 F12
Location: S of city center on US 93. 409 S 1st St (US 93) 59840. Fax: 406/363-2142. **Facility:** 36 rooms. Park at many rooms. Close to city center & shopping. 1-2 stories; exterior corridors; designated smoking area; whirlpool. **Dining:** Restaurant nearby. **Services:** winter plug-ins. **All Rooms:** extended cable TV. **Cards:** AE, CB, DI, DS, MC, VI. **Special Amenities: Free breakfast and free local telephone calls.**

COMFORT INN OF HAMILTON

Phone: (406)363-6600

AAA SAVE
◆◆
Motel

7/1-8/31 [CP]   1P: $45- 63 2P/1B: $50- 68 2P/2B: $50- 68 XP: $5   F18
5/1-6/30 [CP]   1P: $43- 61 2P/1B: $48- 66 2P/2B: $48- 66 XP: $5   F18
3/1-4/30 & 9/1-2/29 [CP] 1P: $41- 59 2P/1B: $46- 64 2P/2B: $46- 64 XP: $5   F18
Location: N of city center on US 93. 1113 N First St 59840. Fax: 406/363-5644. **Terms:** Weekly/monthly rates; pets, $4 extra charge. **Facility:** 65 rooms. Located in the scenic Bitterroot Valley. Lucky Lil's Casino & Lounge off lobby & 24 hr convenience store/gas station. 2 stories; interior corridors; sauna, whirlpool. **Dining:** Restaurant nearby. **Services:** winter plug-ins. **Recreation:** video movie rentals. **All Rooms:** combo or shower baths, extended cable TV. **Cards:** AE, DI, DS, MC, VI. **Special Amenities: Free breakfast and free local telephone calls.**

HAMILTON SUPER 8 MOTEL

Phone: (406)363-2940

AAA SAVE
◆◆
Motel

4/16-9/15 [EP] 1P: $49- 59 2P/1B: $54- 64 2P/2B: $56- 66 XP: $5   F12
9/16-2/29 [EP] 1P: $44- 54 2P/1B: $46- 56 2P/2B: $48- 58 XP: $5   F12
3/1-4/15 [CP]   1P: $42- 52 2P/1B: $44- 54 2P/2B: $46- 56 XP: $5   F12
Location: US 93, n edge of town. 1325 N 1st St 59840. Fax: 406/363-2940. **Terms:** Weekly rates; mountain rates. **Facility:** 40 rooms. Contemporary rooms. 2 stories; interior corridors; designated smoking area; mountain view. **Services:** winter plug-ins. **All Rooms:** extended cable TV. **Some Rooms:** whirlpools. **Cards:** AE, CB, DI, DS, MC, VI.

STARFIRE FARM LODGE   Phone: (406)363-6240

(AAA) [SAVE]

5/15-9/30 [BP]   1P: $75- 95   2P/1B: $75- 95 2P/2B: $75
3/1-5/14 & 10/1-2/29 [BP]   1P: $68- 86   2P/1B: $68- 86 2P/2B: $68

◆◆◆
Bed &
Breakfast

Location: 8 mi s on US 93, 0.6 mi w on Camas Creek Rd, 0.8 mi sw on Hayes Creek Rd, 0.5 mi s. 387 Fleet St 59840 (401 Fleet St). Fax: 406/363-6240. **Terms:** Check-in 4 pm; reserv deposit, 30 day notice; handling fee imposed; weekly/monthly rates. **Facility:** 5 rooms. Secluded retreat nestled in wooded area with gazebo for relaxing, adjacent to Hayes Creek & stocked pond. 2 stories; interior corridors; designated smoking area. **Recreation:** fishing; gas grill. **Special Amenities:** Early check-in/late check-out and free local telephone calls.

🛅 🖳 🗙 📺 🖵 🗔 🖅 🕸 🖨 🖬 🗙

TROUT SPRINGS BED & BREAKFAST   Rates Subject to Change   Phone: 406/375-0911

(AAA)

All Year [BP]   1P: $70- 95   2P/1B: $75- 100 2P/2B: $75- 100 XP: $156   D5

◆◆◆
Bed &
Breakfast

Location: 721 Desta St 59840. Fax: 406/375-0988. **Facility:** 6 rooms. 1 two-bedroom unit. 3 stories; interior corridors; designated smoking area. **Dining:** Features gourmet 4-course breakfast including fresh caught trout. Complimentary dessert in the evening; restaurant nearby. **Services:** winter plug-ins. **Recreation:** fishing; bicycles, rec room with ping pong table, exercise bike, horseshoes, bocci ball. **All Rooms:** combo or shower baths. **Some Rooms:** color TV. **Cards:** AE, DS, MC, VI.

🛅 🗙 📺 📼 🕸 🖨 🗙

RESTAURANT

4 B'S RESTAURANT   **Lunch:** $5-$7   **Dinner:** $5-$8   Phone: 406/363-4620

◆
American

Location: US 93S. 1105 N 1st St (US 93) 59840. **Hours:** 24 hrs. Closed: 11/25 & 12/25. **Features:** casual dress; children's menu; senior's menu; carryout. Family restaurant. Pleasant, informal atmosphere. **Cards:** AE, DI, DS, MC, VI.

🗙

HARDIN—2,900

LODGINGS

AMERICAN INN OF HARDIN   Rates Subject to Change   Phone: 406/665-1870

(AAA)

5/1-9/30   1P: $45- 56   2P/1B: $56- 63 2P/2B: $65- 70 XP: $5   F10
3/1-4/30 & 10/1-2/29   1P: $38- 42   2P/1B: $40- 44 2P/2B: $44- 48 XP: $5   F10

◆◆
Motel

Location: I-90, exit 495; just s on SR 47. 1324 N Crawford Ave 59034. Fax: 406/665-1615. **Terms:** Pets, $4 extra charge. **Facility:** 42 rooms. 1 two-bedroom unit. 2 stories; exterior corridors; heated pool, waterslide, whirlpool. **Dining:** Restaurant; 6-10 am, in summer; 7-9 am, in winter; $5-$16. **Services:** winter plug-ins. **Recreation:** barbecue area, swingset, video game room. **All Rooms:** extended cable TV. **Some Rooms:** whirlpools. **Cards:** AE, DI, MC, VI. IMA. (See color ad p 320 & below)

🛅 🐾 🛌 🍴 🍽 🖳 🖨 🗙 🖅

WESTERN MOTEL   Rates Subject to Change   Phone: (406)665-2296

◆◆
Motel

6/1-9/30   1P: $45- 75   2P/1B: $50- 75 2P/2B: $55- 85 XP: $5   F6
3/1-5/31 & 10/1-2/29   1P: $30- 38   2P/1B: $35- 50 2P/2B: $40- 60 XP: $5   F6

Location: E I-90, exit 495; 1.3 mi s on SR 47 & Rt 313, just e; W I-90, exit 497; 0.3 mi w on I-90 business loop, continue straight on 3rd St 0.7 mi. 830 W 3rd St 59034. Fax: 406/665-2298. **Terms:** Reserv deposit; handling fee imposed. **Facility:** 28 rooms. Very clean rooms. 4 two-bedroom units. 2 stories; exterior corridors. **Services:** winter plug-ins. **Cards:** AE, DS, MC, VI.

🛅 🐾 🖵 🖨 🗙

HARLOWTON—1,000

LODGINGS

CORRAL MOTEL   Guaranteed Rates   Phone: 406/632-4331

◆
Motel

All Year   1P: $35- 40   2P/1B: $35- 40 2P/2B: $45- 50 XP: $5

Location: 0.5 mi e at jct US 12 & 191. (PO Box 721, 59036). Fax: 406/632-4748. **Terms:** Reserv deposit. **Facility:** 18 rooms. Budget oriented rooms. Large parking area. 6 two-bedroom units. 3 efficiencies, $5 extra charge; 1 story; exterior corridors. **Services:** winter plug-ins. **All Rooms:** combo or shower baths. **Cards:** AE, DI, DS, MC, VI.

🛏 🍴 🕸 🖨 🗙

COUNTRYSIDE INN   Rates Subject to Change   Phone: (406)632-4119

◆
Motel

All Year   1P: $38   2P/1B: $45- 47 2P/2B: $47- 49

Location: US 12E. 309 3rd St NE 59036. **Facility:** 15 rooms. Very clean. Outside patio area. 1 story; exterior corridors; designated smoking area. **Services:** winter plug-ins. **All Rooms:** combo or shower baths. **Cards:** AE, DS, MC, VI.

[ASK] 🛅 🛏 🖅 🕸 🖨 🗙

HAVRE—10,200

LODGING

TOWNHOUSE INN OF HAVRE   Phone: (406)265-6711
AAA SAVE   6/1-9/30   1P: $57- 72   2P/1B: $61- 76   2P/2B: $65- 80   XP: $5   F12
   3/1-5/31 & 10/1-2/29   1P: $52- 67   2P/1B: $56- 71   2P/2B: $60- 75   XP: $5   F12
◆◆   **Location:** Just w on US 2. 601 W 1st St 59501. Fax: 406/265-6213. **Terms:** Pets, $4 extra charge.
Motel   **Facility:** 104 rooms. Convenient location. Clean, comfortable rooms. Mini-fridges & microwaves avail, extra
   charge; 2 stories; interior corridors; small heated indoor pool, sauna, whirlpool. **Dining:** Restaurant nearby.
Services: area transportation, Amtrak; winter plug-ins. **Some Rooms:** 3 kitchens. **Cards:** AE, DI, DS, MC, VI.
Special Amenities: Free local telephone calls and free room upgrade **(subject to availability with advanced reservations).**

RESTAURANT

4 B'S RESTAURANT & BLACK ANGUS CASINO   **Lunch:** $4-$7   **Dinner:** $6-$9   **Phone:** 406/265-9721
◆   **Location:** Just e on US 2 from e entrance of town. 604 W 1st St 59501. **Hours:** 24 hrs; casino 8 am-2 am.
American   Closed: 11/25 & 12/25. **Features:** casual dress; children's menu; cocktails & lounge; a la carte. Family
   restaurant & casino. **Cards:** AE, DI, DS, MC, VI.

HELENA—24,600

LODGINGS

APPLETON INN BED & BREAKFAST   Rates Subject to Change   Phone: (406)449-7492
◆◆◆   All Year [BP]   1P: $70- 90   2P/1B: $75- 105   2P/2B: $75- 105   XP: $15
Historic Bed   **Location:** I-15, exit 193; 1.3 mi n on Cedar St, 1.7 mi w at jct US 12W (Lyndale Ave). 1999 Euclid Ave
& Breakfast   59601. Fax: 406/449-1261. **Terms:** Check-in 4 pm; reserv deposit, 14 day notice; handling fee imposed.
   Facility: 5 rooms. Lovely Victorian style home built in 1890. Romantic guest rooms. 3 stories; interior corridors;
smoke free premises. **Services:** winter plug-ins. **All Rooms:** combo or shower baths. **Cards:** AE, DI, DS, MC, VI.

BARRISTER BED & BREAKFAST   Rates Subject to Change   Phone: (406)443-7330
◆◆◆   All Year [BP]   1P: $85- 100   2P/1B: $85- 100   XP: $15   F18
Historic Bed   **Location:** 0.4 mi from Last Chance Gulch, 0.9 mi w of State Capitol on 6th Ave, just n. 416 N Ewing 59601.
& Breakfast   Fax: 406/442-7964. **Terms:** Age restrictions may apply; check-in 4 pm. **Facility:** 5 rooms. 1874 Victorian man-
   sion. Spacious eloquent bedrooms with ornate fireplace offer intimate elegance. Phones avail, VCR avail with
limited selection of movies; 3 stories, no elevator; interior corridors; smoke free premises. **Services:** winter plug-ins.
All Rooms: combo or shower baths. **Cards:** AE, DI, MC, VI.

BEST WESTERN COLONIAL INN   Rates Subject to Change   Phone: 406/443-2100
◆◆◆   All Year   1P: $69- 86   2P/1B: $79- 97   2P/2B: $79- 97   XP: $8   F18
Motor Inn   **Location:** Jct I-15, US 12 & 287; I-15, Capitol exit southbound, US 12W business district exit northbound.
   2301 Colonial Dr 59601. Fax: 406/442-0181. **Facility:** 149 rooms. Large rooms. Attractive public areas. All
rooms with iron, ironing board & hair dryer. 4 rms with electric fireplace; 4 whirlpool rms, extra chrage; 2 stories; interior corridors; small heated indoor/outdoor pool. **Services:** giftshop; winter plug-ins. **Cards:** AE, CB, DI, DS, MC, VI.

COMFORT INN OF HELENA   Rates Subject to Change   Phone: (406)443-1000
◆◆◆   5/1-10/1   1P: $60- 65   2P/1B: $65- 70   2P/2B: $65- 70   XP: $5   F18
Motel   3/1-4/30 & 10/2-2/29   1P: $45- 50   2P/1B: $50- 55   2P/2B: $50- 55
   Location: I-15, exit 192; just n. 750 N Fee St 59601. Fax: 406/443-1000. **Facility:** 56 rooms. Convenient off
interstate location. 2 stories; interior corridors; designated smoking area; small heated indoor pool. **Services:** winter plug-ins.
Cards: AE, DI, DS, MC, VI.

DAYS INN HELENA   Rates Subject to Change   Phone: (406)442-3280
◆◆   All Year [BP]   1P: $48- 65   2P/1B: $58- 80   2P/2B: $63- 80   XP: $5   F17
Motel   **Location:** I-15, exit 192; just w. 2001 Prospect Ave 59601. Fax: 406/442-3280. **Facility:** 93 rooms. Newly re-
   molded. Very clean rooms. 2 stories; interior corridors; designated smoking area. **Services:** winter plug-ins.
All Rooms: combo or shower baths. **Cards:** AE, CB, DI, DS, MC, VI.

ELKHORN MOUNTAIN INN   Phone: (406)442-6625
AAA SAVE   6/1-9/30 [CP]   1P: $57   2P/1B: $62   2P/2B: $67   XP: $6   F12
   3/1-5/31 & 10/1-2/29 [CP]   1P: $52   2P/1B: $57   2P/2B: $62   XP: $6   F12
◆◆◆   **Location:** 5 mi s, I-15, exit 187 (Montana City); just w. 1 Jackson Creek 59634. Fax: 406/449-8797.
Motel   **Terms:** Check-in 4 pm; weekly rates; pets, $5 extra charge. **Facility:** 22 rooms. Contemporary rustic appeal.
   2 mini-fridge avail. 1 whirlpool rm, extra charge; 2 stories; interior corridors; designated smoking area.
Services: giftshop; winter plug-ins. **All Rooms:** combo or shower baths, extended cable TV. **Cards:** AE, CB, DS, JC, MC,
VI. **Special Amenities:** Free local telephone calls and free newspaper.

FAIRFIELD INN BY MARRIOTT   Rates Subject to Change   Phone: (406)449-9944
◆◆◆   6/1-9/30 [CP]   1P: $69- 79   2P/1B: $74- 84   2P/2B: $74- 84   XP: $5   F12
Motel   3/1-5/31 & 10/1-2/29 [CP]   1P: $62- 72   2P/1B: $65- 75   2P/2B: $65- 75   XP: $5   F12
   Location: 2150 11th Ave 59601. Fax: 406/449-9949. **Facility:** 60 rooms. Brand new property. Lovely. Contem-
porary rooms. 3 stories; interior corridors; designated smoking area; small heated pool. **Services:** winter plug-ins.
All Rooms: combo or shower baths. **Cards:** AE, CB, DI, DS, JC, MC, VI. *(See color ad p 232)*

HOLIDAY INN EXPRESS   Phone: (406)449-4000
AAA SAVE   6/1-10/1 [CP]   1P: $70- 80   2P/1B: $70- 80   2P/2B: $70- 80   XP: $5   F19
   3/1-5/31 & 10/2-2/29 [CP]   1P: $61- 69   2P/1B: $61- 69   2P/2B: $61- 69   XP: $5   F19
◆◆◆   **Location:** I-15, exit 192B; just w on US 12, jct US 12 & I-15. 701 Washington St 59601. Fax: 406/449-4522.
Motel   **Facility:** 75 rooms. Convenient off interstate location. New property with contemporary rooms. All rooms with
   iron, ironing board & hair dryer. 4 stories; interior corridors; smoke free premises. **Services:** winter plug-ins.
All Rooms: combo or shower baths, extended cable TV. **Cards:** AE, CB, DI, DS, MC, VI. **Special Amenities:** Free
breakfast and free local telephone calls. *(See color ad opposite title page)*

JORGENSON'S HOLIDAY MOTEL
Phone: (406)442-1770

(AAA) (SAVE)
◆◆◆
Motor Inn

6/1-9/30   1P: $46- 94   2P/1B: $51- 99   2P/2B: $51- 99   XP: $5   F12
3/1-5/31 & 10/1-2/29   1P: $44- 89   2P/1B: $49- 94   2P/2B: $49- 94   XP: $5   F12
Location: Just w of I-15 & US 287, exit 192 (Townsend/Capitol). 1714 11th Ave 59624 (PO Box 857)
Fax: 406/449-0155. **Facility:** 117 rooms. Next to shopping mall in historic capital district. 3 two-bedroom units
2 rms with fax machines; suites with iron & ironing board; 1-3 stories; interior/exterior corridors; designated
smoking area; small heated indoor pool. **Dining:** Jorgenson's Restaurant & Lounge, see separate listing. **Services:** winter
plug-ins. **Recreation:** exercise machines. **All Rooms:** combo or shower baths, extended cable TV.
Some Rooms: whirlpools. **Cards:** AE, DI, DS, MC, VI. **Special Amenities:** Free local telephone calls.

KNIGHTS REST INN
Phone: (406)442-6384

(AAA) (SAVE)
◆
Motel

6/1-10/1   1P: $40   2P/1B: $43   2P/2B: $44   XP: $5   F11
3/1-5/31 & 10/2-2/29   1P: $30   2P/1B: $35   2P/2B: $40   XP: $5   F11
Location: I-15, exit 193; 1.3 mi w on Cedar St, w at jct US 12W (Lyndale Ave) 1.5 mi. 1831 Euclid 59601
Fax: 406/449-4560. **Terms:** Weekly/monthly rates, 10/1-3/31; pets. **Facility:** 12 rooms. 3 two-bedroom units. 1
story; exterior corridors; designated smoking area. **Services:** winter plug-ins. **All Rooms:** combo or shower
baths, extended cable TV. **Some Rooms:** kitchen. **Cards:** AE, DS, MC, VI. **Special Amenities:** Early check-in/late
check-out and free local telephone calls.

LAMPLIGHTER MOTEL
Phone: (406)442-9200

(AAA) (SAVE)
◆
Cottage

All Year   1P: $36- 39   2P/1B: $39- 42   2P/2B: $42- 54   XP: $6
Location: Hwy 12W, just s of Lundy Shopping Center. 1006 Madison 59601. **Facility:** 16 rooms. Modest cottages. 1 three-bedroom unit, 3 two-bedroom units. 10 kitchens & 2 efficiencies, extra charge; 1 story; exterior
corridors; designated smoking area. **Services:** winter plug-ins. **All Rooms:** combo or shower baths,
extended cable TV. **Cards:** AE, DS, JC, MC, VI. **Special Amenities:** Free local telephone calls and
preferred room (subject to availability with advanced reservations).

THE SANDERS-HELENA'S BED & BREAKFAST
Guaranteed Rates   **Phone: 406/442-3309**

◆◆◆
Historic Bed
& Breakfast

All Year [BP]   1P: $80- 90   2P/1B: $90- 105   2P/2B: $100- 110
Location: 0.3 mi from Last Chance Gulch, 0,8 mi w of State Capitol on 6th Ave, just n. 328 N Ewing St
59601. Fax: 406/443-2361. **Terms:** Check-in 4 pm; reserv deposit, 14 day notice; handling fee imposed.
Facility: 7 rooms. Restored 1875 mansion 1 block from original Governor's Mansion, featuring period furnishings. Hairdryers avail. 3 stories; interior corridors; smoke free premises. **Services:** winter plug-ins. **All Rooms:** combo or
shower baths. **Cards:** AE, DI, DS, MC, VI.

SHILO INN
Phone: (406)442-0320

(AAA) (SAVE)
◆◆
Motel

All Year [CP]   1P: $59- 89   2P/1B: $59- 89   2P/2B: $59- 89   XP: $10   F12
Location: 2 mi e, just w of I-15 interchange, enter from e on Prospect Ave; I-15, exit 192 (Capitol). 2020
Prospect Ave 59601-3298. Fax: 406/449-4426. **Terms:** Pets, $7 extra charge. **Facility:** 47 rooms. Small cozy
rooms. All rooms with iron & ironing board. 3 kitchen units, $9 extra charge; video rentals; 3 stories, no elevator;
interior corridors; designated smoking area; small heated indoor pool, sauna, steamroom, whirlpool.
Dining: Restaurant nearby. **Services:** winter plug-ins. **All Rooms:** extended cable TV. **Cards:** AE, CB, DI, DS, JC, MC, VI.
Special Amenities: Free local telephone calls and free newspaper. (See ad p 183)

SUPER 8 MOTEL
Phone: (406)443-2450

(AAA) (SAVE)
◆◆
Motel

5/28-9/30 [CP]   1P: $52- 62   2P/1B: $60- 70   2P/2B: $64- 74   XP: $5   F12
3/1-5/27 & 10/1-2/29 [CP]   1P: $47- 57   2P/1B: $53- 63   2P/2B: $57- 67   XP: $5   F12
Location: Southbound on I-15, Capitol(area)exit; w or northbound, exit w business district on US 12. 2200
11th Ave 59601. Fax: 406/443-2450. **Terms:** Weekly rates; pets, $25 dep req. **Facility:** 102 rooms. Conven-
ient off interstate location & close to capital area. Some new executive king rooms. Newly renovated. Microwaves & refrigerators avail, extra charge; 3 stories, no elevator; interior corridors; designated smoking area.
Dining: Restaurant nearby. **Services:** winter plug-ins. **All Rooms:** combo or shower baths, extended cable TV. **Cards:** AE,
CB, DI, DS, MC, VI. **Special Amenities:** Free breakfast and free local telephone calls.

RESTAURANTS

4 J'S CASINO & RESTAURANT   **Lunch:** $6-$17   **Dinner:** $9-$17   **Phone:** 406/443-0850
◆
American
Location: I-15, exit 192 (Capitol). 1827 Prospect Ave 59601. **Hours:** 8 am-10 pm, Sun-9 pm. Closed: 12/25.
Features: casual dress; carryout; cocktails & lounge. **Cards:** MC, VI.

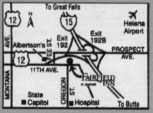

JADE GARDEN **Lunch:** $6-$10 **Dinner:** $8-$19 **Phone:** 406/443-8899
◆◆
Chinese **Location:** I-15, exit 92; 0.9 mi w on Prospect Ave, 1.8 mi n. 3128 N Montana Ave 59602. **Hours:** 11 am-9:30 pm, Fri & Sat-10 pm. **Closed:** 11/25 & 12/25. **Features:** casual dress; children's menu; carryout; beer & wine only. Traditional Chinese menu specializing in Cantonese cooking. Inviting, contemporary atmosphere. Smoke free premises. **Cards:** DS, MC, VI.

JORGENSON'S RESTAURANT & LOUNGE **Lunch:** $5-$7 **Dinner:** $7-$17 **Phone:** 406/442-6380
△△△ **Location:** Just w of I-15 & US 287, exit 192 (Townsend/Capitol); in Jorgenson's Holiday Motel. 1720 11th Ave 59601. **Hours:** 6:30 am-10 pm, Sun-9 pm. Closed major holidays. **Features:** casual dress; children's menu; cocktails & lounge. Popular family restaurant. Near shopping mall. **Cards:** AE, DI, DS, MC, VI.
◆◆
American

MONTANA CITY GRILL AND SALOON **Lunch:** $5-$7 **Dinner:** $6-$19 **Phone:** 406/449-8890
◆ **Location:** 4 mi s via I-15, exit 187; just w. 224 12th Ave 59601. **Hours:** 11 am-10 pm, Sat & Sun from 8 am. Closed: 12/25. **Features:** casual dress; carryout; cocktails & lounge. Casual dining featuring "Rocky Mountain Oysters", steak, seafood & chicken. **Cards:** MC, VI.
◆
American

OVERLAND EXPRESS **Lunch:** $6-$21 **Dinner:** $6-$21 **Phone:** 406/449-2635
◆ **Location:** S on I-15, Capital(area) exit; w or n, exit w business district on US 12. 2250 11th Ave 59601.
Steak and **Hours:** 11 am-10 pm, Sun from 9 am. Closed: 11/25 & 12/25. **Reservations:** suggested. **Features:** casual
Seafood dress; children's menu; carryout; cocktails & lounge. **Cards:** AE, DI, DS, MC, VI.

ROSE'S CANTINA **Lunch:** $4-$12 **Dinner:** $4-$12 **Phone:** 406/442-5221
◆ **Location:** Historic Last Chance Gulch. 314 N Last Chance Gulch 59601. **Hours:** 11 am-9 pm, Fri-9:30 pm,
Mexican Sat 5 pm-9:30 pm. Closed major holidays & Sun. **Features:** casual dress; children's menu; carryout; cocktails & lounge; street parking. Bustling Mexican eatery serving traditional favorites. **Cards:** AE, MC, VI.

YAT SON **Dinner:** $6-$13 **Phone:** 406/442-5405
◆◆ **Location:** Downtown; Main & Broadway. Last Chance Mall 59601. **Hours:** 4 pm-10 pm, Sun-9 pm. Closed
Chinese major holidays & Mon. **Reservations:** suggested. **Features:** casual dress; carryout; beer & wine only; street parking; a la carte. Also American cuisine, served in an enjoyable atmosphere. Smoke free premises.
Cards: AE, DS, MC, VI.

HUNGRY HORSE—900—See also GLACIER NATIONAL PARK.

LODGINGS

MINI GOLDEN INNS MOTEL **Phone:** (406)387-4313
△△△ [SAVE]

	1P:		2P/1B:		2P/2B:		XP:	
5/1-10/31 [CP]	$63-	70	$70-	76	$80-	86	$6	F12
3/1-4/30 & 11/1-2/29 [CP]	$48-	54	$54-	60	$60-	66	$6	F12

Motel **Location:** E end of town. 8955 US 2E 59919. Fax: 406/387-4317. **Terms:** Reserv deposit, 3 day notice; small pets only. **Facility:** 38 rooms. Contemporary rooms; park at room. Oversize parking avail. 4 two-bedroom units. 1 story; exterior corridors; designated smoking area; mountain view. **Dining:** Restaurant nearby.
Services: area transportation, to train or bus; winter plug-ins. **All Rooms:** combo or shower baths. **Some Rooms:** 11 efficiencies. **Cards:** AE, DI, DS, JC, MC, VI. **Special Amenities: Free breakfast and free local telephone calls.**

TAMARACK LODGE & MOTEL **Phone:** (406)387-4420
△△△ [SAVE]

	1P:		2P/1B:		2P/2B:		XP:	
6/1-9/15 [CP]	$60-	65	$65-	70	$75-	80	$5-10	D12
3/1-5/31 & 9/16-2/29 [CP]	$36-	42	$39-	45	$46-	52	$3-6	D12

◆◆ **Location:** 1.6 mi n on US 2. 9549 US 2E 59919 (PO Box 190236). Fax: 406/387-4425. **Terms:** Handling fee
Historic Motel imposed. **Facility:** 8 rooms. Log lodge & motel rooms with parking at rooms. 1 story; exterior corridors; designated smoking area; mountain view. **Recreation:** fishing; hiking trails, bike trails. **All Rooms:** combo or shower baths. **Cards:** AE, DS, MC, VI. **Special Amenities: Early check-in/late check-out and free breakfast.**

KALISPELL—11,900—See also GLACIER NATIONAL PARK.

LODGINGS

AERO INN **Phone:** (406)755-3798
△△△ [SAVE]

	1P:		2P/1B:		2P/2B:		XP:	
6/12-9/13 & 12/25-1/6 [CP]	$63-	67	$68-	72	$68-	72	$5	F5
3/19-6/11 & 9/14-10/17 [CP]	$39-	43	$44-	48	$48		$5	F5
3/1-3/18, 10/18-12/24 &								
1/7-2/29 [CP]	$31		$31		$39		$5	F5

Motel **Location:** 1 mi s on US 93 from jct of US 2. 1830 US 93S 59901. Fax: 406/752-1304. **Terms:** Pets, $10 dep req; in smoking rooms only. **Facility:** 62 rooms. Contemporary rooms with desk & good lighting. 1 two-bedroom unit. A frame cabin with 1 bedroom loft, avail daily in season; monthly off season; 2 stories; interior corridors; designated smoking area; small indoor pool, sauna, whirlpool. **Dining:** Restaurant nearby. **Services:** winter plug-ins. **All Rooms:** combo or shower baths, extended cable TV. **Some Rooms:** efficiency, kitchen, no utensils. **Cards:** AE, CB, DI, DS, MC, VI. **Special Amenities: Free breakfast and free local telephone calls.**

BEST WESTERN CAVANAUGHS OUTLAW HOTEL **Phone:** (406)755-6100
△△△ [SAVE]

	1P:		2P/1B:		2P/2B:		XP:	
6/1-9/15	$105-	120	$115-	140	$115-	140	$10	F17
4/1-5/31 & 9/16-10/31	$95-	110	$105-	130	$105-	130	$10	F17
11/1-2/29	$81-	115	$81-	115	$81-	115	$10	F17
3/1-3/31	$79-	110	$79-	110	$79-	110	$10	F17

Motor Inn **Location:** 1.4 mi s on US 93 from jct US 2. 1701 Hwy 93S 59901. Fax: 406/756-8994. **Terms:** Small pets only, $10 dep req. **Facility:** 220 rooms. Varied room decor & sizes; Western Art Gallery; small casino; cigar shop, barber & beauty shops. 2-3 stories; interior corridors; designated smoking area; small heated indoor pool, wading pool, sauna, whirlpools; racquetball court, 1 lighted tennis court; playground. **Dining:** Dining room; 6 am-10 pm; $7-$18; cocktails. **Services:** giftshop; winter plug-ins. **Some Rooms:** whirlpools. **Cards:** AE, DI, DS, MC, VI. **Special Amenities: Free newspaper and preferred room (subject to availability with advanced reservations).**

CAVANAUGHS AT KALISPELL CENTER
Phone: (406)752-666

(AAA) (SAVE)

| | 6/1-9/15 | 1P: $108- 190 | 2P/1B: $118- 190 | 2P/2B: $118- 190 | XP: $10 | F1 |
| | 4/1-5/31 & 9/16-10/31 | 1P: $98- 170 | 2P/1B: $108- 170 | 2P/2B: $108- 170 | XP: $10 | F1 |
◆◆◆ | 3/1-3/31 & 11/1-2/29 | 1P: $82- 160 | 2P/1B: $82- 160 | 2P/2B: $82- 160 | XP: $10 | F1 |

Motor Inn **Location:** Just s on US 93 from jct of US 2; e end of Kalispell Center. 20 N Main 59901. Fax: 406/752-662 **Terms:** Check-in 4 pm; small pets only. **Facility:** 132 rooms. Spacious rooms. Connected to large downtow shopping mall with adjacent limited gaming facility. 3 stories; interior corridors; designated smoking area; heated indoor poc sauna, whirlpools. **Dining:** Dining room; 6:30 am-10 pm; Fri & Sat-11 pm; Sun-9 am-9 pm; $9-$18; cocktails. **Recreatio** Fee: video games. **All Rooms:** extended cable TV. **Some Rooms:** 2 efficiencies, 4 kitchens. **Cards:** AE, DI, DS, MC, VI.

CRESTON INN BED & BREAKFAST
Phone: (406)755-751

◆◆ | 5/15-9/15 [BP] | Guaranteed Rates | 1P: $65- 75 | 2P/1B: $80- 95 |

Bed & Breakfast **Location:** 9.5 mi e on SR 35 from jct of US 2; just n on Creston Rd. 70 Creston Rd. 59901. **Terms:** Ope 5/15-9/15; age restrictions may apply; check-in 4 pm; reserv deposit, 14 day notice; handling fee impose **Facility:** 4 rooms. 1920's farmhouse in pastoral setting in Flathead Valley with majestic mountain views, creek side grounds & large modern baths. Dietary restrictions accommodated. 2 stories; interior corridors; designated smoking are mountain view. **All Rooms:** combo or shower baths. **Cards:** MC, VI.

DAYS INN KALISPELL
Phone: (406)756-322

◆◆ | 6/15-9/30 [CP] | 1P: $64 | 2P/1B: $69 | 2P/2B: $74 | XP: $5 | F1 |
Motel | 5/15-6/14 [CP] | 1P: $45 | 2P/1B: $50 | 2P/2B: $55 | XP: $5 | F1 |
| 3/1-5/14 & 10/1-2/29 [CP] | 1P: $40 | 2P/1B: $45 | 2P/2B: $45 | XP: $5 | F1 |

Location: 1.3 mi n on US 93 from jct of US 2. 1550 Hwy 93N 59901. Fax: 406/756-3277. **Facility:** 53 rooms. Contempora rooms; easy highway access; hospital across street. 3 suites, $60-$85; 2 stories; interior corridors; designated smoking are **Services:** winter plug-ins. **Cards:** AE, CB, DI, DS, JC, MC, VI.

FOUR SEASONS MOTOR INN
Phone: 406/755-612

(AAA) (SAVE)

| | 6/16-9/15 | 1P: $55- 65 | 2P/1B: $66- 76 | 2P/2B: $70- 78 | XP: $6 | F1 |
| | 5/16-6/15 & 9/16-10/15 | 1P: $47- 57 | 2P/1B: $58- 68 | 2P/2B: $63- 71 | XP: $6 | F1 |
◆◆ | 3/1-5/15 & 10/16-2/29 | 1P: $39- 49 | 2P/1B: $50- 60 | 2P/2B: $56- 64 | XP: $6 | F1 |

Motor Inn **Location:** On US 93; just n of jct US 2. 350 N Main St 59901. Fax: 406/755-1604. **Terms:** Pets. **Facility:** 10 rooms. Convenient location to hwys & shopping mall. 2 stories; interior/exterior corridors; whirlpoc **Dining:** Restaurant; 6 am-7 pm; to 10 pm, 6/1-9/15; closed major holidays; $5-$11. **Services:** winter plug-in **All Rooms:** extended cable TV. **Cards:** AE, CB, DI, DS, MC, VI.

GLACIER GATEWAY MOTEL
Phone: 406/755-333

(AAA) (SAVE)

| | 6/1-9/1 | 1P: $48- 53 | 2P/1B: $45- 53 | 2P/2B: $60- 75 | XP: $4 |
◆ | 3/1-5/31 & 9/2-2/29 | 1P: $30- 35 | 2P/1B: $30- 35 | 2P/2B: $35- 40 | XP: $4 |

Motel **Location:** Nw corner of jct US 2 & 93. 264 N Main St 59901. **Terms:** Weekly rates, in winter; pets, dog only. **Facility:** 14 rooms. Park at some rooms. 8 efficiencies, $4 extra charge; 2 stories; exterior corridors; des ignated smoking area. **Dining:** Restaurant nearby. **Services:** winter plug-ins. **All Rooms:** extended cabl TV. **Cards:** AE, CB, DI, DS, MC, VI.

HAMPTON INN-KALISPELL
Phone: (406)755-790

◆◆◆ | 3/1-9/30 [CP] | 1P: $88 | 2P/1B: $98 | 2P/2B: $98 |
Motel | 10/1-2/29 [CP] | 1P: $68 | 2P/1B: $78 | 2P/2B: $78 |

Location: 0.9 mi w on US 2 from jct US 93. 1140 Hwy 2 W 59901. Fax: 406/755-5056. **Terms:** Check-in pm. **Facility:** 120 rooms. Spacious rooms & recreational facilities. Rooms with iron, ironing board & hairdryer. 3 stories; inte rior corridors; designated smoking area; mountain view; heated indoor pool. **Services:** giftshop; winter plug-ins **All Rooms:** combo or shower baths. **Cards:** AE, DI, DS, MC, VI. (See color ad below)

KALISPELL GRAND HOTEL
Phone: (406)755-810

(AAA) (SAVE)

| | 7/1-8/31 [CP] | 1P: $65- 74 | 2P/1B: $75- 115 | 2P/2B: $75- 91 | XP: $7 | F1 |
◆◆ | 3/1-6/30 & 9/1-2/29 [CP] | 1P: $54- 63 | 2P/1B: $64- 98 | 2P/2B: $64- 60 | XP: $7 | F1 |

Historic Hotel **Location:** Downtown; on US 93. 100 Main St 59901. Fax: 406/752-8012. **Terms:** Reserv deposit; small pe only. **Facility:** 40 rooms. Renovated 1912 historic hotel in heart of Kalispell with various room sizes. 2 tw bedroom units. 3 stories, no elevator; interior corridors; designated smoking area. **Dining:** Restaurant; am-2:30 pm, Tues-Thurs 5 pm-9 pm, Fri & Sat-9:30 pm; $6-$12; cocktails; also, The Alley Connection, see separate listin **Recreation:** casino. **All Rooms:** combo or shower baths, extended cable TV. **Cards:** AE, DI, DS, MC, VI. **Special Amenities:** Free breakfast and free local telephone calls.

TEL 6 KALISPELL - 290

Rates Subject to Change | Phone: 406/752-6355

			1P:		2P/1B:			2P/2B:			XP:		
7/1-9/15			1P:	$47- 52	2P/1B:	$52-	57	2P/2B:	$52-	57	XP:	$3	F17
5/27-6/30 & 9/16-10/3			1P:	$42- 52	2P/1B:	$47-	57	2P/2B:	$47-	57	XP:	$3	F17
3/1-5/26 & 10/4-2/29			1P:	$36- 41	2P/1B:	$42-	47	2P/2B:	$42-	47	XP:	$3	F17

Location: 1.2 mi s on US 93 from jct of US 2. 1540 Hwy 93S 59901. Fax: 406/752-6358. Terms: Check-in 4 pm; small pets only. Facility: 114 rooms. Clean rooms in various sizes; park at some rooms. 2 stories; exterior idors; designated smoking area; heated pool. Dining: Restaurant nearby. All Rooms: shower baths. Cards: AE, CB, DI, MC, VI.

D LION INN KALISPELL

Phone: (406)755-6700

			1P:		2P/1B:			2P/2B:			XP:		
6/16-9/30 [CP]			1P:	$89- 94	2P/1B:	$89-	104	2P/2B:	$89-	104	XP:	$5	F19
4/1-6/15 [CP]			1P:	$84- 89	2P/1B:	$84-	99	2P/2B:	$84-	99	XP:	$5	F19
3/1-3/31 & 10/1-2/29 [CP]			1P:	$79- 84	2P/1B:	$79-	84	2P/2B:	$79-	84	XP:	$5	F19

Location: 1 mi w on US 2 from jct of US 93. 1330 Hwy 2W 59901. Fax: 406/755-6717. Terms: Monthly rates; pets. Facility: 64 rooms. Spacious rooms with iron, ironing board & 2 phones; some with balcony & o. Small casino on property. 3 two-bedroom units. 2 stories; interior corridors; heated pool, whirlpool. Dining: Restaurant; am-2 & 4:30-10 pm; cocktails. Services: winter plug-ins. All Rooms: extended cable TV. Cards: AE, CB, DI, DS, MC, VI. Special Amenities: Early check-in/late check-out and preferred room (subject to availability with advanced ervations). (See color ad below)

REE LODGE BED & BREAKFAST

Rates Subject to Change | Phone: 406/257-5770

			1P:		2P/1B:		2P/2B:	
5/15-10/31 [BP]			1P:	$120	2P/1B:	$120	2P/2B:	$120
3/1-5/14 & 11/1-2/29 [BP]			1P:	$105	2P/1B:	$105	2P/2B:	$105

Location: 12 mi se on SR 35 from jct of US 2 & SR 35, 1 mi e on Lindsey Ln. 10 Sky Ln 59901. Fax: 406/257-5771. Terms: Reserv deposit, 15 day notice. Facility: 4 rooms. Beautiful large cedar home in ene wooded setting close to Flathead Lake with easy hwy access. 3 stories; interior corridors. Services: area sportation. Recreation: cross country skiing; hiking trails. Some Rooms: combo or shower baths, shared bathrooms. ds: AE, DS, MC, VI.

PER 8 MOTEL-KALISPELL

Rates Subject to Change | Phone: (406)755-1888

			1P:		2P/1B:			2P/2B:			XP:		
5/14-9/30			1P:	$60- 65	2P/1B:	$67-	72	2P/2B:	$70-	75	XP:	$5-7	F12
4/1-5/13			1P:	$42- 47	2P/1B:	$47-	54	2P/2B:	$52-	57	XP:	$5-7	F12
3/1-3/31 & 10/1-2/29			1P:	$40- 45	2P/1B:	$47-	52	2P/2B:	$50-	55	XP:	$5-7	F12

ation: 1.2 mi s on US 93 from jct of US 2. 1341 1st Ave E 59901. Fax: 406/755-1888. Facility: 74 rooms. Contemporary ms with good lighting. 3 stories; interior corridors; designated smoking area. Services: winter plug-ins. Cards: AE, CB, DS, MC, VI.

ITE BIRCH MOTEL

Rates Subject to Change | Phone: 406/752-4008

			1P:		2P/1B:			2P/2B:			XP:	
6/1-9/30			1P:	$40- 50	2P/1B:	$45-	48	2P/2B:	$48-	52	XP:	$5
3/1-5/31 & 10/1-2/29			1P:	$25- 30	2P/1B:	$28-	35	2P/2B:	$31-	40	XP:	$5

Location: 0.4 mi e on SR 35 from jct US 2. 17 Shady Ln 59901. Fax: 406/752-1106. Terms: Reserv deposit; monthly rates; pets. Facility: 8 rooms. Very clean rooms in varied sizes with pine furnishings surround shaded lawn area; park at rooms. 2 efficiencies, $70. 1 two-bedroom efficiency, $80; 1 story; exterior corridors; Bas-ball court; playground. Dining: Restaurant nearby. All Rooms: extended cable TV. Cards: AE, DS, MC, VI.

RESTAURANTS

E ALLEY CONNECTION

Lunch: $3-$5 | Dinner: $7-$13 | Phone: 406/752-7077

Location: Downtown; on US 93; in Kalispell Grand Hotel. 22 1st St W 59901. Hours: 11 am-2:30 & 5-9 pm, Fri-9:30 pm, Sat noon-2:30 & 5-9:30 pm. Closed major holidays, Sun, Mon & 11/1-11/30. Features: casual dress; cocktails; a la carte. A variety of Oriental cuisine. Steak, seafood & poultry dishes. Cards: AE, DS, VI.

S AMIGOS

Lunch: $5-$9 | Dinner: $5-$15 | Phone: 406/752-2711

Location: Downtown. 25 2nd Ave W 59901. Hours: 11 am-10 pm. Closed: 11/25 & 12/25. Features: casual dress; children's menu; beer & wine only; a la carte. Traditional & unique Mexican dinner menu only on Sun. Cards: AE, DS, MC, VI.

NDERS RESTAURANT

Lunch: $5-$8 | Dinner: $10-$17 | Phone: 406/752-3000

Location: 7.8 mi n on US 93 from jct of US 2. 4090 Hwy 93 N 59901. Hours: 11 am-10 pm, Sun noon-10 pm. Features: casual dress; children's menu; cocktails & lounge. Country setting with view of the Flathead Valley & featuring steak, seafood & panfried chicken on Sun. Antique car booths. Cards: AE, MC, VI.

ak and food

ROCCO'S
◆◆
Italian

MC, VI.

Dinner: $10-$19

Phone: 406/756-5

Location: 8 mi n on US 2E from jct of US 93. 3796 Hwy 2E 59901. **Hours:** 5 pm-9:30 pm; winter-9 pm & Sat-10 pm. Closed: 11/25, 12/25 & Mon. **Features:** casual dress; children's menu; cocktails & lounge; carte. Casual family atmosphere featuring traditional dishes plus seafood & steak entrees. **Cards:** AE,

LAKESIDE—600

LODGINGS

ANGEL POINT GUEST SUITES
◆◆◆
Bed &
Breakfast

Guaranteed Rates

Phone: (406)844-2

6/1-9/30 [BP]	1P: $110- 125	2P/1B: $110- 125			XP: $40	
3/1-5/31 & 10/1-2/29 [BP]	1P: $95- 110	2P/1B: $95- 110			XP: $40	

Location: 1.7 mi s on US 93, 2 mi e (stay right on paved road). 829 Angel Point Rd 59922 (PO Box 7 **Terms:** Reserv deposit, 15 day notice; 3 night min stay. **Facility:** 2 rooms. Majestic home on Flathead L with panoramic views with lakeside gazebo picnic areas with grill & bench swings. Spacious guest suites with view of lak mountains. 2 stories; exterior corridors; smoke free premises; boat dock. **Services:** winter plug-ins. **Recreation:** swimm canoeing, fishing. **All Rooms:** kitchens.

BAYSHORE MOTEL
AAA SAVE
◆◆
Motel

Phone: (406)844-3

7/1-9/15	1P: $50- 65	2P/1B: $68- 75	2P/2B: $78- 88	XP: $7
3/1-6/30 & 9/16-2/29	1P: $40- 47	2P/1B: $48- 60	2P/2B: $55- 75	XP: $7

Location: Center; on US 93. 616 Lakeside Blvd 59922 (PO Box 375). **Fax:** 406/844-2000. **Facility:** 12 roc On Flathead Lake with good beach access; family style units with kitchens & views; park at many room two-bedroom units. 2 stories; exterior corridors; beach; boat dock. **Dining:** Restaurant nea **Services:** winter plug-ins. **Recreation:** swimming, charter fishing, fishing; Adjacent boat rentals. **All Rooms:** kitch extended cable TV. **Cards:** AE, DS, MC, VI. **Special Amenities:** Free local telephone calls and free room upg (subject to availability with advanced reservations).

LAKE SHORE MOTEL
◆
Cottage

Rates Subject to Change

Phone: 406/844-2

7/2-9/30	1P: $50- 60	2P/1B: $60- 70	2P/2B: $70- 80	XP: $5
6/1-7/1	1P: $40- 50	2P/1B: $50- 60	2P/2B: $50- 60	XP: $5

Location: Center; on US 93. 7175 US 93S 59922 (PO Box 279). **Terms:** Open 6/1-9/30; reserv deposit day notice; handling fee imposed. **Facility:** 7 rooms. Cottages fronting Flathead Lake with full view of lake & mountains f cottage window. 4 two-bedroom units. 1 story; exterior corridors; designated smoking area; boat d **Recreation:** swimming, fishing. **Some Rooms:** 5 efficiencies.

SUNRISE VISTA INN
AAA SAVE
◆◆
Motel

Phone: (406)844-3

6/15-8/31	1P: $55- 60	2P/1B: $55- 60	2P/2B: $60- 70	XP: $7
5/15-6/14 & 9/1-10/31	1P: $48	2P/1B: $48	2P/2B: $54	XP: $7

Location: N edge of town on US 93. 7005 US 93 59922 (PO Box 374). **Terms:** Open 5/15-10/31; re deposit, 3 day notice; CP avail, groups only; small pets only, $20 dep req. **Facility:** 9 rooms. Family atr phere with antique furniture & offers outstanding views of Flathead Lake & Mission Mountains. 1 two-bedr unit. 1 kitchen unit, $10 extra charge; 1 story; exterior corridors; designated smoking area; beach; boat d **Recreation:** swimming, fishing. **All Rooms:** combo or shower baths. **Cards:** MC, VI. **Special Amenities:** Free l telephone calls.

LEWISTOWN—6,100

LODGING

B & B MOTEL
AAA SAVE
◆
Motel

Phone: (406)538-5

6/1-11/15	1P: $38	2P/1B: $43	2P/2B: $46	XP: $3
3/1-5/31 & 11/16-2/29	1P: $34	2P/1B: $38	2P/2B: $41	XP: $3

Location: Downtown. 520 E Main St 59457. **Terms:** Reserv deposit; weekly rates; pets, $3 extra cha **Facility:** 36 rooms. Very clean, budget oriented rooms. 1 two-bedroom unit. 2 stories; exterior corridors; ignated smoking area. **Dining:** Restaurant nearby. **Services:** winter plug-ins. **All Rooms:** combo or show baths, extended cable TV. **Some Rooms:** 4 kitchens. **Cards:** AE, DI, DS, MC, VI. **Special Amenities:** Free l telephone calls. IMA. *(See color ad p 320)*

RESTAURANT

THE WHOLE FAMDAMILY
◆◆
American

Smoke free premises. **Cards:** AE, DS, MC, VI.

Lunch: $4-$8

Dinner: $4-$8

Phone: 406/538-5

Location: Downtown. 206 W Main St 59457. **Hours:** 11 am-8 pm, Sat-5 pm. Closed major holidays & **Features:** casual dress; health conscious menu; carryout; beer & wine only; street parking; a la ca Whopping sandwiches made with fresh ingredients. Rich, homemade soup & salad. Homey atmosph

LIBBY—2,500

LODGINGS

SUPER 8 MOTEL
AAA SAVE
◆◆
Motel

Phone: (406)293-2

6/1-9/30	1P: $50	2P/1B: $56	2P/2B: $66	XP: $5
5/1-5/31	1P: $43	2P/1B: $49	2P/2B: $57	XP: $5
10/1-2/29	1P: $41	2P/1B: $47	2P/2B: $53	XP: $5
3/1-4/30	1P: $40	2P/1B: $46	2P/2B: $52	XP: $2

Location: Just w on US 2 from jct SR 37. 448 US 2W 59923. **Fax:** 406/293-9871. **Terms:** Pets, $5 e charge. **Facility:** 42 rooms. 2 stories; interior corridors; designated smoking area; mountain view; small heated indoor p **Dining:** Restaurant nearby. **Services:** winter plug-ins. **All Rooms:** extended cable TV. **Cards:** AE, DI, DS, MC. **Special Amenities:** Early check-in/late check-out and free local telephone calls.

NTURE MOTOR INN Phone: (406)293-7711

6/1-9/30	1P:	$54-	60	2P/1B:	$60-	69	2P/2B:	$69- 75 XP: $6
3/1-5/31 & 10/1-2/29	1P:	$48-	54	2P/1B:	$54-	62	2P/2B:	$62- 68 XP: $6

Location: Just w on US 2 from jct SR 37. 443 US 2W 59923. **Fax:** 406/293-3326. **Facility:** 72 rooms. Varied styles of rooms. 3 stories; interior corridors; designated smoking area; mountain view; small indoor pool, whirlpool. **Dining:** Restaurant; 6 am-9 pm, Sat from 8 am, Sun 8 am-3 pm; $6-$16. **Services:** winter plug-ins. **Rooms:** extended cable TV. **Cards:** AE, CB, DI, DS, MC, VI. **Special Amenities:** Free local telephone calls and free newspaper.

RESTAURANTS

'S RESTAURANT **Lunch:** $5-$8 **Dinner:** $5-$8 Phone: 406/293-8751

Location: 0.5 mi w on US 2 from jct Hwy 37. 442 US 2W 59923. **Hours:** 6 am-midnight, Fri & Sat-1 am. Closed: 11/25 & 12/25. **Features:** casual dress; children's menu; senior's menu; a la carte. Family restaurant. Pleasant, informal atmosphere. **Cards:** AE, DI, DS, MC, VI.

NRY'S **Lunch:** $4-$12 **Dinner:** $4-$12 Phone: 406/293-7911

Location: Just w on US 2 from jct SR 37. 405 W 9th St 59923. **Hours:** 6 am-10 pm; to 9 pm, in winter. Closed: 11/25 & 12/25. **Features:** casual dress; children's menu; senior's menu; carryout; salad bar; a la carte. An informal coffeeshop & adjoining dining room with antique decor. **Cards:** MC, VI.

DEN CHAPEL Historical **Lunch:** $6-$7 **Dinner:** $10-$20 Phone: 406/293-2928

Location: Just e on US 2 from jct SR 37, just s. 1207 Utah Ave 59923. **Hours:** 11 am-2 & 5-10 pm, Sat & Sun from 5 pm. Closed: 1/1, 11/25 & 12/25. **Reservations:** suggested; holidays. **Features:** casual dress; Sunday brunch; children's menu; health conscious menu items; beer & wine only; street parking; a la carte. orian decor compliments 1900's quaint neighborhood church with seasonal patio dining. Lunch features sandwiches, p, salad; dinner features beef, pasta, fresh seafood & chicken entres. **Cards:** MC, VI.

LINCOLN—500

LODGINGS

E BLACKFOOT RIVER INN MOTEL Rates Subject to Change Phone: 406/362-4948

All Year	1P:	$45	2P/1B:	$45	2P/2B: $45

Location: 5 mi e on SR 200. Hwy 200 59639 (PO Box 185). **Terms:** Reserv deposit; handling fee imposed. **Facility:** 16 rooms. Budget oriented clean rooms. 1/4 mi from Blackfoot River. 1 story; interior corridors. creation: hiking trails. **All Rooms:** shower baths. **Cards:** AE, DS, MC, VI.

EPER'S MOTEL Phone: (406)362-4333

All Year [CP]	1P:	$35- 37	2P/1B:	$41- 46	2P/2B:	$48 XP: $4

Location: Just w on SR 200. Hwy 200 & 1st Ave 59639 (PO Box 611). **Fax:** 406/362-4261. **Terms:** Pets, $5 extra charge. **Facility:** 15 rooms. Ponderosa pine setting. Very clean rooms. 4 efficiencies, $4 extra charge; 1 story; exterior corridors; designated smoking area; sauna, whirlpool. **Services:** winter plug-ins. **All Rooms:** combo or shower baths, extended cable TV. **Cards:** AE, DS, MC, VI. **Special Amenities:** Free al telephone calls and preferred room (subject to availability with advanced reservations).

RESTAURANT

P RANCH SUPPER CLUB **Lunch:** $6-$14 **Dinner:** $15-$21 Phone: 406/362-4255

Location: 5 mi e on SR 200. **Hours:** 5 pm-10 pm, 4/4-12/31; Sun 4 pm-10 pm; Fri-Sun 5 pm-10 pm, 1/1-4/3. Closed: 11/25, 12/24 & 12/25. **Features:** casual dress; children's menu; salad bar; cocktails & lounge. Nice selection of steak, barbecued ribs & seafood served in rustic western atmosphere. Prime rib served on Fri & Sat nights. **Cards:** AE, DS, MC, VI.

LIVINGSTON—6,700

LODGINGS

ST WESTERN YELLOWSTONE INN Guaranteed Rates Phone: (406)222-6110

5/15-9/15	1P:	$72-	79	2P/1B:	$75-	83	2P/2B:	$83 XP: $7		F12
3/1-5/14 & 9/16-2/29	1P:	$54-	59	2P/1B:	$60-	67	2P/2B:	$67- 73 XP: $7		F12

Location: I-90, exit 33; just n on US 89. 1515 W Park 59047. **Fax:** 406/222-3976. **Terms:** Check-in 4 pm. lity: 99 rooms. Southwestern lobby. Spacious rooms. Large garage parking. 2-3 stories; interior corridors; king area; small heated indoor pool. **Services:** winter plug-ins. **Some Rooms:** kitchen. **Cards:** AE, CB, DI, DS, JC, MC,

DGET HOST PARKWAY MOTEL Phone: (406)222-3840

6/6-9/1	1P:	$52-	56	2P/1B:	$55-	59	2P/2B:	$64- 69 XP: $5 F12
5/1-6/5 & 9/2-11/1	1P:	$36-	40	2P/1B:	$42-	46	2P/2B:	$48- 56 XP: $5 F12
3/1-4/30 & 11/2-2/29	1P:	$34-	40	2P/1B:	$40		2P/2B:	$42- 46 XP: $4 F12

Location: US 89, 0.5 mi n jct I-90, exit 333. 1124 W Park 59047. **Fax:** 406/222-7948. **Terms:** Reserv deposit, 3 day notice; weekly/monthly rates, 10/1-4/30; pets, $3 extra charge. **Facility:** 28 rooms. Small rooms. ficiencies, $10 extra charge; 6 two-bedroom units, $10-$20 extra charge; 1 story; exterior corridors; small heated pool. vices: winter plug-ins. **All Rooms:** combo or shower baths, extended cable TV. **Cards:** AE, CB, DI, DS, MC, VI. e color ad p 206)

L MAR MOTEL INC Phone: (406)222-3120

6/2-9/1	1P:	$49-	70	2P/1B:	$49-	70	2P/2B:	$54- 70 XP: $5 F12
5/1-6/1 & 9/2-11/1	1P:	$38-	58	2P/1B:	$38-	58	2P/2B:	$44- 58 XP: $5 F12
3/1-4/30 & 11/2-2/29	1P:	$32		2P/1B:	$31-	50	2P/2B:	$38- 50 XP: $5 F12

Location: Just w of jct US 89, on I-90 business loop. (PO Box 636, 59047). **Fax:** 406/222-5474. **Terms:** Reserv deposit; weekly rates, 10/15-5/15; pets, $5 extra charge. **Facility:** 32 rooms. Nicely landscaped uiet location. 3 two-bedroom units, $10-$20 extra charge; 1 story; exterior corridors; designated smoking area; heated pool, l open 6/1-8/31; playground. **Services:** winter plug-ins. **All Rooms:** extended cable TV. **Cards:** AE, DI, DS, MC, VI. cial Amenities: Free room upgrade and preferred room (each subject to availability with advanced reservations).

ECONO LODGE

Phone: (406)222-0

	5/1-9/30 [CP]	1P:	$46- 69	2P/1B:	$69- 89	2P/2B:	$69- 89	XP: $5
	3/1-4/30 & 10/1-2/29 [CP]	1P:	$35- 45	2P/1B:	$46- 59	2P/2B:	$46- 59	XP: $5

◆◆◆ **Location:** I-90 exit 333, just n on US 89, then just w. 111 Rogers Ln 59047 (PO Box 13
Motel   Fax: 406/222-9588. **Terms:** Reserv deposit; pets, $5 extra charge. **Facility:** 50 rooms. Brand new prop
Very clean, contemporary rooms. Designated smoking area; heated pool, whirlpool. **Dining:** Restau
nearby. **All Rooms:** combo or shower baths, extended cable TV. **Cards:** AE, CB, DI, DS, MC, VI. **Special Amenities:** F
breakfast and free local telephone calls. 🅢 🐕 🈲 🛎 🕎 🆑 🌂 🎿 🖵 🖨 🖴 🛄 📶 🛗 🅇

LIVINGSTON COMFORT INN

Phone: (406)222-4

	Rates Subject to Change			Phone: (406)222-4
◆◆◆ 7/1-8/20 [CP]	1P: $80	2P/1B: $85	2P/2B: $90	XP: $5
Motel 8/21-2/29 [CP]	1P: $65	2P/1B: $70	2P/2B: $75	XP: $5
3/1-6/30 [CP]	1P: $62	2P/1B: $67	2P/2B: $72	XP: $5

Location: I-90, exit 333; just s on US 89, just w. 114 Loves Ln 59047. Fax: 406/222-7658. **Terms:** Reserv dep
Facility: 49 rooms. Contemporary room decor. Convenient location. 2 stories; interior/exterior corridors; designated smo
area; small heated indoor pool. **Services:** winter plug-ins. **Cards:** AE, CB, DI, DS, MC, VI.
🆂🅰🆅🅴 🅢 🈲 🛎 🕎 🆑 🌂 🎿 🖵 📶 🛗

PARADISE INN

Phone: (406)222-6

	5/15-9/30	2P/1B: $77	2P/2B: $87	XP: $5
	3/1-5/14 & 10/1-2/29	2P/1B: $43	2P/2B: $53	XP: $5

◆◆ **Location:** US 89, n of jct I-90 & US 191. Park Rd & Rogers Ln 59047 (PO Box 14
Motor Inn   Fax: 406/222-2481. **Terms:** Reserv deposit; pets, $5 extra charge. **Facility:** 43 rooms. Very clean, comfort
rooms. Suites, extra charge; 1 whirlpool rm, extra charge; 1 story; interior/exterior corridors; heated indoor p
Dining: Restaurant; 6 am-11 pm, in summer; to 10 pm, in winter; $5-$15; cocktails. **Services:** winter plug
All Rooms: extended cable TV. **Cards:** AE, MC, VI. 🛏 🛎 🕎 🍸 🎿

SUPER 8 MOTEL

	Rates Subject to Change			Phone: 406/222-7
◆◆ 6/1-9/30	1P: $52	2P/1B: $56	2P/2B: $60	XP: $4
Motel 5/1-5/31 & 10/1-10/31	1P: $46	2P/1B: $50	2P/2B: $54	XP: $4
3/1-4/30 & 11/1-2/29	1P: $40	2P/1B: $44	2P/2B: $48	XP: $4

Location: I-90 exit 333, just s on US 89. 105 Centennial Dr 59047 (PO Box 1385). Fax: 406/222-7711. **Facility:** 36 roo
New property. Convenient location. 2 stories; interior corridors; designated smoking area. **Cards:** AE, DI, DS, MC, VI.
🕎 🌂 🎿

RESTAURANT

UNCLE LOOIE'S
Lunch: $7-$9   **Dinner:** $9-$20   **Phone:** 406/222-7

◆◆ **Location:** Downtown; opposite train station. 119 W Park Rd. **Hours:** 11:30 am-2 & 5:30-9:30 pm, Sat &
Italian   5:30pm-9:30 pm. Closed: 11/25 & 12/25. **Reservations:** suggested. **Features:** casual dress; carry
cocktails & lounge; street parking. Italian & continental cuisine served in a Mediterranean atmosph
Smoke free premises. **Cards:** AE, DI, DS, MC, VI.

MALTA—2,300

LODGINGS

EDGEWATER INN

	Rates Subject to Change			Phone: 406/654-1
◆ All Year	1P: $40- 46	2P/1B: $50	2P/2B: $46- 51	XP: $5

Motel   **Location:** Between jct SR 242N & US 191S. 101 Hwy 2W 59538 (PO Box 1630). Fax: 406/654-7
Terms: Reserv deposit. **Facility:** 32 rooms. Small, cozy rooms. 1 story; exterior corridors; designated smo
area; heated indoor pool. **Services:** winter plug-ins. **All Rooms:** combo or shower baths. **Cards:** AE, CB, DI, DS, MC, V
🌂 🕎 🎿 🖵 📶

MALTANA MOTEL

	Guaranteed Rates			Phone: 406/654-2
ⒶⒶⒶ All Year	1P: $35- 38	2P/1B: $40- 43	2P/2B: $44- 47	XP: $3

◆◆ **Location:** Just s of US 2, via US 191, then just w. 138 S 1st Ave W 59538 (PO Box 1807). **Facility:** 19 roo
Motel   Very clean, cozy rooms. 1 story; exterior corridors. **Services:** winter plug-ins. **Cards:** AE, CB, DI, DS,
VI. 🔜 🖵 📶

MARYSVILLE

RESTAURANT

THE MARYSVILLE HOUSE

◆   **Dinner:** $11-$31
Location: SR 279, s at sign, 6 mi on gravel road, just n. **Hours:** Wed-Sat 5 pm-9 pm, in winter; Tues-S
Steak and   pm-10 pm, in summer. Closed major holidays , Sun & Mon. **Features:** No A/C; casual dress; cocktai
Seafood   lounge; street parking. A step back in time. Very rustic, unique dining in old ghost town. Enjoy T-Bone st
shrimp, oysters, grilled chicken, crab legs, & lobster.

MILES CITY—8,500

LODGINGS

BEST WESTERN WAR BONNET INN

Phone: (406)232-4

	3/1-4/30 & 1/1-2/29 [CP]	1P:	$50- 66	2P/1B:	$56- 74	2P/2B:	$56- 74	XP: $6
	5/1-12/31 [CP]	1P:	$49- 65	2P/1B:	$55- 73	2P/2B:	$55- 73	XP: $6

◆◆◆ **Location:** SR 59, 0.3 mi n jct I-94, exit 138 (Broadus). 1015 S Haynes Ave 59301 (PO Box 10
Motel   Fax: 406/232-0363. **Terms:** Pets. **Facility:** 54 rooms. Spacious contemporary styled rooms. 4 two-room u
$90-$95; 2 stories; exterior corridors; designated smoking area; small heated pool, sauna, whirl
Dining: Restaurant nearby. **Services:** winter plug-ins. **All Rooms:** extended cable TV. **Cards:** AE, CB, DI, MC.
Special Amenities: Free breakfast and free local telephone calls. 🅢 🐕 🕎 🌂 🛎 🎿 🍸 🖵 📶 🛄

UDGET HOST CUSTER'S INN

Rates Subject to Change

Phone: 406/232-5170

| | 1P: $35 | 2P/1B: $39 | 2P/2B: $43 | XP: $4 | F12 |

All Year
Location: SR 59, just n jct I-94, exit 138 (Broadus). 1209 S Haynes Ave 59301 (PO Box 1235).
Fax: 406/232-5170. **Terms:** Pets, $20 dep req. **Facility:** 56 rooms. Very clean budget oriented rooms. 2 stories; exterior corridors; heated indoor pool, saunas. **Dining:** Restaurant nearby. **Services:** winter plug-ins.
All Rooms: combo or tub baths. **Cards:** AE, CB, DI, DS, MC, VI. *(See color ad p 206)*

OMFORT INN

Rates Subject to Change

Phone: 406/232-3141

| 5/13-2/29 [BP] | 1P: $54- 60 | 2P/1B: $58- 65 | 2P/2B: $63- 70 | XP: $5 | F18 |
| 3/1-5/12 [BP] | 1P: $45- 50 | 2P/1B: $50- 55 | 2P/2B: $54- 60 | XP: $5 | F18 |

Location: I-94, exit 138; just s. 1615 S Haynes Ave 59301. Fax: 406/232-2924. **Facility:** 49 rooms. Very clean, ntemporary style rooms. 1 suite, $57-$62; 2 stories; interior corridors; designated smoking area; small heated indoor pool.
ervices: winter plug-ins. **Cards:** AE, DI, DS, MC, VI.

AYS INN

Phone: (406)232-3550

| | 1P: $33- 40 | 2P/1B: $38- 48 | 2P/2B: $48- 60 | XP: $5 | F12 |

All Year [CP]
Location: SR 59, 0.3 mi n jct I-94, exit 138 (Broadus). 1006 S Haynes Ave 59301. Fax: 406/232-3550.
Terms: Weekly/monthly rates; pets, $5 extra charge. **Facility:** 57 rooms. Cozy Continental breakfast area.
Convenient drive up parking. Mini fridges & mini microwaves avail, extra charge; 1 story; exterior corridors;
designated smoking area; small heated pool. **Dining:** Restaurant nearby. **Services:** winter plug-ins.
l Rooms: combo or shower baths, extended cable TV. **Cards:** AE, DS, MC, VI. **Special Amenities: Free breakfast and
ee local telephone calls.**

OLIDAY INN EXPRESS MILES CITY

Phone: (406)232-1000

| 5/9-9/11 [CP] | 1P: $69- 75 | 2P/1B: $69- 75 | 2P/2B: $69- 75 |
| 3/1-5/8 & 9/12-2/29 [CP] | 1P: $59- 63 | 2P/1B: $59- 63 | 2P/2B: $59- 63 |

Location: I-94, exit 138; just s. 1720 S Haynes Ave 59301. Fax: 406/232-1365. **Facility:** 52 rooms. New property. Attractive, contemporary rooms & lobby. Some rooms with iron & ironing board. 2 stories; interior corridors; designated smoking area; small heated indoor pool, whirlpool. **Dining:** Restaurant nearby.
ervices: combo or shower baths, extended cable TV. **Some Rooms:** whirlpools. **Cards:** AE,
, DS, JC, MC, VI. **Special Amenities: Free breakfast and free local telephone calls.**
ee color ad opposite title page)

RESTAURANT

B'S RESTAURANT   **Lunch:** $5-$8   **Dinner:** $5-$8   Phone: 406/232-5772
Location: Adjacent to & n of I-94, exit 138; on US 12, Miles City Broadus exit. 1406 S Haynes Ave 59301.
merican   **Hours:** 24 hrs. Closed: 11/25 & 12/25. **Features:** casual dress; children's menu; salad bar; a la carte. Family
restaurant. **Cards:** AE, DI, DS, MC, VI.

MISSOULA—42,900

LODGINGS

EL AIRE MOTEL

Rates Subject to Change

Phone: (406)543-3183

| 5/13-9/15 [CP] | 1P: $40- 50 | 2P/1B: $40- 50 | 2P/2B: $50- 60 | XP: $5 |
| 3/1-5/12 & 9/16-2/29 [CP] | 1P: $30- 40 | 2P/1B: $35- 45 | 2P/2B: $38- 50 | XP: $5 |

Location: I-90, Van Buren exit; just s to Broadway, 0.3 mi w. 300 E Broadway 59802. Fax: 406/543-0391.
Terms: Reserv deposit; weekly rates, in winter; small pets only, $5 extra charge. **Facility:** 52 rooms. Convenient to downtown businesses & shopping. 1 two-bedroom unit. 2 stories; exterior corridors; heated indoor pool,
hirlpool. **Dining:** Restaurant nearby. **Some Rooms:** 4 efficiencies. **Cards:** AE, DS, MC, VI. *(See color ad p 240)*

EST WESTERN EXECUTIVE INN

Phone: (406)543-7221

7/1-8/31	1P: $57	2P/1B: $62	2P/2B: $67	XP: $5	F12
5/16-6/30 & 9/1-9/30	1P: $52	2P/1B: $57	2P/2B: $62	XP: $5	F12
3/1-5/15 & 10/1-2/29	1P: $47	2P/1B: $52	2P/2B: $57	XP: $5	F12

otor Inn   **Location:** I-90, exit 104 (Orange St); 0.5 mi s to Broadway, 0.5 mi e to Washington, just s to Main St, just w.
201 E Main St 59802. Fax: 406/543-7225. **Terms:** Pets, $50 dep req. **Facility:** 51 rooms. Convenient to businesses & shopping. Some covered parking; 2 stories; exterior corridors; heated pool. **Dining:** Coffee shop; 7 am-2 pm.
ervices: winter plug-ins. **All Rooms:** extended cable TV. **Cards:** AE, CB, DI, DS, MC, VI. **Special Amenities: Free local
lephone calls and free newspaper.**

EST WESTERN GRANT CREEK INN

Phone: (406)543-0700

| 6/15-9/15 [CP] | 1P: $89- 119 | 2P/1B: $89- 119 | 2P/2B: $89- 119 | XP: $10 | F16 |
| 3/1-6/14 & 9/16-2/29 [CP] | 1P: $79- 99 | 2P/1B: $79- 99 | 2P/2B: $79- 99 | XP: $10 | F16 |

Location: Just n of I-90, exit 101. 5280 Grant Creek Rd 59808. Fax: 406/543-0777. **Terms:** Small pets only.
Facility: 126 rooms. Unique large rooms. 4 stories; interior corridors; heated indoor pool, sauna, steamroom,
indoor whirlpool. **Services:** giftshop; area transportation, to the mall & university. **Cards:** AE, CB, DI, DS,
, VI. **Special Amenities: Free breakfast and free local telephone calls.**

ROOKS STREET MOTOR INN

Phone: (406)549-5115

| 5/1-9/30 [CP] | 1P: $44- 55 | 2P/1B: $47- 60 | 2P/2B: $50- 70 | XP: $5 | F12 |
| 3/1-4/30 & 10/1-2/29 [CP] | 1P: $35- 45 | 2P/1B: $39- 50 | 2P/2B: $50- 70 | XP: $5 | F12 |

Location: I-90, Reserve St exit; 5 mi s, just e. 3333 Brooks St 59801. Fax: 406/549-5115. **Facility:** 61 rooms.
Very clean rooms. Close to shopping mall & movie theater. 2 stories; interior/exterior corridors.
Dining: Restaurant nearby. **Services:** winter plug-ins. **All Rooms:** extended cable TV.
me Rooms: whirlpools. **Cards:** AE, DS, MC, VI. **Special Amenities: Free local telephone calls.**

AMPUS INN

Rates Subject to Change

Phone: 406/549-5134

| 5/15-9/15 | 1P: $49 | 2P/1B: $50 | 2P/2B: $59 | XP: $3 | F16 |
| 3/1-5/14 & 9/16-2/29 | 1P: $39 | 2P/1B: $40 | 2P/2B: $59 | XP: $3 | F16 |

Location: I-90, exit 105 (Van Buren St); just s to Broadway, just w. 744 E Broadway 59802. **Facility:** 82 rooms.
cated near creek & University Campus. 2 stories; interior/exterior corridors; small heated pool. **Services:** winter plug-ins.
ards: AE, DI, DS, MC, VI.

CITY CENTER MOTEL

Rates Subject to Change   Phone: 406/543-31
6/1-8/31   2P/1B: $38   2P/2B: $40   XP: $3
3/1-5/31 & 9/1-2/29   2P/1B: $32   2P/2B: $36   XP: $3
Location: I-90, exit 105 (Van Buren St); just s to Broadway, just w. 338 E Broadway 59802. **Terms:** Res
deposit. **Facility:** 15 rooms. Near downtown. Array of antiques displayed in lobby. 2 stories; interior/exte
corridors. **Dining:** Restaurant nearby. **All Rooms:** combo or shower baths, extended cable TV. **Cards:**
CB, DI, DS, MC, VI.

Motel

COMFORT INN
All Year [CP]   Rates Subject to Change   Phone: (406)542-08
Motel   1P: $60- 150   2P/1B: $70- 150 2P/2B: $70- 150 XP: $10   F
Location: 0.5 mi s of I-90, exit 101. 4545 N Reserve St 59802. Fax: 406/543-6247. **Facility:** 52 rooms. 2 s
ries; interior corridors; designated smoking area; small heated indoor pool. **Services:** winter plug-i
All Rooms: combo or shower baths. **Cards:** AE, CB, DI, DS, MC, VI.

THE CREEKSIDE INN

7/1-8/31   1P: $52   2P/1B: $57   2P/2B: $62   XP: $5   F
5/16-6/30 & 9/1-9/30   1P: $47   2P/1B: $52   2P/2B: $57   XP: $5   F
3/1-5/15 & 10/1-2/29   1P: $42   2P/1B: $47   2P/2B: $52   XP: $5   F
Motel
Location: I-90, exit 105 (Van Buren St); just s to Broadway, then w. 630 E Broadway 59802. **Terms:** Mont
rates; pets, $25 dep req. **Facility:** 30 rooms. 2 two-bedroom units. 2-3 stories, no elevator; exterior corrido
heated pool. **Dining:** Restaurant nearby. **All Rooms:** extended cable TV. **Cards:** AE, CB, DI, DS, MC,
Special Amenities: Free local telephone calls and free newspaper.

DAYS INN/WESTGATE

5/15-9/30 [CP]   1P: $56   2P/1B: $61   2P/2B: $66   XP: $5   F
3/1-5/14 & 10/1-2/29 [CP]   1P: $43   2P/1B: $47   2P/2B: $51   XP: $5   F
Motel
Location: Just n of I-90, exit 96. 8600 Truck Stop Rd 59808. Fax: 406/721-9781. **Terms:** Reserv depo
pets, $5 extra charge. **Facility:** 69 rooms. Adjacent to truck parking lot for oversized vehicles. 2 stories; in
rior corridors; whirlpool. **Dining:** Restaurant nearby. **Services:** winter plug-ins. **Recreation:** video mo
rentals. **Cards:** AE, CB, DI, DS, JC, MC, VI. **Special Amenities:** Free local telephone calls and free room upgra
(subject to availability with advanced reservations).

DOUBLETREE HOTEL MISSOULA/EDGEWATER

Rates Subject to Change — Phone: (406)728-3100

◆◆ Motor Inn

6/1-9/30	1P: $100- 129	2P/1B: $100- 129	2P/2B: $100- 129	XP: $10	F17
10/1-2/29	1P: $84- 95	2P/1B: $84- 95	2P/2B: $84- 95	XP: $10	F17
3/1-5/31	1P: $79- 89	2P/1B: $79- 89	2P/2B: $79- 89	XP: $10	F17

Location: I-90, exit 105 (Van Buren St); just s, then w on Front St. 100 Madison 59802. Fax: 406/728-2530. **Terms:** Handling fee imposed. **Facility:** 171 rooms. Large, stylish rooms. Some rooms facing Clark Fork River. Iron & ironing board in each room. 1 two-bedroom unit. 3 stories; interior corridors; heated pool. **Services:** giftshop; winter plug-ins. **All Rooms:** combo or shower baths. **Cards:** ASK, DI, DS, MC, VI.

DOWNTOWN MOTEL

Guaranteed Rates — Phone: 406/549-5191

[AAA] Motel

6/1-10/31	1P: $34	2P/1B: $36	2P/2B: $39	XP: $5
4/1-5/31	1P: $32	2P/1B: $34	2P/2B: $37	XP: $3
3/1-3/31 & 11/1-2/29	1P: $28	2P/1B: $30	2P/2B: $32	XP: $3

Location: I-90, just w of exit 105 (Van Buren St). 502 E Broadway 59801. **Terms:** Weekly rates; pets, $6 extra charge. **Facility:** 22 rooms. Comfortable rooms in residential neighborhood. 1 two-bedroom unit. 1 story; exterior corridors. **Services:** winter plug-ins. **All Rooms:** combo or shower baths, extended cable TV. **Cards:** MC, VI.

FAMILY INN

Phone: (406)543-7371

[AAA] [SAVE]
◆ Motel

5/15-9/1   1P: $42- 46   2P/1B: $46- 51   2P/2B: $50- 56   XP: $4-6

Location: Just s of I-90, exit 105; just e. 512 E Broadway 59802. **Terms:** Open 5/15-9/1; reserv deposit. **Facility:** 30 rooms. Small comfortable rooms. Easy freeway access; close to university and river. Kitchens, $5 extra charge; 2 stories; exterior corridors; small heated pool. **Dining:** Restaurant nearby. **All Rooms:** shower baths, extended cable TV. **Cards:** AE, DS, MC, VI. **Special Amenities:** Early check-in/late check-out and free local telephone calls.

B'S INN NORTH

Guaranteed Rates — Phone: (406)542-7550

◆◆ Motel

5/15-9/30	1P: $62	2P/1B: $62	2P/2B: $73
10/1-2/29	1P: $50	2P/1B: $50	2P/2B: $60
3/1-5/14	1P: $46	2P/1B: $46	2P/2B: $58

Location: W on I-90, exit 101; just s. 4953 N Reserve St 59808. Fax: 406/721-5931. **Facility:** 67 rooms. Convenient off-interstate location. Very clean, contemporary rooms. 4 deluxe rms, $59.95-$69.95; 3 stories; interior corridors. **Services:** winter plug-ins. **All Rooms:** combo or shower baths. **Cards:** AE, CB, DI, DS, MC, VI.

B'S INN SOUTH

Phone: (406)251-2665

[AAA] [SAVE]
◆◆◆ Motel

5/15-9/30	1P: $62	2P/1B: $62	2P/2B: $73
10/1-2/29	1P: $50	2P/1B: $50	2P/2B: $60
3/1-5/14	1P: $46	2P/1B: $46	2P/2B: $58

Location: I-90, exit 101; to Reserve St, 5 mi s to Hwy 93, just w. 3803 Brooks St 59804. Fax: 406/251-5733. **Terms:** Reserv deposit, 10 day notice; weekly/monthly rates, 9/30-5/14; pets. **Facility:** 91 rooms. Comfortable rooms, attractive whirlpool room. Deluxe rms, $66.95-$69.95; 3 stories; interior corridors; whirlpool. **Dining:** Restaurant nearby. **Services:** area transportation, community hospital; winter plug-ins. **All Rooms:** combo or shower baths. **Cards:** AE, CB, DI, DS, MC, VI. **Special Amenities:** Free local telephone calls and free newspaper.

GOLDSMITH'S INN

Guaranteed Rates — Phone: (406)721-6732

◆◆◆ Bed & Breakfast

3/1-4/30 & 10/1-2/29 [BP]	1P: $69- 99	2P/1B: $79- 109	2P/2B: $109- 139	XP: $15	F10
5/1-9/30 [BP]	1P: $85- 119	2P/1B: $95- 129		XP: $15	F10

Location: I-90, exit 105; 2 blks s, just w. 809 E Front St 59802. Fax: 406/543-0045. **Terms:** Reserv deposit, 10 day notice. **Facility:** 7 rooms. On Clark Fork River. Restored 1911 former home of university president. 2 stories, no elevator; interior corridors; smoke free premises. **All Rooms:** combo or shower baths. **Some Rooms:** color TV. **Cards:** AE, DS, MC, VI.

HAMPTON INN

Rates Subject to Change — Phone: (406)549-1800

◆◆◆ Motel

6/13-9/18 [CP]	1P: $71- 81	2P/1B: $83- 89	2P/2B: $79- 81	
5/2-6/12 [CP]	1P: $63- 73	2P/1B: $73- 77	2P/2B: $69- 71	
9/19-2/29 [CP]	1P: $59- 65	2P/1B: $65- 69	2P/2B: $63- 65	
3/1-5/1 [CP]	1P: $57- 63	2P/1B: $63- 67	2P/2B: $61- 63	

Location: Just s of I-90, exit 101. 4805 N Reserve St 59802. Fax: 406/549-1737. **Facility:** 60 rooms. Adjacent to Grant Creek; access to adjacent coin laundry & outdoor pool. 4 stories; interior corridors; designated smoking area; small heated indoor pool. **All Rooms:** combo or shower baths. **Cards:** AE, CB, DI, DS, MC, VI.

HOLIDAY INN EXPRESS-RIVERSIDE

Rates Subject to Change — Phone: (406)549-7600

◆◆◆ Motel

5/16-10/15 [CP]	1P: $79	2P/1B: $79	2P/2B: $79
3/1-5/15 & 10/16-2/29 [CP]	1P: $65	2P/1B: $65	2P/2B: $65

Location: I-90, exit 105; just s & e. 1021 E Broadway 59802. Fax: 406/543-2223. **Terms:** Check-in 4 pm. **Facility:** 95 rooms. Adjacent to Clark Fork River; easy freeway access; close to university & downtown. Rooms with river view; phones, hairdryers & some with balcony. 4 whirlpool/deluxe suites, $85-$99; interior corridors; mountain view. **All Rooms:** combo or shower baths. **Cards:** AE, CB, DI, DS, MC, VI. (See color ad opposite title page)

HOLIDAY INN MISSOULA-PARKSIDE

Phone: (406)721-8550

[AAA] [SAVE]
◆◆◆ Motel

6/1-10/31	1P: $89	2P/1B: $89	2P/2B: $89
3/1-5/31 & 11/1-2/29	1P: $79	2P/1B: $79	2P/2B: $79

Location: I-90, Orange St exit; 0.5 mi s to Broadway, just e to Pattee St, just s. 200 S Pattee St 59802. Fax: 406/721-7427. **Terms:** Check-in 4 pm; pets. **Facility:** 200 rooms. Spacious rooms. 3 stories; interior corridors; heated indoor pool, sauna, whirlpool. **Dining:** Dining room, coffee shop; 6:30 am-2 & 5:30-10 pm; $11-$25. **Services:** giftshop. **Cards:** AE, CB, DI, DS, JC, MC, VI. (See color ad p 242 & opposite title page)

HUBBARD'S PONDEROSA LODGE

Phone: (406)543-310

| | 5/1-10/1 | 1P: $47 | 2P/1B: $55 | 2P/2B: $60 | XP: $4 |
| | 3/1-4/30 & 10/2-2/29 | 1P: $40 | 2P/1B: $49 | 2P/2B: $54 | XP: $4 |

Location: I-90, exit 105 (Van Buren St); just s to Broadway, then w. 800 E Broadway 59802. **Terms:** Pet with permission. **Facility:** 40 rooms. Budget oriented rooms. Close to university. 2 stories; interior/exterior co ridors. **Dining:** Restaurant nearby. **Services:** winter plug-ins. **All Rooms:** extended cable TV. **Cards:** A DS, MC, VI. **Special Amenities:** Free local telephone calls and preferred room (subject to availability with advance reservations). IMA. *(See color ad p 320)*

ORANGE STREET BUDGET MOTOR INN

Rates Subject to Change   Phone: (406)721-361

| | All Year [CP] | 1P: $43 | 2P/1B: $47 | 2P/2B: $49 | |

Location: Just s of I-90, exit 104. 801 N Orange St 59802. Fax: 406/721-8875. **Terms:** Pets, $5 ext charge, in 4 rooms. **Facility:** 81 rooms. 6 rms with waterbed; 3 stories; interior corridors. **Services:** wint plug-ins. **All Rooms:** extended cable TV. **Cards:** AE, CB, DI, DS, MC, VI.

RED LION INN

Phone: (406)728-330

	6/16-8/31 [CP]	1P: $84- 89	2P/1B: $84- 89	2P/2B: $84- 89	XP: $5	F1
	4/1-6/15 & 9/1-10/31 [CP]	1P: $79- 84	2P/1B: $79- 84	2P/2B: $79- 84	XP: $5	F1
	3/1-3/31 & 11/1-2/29 [CP]	1P: $69- 74	2P/1B: $69- 74	2P/2B: $69- 74	XP: $5	F1

Location: I-90, Orange St exit; just w. 700 W Broadway 59802. Fax: 406/728-4441. **Terms:** Pets, $5 ext charge. **Facility:** 76 rooms. Contemporary styled rooms. 2 stories; exterior corridors; heated pool, whirlpoo **Dining:** Restaurant nearby. **Services:** winter plug-ins. **All Rooms:** combo or shower baths, extended cable TV. **Cards:** A CB, DI, DS, MC, VI. **Special Amenities:** Early check-in/late check-out and preferred room (subject to availability wi advanced reservations). *(See color ad below)*

REDWOOD LODGE

Phone: (406)721-211

| | 5/1-9/14 | 1P: $49 | 2P/1B: $49 | 2P/2B: $54 | XP: $4 |
| | 3/1-4/30 & 9/15-2/29 | 1P: $40- 45 | 2P/1B: $45- 59 | 2P/2B: $49- 54 | XP: $4 |

Location: Just s of I-90, exit 96. 8060 Hwy 93 59808. Fax: 406/721-2110. **Terms:** Pets. **Facility:** 40 room Adjacent truck parking lot for oversized vehicles. 3 waterbeds avail; 2 stories; exterior corridors; designate smoking area; whirlpool. **Dining:** Restaurant nearby. **All Rooms:** combo or shower baths. **Cards:** AE, CI DI, DS, JC, MC, VI. **Special Amenities:** Free breakfast and free local telephone calls.

DIAMONDS tell the story—read The ⟨AAA⟩ Diamonds.

RODEWAY INN SOUTHGATE
Phone: (406)251-2250

5/1-9/15 [CP]	1P:	$55- 75	2P/1B:	$59- 79	2P/2B:	$69- 89	
3/1-4/30 & 9/16-2/29 [CP]	1P:	$42- 59	2P/1B:	$49- 69	2P/2B:	$42- 79	

Location: I-90, exit 101 (Reserve St); 5 mi s to Brooks St, just e. 3530 Brooks St 59801. Fax: 406/251-2006. **Terms:** Weekly rates, in winter; package plans. **Facility:** 81 rooms. Comfortable rooms, convenient to shopping mall & movie theaters. 2 stories; exterior corridors; designated smoking area; heated pool, sauna, whirlpool. **Dining:** Restaurant nearby. **Services:** winter plug-ins. **All Rooms:** combo or shower baths. **Some Rooms:** whirlpools. **Cards:** AE, DI, DS, MC, VI. **Special Amenities: Free breakfast and free local telephone calls.**

ROYAL MOTEL
Rates Subject to Change **Phone:** 406/542-2184

6/15-9/7	1P:	$38- 46	2P/1B:	$42	2P/2B:	$46	XP: $3
5/1-6/14 & 9/8-10/15	1P:	$29- 38	2P/1B:	$34	2P/2B:	$38	XP: $3
3/1-4/30 & 10/16-2/29	1P:	$25- 32	2P/1B:	$29	2P/2B:	$32	XP: $3

Location: I-90, exit 105; just s on Van Buren, 0.5 mi w on Broadway. 338 Washington St 59802. **Terms:** Reserv deposit; weekly rates, winter; pets, $3 extra charge. **Facility:** 12 rooms. Clean, comfortable rooms close to downtown with 2 free movie channels. 4 two-bedroom units. 1 story; exterior corridors; designated smoking area. **Services:** winter plug-ins. **All Rooms:** extended cable TV. **Cards:** AE, CB, DI, DS, MC, VI. *(See color ad below)*

RUBY'S INN & CONVENTION CENTER
Phone: (406)721-0990

5/1-9/30 [AP]	1P:	$66- 76	2P/1B:	$66- 76	2P/2B:	$76- 86	XP: $4 F17
3/1-4/30 & 10/1-2/29 [AP]	1P:	$56- 66	2P/1B:	$56- 66	2P/2B:	$66- 76	XP: $4 F17

Location: Just s of I-90, exit 101. 4825 N Reserve St 59808. Fax: 406/721-0990. **Terms:** Pets. **Facility:** 127 rooms. Adjacent to Grant Creek, many creekside units. Picnic area next to creek with barbecue grills. 2 stories; interior/exterior corridors; designated smoking area; heated pool, sauna, creekside hot tub, access to indoor pool, whirlpool. **Dining:** Restaurant; 6 am-2 pm; closed Sat & Sun. **Services:** winter plug-ins. **Recreation:** horseshoe pit, access to exercise room. **All Rooms:** combo or shower baths. **Some Rooms:** kitchen, whirlpools. **Cards:** AE, CB, DI, DS, MC, VI. **Special Amenities: Free breakfast and free local telephone calls.** *(See color ad below)*

SLEEP INN
Rates Subject to Change **Phone:** (406)543-5883

5/1-9/1 [CP]	1P:	$51- 81			2P/2B:	$56- 91	XP: $5 F18
9/2-10/31 [CP]	1P:	$46- 59			2P/2B:	$51- 61	XP: $5 F18
11/1-1/1 [CP]	1P:	$43- 56			2P/2B:	$50- 60	XP: $5 F18
3/1-4/30 & 1/2-2/29 [CP]	1P:	$45- 58			2P/2B:	$50- 60	XP: $5 F18

Location: I-90, exit 101; 5 mi on Reserve St, just e on Brooks St. 3425 Dore Ln 59801. Fax: 406/543-5883. **Facility:** 59 rooms. Close to shopping & movie theatres; complimentary newspaper. 3 stories; interior corridors; designated smoking area; small heated indoor pool. **Services:** winter plug-ins. **All Rooms:** combo or shower baths. **Cards:** AE, CB, DI, DS, JC, MC, VI.

SUPER 8-BROOK ST
◆◆ Motel

Rates Subject to Change

5/1-9/30	1P: $46- 48	2P/1B: $51- 53	2P/2B: $56- 58	XP: $3	F1
3/1-4/30 & 10/1-2/29	1P: $40	2P/1B: $44	2P/2B: $48	XP: $3	F1

Phone: 406/251-2255

Location: 5 mi s of I-90, exit 101; just w. 3901 Brooks St 59801. Fax: 406/251-2989. **Facility:** 103 rooms. Close to mall & golf course. 3 stories, no elevator; interior corridors; designated smoking area. **Services:** winter plug-ins. **Cards:** AE, CB, DI, DS, MC, VI.

SUPER 8 MOTEL-RESERVE ST
◆◆ Motel

Rates Subject to Change

5/1-9/30	1P: $54	2P/1B: $58	2P/2B: $62	XP: $3	F12
3/1-4/30 & 10/1-2/29	1P: $45		2P/2B: $48	XP: $3	F12

Phone: 406/549-1199

Location: 0.4 mi s of I-90, exit 101. 4703 N Reserve St 59802. Fax: 406/549-0677. **Terms:** Weekend rates avail. **Facility:** 58 rooms. Oversize parking area avail. 3 stories; interior corridors; designated smoking area. **Services:** winter plug-ins. **All Rooms:** combo or shower baths. **Cards:** AE, CB, DI, DS, MC, VI.

THUNDERBIRD MOTEL
AAA SAVE
◆◆ Motel

5/12-9/15	1P: $60	2P/1B: $60	2P/2B: $65	XP: $5	
3/1-5/11 & 9/16-2/29	1P: $50	2P/1B: $50	2P/2B: $55	XP: $5	

Phone: (406)543-7251

Location: I-90, exit 105 (Van Buren St); just s to Broadway, then e. 1009 E Broadway 59802. Fax: 406/543-7251. **Terms:** Reserv deposit. **Facility:** 27 rooms. 4 two-bedroom units. 1 whirlpool rm, $80; 2 stories; exterior corridors; heated indoor pool, sauna, whirlpool. **Services:** winter plug-ins. **Some Rooms:** whirlpools. **Cards:** AE, DS, MC, VI. **Special Amenities:** Early check-in/late check-out and free local telephone calls. (See color ad below)

TRAVELERS INN MOTEL
AAA SAVE
◆ Motel

6/1-8/31	1P: $50	2P/1B: $50	2P/2B: $59	XP: $5	F12
4/16-5/31 & 9/1-10/31	1P: $43	2P/1B: $46	2P/2B: $52	XP: $3	F12
3/1-4/15 & 11/1-2/29	1P: $35	2P/1B: $41	2P/2B: $45	XP: $3	F12

Phone: (406)728-8330

Location: W on I-90, exit 101 (Reserve St); just s. 4850 N Reserve St 59802 (5453 Prospect Dr). Fax: 406/728-4435. **Terms:** Weekly rates, 10/15-4/15; small pets only. **Facility:** 29 rooms. Small, very clean rooms. Convenient off-interstate location. 1 story; exterior corridors. **Dining:** Restaurant nearby. **Services:** winter plug-ins. **All Rooms:** combo or shower baths. **Cards:** AE, CB, DI, DS, MC, VI. **Special Amenities:** Free local telephone calls.

TRAVELODGE
◆◆ Motel

Guaranteed Rates

6/6-9/18	1P: $52- 60	2P/1B: $56- 60	2P/2B: $62- 64	XP: $2	F17
6/1-6/5 & 9/19-2/29	1P: $47- 55	2P/1B: $51- 55	2P/2B: $57- 59		

Location: I-90, exit 104; 0.5 mi s on Orange St, just w on Broadway. 420 W Broadway 59802. Fax: 406/543-8118. **Facility:** 60 rooms. Pleasant accommodations close to downtown businesses, shopping & hospital with some covered parking. 1 two-bedroom unit. Microwave & mini fridges avail, extra charge; 3 stories; interior/exterior corridors; designated smoking area. **Services:** winter plug-ins. **All Rooms:** combo or shower baths. **Cards:** AE, CB, DI, DS, MC, VI.

UPTOWN MOTEL
AAA SAVE
◆ Motel

6/15-9/15	1P: $38- 46	2P/1B: $42	2P/2B: $46	XP: $4	F12
5/1-6/14 & 9/16-10/15	1P: $32	2P/1B: $36	2P/2B: $38	XP: $4	F12
3/1-4/30 & 10/16-2/29	1P: $25	2P/1B: $32	2P/2B: $36	XP: $4	F12

Phone: 406/549-5141

Location: I-90 exit 104 (Orange St) to Pine, west to Woody St s. 329 Woody St 59802. Fax: 406/728-3796. **Terms:** Small pets only, dogs. **Facility:** 12 rooms. Small comfortable rooms, close to downtown shopping easy Interstate access. 5 two-bedroom units. 1 story; exterior corridors; designated smoking area. **Dining:** Restaurant nearby. **All Rooms:** combo or shower baths, extended cable TV. **Some Rooms:** efficiency. **Cards:** AE, DS, MC, VI.

VAL-U-INN
◆◆ Motel

Guaranteed Rates

6/1-9/1 [CP]	1P: $50- 60	2P/1B: $56- 60	2P/2B: $68- 75	XP: $6	F
3/1-5/31 & 9/2-2/29 [CP]	1P: $42- 50	2P/1B: $50- 56	2P/2B: $60- 70		

Phone: (406)721-9600

Location: I-90, exit 101 (Reserve St); 5 mi s to Hwy 93, 0.7 mi s. 3001 Brooks St 59801. Fax: 406/721-7208. **Facility:** 84 rooms. Pleasant & clean rooms close to shopping mall. 3 stories; interior corridors; designated smoking area. **Services:** winter plug-ins. **Cards:** AE, CB, DI, MC, VI. (See color ad p 240)

RESTAURANTS

THE DEPOT Historical
◆◆
American
Dinner: $11-$20   **Phone:** 406/728-7007
Location: I-90, exit 104; just s on Orange St, e on Spruce, n on Ryman. 201 W Railroad St 59802.
Hours: 5:30 pm-10:30 pm. Closed: 11/25, 12/25 & Super Bowl Sun. **Reservations:** accepted.
Features: casual dress; children's menu; salad bar; cocktails & lounge; a la carte. Historic railroad hotel offers casual dining in pub or dining room featuring fresh seafood, hardcut steak, choice prime rib; seasonal patio.
Cards: AE, DI, DS, MC, VI.   (f) [X]

MCKAY'S ON THE RIVER   **Lunch:** $5-$9   **Dinner:** $8-$18   **Phone:** 406/728-0098
(AAA)
◆◆
American
Location: I-90, exit 105; just s to Broadway, then e. 1111 E Broadway 59802. **Hours:** 11 am-10 pm. Closed major holidays. **Reservations:** suggested; dinner & wknds. **Features:** casual dress; Sunday brunch; children's menu; senior's menu; health conscious menu; carryout; salad bar; cocktails & lounge; a la carte. Casual dining amidst early 1900's memorabilia with spacious view of Clark Fork River; patio dining. Fine selection of seafood, steak & pasta entrees. **Cards:** AE, DS, MC, VI.   [X]

MING'S RESTAURANT   **Lunch:** $4-$5   **Dinner:** $5-$16   **Phone:** 406/728-9000
(AAA)
◆
Chinese
Location: 1.8 mi s of Broadway via Orange St & Stephens to Brooks St, just e on Central, corner of Regent. 1049 W Central 59801. **Hours:** 11:30 am-9:30 pm. Closed major holidays & Mon. **Features:** casual dress; children's menu; carryout; beer & wine only; a la carte. Traditional Chinese cuisine. Also serving American dishes. **Cards:** MC, VI.

MURALT'S PLAZA CAFE   **Lunch:** $4-$17   **Dinner:** $5-$17   **Phone:** 406/728-8182
◆
American
Location: Just n of I-90, exit 96. 8800 Truck Stop Rd 59802. **Hours:** 24 hrs. **Features:** casual dress; children's menu; a la carte. Truck stop cafe with family dining & 24 hr breakfast. **Cards:** AE, DI, DS, MC, VI.   [&] [X]

THE MUSTARD SEED   **Lunch:** $5-$9   **Dinner:** $7-$14   **Phone:** 406/728-7825
(AAA)
◆◆
Ethnic
Location: Just w on I-90, Orange St exit; 0.7 mi s to Front, just w. 419 W Front 59802. **Hours:** 11 am-2:30 & 5-9:30 pm, Fri-10 pm, Sat noon-10 pm, Sun noon-9:30 pm; 11:30 am-2:30 & 5-9 pm, Fri-10 pm, Sat noon-10 pm, Sun noon-9 pm, in winter. Closed major holidays. **Features:** casual dress; health conscious menu; carryout; beer & wine only; a la carte. Contemporary Asian cuisine with original recipes. Smoke free premises. **Cards:** AE, DI, DS, MC, VI.   [X]

PRIME TIME ON BROADWAY   **Lunch:** $4-$6   **Dinner:** $9-$18   **Phone:** 406/543-6192
◆
Steak and
Seafood
Location: 1 mi w on US 10 & 93; I-90, Orange St; 0.5 mi s to Broadway, then 0.7 mi w. 1210 W Broadway 59802. **Hours:** 7 am-10 pm. Closed: 11/25 & 12/25. **Features:** casual dress; carryout; cocktails & lounge. Pleasant, informal atmosphere. Nice selection of premium wine by glass, steak, chicken & seafood. **Cards:** AE, DI, DS, MC, VI.

THE SHACK RESTAURANT   **Lunch:** $5-$9   **Dinner:** $7-$16   **Phone:** 406/549-9903
(AAA)
◆◆
American
Location: Downtown. 222 W Main St 59801. **Hours:** 7 am-3 pm; Wed & Thurs also 5:30 pm-9 pm; Fri & Sat also 5:30 pm-9:30 pm; Sun 7 am-8 pm. Closed: 7/4, 11/25 & 12/25. **Features:** casual dress; children's menu; health conscious menu; carryout; beer & wine only; street parking. Innovative freshly prepared foods; exceptional breakfast items; summer patio seating. Smoke free premises. **Cards:** MC, VI.   [X]

OVANDO—100

LODGING

LAKE UPSATA GUEST RANCH
(AAA)
◆◆◆
Ranch

Rates Subject to Change   **Phone:** (406)793-5890

	1P	2P/1B	2P/2B	XP	
6/1-9/30 [AP]	$220	$440	$440	$220	F4
5/1-5/31 & 10/1-10/31 [AP]	$100	$200	$200		

Location: 7.5 mi w on SR 200 to MM 38, 3.4 mi n on Woodworth Rd, 1 mi e. 135 Lake Upsata Rd 59854 (PO Box 6). Fax: 406/793-5894. **Terms:** Open 5/1-10/31; reserv deposit, 90 day notice; handling fee imposed; 3 night min stay; pets. **Facility:** 8 rooms. Guest ranch with charming cabins located on Lake Upsata near picturesque Bob Marshall wilderness; barbecues; campfires; entertainment. Childrn, $190, 6/1-9/30. 5/1-5/30 & 10/1-10/31 limited services; 1 story; exterior corridors; designated smoking area; golf course nearby; beach, whirlpool; boat dock. **Services:** complimentary evening beverages. Fee: massage. **Recreation:** swimming, boating, canoeing, fishing, paddleboats, fly fishing lessons, inner tubing, kayaking; bicycles, hiking trails, horseback riding, horseshoes, volleyball, ghost town tour. **All Rooms:** shower baths. **Some Rooms:** efficiency.   (pet) (spray) (-K-) (f) [X] (cw) [▭] (Z) (X) [B] [X]

POLSON—3,300

LODGINGS

BEST WESTERN KWATAQNUK RESORT
(AAA) [SAVE]
◆◆◆
Motor Inn

        Phone: (406)883-3636

	1P		2P/1B		2P/2B		XP	
6/16-9/15	$88-	114	$98-	124	$98-	124	$10	F12
4/16-6/15 & 9/16-10/31	$64-	81	$74-	91	$74-	91	$10	F12
3/1-4/15 & 11/1-2/29	$54-	73	$64-	83	$64-	83	$10	F12

Location: Just s of downtown on US 93. 303 US Hwy 93E 59860. Fax: 406/883-5392. **Terms:** Reserv deposit, 3 day notice, 6/16-9/15; handling fee imposed. **Facility:** 112 rooms. On south shore of Flathead Lake with views of Mission Mountains. Casino & art gallery. 1 whirlpool suite, $179; 2-3 stories; interior corridors; whirlpool; boat dock, boat ramp. Fee: marina. **Dining:** Dining room; 6 am-2 & 5-10 pm; 8 am-2 & 5-9 pm, in winter; $6-$18; cocktails; Sun brunch 10 am-3 pm. **Services:** winter plug-ins. **Recreation:** waterskiing. Fee: jet skis & lake cruises. Rental: boats, canoes. **All Rooms:** extended cable TV. **Cards:** AE, CB, DI, DS, MC, VI. *(See ad p 246)*   (S) (spray) (≈) (TT) (Y) (X) (pet) (VCR) (▭) (B) (f) (X)

DAYS INN
◆◆
Motel

	Rates Subject to Change				Phone: 406/883-3120
6/1-9/30 [CP]	1P: $65	2P/1B: $70	2P/2B: $70	XP: $5	F17
3/1-5/31 & 10/1-2/29 [CP]	1P: $37	2P/1B: $39	2P/2B: $39	XP: $5	F17

Location: S of downtown on US 93. 914 Hwy 93 59860. Fax: 406/883-2325. **Facility:** 25 rooms. Many rooms overlooking scenic Flathead Lake & mountains. 2 stories; exterior corridors. **Services:** winter plug-ins. **Cards:** AE, DI, DS, MC, VI.

PORT POLSON INN
ⒶⒶⒶ
◆◆◆
Motel

	Rates Subject to Change				Phone: (406)883-5385
6/1-9/15 [CP]	1P: $69	2P/1B: $79	2P/2B: $84	XP: $5	F12
3/16-5/31 & 9/16-10/31 [CP]	1P: $49	2P/1B: $54	2P/2B: $59	XP: $5	F12
3/1-3/15 & 11/1-2/29 [CP]	1P: $40	2P/1B: $48	2P/2B: $53	XP: $5	F12

Location: Just s of downtown on US 93. 502 Hwy 93 59860 (PO Box 1411). Fax: 406/883-3998. **Facility:** 43 rooms. Overlooks Flathead Lake with some themed rooms. 2 stories; interior/exterior corridors; designated smoking area; mountain view; sauna, whirlpools. **Services:** extended cable TV. **Some Rooms:** 5 efficiencies, 2 kitchens. **Cards:** AE, DI, DS, MC, VI. IMA. *(See color ad p 320 & below)*

RED LODGE—2,000—See also YELLOWSTONE NATIONAL PARK.

LODGINGS

BEST WESTERN LU PINE INN
◆◆
Motel

	Rates Subject to Change			Phone: (406)446-1321
6/20-8/28 [CP]	1P: $75- 85	2P/1B: $75- 85	2P/2B: $79- 89	
3/1-4/9, 5/28-6/19 & 8/29-9/25 [CP]	1P: $59- 69	2P/1B: $59- 69	2P/2B: $69- 79	
4/10-5/27 & 9/26-2/29 [CP]	1P: $49- 59	2P/1B: $49- 59	2P/2B: $59- 69	

Location: 0.4 mi s, just w of US 212. 702 S Hauser 59068 (PO Box 30). Fax: 406/446-1465. **Facility:** 46 rooms. Close to winter skiing. 1 two-bedroom unit. 6 efficiencies, $4 extra charge; 2 stories; interior corridors; designated smoking area; small heated indoor pool. **Services:** winter plug-ins. **All Rooms:** combo or shower baths. **Some Rooms:** 6 efficiencies. **Cards:** AE, CB, DI, DS, MC, VI.

COMFORT INN OF RED LODGE
◆◆◆
Motel

	Rates Subject to Change			Phone: (406)446-4469
6/1-9/15 [CP]	1P: $79- 89	2P/1B: $79- 109	2P/2B: $79- 109	XP: $10-20	F18
3/1-4/15 & 12/1-2/29 [CP]	1P: $59- 69	2P/1B: $59- 89	2P/2B: $59- 89	XP: $10-20	F18
4/16-5/31 & 9/16-11/30 [CP]	1P: $49- 69	2P/1B: $49- 79	2P/2B: $49- 79	XP: $5-10	F18

Location: Jct US 1212 & SR 78, n entrance. 612 N Broadway 59068 (PO Box 1970). Fax: 406/446-4469. **Facility:** 55 rooms. New property. Attractive lobby. Small, contemporary rooms. 2 stories; interior corridors; designated smoking area; small heated indoor pool. **Services:** winter plug-ins. **All Rooms:** combo or shower baths. **Cards:** AE, CB, DI, DS, JC, MC, VI.

THE POLLARD
◆◆◆ All Year [BP]
Historic Hotel
Rates Subject to Change
1P: $75- 235 2P/1B: $75- 235 2P/2B: $105- 235
Phone: (406)446-0001
Location: Downtown; US 212 (N Broadway). 2 N Broadway 59068 (PO Box 650). Fax: 406/446-0002.
Terms: Check-in 4 pm; reserv deposit, 7 day notice. **Facility:** 38 rooms. Sophisticated decor in historic hotel.
Originally built in 1893; history room. 4 stories; interior/exterior corridors; smoke free premises; racquetball courts.
Services: winter plug-ins. **All Rooms:** combo or shower baths. **Cards:** AE, DS, MC, VI. *(See color ad below)*

ROCK CREEK RESORT
◆◆◆ All Year
Resort
Complex
Rates Subject to Change
1P: $88- 125 2P/1B: $88- 125 2P/2B: $88 XP: $20 F10
Phone: 406/446-1111
Location: 5.8 mi s on US 212. Rt 2, US 212 59068 (HC 49, Box 3500). Fax: 406/446-3688.
Terms: Handling fee imposed. **Facility:** 87 rooms. Rustic smartly appointed rooms; Rocky Creek borders this
wilderness area. All rooms with voice mail. 2 three-bedroom units. 2 townhouses, $250; efficiencies & kitchens,
extra charge; cottage; 3-5 stories; interior/exterior corridors; heated indoor pool; 4 tennis courts. **Services:** giftshop.
Recreation: fishing; cross country skiing. Rental: bicycles. **All Rooms:** combo or shower baths. **Some Rooms:** 21
efficiencies, 19 kitchens. **Cards:** AE, DI, DS, MC, VI. *(See color ad p 248)*

SUPER 8 OF RED LODGE
Phone: (406)446-2288
AAA SAVE
◆◆ Motel

3/1-4/15, 6/11-8/31 & 12/15-1/3 [CP]	1P: $69- 99	2P/1B: $69- 99	2P/2B: $69- 99	XP: $5	F12
5/22-6/10, 9/1-9/30 & 1/4-2/29 [CP]	1P: $59- 89	2P/1B: $59- 89	2P/2B: $59- 89	XP: $5	F12
4/16-5/21 & 10/1-12/14 [CP]	1P: $49- 69	2P/1B: $49- 69	2P/2B: $49- 69	XP: $5	F12

Location: Just s on US 212. 1223 S Broadway Ave 59068. Fax: 406/446-3162. **Terms:** Pets. **Facility:** 50 rooms. Close to
winter skiing. Ski wax room for guest use. 6 one-rm suites with whirlpool, $79-$129; 2 stories; interior/exterior corridors; designated smoking area; heated indoor pool, whirlpools. **Services:** winter plug-ins. **All Rooms:** extended cable TV.
Some Rooms: 2 kitchens. **Cards:** AE, CB, DI, DS, MC, VI. **Special Amenities:** Free breakfast and free local telephone
calls.

YODELER MOTEL
Phone: (406)446-1435
AAA SAVE
◆◆ Motel

6/11-9/1 & 12/24-12/31 3/1-4/11, 9/2-9/25 &	1P: $45	2P/1B: $45	2P/2B: $58- 66
2/11-2/29 11/26-12/23 & 1/1-2/10	1P: $39	2P/1B: $39	2P/2B: $49- 59
4/12-6/10 & 9/26-11/25	1P: $37	2P/1B: $37	2P/2B: $44- 54
	1P: $35	2P/1B: $35	2P/2B: $41- 48

Location: Just s on US 212. 601 S Broadway 59068 (PO Box 1336). Fax: 406/446-1020. **Terms:** Pets. **Facility:** 22 rooms.
Quaint Scandanavian lobby. Very clean rooms. 5 two-bedroom units. 1 two-bedroom kitchen unit, $79. 18 rms with steam bath.
2 whirlpool rms, $75; 2 stories; exterior corridors; whirlpool. **Services:** winter plug-ins. **Recreation:** ski wax room.
All Rooms: extended cable TV. **Cards:** AE, CB, DI, DS, MC, VI. **Special Amenities:** Free local telephone calls.
(See color ad below)

RESTAURANTS

BOGART'S
◆
American

Lunch: $6-$17　　　　　　　　**Dinner:** $6-$17　　　　　　　　**Phone:** 406/446-1784
Location: City center. 11 S Broadway Ave 59068. **Hours:** 11:30 am-9 pm, in winter; 11:30 am to 10 pm, in summer. Closed: 11/25 & 12/25. **Features:** No A/C; casual dress; children's menu; carryout; cocktails; street parking; a la carte. Local favorite serving specialty pizza, Mexican dishes, standard American cuisine amidst Humphrey Bogart memorabilia & a variety of antiques. Large portions. **Cards:** MC, VI.

GREENLEE'S AT THE POLLARD
◆◆◆
American

Lunch: $5-$9　　　　　　　　**Dinner:** $17-$21　　　　　　　　**Phone:** 406/446-0001
Location: Downtown; US 212 (N Broadway); in The Pollard. 2 N Broadway 59068. **Hours:** 7 am-2 & 5:30-9:30 pm. **Reservations:** suggested; dinner. **Features:** casual dress; health conscious menu; cocktails; street parking; a la carte. Traditional casual dining in intimate atmosphere. Specializing in beef, seafood, fowl & lamb. Smoke free premises. **Cards:** AE, DS, MC, VI.

NATALI ITALIAN PASTA & STEAKHOUSE
◆◆
Italian

Dinner: $5-$25　　　　　　　　**Phone:** 406/446-3333
Location: City center. 119 S Broadway 59068. **Hours:** 4 pm-10 pm, in summer; 5 pm-9 pm, in winter. **Features:** casual dress; carryout; cocktails; street parking. Traditional Italian menu, steak & seafood dishes. Nightly specials. Smoke free premises. **Cards:** MC, VI.

OLD PINEY DELL
◆◆
American

Dinner: $17-$22　　　　　　　　**Phone:** 406/446-1196
Location: 5.8 mi s on US 212; in Rock Creek Resort. Rt 2, US 212 59068. **Hours:** 5:30 pm-9 pm, Fri & Sat-10 pm, 6/1-9/30; hrs may vary in winter. **Reservations:** suggested. **Features:** No A/C; casual dress; Sunday brunch; children's menu; cocktails & lounge. Steak, seafood, chicken, pork & pasta served in rustic 1920 log cabin adjacent to creek. Smoke free premises. **Cards:** AE, DI, DS, MC, VI. *(See color ad below)*

RONAN—1,500

LODGING

STARLITE MOTEL
◆
Motel

Rates Subject to Change　　　　　　　　**Phone:** 406/676-7000
6/15-9/15　　　1P:　$42　　2P/1B:　$49　　2P/2B:　$52　　XP:　$5　　F12
3/1-6/14 & 9/16-2/29　1P:　$37　　2P/1B:　$44　　2P/2B:　$47　　XP:　$5　　F12
Location: Just w of intersection of US 93 & Main. 18 Main St SW 59864. **Terms:** Reserv deposit.
Facility: 15 rooms. Easy hwy access; park at some rooms. 2 stories; exterior corridors. **Services:** winter plug-ins.
Cards: AE, DI, DS, MC, VI.

ROSCOE—100

RESTAURANT

GRIZZLY BAR
AAA
◆
American

Lunch: $4-$22　　　　　　　　**Dinner:** $4-$22　　　　　　　　**Phone:** 406/328-6789
Location: Just off SR 78. Main St 59071. **Hours:** 11 am-10 pm, winter-9 pm. Closed: 11/25, 12/24 & 12/25. **Features:** No A/C; casual dress; children's menu; cocktails & lounge; a la carte. Rustic, homey atmosphere. Specializing in steak & seafood. **Cards:** AE, DS, MC, VI.

ROUNDUP—1,800

RESTAURANT

BUSY BEE RESTAURANT & GIFT SHOP
AAA
◆
American

Lunch: $4-$14　　　　**Dinner:** $4-$14　　　　**Phone:** 406/323-2204
Location: S edge of city on US 12 & 87. 317 1st Ave W 59072. **Hours:** 5 am-10:30 pm, Fri & Sat 24 hrs. Closed: 1/1, 12/24 & 12/25. **Features:** Sunday brunch; children's menu; health conscious menu; carryout; salad bar; beer & wine only; a la carte. Family dining in Honeycomb or Fireside dining rooms. Breakfast buffet; Fri night Western buffet. **Cards:** AE, DS, MC, VI.

ST. IGNATIUS—800

LODGINGS

STONEHEART INN
AAA SAVE
Bed & Breakfast

Rates Subject to Change
All Year [BP]   1P: $40- 60   2P/1B: $40- 60
Location: US 93 s on Main. 26 N Main 59865 (PO Box 236). **Terms:** Small pets only, kennel for large cats. **Facility:** 4 rooms. Charming decorated, themed rooms in turn of the century house. $5 extra charge for tipi in dream catcher rm; 2 stories; interior corridors. **All Rooms:** combo or shower baths. **Cards:** MC, VI.
Phone: 406/745-4999
XP: $5
🐾 📺 🅿 ⊠

SUNSET MOTEL
AAA
◆
Motel

Rates Subject to Change
5/1-11/1   1P: $55   2P/1B: $57   2P/2B: $59
Location: Just s of downtown exit on US 93. 32670 Hwy 93 59865 (PO Box 566). Fax: 406/745-3900. **Terms:** Open 5/1-11/1; reserv deposit; pets, $5 extra charge, dogs only. **Facility:** 10 rooms. Contemporary theme rooms with ceiling fan & mountain view. 2 stories; designated smoking area. **All Rooms:** extended cable TV. **Cards:** DS, MC, VI.
Phone: 406/745-3900
XP: $5
ASK 🐾 🅧 🛎 ⊠

SEELEY LAKE—900

LODGINGS

THE EMILY A
AAA
◆◆◆
Bed & Breakfast

Rates Subject to Change
All Year [BP]   1P: $115   2P/1B: $115   2P/2B: $115- 150   XP: $15   D
Location: 5 mi n on SR 83 (just n of MM 20). SR 83 N, MM 20 59868 (PO Box 350). Fax: 406/677-3474. **Terms:** Reserv deposit, 7 day notice; weekly/monthly rates; pets, advanced notice req, horses $10 extra charge. **Facility:** 5 rooms. Elegant spacious log home overlooking private lake on the Clearwater River. 2 stories; interior corridors; smoke free premises. **Services:** winter plug-ins. **Recreation:** canoeing, fishing; hiking trails. **Some Rooms:** combo or shower baths, shared bathrooms. **Cards:** MC, VI.
Phone: (406)677-3474
🐄 🛏 ⊠ 📺 🅿 🅧 🖨 ⊠

WILDERNESS GATEWAY INN
AAA SAVE
◆◆
Motel

5/15-10/15   1P: $48   2P/1B: $51   2P/2B: $54   XP: $3   F16
3/1-5/14 & 10/16-2/29   1P: $38   2P/1B: $41   2P/2B: $44   XP: $3   F16
Location: S end of town on SR 83. SR 83 59868 (PO Box 661). Fax: 406/677-2095. **Terms:** Reserv deposit; handling fee imposed; pets, $5.20 extra charge. **Facility:** 19 rooms. In scenic valley nestled between 3 wilderness areas. 2 stories; exterior corridors; designated smoking area; whirlpool. **Services:** winter plug-ins.
Cards: DS, MC, VI. **Special Amenities:** Free local telephone calls and preferred room (subject to availability with advanced reservations).
Phone: (406)677-2095
XP: $3   F16
🆂 🐾 🅧 ⊠

RESTAURANT

LINDEY'S PRIME STEAK HOUSE
AAA
◆◆
Steakhouse

Lunch: $4   **Dinner:** $14-$19   Phone: 406/677-9229
Location: Just s on SR 83. SR 83 59868. **Hours:** 5 pm-10 pm. Closed: 4/15-4/30 & Tues-Wed 10/1-4/30. **Features:** casual dress; cocktails & lounge. Overlooking Seeley Lake with northwoods atmosphere featuring aged prime sirloin. "Dinner sharing" avail. Summer dining at very casual outdoor lakeside seating featuring thick bayburgers.
⊠

SHELBY—2,800

LODGINGS

COMFORT INN OF SHELBY
AAA SAVE
◆◆◆
Motel

7/1-8/31 [CP]   1P: $62- 80   2P/1B: $66- 84 2P/2B: $66- 84 XP: $5   F18
5/1-6/30 [CP]   1P: $58- 76   2P/1B: $61- 79 2P/2B: $61- 79 XP: $5   F18
3/1-4/30 & 9/1-2/29 [CP]   1P: $56- 74   2P/1B: $59- 77 2P/2B: $59- 77 XP: $5   F18
Location: I-15, exit 363; just w, just s on McKinley Ave; from US 2, just s on McKinley Ave. 50 Frontage Rd 59474. Fax: 406/434-2493. **Terms:** Weekly/monthly rates; pets, $5 extra charge. **Facility:** 72 rooms. New contemporary styled rooms; convenient off interstate access. 3 stories; interior corridors; sauna, whirlpool, swim spa. **Dining:** Restaurant nearby. **Services:** winter plug-ins. **All Rooms:** combo or shower baths, extended cable TV. **Some Rooms:** 4 efficiencies, 2 kitchens, whirlpools. **Cards:** AE, DI, DS, MC, VI. **Special Amenities:** Free breakfast and free local telephone calls.
Phone: (406)434-2212
🆂 🐾 🅧 🍴 🛏 🕊 🐾 🖥 🖥 🛎 🎱 ⊠

CROSSROADS INN

AAA SAVE

◆◆◆
Motel

Phone: (406)434-5134

| | 6/1-8/31 | 1P: $50 | 2P/1B: $58 | 2P/2B: $64 | XP: $6 | F16 |
| | 3/1-5/31 & 9/1-2/29 | 1P: $46 | 2P/1B: $53 | 2P/2B: $59 | XP: $9 | F16 |

Location: US 2. (PO Box 926, 59474). Fax: 406/434-2937. **Terms:** Small pets only, $5 fee, smoking rooms only. **Facility:** 52 rooms. Spacious rooms, near Canadian border. 2 stories; interior corridors; designated smoking area; small heated indoor pool, whirlpool. **Dining:** Restaurant nearby. **Services:** winter plug-ins. **Cards:** AE, DI, DS, MC, VI.

O'HAIRE MANOR MOTEL

AAA SAVE

◆◆
Motel

Phone: (406)434-5555

| | 5/1-9/30 | 1P: $35 | 2P/1B: $45 | 2P/2B: $50 | XP: $5 |
| | 3/1-4/30 & 10/1-2/29 | 1P: $32 | 2P/1B: $40 | 2P/2B: $44 | XP: $4 |

Location: Just s of Main St via Maple St. 204 2nd St S 59474. Fax: 406/434-2702. **Terms:** Weekly rates; small pets only, $5 extra charge. **Facility:** 40 rooms. Clean, cozy rooms. 4 two-bedroom units. 5 rooms with 3-4 beds; 2 stories; exterior corridors; designated smoking area; whirlpool. **Dining:** Restaurant nearby. **Services:** area transportation, Amtrak & bus station; winter plug-ins. **All Rooms:** combo or shower baths. **Cards:** AE, CB, DI, DS, MC, VI. **Special Amenities:** Free local telephone calls and preferred room (subject to availability with advanced reservations).
(See color ad p 249)

WILLIAMS COURT

AAA SAVE

◆◆
Motel

Phone: (406)434-2254

| | All Year | | 2P/1B: $38- 43 | 2P/2B: $43- 47 | XP: $2 |

Location: Just s of US 2, between 5th & 6th aves. 525 1st St S 59474 (PO Box 590). **Terms:** Reserv deposit. **Facility:** 7 rooms. Residential area. Very well kept rooms. 1 two-bedroom unit. 1-2 stories; exterior corridors; designated smoking area. **Services:** winter plug-ins. **All Rooms:** combo or shower baths. **Some Rooms:** 5 kitchens. **Cards:** MC, VI.

STEVENSVILLE—1,200

LODGING

BIG CREEK PINE'S BED & BREAKFAST

AAA

◆◆◆
Bed &
Breakfast

Rates Subject to Change   Phone: (406)642-6475

| | All Year [BP] | 1P: $70 | 2P/1B: $80 | 2P/2B: $80 | XP: $15 |

Location: 4.7 mi s on US 93, between MM 62 & 63. 2986 US 93N 59870. **Terms:** Reserv deposit, 15 day notice; handling fee imposed. **Facility:** 4 rooms. Relaxing Bitterroot Valley countryside setting adjacent to Big Creek & each unique room accessorized with ceiling fans. 2 stories; interior corridors; designated smoking area; mountain view. **Services:** complimentary evening beverages. **Cards:** MC, VI.

SUPERIOR—900

LODGING

BUDGET HOST BIG SKY MOTEL

AAA SAVE

◆◆
Motel

Phone: (406)822-4831

| | 6/1-10/31 | 1P: $44- 48 | 2P/1B: $48- 54 | 2P/2B: $52- 58 | XP: $4 | F12 |
| | 3/1-5/31 & 11/1-2/29 | 1P: $40- 44 | 2P/1B: $44- 46 | 2P/2B: $46- 50 | XP: $4 | F12 |

Location: Just n of I-90, exit 47. 103 4th Ave E 59872 (PO Box 458). Fax: 406/822-4371. **Terms:** Weekly rates, in winter; pets. **Facility:** 24 rooms. Large comfortable, contemporary rooms. Easy freeway access; close to river, city park with pool & mountain bike trails. 1 two-bedroom unit. 2 stories; exterior corridors; designated smoking area. **Dining:** Restaurant nearby. **Services:** winter plug-ins. **Cards:** AE, DS, MC, VI. **Special Amenities:** Free breakfast and free local telephone calls. *(See color ad p 206)*

THOMPSON FALLS—1,300

LODGING

THE RIVERFRONT

◆◆
Motel

Rates Subject to Change   Phone: 406/827-3460

| | All Year | 1P: $45- 59 | 2P/1B: $49- 59 | 2P/2B: $59- 79 | XP: $5 | F6 |

Location: 1 mi w of city center. 4907 Scenic SR 200 W 59873 (PO Box 22). **Facility:** 8 rooms. Some with enclosed porches. 2 stories; exterior corridors; designated smoking area; mountain view. **Services:** giftshop. **Recreation:** fishing. **All Rooms:** comb, shower or tub baths. **Some Rooms:** efficiency, color TV. **Cards:** AE, DI, DS, MC, VI.

THREE FORKS—1,200

LODGINGS

BROKEN SPUR MOTEL INC

◆◆
Motel

Rates Subject to Change   Phone: 406/285-3237

| | 5/15-9/15 [CP] | 1P: $42 | 2P/1B: $46 | 2P/2B: $48 | XP: $4 | F11 |
| | 3/1-5/14 & 9/16-2/29 [CP] | 1P: $38 | 2P/1B: $42 | 2P/2B: $44 | XP: $4 | F11 |

Location: I-90; exit 278 westbound, 1.3 mi sw on SR 2; exit 274 eastbound, 1 mi s on Hwy 287 to jct Hwy 2, 3 mi se on SR 2. 124 West Elm 59752 (PO Box 1009). Fax: 406/285-4133. **Facility:** 24 rooms. Gifts avail at front desk. 2 stories; exterior corridors. **Services:** winter plug-ins. **All Rooms:** combo or shower baths. **Some Rooms:** 2 kitchens. **Cards:** AE, DI, DS, MC, VI.

FORT THREE FORKS MOTEL INC

AAA

◆◆
Motel

Rates Subject to Change   Phone: (406)285-3233

| | 5/15-9/15 [CP] | 1P: $42 | 2P/1B: $46 | 2P/2B: $48 | XP: $4 | F11 |
| | 3/1-5/14 & 9/16-2/29 [CP] | 1P: $38 | 2P/1B: $42 | 2P/2B: $44 | XP: $4 | F11 |

Location: I-90, exit 274 & Hwy 287. 10776 Hwy 287 59752 (PO Box 970). Fax: 406/285-4362. **Terms:** Reserv deposit; monthly rates; small pets only, $5 extra charge. **Facility:** 24 rooms. Replica of late 1800's fort; ample truck parking. Montana made gifts. 3 coffeemakers avail; 2 stories; exterior corridors. **Dining:** Restaurant nearby. **Services:** winter plug-ins. **All Rooms:** combo or shower baths, extended cable TV. **Cards:** AE, DI, DS, MC, VI.

SACAJAWEA INN

AAA

◆◆◆
Historic Bed
& Breakfast

Rates Subject to Change   Phone: (406)285-6515

| | 4/1-10/31 | 1P: $69- 79 | 2P/1B: $69- 79 | 2P/2B: $79- 99 | XP: $10 | F12 |

Location: I-90, exit 278; 1 mi s on Hwy 2. 5 N Main St 59752 (PO Box 648). Fax: 406/285-4210. **Terms:** Open 4/1-10/31; check-in 4 pm; reserv deposit. **Facility:** 32 rooms. Historic building built in 1910. Old fashioned charming rooms. Listed on National Register of Historic Places. 3 stories, no elevator; interior corridors; smoke free premises. **Services:** giftshop. **All Rooms:** combo or shower baths. **Cards:** AE, DS, MC, VI.

WEST GLACIER—300—*See also GLACIER NATIONAL PARK.*

LODGINGS

GREAT NORTHERN WHITEWATER RESORT   Rates Subject to Change   Phone: (406)387-5340

7/1-9/15	1P: $162- 212	2P/1B: $162- 212	2P/2B: $162- 212
6/15-6/30 & 9/16-9/30	1P: $147- 197	2P/1B: $147- 197	2P/2B: $147- 197
4/1-6/14 & 10/1-10/31	1P: $105- 165	2P/1B: $105- 165	2P/2B: $105- 165

Cottage
Location: 1 mi w on US 2. 12127 US 2 59936 (PO Box 278). Fax: 406/387-9007. **Terms:** Open 4/1-10/31; reserv deposit, 45 day notice; handling fee imposed. **Facility:** 5 rooms. Log chalets surrounding pond with mountain range views. 3 two-bedroom units. 3 rms with fireplace; max occupancy applies to chalets; 2 stories; exterior corridors; mountain view; swim spa. **Dining:** Restaurant nearby. **Services:** area transportation, West Glacier Train Depot. **Recreation:** fly fishing trips & lessons, river rafting;; volleyball court. **All Rooms:** combo or shower baths. **Some Rooms:** efficiency, 4 kitchens. **Cards:** AE, DS, MC, VI. *(See color ad p 93)*

SILVERWOLF CHALETS   Phone: 406/387-4448

7/1-8/18 [CP]	1P: $120- 134	2P/1B: $120- 134
6/15-6/30 & 8/19-9/15 [CP]	1P: $115- 128	2P/1B: $115- 128
4/14-6/14 & 9/16-10/10 [CP]	1P: $88- 102	2P/1B: $102

Cottage
Location: 6 mi w of West Glacier on US 2. 160 Gladys Glen Rd 59936 (PO Box 115). **Terms:** Open 4/14-10/10; age restrictions may apply; reserv deposit, 30 day notice; handling fee imposed. **Facility:** 10 rooms. Log cabins for 2 with covered porch in a landscaped forest setting. Cabins finished with crafted lodgepole furniture, handmade quilt & gas log fireplace. 1 story; exterior corridors; smoke free premises. **Recreation:** barbecue grill & picnic table at each chalet. **All Rooms:** shower baths. **Cards:** DS, MC, VI.

WEST YELLOWSTONE—900

LODGINGS

ALPINE MOTEL   Phone: (406)646-7544

6/7-9/20	1P: $45- 53	2P/1B: $45- 53	2P/2B: $53- 62	XP: $3	F
5/1-6/6 & 9/21-10/31	1P: $28- 36	2P/1B: $28- 36	2P/2B: $34- 42	XP: $2	F

Motel
Location: Just w from park entrance. 120 Madison 59758 (PO Box 1497). **Terms:** Open 5/1-10/31; reserv deposit, 3 day notice; handling fee imposed. **Facility:** 12 rooms. Charming well-kept rooms. 1 story; exterior corridors; smoke free premises. **Dining:** Restaurant nearby. **All Rooms:** shower baths. **Cards:** AE, MC, VI.

AL'S WESTWARD HO MOTEL

Rates Subject to Change

Phone: 406/646-733

6/11-9/20	2P/1B:	$40-	48	2P/2B:	$52-	56	XP:	$4
5/1-6/10 & 9/21-11/1	2P/1B:	$30-	36	2P/2B:	$42-	48	XP:	$4

Motel

Location: Just n of park entrance. 16 Boundary St 59758 (PO Box 49). **Terms:** Open 5/1-11/1; reser deposit, 5 day notice. **Facility:** 33 rooms. Quiet secluded location. Spacious rooms. No telephones. 3 two bedroom units. 5 kitchens, $3 extra charge; 1-2 stories; interior/exterior corridors; designated smoking area **All Rooms:** no utensils, combo or shower baths, extended cable TV. **Cards:** DS, MC, VI.

BEST WESTERN CROSS WINDS MOTOR INN

Phone: (406)646-955

6/10-8/25 [CP]	1P:	$89-	98	2P/1B:	$89-	98	2P/2B:	$99- 109
5/27-6/9 & 8/26-9/30 [CP]	1P:	$66-	82	2P/1B:	$66-	82	2P/2B:	$76- 92
3/1-3/19 & 12/20-2/29 [CP]	1P:	$64-	74	2P/1B:	$64-	74	2P/2B:	$70- 80
3/20-5/26 & 10/1-12/19 [CP]	1P:	$59	59	2P/1B:	$59-	59	2P/2B:	$65- 65

Motel

Location: Just w of US 191 & 287, on US 20 at Dunraven St & Firehole Ave; at end of city park. 20 Firehole Ave 59758 (PO Box 340). Fax: 406/646-9592. **Terms:** Reserv deposit, 3 day notice; pets. **Facility:** 70 rooms. Spa cious rooms; city park adjacent. 2 stories; exterior corridors; designated smoking area; small heated indoor pool, whirlpool **Services:** winter plug-ins. **Cards:** AE, CB, DI, DS, MC, VI. **Special Amenities:** Free breakfast.

BEST WESTERN DESERT INN

Phone: (406)646-737

6/10-8/25 [CP]	1P:	$99- 155		2P/1B:	$99- 155		2P/2B:	$99- 155
5/27-6/9 & 8/26-9/30 [CP]	1P:	$75- 95		2P/1B:	$75- 95		2P/2B:	$75- 105
3/1-3/19 & 12/20-2/29 [CP]	1P:	$70- 90		2P/1B:	$70- 90		2P/2B:	$70- 90
3/20-5/26 & 10/1-12/19 [CP]	1P:	$39- 69		2P/1B:	$39- 69		2P/2B:	$39- 69

Motel

Location: US 191 at jct US 20, corner of Canyon & Firehole aves. 133 Canyon Ave 59758 (PO Box 340) Fax: 406/646-7759. **Terms:** Check-in 4 pm; reserv deposit, 3 day notice; pets. **Facility:** 76 rooms. 3 stories; interior corridors heated indoor pool, whirlpool. **All Rooms:** extended cable TV. **Some Rooms:** 2 kitchens. **Cards:** AE, CB, DI, DS, MC, VI **Special Amenities:** Free breakfast.

BEST WESTERN WESTON INN

Rates Subject to Change

Phone: 406/646-7373

6/17-9/16	1P:	$60		2P/1B:	$75-	85	2P/2B:	$75- 85	XP: $5	F12
3/1-3/16, 5/17-6/16,								
9/17-10/16 & 12/17-2/29	1P:	$45		2P/1B:	$47-	65	2P/2B:	$47- 65	XP: $5	F12
3/17-5/16 & 10/17-12/16	1P:	$30		2P/1B:	$35-	45	2P/2B:	$35- 45	XP: $5	F12

Motel

Location: US 191 at corner of Canyon Ave & Gibbon St. 103 Gibbon St 59758. Fax: 406/646-7572. **Facility:** 65 rooms. 2-3 stories, no elevator; interior/exterior corridors. **Services:** winter plug-ins. **Cards:** AE, DI, DS, MC, VI.

BIG WESTERN PINE MOTEL

Rates Subject to Change

Phone: 406/646-7622

6/15-8/26 [CP]	1P:	$55-	65	2P/1B:	$63-	75	2P/2B:	$65- 85	XP: $5
12/20-2/29 [CP]	1P:	$53-	59	2P/1B:	$55-	65	2P/2B:	$57- 75	XP: $5
3/1-3/20, 5/28-6/14 &								
8/27-9/30 [CP]	1P:	$48-	55	2P/1B:	$53-	60	2P/2B:	$55- 65	XP: $5
3/21-5/27 & 10/1-12/19 [CP]	1P:	$25-	45	2P/1B:	$35-	47	2P/2B:	$39- 50

Motor Inn

Location: Just w of Canyon Ave, corner Firehole Ave & Electric St; on US 20 & 191. 234 Firehole Ave 59758 (PO Box 67). Fax: 406/646-9443. **Terms:** Handling fee imposed; pets, $5 extra charge. **Facility:** 45 rooms. Close to restaurants & shopping. 7 two-bedroom units. Kitchens & efficiencies, $10-$20 extra charge; 1-2 stories; interior/exterior corridors; small heated pool, whirlpool. **Dining:** Rustler's Roost, see separate listing. **Services:** winter plug-ins. **Recreation:** Fee: guided snowmobile tours, heated snowcoach, dog sleds. **Cards:** AE, CB, DI, DS, MC, VI. *(See color ad below)*

BRANDIN' IRON INN

Guaranteed Rates

Phone: (406)646-9411

6/7-9/20 [CP]	1P:	$80		2P/1B:	$90		2P/2B:	$90	XP: $6	F12
3/1-3/16 & 12/24-2/29 [CP]	1P:	$70		2P/1B:	$80		2P/2B:	$80	XP: $6	F12
3/17-6/6 & 9/21-12/23 [CP]	1P:	$53		2P/1B:	$63		2P/2B:	$63	XP: $6	F12

Motel

Location: Just w & n of park entrance. 201 Canyon Ave 59758 (PO Box 978). Fax: 406/646-9436. **Terms:** Check-in 4 pm; reserv deposit, 14 day notice, in winter. **Facility:** 79 rooms. New breakfast room, re modeled facility. 2 stories; exterior corridors; whirlpools. **Dining:** Restaurant nearby. **Services:** winter plug-ins. **Recreation:** guided snowmobile tours; summer park tours, guided fly fishing. Fee: snowmobiling. **All Rooms:** combo or shower baths, extended cable TV. **Cards:** AE, DI, JC, MC, VI. *(See color ad p 253)*

UCKBOARD MOTEL · Phone: (406)646-9020

3/1-3/24, 6/6-9/21 & 12/11-2/29	1P: $60- 68	2P/1B: $60- 70	2P/2B: $65- 88		
3/25-6/5 & 9/22-12/10	1P: $32- 42	2P/1B: $32- 46	2P/2B: $38- 50		

Location: Just nw of park entrance, w off US 191 at Electric St & Madison Ave. 119 Electric St 59758 (PO Box 186). Fax: 406/646-7263. **Terms:** Package plans. **Facility:** 25 rooms. Very clean, small rooms. 1 two-bedroom unit. 2 stories; exterior corridors; whirlpool. **Dining:** Restaurant nearby. **Services:** winter plug-ins. All Rooms: combo or shower baths. **Cards:** DS, MC, VI. **Special Amenities: Free local telephone calls.**

TY CENTER MOTEL · Phone: (406)646-7337

6/11-8/21	1P: $69	2P/1B: $69	2P/2B: $89	XP: $10
5/20-6/10 & 8/22-9/23	1P: $59	2P/1B: $59	2P/2B: $79	XP: $10
12/18-2/29	1P: $59	2P/1B: $59	2P/2B: $69	XP: $10
3/1-5/19 & 9/24-12/17	1P: $39	2P/1B: $39	2P/2B: $49	XP: $10

Location: Just nw of park entrance, w off US 191 at Madison Ave & Dunraven St. 214 Madison Ave 59758 PO Box 580). Fax: 406/646-7337. **Terms:** Reserv deposit, 3 day notice, 20 days 11/1-3/31, 3 days 5/1-9/30. **Facility:** 25 ooms. Daily narrative bus tours in summer. Meeting room with full kitchen & big screen TV. 2- & 3-bedroom units, $10-$25 xtra charge; 1-2 stories; exterior corridors; designated smoking area; whirlpool. **Dining:** Restaurant nearby. **Recreation:** ee: snowmobiling. All Rooms: combo or shower baths. **Cards:** AE, MC, VI. *(See color ad p 254)*

COMFORT INN

6/1-9/30 [CP]	1P:	$79- 129	2P/1B:	$79- 129	2P/2B:	$79- 129	XP:	$8	F
3/1-3/20 & 12/20-2/29 [CP]	1P:	$69- 99	2P/1B:	$69- 99	2P/2B:	$69- 99	XP:	$8	F
3/21-5/31 & 10/1-12/19 [CP]	1P:	$49- 79	2P/1B:	$49- 79	2P/2B:	$49- 79	XP:	$8	F

Phone: (406)646-42

Motel

Location: US 191, 0.6 mi w on Madison Ave; e from Hwy 20, 0.4 mi s on Iris St. 638 Madison Ave 59758 (F Box 1050). Fax: 406/646-4212. **Terms:** Reserv deposit, 3 day notice, 14 day notice, 3/1-3/30 & 12/1-2/2 package plans. **Facility:** 78 rooms. Very clean, modern property. Attractive pool room. 10 large family rms, up to 6 persons; 3 s ries; interior corridors; designated smoking area; heated indoor pool, whirlpool. **Services:** winter plug-ins. **Recreation:** exerci equipment. **All Rooms:** extended cable TV. **Cards:** AE, CB, DI, DS, MC, VI. **Special Amenities:** Free breakfast and fr local telephone calls. (See color ad below)

/S INN WEST YELLOWSTONE   **Phone: (406)646-7656**

SAVE

3/1-3/20, 6/7-10/1 & 12/15-2/29	1P:	$82- 105	2P/1B:	$89- 105	2P/2B:	$89- 105	XP:	$8	F13
3/21-6/6 & 10/2-12/14	1P:	$42- 52	2P/1B:	$45- 55	2P/2B:	$45- 60	XP:	$8	F13

Location: Just nw of park entrance, w off US 191. 118 Electric St 59758. Fax: 406/646-7965. **Terms:** Reserv deposit, 14 day notice, in winter; handling fee imposed; small pets only, $5 extra charge. **Facility:** 70 rooms. good housekeeping. 1 kitchen suite, $152. Whirlpool rms, $95-$155; 2 stories; interior/exterior corridors; small heated in- r pool, saunas, whirlpools. **Dining:** Restaurant nearby. **Services:** winter plug-ins. **Recreation:** Fee: snowmobiling. **Rooms:** extended cable TV. **Cards:** AE, CB, DI, DS, JC, MC, VI.

RGREEN MOTEL   Rates Subject to Change   **Phone: (406)646-7655**

7/1-8/31	2P/1B:	$59	2P/2B:	$69	XP:	$3
6/10-6/30 & 9/1-9/30	2P/1B:	$49	2P/2B:	$59	XP:	$3
3/1-3/20 & 12/20-2/29	2P/1B:	$45	2P/2B:	$55	XP:	$3
3/21-6/9 & 10/1-12/19	2P/1B:	$29	2P/2B:	$39	XP:	$3

Location: Just w of Canyon, on US 20 & 191. 229 Firehole Ave 59758 (PO Box 631). Fax: 406/646-0060. **ns:** Reserv deposit, 14 day notice; handling fee imposed; small pets only, $10 extra charge. **Facility:** 16 rooms. 0.5 mi Yellowstone Park entrance. Very clean rooms. Locally owned & operated. 2 two-bedroom units. 3 kitchens, extra charge; ory; exterior corridors; designated smoking area. **Dining:** Restaurant nearby. **All Rooms:** combo or shower baths, nded cable TV. **Cards:** AE, DS, MC, VI.

RFIELD INN   Rates Subject to Change   **Phone: (406)646-4892**

6/13-9/30 [CP]	1P:	$95- 105	2P/1B:	$99- 109	2P/2B:	$99- 109	XP:	$8	F16
3/1-3/17 & 12/24-2/29 [CP]	1P:	$85- 95	2P/1B:	$86- 91	2P/2B:	$86- 91	XP:	$8	F16
5/16-6/12 & 10/1-10/31 [CP]	1P:	$60- 70	2P/1B:	$65- 80	2P/2B:	$65- 80	XP:	$8	F16
3/18-5/15 & 11/1-12/23 [CP]	1P:	$50- 60	2P/1B:	$50- 60	2P/2B:	$50- 60	XP:	$8	F16

ation: Just w of Yellowstone Park entrance; just sw of jct US 191, 187 & 20. 105 S Electric St 59758 (PO Box 1745). : 406/646-4893. **Facility:** 77 rooms. New property. Contemporary, attractive rooms & public areas. 4 whirlpool rms, $30-$40 a charge; 3 stories; interior corridors; designated smoking area; small heated indoor pool. **Cards:** AE, CB, DI, DS, JC, VI. *(See color ad below)*

AY WOLF INN & SUITES   **Phone: (406)646-0000**

SAVE

3/1-3/19 & 6/14-9/6 [CP]	1P:	$89- 129	2P/1B:	$89- 129	2P/2B:	$89- 129	XP:	$10	F16
9/7-9/30 & 12/22-2/29 [CP]	1P:	$69- 89	2P/1B:	$69- 89	2P/2B:	$69- 89	XP:	$10	F16
5/16-6/13 & 10/1-10/30 [CP]	1P:	$59- 79	2P/1B:	$59- 79	2P/2B:	$59- 79	XP:	$10	F16
3/20-5/15 & 10/31-12/21 [CP]	1P:	$49- 69	2P/1B:	$49- 69	2P/2B:	$49- 69	XP:	$10	F16

Location: Just w of Yellowstone National Park entrance. 250 S Canyon St 59758 (PO Box 1449). : 406/646-4232. **Facility:** 102 rooms. New property. Attractive public areas. Stylish rooms. Underground heated parking age. All rooms with hair dryer & voice mail. 2 two-bedroom units. 18 suites; 3 stories; interior corridors; designated smoking a; small heated indoor pool, sauna, whirlpool. **Dining:** Restaurant nearby. **Some Rooms:** 16 kitchens. **Cards:** AE, DI, MC, VI. **Special Amenities:** Free breakfast and free local telephone calls. *(See color ad p 256)*

LLY INN   **Phone: (406)646-4544**

SAVE

6/13-9/30 [CP]	1P:	$95- 105	2P/1B:	$99- 109	2P/2B:	$99- 109	XP:	$8	F16
3/1-3/17 & 12/24-2/29 [CP]	1P:	$85- 95	2P/1B:	$86- 91	2P/2B:	$86- 91	XP:	$8	F16
5/16-6/12 & 10/1-10/31 [CP]	1P:	$60- 70	2P/1B:	$65- 80	2P/2B:	$65- 80	XP:	$8	F16
3/18-5/15 & 11/1-12/23 [CP]	1P:	$50- 60	2P/1B:	$50- 60	2P/2B:	$50- 60	XP:	$8	F16

Location: Just w of Yellowstone Park entrance; s of jct US 191, 287 & 20. 104 S Canyon St 59758 (PO Box 2). Fax: 406/646-9838. **Terms:** Check-in 4 pm; pets, $20 dep req. **Facility:** 78 rooms. Well lit contemporary rooms; attrac- public areas; close to Yellowstone Park entrance. 3 stories; interior/exterior corridors; designated smoking area; small ted indoor pool, sauna, whirlpool. **Dining:** Restaurant nearby. **Services:** winter plug-ins. **All Rooms:** combo or shower as. **Some Rooms:** whirlpools. **Cards:** AE, CB, DI, DS, JC, MC, VI. **Special Amenities:** Free breakfast. e color ad p 281)

LAZY G MOTEL
(AAA)

◆ ◆
Motel

Guaranteed Rates

3/1-3/15, 6/1-9/30 & 12/15-2/29		2P/1B:	$43	2P/2B:	$53	XP: $5
3/16-3/31, 5/1-5/31 & 10/1-12/14		2P/1B:	$32	2P/2B:	$40	XP: $5

Phone: 406/646-7

Location: 0.6 mi w of park entrance on Yellowstone Ave, n on Hayden St; eastbound via US 20, then j 123 Hayden St 59758 (PO Box 218). **Terms:** Open 3/1-3/31 & 5/1-2/29; reserv deposit, 5 day notice, 21 day noti winter; handling fee imposed; 2 night min stay, efficiencies. **Facility:** 15 rooms. Cozy, quiet exceptionally clean ro Summer picnic area with gas grill and tables. 5 efficiencies, $10 extra charge; 1-2 stories; exterior corridors; designer smoking area. **Services:** winter plug-ins. **Recreation:** fish cleaning & freezing facilities. **All Rooms:** combo or shower b **Cards:** DS, MC, VI.

ONE HORSE MOTEL
(AAA)

◆
Motel

Guaranteed Rates

7/1-8/31	2P/1B:	$59	2P/2B:	$69	XP:	$3
3/1-3/20 & 12/20-2/29	2P/1B:	$55	2P/2B:	$65	XP:	$3
6/10-6/30 & 9/1-9/30	2P/1B:	$49	2P/2B:	$59	XP:	$3
3/21-6/9 & 10/1-12/19	2P/1B:	$29	2P/2B:	$39	XP:	$3

Phone: (406)646-7

Location: Just w of US 191 & 287, on US 20 at Dunraven St & Firehole Ave; at end of city park. Dunraven St 59758 (PO Box 878). Fax: 406/646-0060. **Terms:** Reserv deposit, 14 day notice; small pets only, $10 charge. **Facility:** 19 rooms. Small, cozy rooms. Adjacent to city park. Closed 3/26-4/15 & 10/31-12/20. Locally owned & ated. Family units, extra charge; 1 story; exterior corridors; designated smoking area; whirlpool open 12/1- **Dining:** Restaurant nearby. **Services:** winter plug-ins. **All Rooms:** extended cable TV. **Cards:** AE, DS, MC, VI.

ROUNDUP MOTEL & DUDE MOTOR INN
(AAA) (SAVE)

◆ ◆ ◆
Motel

7/1-8/15 [CP]	2P/1B:	$70-	78	2P/2B:	$75-	84	XP: $6
9/2-9/25 [EP]	2P/1B:	$59-	66	2P/2B:	$68-	76	XP: $6
8/16-9/1 & 12/20-2/29 [EP]	2P/1B:	$59-	66	2P/2B:	$66-	74	XP: $6
5/10-6/30 & 9/26-10/15 [EP]	2P/1B:	$56-	62	2P/2B:	$58-	66	XP: $6

Phone: 406/646-7

Location: Just n of park entrance. 3 Madison Ave 59758 (PO Box 709). Fax: 406/646-4261. **Terms:** C 5/10-10/15 & 12/20-2/29; reserv deposit, 5 day notice. **Facility:** 60 rooms. Very close to Yellowstone Park entrance. Cl 3/20-4/30 & 10/16-12/14. Large contempary style rooms. 3 two-bedroom units. 1-2 stories; exterior corridors; designer smoking area; small heated pool, whirlpools. **Dining:** Restaurant nearby. **Services:** winter plug-ins. **All Rooms:** exte cable TV. **Some Rooms:** 3 kitchens. **Cards:** JC, MC, VI.

AAA CampBooks—valuable additions for members who enjoy outdoor vacations.

GE COACH INN

Phone: (406)646-7381

		Guaranteed Rates					
6/18-9/25	1P: $75- 122	2P/1B: $79- 128	2P/2B: $79- 128	XP: $6	F12
3/1-3/20 & 12/17-2/29	1P: $69- 104	2P/1B: $76- 110	2P/2B: $76- 110	XP: $6	F12
5/14-6/17	1P: $55- 86	2P/1B: $61- 92	2P/2B: $61- 92	XP: $6	F12
3/21-5/13 & 9/26-12/16	1P: $37- 54	2P/1B: $43- 60	2P/2B: $43- 60	XP: $6	F12

Location: Just nw of park entrance, w off US 191 at Madison Ave & Dunraven St. 209 Madison Ave 59758 (PO Box 169). Fax: 406/646-9575. **Terms:** Check-in 5 pm; reserv deposit, 14 day notice, in winter; package plans. **...lity:** 84 rooms. Contemporary rustic rooms, underground parking. Wheelchair avail; 2 stories; interior corridors; designated ...king area; sauna, whirlpools. **Dining:** Live entertainment 12/28-3/18, 6/15-9/15. **Services:** giftshop; winter plug-ins. **...reation:** Fee: snowcoach guided tours. **All Rooms:** combo or shower baths, extended cable TV. **Cards:** AE, CB, DI, VI. *(See color ad p 253)*

...ER 8 WEST YELLOWSTONE LIONSHEAD RESORT

Phone: (406)646-9584

3/18-3/31, 5/16-9/30, 12/21-1/3 & 2/1-2/29	1P: $70- 76	2P/1B: $70- 76	2P/2B: $74- 86	XP: $5	F12
3/1-5/15, 4/1-5/15, 10/1-12/20 & 1/4-1/31	1P: $37- 48	2P/1B: $39- 50	2P/2B: $47- 54	XP: $5	F12

Location: 8 mi w of w park entrance, on US 20. 1545 Targhee Pass Hwy 59758. Fax: 406/646-7404. **...ns:** Check-in 4 pm. **Facility:** 44 rooms. In scenic valley. Satellite TV. 2 stories; interior corridors; sauna, whirlpool; play-...nd. **Dining:** Restaurant nearby. **Services:** winter plug-ins. **Recreation:** square dancing. Fee: fishing; snowmobiling. **...ds:** AE, DI, DS, MC, VI. **Special Amenities:** Free local telephone calls.

...REE BEAR LODGE ANNEX

Phone: 406/646-7353

6/11-8/20, 9/3-9/17 & 12/15-2/29 [EP]	1P: $63	2P/1B: $68- 78	2P/2B: $83- 88	XP: $5
5/23-6/10, 8/21-9/2 & 9/18-9/30 [CP]	1P: $53	2P/1B: $58- 68	2P/2B: $73- 78	XP: $5
4/30-5/22 & 10/1-10/16 [CP]	1P: $43	2P/1B: $43- 53	2P/2B: $58- 63	XP: $5

...ation: Just w of park entrance. 24 Dunraven St 59758 (PO Box 1590). Fax: 406/646-4567. **Terms:** Open 4/30-10/16 & ...5-2/29; small pets only, $5 extra charge. **Facility:** 15 rooms. Contemporary styled rooms. 1 story; exterior corridors; des-...ted smoking area; whirlpools, summer heated pool. **Services:** winter plug-ins. **All Rooms:** extended cable TV. **...ds:** DS, MC, VI. *(See color ad p 251)*

...REE BEAR MOTOR LODGE

Phone: 406/646-7353

6/11-9/17 & 12/15-2/29 [EP]	1P: $68	2P/1B: $73- 83	2P/2B: $88- 93	XP: $5
5/22-6/10 & 9/18-9/30 [EP]	1P: $58	2P/1B: $63- 73	2P/2B: $78- 83	XP: $5
4/30-5/21 & 10/1-10/16 [EP]	1P: $48	2P/1B: $53- 63	2P/2B: $68- 73	XP: $5

Location: Just w of park entrance. 217 Yellowstone Ave 59758 (PO Box 1590). Fax: 406/646-4567. **Terms:** Open 4/30-10/16 & 12/15-2/29; small pets only, $5 extra charge. **Facility:** 59 rooms. Stylish rooms. ...se to Yellowstone Park entrance. 11 two-bedroom units. 1-2 stories; interior/exterior corridors; designated smoking area; ...lpools, small summer heated pool. **Dining:** Restaurant, see separate listing. **Services:** winter plug-ins. **Recreation:** ... guided snowmobile tours. **All Rooms:** extended cable TV. **Some Rooms:** whirlpools. **Cards:** DS, MC, VI. *...e color ad p 251)*

...AVELERS LODGE

Phone: (406)646-9561

3/1-3/20, 5/25-10/1 & 12/20-2/29 [CP]	1P: $65- 72	2P/1B: $70- 82	2P/2B: $75- 89	XP: $6	F12
3/21-5/24 & 10/2-12/19 [EP]	1P: $39- 42	2P/1B: $44- 56	2P/2B: $49- 62	XP: $4	F12

Location: Just w of park entrance. 225 Yellowstone Ave 59758 (PO Box 1110). Fax: 406/646-4478. **Terms:** Reserv deposit, 14 day notice, in winter; handling fee imposed; package plans, in winter; small pets ... $6 extra charge. **Facility:** 46 rooms. Some small rooms conveniently located near park entrance, recreation room with ...en. 2 two-bedroom units. Family units, $129-$149 for 1-8 persons. King bed, $78; king suite, $82; 2 stories; exterior cor-...rs; small heated pool, sauna, whirlpool. **Recreation:** Fee: snowmobiling. **All Rooms:** combo or shower baths, extended ...e TV. **Cards:** DI, DS, JC, MC, VI. **Special Amenities:** Free local telephone calls and preferred room (subject to ...lability with advanced reservations).

For **guaranteed** rates, you MUST show your membership card.

THE WEST YELLOWSTONE CONFERENCE HOTEL
HOLIDAY INN SUNSPREE RESORT

Phone: (406)646-7

⬡ SAVE	6/11-9/18	1P: $139- 200	2P/1B: $139- 200	2P/2B: $139- 200	XP: $8
	3/1-3/22 & 12/12-2/29	1P: $109- 190	2P/1B: $109- 190	2P/2B: $109- 190	XP: $8
◆ ◆ ◆	5/14-6/10	1P: $89- 185	2P/1B: $89- 185	2P/2B: $89- 185	XP: $8
Hotel	3/23-5/13 & 9/19-12/11	1P: $69- 185	2P/1B: $69- 185	2P/2B: $69- 185	XP: $8

Location: Just w of park entrance. 315 Yellowstone Ave 59758 (PO Box 470). Fax: 406/646-4
Terms: Check-in 4 pm. **Facility:** 123 rooms. Large stylish rooms. 1903 executive railroad car with museum. In room v
games. 13 two-bedroom units. 3 rms with fireplace; 3 stories; interior corridors; designated smoking area; small heated in
pool, sauna, whirlpool. **Dining:** Dining room; $8-$21. **Services:** giftshop; winter plug-ins. Fee: area transporta
All Rooms: extended cable TV. **Some Rooms:** whirlpools. **Cards:** AE, CB, DI, DS, JC, MC, VI. **Special Amenities:** I
local telephone calls. (See color ad below & opposite title page)

⬡ ⬡ ⬡ ⬡ ⬡ ⬡ ⬡ ⬡ ⬡ ⬡ ⬡ ⬡ ⬡ ⬡ ⬡ ⬡ ⬡ ⬡ ⬡

YELLOWSTONE LODGE

Phone: 406/646-0

FYI   Under construction. **Location:** 250 Electric St 59758. Fax: 406/646-4232. **Facility:** 79 rooms. Schedule
open May, 1999.

RESTAURANTS

ALICE'S RESTAURANT   **Dinner:** $6-$14   Phone: 406/646-7
⬡
   Location: 8 mi w of park west entrance on US 20. 1545 Targhee Pass Hwy 59758. **Hours:** 6:30 am-
◆   5-9:30 pm, 7 am-9 pm, in winter. **Reservations:** suggested. **Features:** casual dress; cocktails & lounge;
American   carte. Mountainous setting. Chicken, steak & fresh rainbow trout. **Cards:** DI, DS, MC, VI.

CHINATOWN RESTAURANT   **Lunch:** $5-$6   **Dinner:** $6-$13   Phone: 406/646-7
◆   **Location:** Just w of park entrance. 124 Madison Ave 59758. **Hours:** 11 am-10 pm. Closed: 4/1-4/3
Chinese   11/1-12/15. **Features:** casual dress; carryout; street parking. Traditional Chinese cuisine to include Pe
Hunan, Szechuan & Cantonese dishes. Smoke free premises. **Cards:** AE, DS, MC, VI.

RUNNING BEAR PANCAKE HOUSE   **Lunch:** $4-$7   Phone: 406/646-7
⬡   **Location:** 0.6 mi w of park entrance on Yellowstone Ave, right at lumber company, corner Hayde
◆ ◆   Madison Ave. 538 Madison Ave 59758. **Hours:** 7 am-2 pm. Closed: 4/1-4/30, 11/1-11/30 & 12
American   **Features:** casual dress; children's menu; carryout. Specializes in pancakes & many other homemade ite
Cards: DS, MC, VI.

RUSTLER'S ROOST   **Lunch:** $3-$6   **Dinner:** $5-$18   Phone: 406/646-7
⬡   **Location:** Just w of Canyon Ave, corner Firehole Ave & Electric St; on US 20 & 191; in Big Western
◆ ◆   Motel. 234 Firehole Ave 59758. **Hours:** 6:30 am-10 pm. **Features:** casual dress; children's menu; carr
American   cocktails & lounge; street parking; a la carte. Pleasant restaurant specializing in prime rib, seafood,
buffalo & home baked goods. Meals served in lounge during off season. **Cards:** AE, DI, DS, MC, VI.
(See color ad p 252)

THREE BEAR RESTAURANT   **Dinner:** $8-$21   **Phone:** 406/646-7811
Location: Just w of park entrance; in Three Bear Motor Lodge. 205 Yellowstone Ave 59758. **Hours:** Open 5/15-10/15 & 12/1-2/29; 7 am-11 & 5-10 pm; 7 am-10:30 & 5-9:30 pm, in winter. **Features:** casual dress; children's menu; health conscious menu; carryout; salad bar; cocktails & lounge; street parking; a la carte. Family dining room with historic decor, specializing in prime rib & home baked pastry. Smoke free premises.
Cards: DS, MC, VI. *(See color ad p 251)*

WHITEFISH—4,400—See also GLACIER NATIONAL PARK.

LODGINGS

ANAPURNA CONDOMINIUMS   **Phone:** (406)862-3687

12/18-1/2 & 2/12-2/20	1P: $207- 250	2P/1B: $207- 250	2P/2B: $207- 250	XP: $20	F12
3/1-3/27, 1/3-2/11 &					
2/21-2/29	1P: $145- 175	2P/1B: $145- 175	2P/2B: $145- 175	XP: $20	F12
3/28-4/10 & 11/26-12/17	1P: $123- 149	2P/1B: $123- 149	2P/2B: $123- 149	XP: $20	F12
4/11-11/25	1P: $72- 120	2P/1B: $72- 120	2P/2B: $72- 120	XP: $10	F12

Location: Jct of US 93/SR 487, 2.4 mi n on SR 487, 5.2 mi n at flashing light. 3840 Big Mountain Rd 59937 (PO Box 55). Fax: 406/862-0586. **Terms:** Check-in 4 pm; reserv deposit, 30 day notice; handling fee imposed; weekly/monthly rates, in summer; package plans. **Facility:** 5 rooms. Registration at Management Co office at 3840 Big Mountain Rd. Firplace, ski locker/dryer; ceiling fan & voicemail for each unit. 2 two-bedroom units, 2 three-bedroom units. 3 stories, no elevator; interior corridors; access to adjacent small indoor heated pool & whirlpool. **All Rooms:** kitchens, combo or shower baths, extended cable TV. **Cards:** AE, DS, MC, VI. *(See color ad below)*

BEST WESTERN ROCKY MOUNTAIN LODGE   **Phone:** (406)862-2569

7/1-8/31 & 12/17-1/2 [CP]	1P: $89- 159	2P/1B: $89- 159	2P/2B: $89- 159	XP: $10	F12
6/12-6/30 & 9/1-9/19 [CP]	1P: $79- 139	2P/1B: $79- 139	2P/2B: $79- 139	XP: $10	F12
3/1-4/11, 6/1-6/11 & 1/3-2/29					
[CP]	1P: $59- 99	2P/1B: $59- 99	2P/2B: $59- 99	XP: $10	F12
4/12-5/31 & 9/20-12/16 [CP]	1P: $49- 99	2P/1B: $49- 99	2P/2B: $49- 99	XP: $10	F12

Location: 1.3 mi s on US 93 from jct of SR 487. 6510 Hwy 93S 59937. Fax: 406/862-1154. **Terms:** Small pets only, $10 fee, in designated rooms. **Facility:** 79 rooms. Spacious rooms with a few smaller units avail. 2-3 stories; interior/exterior corridors; designated smoking area; heated pool, small heated pool, whirlpool. **Dining:** Restaurant nearby. **Services:** area transportation, Amtrak, by reservation. **All Rooms:** combo or shower baths, extended cable TV. **Some Rooms:** whirlpools. **Cards:** AE, CB, DI, DS, MC, VI. **Special Amenities:** Free breakfast and free local telephone calls.

BITTERROOT CONDOMINIUMS   Rates Subject to Change   **Phone:** (406)862-3687

12/18-1/2 & 2/12-2/20	1P: $271- 293	2P/1B: $271- 293	2P/2B: $271- 293	XP: $20	
3/1-3/27, 1/3-2/11 &					
2/21-2/29	1P: $190- 205	2P/1B: $190- 205	2P/2B: $190- 205	XP: $20	F12
3/28-4/10 & 11/26-12/17	1P: $162- 174	2P/1B: $162- 174	2P/2B: $162- 174	XP: $20	F12
4/11-11/25	1P: $97- 135	2P/1B: $97- 135	2P/2B: $97- 135	XP: $10	F12

Location: Jct of US 93 & SR 487, 2.4 mi n on SR 487, 5.2 mi n at flashing light. 3860 Gelande St 59937 (PO Box 55). Fax: 406/862-0586. **Terms:** Check-in 4 pm; reserv deposit, 30 day notice; handling fee imposed. **Facility:** 11 rooms. Registration at Management Co office at 3840 Big Mountain Rd. Gas fireplace, ski locker/ dryer, washer/dryer & voicemail for each unit. two-bedroom units. 4 stories, no elevator; interior corridors; smoke free premises. **Services:** winter plug-ins. **All Rooms:** kitchens. **Cards:** AE, DS, MC, VI.

CHALET MOTEL   Rates Subject to Change   **Phone:** (406)862-5581

6/15-9/30 & 12/23-1/5	1P: $73	2P/1B: $84	2P/2B: $84	XP: $5	F11
3/1-6/14, 10/1-12/22 &					
1/6-2/29	1P: $37	2P/1B: $45	2P/2B: $45	XP: $5	F11

Location: 1 mi n on US 93 from jct SR 40. 6430 US 93S 59937. Fax: 406/862-5581. **Terms:** Pets, $5 extra charge; limited rooms. **Facility:** 33 rooms. Contemporary; park at some rooms. 2 stories; exterior corridors; designated smoking area; small heated indoor pool, whirlpool. **Dining:** Restaurant nearby. **Services:** winter plug-ins. **All Rooms:** combo or shower baths, extended cable TV. **Cards:** AE, DS, MC, VI.

DUCK INN LODGE   Rates Subject to Change   **Phone:** (406)862-3825
All Year [CP]   1P: $59- 89   2P/1B: $59- 89   2P/2B: $59- 89   XP: $5-10
Location: 1.5 mi n on US 93 of jct SR 40, just e at Columbia Ave (Conoco Station). 1305 Columbia Ave 59937. **Terms:** Check-in 4 pm; reserv deposit, 7 day notice. **Facility:** 10 rooms. Quiet setting on Whitefish River & most rooms with fireplace, balcony & mountain views. 2 stories; interior corridors; designated smoking area. **Services:** area transportation. **Cards:** AE, CB, DI, DS, JC, MC, VI. *(See color ad p 260)*

EDELWEISS CONDOMINIUMS
◆◆   11/20-2/29   Rates Subject to Change   **Phone:** 406/862-52▮
Condominium   3/1-11/19   1P: $140- 205   2P/1B: $140- 205   2P/2B: $203- 300
                              1P: $77- 95   2P/1B: $77- 95   2P/2B: $95- 117
Location: US 93 & SR 487; 2.4 mi n on SR 487; 5.2 mi n. 3898 Big Mountain Rd 59937 (PO Box 84▮
Fax: 406/862-3009. **Terms:** Check-in 4 pm; reserv deposit, 30 day notice, in season, 14 day for off season. **Facility:** 47 room▮
Ski-in condo's in the base area of Big Mountain ski resort with excellent view. 15 two-bedroom units. 3 night min stay,
season; 2 night min stay, off season; 3 stories; interior/exterior corridors; 2 tennis courts. **Recreation:** fishing; ice skatir▮
tobogganing; bicycles, hiking trails, jogging. Fee: downhill & cross country skiing, snowmobiling; horseback ridir▮
All Rooms: kitchens. **Cards:** AE, DS, MC, VI.

GOOD MEDICINE LODGE
(AAA)   All Year [BP]   1P: $75- 105   2P/1B: $95- 145   2P/2B: $95- 115   XP: $30   F
            Location: Jct US 93 & SR 487, 0.5 mi n on SR 487. 537 Wisconsin Ave 59937. Fax: 406/862-548▮
◆◆◆   **Terms:** Reserv deposit, 14 day notice. **Facility:** 9 rooms. Cozy cedar lodge located on road to Big Mounta▮
Bed &   with custom made lodge pole beds, many with balcony & all with ceiling fan or a/c. 2 stories; interior corrido▮
Breakfast   designated smoking area; whirlpool. **Services:** Fee: area transportation, train & ski area. **Recreation:** ▮
            room with boot & glove dryer. **All Rooms:** combo or shower baths. **Cards:** AE, DS, MC, VI.

GROUSE MOUNTAIN LODGE
◆◆◆   6/1-10/31, 12/19-1/1 &   Rates Subject to Change   **Phone:** (406)862-30▮
Lodge   2/11-2/29   1P: $140- 190   2P/1B: $140- 190   2P/2B: $140- 190   XP: $10   F
            3/1-3/28 & 1/2-2/10   1P: $92- 162   2P/1B: $92- 162   2P/2B: $92- 162   XP: $10   F
            3/29-5/31 & 11/1-12/18   1P: $72- 162   2P/1B: $72- 162   2P/2B: $72- 162   XP: $10   F
Location: 1 mi w on US 93 from jct of SR 487. 2 Fairway Dr 59937. Fax: 406/862-0326. **Terms:** Check-in 4 pm; rese▮
deposit, 3 day notice. **Facility:** 145 rooms. Unique room styles offered in scenic resort property adjacent to golf course.
two-bedroom units. 3 stories; interior corridors; mountain view; heated indoor pool. **Services:** giftshop; area transportatic▮
winter plug-ins. **Some Rooms:** 10 kitchens. **Cards:** AE, CB, DS, MC, VI.

KANDAHAR LODGE
Phone: (406)862-6098

	1P	2P/1B	2P/2B	XP
12/17-1/8 & 2/11-2/29	1P: $139- 151	2P/1B: $151- 312	2P/2B: $151- 312	XP: $12
3/1-3/25 & 1/9-2/10	1P: $127- 151	2P/1B: $139- 275	2P/2B: $139- 275	XP: $12
3/26-12/16	1P: $125- 139	2P/1B: $125- 199	2P/2B: $125- 199	XP: $12

Lodge
Location: Jct of US 93 & SR 487; 2.4 mi n on SR 487, 5.2 mi n at flashing light. 3824 Big Mountain Rd 59937 (PO Box 1659). Fax: 406/862-6095. **Terms:** Check-in 4 pm; reserv deposit, 30 day notice. **Facility:** 48 rooms. Spacious rooms in a mountain retreat nestled in the trees. Closed 4/10-5/27 & 10/24-11/24. 16 kitchens, $10 extra charge; 4 stories, no elevator; interior corridors; sauna, steamroom, whirlpool. **Dining:** Restaurant; 7:30 am-10:30 & 5:30-9:30 pm; closed 4/19-5/20 & 10/10-11/20; $12-$20; cocktails. **Services:** area transportation, ski area, in winter. **Recreation:** ski in & out; bicycles, hiking trails. Fee: downhill & cross country skiing. **All Rooms:** extended cable TV. **Cards:** AE, DS, MC, VI. **Special Amenities:** Free local telephone calls. (See ad p 260)

KRISTIANNA CONDOMINIUMS
Phone: (406)862-2860

	1P	2P/1B	2P/2B	XP	
12/18-1/2 & 2/12-2/20	1P: $300- 660	2P/1B: $300- 660	2P/2B: $300- 660	XP: $20	F12
3/1-4/11, 11/25-12/17,					
1/3-2/11 & 2/21-2/29	1P: $225- 660	2P/1B: $225- 660	2P/2B: $225- 660	XP: $20	F12
7/1-9/4	1P: $135- 325	2P/1B: $135- 325	2P/2B: $135- 325	XP: $10	F12
4/12-6/30 & 9/5-11/24	1P: $125- 325	2P/1B: $125- 325	2P/2B: $125- 325	XP: $10	F12

Condominium
Location: Jct of US 93 & SR 487; 2.4 mi n on SR 487, at flashing light go 5.2 mi on Big Mountain Rd, just n on Gelande, just w on Kristanna Close. 3842 Winter Lane 59937 (PO Box 1545). Fax: 406/862-0782. **Terms:** Check-in 4 pm; reserv deposit, 30 day notice; handling fee imposed; weekly rates. **Facility:** 9 rooms. Swiss style 2 story condo unit, with 2.5 baths, on Big Mountain. In quiet alpine setting with separate sleeping & living levels with wood stove. 7 two-bedroom units, 2 three-bedroom units. Max occupancy: 2 bedroom-8 persons (over 4 persons, $10-$20 extra charge), 3 bedroom-10 persons (over 6 persons, $10-$20 extra charge). Handling f; 4 stories, no elevator; interior/exterior corridors; designated smoking area; mountain view; sauna, whirlpool. **Dining:** Restaurant nearby. **Services:** winter plug-ins. **Recreation:** adjacent to Chair 3 with ski in/ski out access; hiking trails, mountain biking trails. Fee: downhill & cross country skiing, snowmobiling; horseback riding. **All Rooms:** kitchens, extended cable TV. **Cards:** AE, DS, MC, VI. **Special Amenities:** Free local telephone calls.

LA VILLA MONTANA BED & BREAKFAST
Rates Subject to Change
Phone: 406-863-9339

	1P	2P/1B	2P/2B	XP
5/1-10/1 [BP]	1P: $75- 90	2P/1B: $95- 125	2P/2B: $95- 125	XP: $25
3/1-4/30 & 10/2-2/29 [BP]	1P: $65- 85	2P/1B: $85- 115	2P/2B: $85- 115	XP: $25

Bed & Breakfast
Location: 2.8 mi e on SR 40 from jct of US 93. 3800 SR 40 W 59937 (PO Box 4390). Fax: 406/892-0690. **Terms:** Age restrictions may apply; check-in 4 pm; reserv deposit, 14 day notice; handling fee imposed. **Facility:** 4 rooms. Spacious air conditioned chalet with Western decor in valley setting with panoramic mountain views; signature breakfast. 2 stories; interior/exterior corridors; smoke free premises. **Services:** winter plug-ins. **All Rooms:** combo or shower baths. **Cards:** AE, MC, VI.

LOTUS CONDOMINIUM
Rates Subject to Change
Phone: (406)862-3687

	1P	2P/1B	2P/2B	XP	
12/18-1/2 & 2/12-2/20	1P: $336	2P/1B: $336	2P/2B: $336	XP: $20	F12
3/1-3/27, 1/3-2/11 & 2/21-2/29	1P: $235	2P/1B: $235	2P/2B: $235	XP: $20	F12
3/28-4/10 & 11/26-12/17	1P: $200	2P/1B: $200	2P/2B: $200	XP: $20	F12
4/11-11/25	1P: $111- 155	2P/1B: $111- 155	2P/2B: $111- 155	XP: $20	F12

Condominium
Location: Jct of US 93 & SR 487; 2.4 mi n on SR 487, 5.2 mi n at flashing light. 3858 Winter Ln 59937 (PO Box 55). Fax: 406/862-0586. **Terms:** Check-in 4 pm; reserv deposit, 30 day notice; handling fee imposed. **Facility:** 5 rooms. Registration at Management Co office at 3840 Big Mountain Rd. Parking garage. Heated ski locker, voice mail for each unit. Fireplace in all units. 2 two-bedroom units, 3 three-bedroom units. 3 stories, no elevator; interior corridors. **Services:** winter plug-ins. **All Rooms:** kitchens. **Cards:** AE, DS, MC, VI.

NORTH FORTY RESORT
Guaranteed Rates
Phone: (406)862-7740

	1P	2P/1B	2P/2B	XP	
6/11-9/19 & 12/18-1/4	1P: $105- 125	2P/1B: $105- 125	2P/2B: $105- 125	XP: $10	F13
3/1-6/10, 9/20-12/17 & 1/5-2/29	1P: $59- 89	2P/1B: $59- 89	2P/2B: $59- 89	XP: $10	F13

Cottage
Location: 2.5 mi e on SR 40 from jct of US 93. 3765 Hwy 40W 59912 (PO Box 4250, 59903). Fax: 406/862-7741. **Terms:** Check-in 4 pm; reserv deposit, 14 day notice. **Facility:** 22 rooms. Cabins in 40 acre secluded wooded setting with paved parking at each cabin, gas log fireplace; all with 2 phones & 2 TV's. 8 two-bedroom units. 1 story; exterior corridors; designated smoking area; sauna, whirlpools. **Services:** winter plug-ins. **Recreation:** hiking trails. **All Rooms:** efficiencies, extended cable TV. **Cards:** AE, DS, MC, VI.

QUALITY INN PINE LODGE
Phone: (406)862-7600

	1P	2P/1B	2P/2B
All Year [CP]	1P: $53- 108	2P/1B: $63- 118	2P/2B: $63- 118

Motel
Location: 1 mi s on US 93. 920 Spokane Ave 59937. Fax: 406/862-7616. **Terms:** Check-in 4 pm; pets. **Facility:** 76 rooms. Adjacent to Whitefish River with spacious rooms & some river view rooms with balcony. 3 stories; interior corridors; designated smoking area; small heated indoor/outdoor pool, whirlpool. **Services:** winter plug-ins. **All Rooms:** combo or shower baths, extended cable TV. **Some Rooms:** 2 kitchens, whirlpools. **Cards:** AE, CB, DI, DS, MC, VI. **Special Amenities:** Free breakfast and free local telephone calls.

SHERPA CONDOMINIUMS
Rates Subject to Change
Phone: (406)862-3687

	1P	2P/1B	2P/2B	XP	
12/18-1/2 & 2/12-2/20	1P: $171- 207	2P/1B: $171- 207	2P/2B: $320- 336	XP: $20	F12
3/1-3/27, 1/3-2/11 & 2/21-2/29	1P: $120- 145	2P/1B: $120- 145	2P/2B: $224- 235	XP: $20	F12
3/28-4/10 & 11/26-12/17	1P: $102- 123	2P/1B: $102- 123	2P/2B: $192- 200	XP: $20	F12
4/11-11/25	1P: $65- 100	2P/1B: $65- 100	2P/2B: $104- 155	XP: $10	F12

Condominium
Location: Jct of US 93 & SR 487; 2.4 mi n on SR 487, 5.2 mi n at flashing light. 3832 Big Mountain Rd 59937 (PO Box 55). Fax: 406/862-0586. **Terms:** Check-in 4 pm; reserv deposit, 30 day notice; handling fee imposed. **Facility:** 10 rooms. Registration at Management Co office at 3840 Big Mountain Rd. Parking garage. Wood burning fireplace, heated ski locker, voice mail & washer/dryer for each unit. 6 two-bedroom units, 2 three-bedroom units. 3 stories, no elevator; interior corridors; small heated indoor pool. **Services:** winter plug-ins. **All Rooms:** kitchens. **Cards:** AE, DS, MC, VI.

SUPER 8 MOTEL   Phone: 406/862-825

AAA SAVE
◆◆
Motel

7/2-8/28 [CP]	1P: $75	2P/1B: $80	2P/2B: $80	XP: $5	F1
6/12-7/1 [CP]	1P: $50	2P/1B: $55	2P/2B: $55	XP: $5	F1
8/29-9/30 [CP]	1P: $45	2P/1B: $50	2P/2B: $50	XP: $5	F1
3/1-6/11 & 10/1-2/29 [CP]	1P: $37- 40	2P/1B: $42- 45	2P/2B: $42- 45	XP: $5	F1

Location: 1 mi s on US 93 from jct of SR 487. 800 Spokane Ave 59937. Fax: 406/862-8255. **Terms:** Pet $5 extra charge. **Facility:** 40 rooms. Adjacent to Whitefish River with contemporary large rooms. 2 stories; interior corridor designated smoking area; whirlpool. **Services:** winter plug-ins. **All Rooms:** extended cable TV. **Cards:** AE, DI, DS, MC, VI

SWANSON'S CONDOMINIUM   Rates Subject to Change   Phone: (406)862-368
◆◆◆
Condominium

12/18-1/2 & 2/12-2/20	1P: $207	2P/1B: $207	2P/2B: $364	XP: $20	F1
3/1-3/29, 1/3-2/11 & 2/21-2/29	1P: $145	2P/1B: $145	2P/2B: $255	XP: $20	F1
3/30-4/10 & 11/26-12/17	1P: $123	2P/1B: $123	2P/2B: $217	XP: $20	F1
4/11-11/25	1P: $97- 135	2P/1B: $97- 135	2P/2B: $111- 155	XP: $10	F1

Location: Jct of US 93 & SR 487, 2.4 mi n on SR 487, 5.2 mi n at flashing light. 3835 Alpine Glow Ave 59937 (PO Box 58 Fax: 406/862-0586. **Terms:** Check-in 4 pm; reserv deposit, 30 day notice; handling fee imposed. **Facility:** 4 rooms. Registration at Management Co office at 3840 Big Mountain Rd. Fireplace, ski locker & voice mail for each unit. 2 three-bedroom unit 2 stories, no elevator; interior/exterior corridors; smoke free premises. **Cards:** AE, DS, MC, VI. combo or shower baths.

WHITEFISH LAKE LODGE   Phone: (406)862-292
AAA SAVE
◆◆◆
Complex

6/11-9/6 & 12/17-2/29 3/1-3/31, 5/14-6/10 &	1P: $85- 200	2P/1B: $85- 200	2P/2B: $200- 260		
9/7-9/30	1P: $75- 150	2P/1B: $75- 150	2P/2B: $150- 190		
4/1-5/13 & 10/1-12/16	1P: $65- 125	2P/1B: $65- 125	2P/2B: $125- 170		

Location: Jct US 93 & SR 487, 1.5 mi n on SR 487. 1400 Wisconsin Ave 59937 (1399 Wisconsin Ave Fax: 406/862-3550. **Terms:** Check-in 4 pm; reserv deposit, 45 day notice; handling fee imposed; weekly/monthly rates, r monthly 7/1-8/31. **Facility:** 32 rooms. Contemporary appealing condos & most with fireplace & private balcony overlookir Whitefish Lake. Motel rooms without kitchens, balcony & fireplace also avail. 23 two-bedroom units, 9 three-bedroom units. stories; exterior corridors; designated smoking area; beach, heated pool, whirlpools; boat dock. **Dining:** Restaurant nearb **Services:** winter plug-ins. **Recreation:** swimming, fishing, waterskiing. Fee: pontoons, waverunners, water ski equipmer Rental: boats, canoes, paddleboats. **All Rooms:** kitchens, extended cable TV. **Cards:** MC, VI.

RESTAURANTS

LOGAN'S   Lunch: $7-$12   Dinner: $12-$21   Phone: 406/862-300
◆◆◆
Continental

Location: 1 mi w on US 93 from jct of SR 487; in Grouse Mountain Lodge. 2 Fairway Dr 59937. **Hours:** am-2 & 5:30-9:30 pm. **Reservations:** suggested. **Features:** casual dress; children's menu; cocktails lounge. Fine dining in a mountain resort atmosphere. **Cards:** AE, DI, DS, MC, VI.

POLLO GRILL   Dinner: $8-$14   Phone: 406/863-940
◆◆
American

Location: 2 mi n on Wisconsin Ave; following signs to Big Mountain Rd. 1705 Wisconsin Ave 5993 **Hours:** 5 pm-10 pm. Closed: 11/25. **Reservations:** suggested. **Features:** casual dress; children's men beer & wine only; a la carte. Variety of entrees, many prepared on rotisserie grill. Casual rural settin Smoke free premises. **Cards:** AE, DS, MC, VI.

WHITE SULPHUR SPRINGS—1,000

LODGING

FOXWOOD INN   Rates Subject to Change   Phone: 406/547-222
◆◆
Historic Bed & Breakfast

All Year [BP]   1P: $42   2P/1B: $52   2P/2B: $56   XP: $10   F

Location: US 12 & US 89, w on SR 360 0.3 mi, just s on SW 10th Ave, 0.5 mi w on gravel road. 52 Mille Rd 59645 (PO Box 368). Fax: 406/547-3380. **Terms:** Check-in 4 pm; reserv deposit. **Facility:** 14 room Quaint home built in 1890. Cozy guest rooms. 1 two-bedroom unit. 2 stories; interior corridors; designate smoking area. **Cards:** DS, MC, VI.

Wyoming

AFTON—1,400

LODGINGS

BEST WESTERN HI COUNTRY INN   Phone: (307)886-38
(AAA) (SAVE)   All Year   1P: $45   2P/1B: $50   2P/2B: $55   XP: $5
◆◆◆   **Location:** 0.8 mi s on US 89. 689 S Washington 83110-0907 (PO Box 0907). Fax: 307/886-93
Motel   unit. 1 story; exterior corridors; mountain view; heated pool, whirlpool. **Dining:** Restaurant nea
Services: winter plug-ins. **Recreation:** cross country skiing, snowmobiling. **All Rooms:** extended cable
Cards: AE, CB, DI, DS, MC, VI. **Special Amenities: Free local telephone calls and free newspaper.** Best West
Motels.

THE CORRAL   Guaranteed Rates   Phone: 307/886-54
◆◆   4/15-11/1   1P: $35   2P/1B: $40   2P/2B: $50   XP: $5
Cottage   **Location:** City center; on US 89. 161 Washington 83110 (PO Box 442). Fax: 307/886-5464. **Terms:** O
4/15-11/1; reserv deposit. **Facility:** 15 rooms. Charming small log cabins built in the 1940's & maintaine
pristine condition. Well cared for grounds. 4 two-bedroom units. 2 efficiencies, $5 extra charge; no utensils; 1 story; exte
corridors; smoke free premises. **All Rooms:** combo or shower baths. **Cards:** AE, CB, DI, DS, MC, VI.

MOUNTAIN INN   Rates Subject to Change   Phone: 307/886-31
◆◆   5/15-9/15   1P: $45- 55   2P/1B: $50- 60   2P/2B: $55- 65   XP: $5
Motel   3/1-5/14 & 9/16-2/29   1P: $45- 50   2P/1B: $50- 55   2P/2B: $50- 55   XP: $5
Location: 1.5 mi s on US 89. 83542 Hwy 89 83110. **Facility:** 20 rooms. Large comfortable rooms. 1 story;
terior corridors; heated pool. **Services:** winter plug-ins. **All Rooms:** combo or shower baths. **Cards:** AE, CB, DI, DS, .
MC, VI.

ALPINE—200

LODGINGS

ALPEN HAUS HOTEL & RESORT   Phone: (307)654-75
(AAA) (SAVE)   All Year [BP]   1P: $42- 109   2P/1B: $55- 120   2P/2B: $67- 120   XP: $7-15
◆◆   **Location:** Jct US 26 & 89. 50 W US Hwy 26 83128 (PO Box 3250). Fax: 307/654-7287. **Terms:** Check-i
Motor Inn   pm; weekly/monthly rates, off season; package plans; small pets only, $10 extra charge. **Facility:** 45 roor
European style inn. Some large rooms. 3 stories; interior corridors; designated smoking area; whirlpool; pl
ground. **Dining:** Restaurant; 6:30 am-9:30 pm, ice cream shop, in summer; $8-$15; cockta
Recreation: horseshoe pits, horse corrals. Fee: horseback riding in summer. **All Rooms:** combo or shower bat
Cards: AE, CB, DI, DS, MC, VI. **Special Amenities: Free breakfast and free local telephone calls.**
(See color ad below)

EST WESTERN FLYING SADDLE LODGE   Rates Subject to Change   **Phone:** (307)654-7561
5/27-10/1   1P: $60- 160   2P/1B: $60- 160   2P/2B: $65- 135   XP: $10   F
Location: 0.5 mi e of jct US 26 & 89. 118878 Jct US 26 & 89 83128 (PO Box 3227). Fax: 307/654-7563.
Terms: Open 5/27-10/1; reserv deposit; handling fee imposed. **Facility:** 26 rooms. Superbly decorated & finely
otor Inn   appointed rooms & cottage suites. Wildlife routinely visits property. River view. 1 story; exterior corridors; des-
♦♦♦   ignated smoking area; mountain view; heated pool, whirlpools; 1 tennis court. **Dining:** $10-$32; cocktails;
ning room, see separate listing. **Recreation:** charter fishing, fishing; hiking trails, jogging. **Some Rooms:** whirlpools.
ards: AE, CB, DI, DS, JC, MC, VI. *(See color ad below)*   🛗 📶 🏊 ⛽ 🍴 🛎 🅿️ ✖️ 🎾 VCR 🖥️ 🔌 ✖️

RESTAURANTS

HE FLYING SADDLE LODGE DINING ROOM   **Dinner:** $10-$32   **Phone:** 307/654-7561
Location: 0.5 mi e of jct US 26 & 89; in the Best Western Flying Saddle Lodge. Jct US 26 & 89 83128.
Hours: Open 5/27-10/1; 7 am-11 & 5-10 pm. **Reservations:** suggested. **Features:** casual dress; children's
merican   menu; senior's menu; health conscious menu; carryout; cocktails. Small intimate dining room with player
piano. Smoke free premises. **Cards:** AE, CB, DI, DS, JC, MC, VI. *(See color ad below)*   ♿ ✖️

UNNAR'S PIZZA   **Lunch:** $5-$8   **Dinner:** $5-$8   **Phone:** 307/654-7778
Location: Center. SR #89 83128. **Hours:** 11 am-10 pm. **Features:** casual dress; carryout; beer only.
merican   Wonderful bread, salad, soup & subs. Smoke free premises.   ✖️

ALTA—300

LODGING

RAND TARGHEE RESORT   **Phone:** (307)353-2300
3/1-3/19   1P: $109- 213   2P/1B: $109- 213   2P/2B: $109- 405   XP: $11-25   F14
3/20-6/10   1P: $65- 266   2P/1B: $65- 266   2P/2B: $65- 329   XP: $10-15   F14
7/1-2/29   1P: $84- 225   2P/1B: $84- 225   2P/2B: $84- 225
esort Lodge   6/11-6/30   1P: $65- 176   2P/1B: $65- 176   2P/2B: $65- 176
Location: 12 mi e on Little Ave; following signs. (PO Box SKI, 83422). Fax: 307/353-8148. **Terms:** Reserv
eposit, 30 day notice, in winter; package plans. **Facility:** 96 rooms. In Targhee National Forest at the base of Grand Targhee
ki Area. Family oriented. Closed 9/6-11/18 & 4/11-6/10. Adobe style fireplaces in apartments. 16 two-bedroom units. Apartment units avail for up to 8 persons, 3 night min stay; 2-4 stories, no elevator; interior/exterior corridors; designated smoking
rea; mountain view; small heated pool, sauna, whirlpools; 2 tennis courts. **Dining:** Dining room, 2 restaurants, 2 cafeterias;
am-10 pm; $7-$14; cocktails; entertainment 11/20-4/12. **Services:** giftshop. Fee: massage. **Recreation:** cross country
kiing; hiking trails, climbing wall. Fee: children, nature & recreation programs; downhill skiing, dog sledding, snowboarding;
icycles, horseback riding, yoga classes, sleighride & Dutch oven cook-out's. **All Rooms:** combo or shower baths, extended
able TV. **Some Rooms:** 32 efficiencies. **Cards:** AE, DS, MC, VI. **Special Amenities:** Free local telephone calls.
🆓 🛗 🏊 🍴 ⛽ 🐾 🅿️ ✖️ 🛗 VCR 🖥️ 🎾 ✖️

BIG HORN—200

LODGING

PAHN'S BIG HORN MOUNTAIN BED & BREAKFAST LLC   Rates Subject to Change   **Phone:** 307/674-8150
6/20-8/20 [BP]   1P: $90- 140   2P/1B: $90- 140   2P/2B: $90- 140   XP: $25
5/20-6/19 & 8/21-10/19 [BP]   1P: $85- 120   2P/1B: $85- 120   2P/2B: $85- 120   XP: $15
ed &   4/1-5/19 & 10/20-11/1 [BP]   1P: $75- 100   2P/1B: $75- 100   2P/2B: $75- 100   XP: $15
reakfast   **Location:** 6 mi w of Big Horn, last 1.4 mi on gravel road; in the Big Horn Mountains (call for directions). 70
Upper Hideaway Ln 82833 (PO Box 579). **Terms:** Open 4/1-11/1; check-in 4 pm; reserv deposit, 21 day notice. **Facility:** 5
ooms. Advance reservations strongly advised. 3 rooms in contemporary log house & 2 cabin units; 1 reached only by hiking
.1 mi. Excellent views, binoculars served with breakfast. 1 two-bedroom unit. Depending on road conditions, open in winter;
-4 stories; interior/exterior corridors; smoke free premises; valley view. **All Rooms:** shower baths. **Some Rooms:** kitchen.
📺 🅿️ 🔌 🔌 ✖️

BUFFALO—3,300

LODGINGS

ARROWHEAD MOTEL
Rates Subject to Change
Phone: (307)684-94█

6/15-8/31	1P:	$34-	40	2P/1B:	$36-	40	2P/2B:	$42-	60	XP: $5	D█
3/1-6/14 & 9/1-10/31	1P:	$30-	36	2P/1B:	$30-	36	2P/2B:	$38-	50	XP: $3	D█
11/1-2/29	1P:	$24		2P/1B:	$28		2P/2B:	$36		XP: $3	D█

Motel   **Location:** Jct US 16, 87 & Business Loop 75, 0.6 mi w. 749 Fort St 82834. **Terms:** Weekly/monthly rates, winter; pets, $5 extra charge. **Facility:** 13 rooms. Budget oriented, clean rooms. 4 efficiencies, $5 extra charg█ 1 story; exterior corridors; designated smoking area. **Dining:** Restaurant nearby. **Services:** winter plug-in█ **All Rooms:** combo or shower baths. **Some Rooms:** 4 efficiencies. **Cards:** DS, MC, VI.

BIG HORN MOTEL
Rates Subject to Change
Phone: 307/684-782█

7/1-10/31	1P:	$46-	54	2P/1B:	$48-	58	2P/2B:	$62-	72	XP: $4
4/16-6/30	1P:	$34-	44	2P/1B:	$36-	48	2P/2B:	$48-	60	XP: $4
3/14/15 & 11/1-2/29	1P:	$32-	38	2P/1B:	$34-	40	2P/2B:	$40-	46	XP: $4

Motel   **Location:** On US 16, downtown. 209 N Main St 82834. **Facility:** 20 rooms. Very clean rooms. 1 story; exterior corridors; de█ ignated smoking area. **All Rooms:** combo or shower baths. **Cards:** AE, DI, DS, MC, VI.

CANYON MOTEL
Phone: (307)684-295█

5/15-10/31	1P:	$36		2P/1B:	$38-	42	2P/2B:	$42-	50	XP: $3
3/1-5/14 & 11/1-2/29	1P:	$30-	34	2P/1B:	$30-	36	2P/2B:	$38-	48	XP: $3

Motel   **Location:** Jct US 16/87/Business Loop 25, 0.9 mi w on US 16. 997 Fort St 82834 (PO Box 5█ **Terms:** Weekly rates; pets, $3 extra charge. **Facility:** 18 rooms. Very clean rooms. 2 two-bedroom units. mini-refrigerators avail; 1 story; exterior corridors. **Services:** winter plug-ins. **All Rooms:** combo or show█ baths. **Some Rooms:** 2 efficiencies, kitchen, no utensils. **Cards:** AE, DS, MC, VI. **Special Amenities:** Free local telepho█ **calls and preferred room (subject to availability with advanced reservations).**

CLOUD PEAK INN BED & BREAKFAST
Guaranteed Rates
Phone: (307)684-579█

5/15-9/15 [BP]	1P:	$50-	70	2P/1B:	$60-	80	2P/2B:	$60	XP: $5
3/1-5/14 & 9/16-2/29 [BP]	1P:	$40-	60	2P/1B:	$50-	70	2P/2B:	$50	XP: $5

Bed &   **Location:** Jct US 16, 87 & Business Loop 25, just w on Fort St, 0.4 mi n. 590 N Burritt 8283█
Breakfast   Fax: 307/684-7653. **Terms:** Check-in 5 pm; reserv deposit, 3 day notice. **Facility:** 5 rooms. Located in res█ residential area. Various sized very clean rooms. 2 stories; interior corridors; smoke free premises. **Services:** wint█ plug-ins. **Cards:** AE, MC, VI.

COMFORT INN
Rates Subject to Change
Phone: (307)684-956█

7/1-8/15 [CP]	1P:	$85-	110	2P/1B:	$85-	110	2P/2B:	$85-	110	XP: $5	F█
5/20-6/30 [CP]	1P:	$55-	75	2P/1B:	$55-	75	2P/2B:	$55-	75	XP: $5	F█
8/16-10/31 [CP]	1P:	$45-	65	2P/1B:	$45-	65	2P/2B:	$45-	65	XP: $5	F█
3/1-5/19 & 11/1-2/29 [CP]	1P:	$40-	50	2P/1B:	$40-	50	2P/2B:	$40-	50	XP: $5	F█

Motel   **Location:** US 16, just e of I-25, exit 299; 1.3 mi w of I-90, exit 58. 65 Hwy 16E 82834. Fax: 307/684-9564. **Facility:** 41 room█ Exceptional housekeeping. 2 stories; interior/exterior corridors; designated smoking area. **Services:** winter plug-in█ **Cards:** AE, CB, DI, DS, JC, MC, VI.

HISTORIC MANSION HOUSE INN AND MOTEL
Phone: (307)684-221█

6/15-8/31 [CP]	1P:	$45	2P/1B:	$60	2P/2B:	$64	XP: $4	F█
5/15-6/14 & 9/1-10/31 [CP]	1P:	$38	2P/1B:	$46	2P/2B:	$50	XP: $4	F█
3/1-5/14 & 11/1-2/29 [CP]	1P:	$30	2P/1B:	$38	2P/2B:	$42	XP: $4	F█

Motel   **Location:** US 16, downtown. 313 N Main St 82834. **Terms:** Check-in 4 pm. **Facility:** 18 rooms. Rooms house built in 1903 & adjacent motel section. 1-2 stories; interior/exterior corridors; designated smoking are█ **Dining:** Restaurant nearby. **Services:** winter plug-ins. **All Rooms:** combo or shower baths. **Cards:** DS, MC, █ **Special Amenities: Free breakfast and free local telephone calls.** (See color ad below)

SUPER 8 MOTEL OF BUFFALO
Phone: (307)684-253█

6/1-8/31 [BP]	1P:	$65	2P/1B:	$65	2P/2B:	$70	XP: $6
9/1-10/26 [BP]	1P:	$50	2P/1B:	$50	2P/2B:	$54	XP: $6
5/1-5/31 [BP]	1P:	$46	2P/1B:	$46	2P/2B:	$51	XP: $6
3/1-4/30 & 10/27-2/29 [EP]	1P:	$40	2P/1B:	$40	2P/2B:	$46	XP: $6

Motel   **Location:** Just w of I-25, exit 299; on US 16, 1.3 mi w of I-90, exit 58. 655 E Hart St 8283█ Fax: 317/684-7954. **Terms:** Pets, $5.25 extra charge. **Facility:** 50 rooms. Very good housekeeping. 2 two-bedroom units. █ stories; interior corridors; designated smoking area. **Fee:** miniature golf. **Dining:** Restaurant nearby. **Services:** wint█ plug-ins. **All Rooms:** extended cable TV. **Some Rooms:** color TV. **Cards:** AE, DI, DS, MC, VI. **Special Amenities: Fr█ breakfast and free local telephone calls.** (See color ad p 267)

WYOMING MOTEL   Rates Subject to Change   Phone: (307)684-5505

	6/7-8/20	1P: $62- 67	2P/1B: $62- 67	2P/2B: $65- 89	XP: $8
	5/1-6/6 & 8/21-9/30	1P: $36- 51	2P/1B: $36- 51	2P/2B: $43- 75	XP: $8
	3/1-4/30 & 10/1-2/29	1P: $22- 38	2P/1B: $22- 38	2P/2B: $30- 55	XP: $8

Motel   **Location:** US 16, just w of I-25, exit 299; 1.3 mi w of I-90, exit 58. 610 E Hart St 82834. Fax: 307/684-5442.
Terms: Weekly rates, off season; pets. **Facility:** 27 rooms. Comfortable, modern rooms. 5 large units with ef-
ficiencies, $75-$145; 1 story; exterior corridors; designated smoking area; small heated pool, whirlpool; playground.
Dining: Restaurant nearby. **Services:** winter plug-ins. **All Rooms:** extended cable TV. **Some Rooms:** 5 efficiencies.
Cards: AE, DI, DS, MC, VI. *(See color ad below)*

Z-BAR MOTEL IMA   Phone: 307/684-5535

	6/11-9/30	1P: $45- 54	2P/1B: $49- 58	2P/2B: $54- 63	XP: $4	D10
	10/1-11/15	1P: $43- 52	2P/1B: $47- 56	2P/2B: $52- 61	XP: $4	D10
	5/21-6/10	1P: $42- 51	2P/1B: $46- 55	2P/2B: $50- 59	XP: $4	D10
Cottage	3/1-5/20 & 11/16-2/29	1P: $32- 40	2P/1B: $36- 44	2P/2B: $42- 50	XP: $4	D10

Location: Jct US 16, 87 & Business Loop 25, 0.5 mi w on US 16. 626 Fort St 82834. Fax: 307/684-5538.
Terms: Reserv deposit; pets, $4 extra charge. **Facility:** 20 rooms. Modern Western style log cabins. 6 kitchen units, $5 extra
charge; 1 story; exterior corridors; designated smoking area. **Dining:** Restaurant nearby. **Services:** winter plug-ins.
All Rooms: extended cable TV. **Cards:** AE, DI, DS, MC, VI. IMA. *(See color ad p 320 & below)*

RESTAURANTS

COLONEL BOZEMAN'S
AAA

♦♦
American

Lunch: $3-$14   **Dinner:** $3-$14   Phone: 307/684-555
Location: Just w of I-25, exit 299. 655 E Hart 82834. **Hours:** 6 am-10 pm; 7 am-9 pm, 10/1-5/31. Close
12/25. **Features:** casual dress; children's menu; carryout; cocktails & lounge. Family oriented. Western
Plains Indian decor. **Cards:** AE, CB, DI, DS, MC, VI. *(See color ad p 267)*

THE STAGECOACH INN
AAA

♦♦
American

Lunch: $5-$9   **Dinner:** $10-$20   Phone: 307/684-250
Location: 0.8 mi w on US 16. 845 Fort St 82834. **Hours:** 11:30 am-2 & 5-9 pm, Sat from 5 pm. Closed
12/25, Sun; Mon 12/1-5/31. **Reservations:** suggested. **Features:** casual dress; children's menu; cocktails
lounge. Hearty, casual dining in Western atmosphere. Very popular & family operated. **Cards:** DS, MC, VI.

CASPER—46,700

LODGINGS

BEST WESTERN CASPER
AAA [SAVE]

Motel

Phone: (307)234-354

	1P:		2P/1B:		2P/2B:		XP:		
5/16-9/15 [CP]	$54-	59	$59-	69	$69-	69	$5		F1
3/1-5/15 & 9/16-2/29 [CP]	$47-	57	$49-	59	$59-	69	$5		F1

Location: Just s of I-25, exit 186; just s on Beverly, then e. 2325 E Yellowstone Hwy 82609
Fax: 307/266-5850. **Terms:** Pets, $8 extra charge. **Facility:** 42 rooms. Very good housekeeping. 4 two
bedroom units. Spacious rooms in 2-story, $69-$74; 1-2 stories; interior/exterior corridors; designated smokin
area; heated indoor pool. **Dining:** Restaurant nearby. **Services:** winter plug-ins. **All Rooms:** combo or shower baths
extended cable TV. **Some Rooms:** 2 kitchens. **Cards:** AE, CB, DI, DS, JC, MC, VI. **Special Amenities:** Free breakfas
and free local telephone calls.

CASPER DAYS INN
♦♦
Motel

Phone: (307)234-1159

Rates Subject to Change

	1P:		2P/1B:		2P/2B:		XP:		
6/1-9/30 [EP]	$48-	53	$53-	58	$53-	58	$5		F1
3/1-5/31 & 10/1-2/29 [CP]	$43-	48	$48-	53	$48-	53	$5		F1

Location: I-25, exit 188A (Center St). 301 East E St 82601. **Fax:** 307/265-0829. **Facility:** 122 rooms. Impres
sive housekeeping. Attractive lobby. 2 stories; interior corridors; designated smoking area; heated pool. **Services:** winter
plug-ins. **Cards:** AE, DI, DS, MC, VI.

CASPER HILTON INN
♦♦♦
Hotel

Phone: (307)266-6000

Rates Subject to Change

	1P:	2P/1B:	2P/2B:	XP:	
All Year	$69	$69	$69	$10	F

Location: N of I-25, exit 188B (SR 220). 800 N Poplar St 82602 (PO Box 224). **Fax:** 307/473-1010
Facility: 229 rooms. Indoor atrium. 6 stories; interior corridors; heated indoor pool. **Services:** giftshop; winte
plug-ins. **All Rooms:** combo or shower baths. **Cards:** AE, CB, DI, DS, JC, MC, VI. *(See color ad p 269)*

DURBIN STREET INN BED & BREAKFAST
♦♦
Bed &
Breakfast

Phone: (307)577-5774

Guaranteed Rates

	1P:		2P/1B:		2P/2B:		XP:
5/15-9/15 [BP]	$60-	80	$75-	95	$125-	145	$20
3/1-5/14 & 9/16-2/29 [BP]	$45-	65	$60-	75	$100-	125	$10

Location: 0.7 mi s of downtown; I-25, Center St exit; s to 9th St, just e. 843 S Durbin 82601
Fax: 307/266-5441. **Terms:** Age restrictions may apply; reserv deposit, 5 day notice. **Facility:** 5 rooms. In resi
dential area downtown. 2 stories; interior corridors; designated smoking area. **Cards:** AE, DI, MC, VI.

HAMPTON INN
♦♦♦
Motor Inn

Phone: (307)235-6668

Rates Subject to Change

	1P:	2P/1B:	2P/2B:
All Year [CP]	$75	$75	$75

Location: Just n of I-25, between exits 188A & 188B. 400 West F St 82601. **Fax:** 307/235-2027
Facility: 122 rooms. Very clean rooms. Contemporary decor, all rooms with iron & ironing board. 2 stories; in
terior corridors; designated smoking area; heated pool. **Services:** winter plug-ins. **Cards:** AE, CB, DI, DS, MC, VI.
(See color ad p 269)

HOLIDAY INN
♦♦♦
Motor Inn

Phone: (307)235-2531

Rates Subject to Change

	1P:		2P/1B:		2P/2B:	
6/1-9/30 & 1/1-2/29	$99-	175	$99-	175	$99-	175
3/1-5/31 & 10/1-12/31	$89-	175	$89-	175	$89-	175

Location: Just n of I-25, between exits 188A & 188B. 300 West F St 82601. **Fax:** 307/473-3100.
Facility: 200 rooms. Many rooms with view of atrium. 2 stories; interior corridors; heated indoor pool. **Services:** winter
plug-ins. **Some Rooms:** 3 kitchens. **Cards:** AE, CB, DI, DS, JC, MC, VI. *(See color ad p 270 & opposite title page)*

KELLY INN
◆◆
Motel

Rates Subject to Change
Phone: (307)266-2400
All Year [CP]   1P: $46- 54   2P/1B: $50- 56   2P/2B: $52- 58   XP: $6   F18
Location: N of I-25, exit 188B (SR 220). 821 N Poplar St 82601. **Fax:** 307/266-1146. **Facility:** 103 rooms. Off Interstate location. 2 stories; interior/exterior corridors. **Services:** winter plug-ins. **All Rooms:** combo or shower baths. **Cards:** AE, CB, DI, DS, JC, MC, VI. *(See color ad p 281)*

(ASK) 🅢 🛏 🍽 🛗 🖚 ⬜ 🐕 🖨 📧 ✕

NATIONAL 9 INN SHOWBOAT
ⓐⓐⓐ SAVE

Motel

Phone: (307)235-2711
4/16-9/15 [CP]   1P: $34- 39   2P/1B: $44   2P/2B: $44- 49   XP: $6   F10
3/1-4/15 & 9/16-2/29 [CP]   1P: $29- 34   2P/1B: $34- 39   2P/2B: $39- 44   XP: $5   F10
Location: Just n of I-25, exit 188A (Center St). 100 West F St 82601-1440. **Fax:** 307/235-2711. **Terms:** Reserv deposit; weekly rates; small pets only, $10 dep req, $5 extra charge. **Facility:** 46 rooms. Quiet rooms close to river. 2 stories; interior corridors. **Dining:** Restaurant nearby. **Services:** winter plug-ins.
All Rooms: extended cable TV. **Cards:** AE, DS, MC, VI. **Special Amenities:** Early check-in/late check-out and free breakfast. *(See color ad p 270)*

🅢 🛏 🛗 🐕 (VCR) 📧 🖥 ✕

PARKWAY PLAZA HOTEL & CONVENTION CENTRE
ⓐⓐⓐ SAVE
◆◆
Hotel

Phone: (307)235-1777
All Year   1P: $50   2P/1B: $50   2P/2B: $50
Location: Just s of I-25, exit 188A (Center St). 123 West E St 82601. **Fax:** 307/235-8068. **Terms:** BP avail; pets, $25 dep req. **Facility:** 232 rooms. Spacious public areas. Various rooms, from luxury suites & modern rooms to more modest rooms yet to be remodeled. Rates for up to 4 persons. A few luxury suites $175; 2-4 stories; interior/exterior corridors; heated pool, whirlpool. **Dining:** Restaurant; 6 am-10 pm; $6-$18; cocktails.
Services: giftshop; winter plug-ins. **All Rooms:** extended cable TV. **Some Rooms:** kitchen, no utensils, whirlpools. **Cards:** AE, CB, DI, DS, MC, VI. **Special Amenities:** Free local telephone calls and free newspaper. *(See color ad p 268)*

🅢 🛏 🍽 📶 ⇄ 🍴 🍸 🖚 ⬜ 🐕 🖥 ▢ 🖨 🐕 🏠 ✕

SUPER 8 MOTEL
◆◆
Motel

Rates Subject to Change
Phone: 307-266-3480
All Year [BP]   1P: $45   2P/1B: $55   2P/2B: $610   XP: $4   F12
Location: 3 mi sw, on SR 220. 3838 Cy Ave 82604. **Fax:** 307/266-3480. **Facility:** 66 rooms. Very clean rooms. 3 stories, no elevator; interior corridors; designated smoking area. **Services:** winter plug-ins. **Cards:** AE, CB, DI, DS, MC, VI.

(ASK) 🅢 🛏 🍽 🛗 ⬜ 🖚 🐕 📧 🖨 ✕

WESTRIDGE MOTEL

All Year · 1P: $36- 41 · 2P/1B: $36- 41 · 2P/2B: $42- 53 · XP: $6 · F1
Phone: (307)234-891
Location: I-25, S Poplar St exit, 1 mi sw on SR 220. 955 Cy Ave 82601. Fax: 307/234-8917. **Terms:** Week
rates; small pets only, $5 extra charge. **Facility:** 28 rooms. Very clean rooms. 2 two-bedroom units. 2 stories
Motel · exterior corridors; designated smoking area. **Dining:** Restaurant nearby. **Services:** winter plug-in
All Rooms: combo or shower baths, extended cable TV. **Cards:** AE, DI, MC, VI. **Special Amenities:** Fre
local telephone calls and preferred room (subject to availability with advanced reservations).

RESTAURANTS

ANTHONY'S ITALIAN RESTAURANT · **Lunch:** $5-$9 · **Dinner:** $9-$18 · **Phone:** 307/237-968
◆◆
Italian
DS, MC, VI.
Location: I-25, exit 185; 0.7 mi s on Wyoming Blvd, just e on Carriage Ln. 621 SE Wyoming Blvd 82609
Hours: 11 am-2 & 5-9 pm, Sun 5 pm-9 pm. Closed: 11/25, 12/25, 1/1 & Mon. **Features:** casual dress
cocktails. Intimate dining atmosphere featuring freshly made pasta. Smoke free premises. **Cards:** AE, D

RMOR'S SILVER FOX RESTAURANT & LOUNGE   **Dinner:** $9-$24   **Phone:** 307/235-3000
◆◆◆   **Location:** I-25, exit 188B; 4.2 mi sw on SR 220. 3422 S Energy Ln 82604. **Hours:** 5 pm-9:30 pm, Fri &
Continental   Sat-10 pm, Sun-9 pm. Closed major holidays. **Reservations:** suggested. **Features:** casual dress; children's
menu; cocktails & lounge. Well prepared dishes served in attractive setting. **Cards:** AE, CB, DI, DS, MC, VI.   ☒

OSCO'S ITALIAN RESTAURANT   **Lunch:** $4-$8   **Dinner:** $8-$17   **Phone:** 307/265-9658
◆◆   **Location:** 0.3 mi s of I-25, between Center & McKinley sts; I-25, exit 187; just s on McKinley St, just w on
alian   East A St, Corner of Jefferson & East A St. 847 East A St 82601. **Hours:** 11 am-2 & 5-10 pm, Sat for dinner
hildren's menu; health conscious menu items; carryout; cocktails; street parking. Small, very casual dining. Difficult to find,
ut worth it. Seating may be a problem at this local favorite. Smoke free premises. **Cards:** AE, CB, DI, DS, MC, VI.   ☒

SOUTH SEA CHINESE RESTAURANT   **Lunch:** $5-$7   **Dinner:** $5-$12   **Phone:** 307/237-4777
◆   **Location:** 1.5 mi e on 2nd St. 2025 E 2nd St 82609. **Hours:** 11 am-2:30 & 4:30-8:30 pm. Closed: 12/25 &
Chinese   Sun. **Features:** cocktails. Informal atmosphere, some American dishes. **Cards:** AE, DI, MC, VI.   ☒

CHEYENNE—50,000

LODGINGS

DRUMMOND'S RANCH BED & BREAKFAST   Guaranteed Rates   **Phone:** (307)634-6042
◆◆◆   All Year [BP]   1P: $60- 150   2P/1B: $65- 175   2P/2B: $65- 175   XP:$15-20   F10
Bed &   **Location:** I-25N, exit 10B; 22.4 mi w on SR 210 (Happy Jack Rd), then s on private road. 399 Happy Jack
Breakfast   Rd 82007. Fax: 307/634-6042. **Terms:** Check-in 4 pm; reserv deposit, 14 day notice. **Facility:** 4 rooms. Quiet,
gracious retreat on 120 acres. Incredible view, some rooms with private outdoor hot tubs. Reservations required. Halfway between Laramie & Cheyenne. TV on request. One suite with private entrance, fireplace & whirlpool, $125-
150; 1-2 stories; interior/exterior corridors; smoke free premises. **Services:** winter plug-ins. **Recreation:** fishing; cross
country skiing; bicycles; hiking trails. Fee: horseback riding. **Some Rooms:** combo or shower baths, shared bathrooms,
color TV. **Cards:** DS, MC, VI.

BEST WESTERN HITCHING POST INN   **Phone:** (307)638-3301
🆎🆎🆎 SAVE   6/1-9/30   1P: $79- 95   2P/1B: $85- 105   2P/2B: $85- 105   XP: $10   F16
   3/1-5/31 & 10/1-2/29   1P: $65- 85   2P/1B: $71- 95   2P/2B: $71- 95   XP: $10   F16
◆◆◆   **Location:** 1 mi w on I-80 business loop & US 30; 1 mi e of jct I-25 & I-80, W Lincolnway exit. 1700 W
Motor Inn   Lincolnway 82001 (PO Box 1769). Fax: 307/778-7194. **Terms:** Pets. **Facility:** 166 rooms. Spacious public
areas. Excellent food at any price range. Various room sizes & decor. 2 stories; interior/exterior corridors;
heated indoor pool, saunas, whirlpool, outside pool & playground at Lincoln Court next door. **Dining:** 2 restaurants, coffee
shop; 6 am-11 pm; to 10 pm, in winter; package good store; also, Carriage Court, The Cheyenne Cattle Company, see
separate listing. **Services:** giftshop; winter plug-ins. **All Rooms:** extended cable TV. **Cards:** AE, CB, DI, DS, JC, MC, VI.
Best Western Motels. *(See ad below)*

COMFORT INN   Rates Subject to Change   **Phone:** (307)638-7202
◆◆   7/16-7/31 [CP]   1P: $125   2P/1B: $125   2P/2B: $125   XP: $10   F18
Motel   5/15-7/15 & 8/1-8/15 [CP]   1P: $69   2P/1B: $69   2P/2B: $69   XP: $5   F18
   3/1-5/14 & 8/16-2/29 [CP]   1P: $59   2P/1B: $59   2P/2B: $59   XP: $5   F18
Location: I-25, exit 7 (College Dr); 1 mi s of I-80; at Flying J Plaza. 2245 Etchepare Dr 82007. Fax: 307/635-8560.
Facility: 77 rooms. Modern rooms with thoughtful amenities. 2 stories; interior corridors; designated smoking area; small
heated pool. **Cards:** AE, DI, DS, MC, VI. *(See color ad p 272)*

DAYS INN CHEYENNE
◆◆ Motel
Rates Subject to Change
Phone: 307/778-887
5/1-9/30 [CP]   1P: $60- 65   2P/1B: $65- 70   2P/2B: $72- 75   XP: $5   F!
3/1-4/30 & 10/1-2/29 [CP]   1P: $44   2P/1B: $49   2P/2B: $55   XP: $5   F!
Location: 1.5 mi w on I-80 business loop & US 30 at jct I-25. 2360 W Lincolnway 82001 (PO Box 128 82003). Fax: 307/778-8697. **Terms:** Reserv deposit. **Facility:** 72 rooms. Nicely furnished, spacious rooms. 2 stories; interi corridors; designated smoking area. **Services:** winter plug-ins. **All Rooms:** combo or shower baths. **Cards:** AE, CB, DI, D JC, MC, VI.

ECONOLODGE OF CHEYENNE
◆◆ Motel
Rates Subject to Change
Phone: 307/632-755
6/1-9/1 [CP]   1P: $35- 45   2P/1B: $41- 51   2P/2B: $46- 69   XP: $6   F1
4/30-5/31 [CP]   1P: $34- 45   2P/1B: $40- 51   2P/2B: $45- 56   XP: $6   F1
3/1-4/29 & 9/2-2/29 [CP]   1P: $30- 40   2P/1B: $36- 46   2P/2B: $41- 51   XP: $6   F1
Location: 2 mi w on I-80 business loop & US 30 at jct I-25. 2512 W Lincolnway 82001. Fax: 307/635-9141. **Terms:** Rese deposit. **Facility:** 60 rooms. Convenient off interstate location. Rental fee for 1 VCR; 2 stories; interior corridors; designate smoking area; small heated indoor pool. **Services:** winter plug-ins. **Cards:** AE, CB, DI, DS, MC, VI. *(See ad below)*

FAIRFIELD INN BY MARRIOTT
◆◆◆ Motel
Rates Subject to Change
Phone: 307/637-407
5/15-10/1 [CP]   1P: $52- 62   2P/1B: $58- 79   2P/2B: $58- 79   XP: $6   F1
3/1-5/14 & 10/2-2/29 [CP]   1P: $48- 54   2P/1B: $52- 62   2P/2B: $52- 62   XP: $6   F1
Location: Intersection of Dell Range Blvd & Stillwater Dr; on n side of airport. 1415 Stillwater Ave 8200 Fax: 307/637-4070. **Facility:** 62 rooms. Modern rooms. Close to shopping. 3 stories; interior corridors; designated smokin area; small heated indoor pool. **Services:** winter plug-ins. **All Rooms:** combo or shower baths. **Cards:** AE, DI, DS, MC, VI.

FLEETWOOD MOTEL
Ⓐ SAVE
◆ Motel
Phone: (307)638-890
6/1-9/7   1P: $38   2P/1B: $44   2P/2B: $48   XP: $3
3/1-5/31 & 9/8-2/29   1P: $34   2P/1B: $40   2P/2B: $43   XP: $3
Location: I-80, exit 364; n on College Dr (SR 212). 3800 E Lincolnway 82001. **Terms:** Weekly rate seasonal; pets, $3 extra charge. **Facility:** 21 rooms. Quiet, convenient location. Very clean, budget oriente rooms. 2 stories; exterior corridors; designated smoking area; small heated pool. **Services:** winter plug-ins **All Rooms:** extended cable TV. **Cards:** AE, DI, DS, MC, VI. **Special Amenities:** Free local telephone calls and preferre **room (subject to availability with advanced reservations).**

LA QUINTA INN
◆◆◆ Motel
Rates Subject to Change
Phone: (307)632-711
5/1-8/31 [CP]   1P: $65- 80   2P/1B: $75- 90   2P/2B: $75- 90   XP: $10   F1
3/1-4/30 & 9/1-2/29 [CP]   1P: $50- 65   2P/1B: $60- 75   2P/2B: $60- 75   XP: $10   F1
Location: 2 mi w on I-80 business loop & US 30 at jct I-25. 2410 W Lincolnway 82001. Fax: 307/638-7807 **Facility:** 105 rooms. Newly renovated. Attractive lobby. Mini-microwaves & refrigerators avail; 3 stories; interior corridors; des ignated smoking area; small heated pool. **Services:** winter plug-ins. **Cards:** AE, CB, DI, DS, MC, VI.

LINCOLN COURT

Phone: (307)638-3302

AAA [SAVE]

◆◆
Motel

		1P:		2P/1B:		2P/2B:		XP:		
6/1-9/30 [CP]		1P:	$51- 56	2P/1B:	$57- 63	2P/2B:	$57- 63	XP:	$10	F16
3/1-5/31 & 10/1-2/29 [CP]		1P:	$39- 47	2P/1B:	$46- 51	2P/2B:	$46- 51	XP:	$10	F16

Location: 1 mi w on I-80 business loop & US 30; 1 mi e of jct I-25 & I-80, W Lincolnway exit. 1720 W Lincolnway 82001 (PO Box 1769). Fax: 307/778-7194. **Terms:** Reserv deposit; pets. **Facility:** 67 rooms. Some large rooms. Near railroad tracks. Barbecue & picnic tables in center court. Family units, $60-$75 for up to 8 persons; 1 story; interior/exterior corridors; playground. **Dining:** Restaurant nearby. **Recreation:** recreational facility privileges at Best Western Hitching Post next door. **All Rooms:** extended cable TV. **Cards:** AE, CB, DI, DS, JC, MC, VI. **Special Amenities:** Early check-in/late check-out and preferred room (subject to availability with advanced reservations).

LITTLE AMERICA HOTEL

Phone: (307)775-8400

AAA [SAVE]

◆◆
Motel

		1P:		2P/1B:		2P/2B:		XP:		
6/15-9/30		1P:	$75- 89	2P/1B:	$85- 99	2P/2B:	$89	XP:	$10	F12
5/1-6/14 & 10/1-2/29		1P:	$69- 85	2P/1B:	$79- 95	2P/2B:	$85	XP:	$10	F12
3/1-4/30		1P:	$62- 82	2P/1B:	$72- 92	2P/2B:	$82			

Location: 2 mi w at jct I-25 & I-80. 2800 W Lincolnway 82001 (PO Box 1529, 82003). Fax: 307/775-8425. **Facility:** 188 rooms. Spacious rooms & suites secluded on 80 acres. 4 executive/presidential suites, $96-$135; 2-3 stories; interior/exterior corridors; putting green; heated pool. Fee: 9 holes golf. **Dining:** Coffee shop; 24 hrs; $5-$16. **Services:** giftshop; area transportation, bus station. **Recreation:** jogging, volleyball, croquet & badminton. Fee: stationary bike. **All Rooms:** extended cable TV. **Cards:** AE, CB, DI, DS, MC, VI. *(See color ad below)*

LUXURY INN

Phone: (307)638-2550

AAA [SAVE]

◆◆
Motel

		1P:		2P/1B:		2P/2B:		XP:		
5/1-8/31 [CP]		1P:	$40- 44	2P/1B:	$47- 50	2P/2B:	$50- 53	XP:	$8	F13
4/1-4/30 & 10/1-10/31 [CP]		1P:	$36- 39	2P/1B:	$40- 43	2P/2B:	$44- 47	XP:	$7	F13
3/1-3/31, 9/1-9/30 &										
11/1-11/30 [CP]		1P:	$30- 36	2P/1B:	$38- 41	2P/2B:	$42- 45	XP:	$7	F13
12/1-2/29 [CP]		1P:	$28- 30	2P/1B:	$42- 45	2P/2B:	$33- 36	XP:	$7	F13

Location: 0.7 mi n of jct I-25 & I-80, exit 10 (Missile Dr); just e. 1805 Westland Rd 82001. Fax: 307/778-8113. **Terms:** Reserv deposit; weekly/monthly rates. **Facility:** 32 rooms. Budget oriented rooms. 2 stories; interior corridors; designated smoking area. **Services:** winter plug-ins. **All Rooms:** extended cable TV. **Cards:** AE, CB, DI, DS, VI. **Special Amenities:** Free breakfast and free local telephone calls. *(See ad p 272)*

NAGLE WARREN MANSION B & B

Rates Subject to Change

Phone: 307-637-3333

◆◆◆◆
Bed & Breakfast

		2P/1B:		
3/1-7/15 & 2/25-2/29 [BP]		2P/1B:	$105- 115	
7/16-2/24 [BP]		2P/1B:	$85	

Location: I-80, exit 362, downtown. 222 E 17th St 82001. Fax: 307/638-6835. **Terms:** Age restrictions may apply; reserv deposit, 3-30 day notice. **Facility:** 12 rooms. Circa 1888, elegant with contemporary comfort & rich with Western history, close by capitol, state offices & shopping. 3 stories; interior corridors; smoke free premises; street parking only. **Services:** Fee: massage. **Cards:** AE, MC, VI.

PORCH SWING BED & BREAKFAST
◆◆
Historic Bed
& Breakfast

| | 7/24-8/1 [BP] | 1P: $66 | 2P/1B: $70 | 2P/2B: $85 | XP: $15 |
| 3/1-7/23 & 8/2-2/29 [BP] | 1P: $43- 49 | 2P/1B: $49- 59 | 2P/2B: $59- 64 | XP: $15 |

Rates Subject to Change

Phone: 307/778-718

Location: Downtown. 712 E 20th St 82001. Fax: 307/778-7182. **Terms:** Check-in 4 pm; reserv deposit, day notice, 30 day notice 7/22-7/31. **Facility:** 3 rooms. Rooms in 1907 historic home. European style person attention, breakfast made from scratch. 2 stories; interior corridors; smoke free premises. **Services:** area transportatio **Recreation:** bicycles. **Some Rooms:** shower or tub baths, shared bathrooms. **Cards:** MC, VI.

STAGE COACH MOTEL
(AAA) (SAVE)

Motel

	7/15-8/1	1P: $85- 102	2P/1B: $105- 120	2P/2B: $115- 135	XP: $5-10	D1
5/15-7/14 & 8/2-9/30	1P: $35- 40	2P/1B: $45- 50	2P/2B: $55- 75	XP: $10	D1
3/1-5/14 & 10/1-2/29	1P: $25- 35	2P/1B: $35- 40	2P/2B: $40- 55	XP: $5-10	D1

Phone: (307)634-449

Location: 1 mi w on I-80 business loop & US 30; 1 mi e of jct I-25 & I-80. 1515 W Lincolnway 8200 Fax: 307/634-3288. **Terms:** Reserv deposit; weekly rates. **Facility:** 25 rooms. Good housekeeping. 1 twe bedroom unit. 1 story; exterior corridors. **Dining:** Restaurant nearby. **Services:** winter plug-ins. **All Rooms:** extended cab TV. **Cards:** AE, CB, DI, DS, MC, VI. *(See ad below)*

VINDY HILLS GUEST HOUSE Rates Subject to Change Phone: 307/632-6423
◆◆◆ All Year [BP] 1P: $75 2P/1B: $75- 150 2P/2B: $90 XP: $20 F12
Red & **Location:** I-25, exit 10B; then 22.4 mi w on SR 210 (Happy Jack Rd), 1 mi s on private dirt road; 23 mi e of
Breakfast Laramie. 393 Happy Jack Rd 82007. Fax: 307/632-8906. **Terms:** Check-in 4 pm; reserv deposit, 30 day
notice; handling fee imposed. **Facility:** 7 rooms. Beautiful guest house overlooking scenic Granite Lake. Winter
garage parking. Halfway between Laramie & Cheyenne. 3 rooms with fireplace. 1 story; exterior corridors; smoke free prem-
ses; mountain view; boat dock. **Services:** area transportation. **Recreation:** fishing; cross country skiing. Fee: bicycles.
All Rooms: combo or shower baths. **Some Rooms:** color TV. **Cards:** DS, MC, VI.

RESTAURANTS

CARRIAGE COURT Dinner: $22-$45 Phone: 307/638-3301
◆◆◆ **Location:** 1 mi w on I-80 business loop & US 30; 1 mi e of jct I-25 & I-80, W Lincolnway exit; in Best
American Western Hitching Post Inn. 1700 W Lincolnway 82001. **Hours:** 6 pm-10 pm. Closed: 12/25 & Sun.
Reservations: suggested. **Features:** casual dress; health conscious menu items; cocktails & lounge; a la
carte. Intimate dining in casual elegance, ample portions, tableside preparation of many dishes by friendly & capable wait
staff. Martini/cigar patio. **Cards:** AE, DI, DS, JC, MC, VI. (See ad p 271)

THE CHEYENNE CATTLE COMPANY Dinner: $11-$27 Phone: 307/638-3301
◆◆ **Location:** 1 mi w on I-80 business loop & US 30; 1 mi e of jct I-25 & I-80, W Lincolnway exit; in Best
Steakhouse Western Hitching Post Inn. 1700 W Lincolnway 82001. **Hours:** 11 am-1:30 & 5:30-10 pm.
Reservations: accepted. **Features:** casual dress; health conscious menu items; cocktails & lounge; buffet.
Luncheon buffet. Casual dining, ample portions. Smoke free premises. **Cards:** AE, DI, DS, JC, MC, VI. (See ad p 271)

LOS AMIGOS RESTAURANT Lunch: $3-$10 Dinner: $3-$10 Phone: 307/638-8591
AAA **Location:** 0.6 mi on Central Ave; on frontage road. 620 Central Ave 82007. **Hours:** 11 am-8:30 pm, Fri &
Sat-9 pm. Closed major holidays & Sun. **Features:** casual dress; children's menu; carryout; cocktails; a la
Mexican carte. Authentic recipes. **Cards:** AE, DI, DS, MC, VI.

OWL INN RESTAURANT Lunch: $6-$17 Dinner: $6-$17 Phone: 307/638-8578
AAA **Location:** 1.3 mi n. 3919 Central Ave 82001. **Hours:** 6:30 am-9 pm, Fri & Sat-10 pm. Closed: 11/25 &
12/25. **Features:** casual dress; children's menu; senior's menu; carryout; cocktails. Well-prepared home style
◆◆ food served in relaxed atmosphere. Some Mexican & Italian specialties. **Cards:** AE, DS, MC, VI.
American

POOR RICHARDS Lunch: $5-$9 Dinner: $10-$25 Phone: 307/635-5114
AAA **Location:** 1.5 mi e on I-80 business loop & US 30. 2233 E Lincolnway 82001. **Hours:** 11 am-2:30 & 5-10
pm, Fri & Sat-11 pm. Closed: 11/26, 12/25 & Superbowl Sun. **Features:** casual dress; children's menu;
◆◆ carryout; salad bar; cocktails & lounge. Prime rib & seafood varieties served in early American atmosphere.
American Sat brunch. Smoke free premises. **Cards:** AE, CB, DI, DS, MC, VI.

SENATOR'S AT TERRY BISON RANCH Lunch: $5-$7 Dinner: $11-$26 Phone: 307/634-5347
AAA **Location:** S on I-25, exit 2; se on Terry Ranch Rd to entrance. 51 I-25 Service Rd E 82007. **Hours:** 7 am-9
pm in summer, Fri & Sat from 5 pm, Sun 10 am-3 pm off season. Closed: 1/1, 11/25 & 12/25.
◆◆ **Reservations:** suggested. **Features:** casual dress; Sunday brunch; children's menu; salad bar; cocktails &
Steakhouse lounge; entertainment. Rustic pine dining room. Featuring American bison & beef. **Cards:** DS, MC, VI.
(See color ad p 99)

WESTERN GOLD DINING ROOM Lunch: $7-$9 Dinner: $12-$32 Phone: 307/775-8404
◆◆◆ **Location:** 2 mi w at jct I-25 & I-80; in Little America Hotel. 2800 W Lincoln Way 82001. **Hours:** 11 am-2 &
Continental 5-10 pm. **Reservations:** accepted. **Features:** casual dress; Sunday brunch; children's menu; health
conscious menu; carryout; cocktails & lounge; also prix fixe. Attractive dining room with well-prepared variety
of menu selections. Buffet luncheon. Summer entertainment. **Cards:** AE, DI, DS, MC, VI.

CHUGWATER—200

LODGING

CHUGWATER SUPER 8 Rates Subject to Change Phone: 307/422-3248
◆◆ 6/1-8/15 1P: $49 2P/1B: $53 2P/2B: $59 XP: $2
Motor Inn 3/1-5/31 & 8/16-2/29 1P: $37 2P/1B: $39 2P/2B: $47 XP: $2
Location: Just ne of I-25, exit 54. 100 Buffalo Dr 82210. Fax: 307/834-2494. **Facility:** 23 rooms. Loft-style
rooms on 2nd floor. Charming, country lobby. 2 stories; interior corridors; small pool. **Services:** giftshop; winter plug-ins.
All Rooms: combo or shower baths. **Cards:** AE, DS, MC, VI.

CODY—7,900—See also YELLOWSTONE NATIONAL PARK.

LODGINGS

BEST WESTERN SUNRISE MOTOR INN Guaranteed Rates Phone: (307)587-5566
◆◆ 6/14-8/22 [CP] 1P: $85 2P/1B: $85 2P/2B: $99 XP: $5 F12
Motel 8/23-10/25 [CP] 1P: $51- 55 2P/1B: $51- 55 2P/2B: $51- 85 XP: $5 F12
5/31-6/13 [CP] 1P: $55 2P/1B: $55 2P/2B: $69 XP: $5 F12
5/1-5/30 [CP] 1P: $42 2P/1B: $42 2P/2B: $51 XP: $5 F12
Location: 0.8 mi w on US 14, 16 & 20. 1407 8th St 82414. Fax: 307/587-0217. **Terms:** Open 5/1-10/25. **Facility:** 40 rooms.
Quiet location. Close to area attractions. 1 story; exterior corridors; small heated pool. **Cards:** AE, DI, DS, MC, VI.
(See ad p 276)

BEST WESTERN SUNSET MOTOR INN

Phone: (307)587-426

(AAA) (SAVE)	6/14-8/21	1P: $105	2P/1B: $105	2P/2B: $119	XP: $10	F1
	5/24-6/13 & 8/22-9/25	1P: $75- 99	2P/1B: $75- 99	2P/2B: $85- 105	XP: $10	F1
◆ ◆ ◆	5/10-5/23 & 9/26-10/16	1P: $55- 65	2P/1B: $55- 65	2P/2B: $65- 75	XP: $10	F1
Motor Inn	3/1-5/9 & 10/17-2/29	1P: $49	2P/1B: $49	2P/2B: $59	XP: $10	F1

Location: 0.8 mi w on US 14, 16 & 20. 1601 8th St 82414 (PO Box 1720). Fax: 307/587-902
Terms: Small pets only. **Facility:** 120 rooms. Various room sizes, from cozy well maintained rooms to large, luxury accommodations. 1 two-bedroom unit. 1 full kitchen unit avail; 1-2 stories; interior/exterior corridors; heated indoor pool, whirlpool; playground. **Dining:** Restaurant; 6 am-10 pm; 7 am-9 pm, in winter; $5-$15; cocktails. **Services:** winter plug-ins
All Rooms: combo or shower baths, extended cable TV. **Cards:** AE, CB, DI, DS, MC, VI. *(See ad p 277)*

BIG BEAR MOTEL

Rates Subject to Change

Phone: 307/587-311

(AAA)	6/14-8/21		2P/1B: $45- 49	2P/2B: $52- 56	XP: $4
	5/29-6/13 & 8/22-9/18		2P/1B: $33- 36	2P/2B: $38- 44	XP: $4
◆	5/1-5/28 & 9/19-9/30		2P/1B: $29	2P/2B: $34	XP: $4

Motel **Location:** 2 mi w on US 14, 16 & 20; from city center. 139 W Yellowstone Hwy 82414. **Terms:** Ope
5/1-9/30; pets. **Facility:** 42 rooms. Very clean rooms. Close to rodeo grounds. 2 family units, $79 for up to
persons; 1 story; exterior corridors; heated pool. **Dining:** Restaurant nearby. **All Rooms:** extended cable TV. **Cards:** DS
MC, VI. *(See color ad p 277)*

AAA Plus® provides you extended services, such as up to 100 miles of free towing.

BUFFALO BILL VILLAGE RESORT
Phone: (307)587-5544

Mon-Thurs 6/16-9/1	1P:	$79-89	2P/1B:	$89-99	2P/2B:	$89-99	XP: $10-20	F19
Fri-Sun 6/16-9/1	1P:	$69-79	2P/1B:	$79-89	2P/2B:	$79-99	XP: $10	F19
Mon-Thurs 5/1-6/15 & 9/2-9/30	1P:	$49-79	2P/1B:	$59-89	2P/2B:	$59-89	XP: $10	F19
Fri-Sun 5/1-6/15 & 9/2-9/30	1P:	$39-59	2P/1B:	$49-69	2P/2B:	$49-79	XP: $10	F19

Historic Cottage

Location: US 14, 16 & 20 & SR 120, just e of n jct SR 120. 1701 Sheridan Ave 82414. Fax: 307/527-7757. **Terms:** Open 5/1-9/30; reserv deposit. **Facility:** 83 rooms. Complex of closely spaced log cabins built between 1920 & 1923. Guests can use all facilities of the Holiday Inn next door. 23 two-bedroom units. 1 story; exterior corridors; small heated pool. **Dining:** 3 restaurants, coffee shop; 6 am-10 pm; $7-$20; cocktails. **Services:** giftshop. **Recreation:** Fee: rafting, day tours of Yellowstone. **Cards:** AE, DI, DS, JC, MC, VI. **Special Amenities:** Free local telephone calls and free room upgrade **(subject to availability with advanced reservations).** *(See ad p 278)*

BURL INN

AAA SAVE
◆ ◆
Motel

Phone: (307)587-2084

6/19-8/20	1P:	$80	2P/1B:	$85	2P/2B:	$85	XP:	$5	F6
5/1-6/18 & 8/21-10/31	1P:	$60	2P/1B:	$65	2P/2B:	$65	XP:	$5	F6
3/1-4/30 & 11/1-2/29	1P:	$40	2P/1B:	$45	2P/2B:	$45	XP:	$5	F6

Location: Just e of jct US 14, 16 & 20. 1213 17th St 82414. Fax: 307/587-3031. **Terms:** Reserv deposit. **Facility:** 40 rooms. All rooms with handmade, wood furniture. Very clean rooms. 2 stories; interior corridors; designated smoking area. **Dining:** Restaurant nearby. **All Rooms:** combo or tub baths, extended cable TV **Some Rooms:** whirlpools. **Cards:** AE, DS, MC, VI. **Special Amenities:** Free local telephone calls. *(See color ad below)*

CARRIAGE HOUSE

AAA
◆
Historic
Cottage

Guaranteed Rates   Phone: 307/587-2572

6/7-8/20	1P:	$50- 55	2P/1B:	$50- 55	2P/2B:	$58- 65	XP: $5
4/15-6/6 & 8/21-9/9			2P/1B:	$32- 38	2P/2B:	$38- 40	XP: $5
9/10-10/15			2P/1B:	$24	2P/2B:	$28	XP: $5

Location: Just w of Buffalo Bill Historical Center on US 14 & 20. 1816 8th St 82414. Fax: 307/587-2572 **Terms:** Open 4/15-10/15; reserv deposit. **Facility:** 24 rooms. Small duplex log cabins built in the 1920's. 1 three-bedroom unit, 2 two-bedroom units. 1 story; exterior corridors; smoke free premises; playground. **Dining:** Restaurant nearby. **All Rooms:** combo or shower baths. *(See color ad p 279)*

COMFORT INN AT BUFFALO BILL VILLAGE RESORT

AAA SAVE
◆ ◆ ◆
Motel

Phone: (307)587-5556

6/16-9/30	1P:	$89- 129	2P/1B:	$89- 129	2P/2B:	$89- 129	XP: $10
5/1-6/15 & 10/1-10/31	1P:	$69- 99	2P/1B:	$69- 99	2P/2B:	$69- 99	XP: $10
3/1-4/30 & 11/1-2/29	1P:	$39- 69	2P/1B:	$39- 69	2P/2B:	$39- 69	XP: $10

Location: US 14, 16 & 20 & SR 120. 1601 Sheridan Ave 82414 (PO Box 30). Fax: 307/527-7757. **Terms:** Reserv deposit. **Facility:** 75 rooms. Two buildings side by side. Guests can use all facilities of the resort. 1 suite, $50-$115 for 2 persons; 2 stories; interior corridors; designated smoking area; pool privileges. **Dining:** Restaurant nearby. **Services:** winter plug-ins. **Recreation:** Fee: rafting; scenic flights, day tour of Yellowstone. **All Rooms:** extended cable TV. **Cards:** AE, DI, DS, JC, MC, VI. **Special Amenities:** Free breakfast and free local telephone calls. *(See ad p 280)*

PATRONIZE ESTABLISHMENTS

DAYS INN

AAA SAVE

◆◆◆
Motel

6/2-10/1 [CP]	1P: $85- 115	2P/1B: $95- 125	2P/2B: $95- 125	XP: $10	F12
4/1-6/1 [CP]	1P: $45	2P/1B: $55	2P/2B: $61	XP: $6	F12
3/1-3/31 & 10/2-2/29 [CP]	1P: $35	2P/1B: $45	2P/2B: $51	XP: $6	F12

Phone: (307)527-6604

Location: 1.8 mi w on US 14,16 & 20 from jct US 14, 16 & 20 & SR 128. 524 Yellowstone 82414. Fax: 307/527-7341. **Terms:** Reserv deposit. **Facility:** 52 rooms. Close to rodeo grounds. Fifty-two miles east of park entrance. 2 suites with whirlpool, $85-$145; 2 stories; interior corridors; designated smoking area; heated indoor pool, whirlpool. **Dining:** Restaurant nearby. **Services:** winter plug-ins. **All Rooms:** combo or shower baths, extended cable TV. **Some Rooms:** whirlpools. **Cards:** AE, CB, DI, DS, MC, VI. *(See ad p 280)*

HOLIDAY INN IN BUFFALO BILL VILLAGE RESORT

◆◆◆
Motor Inn

Rates Subject to Change

6/16-9/30	1P: $99- 129	2P/1B: $99- 129	2P/2B: $99- 129	XP: $10	F19
5/1-6/15 & 10/1-10/31	1P: $69- 99	2P/1B: $69- 99	2P/2B: $69- 99	XP: $10	F19
3/1-4/30 & 11/1-2/29	1P: $49- 69	2P/1B: $49- 69	2P/2B: $49- 69	XP: $10	F19

Phone: (307)587-5555

Location: US 14, 16 & 20 & SR 120. 1701 Sheridan Ave 82414. Fax: 307/527-7757. **Terms:** Reserv deposit. **Facility:** 190 rooms. Large property. Close to shopping & businesses. Phones with voice mail. 1 two-bedroom unit. 2 stories; interior corridors; heated pool. **Services:** winter plug-ins. **All Rooms:** combo or shower baths. **Cards:** AE, DI, DS, JC, MC, VI. *(See ad p 281 & color ad opposite title page)*

HOLIDAY MOTEL

								Phone: 307/587-425■
	6/12-8/27	1P:	$45	2P/1B:	$48	2P/2B:	$58	XP: $3
	5/29-6/11 & 8/28-9/20	1P:	$30	2P/1B:	$33	2P/2B:	$40	XP: $3
	9/21-11/14	1P:	$27	2P/1B:	$30	2P/2B:	$38	XP: $3
Motel	3/1-5/28 & 11/15-2/29	1P:	$25	2P/1B:	$28	2P/2B:	$32	XP: $3

Guaranteed Rates

Location: 0.4 mi e. 1807 Sheridan Ave 82414. Fax: 307/527-6990. **Terms:** Reserv deposit. **Facility:** 21 rooms. Quiet location. Very clean newly renovated rooms. 1 two-bedroom unit. 1 two-bedroom family unit, extra charge; 1 story; exterior corridors; designated smoking area. **Dining:** Restaurant nearby. **Services:** winter plug-ins. **All Rooms:** combo c shower baths, extended cable TV. **Cards:** AE, DS, MC, VI. IMA. *(See color ad p 320 & p 281)*

KELLY INN OF CODY

								Phone: (307)527-5505
	6/1-9/15 [CP]	1P:	$89	2P/1B:	$99	2P/2B:	$99	XP: $5 F12
	5/1-5/31 & 9/16-10/31 [CP]	1P:	$59	2P/1B:	$69	2P/2B:	$69	XP: $5 F12
	3/1-4/30 & 11/1-2/29 [CP]	1P:	$49	2P/1B:	$59	2P/2B:	$59	XP: $5 F12
Motel								

Location: 1.5 mi e on US 14, 16 & 20. 2513 Greybull Hwy 82414 (PO Box 216). Fax: 307/527-5001 **Terms:** Weekly/monthly rates, in winter only; pets. **Facility:** 50 rooms. Quiet location, adjacent to lake. 2 family units for up to 6 persons. 5 microwaves & refrigerators avail; 2 stories; interior/exterior corridors; designated smoking area, sauna, whirlpool. **Services:** winter plug-ins. **All Rooms:** extended cable TV. **Some Rooms:** whirlpools. **Cards:** AE, CB, DI DS, JC, MC, VI. **Special Amenities:** Free breakfast. *(See color ad p 281)*

ABSAROKA MOUNTAIN LODGE
1231 East Yellowstone Hwy. • Cody, WY 82414
307-587-3963 • Fax 307-527-9628

Historic lodge built in 1910 minutes from Yellowstone National Park. Log cabins located along "Gunbarrel Creek" with stunning views of Gunbarrel Canyon. Come experience the West at its best. Horseback rides into the spectacular Absaroka Wilderness available. Fine dining, hiking, nightly campfires. Nightly rates for cabins and package plans available.

See us on the internet @ www.absarokamtlodge.com

Comfort Inn®
AT THE BUFFALO BILL VILLAGE RESORT
Deluxe Accommodations • Swimming
FREE Continental Breakfast
Kids stay FREE in same room with parents

1601 Sheridan Ave. • Cody, Wyoming 82414 • 1-800-527-5544

DAYS INN.

Days Inn
524 Yellowstone Ave.
Cody, Wyoming 82414
Ph (307) 527-6604
Fax (307) 527 - 7341

• Continental Breakfast
• King & Queen Beds
• Indoor Hot Tub
• Outdoor Pool • HBO
• Family Suite
• Special Rate Subject to Availability

PARSON'S PILLOW BED & BREAKFAST

◆◆
Bed & Breakfast

Rates Subject to Change

5/16-10/15 [BP]	1P: $80	2P/1B: $85
3/1-5/15 & 10/16-2/29 [BP]	1P: $70	2P/1B: $75

Phone: 307/587-2382

Location: Just s of US 14, 16 & 20. 1202 14th St 82414. **Terms:** Age restrictions may apply; reserv deposit, 30 day notice; handling fee imposed. **Facility:** 4 rooms. Small, cozy rooms in renovated 1902 church. Close to public pool. Public refrigerator; 2 stories; interior corridors; smoke free premises; street parking only. **Services:** winter plug-ins. **All Rooms:** combo or tub baths. **Cards:** DS, MC, VI.

ASK ⊁ 📺 📞 🖥 ⊠

RAINBOW PARK MOTEL

AAA
◆
Motel

Guaranteed Rates

6/10-8/31	1P: $44	2P/1B: $47	2P/2B: $60	XP: $3
9/1-10/31	1P: $31	2P/1B: $34	2P/2B: $40	XP: $3
3/1-6/9 & 11/1-2/29	1P: $25	2P/1B: $28	2P/2B: $32	XP: $3

Phone: 307/587-6251

Location: Just e on US 14, 16, 20 & SR 120. 1136 17th St 82414. **Terms:** Reserv deposit; handling fee imposed. **Facility:** 39 rooms. Budget oriented rooms. 2 two-bedroom units. 1 story; exterior corridors; designated smoking area; playground. **Dining:** Restaurant nearby. **Services:** winter plug-ins. **All Rooms:** combo or shower baths, extended cable TV. **Some Rooms:** 5 kitchens, no utensils. **Cards:** AE, CB, DI, DS, MC, VI. IMA.
(See color ad p 320)

🛏 ⊠ 🍴 🔌 ⊠

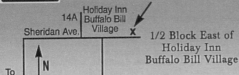

RIVERSIDE INN & CAMPGROUND
◆◆
Motel

Rates Subject to Change
5/1-11/30   2P/1B: $38- 40 2P/2B: $40- 44 XP: $2-4

Phone: 307/455-2337

Location: 2.7 mi e of town center. 5810 US Hwy 26 82513 (PO Box 642, DUBOIS). **Terms:** Open 5/1-11/30 reserv deposit. **Facility:** 14 rooms. Log cabins with view of wind river mountains, no phones or TV's. 1 two bedroom housekeeping unit, $65-$80 for up to 7 persons; 1 story; exterior corridors; playground. **Recreation:** fishing; hiking trails. Fee: horseback riding. **All Rooms:** combo or shower baths. **Some Rooms:** 5 efficiencies. **Cards:** DS, MC, VI.

SKYLINE MOTOR INN

6/13-8/24	1P: $48	2P/1B: $54	2P/2B: $60	XP: $4	
5/28-6/12 & 8/25-9/16	1P: $32	2P/1B: $38	2P/2B: $48	XP: $4	
3/1-5/27 & 9/17-2/29	1P: $28	2P/1B: $32	2P/2B: $36- 38	XP: $4	

Rates Subject to Change

Phone: 307/587-4201

◆◆
Motel

Location: 0.8 mi e on US 14, 16, 20 & SR 120. 1919 17th St 82414. **Terms:** Reserv deposit weekly/monthly rates; pets. **Facility:** 46 rooms. Very clean, large rooms. 1-2 stories; exterior corridors; designated smoking area; small heated pool; playground. **Dining:** Restaurant nearby. **Services:** winter plug-ins. **All Rooms:** extended cable TV. **Cards:** AE, MC, VI. *(See color ad p 276)*

RESTAURANTS

FRANCA'S ITALIAN DINING   **Dinner:** $14-$26   Phone: 307/587-5354
◆◆◆
Northern
Italian

Location: Just n off Sheridan Ave at 14th St. 1421 Rumsey Ave 82414. **Hours:** Open 5/15-1/15; 6 pm-10 pm. Closed: 1/16-5/14. **Reservations:** required. **Features:** casual dress; cocktails; street parking; prix fixe Gourmet Italian cuisine. Award-winning wine list. 2 menu choices, with different menu each night. Smoke free premises.

LA COMIDA   **Lunch:** $5-$12   **Dinner:** $5-$12   Phone: 307/587-9556
◆◆
Mexican

Location: On US 14, 16 & 20. 1385 Sheridan Ave 82414. **Hours:** 11 am-8 pm, Fri & Sat-9 pm; 11 am-10 pm, Sun noon-10 pm, in summer. Closed: 1/1, 11/25 & 12/25. **Reservations:** suggested; wkends & summer. **Features:** casual dress; children's menu; carryout; cocktails; street parking. Light menu. Some American dishes, daily homemade soup. Italian cuisine served also in winter. Patio dining in summer. Smoke free premises. **Cards:** AE, DS, MC, VI.

DIAMONDVILLE—900

LODGING

ENERGY INN
◆◆
Motel

Rates Subject to Change
All Year   1P: $34   2P/1B: $43   2P/2B: $43   XP: $5

Phone: 307/877-6901

Location: Jct US 30 & 189. (PO Box 494, 83116). Fax: 307/877-6901. **Facility:** 43 rooms. Modest, very clean rooms. 1-2 stories; interior/exterior corridors. **Services:** winter plug-ins. **All Rooms:** combo or shower baths. **Some Rooms:** 11 kitchens. **Cards:** AE, CB, DI, JC, MC, VI.

DOUGLAS—5,100

LODGINGS

ALPINE INN   Phone: (307)358-4780
(AAA) (SAVE)   6/1-9/30   1P: $35   2P/1B: $40   2P/2B: $40   XP: $3
            3/1-5/31 & 10/1-2/29   1P: $28   2P/1B: $32   2P/2B: $32   XP: $4
◆   **Location:** I-25, exit 135. 2310 E Richard St 82633. Fax: 307/358-5799. **Terms:** Reserv deposit, 7 day
Motel   notice; pets, $5 extra charge. **Facility:** 40 rooms. Budget rooms. 2 stories; exterior corridors.
            Dining: Restaurant nearby. **Services:** winter plug-ins. **All Rooms:** extended cable TV. **Cards:** AE, CB, DI,
DS, MC, VI. **Special Amenities:** Free local telephone calls.

BEST WESTERN DOUGLAS INN & CONFERENCE CENTER   Phone: (307)358-9790
(AAA) (SAVE)   6/1-8/31   1P: $61- 71   2P/1B: $71- 81   2P/2B: $71- 81
            9/1-2/29   1P: $59- 69   2P/1B: $69- 79   2P/2B: $69- 79   XP: $8   F18
◆◆◆   3/1-5/31   1P: $53- 63   2P/1B: $61- 71   2P/2B: $61- 71
Motor Inn   **Location:** I-25, exit 140. 1450 Riverbend Dr 82633. Fax: 307/358-6251. **Terms:** Package plans; pets, in
            designated rooms. **Facility:** 116 rooms. Attractive public areas. 2 stories; interior corridors; heated indoor pool,
saunas, whirlpool. **Dining:** $6-$29; also, Chutes Eatery & Saloon, see separate listing. **Services:** winter plug-ins.
Recreation: dart boards in lounge, pool tables. **All Rooms:** extended cable TV. **Cards:** AE, CB, DI, DS, MC, VI.
**Special Amenities: Free local telephone calls and free room upgrade (subject to availability with advanced
reservations).**

SUPER 8 MOTEL   Phone: (307)358-6800
(AAA) (SAVE)   All Year   1P: $41   2P/1B: $50   2P/2B: $55   XP: $6
◆   **Location:** I-25, exit 140. 314 Russell Ave 82633. Fax: 307/358-6800. **Terms:** Reserv deposit. **Facility:** 37
Motel   rooms. Simply furnished rooms with modern TV's. 2 stories; interior corridors; designated smoking area.
            Dining: Restaurant nearby. **Services:** winter plug-ins. **All Rooms:** extended cable TV. **Cards:** AE, CB, DI,
            DS, MC, VI. **Special Amenities:** Early check-in/late check-out and free local telephone calls.

RESTAURANT

CHUTES EATERY & SALOON   **Lunch:** $5-$8   **Dinner:** $6-$29   Phone: 307/358-9790
◆◆   **Location:** I-25, exit 140; in Best Western Douglas Inn & Conference Center. 1450 River Bend Dr 82633.
American   **Hours:** 6 am-2 & 5-10 pm. **Features:** casual dress; children's menu; salad bar; cocktails & lounge. Relaxed
            dining in a contemporary Western atmosphere. **Cards:** AE, CB, DI, DS, MC, VI.

DUBOIS—900

LODGINGS

BALD MOUNTAIN INN   Rates Subject to Change   Phone: 307/455-2844
◆◆   3/1-3/5 & 5/15-2/29 1P: $40- 50   2P/1B: $45- 58   2P/2B: $45- 58   XP: $5-10   F12
Motel   **Location:** 1.6 mi w on US 26 & 287. 1349 W Ramshorn St 82513. Fax: 307/455-3167. **Terms:** Open 3/1-3/5
            & 5/15-2/29; reserv deposit. **Facility:** 15 rooms. 7 two-bedroom units. Suites with fireplace, $75-$85 for up to
6 persons; 2 stories; exterior corridors; designated smoking area; playground. **Some Rooms:** 10 kitchens. **Cards:** AE, CB,
DI, DS, MC, VI.

BLACK BEAR COUNTRY INN   Phone: (307)455-2344
(AAA) (SAVE)   6/10-9/26   1P: $34- 48   2P/1B: $44- 50   2P/2B: $44- 50   XP: $4   F12
            5/1-6/9 & 9/27-11/30 1P: $32- 46   2P/1B: $40- 50   2P/2B: $42- 50   XP: $4   F12
◆   **Location:** 0.5 mi w on US 26 & 287. 505 N Ramshorn 82513 (PO Box 595). **Terms:** Open 5/1-11/30; reserv
Motel   deposit; pets, no cats. **Facility:** 15 rooms. 1 two-bedroom unit. 1 kitchen unit for up to 5 persons, $55; no uten-
            sils; 1 story; exterior corridors. **Services:** giftshop; winter plug-ins. **Recreation:** fishing. **All Rooms:** combo
or shower baths. **Cards:** AE, CB, DI, DS, MC, VI. **Special Amenities: Free local telephone calls and preferred room
(subject to availability with advanced reservations).**

BRANDING IRON INN   Phone: (307)455-2893
(AAA) (SAVE)   6/15-11/15   1P: $48   2P/1B: $53- 63   2P/2B: $58- 68   XP: $5   F14
            3/1-6/14 & 11/16-2/29   1P: $35   2P/1B: $45- 55   2P/2B: $45- 55   XP: $5   F14
◆◆   **Location:** 0.3 mi w on US 26 & 287. 401 W Ramshorn 82513 (PO Box 705). Fax: 307/455-2446.
Cottage   **Terms:** Reserv deposit, 3 day notice; pets. **Facility:** 23 rooms. Duplex log cabin units. Horse corrals on prem-
            ises. 3 efficiencies, $6 extra charge; 1 story; exterior corridors; designated smoking area. **Dining:** Restaurant
nearby. **Services:** winter plug-ins. **All Rooms:** combo or shower baths, extended cable TV. **Some Rooms:** 3 kitchens, no
utensils. **Cards:** AE, DI, MC, VI. *(See color ad p 320)*

CHINOOK WINDS MT LODGE   Phone: (307)455-2987
(AAA) (SAVE)   5/10-11/15 [CP]   1P: $50- 80   2P/1B: $50- 80   2P/2B: $80   XP: $5   F12
◆◆◆   **Location:** 0.8 mi s on US 26 & 287. 640 S First St 82513 (PO Box 1497). **Terms:** Open 5/10-11/15; weekly
Motel   rates; pets, $5 extra charge. **Facility:** 18 rooms. Attractive rustic Western decor; 1 story log unit & 2 story
            Western facade unit. 1 bedroom cabin, $120; 1-2 stories; exterior corridors; designated smoking area.
            Services: winter plug-ins. **Recreation:** fishing; volleyball net, games & puzzles, horse & wagon rides.
All Rooms: combo or shower baths. **Some Rooms:** efficiency, kitchen, no utensils, whirlpools. **Cards:** AE, DS, MC, VI.
Special Amenities: Early check-in/late check-out and free local telephone calls.

MOUNTAIN TOP BED & BREAKFAST   Rates Subject to Change   Phone: 307/455-2304
◆   All Year [BP]   1P: $95- 105 2P/1B: $95- 105 2P/2B: $95- 105 XP: $20   D18
Bed &   **Location:** 6 mi w on US 26/287, s at Stoney Point Ranch, 0.3 mi follow s on gravel road, 1.1 mi se, 0.7 mi
Breakfast   e. 177 Uphill Rd 82513 (PO Box 538). Fax: 307/455-2304. **Facility:** 5 rooms. Located 8,000 feet above sea
            level with views of the Absaroka Mountains & Wind River Valley. 1-2 stories; interior/exterior corridors; smoke
free premises. **Recreation:** hiking trails. **All Rooms:** combo or shower baths. **Cards:** MC, VI.

PINNACLE BUTTES LODGE & CAMPGROUND   Phone: (307)455-2506
(AAA) (SAVE)   5/28-9/5 & 12/16-2/29   1P: $55   2P/1B: $70   2P/2B: $70   XP: $5   F
                3/1-5/27 & 9/6-12/15   1P: $45   2P/1B: $50   2P/2B: $50
◆◆   **Location:** 20 mi w on US 26 & 287; in Shoshone National Forest. 3577 US Hwy 26W 82513.
Motel   **Fax:** 307/455-3874. **Terms:** Pets, $50 dep req. **Facility:** 13 rooms. Quiet location simple modern rooms; 3
cabins. Cabins, $70-$90; 1 story; exterior corridors; heated pool, whirlpool. **Dining:** Restaurant; 8 am-10 pm;
$4-$19. **Services:** giftshop. **Recreation:** fishing; cross country skiing; video rentals. **Fee:** snowmobiling. **All Rooms:** combo
or shower baths, extended cable TV. **Some Rooms:** 2 efficiencies. **Cards:** DS, MC, VI. **Special Amenities:** Early
check-in/late check-out.   🛏 ⌚ ⍟ 🍴 ⊠ 🐾 VCR 💻 🖨 🎁 🗝

STAGECOACH MOTOR INN   Phone: (307)455-2303
(AAA) (SAVE)   5/1-9/30   1P: $38- 48   2P/1B: $46- 56   2P/2B: $50- 60   XP: $5   F5
                3/1-4/30 & 10/1-2/29   1P: $32- 44   2P/1B: $40- 50   2P/2B: $44- 52   XP: $5   F5
◆◆◆   **Location:** Center; on US 26 & 287. 103 Ramshorn 82513 (PO Box 216). **Fax:** 307/455-3903. **Terms:** Reserv
Motel   deposit; small pets only, $5 extra charge. **Facility:** 50 rooms. Quiet location, with modern rooms & contempo-
rary decors. 2 two-bedroom units. 2 two-bedroom units with kitchen; 1-2 stories; exterior corridors; heated pool;
playground. **Dining:** Restaurant nearby. **Services:** giftshop; winter plug-ins. **Fee:** area transportation. **Recreation:** fishing;
horseshoes, tennis at park, tee pee at play area. **All Rooms:** combo or shower baths. **Some Rooms:** 4 kitchens.
Cards: AE, DI, DS, MC, VI. **Special Amenities:** Free local telephone calls and preferred room (subject to availability
with advanced reservations). *(See color ad below)*   🛏 🐕 ⌚ 🍴 ⊞ ⊞ 🛌 ⊠ 🚗 💻 🖨 🗝 🎁 🚫 ⊠

TRAIL'S END MOTEL   Phone: (307)455-2540
(AAA) (SAVE)   7/1-8/25   1P: $36   2P/1B: $42   2P/2B: $44   XP: $3-6   D12
                3/1-6/30 & 8/26-2/29   1P: $26   2P/1B: $32   2P/2B: $34   XP: $3-6   D12
◆◆   **Location:** 0.5 mi w on US 26 & 287. 511 Ramshorn 82513 (PO Box 1730). **Facility:** 20 rooms. Handsome log
Motel   building with a few large family style units. Excellent housekeeping. River front units, door front parking. 2 two-
bedroom units. 1 story; exterior corridors; designated smoking area. **Dining:** Restaurant nearby. **All Rooms:** combo or
shower baths, extended cable TV. **Some Rooms:** kitchen. **Cards:** AE, DS, MC, VI. **Special Amenities:** Early check-in/late
check-out and free local telephone calls.   🚗 ⊞ ⊞ ⊠ 🐾 🎁 💻 🖨 🗝 🖼 🗝 ⊠

RESTAURANT

OLD YELLOWSTONE GARAGE   **Lunch:** $5   **Dinner:** $25-$40   Phone: 307/455-3666
◆◆   **Location:** Center. 106 Ramshorn 82513. **Hours:** 5 pm-10 pm. Closed: 4/1-4/30 & 11/1-11/30.
Italian **Reservations:** accepted. **Features:** No A/C; casual dress; cocktails; street parking. Casual dining with daily
changing menu. Family style avail. **Cards:** AE, DS, MC, VI.   ⊠

EVANSTON—10,900

LODGINGS

BEST WESTERN DUNMAR INN   Phone: (307)789-3770
(AAA) (SAVE)   5/28-9/6   1P: $69- 89   2P/1B: $75- 95   2P/2B: $79- 109   XP: $6   F18
                Mon-Thurs 3/1-5/27 &
◆◆◆   9/7-2/29   1P: $59- 79   2P/1B: $65- 85   2P/2B: $69- 99   XP: $6   F18
Motor Inn   Fri-Sun 3/1-5/27 & 9/7-2/29   1P: $50   2P/1B: $50   2P/2B: $60   XP: $6   F18
Location: I-80, exit 3. 1601 Harrison Dr 82930 (PO Box 0768, 82931). **Fax:** 307/789-3758. **Facility:** 166
rooms. Located on over 10 acres. Complex of buildings; newly remodeled facilities & luxurious rooms. Excellent dollar value.
Hair dryer in all rooms. Executive & honeymoon suites, $95-$195. Mini-fridges avail; 1 story; exterior corridors; heated pool,
sauna. **Dining:** Dunmar's Legal Tender Dining & Lounge, see separate listing. **Services:** giftshop; winter plug-ins.
All Rooms: extended cable TV. **Some Rooms:** 2 efficiencies, no utensils, whirlpools. **Cards:** AE, CB, DI, DS, JC, MC, VI.
Special Amenities: Early check-in/late check-out and free local telephone calls. Best Western Motels.
(See color ad p 285)   🆂 🐕 🚐 ⌚ 🍴 🍸 ⊞ 🛌 🐾 🎿 💲 🖨 🖼 ⊞ 🏠 ⊠ 🗝

DAYS INN EVANSTON   Phone: (307)789-2220
(AAA) (SAVE)   5/28-9/8 [CP]   1P: $69- 79   2P/1B: $74- 84   2P/2B: $79- 89
                3/1-5/27 & 9/9-2/29 [CP] 1P: $59- 69   2P/1B: $64- 74   2P/2B: $69- 79
◆◆◆   **Location:** Just n of I-80, exit 3 (Harrison Rd n to Wasatch Rd). 339 Wasatch Rd 82930. **Fax:** 307/789-4122.
Motor Inn   **Terms:** Weekly rates; small pets only. **Facility:** 116 rooms. Contemporary rooms; espresso bar. Outside patio.
Weekend rates $10 extra charge; mini fridges avail, extra charge; 3 stories, no elevator; interior corridors; whirl-
pool. **Dining:** Restaurant; 6 am-10 pm; $8-$17; cocktails. **Services:** winter plug-ins. **All Rooms:** extended cable TV.
Some Rooms: 7 efficiencies, whirlpools. **Cards:** AE, CB, DI, DS, JC, MC, VI. **Special Amenities:** Free breakfast and free
local telephone calls. *(See color ad p 285)*   🆂 🛏 🐕 🚐 🍴 🍸 🛌 🐾 🖨 ⊞ 🏠 ⊠

EVANSTON SUPER 8 MOTEL
◆
Motel

Rates Subject to Change
4/1-9/30 [CP]   1P: $35   2P/1B: $40   2P/2B: $40
3/1-3/31 & 10/1-2/29 [EP]   1P: $33   2P/1B: $38   2P/2B: $38

Phone: 307/789-7510
XP: $4   F12

Location: I-80 exit 6, w on Bear River Dr 1.4 mi. 70 Bear River Dr 82930. Fax: 307/789-1200.
Terms: Reserv deposit. **Facility:** 89 rooms. Economical lodging. Mini refrigerator, $6; 2 stories; interior corridors; smoke free premises. **Cards:** AE, DI, DS, MC, VI. 🐾 📺 🖨 ✕

PINE GABLES B & B INN
◆◆◆
Historic Bed
& Breakfast

Rates Subject to Change
All Year [BP]   1P: $45- 50   2P/1B: $55- 70   2P/2B: $70- 80   XP: $10-20

Phone: (307)789-2069

Location: I-80, exit 3; 0.6 mi ne on Harrison Rd. 1049 Center St 82930. **Terms:** Age restrictions may apply; check-in 4 pm. **Facility:** 4 rooms. Built in 1883. Charming, elegant rooms. Antiques throughout. Close to golf course & tennis courts. All rooms with ceiling fans. Check-in between 4 pm-7 pm. 2 stories; interior corridors; smoke free premises; street parking only. **All Rooms:** combo or shower baths. **Cards:** AE, DS, MC, VI. 🛇 🔧 🖨 ✕

PRAIRIE INN
🔺🔺🔺
◆◆
Motel

Guaranteed Rates
All Year [CP]   2P/1B: $45- 50   2P/2B: $50- 60   XP: $6

Phone: (307)789-2920
F11

Location: 0.3 mi n of I-80, exit 6. 264 Bear River Dr 82930. **Terms:** Pets, $5 extra charge. **Facility:** 31 rooms. Spacious rooms. 1 story; interior/exterior corridors; designated smoking area. **Dining:** Restaurant nearby. **Services:** winter plug-ins. **All Rooms:** extended cable TV. **Cards:** AE, CB, DI, DS, MC, VI. 🐾 🍴 📺 🖨 ✕

RESTAURANT

DUNMAR'S LEGAL TENDER DINING & LOUNGE   **Lunch:** $5-$8   **Dinner:** $8-$25   **Phone:** 307/789-3770
Ⓐ
Location: I-80, exit 3; in Best Western Dunmar Inn. 1601 Harrison Dr 82930. **Hours:** 5:30 am-10 pm.
Reservations: accepted. **Features:** casual dress; children's menu; health conscious menu items; salad bar;
◆◆◆   cocktails & lounge; entertainment. Attractively appointed dining room. Daily lunch & dinner specials.
Continental   **Cards:** AE, CB, DI, DS, JC, MC, VI. *(See color ad p 285)*   ⓕ ☒

EVANSVILLE—1,400

LODGINGS

CASPER COMFORT INN   Rates Subject to Change   **Phone:** 307/235-3038
◆◆◆   6/1-8/31 [CP]   1P: $70- 90   2P/1B: $75- 85   2P/2B: $75- 85   XP: $5   F18
Motel   3/1-5/31 & 9/1-2/29 [CP]   1P: $55- 75   2P/1B: $60- 80   2P/2B: $60- 80   XP: $5   F18
Location: Just n of I-25, exit 185. 480 Lathrop Rd 82636 (PO Box 399). Fax: 307/235-3038. **Facility:** 56
rooms. Close to mall. Property still appears new. 2 stories; interior corridors; designated smoking area; small heated indoor
pool. **Services:** winter plug-ins. **All Rooms:** combo or shower baths. **Cards:** AE, CB, DI, DS, MC, VI.
SAVE ⑤ 🐾 ➦ 🍴 🍽 ☐ 🖨 🛢 ⌨ ♿ ☒ 🏊

SHILO INN-CASPER/EVANSVILLE   All Year [BP]   1P: $59- 99   2P/1B: $59- 99   2P/2B: $59- 99   XP: $8   F12
Ⓐ SAVE   **Location:** Just n of I-25, exit 185 (East Casper). I-25 & Curtis Rd 82636-0246 (PO Box 246).
◆◆   Fax: 307/577-7429. **Terms:** Pets, $7 extra charge. **Facility:** 101 rooms. Close to shopping mall. Very clean
Motor Inn   rooms. 2 stories; interior corridors; heated indoor pool, sauna, steamroom, whirlpool. **Dining:** Restaurant; 6
am-10 pm; $6-$19; cocktails. **Services:** winter plug-ins. **All Rooms:** combo or shower baths, extended cable
TV. **Cards:** AE, CB, DI, DS, JC, MC, VI. **Special Amenities:** Free local telephone calls and free newspaper.
⑤ 🐾 🛏 ♿ 🍽 ➦ 🍴 🍽 🛳 🖨 VCR ☐ 🖨 🛢 ⌨ ☒

GILLETTE—17,600

LODGING

HOLIDAY INN OF GILLETTE   Rates Subject to Change   **Phone:** (307)686-3000
◆◆◆   5/30-9/11   1P: $84- 93   2P/1B: $84- 93   2P/2B: $84- 93
Motor Inn   3/14-5/29 & 9/12-2/29   1P: $68- 75   2P/1B: $68- 75   2P/2B: $68- 75
3/1-3/13   1P: $64- 71   2P/1B: $64- 71   2P/2B: $64- 71
Location: Just se of I-90, exit 126. 2009 S Douglas Hwy 59 82718. Fax: 307/686-4018. **Facility:** 158 rooms. Spacious public
areas; many rooms with inside balcony. Suites, $108 for 2 persons; 3 stories; interior/exterior corridors; heated indoor pool;
playground. **Services:** giftshop; winter plug-ins. **Cards:** AE, CB, DI, DS, JC, MC, VI.
ASK ⑤ 🛏 ♿ 🐾 ➦ 🍴 🍽 🛳 🖨 ☒ 🏊 🍽 ☐ 🖨 🛢 ☒ 🏊

RESTAURANT

BAILEY'S BAR & GRILL   Historical   **Lunch:** $4-$8   **Dinner:** $6-$15   **Phone:** 307/686-7678
Ⓐ   **Location:** Center. 301 S Gillette 82716. **Hours:** 8 am-10 pm, Sat from 10 am. Closed major holidays & Sun.
Features: casual dress; children's menu; cocktails; street parking. Casual dining in restored 1935 post office,
◆◆   featuring light meals & homemade pie. **Cards:** AE, DS, MC, VI.   ☒
American

GLENROCK—2,200

LODGINGS

ALL AMERICAN INN   All Year   **Phone:** (307)436-2772
Ⓐ SAVE   1P: $29   2P/1B: $33   2P/2B: $39   XP: $5   F15
Location: I-25, exit 165; 2.4 mi n. 500 W Aspen St 82637. **Terms:** Pets, $20 dep req. **Facility:** 21 rooms. Very
◆◆   clean, spacious rooms. 1-2 stories; exterior corridors. **Dining:** Restaurant. **Services:** winter plug-ins.
Motel   **Cards:** AE, DS, MC, VI. **Special Amenities:** Early check-in/late check-out and free local telephone
calls.   🛏 🍴 🍽 ☐ 🛢

HOTEL HIGGINS   Rates Subject to Change   **Phone:** 307/436-9212
◆◆   All Year [BP]   1P: $46- 56   2P/1B: $60- 70   2P/2B: $60- 84   XP: $15-30
Historic   **Location:** I-25, exit 165; 2 mi n on 4th St to Birch St. 416 W Birch St 82637. Fax: 307/436-9213. **Facility:** 9
Country Inn   rooms. 1916 hotel, turn-of-the-century decor, with personalized service. 2 suites, $70 for up to 2 persons; 2
stories; interior corridors; street parking only. **Services:** winter plug-ins. **All Rooms:** shower or tub baths.
Some Rooms: color TV. **Cards:** CB, DI, DS, MC, VI.   🍽 🍴 🍽 🍽 🏊

RESTAURANT

THE PAISLEY SHAWL   **Lunch:** $4-$8   **Dinner:** $16-$28   **Phone:** 307/436-9212
◆◆◆   **Location:** I-25, exit 165; 2 mi n on 4th St to Birch St; in Hotel Higgins. 416 W Birch 82637. **Hours:** 11:30
American   am-1:30 & 6-9:30 pm. Closed major holidays, Sun & Mon in winter. **Reservations:** suggested.
Features: casual dress; cocktails & lounge; street parking; also prix fixe. Elegant Victorian atmosphere;
offering continental dining. Excellent prime rib & steak. **Cards:** CB, DI, DS, MC, VI.

GRAND TETON NATIONAL PARK—*See also DRIGGS, JACKSON, MORAN & TETON VILLAGE.*

LODGINGS

COLTER BAY VILLAGE & CABINS
Rates Subject to Change
Phone: (307)543-2828
[FYI]
5/21-9/26
1P: $61- 117 2P/1B: $61- 117 2P/2B: $61- 117 XP: $9   F11
Has not been inspected. **Location:** 10 mi nw of Moran, jct US 89 & 287. (PO Box 240, MORAN, 83013).
Resort Fax: 307/543-3029. **Terms:** Open 5/21-9/26; check-in 4 pm; reserv deposit; handling fee imposed.
Cottage **Facility:** 208 rooms. Rustic log cabins on spacious grounds, some with view of Teton Range. Meets AAA fire safety requirements. 31 two-bedroom units. 42 two-bedroom cabins, $79-$99 for 1-4 persons; 9 rooms with shared bath, $27; 1 story; exterior corridors; designated smoking area; boat dock, boat ramp. Fee: marina.
Services: giftshop. Fee: area transportation. **Recreation:** swimming, fishing. Fee: horseback riding. Rental: boats, canoes.
Cards: AE, DI, MC, VI. *(See color ad p 142)*
🛏️ 📶 🍴 🛬 🛋️ 🏊 ⊗ 📷 🎿 🛎️ 📱 ⊗

COWBOY VILLAGE RESORT AT TOGWOTEE
Rates Subject to Change
Phone: (307)543-2847
(AAA)
3/1-4/12 [MAP]
1P: $199
2P/2B: $211- 260
◆◆◆
6/25-8/20 [EP]
1P: $99- 154
2P/2B: $99- 154 XP: $8   F12
Lodge
6/1-6/24 & 8/21-10/15 [EP] 1P: $89- 144
2P/2B: $89- 144 XP: $8   F12
Location: 16.5 mi e of Moran, jct US 26 & 287. (PO Box 91, MORAN, 83013). Fax: 307/543-2391.
Terms: Open 3/1-4/12 & 6/1-10/15; check-in 4 pm; reserv deposit, 7 day notice; handling fee imposed; weekly rates; package plans, in winter. **Facility:** 89 rooms. Wooded & mountainous national forest area. Closed 4/15-6/2 & 10/21-11/20. Fireside lounge for evening get togethers. 7 two-bedroom units. 3 stories, no elevator; interior corridors; whirlpools; playground. **Dining:** Dining room; 7 am-9:30 pm; dining room, see separate listing. **Services:** complimentary evening beverages, in winter. Fee: massage. **Recreation:** fishing; cross country skiing, tobogganing. **Services:** snowmobiling; dogsledding; horseback riding. **Some Rooms:** whirlpools. **Cards:** AE, DI, MC, VI. *(See color ad below)*
ASK 📶 📶 🍴 🍷 🏊 ⊗ 📷 🎿 🖥️ 🍴 📱 🛎️ ⊗

FLAGG RANCH VILLAGE
Rates Subject to Change
Phone: (307)543-2861
(AAA)
3/16-12/14
2P/1B: $94- 125 2P/2B: $94- 125 XP: $5
◆◆
3/1-3/15 & 12/15-2/29
2P/1B: $77- 105 2P/2B: $77- 105 XP: $5
Motor Inn
Location: Hwy 89 & US 191, 2 mi s of Yellowstone National Park s entrance, 5 mi n of Grand Teton National park n entrance. (PO Box 187, MORAN, 83013). Fax: 307/543-2356. **Terms:** Check-in 4 pm; reserv deposit, 14 day notice, in winter; handling fee imposed; package plans, in winter; pets, $5 extra charge.
Facility: 92 rooms. Motel units on banks of Snake River. Newly built cabins some with view of Tetons. Closed 3/15-5/14 & 11/1-12/14. 1 story; exterior corridors. **Dining:** Restaurant, deli; 7 am-10 pm; store & deli 6 am-10 pm; $7-$14.
Services: giftshop; area transportation. **Recreation:** fishing; cross country skiing, snowshoeing; hiking trails, jogging. Fee: float trips; snowmobiling; horseback riding, snow coach tours, whitewater rafting. **Cards:** AE, DS, MC, VI.
(See color ad p 320)
🛏️ 📶 🍴 🍷 🛬 ⊗ 📷 📱 🛎️ 🍴 🛎️ 🛋️ ⊗ 📱

HATCHET MOTEL
Rates Subject to Change
Phone: 307/543-2413
◆
6/19-9/2
1P: $80
2P/1B: $80
2P/2B: $80   XP: $5
Motor Inn
6/6-6/18 & 9/3-9/28
1P: $70
2P/1B: $70
2P/2B: $70   XP: $5
Location: 7.5 mi e, on US 26 & 287, from Moran Jct. (PO Box 316, MORAN, 83013). Fax: 307/543-2413.
Terms: Open 6/6-9/28; check-in 4 pm; reserv deposit; handling fee imposed. **Facility:** 22 rooms. Rustic log building on landscaped grounds with scenic mountain view. 1 story; exterior corridors; designated smoking area; playground.
Recreation: hiking trails. **All Rooms:** shower baths. **Cards:** DS, MC, VI.
🛏️ 🍴 ⊗ 📷 🎿 🍴 🛎️ ⊗

THE INN AT BUFFALO FORK
◆◆◆
Bed &
Breakfast
Rates Subject to Change
5/1-9/30 [BP]   1P: $140- 190   2P/1B: $150- 210 2P/2B: $150   XP: $20   F10
3/1-4/30 & 10/1-2/29 [BP] 1P: $120- 160   2P/1B: $125- 180 2P/2B: $125   XP: $20   F10
Location: 6.5 mi e of Moran jct on US 26 & 287. 18200 E US 287 (PO Box 311, MORAN, 83013).
Fax: 307/543-0935. **Terms:** Check-in 4 pm; reserv deposit, 30 day notice; handling fee imposed. **Facility:** 5
rooms. 2 stories; interior corridors; smoke free premises. **Services:** winter plug-ins. **Recreation:** charter fishing.
Fee: horseback riding. **All Rooms:** combo or shower baths. **Some Rooms:** color TV. **Cards:** DS, MC, VI.
Phone: 307/543-2010

JACKSON LAKE LODGE
◆◆◆
Resort Hotel
Rates Subject to Change
5/16-10/13   1P: $99- 190   2P/1B: $99- 190   2P/2B: $99- 190 XP: $9   F11
Location: 5 mi nw of Moran, jct US 89 & 287. (PO Box 240, MORAN, 83013). Fax: 307/543-3143.
Terms: Open 5/16-10/13; check-in 4 pm; reserv deposit; handling fee imposed; 15% service charge.
Facility: 385 rooms. Spacious, landscaped grounds overlooking Grand Teton & Jackson Lake. Some units with Grand Teton
view. 1-3 stories; interior/exterior corridors; designated smoking area; heated pool; playground. **Services:** giftshop. Fee: area
transportation. **Recreation:** fishing; hiking trails. Fee: horseback riding. **Cards:** AE, DI, MC, VI. *(See color ad p 142)*
Phone: (307)543-2811

JENNY LAKE LODGE
Ⓐ
◆◆◆◆
Resort
Cottage
Rates Subject to Change
5/28-10/3 [MAP]   1P: $300   2P/1B: $375   2P/2B: $375   XP: $110
Location: 3 mi off Interpark Rd, jct N Jenny Lake. (PO Box 240, MORAN, 83013). Fax: 307/733-0324.
Terms: Open 5/28-10/3; check-in 4 pm; reserv deposit, 21 day notice; handling fee imposed. **Facility:** 37
rooms. Individual & duplex, log cabins in a scenic, quiet, pine shaded setting at foot of Tetons. 6 cottages with
fireplace, $455; 1 story; exterior corridors; smoke free premises; mountain view. **Dining:** Dining room; 7:30
am-9, noon-1:30 & 6-9 pm, Sun 5:15 pm-8:45 pm; $40; cocktails; reservations req for dinner, jackets
suggested; Sun buffet. **Recreation:** bicycles, hiking trails, horseback riding, lawn games. Fee: fishing.
Some Rooms: whirlpools. **Cards:** AE, DI, MC, VI. *(See color ad p 142)*
Phone: 307/733-4647

SIGNAL MOUNTAIN LODGE
Ⓐ [SAVE]
◆◆◆
Resort
Complex
5/8-10/10   1P: $80- 175   2P/1B: $80- 175   2P/2B: $80- 175 XP: $8   F
Location: Teton Park Rd, 2 mi s of US 89, 191 & 287. (PO Box 50, MORAN, 83013). Fax: 307/543-2569.
Terms: Open 5/8-10/10; reserv deposit, 4 day notice; pets. **Facility:** 79 rooms. Older property on Jackson Lake
with excellent view of Grand Tetons. Motel rooms & 34 rustic log cabins. 2 stories; exterior corridors; ocean-
front; beach; boat ramp, marina. **Dining:** Dining room, coffee shop; 7 am-10 pm; $10-$20; cocktails.
Services: giftshop. **Recreation:** swimming, fishing, waterskiing; bicycles, hiking trails. Rental: boats, canoes.
Some Rooms: 30 efficiencies, no utensils. **Cards:** AE, DS, MC, VI.
Phone: (307)543-2831

RESTAURANTS

ASPENS RESTAURANT
◆◆
American
Lunch: $7-$12   **Dinner:** $10-$20   **Phone:** 307/543-2831
Location: Teton Park Rd, 2 mi s of US 89, 191 & 287; in the Signal Mountain Lodge. **Hours:** Open
5/17-10/16; 7 am-10 pm; 9/25-10/16. **Features:** No A/C; casual dress; children's menu; carryout;
cocktails & lounge. On Jackson Lake with excellent view of Grand Tetons. Varied menu with seafood
specialties. Smoke free premises. **Cards:** AE, DS, MC, VI.

COWBOY VILLAGE RESORT AT TOGWOTEE
◆◆
American
Lunch: $5-$7   **Dinner:** $7-$21   **Phone:** 307/543-2847
Location: 16.5 mi e of Moran jct, on US 26 & 287; in Togwotee Mountain Lodge. **Hours:** 7-9:30 am,
11:30-3:30 & 5:30-9:30 pm; 7 am-4 & 5:30-9:30 pm, 6/3-10/21. **Features:** casual dress; children's menu;
senior's menu; carryout; salad bar; cocktails & lounge; a la carte. Family dining in mountain lodge, featuring
varied menu. Located in National Forest. Smoke free premises. **Cards:** AE, DS, MC, VI.

THE MURAL ROOM
◆◆◆
American
Lunch: $5-$8   **Dinner:** $15-$30   **Phone:** 307/543-2811
Location: 5 mi nw of Moran, jct US 89 & 287; in Jackson Lake Lodge. 83013. **Hours:** Open 5/17-10/14; 7
am-9:30, noon-1:30 & 6-9:30 pm. **Reservations:** suggested. **Features:** casual dress; children's menu; health
conscious menu; cocktails & lounge; a la carte. Wall murals portray history of Jackson Hole. Magnificent
view of the Tetons. Outdoor barbecue nightly. Smoke free premises. **Cards:** AE, DI, MC, VI.

GREEN RIVER—12,700

LODGINGS

COACHMAN INN MOTEL
Ⓐ
◆◆
Motel
Guaranteed Rates   **Phone:** (307)875-3681
5/1-9/30   1P: $31- 36   2P/1B: $36- 40   2P/2B: $40- 47 XP: $5   D5
3/1-4/30 & 10/1-2/29   1P: $30- 36   2P/1B: $34- 38   2P/2B: $38- 46 XP: $5   D5
Location: Just e on I-80 business loop. 470 E Flaming Gorge Way 82935. **Facility:** 18 rooms. Some remodeled rooms. Very clean rooms. Microwaves & mini refrigerators avail, extra charge; 1 story; exterior corridors;
designated smoking area. **Dining:** Restaurant nearby. **Cards:** AE, DI, DS, JC, MC, VI.

SUPER 8 MOTEL GREEN RIVER
◆◆
Motel
Rates Subject to Change   **Phone:** 307/875-9330
6/1-9/30   1P: $37   2P/1B: $42   2P/2B: $46   XP: $5
3/1-5/31 & 10/1-2/29   1P: $33   2P/1B: $37   2P/2B: $43   XP: $5
Location: Just w on US 30 & I-80 business loop. 280 W Flaming Gorge Way 82935. Fax: 307/875-7636.
Facility: 37 rooms. Economy lodging. 3 stories, no elevator; interior corridors. **Services:** winter plug-ins. **Cards:** AE, CB, DI,
DS, MC, VI.

RESTAURANT

EMBERS FAMILY RESTAURANT
◆
American
Lunch: $4-$13   **Dinner:** $4-$13   **Phone:** 307/875-9983
Location: Just s of I-80 business loop, on N First East St. 95 E Railroad 82935. **Hours:** 6 am-10 pm.
Closed: 12/25. **Features:** carryout; cocktails; street parking; a la carte. Casual diner with wide menu
selection, including some Mexican dishes. **Cards:** AE, DS, MC, VI.

GREYBULL—1,800

LODGINGS

ANTLER MOTEL — Rates Subject to Change — **Phone: 307/765-4404**
◆
Motel

	1P:		2P/1B:			2P/2B:		XP:		
6/15-9/1	$30-	35	$30-	35		$40-	50	$3		F12
9/2-11/1	$30		$32			$40		$3		F12
3/1-6/14 & 11/2-2/29	$27		$30			$35		$2		F12

Location: 0.8 mi w on US 14, 16 & 20. 1116 N 6th St 82426. **Facility:** 14 rooms. Quiet, economical lodging. 1 two-bedroom unit. 1 story; exterior corridors; playground. **Services:** winter plug-ins. **All Rooms:** combo or shower baths. **Some Rooms:** 5 efficiencies. **Cards:** AE, DS, MC, VI.

K-BAR MOTEL — **Phone: (307)765-4426**
AAA SAVE
◆
Motel

	1P:		2P/1B:			2P/2B:		XP:		
6/1-9/15	$40-	48	$45-	53		$60-	66	$5		F18
3/1-5/31 & 9/16-2/29	$35-	40	$38-	45		$50-	55	$4		F18

Location: 0.3 mi e on US 14. 300 Greybull Ave 82426. Fax: 307/765-9344. **Terms:** Small pets only, $4 extra charge. **Facility:** 19 rooms. A few family rooms. 3 two-bedroom units, $50 for up to 5 persons; 1 story; exterior corridors. **Dining:** Restaurant nearby. **Services:** winter plug-ins. **Recreation:** picnic area. **All Rooms:** combo or shower baths, extended cable TV. **Cards:** AE, DS, MC, VI. **Special Amenities:** Free local telephone calls.

SAGE MOTEL — **Phone: (307)765-4443**
AAA SAVE
◆
Motel

	1P:		2P/1B:			2P/2B:		XP:	
6/30-9/1	$32-	36	$38-	42		$44-	48	$4	
3/1-6/29 & 9/2-2/29	$25		$28			$34		$4	

Location: 0.8 mi nw on US 14, 16 & 20. 1135 N 6th St 82426. Fax: 307/765-4794. **Terms:** Weekly/monthly rates; package plans, in winter; small pets only, $5 extra charge, $50 dep req. **Facility:** 17 rooms. Well maintained rooms. 2 family units, $60-$65; 1 story; exterior corridors; designated smoking area. **Dining:** Restaurant nearby. **Services:** winter plug-ins. **All Rooms:** combo or shower baths, extended cable TV. **Cards:** AE, DS, MC, VI. **Special Amenities:** Early check-in/late check-out and free local telephone calls.

YELLOWSTONE MOTEL — **Phone: (307)765-4456**
AAA SAVE
◆◆
Motel

	1P:		2P/1B:			2P/2B:		XP:	
5/23-8/31	$45-	50	$55-	66		$60-	70	$6	
3/1-5/22 & 9/1-2/29	$34-	40	$38-	45		$42-	52	$6	

Location: 0.4 mi e on US 14. 247 Greybull Ave 82426. Fax: 307/765-2108. **Terms:** Reserv deposit, 3 day notice; small pets only, $5 extra charge. **Facility:** 34 rooms. Large rooms. 2 two-bedroom units, $60-$80; 1 story; exterior corridors; putting green; small heated pool. **Dining:** Restaurant nearby. **Services:** winter plug-ins. **All Rooms:** combo or shower baths, extended cable TV. **Some Rooms:** kitchen. **Cards:** AE, DS, MC, VI.

RESTAURANT

LISA'S — **Lunch:** $4-$8 — **Dinner:** $8-$16 — **Phone:** 307/765-4765
AAA
◆◆
American

Location: 0.4 mi e on US 14. 200 Greybull Ave 82426. **Hours:** 11 am-10 pm, from 6 am 7/1-8/31. Closed major holidays & Sun 11/1-5/31. **Features:** casual dress; children's menu; carryout; cocktails & lounge. Tex-Mex meals, steak, pasta, salad & dessert. **Cards:** DS, MC, VI.

GUERNSEY—1,200

LODGING

THE BUNKHOUSE MOTEL — Rates Subject to Change — **Phone:** 307/836-2356
◆◆
Motel

	1P:	2P/1B:	2P/2B:
Fri & Sat	$51	$62	$63
Sun-Thurs	$40	$41	$42

Location: Just w on US 26. 350 W Whalen 82214 (PO Box 310). Fax: 307/836-2328. **Facility:** 31 rooms. Unique, rustic western decor. 1 story; exterior corridors; designated smoking area. **Services:** winter plug-ins. **Cards:** AE, DI, DS, MC, VI.

HULETT—400

LODGING

HULETT MOTEL — Rates Subject to Change — **Phone:** 307/467-5220
AAA
◆
Motel

	1P:		2P/1B:		2P/2B:		XP:	
4/20-12/1	$35-	45	$45-	60	$45-	60	$6-10	

Location: SR 24 at n end of town. 202 Main St 82720 (PO Box 489). **Terms:** Open 4/20-12/1; reserv deposit; pets. **Facility:** 11 rooms. Adjacent Belle Fourche river. Very clean rooms. Espresso & ice cream bar. 4 two-bedroom units. Mini refrigerators avail; 1 story; exterior corridors; designated smoking area; gazebo, sundeck. **Services:** giftshop. **All Rooms:** combo or shower baths. **Cards:** DS, MC, VI.

JACKSON—4,500—See also GRAND TETON NATIONAL PARK & YELLOWSTONE NATIONAL PARK.

LODGINGS

THE ALPINE HOUSE — Rates Subject to Change — **Phone:** 307/739-1570
◆◆
Bed &
Breakfast

	1P:	2P/1B:	2P/2B:	XP:
7/1-8/31 [BP]	$120	$120	$120	$20
6/1-6/30 & 9/1-9/30 [BP]	$110	$110	$110	$20
3/1-3/31 & 12/15-2/29 [BP]	$95	$95	$95	$20
4/1-5/31 & 10/1-12/14 [BP]	$80	$80	$80	$20

Location: 0.3 mi n, turn n on Glenwood or w on Mercil Ave from US 26/89/191. 285 N Glenwood 83001 (PO Box 20245). Fax: 307/734-2850. **Terms:** Check-in 4 pm; reserv deposit, 30 day notice; handling fee imposed. **Facility:** 7 rooms. Downtown, cedar-sided house with large open dining area. Norwegian Inn decor, all rooms with private balcony. 2 stories; interior/exterior corridors; smoke free premises. **Services:** winter plug-ins. **Cards:** MC, VI.

ANGLER'S INN

AAA SAVE

Phone: (307)733-3682

6/1-9/30	1P:	$95	2P/1B:	$95	2P/2B:	$100- 105	XP: $5	F12
3/1-5/31 & 10/1-2/29	1P:	$60	2P/1B:	$60	2P/2B:	$65- 70	XP: $5	F12

◆◆
Motel

Location: Just nw of town square, n on Millward or w on Mercil from US 26/89/191. 265 N Millward 83001 (PO Box 1247). Fax: 307/733-8662. **Terms:** Reserv deposit, 3 day notice. **Facility:** 28 rooms. Appropriately & tastefully decorated rooms, custom made furniture, good room lighting. 2 stories; exterior corridors; designated smoking area. **Dining:** Restaurant nearby. **Services:** winter plug-ins. **All Rooms:** extended cable TV. **Cards:** AE, DS, MC, VI. **Special Amenities:** Free local telephone calls and free newspaper.

BEST WESTERN-THE LODGE AT JACKSON HOLE

AAA SAVE

Phone: (307)739-9703

6/19-9/7 [BP]	1P:	$199	2P/1B:	$199	2P/2B:	$199	XP: $10	F12
3/1-4/12 & 1/1-2/29 [BP]	1P:	$109- 159	2P/1B:	$159	2P/2B:	$159	XP: $10	F12
5/22-6/18 [BP]	1P:	$129- 159	2P/1B:	$159	2P/2B:	$159	XP: $10	F12
4/13-5/21 & 9/8-12/31 [BP]	1P:	$79- 199					XP: $10	F12

◆◆◆
Motor Inn

Location: 0.3 mi sw, just e of US 26/89/191. 80 Scott Ln 83001 (PO Box 7478, 83002). Fax: 307/739-9168. **Terms:** Check-in 4 pm; reserv deposit, 7 day notice, 30 day in winter. **Facility:** 154 rooms. Attractive lodge pole decor. Unique animal wood carvings at entrance. Large, modern rooms, most with fireplace. 3 stories; interior corridors; designated smoking area; heated indoor/outdoor pool, sauna, whirlpools. **Dining:** Limited grill, happy hour & full cocktails. **Services:** giftshop; complimentary evening beverages; area transportation, town center; winter plug-ins. **Recreation:** ski lockers; fun stop coupons, privileges to local health club. **All Rooms:** combo or shower baths, extended cable TV. **Some Rooms:** whirlpools. **Cards:** AE, DI, DS, JC, MC, VI. **Special Amenities:** Free breakfast and free local telephone calls.

BUCKRAIL LODGE

AAA

Guaranteed Rates

Phone: 307/733-2079

6/4-9/5			2P/2B:	$75- 110	XP: $5	D8
9/6-9/26			2P/2B:	$65- 80	XP: $5	D8
5/7-6/3			2P/2B:	$50- 60	XP: $5	D8
5/1-5/6 & 9/27-10/16			2P/2B:	$45- 50	XP: $5	D8

◆◆◆
Motel

Location: Just s & e of US 26/89/187/189; 0.3 mi s of Town Square via King St, at jct of Karns Ave & King St. 110 E Karns Ave 83001 (PO Box 23). Fax: 307/734-1663. **Terms:** Open 5/1-10/16; reserv deposit, 7 day notice; handling fee imposed. **Facility:** 12 rooms. Cedar logged motel in quiet residential area close to downtown at base of Snow King Mountain. Well-kept rooms with Western touches. Inviting yard area with tables & shade trees. 1 story; exterior corridors; designated smoking area; whirlpool. **Dining:** Restaurant. **All Rooms:** combo or shower baths, extended cable TV. **Cards:** AE, DS, MC, VI. *(See color ad below)*

Our **bold type** listings have a special interest in serving you!

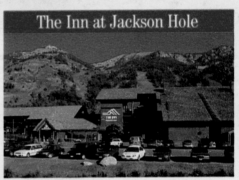

CACHE CREEK MOTEL

Phone: (307)733-7781

3/1-4/10, 6/15-9/10 & 12/20-2/29

4/11-6/14 & 9/11-12/19

1P:	$88-	97	2P/1B:	$88-	97	2P/2B:	$95- 105	XP:	$6	F5
1P:	$55-	65	2P/1B:	$55-	65	2P/2B:	$62- 72	XP:	$6	F5

Apartment Motel

Location: Just n, n on Glenwood or w on Perry from US 26/89/191. 390 N Glenwood 83001 (PO Box 918). **Fax:** 307/733-4652. **Terms:** Reserv deposit, 15 day notice; package plans. **Facility:** 37 rooms. Good size rooms. Close to restaurants/shopping. 9 two-bedroom units. 19 suites, $150 for up to 2 persons; 3 stories, no elevator; exterior corridors; designated smoking area; whirlpool. **Services:** winter plug-ins. **Recreation:** ski lockers. **All Rooms:** efficiencies, extended cable TV. **Cards:** AE, CB, DI, DS, MC, VI. *(See color ad p 290)*

- Log Cabin Resort in Jackson Hole
- Kitchenettes
- Hot Tubs
- Covered Decks
- Air Conditioning
- 4 1/2 blocks from Town Square

COWBOY VILLAGE RESORT

800-962-4988

120 S. Flatcreek Dr.
Jackson, WY 83001

COWBOY VILLAGE RESORT

Phone: (307)733-3121

◆◆◆ Cottage

	Rates Subject to Change				
6/17-8/17	1P: $139	2P/1B: $139	2P/2B: $139- 159	XP: $5	F12
6/10-6/16 & 8/18-9/14	1P: $119	2P/1B: $119	2P/2B: $119- 149	XP: $5	F12
5/13-6/9 & 9/15-10/4	1P: $99	2P/1B: $99	2P/2B: $99- 129	XP: $5	F12
3/1-5/12 & 10/5-2/29	1P: $89	2P/1B: $89	2P/2B: $89- 109	XP: $5	F12

Location: 0.3 mi w on Broadway to Flat Creek Dr, just s. 120 S Flat Creek Dr 83001 (PO Box 1747). Fax: 307/739-1955. **Terms:** Reserv deposit, 10 day notice, in winter; handling fee imposed. **Facility:** 82 rooms. A small village of log cabins downtown near ski lift, each with picnic table & barbecue grill. 1 story; exterior corridors; designated smoking area. **Services:** winter plug-ins. **Recreation:** Fee: downhill skiing, snowmobiling; bicycles, horseback riding. **All Rooms:** kitchens. **Cards:** AE, DI, DS, MC, VI. *(See color ad p 292)*

DAVY JACKSON INN

Phone: (307)739-2294
XP: $15   F12

Ⓐ Ⓢ
◆◆◆
Bed & Breakfast

6/15-9/30 [BP]	1P: $169- 229	2P/1B: $169- 229	
3/1-6/14 & 10/1-2/29 [BP]	1P: $139- 179	2P/1B: $139- 179	

Location: Just n & w from town square. 85 Perry Ave 83001 (PO Box 20147). Fax: 307/733-9704. **Terms:** Reserv deposit, 30 day notice; handling fee imposed. **Facility:** 12 rooms. Newly built Victorian house; European Inn style of operation. Luxurious room accommodations & decor. 1 two-bedroom unit. 3 rms with fireplace; 3 rms with steam shower; 3 stories, no elevator; interior corridors; designated smoking area; whirlpool. **Dining:** Afternoon tea. **All Rooms:** extended cable TV. **Some Rooms:** kitchen, whirlpools. **Cards:** AE, DS, MC, VI. **Special Amenities:** Free breakfast and free local telephone calls.

DAYS INN OF JACKSON HOLE

Phone: (307)733-0033

Ⓐ Ⓢ
◆◆◆
Motel

5/28-10/2 [CP]	1P: $159- 219	2P/1B: $159- 219	2P/2B: $159- 219	XP: $5-10	F12
12/24-1/1 [CP]	1P: $119- 199	2P/1B: $119- 199	2P/2B: $119- 199	XP: $5-10	F12
3/1-4/3 & 1/2-2/29 [CP]	1P: $99- 179	2P/1B: $99- 179	2P/2B: $99- 179	XP: $5-10	F12
4/4-5/27 & 10/3-12/23 [CP]	1P: $79- 159	2P/1B: $79- 159	2P/2B: $79- 159	XP: $5-10	F12

Location: 1.5 mi s on US 26/89/191. 350 S Hwy 89 83001 (PO Box 2986). Fax: 307/733-0044. **Terms:** Reserv deposit, 3 day notice. **Facility:** 91 rooms. Attractive public areas. 12 very luxurious suites, some with whirlpool & fireplace, $195-$250; 3 stories; interior corridors; designated smoking area; sauna, whirlpool. **Dining:** Restaurant nearby. **Services:** winter plug-ins. **Recreation:** ski racks. **All Rooms:** extended cable TV. **Some Rooms:** whirlpools. **Cards:** AE, CB, DI, DS, MC, VI. **Special Amenities:** Free breakfast and free local telephone calls.

ELK REFUGE INN

Phone: (307)733-3582

Ⓐ
◆◆
Motel

	Rates Subject to Change				
6/15-9/10	1P: $89	2P/1B: $94	2P/2B: $94- 110	XP: $6	F10
5/23-6/14 & 9/11-10/31	1P: $60	2P/1B: $65	2P/2B: $65- 75	XP: $6	F10
3/1-5/22 & 11/1-2/29	1P: $45	2P/1B: $50	2P/2B: $55- 65	XP: $6	F10

Location: 1.5 mi n on US 26/89/191. 1755 N Hwy 89 83001 (PO Box 2834). Fax: 307/733-6531. **Terms:** Check-in 4 pm; reserv deposit, 3 day notice; handling fee imposed; weekly rates, in winter. **Facility:** 23 rooms. Overlooks Elk Refuge. 2-bedroom suites, $75-$150; 2 stories; exterior corridors; designated smoking area. **Services:** winter plug-ins. **All Rooms:** extended cable TV. **Cards:** AE, DS, MC, VI. *(See color ad below)*

4 WINDS MOTEL

Phone: (307)733-2474

Ⓐ Ⓢ
◆◆
Motel

6/18-9/5	2P/1B: $82- 102	2P/2B: $82- 102	XP: $5	F10
6/1-6/17, 9/6-9/18 & 12/17-1/1	2P/1B: $60- 83	2P/2B: $72- 93	XP: $5	F10
3/1-3/31, 9/19-9/30 & 1/2-2/29	2P/1B: $46- 72	2P/2B: $54- 80	XP: $5	F10
4/1-5/31 & 10/1-12/16	2P/1B: $40- 58	2P/2B: $46- 66	XP: $5	F10

Location: Just n of US 26, 89, 187 & 191. 150 N Millward St 83001 (PO Box 66). **Terms:** Check-in 4 pm; reserv deposit, 3 day notice, 7 days 9/7-6/17; handling fee imposed. **Facility:** 21 rooms. Near downtown area, well-lighted rooms. Across from City Park. 2 stories; exterior corridors. **Dining:** Restaurant nearby. **Services:** winter plug-ins. **All Rooms:** extended cable TV. **Cards:** AE, DI, MC, VI. *(See color ad p 294)*

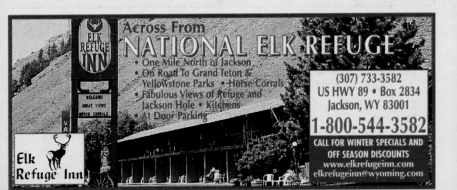

THE GOLDEN EAGLE INN

⬥⬥⬥ SAVE	6/18-9/5		2P/1B:	$84- 102	2P/2B:	$89- 115	XP: $5	F10
⬥⬥⬥ Motel	6/1-6/17, 9/6-9/18 & 12/17-1/1		2P/1B:	$60- 83	2P/2B:	$72- 93	XP: $5	F10
	3/1-3/31, 9/19-9/30 & 1/2-2/29		2P/1B:	$46- 72	2P/2B:	$54- 80	XP: $5	F10
	4/1-5/31 & 10/1-12/16		2P/1B:	$40- 58	2P/2B:	$46- 66	XP: $5	F10

Phone: 307/733-2042

Location: Just e on Broadway. 325 E Broadway 83001 (PO Box 1107). **Terms:** Reserv deposit, 3 day notice, 7 days 9/7-6/17; handling fee imposed. **Facility:** 23 rooms. In quiet residential area with a few very spacious rooms. 1 two-bedroom unit. 1 two-bedroom house, $175-$225; 2 stories; exterior corridors; designated smoking area; heated pool. **Services:** winter plug-ins. **Recreation:** ski lockers. **All Rooms:** extended cable TV. **Some Rooms:** kitchen. **Cards:** AE, DI, MC, VI.
(See color ad below)

HITCHING POST LODGE

Rates Subject to Change

⬥⬥ Cottage	6/15-9/15 & 12/21-1/3 [CP]	1P: $78- 149	2P/1B:	$78- 149	2P/2B:	$88- 179	XP: $5	F5
	3/1-4/10, 12/2-12/20 & 1/4-2/29 [EP]	1P: $52- 119	2P/1B:	$52- 119	2P/2B:	$58- 149	XP: $5	F5
	5/16-6/14 & 9/16-10/10 [CP]	1P: $58- 109	2P/1B:	$58- 109	2P/2B:	$64- 139	XP: $5	F5
	4/11-5/15 & 10/11-12/1 [CP]	1P: $39- 89	2P/1B:	$39- 89			XP: $5	F5

Phone: 307/733-2606

Location: 0.8 mi e of US 26/89/191. 460 E Broadway 83001 (PO Box 4397). Fax: 307/733-8221. **Terms:** Reserv deposit, 14 day notice; handling fee imposed. **Facility:** 33 rooms. Cozy cabins in quiet neighborhood. 1-2 stories; exterior corridors; designated smoking area; heated pool. **Services:** winter plug-ins. **Cards:** DS, MC, VI.

JACKSON HOLE LODGE

Rates Subject to Change

⬥⬥ Condo Complex	5/15-9/30	1P: $105- 175	2P/1B:	$105- 175	2P/2B:	$130- 290	XP: $10-20	F12
	3/1-4/4 & 12/10-2/29	1P: $90- 155	2P/1B:	$90- 155	2P/2B:	$115- 250	XP: $10-20	F12
	4/5-5/14 & 10/1-12/9	1P: $75- 130	2P/1B:	$75- 130	2P/2B:	$100- 210	XP: $10-20	F12

Phone: (307)733-2992

Location: 0.3 mi w on US 26/89/191. 420 W Broadway 83001 (PO Box 1805). Fax: 307/739-2144. **Terms:** Check-in 4 pm; reserv deposit, 14 day notice. **Facility:** 59 rooms. Wide variety of rooms, from original motel units to spacious, well-appointed condos, a few with balconies. No elevator in 3 story condo building. 6 two-bedroom units. 33 condos with full kitchen, fireplace & washer/dryer, $175-$250; 2-3 stories, no elevator; exterior corridors; designated smoking area; heated indoor pool. **Services:** winter plug-ins. **Cards:** AE, CB, DI, DS, JC, MC, VI. *(See color ad below)*

MOTEL 6 OF JACKSON HOLE - 328

Rates Subject to Change

⬥⬥⬥	5/21-9/30	1P: $57	2P/1B: $63	XP: $6	F17
	5/1-5/20	1P: $40	2P/1B: $46	XP: $3	F17
⬥ Motel	3/1-4/30 & 10/1-2/29	1P: $39	2P/1B: $45	XP: $3	F17

Phone: 307/733-1620

Location: Jct US 26/89/189, s 0.4 mi e on US 89. 600 S Hwy 89 83001. Fax: 307/734-9175. **Terms:** Reserv deposit; small pets only. **Facility:** 155 rooms. Budget oriented, very clean rooms. 2 stories; exterior corridors; designated smoking area; small heated pool. **Dining:** Restaurant nearby. **All Rooms:** shower baths, extended cable TV. **Cards:** AE, DI, DS, MC, VI.

NOWLIN CREEK INN

◆◆◆ All Year [BP]

Bed & Breakfast

	Rates Subject to Change			Phone: 307/733-0882	
1P: $185	2P/1B: $160	2P/2B: $275	XP: $25	F18

Location: 0.3 mi e of town square. 660 E Broadway 83001 (PO Box 2766). Fax: 307/733-0106. **Terms:** Age restrictions may apply; check-in 4 pm; reserv deposit, 30 day notice. **Facility:** 6 rooms. Cedar-sided home in quiet, residential area next to Elk Refuge. 1 two-bedroom unit. 1 two-bedroom cabin, with full housekeeping, $185-$210, 5 night min stay in season; 2 stories; interior corridors; smoke free premises; mountain view. **Services:** winter plug-ins. Fee: massage. **Recreation:** cross country skiing, tobogganing; bicycles, hiking trails, jogging. Fee: downhill skiing, ice skating, snowmobiling; horseback riding. **Some Rooms:** color TV. **Cards:** AE, DI, DS, MC, VI.

PAINTED BUFFALO INN

🆎 SAVE

◆◆

Motor Inn

Phone: (307)733-4340

	1P:		2P/1B:		2P/2B:		XP:	
6/17-8/31	$95-	130	$99-	135	$99-	139	$5-10	
5/21-6/16 & 9/1-9/30	$80-	95	$85-	99	$90-	99	$5-10	
3/1-5/20 & 10/1-2/29	$80-	95	$85-	99	$90-	99	$5-10	

Location: Just w of town square. PO Box 2547 83001. Fax: 307/733-7953. **Terms:** Check-in 4 pm; small pets only, $10 extra charge. **Facility:** 136 rooms. Contemporary room decor. Close to shopping & restaurants. Mini refrigerator & microwave avail, extra charge; 2 stories; exterior corridors; designated smoking area; heated indoor pool. **Dining:** Cafe; 7 am-9 pm, closed Sun; $5-$9; wine/beer only. **Services:** Fee: massage. **All Rooms:** extended cable TV. **Cards:** AE, DI, DS, MC, VI. **Special Amenities:** Early check-in/late check-out and free local telephone calls.
(See color ad below)

PARKWAY INN

🆎 SAVE

◆◆◆

Motel

Phone: (307)733-3143

	1P:		2P/1B:		2P/2B:		XP:
6/12-9/25 [CP]	$129-	159	$129-	159	$129-	159	$10
5/29-6/11 & 12/24-1/1 [CP]	$95-	119	$95-	119	$95-	119	$10
3/1-5/28, 9/26-12/23 & 1/2-2/29 [CP]	$75-	99	$75-	99	$75-	99	$10

Location: Just n of jct Broadway & Jackson aves, 0.3 mi w of Town Square. 125 N Jackson Ave, PO Box 494 83001. Fax: 307/733-0955. **Terms:** Reserv deposit, 30 day notice, in winter, 5 day for summer; handling fee imposed; package plans. **Facility:** 49 rooms. Victoria style inn with unique turn-of-the-century decor. Excellent well-equipped exercise room. A few units with private balcony. 2 two-bedroom units. Suites with ski lockers, $85-$185; 2 stories; interior/exterior corridors; designated smoking area; saunas, whirlpools, small heated indoor lap pool. **Dining:** Restaurant nearby. **All Rooms:** extended cable TV. **Cards:** AE, CB, DI, DS, MC, VI. **Special Amenities:** Free local telephone calls.
(See color ad p 296)

PIONEER MOTEL

◆◆

Motel

Phone: 307/733-3673

	Rates Subject to Change							
7/1-9/30	1P: $85-	90	2P/1B: $85-	90	2P/2B: $95-	100	XP: $5	F12
10/1-2/29	1P: $50-	60	2P/1B: $50-	60	2P/2B: $60-	70	XP: $5	F12
5/13-6/30	1P: $60-	65	2P/1B: $60		2P/2B: $70		XP: $5	F12
3/1-5/12	1P: $40-	50	2P/1B: $40-	60	2P/2B: $50-	60	XP: $5	F12

Location: Just n on US 26/89/191. 325 N Cache St 83001 (Box 604). **Terms:** Handling fee imposed. **Facility:** 23 rooms. Comfy rooms with handmade quilts. 2 stories; exterior corridors; smoke free premises. **Cards:** AE, DS, MC, VI.

PONY EXPRESS MOTEL INC   Phone: (307)733-3835

AAA SAVE

	5/26-9/7	1P: $77	2P/1B: $92	2P/2B: $92
	3/1-4/5 & 9/8-2/29	1P: $52	2P/1B: $62	2P/2B: $62
	4/6-5/25	1P: $35	2P/1B: $42	2P/2B: $42

◆◆
Motel   **Location:** Just s of US 26/89/191. 50 S Millward St 83001 (PO Box 972). Fax: 307/739-0149
Terms: Reserv deposit. **Facility:** 18 rooms. Large, budget oriented rooms. Outside patio facing small wooded area & whirlpool. 2 stories; exterior corridors; whirlpool. **Dining:** Restaurant nearby. **Services:** winter plug-ins **All Rooms:** extended cable TV. **Cards:** AE, DS, MC, VI. **Special Amenities:** Free local telephone calls and free newspaper.

IT COULD HAPPEN. Some lodgings require advance payment when you check in, and if your trip is cut short a refund may be impossible.

PROSPECTOR MOTEL

Phone: (307)733-4858

AAA SAVE	6/18-9/12 [EP]	1P:	$90-110	2P/1B:	$90-110	2P/2B:	$100-125	XP:	$5		F10
◆◆	5/28-6/17 & 9/13-10/31 [EP]	1P:	$55-75	2P/1B:	$55-75	2P/2B:	$70-95	XP:	$5		F10
Motel	3/1-3/31, 12/24-1/2 &										
	2/1-2/29 [CP]	1P:	$60-75	2P/1B:	$60-75	2P/2B:	$75-90	XP:	$5		F10
	4/1-5/27, 11/1-12/23 &										
	1/3-1/31 [EP]	1P:	$45-70	2P/1B:	$45-70	2P/2B:	$60-80	XP:	$5		F10

Location: 0.3 mi nw of town square; n on Jackson or w on Gill Ave from US 26/89/191. 155 N Jackson St 83001 (PO Box 2376). **Fax:** 307/733-3133. **Terms:** Reserv deposit, 3 day notice; small pets only. **Facility:** 19 rooms. Quiet location; well-maintained. City park across from motel. 2 stories; exterior corridors; designated smoking area; whirlpool. **Dining:** Restaurant nearby. **Services:** winter plug-ins. **All Rooms:** combo or shower baths, extended cable TV. **Cards:** AE, CB, DI, DS, MC, VI. **Special Amenities:** Free local telephone calls and free newspaper. *(See color ad p 296)*

ROOM RESERVATIONS: Mail in your advance deposit early to make certain that space is held for you.

QUALITY 49'ER INN AND SUITES
Phone: (307)733-7550

Guaranteed Rates

		1P:		2P/1B:		2P/2B:		XP:	
AAA	6/1-9/30	1P:	$84- 188	2P/1B:	$88- 192	2P/2B:	$88- 192	XP: $4-10	F12
◆◆◆	3/1-3/31 & 12/1-2/29	1P:	$66- 154	2P/1B:	$70- 158	2P/2B:	$70- 158	XP: $4-10	F12
	5/1-5/31	1P:	$62- 134	2P/1B:	$66- 140	2P/2B:	$66- 140	XP: $4-10	F12
Motor Inn	4/1-4/30 & 10/1-11/30	1P:	$50- 102	2P/1B:	$54- 106	2P/2B:	$58- 106	XP: $4-10	F12

Location: Just w & just s of town square. 330 W Pearl St 83001 (PO Box 1948). Fax: 307/733-2002.
Terms: $1 service charge; pets. **Facility:** 145 rooms. Large comfortable rooms, some handsomely furnished fireplace suites. Gas & wood fireplaces avail. 2 two-bedroom units. 2 suites with steam showers; 3 stories; interior/exterior corridors; designated smoking area; sauna, whirlpools. **Dining:** Restaurant; 11 am-10 pm; $7-$18; cocktails. **Services:** winter plug-ins. **Recreation:** indoor large Roman bath. **All Rooms:** extended cable TV. **Cards:** AE, CB, DI, DS, JC, MC, VI.
(See color ad p 297)

RAWHIDE MOTEL
Phone: (307)733-1216

		1P:		2P/1B:		XP:	
AAA SAVE	6/15-9/12	1P:	$90- 113	2P/1B:	$98- 117		F16
◆◆	6/1-6/14, 9/13-9/26 &					XP: $6	F16
Motel	12/24-1/3	1P:	$62- 72	2P/1B:	$67- 77	XP: $6	F16
	3/1-5/31, 9/27-12/23 &						
	1/4-2/29	1P:	$48- 60	2P/1B:	$55- 75	XP: $6	F16

Location: Just s of US 26/89/191. 75 S Millward St 83001 (PO Box 3289). Fax: 307/734-1335. **Terms:** Reserv deposit; package plans. **Facility:** 23 rooms. 1 blk from town square. 2 stories; exterior corridors; designated smoking area. **Dining:** Restaurant. **All Rooms:** extended cable TV. **Cards:** AE, CB, DI, DS, MC, VI. **Special Amenities:** Free local telephone calls and free newspaper.

RED LION/ WYOMING INN
Phone: (307)734-0035

		1P:		2P/1B:		2P/2B:		XP:	
AAA SAVE	6/1-9/30 [CP]	1P:	$179- 249	2P/1B:	$179- 249	2P/2B:	$179- 249	XP: $15	F12
◆◆◆	3/1-5/31 & 10/1-2/29 [CP]	1P:	$79- 149	2P/1B:	$79- 149	2P/2B:	$79- 149	XP: $15	F12

Location: 0.5 mi s on US 26, 89 & 191. 930 W Broadway 83001 (PO Box 30505). Fax: 307/734-0037.
Motel **Terms:** Check-in 4 pm; pets, $25 extra charge, by reservation only. **Facility:** 73 rooms. Luxurious, spacious, upscale rooms. Some suites with fireplace, others with kitchen, $179-$359; 1-3 stories; interior corridors; smoke free premises; mountain view. **Dining:** Restaurant nearby. **All Rooms:** extended cable TV. **Some Rooms:** whirlpools. **Cards:** AE, DI, MC, VI. **Special Amenities:** Free breakfast and free local telephone calls.
(See color ad p 297)

RUSTY PARROT LODGE
Phone: (307)733-2000

Rates Subject to Change

		1P:		2P/1B:		2P/2B:		XP:	
AAA	3/1-3/31, 6/11-9/30 &								
	12/3-2/29 [BP]	1P:	$220- 500	2P/1B:	$220- 500	2P/2B:	$220- 500	XP: $30-60	
◆◆◆◆	5/14-6/10 & 10/1-10/31 [BP]	1P:	$145- 450	2P/1B:	$145- 450	2P/2B:	$145- 450	XP: $30-60	
Lodge	4/1-5/13 & 11/1-12/2 [BP]	1P:	$108- 375	2P/1B:	$108- 375	2P/2B:	$108- 375	XP: $30-60	

Location: Just nw from town square. 175 N Jackson 83001 (PO Box 1657). Fax: 307/733-5566.
Terms: Check-in 4 pm; reserv deposit, 21 day notice; handling fee imposed; 5 night min stay, 12/18-1/3. **Facility:** 32 rooms. Modern new lodge with unique pine log beds & southwest decor. Gourmet cooked to order breakfast. Variety of spa therapies avail. 4 rms with double whirlpool bath & fireplace in bedroom, $205. Full payment of lodging is required 45 days prior to arrival; 3 stories, no elevator; interior corridors; smoke free premises; whirlpool. **Dining:** Restaurant nearby. **Fee:** massage. **Recreation:** sundeck at whirlpool. **Services:** complimentary evening beverages; winter plug-ins. **All Rooms:** extended cable TV. **Cards:** AE, CB, DI, DS, MC, VI.

SNOW KING RESORT
Phone: (307)733-5200

AAA [SAVE]

◆◆◆ Resort Complex

		1P		2P/1B		2P/2B		XP		
5/29-9/18 & 12/25-1/2	1P:	$190- 500	2P/1B:	$200- 500	2P/2B:	$200- 500	XP:	$10	F13
3/1-3/27 & 1/29-2/29	1P:	$150- 450	2P/1B:	$160- 450	2P/2B:	$160- 450	XP:	$10	F13
3/28-5/28, 9/19-12/24 & 1/3-1/28	1P:	$110- 340	2P/1B:	$120- 340	2P/2B:	$120- 340	XP:	$10	F13

Location: Just se of town square. 400 E Snow King Ave 83001 (PO Box SKI). Fax: 307/733-4086. **Terms:** Check-in 4 pm; reserv deposit, 3 day notice; handling fee imposed; 3% service charge; AP, BP avail; package plans; small pets only, $50 extra charge, $50 dep req. **Facility:** 254 rooms. At base of Snow King Mountain. 1-4 bedroom condominums, some with fireplace and/or washer & dryer, some with garage. Modest hotel rooms. 14 two-bedroom units, 36 three-bedroom units. 4-7 stories; interior corridors; mountain view; heated pool, sauna, whirlpools; playground. Fee: miniature golf. **Dining:** Restaurant; 6:30 am-10 pm; $7-$19; cocktails. **Services:** giftshop; area transportation, within ski area; winter plug-ins. Fee: massage. **Recreation:** cross country skiing; hiking trails. Fee: downhill skiing, ice skating, ski trails, ski equipment & instruction, enclosed ice skating rink; bicycles, horseback riding, alpine slide. **All Rooms:** extended cable TV. **Some Rooms:** 38 kitchens, whirlpools. **Cards:** AE, CB, DI, DS, JC, MC, VI. (*See color ad p 298 & p 149*)

SPLIT CREEK RANCH
Rates Subject to Change   **Phone: 307/733-7522**

◆◆ Motel

	1P	2P/1B	2P/2B	XP
All Year	1P: $58	2P/1B: $64- 180	2P/2B: $68- 190	XP: $6-10

Location: 7 mi n on US 89 to Gros Ventre jct, 0.5 mi w, then 1.3 mi n to Zenith Dr, 1.7 mi w on gravel road following signs. 240 W Zenith 83001 (PO Box 3463). **Terms:** Reserv deposit, 30 day notice. **Facility:** 9 rooms. All gravel entry road. Reservations advised, please call ahead. Wooded area with picnic tables & grill. Occasional bear sightings. 4 efficiencies, $15 extra charge. 1 honeymoon cottage with whirlpool & fireplace, $180 for up to 2 persons; 1 story; exterior corridors. **Services:** winter plug-ins. **Recreation:** fishing. **Cards:** MC, VI.

SPRING CREEK RESORT
Rates Subject to Change   **Phone: 307/733-8833**

◆◆◆ Resort Complex

		1P		2P/1B		2P/2B		XP
6/1-10/10	1P:	$250-1400	2P/1B:	$250-1400	2P/2B:	$250-1400	XP:	$20
3/1-3/31 & 12/17-2/29	1P:	$195-1400	2P/1B:	$195-1400	2P/2B:	$195-1400		
4/1-5/31 & 10/11-12/16	1P:	$140-1400	2P/1B:	$140-1400	2P/2B:	$140-1400		

Location: 2 mi w on US 89, 189 & 191, 0.8 mi w on Hwy 22, 1 mi n on Spring Gulch Rd, then follow signs. 1800 Spirit Dance Rd 83001 (PO Box 3154). Fax: 307/733-1524. **Terms:** Check-in 4 pm; reserv deposit, 15 day notice; handling fee imposed; 15% service charge. **Facility:** 120 rooms. Resort condomimiums & cottage style hotel rooms with fireplace. World class view. Some units have washer & dryer, a few units have 1 car garage. 2 stories; exterior corridors; mountain view; heated pool; 2 tennis courts. **Services:** giftshop; area transportation; winter plug-ins. **Recreation:** cross country skiing; hiking trails, jogging. Fee: horseback riding. **Cards:** AE, DS, MC, VI.

TETON INN
Phone: (307)733-3883

AAA [SAVE]

◆ Motel

		1P		2P/1B		2P/2B		XP		
6/19-9/18 [EP]	1P:	$90	2P/1B:	$90	2P/2B:	$105	XP:	$5	F10
5/29-6/18 & 9/19-10/31 [EP]	1P:	$53	2P/1B:	$53	2P/2B:	$80	XP:	$5	F10
3/1-4/5 & 2/1-2/29 [CP]	1P:	$60	2P/1B:	$60	2P/2B:	$60	XP:	$5	F10
4/6-5/28 [EP]	1P:	$40	2P/1B:	$40	2P/2B:	$55	XP:	$5	F10

Location: Just nw of US 26, 89 & 191. 165 W Gill 83001 (PO Box 2376). Fax: 307/733-3133. **Terms:** Open 3/1-10/31 & 2/1-2/29; reserv deposit, 3 day notice, 14 day in winter. **Facility:** 14 rooms. 2 stories; exterior corridors; designated smoking area. **Dining:** Restaurant nearby. **All Rooms:** shower or tub baths, extended cable TV. **Cards:** AE, CB, DI, DS, MC, VI. **Special Amenities:** Free local telephone calls and free newspaper.

TRAPPER INN
Phone: (307)733-2648

AAA [SAVE]

◆◆◆ Motel

		2P/1B		2P/2B		XP		
6/18-8/21	2P/1B:	$98- 129	2P/2B:	$117- 129	XP:	$7	F12
8/22-9/30 & 12/25-1/1	2P/1B:	$95- 117	2P/2B:	$106- 117	XP:	$7	F12
5/28-6/17	2P/1B:	$76- 92	2P/2B:	$80- 92	XP:	$7	F12
3/1-5/27, 10/1-12/24 & 1/2-2/29	2P/1B:	$54- 76	2P/2B:	$65- 76	XP:	$7	F12

Location: Downtown; just n on US 26/89/191. 235 N Cache St 83001-1712 (PO Box 1712, 83001). Fax: 307/739-9351. **Terms:** Reserv deposit, 14 day notice, 3/1-4/4 & 1/2-2/29. **Facility:** 53 rooms. A few small, but mostly large comfortable rooms. 2 bedroom/2 bath suite, $230; family rm with 3 beds, $178; 2 stories; exterior corridors; designated smoking area; whirlpools. **Dining:** Restaurant nearby. **Services:** winter plug-ins. **All Rooms:** extended cable TV. **Some Rooms:** whirlpools. **Cards:** AE, CB, DI, MC, VI. **Special Amenities:** Early check-in/late check-out and free local telephone calls. IMA. (*See color ad p 320 & p 300*)

VIRGINIAN LODGE
Phone: 307/733-2792

AAA [SAVE]

◆◆ Motor Inn

		1P		2P/1B		2P/2B		XP		
6/1-9/30	1P:	$95- 105	2P/1B:	$95- 110	2P/2B:	$95- 110	XP:	$7	F11
3/1-5/31 & 10/1-2/29	1P:	$52	2P/1B:	$52	2P/2B:	$61	XP:	$7	F11

Location: Just w. 750 W Broadway, PO Box 1052 83001. Fax: 307/733-0281. **Terms:** Check-in 4 pm. **Facility:** 170 rooms. Basic, cozy lodging in older property. 3 two-bedroom units. Suites avail; 1-2 stories; interior/exterior corridors; designated smoking area; heated pool, whirlpool. **Dining:** Restaurant; 7 am-2 & 5-10 pm; 7 am-2 & 5-9 pm, 9/16-6/14; $10-$19; cocktails. **Services:** winter plug-ins. **All Rooms:** extended cable TV. **Some Rooms:** 8 efficiencies, 13 kitchens, whirlpools. **Cards:** AE, CB, DI, DS, JC, MC, VI. (*See color ad p 300*)

WAGON WHEEL VILLAGE
Phone: (307)733-2357

AAA [SAVE]

◆◆◆ Motor Inn

		1P		2P/1B		2P/2B		XP		
6/15-9/15	1P:	$87	2P/1B:	$92	2P/2B:	$97- 119	XP:	$3-5	F12
5/1-6/14 & 9/16-10/5	1P:	$77	2P/1B:	$87	2P/2B:	$97	XP:	$3-5	F12
3/1-4/30 & 10/6-2/29	1P:	$65	2P/1B:	$71	2P/2B:	$76- 95	XP:	$3-5	F12

Location: 0.5 mi n on US 26, 89, 189 & 191. 435 N Cache St 83001 (PO Box 525). Fax: 307/733-0568. **Terms:** Reserv deposit. **Facility:** 97 rooms. Log cabins in attractively landscaped shaded grounds, across from Elk refuge & close to city recreational facilities; some fireplace. 7 two-bedroom units. 2 stories; exterior corridors; whirlpools. **Dining:** Restaurant; 6 am-10 pm; pizza restaurant noon-midnight; $6-$18; cocktails. **Services:** giftshop. **All Rooms:** combo or shower baths, extended cable TV. **Some Rooms:** 5 efficiencies, no utensils, whirlpools. **Cards:** AE, DS, MC, VI. **Special Amenities:** Free local telephone calls and free newspaper. (*See color ad p 300*)

WORT HOTEL   Phone: (307)733-2190

12/26-1/2 [BP]	1P: $220- 300	2P/1B: $220- 300	2P/2B: $220- 300	XP: $15	F14
6/1-9/30 [EP]	1P: $181- 235	2P/1B: $181- 235	2P/2B: $181- 235	XP: $15	F14
3/1-3/31, 5/16-5/31 &				
1/3-2/29 [BP]	1P: $149- 235	2P/1B: $149- 235	2P/2B: $149- 235	XP: $15	F14
4/1-5/15 & 10/1-12/25 [BP]	1P: $125- 235	2P/1B: $125- 235	2P/2B: $125- 235	XP: $15	F14

Motor Inn
Location: Center. 50 N Glenwood 83001 (PO Box 69). **Fax:** 307/733-2067. **Terms:** Check-in 4 pm; reserv deposit, 14 day notice; $3 service charge. **Facility:** 60 rooms. Established hotel with colorful history. 2 stories; interior corridors; whirlpools. **Dining:** Restaurant; 7 am-10 pm; entertainment, in summer; $15-$25; cocktails. **Services:** giftshop; area transportation, ski transportation; winter plug-ins. **Fee:** massage. **Recreation:** ski lockers. **All Rooms:** extended cable TV. **Some Rooms:** whirlpools. **Cards:** AE, DI, DS, MC, VI. *(See color ad below)*

RESTAURANTS

BAR-T-FIVE COVERED WAGON COOKOUT & WILD WEST SHOW   **Dinner:** $20-$30   **Phone:** 307/733-5386
Location: 1 mi e on Broadway, 0.5 mi s on Redmond, just e. 790 Cache Creek Dr 83001. **Hours:** 5/15-8/31 at 5:30 pm & 6:30 pm; 9/1-9/30 5 pm & 6 pm. **Reservations:** required. **Features:** casual dress. Covered wagon ride into canyon, robust meal, mountain men, Indians & Western music under the pinetrees. Elk sleigh rides, in winter. **Cards:** AE, DS, MC, VI.
American

BLUE LION   **Dinner:** $15-$25   **Phone:** 307/733-3912
Location: Just n of US 26, 89, 189 & 191; opposite Miller Park. 160 N Millward St 83001. **Hours:** 5:30 pm-10 pm, 11/1-5/25 from 6 pm. **Closed:** 11/25. **Reservations:** suggested. **Features:** No A/C; casual dress; cocktails & lounge; street parking; a la carte. Casual intimate atmosphere with outdoor dining featuring game, fresh fish, pasta & fowl. Same owner since 1978, loyal local following, friendly & attentive service. Smoke free premises. **Cards:** AE, DS, MC, VI.
Regional American

BUBBA'S BAR-B-QUE RESTAURANT   **Lunch:** $4-$8   **Dinner:** $4-$12   **Phone:** 307/733-2288
Location: 0.5 mi w on US 26/89/191. 515 W Broadway 83001. **Hours:** 7 am-10 pm; to 9 pm, in winter. **Features:** casual dress; children's menu; salad bar; a la carte. Pit barbecue with homemade sauce. Very popular, expect to sign-in & wait during busy periods. **Cards:** AE, DS, MC, VI.
American

THE BUNNERY, BAKERY & RESTAURANT   **Lunch:** $3-$6   **Dinner:** $5-$12   **Phone:** 307/733-5474
Location: Just n of downtown center. 130 N Cache St 83001. **Hours:** 7 am-3 & 5-9 pm; 7 am-2 pm in winter. **Closed:** 12/25. **Features:** casual dress; children's menu; carryout; beer & wine only; street parking; a la carte. Light meals featuring sandwiches & fresh, all natural bakery items. Smoke free premises. **Cards:** MC, VI.
American

CADILLAC GRILLE
Lunch: $6-$10   **Dinner:** $8-$24   **Phone:** 307/733-3279

Location: US 26, 89 & 187. 55 N Cache St 83001. **Hours:** 11:30 am-10 pm; 11:30 am-10:30 pm, in summer. Closed: Sun in winter. **Features:** casual dress; carryout; cocktails & lounge; street parking. Featuring fresh seafood, game & homemade pasta served in casual setting. **Cards:** AE, MC, VI.

Regional American

GRANARY
Lunch: $6-$10   **Dinner:** $18-$28   **Phone:** 307/733-8833

Location: 2 mi w on US 89, 189 & 191, 0.8 mi w on Hwy 22, 1 mi n on Spring Gulch Rd, then follow signs; in Spring Creek Resort. Spring Gulch Road 83001. **Hours:** 7:30 am-10, noon-2 & 6-10:30 pm. **Reservations:** suggested. **Features:** No A/C; casual dress; children's menu; carryout; cocktails & lounge. Fine upscale dining with world class view. Smoke free premises. **Cards:** AE, DI, DS, MC, VI.

Continental

OFF BROADWAY GRILLE
Dinner: $14-$18   **Phone:** 307/733-9777

Location: Downtown. 30 S King St 83001. **Hours:** 5:30 pm-10 pm. Closed major holidays. **Reservations:** suggested. **Features:** No A/C; casual dress; children's menu; cocktails; street parking; a la carte. Varied menu; fresh seafood, pasta, wild game. Patio dining in summer. Smoke free premises. **Cards:** AE, MC, VI.

Continental

THE RANGE REGIONAL AMERICAN CUISINE
Dinner: $17-$28   **Phone:** 307/733-5481

Location: SR 191/89/26, just n of Gill Ave, opposite public parking. 225 N Cache 83001. **Hours:** 5:30 pm-10 pm. Closed: 4/20-5/14 & 10/15-11/15. **Reservations:** suggested. **Features:** casual dress; health conscious menu; cocktails; a la carte. Progressive & evolving Regional American cuisine with open style kitchen. Very popular, upscale dining room, may be noisy. Smoke free premises. **Cards:** AE, MC, VI.

American

SNAKE RIVER BREWING CO RESTAURANT & BREWERY
Lunch: $5-$7   **Dinner:** $6-$11   **Phone:** 307/739-2337

Location: Just s of Broadway. 265 S Millward St 83001. **Hours:** noon-midnight. Closed: 11/25 & 12/25. **Features:** casual dress; cocktail lounge; beer & wine only. Wood fired oven pizza, calzone, bread, sandwiches, pasta & daily homemade soup. Patio seating, fireplace in winter. **Cards:** AE, MC, VI.

American

STRUTTING GROUSE RESTAURANT
Lunch: $5-$12   **Dinner:** $13-$27   **Phone:** 307/733-7788

Location: 6.8 mi n on US 26, 89 & 191, turn w at Gros Ventre jct at Jackson Hole Golf Course. **Hours:** Open 5/8-10/5; 11:30 am-2:30 & 5:30-9 pm. Closed: Mon for dinner. **Reservations:** suggested. **Features:** casual dress; cocktails & lounge; a la carte. Changing menu revolves around a core of signature items. Artistically presented, fine food. Some game offerings. Excellent view of golf course & the Tetons. **Cards:** AE, DI, MC, VI. *(See color ad p 142)*

Continental

LANDER—7,000

LODGINGS

BLUE SPRUCE INN
Guaranteed Rates   **Phone:** 307/332-8253

| | 1P: | $70 | 2P/1B: | $80 | 2P/2B: | $80 | XP: | $10 |

Location: Jct US 287 & SR 789, 0.3 mi n on US 287, w 0.4 mi. 677 S 3rd St 82520. Fax: 307/332-8253. **Terms:** Age restrictions may apply; check-in 4 pm; reserv deposit, 7 day notice; handling fee imposed. **Facility:** 4 rooms. Built in 1920. Mission style furnishings. Second floor rooms with mountain views. 3 stories; interior corridors; smoke free premises. **Recreation:** bicycles, pool tables, darts, piano. **All Rooms:** combo or shower baths. **Cards:** AE, DS, MC, VI.

Historic Bed & Breakfast

HOLIDAY LODGE NATIONAL 9
Rates Subject to Change   **Phone:** 307/332-2511

		1P:	2P/1B:		2P/2B:		XP:	
4/1-9/30		$37	$42		$47		$3	
3/1-3/31 & 10/1-2/31		$30	$35		$38		$3	

Location: S on US 287 at jct SR 789. 210 McFarlane Dr 82520. Fax: 307/332-2256. **Terms:** Weekly/monthly rates; pets, $5 extra charge. **Facility:** 40 rooms. 7 efficiencies, $5 extra charge; 1-2 stories; exterior corridors; whirlpool. **Dining:** Restaurant nearby. **Services:** winter plug-ins. **All Rooms:** extended cable TV. **Cards:** AE, CB, DI, DS, MC, VI.

Motel

PIECE OF CAKE BED & BREAKFAST
Rates Subject to Change   **Phone:** 307/332-7608

| | 2P/1B: | $90 | XP: | $10 | D18 |

Location: 4.8 mi sw on Baldwin Creek Rd, off US 287 at n side of town. 2343 Baldwin Creek Rd 82520. Fax: 307/332-7608. **Terms:** Check-in 4 pm; reserv deposit, 14 day notice. **Facility:** 6 rooms. Charming Western decor; 4 cabins. Nestled in Red Butte Canyon. 1-2 stories; interior/exterior corridors; smoke free premises. **Recreation:** bicycles, hiking trails. **All Rooms:** combo or shower baths. **Some Rooms:** color TV. **Cards:** MC, VI.

Bed & Breakfast

PRONGHORN LODGE
   Phone: (307)332-3940

		1P:		2P/1B:		2P/2B:		XP:		
5/1-10/31 [CP]		$50		$55		$61		$5		F12
3/1-4/30 & 11/1-2/29 [CP]		$44		$44		$48		$5		F12

Location: Just n on US 287 at jct SR 789. 150 E Main St 82520. Fax: 307/332-2651. **Terms:** Pets, $10 extra charge. **Facility:** 54 rooms. 1-2 stories; exterior corridors; whirlpool. **Dining:** Restaurant; also, The Oxbow, see separate listing. **Services:** winter plug-ins. **All Rooms:** combo or shower baths, extended cable TV. **Some Rooms:** 6 efficiencies. **Cards:** AE, CB, DI, DS, MC, VI. Budget Host. *(See color ad p 264)*

Motel

SILVER SPUR MOTEL
   Phone: (307)332-5189

		1P:		2P/1B:		2P/2B:		XP:	
5/1-9/30		$38		$40		$45		$3	
3/1-4/30 & 10/1-2/29		$28		$30		$37		$3	

Location: 1.5 mi w on US 287 & SR 789. 1240 Main St 82520. Fax: 307/332-9251. **Terms:** Pets, $3 extra charge. **Facility:** 25 rooms. Economy family oriented lodging. 3 two-bedroom units. 2 stories; exterior corridors; heated pool. **Dining:** Outdoor barbecue lunches & dinners summer only; restaurant nearby. **Services:** winter plug-ins. **All Rooms:** combo or shower baths. **Some Rooms:** 2 efficiencies. **Cards:** AE, DI, DS, MC, VI. **Special Amenities:** Free local telephone calls and preferred room (subject to availability with advanced reservations).

Motel

RESTAURANTS

HITCHING RACK   **Dinner:** $8-$22   **Phone:** 307/332-4322
◆◆   **Location:** 0.5 mi s on US 287. 785 E Main 82520. **Hours:** 5:30 pm-10 pm. Closed major holidays & Sun.
American   **Reservations:** accepted. **Features:** salad bar. Steak, seafood, chicken, pasta & prime rib. Numerous micro
brewery beers avail. **Cards:** DS, MC, VI.

THE OXBOW   **Lunch:** $5   **Dinner:** $6-$15   **Phone:** 307/332-0233
◆◆   **Location:** Just n on US 287 at jct SR 789; in Pronghorn Lodge. 170 E Main St 82520. **Hours:** 7 am-10 pm.
American   Closed: 12/25. **Features:** casual dress; carryout; salad bar; cocktails. Home cooked food, daily specials,
some patio seating. **Cards:** AE, CB, DI, DS, MC, VI.   ⊠

THE RANCH BARBECUE & OLD WEST SALOON   **Lunch:** $4-$7   **Dinner:** $4-$17   **Phone:** 307/332-7388
◆◆   **Location:** Center. 148 Main St 82520. **Hours:** 6 am-10:30 & noon-10 pm, Sun 10 am-2 pm. Closed major
American   holidays. **Reservations:** suggested. **Features:** casual dress; Sunday brunch; carryout; cocktails & lounge. All
you can eat breakfast Mon-Fri; Sun champagne brunch, build your own dessert bar, entrees of ribs, prime
rib, salmon, chicken & lots of finger foods. Micro brewery. **Cards:** MC, VI.   ⊠

LARAMIE—26,700

LODGINGS

BEST WESTERN FOSTER'S COUNTRY INN   **Phone:** (307)742-8371

		1P		2P/1B		2P/2B		XP	
AAA SAVE	7/20-7/31 [BP]	1P:	$85	2P/1B:	$93	2P/2B:	$93	XP:	$6	F18
	5/1-7/19 & 8/1-9/15 [BP]	1P:	$52	2P/1B:	$58	2P/2B:	$58	XP:	$6	F18
◆◆	3/1-4/30 & 9/16-2/29 [BP]	1P:	$44	2P/1B:	$50	2P/2B:	$50	XP:	$6	F18

Motor Inn   **Location:** I-80, exit 311 (Snowy Range Rd). 1561 Snowy Range Rd 82070 (PO Box 580).
Fax: 307/742-0884. **Terms:** Reserv deposit; BP avail; package plans, in winter; pets. **Facility:** 112 rooms.
Cozy, clean rooms. 2 stories; exterior corridors; designated smoking area; heated indoor pool, whirlpool. **Dining:** Restaurant;
24 hrs; $8-$14; cocktails. **Services:** giftshop; winter plug-ins. **All Rooms:** extended cable TV. **Cards:** AE, CB, DI, DS, MC,
VI. **Special Amenities:** Free breakfast and free local telephone calls.   🐕 🏋 🛥 🍴 🍸 🌬 🖂 ⊠

BEST WESTERN GAS LITE   Rates Subject to Change   **Phone:** (307)742-6616

		1P		2P/1B		2P/2B		XP	
AAA	7/1-8/31	1P:	$55- 64	2P/1B:	$55- 64	2P/2B:	$63- 79	XP:	$5-10
	9/1-2/29	1P:	$45- 64	2P/1B:	$45- 64	2P/2B:	$59- 69	XP:	$5-10
◆◆	5/1-6/30	1P:	$50- 60	2P/1B:	$49- 63	2P/2B:	$55- 65	XP:	$5-10
Motel	3/1-4/30	1P:	$44- 56	2P/1B:	$49- 63	2P/2B:	$49- 63	XP:	$5-10

Location: I-81, exit 313; 1.7 mi n. 960 N 3rd St 82070. Fax: 307/742-6616. **Terms:** Reserv deposit; pets, $5
extra charge. **Facility:** 30 rooms. Very clean rooms. 2 stories; exterior corridors; small heated indoor pool. **Services:** winter
plug-ins. **All Rooms:** combo or shower baths. **Cards:** AE, DI, DS, MC, VI.   ASK 🛏 🐕 🛥 🍽 ⊠

CAMELOT MOTEL   **Phone:** (307)721-8860

		1P		2P/1B		2P/2B		XP	
AAA	5/1-10/2	1P:	$45- 55	2P/1B:	$55- 65	2P/2B:	$65- 75	XP:	$5	F5
	3/1-4/30 & 10/3-2/29	1P:	$35- 40	2P/1B:	$45- 50	2P/2B:	$52- 57	XP:	$5	F5

◆◆   **Location:** Just s of I-80, exit 311 (Snowy Range Rd). 523 Adams 82070. **Terms:** Reserv deposit; handling
Motel   fee imposed. **Facility:** 33 rooms. Very clean rooms. 2 stories; interior/exterior corridors. **Dining:** Restaurant
nearby. **Cards:** AE, DI, DS, MC, VI. **Special Amenities:** Free local telephone calls and preferred room
(subject to availability with advanced reservations).   🛏 🍴 🛥 ⊠

HOLIDAY INN OF LARAMIE   Rates Subject to Change   **Phone:** (307)742-6611

		1P		2P/1B		2P/2B		XP	
◆◆	3/1-5/1 & 9/6-2/29	1P:	$75- 80	2P/1B:	$75- 80	2P/2B:	$75- 80	XP:	$8-10	F18
Motor Inn	5/2-9/5	1P:	$69- 79	2P/1B:	$69- 79	2P/2B:	$69- 79	XP:	$8-10	F18

Location: I-80, exit 313 (3rd St). 2313 Soldier Springs 82070 (PO Box 580). Fax: 307/745-8371.
Facility: 100 rooms. Attractive public areas. 2 stories; interior/exterior corridors; designated smoking area; heated indoor pool.
Services: giftshop. **Cards:** AE, CB, DI, DS, JC, MC, VI.
ASK 🛏 🐕 🏋 🎱 🛥 🍴 🍸 🌬 🖂 🎾 🖥 🖨 📞 ⊠

1ST INN GOLD   Rates Subject to Change   **Phone:** (307)742-3721

		1P		2P/1B		2P/2B		XP	
AAA SAVE	Fri & Sat 9/1-11/30 [BP]	1P:	$78	2P/1B:	$88	2P/2B:	$88	XP:	$8	F12
	5/1-8/31 & Sun-Thurs									
◆◆	9/1-9/15 [BP]	1P:	$48- 58	2P/1B:	$56- 68	2P/2B:	$58- 69	XP:	$8	F12
Motor Inn	Sun-Thurs 9/16-10/31 [BP]	1P:	$48	2P/1B:	$56	2P/2B:	$59	XP:	$8	F12
	3/1-4/30, Sun-Thurs									
	11/1-11/30 & 12/1-2/29 [BP]	1P:	$38	2P/1B:	$46	2P/2B:	$49	XP:	$8	F12

Location: Just n of I-80, exit 313 (3rd St). 421 Boswell 82070. Fax: 307/742-5473. **Terms:** Reserv deposit; 10 day notice;
weekly/monthly rates; pets, $8 extra charge. **Facility:** 79 rooms. Various room types, from modest to modern. 8 queen suites,
$78; 2 stories; interior/exterior corridors; small heated pool. **Dining:** Restaurant; 6 am-10 pm, Sun-8 pm; $5-$11; cocktails.
Services: winter plug-ins. **All Rooms:** extended cable TV. **Cards:** AE, CB, DI, DS, MC, VI. **Special Amenities:** Free
breakfast and free local telephone calls.   🛏 🐕 🏋 🎱 🛥 🍴 🍸 🌬 🖂 🎾 🖥 🖨 📞 ⊠

SUNSET INN   **Phone:** (307)742-3741

		1P		2P/1B		2P/2B		XP	
AAA SAVE	7/16-7/31	1P:	$75- 80	2P/1B:	$80- 85	2P/2B:	$85	XP:	$10	F16
	5/1-7/15, 7/1-7/18 & 8/1-9/30	1P:	$42- 46	2P/1B:	$52- 58	2P/2B:	$56- 62	XP:	$8	F16
◆◆	3/1-4/30 & 10/1-2/29	1P:	$35- 40	2P/1B:	$40- 45	2P/2B:	$46- 50	XP:	$8	F16

Motel   **Location:** 0.3 mi n of I-80, exit 313 (3rd St). 1104 S 3rd St 82070. Fax: 307/745-9305.
Terms: Weekly/monthly rates, in winter; small pets only. **Facility:** 51 rooms. Large rooms. 2 stories; exterior
corridors; designated smoking area; small heated pool, whirlpool. **Services:** winter plug-ins. **All Rooms:** extended cable TV.
Cards: AE, DI, DS, MC, VI. **Special Amenities:** Free local telephone calls.   🛏 🛥 🎾 🖥 🖨 📞 ⊠

TRAVEL INN   **Phone:** (307)745-4853

		1P		2P/1B		2P/2B		XP	
AAA SAVE	7/15-7/31	1P:	$66- 72	2P/1B:	$66- 72	2P/2B:	$75- 80	XP:	$5	F9
	6/15-7/14 & 8/1-9/15	1P:	$36- 42	2P/1B:	$38- 45	2P/2B:	$44- 49	XP:	$4	F9
◆◆	5/1-6/14 & 9/16-11/20	1P:	$33- 37	2P/1B:	$36- 42	2P/2B:	$44- 49	XP:	$3	F9
Motel	3/1-4/30 & 11/21-2/29	1P:	$31- 34	2P/1B:	$34- 37	2P/2B:	$38- 44	XP:	$3	F9

Location: Just n on I-80 business loop, 1 mi n I-80, exit 313. 262 N 3rd St 82072. Fax: 307/721-4943.
Terms: Weekly/monthly rates, 9/20-4/30. **Facility:** 28 rooms. Well kept. Mini microwave avail; 2 stories; exterior corridors;
small heated pool. **Dining:** Restaurant nearby. **Services:** winter plug-ins. **All Rooms:** combo or shower baths, extended
cable TV. **Cards:** AE, DI, DS, MC, VI. **Special Amenities:** Free local telephone calls.
🛏 🎱 🛥 🍴 🎾 🖥 🖨 📞 ⊠

RESTAURANT

THE CAVALRYMAN SUPPER CLUB

Dinner: $14-$25

Phone: 307/745-555

American

Location: I-80, exit 313; 1.8 mi s on US 287. 4452 S 3rd St 82070. **Hours:** 4:30 pm-10 pm; noon-9 pm 4/4 5/9 & 11/25. **Closed:** 12/24 & 12/25. **Reservations:** accepted. **Features:** casual dress; children's menu salad bar; cocktails & lounge; a la carte. Featuring steak, seafood, prime rib, soup, salad, chicken & barbecue ribs in Western hospitality & atmosphere. **Cards:** AE, CB, DI, DS, MC, VI.

LITTLE AMERICA

LODGING

LITTLE AMERICA HOTEL & TRAVEL CENTER

Phone: (307)875-2406

SAVE	5/1-9/30	1P:	$63-	79	2P/1B:	$69-	75	2P/2B:	$75-	85 XP:	$6 F12
	10/1-2/29	1P:	$59-	73	2P/1B:	$65-	69	2P/2B:	$69-	79 XP:	$6 F12
Motor Inn	3/1-4/30	1P:	$49-	63	2P/1B:	$55-	65	2P/2B:	$65-	69 XP:	$6 F12

Location: I-80, exit 68. I-80 MM 68 82929 (PO Box 1). **Fax:** 307/872-2666. **Facility:** 129 rooms. The original Little America lodging. Various room sizes, from quaint charming rooms to large luxurious accommodations. 12 two-bedroom units. 1-2 stories; interior/exterior corridors; heated pool, spacious deck area. **Dining:** Dining room, coffee shop, 2 delis; 7 am-10 pm dining room; 24 hrs, deli; $5-$15; cocktails. **Services:** giftshop; area transportation, on property shuttle. **All Rooms:** combo or shower baths. **Cards:** AE, CB, DI, DS, MC, VI. **Special Amenities:** Early check-in/late check-out and free local telephone calls. *(See color ad below)*

LOVELL—2,100

LODGINGS

CATTLEMEN MOTEL

Rates Subject to Change

Phone: 307/548-2296

	5/15-9/15	1P:	$36-	40	2P/1B:	$39-	45	2P/2B:	$44-	49 XP:	$5 D10
Motel	3/1-5/14 & 9/16-2/29	1P:	$29-	32	2P/1B:	$31-	34	2P/2B:	$35-	38 XP:	$3 D10

Location: Center; US 310 (Main St), just s. 470 Montana Ave 82431. **Terms:** Reserv deposit. **Facility:** 15 rooms. Quiet, shady residential area. Free coffee in antique shop/lobby. Mini refrigerator & mini microwave avail, extra charge 1 story; exterior corridors. **Services:** winter plug-ins. **All Rooms:** combo or shower baths. **Cards:** AE, DI, DS, MC, VI.

HORSESHOE BEND MOTEL

Phone: (307)548-2221

SAVE	7/1-8/31	1P:	$42-	46	2P/1B:	$46-	49	2P/2B:	$49-	54 XP:	$5
	5/1-6/30	1P:	$35		2P/1B:	$39		2P/2B:	$42	XP:	$5
Motel	3/1-4/30 & 9/1-2/29	1P:	$30		2P/1B:	$33		2P/2B:	$36	XP:	$5

Location: 0.3 mi e on US 14A & 310. 375 E Main St 82431. **Terms:** Reserv deposit, 3 day notice; weekly/monthly rates; pets. **Facility:** 22 rooms. Very clean rooms. 1 story; interior/exterior corridors; designated smoking area; small heated pool. **Dining:** Restaurant nearby. **Services:** winter plug-ins. **All Rooms:** extended cable TV. **Some Rooms:** 4 efficiencies no utensils. **Cards:** AE, CB, DI, DS, MC, VI. **Special Amenities:** Free local telephone calls.

LUSK—1,500

LODGINGS

BEST WESTERN PIONEER COURT   Phone: (307)334-2640

		6/15-8/31	1P:	$53-	75	2P/1B:	$55-	70	2P/2B:	$64-	75	XP:	$4
		4/15-6/14	1P:	$53-	70	2P/1B:	$53-	70	2P/2B:	$60-	75	XP:	$4
		3/1-4/14, 9/1-10/11 &											
		1/1-2/29	1P:	$45-	50	2P/1B:	$43-	50	2P/2B:	$47-	52	XP:	$4
		10/12-12/31	1P:	$43-	47	2P/1B:	$43-	49	2P/2B:	$47-	52	XP:	$4

Location: Just n of jct US 20 & 85. 731 S Main St 82225 (PO Box 87). Fax: 307/334-2642. **Facility:** 30 rooms. 3 two-bedroom units. 1 story; exterior corridors; small heated pool. **Dining:** Restaurant nearby. **Services:** winter plug-ins. **All Rooms:** extended cable TV. **Cards:** AE, CB, DI, DS, JC, MC, VI. **Special Amenities:** Early check-in/late check-out and free local telephone calls.

COVERED WAGON MOTEL   Phone: (307)334-2836

		6/15-8/24 [CP]	1P:	$60	2P/1B:	$69	2P/2B:	$73	XP:	$6
		5/1-6/14 & 8/25-10/5 [EP]	1P:	$47	2P/1B:	$61	2P/2B:	$63	XP:	$4
		3/1-4/30 & 10/6-2/29 [CP]	1P:	$46	2P/1B:	$51	2P/2B:	$53	XP:	$4

Location: Just n of jct US 20 & 85. 730 S Main St 82225 (PO Box 236). Fax: 307/334-2977. **Terms:** Reserv deposit, 15 day notice. **Facility:** 51 rooms. 1-2 stories; interior/exterior corridors; heated indoor pool, sauna, whirlpool; playground. **Dining:** Restaurant nearby. **Services:** winter plug-ins. **Recreation:** exercise equipment. **All Rooms:** extended cable TV. **Cards:** AE, CB, DI, DS, MC, VI. **Special Amenities:** Free room upgrade and preferred room (each subject to availability with advanced reservations). IMA. *(See color ad p 320 & below)*

TOWN HOUSE MOTEL   Rates Subject to Change   Phone: (307)334-2376

| | | 4/1-12/31 | 1P: | $26- | 38 | 2P/1B: | $32- | 48 | 2P/2B: | $36- | 60 | XP: | $3-5 |

Location: In town, on US 20 & 85. 525 S Main St 82225 (PO Box 672). **Terms:** Open 4/1-12/31. **Facility:** 20 rooms. Very clean rooms. 1 story; exterior corridors; designated smoking area. **Services:** winter plug-ins. **Cards:** AE, DS, MC, VI.

TRAIL MOTEL   Phone: (307)334-2530

| | | 6/15-8/25 [CP] | | | 2P/1B: | $52 | 2P/2B: | $60 | XP: | $5 |
| | | 5/1-6/14 & 8/26-10/15 [CP] | | | 2P/1B: | $40 | 2P/2B: | $50 | XP: | $5 |

Location: 0.3 mi sw on US 20; just w of US 85. 305 W 8th St 82225 (PO Box 1087). Fax: 307/334-3136. **Terms:** Open 5/1-10/15; reserv deposit, 7 day notice; handling fee imposed; small pets only, $10 extra charge. **Facility:** 22 rooms. Economy lodging, a few remodeled rooms. 1 two-bedroom unit. 1 story; exterior corridors; small heated pool; playground. **All Rooms:** combo or shower baths, extended cable TV. **Cards:** AE, CB, DI, DS, MC, VI. **Special Amenities:** Free room upgrade and preferred room (each subject to availability with advanced reservations).

RESTAURANT

FIRESIDE INN   **Lunch:** $5-$13   **Dinner:** $5-$13   Phone: 307/334-3477

Location: 0.3 mi se. 904 S Main St 82225. **Hours:** 6 am-9:30 pm; 7 am-9 pm, in winter. Closed: 12/25. **Features:** casual dress; children's menu; cocktails & lounge; a la carte. Traditional menu featuring homemade soup & pastry daily. **Cards:** DS, MC, VI.

American

MEETEETSE—400

LODGING

VISION QUEST MOTEL   Rates Subject to Change   Phone: 307/868-2512

		7/1-12/1	1P:	$40	2P/1B:	$45	2P/2B:	$50	XP:	$5	F6
		5/2-6/30	1P:	$30	2P/1B:	$35	2P/2B:	$40	XP:	$5	F6
		3/1-5/1 & 12/2-2/29	1P:	$25	2P/1B:	$30	2P/2B:	$35	XP:	$5	F6

Location: SR 120, s end of town. 2207 State St 82433 (PO Box 4). Fax: 307/868-2512. **Facility:** 14 rooms. Budget oriented, clean rooms. 1 two-bedroom unit. 1 rm with waterbed; 2 stories; exterior corridors; smoke free premises. **Services:** winter plug-ins. **All Rooms:** shower baths. **Some Rooms:** 12 efficiencies. **Cards:** AE, DS, MC, VI.

MORAN—See also *GRAND TETON NATIONAL PARK & YELLOWSTONE NATIONAL PARK.*

LODGING

LUTON'S LOG CABINS & LODGE
◆◆◆
Cottage

6/15-8/31	2P/1B: $146	XP: $10
9/1-11/30	2P/1B: $136	XP: $10
5/1-6/14	2P/1B: $126	XP: $10

Rates Subject to Change   **Phone: 307/543-248●**

Location: 5 mi e of Moran jct on US 26 & 287, s side of road. (PO Box 48, 83013). Fax: 307/543-2966. **Terms:** Open 5/1-11/30; reserv deposit, 30 day notice; handling fee imposed. **Facility:** 9 rooms. Newly built duplex log cabins in quiet open meadow with spectacular view of Tetons. 5 two-bedroom cabins for up to 6 persons, $227-$257; 1 story; exterior corridors; designated smoking area; mountain view. **Services:** winter plug-ins. **All Rooms:** kitchens. **Cards:** DS, MC, VI.

NEWCASTLE—3,000

LODGINGS

PINES MOTEL
(AAA) SAVE
◆◆
Motel

Phone: (307)746-433●

	1P: $42	2P/1B: $50	2P/2B: $54-	66 XP: $5
5/1-10/31				
3/1-4/30 & 11/1-2/29	1P: $40	2P/1B: $42	2P/2B: $48-	54 XP: $5

Location: Downtown; e on Wentworth St off SR 16, at blue "motels" sign. 248 E Wentworth St 82701. Fax: 307/746-3409. **Terms:** Small pets only. **Facility:** 11 rooms. Cozy, well appointed rooms in quiet residential area. Excellent housekeeping. 1 story; exterior corridors; designated smoking area; whirlpool. **Services:** winter plug-ins. **All Rooms:** combo or shower baths. **Cards:** AE, CB, DI, DS, MC, VI. **Special Amenities:** Free local telephone calls.

SAGE MOTEL
(AAA) SAVE
◆
Motel

Phone: (307)746-272●

All Year   1P: $29- 32   2P/1B: $36- 44   2P/2B: $40- 44   XP: $4

Location: 0.3 mi s of jct US 16 & 85, just w. 1227 S Summit Ave 82701. **Terms:** Reserv deposit, 3 day notice; weekly rates; pets, $5 extra charge. **Facility:** 13 rooms. Cozy rooms in older, budget motel. 1 story; exterior corridors. **Services:** winter plug-ins. **Cards:** MC, VI. **Special Amenities:** Free local telephone calls and free newspaper.

RESTAURANT

FLYING V CAMBRIA INN   Historical   **Dinner: $9-$23**   **Phone: 307/746-209●**
◆◆
American

Location: 8 mi n on US 85. 23726 US Hwy 85 82701. **Hours:** Open 6/1-12/20; 5 pm-10 pm. Closed: Sun. **Features:** No A/C; casual dress; children's menu; senior's menu; cocktails & lounge. Relaxed dining in historic stone building, also featuring steak, seafood, prime rib & Italian. **Cards:** MC, VI.

PAINTER

LODGING

HUNTER PEAK RANCH
◆
Ranch

Guaranteed Rates   **Phone: 307/587-3711**

All Year   1P: $80   2P/1B: $80   2P/2B: $80- 110 XP: $20

Location: WY 296, 5 mi s of US 212; 40 mi n of WY 120. 4027 Crandall Rd 82414 (Box 1731, Painter Rt CODY). **Terms:** Check-out 9 am; reserv deposit, 30 day notice; handling fee imposed. **Facility:** 8 rooms. Rustic cabins & lodge rooms on the Clarksfork River. 6 two-bedroom units. 1 rm sleeps up to 12 persons; 1-2 stories; exterior corridors. **Services:** winter plug-ins. **Recreation:** fishing. Fee: horseback riding. **All Rooms:** kitchens, combo or shower baths. **Cards:** MC, VI.

PINEDALE—1,200

LODGINGS

BEST WESTERN PINEDALE INN
(AAA) SAVE
◆◆◆
Motel

Phone: (307)367-6869

	1P: $59- 99	2P/1B: $59- 99	2P/2B: $59- 99
6/16-9/15 [CP]			
5/16-6/15 [CP]	1P: $49- 89	2P/1B: $49- 89	2P/2B: $49- 89
3/1-5/15 & 9/16-2/29 [CP]	1P: $40- 70	2P/1B: $40- 70	2P/2B: $40- 70

Location: 0.5 mi n on US 191. 850 W Pine St 82941. Fax: 307/367-6897. **Terms:** Pets. **Facility:** 58 rooms. Newer motel. Moderate size rooms, contemporary rooms. 2 stories; interior corridors; designated smoking area; heated indoor pool, whirlpool. **Services:** winter plug-ins. **All Rooms:** extended cable TV. **Cards:** AE, CB, DI, DS, MC, VI. **Special Amenities:** Free breakfast and free local telephone calls.

THE CHAMBERS HOUSE BED & BREAKFAST
◆◆◆
Bed &
Breakfast

Rates Subject to Change   **Phone: 307/367-2168**
All Year [BP]   2P/1B: $75- 105   XP: $20

Location: Just n via Maybelle. 111 W Magnolia St 82941 (PO Box 753). **Terms:** Check-in 4 pm; reserv deposit, 3 day notice. **Facility:** 4 rooms. 2 stories; interior corridors; smoke free premises; street parking only. **Some Rooms:** color TV. **Cards:** AE, DS, MC, VI.

SUN DANCE MOTEL
(AAA)
◆◆
Motel

Rates Subject to Change   **Phone: (307)367-4336**
All Year   1P: $35- 45   2P/1B: $39- 59   2P/2B: $49- 59   XP: $5

Location: US 191, in city center. 148 E Pine St 82941 (PO Box 622). **Terms:** Pets. **Facility:** 19 rooms. Standard motel rooms & 1 cabin. Homemade fudge made in lobby. 3 two-bedroom units, $50-$79. 1 cabin with kitchen; 1 story; exterior corridors. **Services:** giftshop; winter plug-ins. **All Rooms:** combo or shower baths. **Some Rooms:** efficiency. **Cards:** AE, DS, MC, VI.

WAGON WHEEL MOTEL
(AAA)
◆◆
Motel

Rates Subject to Change   **Phone: (307)367-2871**
All Year   1P: $40- 65   2P/1B: $50- 75   2P/2B: $55- 85   XP: $5   D

Location: S end of town on US 191. 407 S Pine St 82941 (PO Box 407). **Terms:** Reserv deposit. **Facility:** 15 rooms. Large attractive rooms, well maintained. Modern motel with contemporary decor. Very clean rooms. 1 story; exterior corridors; designated smoking area. **Dining:** Restaurant nearby. **Services:** winter plug-ins. **All Rooms:** extended cable TV. **Cards:** AE, CB, DI, DS, MC, VI.

WINDOW ON THE WINDS B & B
Guaranteed Rates
Phone: (307)367-2600

◆◆◆
5/1-10/1   1P: $70- 80   2P/1B: $75- 95   XP: $15   F13
3/1-4/30 & 10/2-2/29   1P: $45- 55   2P/1B: $60- 70   XP: $15   F13

Bed & Breakfast

Location: 2 mi n on US 191. 10151 US 191 82941 (PO Box 996). Fax: 307/367-2395. **Terms:** Check-in 4 pm; reserv deposit, 7 day notice. **Facility:** 4 rooms. Rooms with view of Wind River Mountains. Common parlor. 2 stories; interior corridors; smoke free premises. **Services:** winter plug-ins. **Some Rooms:** color TV. **Cards:** AE, DS, MC, VI.

RESTAURANTS

MCGREGORS PUB   Lunch: $4-$6   Dinner: $9-$25   Phone: 307/367-4443

◆◆
American

Location: Just w, then n, back of Cowboy Shop. 21 N Franklin Ave 82941. **Hours:** 11:30 am-2 & 5:30-10:30 pm. Closed: 11/25, 12/25 & Sat-Sun for lunch. **Reservations:** suggested. **Features:** casual dress; children's menu; carryout; cocktails & lounge; a la carte. Varied menu specializing in prime rib & fresh seafood. Contemporary Western atmosphere. Patio dining in summer. **Cards:** CB, DI, DS, MC, VI.

STOCKMENS RESTAURANT   Lunch: $4-$10   Dinner: $7-$17   Phone: 307/367-4563

◆◆
American

Location: Center. 117 W Pine St 82941. **Hours:** 6 am-10:30 pm. Closed: 12/25. **Reservations:** accepted. **Features:** dressy casual; carryout; salad bar; cocktails & lounge; entertainment. Family owned & operated over 40 yrs, specialties are prime rib & lamb. **Cards:** DS, MC, VI.

POWELL—5,300

LODGINGS

BEST WESTERN KINGS INN   Rates Subject to Change   Phone: 307/754-5117

◆◆
Motor Inn
6/10-8/20   1P: $63   2P/1B: $63   2P/2B: $71
3/1-6/9 & 8/21-2/29   1P: $38   2P/1B: $38   2P/2B: $42

Location: 0.3 mi e on US 14A. 777 E 2nd St 82435 (PO Box 933). Fax: 307/754-2198. **Terms:** Reserv deposit. **Facility:** 48 rooms. Large rooms. 2 stories; exterior corridors; heated pool. **Services:** winter plug-ins. **Cards:** AE, DI, DS, MC, VI.

PARK MOTEL   Rates Subject to Change   Phone: 307/754-2233

◆
Motel
6/10-8/20   1P: $49   2P/1B: $49   2P/2B: $59   XP: $5
5/1-6/9 & 8/21-10/1   1P: $36   2P/1B: $36   2P/2B: $42   XP: $2
3/1-4/30 & 10/2-2/29   1P: $32   2P/1B: $35   2P/2B: $38- 40 XP: $2

Location: 0.4 mi e on US 14A. 737 E 2nd St 82435. Fax: 307/754-2233. **Terms:** Reserv deposit. **Facility:** 18 rooms. Very clean rooms. 1 two-bedroom unit. Efficiency, $65 for up to 2 persons; 1 story; exterior corridors; designated smoking area. **Services:** winter plug-ins. **All Rooms:** combo or shower baths. **Some Rooms:** efficiency. **Cards:** AE, DS, MC, VI.

SUPER 8 MOTEL   Rates Subject to Change   Phone: 307/754-7231

◆
Motel
6/10-8/15   1P: $50   2P/1B: $50   2P/2B: $60   XP: $3
3/1-6/9 & 8/16-2/29   1P: $33   2P/1B: $37   2P/2B: $39   XP: $3

Location: US 14, downtown. 845 E Coulter Ave 82435. Fax: 307/754-7231. **Facility:** 35 rooms. 2 waterbeds; 2 mini-refrigerators avail; 2 stories; interior corridors. **Services:** winter plug-ins. **Cards:** AE, CB, DI, DS, MC, VI.

RANCHESTER—700

LODGING

RANCHESTER WESTERN MOTEL   Rates Subject to Change   Phone: 307/655-2212

◆◆◆
◆
Motel
6/1-8/31   1P: $40   2P/1B: $43   2P/2B: $51   XP: $3
9/1-10/31   1P: $33   2P/1B: $35   2P/2B: $43   XP: $3
4/1-5/31   1P: $25   2P/1B: $30   2P/2B: $36   XP: $3
3/1-3/31 & 11/1-2/29   1P: $22   2P/1B: $25   2P/2B: $31   XP: $3

Location: US 14. 350 Dayton St 82839 (PO Box 41). **Terms:** Pets, in smoking rooms only. **Facility:** 18 rooms. 1 story; exterior corridors; designated smoking area; small heated pool. **Services:** winter plug-ins. **Cards:** DS, MC, VI. IMA.

RAWLINS—9,400

LODGINGS

BEST WESTERN COTTONTREE INN   Phone: (307)324-2737

◆◆◆ [SAVE]
◆◆◆
Motor Inn
7/16-7/31   1P: $79- 84   2P/1B: $84- 89   2P/2B: $84- 89 XP: $5   F17
6/1-7/15 & 8/1-10/31   1P: $69- 74   2P/1B: $74- 79   2P/2B: $74- 79 XP: $5   F17
3/1-5/31 & 11/1-2/29   1P: $59- 64   2P/1B: $69- 74   2P/2B: $69- 74 XP: $5   F17

Location: 1.5 mi w on I-80 & US 30 business loop; 0.3 mi e of I-80, exit 211 (Spruce St). 2221 W Spruce St 82301 (PO Box 387). Fax: 307/324-5011. **Terms:** Pets. **Facility:** 122 rooms. Newly renovated. Spacious rooms. All rooms with iron & ironing board. 2 stories; interior/exterior corridors; heated indoor pool, sauna, whirlpool. **Dining:** The Hungry Miner, see separate listing. **Services:** winter plug-ins. **Cards:** AE, CB, DI, DS, MC, VI. **Special Amenities:** Free local telephone calls and free newspaper.

SLEEP INN   Phone: (307)328-1732

◆◆◆ [SAVE]
◆
Motel
7/1-8/31 [CP]   1P: $53- 58   2P/1B: $58- 63   2P/2B: $58- 63 XP: $5   F18
6/1-6/30 & 9/1-9/30 [CP]   1P: $48- 53   2P/1B: $53- 58   2P/2B: $53- 58 XP: $5   F18
3/1-5/31 & 10/1-2/29 [CP] 1P: $44- 49   2P/1B: $49- 54   2P/2B: $49- 54 XP: $5   F18

Location: I-80, exit 214 (Higley Blvd). 1400 Higley Blvd 82301. Fax: 307/328-0412. **Terms:** Pets, in smoking rooms. **Facility:** 81 rooms. Modern rooms; well-maintained. Mini-refrigerator avail, extra charge; 2 stories; interior corridors; sauna. **Dining:** Restaurant nearby. **Services:** winter plug-ins. **All Rooms:** combo or shower baths, extended cable TV. **Some Rooms:** whirlpools. **Cards:** AE, CB, DI, DS, JC, MC, VI. **Special Amenities:** Free local telephone calls and free newspaper.

RESTAURANTS

ASPEN HOUSE RESTAURANT **Lunch:** $4-$9 **Dinner:** $13-$25 Phone: 307/324-478
◆◆ **Location:** 318 5th St 82301. **Hours:** 11 am-2 pm; Mon-Sat 5 pm-9 pm. Closed: 7/4 & 12/2!
American **Reservations:** suggested. **Features:** casual dress; children's menu; health conscious menu; carryou
cocktails. 1905 Victorian House, beef, poultry, pasta are specialties also Indonesian offerings. Smoke fre
premises. **Cards:** AE, MC, VI.

THE HUNGRY MINER **Lunch:** $5-$10 **Dinner:** $7-$16 Phone: 307/328-218
◆ **Location:** 1.5 mi w on I-80 & US 30 business loop; 0.3 mi e of I-80, exit 211 (Spruce St); in Best Wester
American CottonTree Inn. 2221 W Spruce St 82301. **Hours:** 6 am-10 pm; to 9 pm in winter. Closed: 12/2!
Features: casual dress; children's menu; senior's menu; carryout; salad bar; cocktails. Sandwiches, stea
fish & Mexican dishes. Casual dining in frontier decor. **Cards:** AE, DS, MC, VI.

THE PANTRY **Lunch:** $3-$7 **Dinner:** $9-$19 Phone: 307/324-786
(AAA) **Location:** City center; I-80 business loop. 221 W Cedar 82301. **Hours:** 7 am-9 pm. Closed: 1/1, 12/25
Sun. **Features:** casual dress; a la carte. Historic home. Homemade soup & freshly baked bread. **Cards:** AE
◆◆ DS, MC, VI.
American

RIVERTON—9,200

LODGINGS

DAYS INN Rates Subject to Change Phone: (307)856-967
◆◆ 7/1-8/31 [CP] 1P: $45- 50 2P/1B: $50- 55 2P/2B: $60- 65 XP: $5 F1
Motel 6/1-6/30 [CP] 1P: $40- 45 2P/1B: $45- 50 2P/2B: $55- 60 XP: $5 F1
3/1-5/31 & 9/1-2/29 [CP] 1P: $35- 40 2P/1B: $40- 45 2P/2B: $50- 55 XP: $5 F1
Location: 0.5 mi nw on US 26. 909 W Main St 82501. Fax: 307/856-9677. **Facility:** 32 rooms. Well kept large rooms. Truc
parking avail. 2 stories; exterior corridors. **Services:** winter plug-ins. **All Rooms:** combo or shower baths. **Cards:** AE, CE
DI, DS, MC, VI.

HOLIDAY INN CONVENTION CENTER Rates Subject to Change Phone: (307)856-810
◆◆◆ 5/1-9/30 1P: $69- 89 2P/1B: $69- 89 2P/2B: $69- 89 XP: $10 F1
Motor Inn 3/1-4/30 & 10/1-2/29 1P: $59- 79 2P/1B: $59- 79 2P/2B: $59- 79 XP: $10 F1
Location: 0.8 mi n on US 26 & SR 789. 900 E Sunset 82501. Fax: 307/856-0266. **Facility:** 121 rooms. Newl
renovated public areas. Contemporary, very clean rooms. 2 stories; interior corridors; small heated indoor pool
Services: winter plug-ins. **Cards:** AE, DI, DS, JC, MC, VI. *(See ad below & color ad opposite title page)*

PAINTBRUSH MOTEL Rates Subject to Change Phone: 307/856-923
◆ All Year 1P: $37 2P/1B: $40 2P/2B: $46 XP: $3
Motel **Location:** 1.3 mi ne on US 26 & SR 789. 1550 N Federal Blvd 82501. Fax: 307/856-5594. **Facility:** 23 rooms
Excellent housekeeping. 1 story; exterior corridors. **Services:** winter plug-ins. **Cards:** AE, DS, MC, VI.

SUNDOWNER STATION Rates Subject to Change Phone: 307/856-650
◆◆ All Year 1P: $53- 55 2P/1B: $55- 57 2P/2B: $59 XP: $2-4 F1
Motor Inn **Location:** 1.4 mi ne on US 26 & SR 789. 1616 N Federal Blvd 82501. Fax: 307/856-6503. **Facility:** 60 rooms
Very clean rooms. Courtyard with waterfall. 1 suite, $59 for up to 2 persons; 2 stories; interior corridors; des
ignated smoking area. **Services:** winter plug-ins. **Cards:** AE, CB, DI, DS, MC, VI.

SUPER 8 MOTEL Rates Subject to Change Phone: (307)857-2400
◆◆ 7/1-8/31 [CP] 1P: $47 2P/1B: $52 2P/2B: $57 XP: $5 F!
Motel 6/1-6/30 [CP] 1P: $45 2P/1B: $50 2P/2B: $55 XP: $5 F!
3/1-5/31 & 9/1-2/29 [CP] 1P: $36 2P/1B: $41 2P/2B: $46 XP: $5 F!
Location: 1 mi ne on US 26 & SR 789. 1040 N Federal Blvd 82501. Fax: 307/857-2400. **Facility:** 32 rooms. Family unit avail
$69 for up to 6 persons; 2 stories; interior corridors. **Services:** winter plug-ins. **Cards:** AE, DI, DS, MC, VI.

THUNDERBIRD MOTEL   Phone: (307)856-9201
[AAA] [SAVE]   All Year   1P: $30- 36   2P/1B: $36- 42   2P/2B: $40- 46   XP: $4   F12
◆   **Location:** Downtown; just n of US 26. 302 E Fremont 82501. Fax: 307/856-5486. **Terms:** Pets, $4 extra
Motel   charge. **Facility:** 45 rooms. Very clean, budget oriented rooms. 2 stories; exterior corridors; designated
        smoking area. **Services:** winter plug-ins. **All Rooms:** combo or shower baths, extended cable TV.
        Cards: AE, CB, DI, DS, MC, VI. **Special Amenities:** Free local telephone calls.

TOMAHAWK MOTOR LODGE   Phone: (307)856-9205
[AAA] [SAVE]   7/1-9/30   1P: $45   2P/1B: $50   2P/2B: $55   XP: $5   F12
◆   4/1-6/30   1P: $40   2P/1B: $45   2P/2B: $50   XP: $5   F12
◆◆◆   3/1-3/31 & 10/1-2/29   1P: $37   2P/1B: $42   2P/2B: $47   XP: $5   F12
Motel   **Location:** Downtown; on US 26. 208 E Main St 82501. Fax: 307/856-2879. **Terms:** Reserv deposit.
        Facility: 32 rooms. A 1960's gem with some modern furnishings & decor. Exquisitely maintained. 1 two-
bedroom unit. 4 large double rms, $65-$75; 2 stories; interior/exterior corridors. **Dining:** Restaurant nearby. **Services:** winter
plug-ins. **All Rooms:** extended cable TV. **Cards:** AE, CB, DI, DS, MC, VI. **Special Amenities:** Free local telephone calls.
(See ad below)

RESTAURANTS

THE BROKER RESTAURANT   **Lunch:** $6-$14   **Dinner:** $7-$17   Phone: 307/856-0555
◆◆   **Location:** Downtown; on US 26. 203 E Main St 82501. **Hours:** 11 am-2 & 5-9:30 pm. Closed major holidays
American & Sun. **Reservations:** accepted. **Features:** casual dress; children's menu; carryout; cocktails; street parking;
        a la carte. Historic hotel, features prime rib & seafood specialties; also Mexican fare. **Cards:** AE, MC, VI.

THE DEPOT   **Lunch:** $6-$11   **Dinner:** $8-$17   Phone: 307/856-2221
[AAA]   **Location:** Downtown; just s of US 26. 110 S 1st E 82501. **Hours:** 11 am-9 pm, Fri & Sat-10 pm. Closed
◆◆   major holidays & Sun. **Features:** casual dress; children's menu; cocktails. Casual dining in remodeled train
Mexican depot. Outside dining in season. **Cards:** MC, VI.

ROCK SPRINGS—19,100

LODGINGS

BEST WESTERN OUTLAW INN   Phone: (307)362-6623
[AAA] [SAVE]   5/15-9/15   1P: $74- 84   2P/1B: $81- 91   2P/2B: $93-103   XP: $6   F18
◆   3/1-5/14 & 9/16-2/29   1P: $55- 65   2P/1B: $51- 71   2P/2B: $73- 83   XP: $6   F18
Motor Inn   **Location:** Just n of I-80, exit 104 (Elk St). 1630 Elk St 82901 (PO Box 1570). Fax: 307/362-2633.
        Facility: 101 rooms. Large indoor courtyard area. Very clean rooms. 1-2 stories; interior/exterior corridors;
        heated indoor pool. **Dining:** Cocktails; restaurant, see separate listing. **Services:** winter plug-ins.
All Rooms: extended cable TV. **Cards:** AE, CB, DI, DS, MC, VI. **Special Amenities:** Free local telephone calls and free
newspaper. (See ad p 310)

COMFORT INN   Phone: (307)382-9490
[AAA] [SAVE]   4/1-9/30 [CP]   1P: $51- 56   2P/1B: $51- 61   2P/2B: $51- 61   XP: $6   F19
◆◆◆   3/1-3/31 & 10/1-2/29 [CP] 1P: $46- 51   2P/1B: $46- 51   2P/2B: $51- 56   XP: $6   F19
Motel   **Location:** 0.3 mi s of I-80, exit 102 (Dewar Dr); just w. 1670 Sunset Dr 82901. Fax: 307/382-7333.
        Terms: Small pets only, $10 extra charge. **Facility:** 103 rooms. Large continental breakfast room. Contempo-
rary guest rooms. 1 story; exterior corridors; small heated pool, whirlpool; playground. **Dining:** Restaurant
nearby. **Services:** complimentary evening beverages; winter plug-ins. **Recreation:** 2 exercise machines.
All Rooms: extended cable TV. **Cards:** AE, CB, DI, DS, JC, MC, VI. **Special Amenities:** Free breakfast and free local
telephone calls. (See color ad p 311)

ECONO LODGE   Rates Subject to Change   Phone: (307)382-4217
◆◆   5/1-9/30 [CP]   1P: $40- 60   2P/1B: $50- 70   2P/2B: $50- 70   XP: $5   F16
Motor Inn   10/1-10/31 [CP]   1P: $35- 45   2P/1B: $48- 55   2P/2B: $48- 55   XP: $5   F16
        3/1-4/30 & 11/1-2/29 [CP] 1P: $35- 45   2P/1B: $38- 48   2P/2B: $38- 48   XP: $5   F16
Location: Just n of I-80, exit 104 (Elk St). 1635 N Elk St 82901. Fax: 307/362-4150. **Facility:** 96 rooms. 2 stories; exterior
corridors; designated smoking area; small heated pool. **Cards:** AE, DI, DS, MC, VI.

HOLIDAY INN
Phone: (307)382-920█

[AAA] [SAVE]
All Year   1P: $64- 75 2P/1B: $64- 75 2P/2B: $64- 75

◆◆◆
Location: 0.3 mi sw of I-80, exit 102 (Dewar Dr). 1675 Sunset Dr 82901. Fax: 307/362-1064. **Terms:** Pets
Motor Inn
$10 dep req. **Facility:** 114 rooms. Attractive public areas. Very clean rooms. 4 stories; interior/exterior corridors
heated indoor pool, wading pool, whirlpool. **Dining:** Mr. C's, see separate listing. **Services:** winter plug-ins
All Rooms: extended cable TV. **Cards:** AE, CB, DI, DS, JC, MC, VI. **Special Amenities:** Free loca█
telephone calls and free newspaper. *(See color ad p 311 & opposite title page)*

[icons]

THE INN AT ROCK SPRINGS
Rates Subject to Change
Phone: 307/362-960█

◆◆
All Year [CP]   1P: $42- 58 2P/1B: $52- 64 2P/2B: $52- 64 XP: $6   F1
Motor Inn
Location: I-80 at Dewar Dr, exit 102. 2518 Foothill Blvd 82901. Fax: 307/362-8846. **Terms:** Reserv deposi█
Facility: 148 rooms. Some remodeled rooms. Convenient location. 3 stories; interior corridors; designate█
smoking area; small heated indoor pool. **Services:** giftshop; winter plug-ins. **Cards:** AE, DI, DS, MC, VI.

[icons]

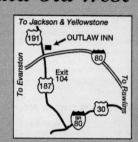

Live a little with our blend of the New and Old West

We offer our guests casual elegance, a relaxed atmosphere with superior service. Fine dining with daily specials, saloon with cocktails & wine and our year around heated indoor pool ensures a comfortable stay. We feature guest rooms on the ground floor with convenient door side parking or rooms located inside our climate controlled atrium, poolside and close to our restaurant. Proudly serving Southwest Wyoming for 33 years!

- Indoor Heated Pool
- Free HBO & Cable TV
- Closest Hotel to Municipal Golf & Tennis
- AAA and Senior Discount (10% off published rates)

- Restaurant 6am - 10pm
- Just 20 Miles From Flaming Gorge National Rec. Area
- Saloon & Package Store
- All Major Credit Cards Accepted

 Best Western Outlaw Inn

1630 Elk Street (I-80 Exit 104, Elk Street & US Hwy 191 North)
Rock Springs, WY 82901 • 307-362-6623

Make reservations at any Best Western or call toll-free 800-528-1234

In the listings, the meal plan included in the rates follows the open dates.

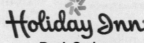

MOTEL 6 - 395
Rates Subject to Change
Phone: 307/362-1850

5/27-2/29   1P: $38- 43   2P/1B: $44- 49   2P/2B: $43- 49   XP: $3   F17

3/1-5/26   1P: $32- 37   2P/1B: $38- 43   2P/2B: $38- 43   XP: $3   F17

Location: I-80, exit 102 (Dewar Dr); n to Foothills Blvd, just e. 2615 Commercial Way 82901
Motel   **Fax:** 307/362-5998. **Terms:** Small pets only. **Facility:** 99 rooms. Modern rooms. Truck parking. 2 stories; exterior corridors; designated smoking area; small heated pool. **Dining:** Restaurant nearby

All Rooms: shower baths. **Cards:** AE, CB, DI, DS, MC, VI.

RAMADA LIMITED
Rates Subject to Change
Phone: (307)362-1770

6/1-9/30 [CP]   1P: $55- 60   2P/1B: $65- 75   2P/2B: $65- 75   XP: $6   F18

Motel   3/1-5/31 & 10/1-2/29 [CP]   1P: $50- 60   2P/1B: $60- 65   2P/2B: $60- 65   XP: $6   F18

Location: Just n of I-80, exit 102 (Dewar Dr). 2717 Dewar Dr 82901. **Fax:** 307/362-2830. **Facility:** 130 rooms. Comfortable clean rooms. Attractive lobby. 2 stories; interior corridors; heated pool. **Services:** winter plug-ins. **Cards:** AE, CB, DI, DS, MC, VI.

RODEWAY INN
Phone: (307)362-6673

All Year   1P: $32- 49   2P/1B: $36- 38   2P/2B: $42- 49   XP: $6   F18

Location: I-80 business loop, 1.3 mi se of I-80, exit 102 (Dewar Dr). 1004 Dewar Dr 82901. **Fax:** 307/362-6673. **Terms:** Weekly rates; pets, $5 extra charge; designated rooms. **Facility:** 32 rooms.
Motel   Various room sizes. Very clean rooms. 1-2 stories; exterior corridors. **Dining:** Restaurant nearby.

Services: winter plug-ins. **All Rooms:** extended cable TV. **Cards:** AE, CB, DI, DS, MC, VI

Special Amenities: Free local telephone calls and free newspaper. *(See color ad below)*

SPRINGS MOTEL
Phone: 307/362-6683

5/1-9/30   1P: $38- 40   2P/1B: $40- 44   2P/2B: $46- 48   XP: $4

3/1-4/30 & 10/1-2/29   1P: $30- 32   2P/1B: $34- 36   2P/2B: $38- 40   XP: $4

Location: I-80, exit 107, 0.3 mi w. 1525 9th St 82901. **Terms:** Small pets only. **Facility:** 23 rooms. Spacious
Motel   & very clean rooms. Two-bedroom unit, $65; 1 story; exterior corridors. **Dining:** Restaurant nearby

Services: winter plug-ins. **All Rooms:** extended cable TV. **Cards:** AE, DS, MC, VI.

RESTAURANTS

THE LOG INN
Dinner: $10-$18
Phone: 307/362-7166

Location: I-80, exit 99; in back of Conoco truck stop. 12 Purple Sage Rd 82901. **Hours:** 5:30 pm-10 pm,
Sun 5 pm-9 pm. Closed major holidays. **Reservations:** accepted. **Features:** casual dress; cocktails &
American   lounge. Pleasant dining in Western atmosphere. **Cards:** AE, CB, DI, DS, MC, VI.

MR. C'S
Lunch: $5-$9   Dinner: $7-$21
Phone: 307/382-9200

Location: 0.3 mi sw of I-80, exit 102 (Dewar Dr); in Holiday Inn. 1675 Sunset Dr 82901. **Hours:** 6 am-2 &
5-10 pm. **Reservations:** accepted. **Features:** casual dress; children's menu; cocktails & lounge; a la carte.
Continental   Cozy dining room. Specialize in steak & seafood. Pleasant staff. **Cards:** AE, CB, DI, DS, MC, VI.

OUTLAW INN RESTAURANT
Lunch: $4-$8   Dinner: $7-$17
Phone: 307/362-6623

Location: Just n of I-80, exit 104 (Elk St); in Best Western Outlaw Inn. 1630 Elk St 82901. **Hours:** 6 am-10
pm. Closed: 12/25. **Features:** casual dress; children's menu; cocktails & lounge; a la carte. Attractive dining
American   room. Steak, seafood & pasta dishes. **Cards:** AE, CB, DI, DS, MC, VI.

SARATOGA—2,000

LODGINGS

FAR OUT WEST BED & BREAKFAST
Rates Subject to Change
Phone: 307/326-5869

5/1-10/31   1P: $80- 110   2P/1B: $95- 125   XP: $15

Bed &   3/1-4/30 & 11/1-2/29   1P: $60- 90   2P/1B: $75- 105
Breakfast   **Location:** Center. 304 N 2nd St 82331-1230 (PO Box 1230, 82331). **Fax:** 307/326-9864. **Terms:** Reserv
deposit. **Facility:** 6 rooms. Charming guest rooms filled with stuffed animals. "Hole in the wall" childrens play
room. Very homey, warm & hospitable atmosphere. VCR in common area. 2 stories; interior/exterior corridors; smoke
free premises. **Cards:** MC, VI.

HACIENDA MOTEL

	Rates Subject to Change						**Phone:** (307)326-5751	
◆◆ 5/1-10/31	1P: $49- 59	2P/1B:	$59-	69	2P/2B:	$59- 69	XP: $6	F11
Motel 3/1-4/30 & 11/1-2/29	1P: $39- 49	2P/1B:	$49-	59	2P/2B:	$49- 59	XP: $6	F11

Location: 0.5 mi s on SR 130; adjacent to airport. 1116 S 1st St 82331 (PO Box 960). Fax: 307/326-5751. **Facility:** 32 rooms. Economy lodging with excellent housekeeping. 1 two-bedroom unit. Suites & family units; 2 stories; interior corridors. **Services:** winter plug-ins. **All Rooms:** combo or shower baths. **Some Rooms:** 5 efficiencies. **Cards:** AE, DI, DS, MC, VI.

ASK 🔊 🐾 🎱 🍴 ▢ 🖨 🔒 ✖

RESTAURANT

HOTEL WOLF RESTAURANT Historical   **Lunch:** $3-$7   **Dinner:** $10-$25   **Phone:** 307/326-5525
  Location: 0.5 mi s on SR 130, adjacent to airport; in downtown historic Hotel Wolf. 101 E Bridge 82331.
◆◆   **Hours:** 11:30 am-2 & 6-10 pm, Sun 5 pm-9 pm. Closed: 1/1 & 12/25. **Reservations:** suggested.
American   **Features:** No A/C; casual dress; children's menu; salad bar; cocktails & lounge; street parking. Featuring steak, seafood, prime rib & chicken. Restored Victorian dining room. **Cards:** AE, CB, DI, MC, VI.

SHERIDAN—13,900

LODGINGS

BEST WESTERN SHERIDAN CENTER

	Rates Subject to Change						**Phone:** (307)674-7421	
◆◆ 6/1-8/31	1P: $69- 89	2P/1B:	$80- 100	2P/2B:	$80- 100	XP: $10		F12
Motor Inn 9/1-9/30	1P: $59- 79	2P/1B:	$65- 90	2P/2B:	$65- 90	XP: $5-10		F12
3/1-5/31 & 10/1-2/29	1P: $49- 69	2P/1B:	$50- 70	2P/2B:	$50- 70	XP: $5-10		F12

Location: I-90, exit 20; 1.7 mi s. 612 N Main St 82801. Fax: 307/672-3018. **Terms:** Reserv deposit. **Facility:** 138 rooms. Mini-refrigerators avail; 2 stories; interior/exterior corridors; heated indoor pool. **Services:** winter plug-ins. **All Rooms:** combo or tub baths. **Cards:** AE, CB, DI, DS, MC, VI.

ASK 🍴 🎱 🏊 🍴 🍸 🎾 🛎 ▢ 🖨 ✖ 🏊

COMFORT INN

	Rates Subject to Change						**Phone:** (307)672-5098
◆◆◆ 7/23-8/14	1P: $85	2P/1B:	$85	2P/2B:	$85	XP: $5	F18
Motel 6/11-7/22 & 8/15-9/9	1P: $70	2P/1B:	$70	2P/2B:	$70	XP: $5	F18
5/21-6/10 & 9/10-9/30	1P: $60	2P/1B:	$60	2P/2B:	$60	XP: $5	F18
3/1-5/20 & 10/1-2/29	1P: $40	2P/1B:	$40	2P/2B:	$40	XP: $5	F18

Location: Just e of I-90, exit 25. 1450 E Brundage Lane 82801. Fax: 307/672-5098. **Facility:** 45 rooms. Newer, clean property. 2 stories; interior/exterior corridors; designated smoking area. **Services:** winter plug-ins. **Cards:** AE, CB, DI, DS, JC, MC, VI.

SAVE 🔊 🐾 🎱 ✖

GUEST HOUSE MOTEL

						Phone: (307)674-7496	
🅰 SAVE 6/1-9/15	1P: $40	2P/1B:	$50	2P/2B:	$55	XP: $5	F10
◆ 3/1-5/31 & 9/16-2/29	1P: $34	2P/1B:	$40	2P/2B:	$45	XP: $5	F10

Motel   **Location:** 0.7 mi s from I-90, exit 20; on I-90 business loop. 2007 N Main St 82801. Fax: 307/674-7687.
Terms: Weekly rates, in winter; pets, $5 extra charge. **Facility:** 44 rooms. Spacious rooms. 1 story; exterior corridors. **Dining:** Restaurant nearby. **Services:** winter plug-ins. **Cards:** AE, DI, DS, JC, MC, VI.
Special Amenities: Early check-in/late check-out and free local telephone calls. *(See color ad below)*

🐾 🍴 🏊 ▢ 🔒 ✖

HOLIDAY INN

						Phone: (307)672-8931	
🅰 SAVE 5/1-10/15	1P: $78- 109	2P/1B:	$84- 119	2P/2B:	$84- 129	XP: $10	F19
◆◆◆ 3/1-4/30 & 10/16-2/29	1P: $49- 75	2P/1B:	$49- 84	2P/2B:	$49- 84	XP: $10	F19

Motor Inn   **Location:** 0.3 mi nw of I-90, exit 25. 1809 Sugarland Dr 82801. Fax: 307/672-6388. **Terms:** Weekly/monthly rates; pets. **Facility:** 212 rooms. Large atrium, some rooms with view of mountains. 5 stories; interior corridors; putting green; small heated indoor pool, saunas, whirlpool; racquetball court. **Dining:** Restaurant; 6 am-10 pm; $10-$19; cocktails. **Services:** giftshop; winter plug-ins. **Recreation:** indoor recreation area. **Cards:** AE, CB, DI, DS, JC, MC, VI. **Special Amenities:** Early check-in/late check-out and free local telephone calls.
(See color ad opposite title page)

🔊 🐾 🎱 🎱 🏊 🍴 🍸 🎾 🏊 ✖ 🛎 ▢ 🖨 🔒 ✖ 🏊

MILL INN
◇◇◇◇
◆ ◆ ◆
Historic Motel

	Rates Subject to Change						
6/1-9/14 [CP]	1P:	$57- 64	2P/1B:	$59-	68	2P/2B:	$68- 78	XP: $5-10
5/1-5/31 [CP]	1P:	$43- 48	2P/1B:	$46-	52	2P/2B:	$52- 58	XP: $5-10
9/15-10/31 [CP]	1P:	$39- 43	2P/1B:	$42-	46	2P/2B:	$49- 54	XP: $5-10
3/1-4/30 & 11/1-2/29 [CP]	1P:	$29- 32	2P/1B:	$32-	35	2P/2B:	$38- 42	XP: $5

Phone: 307/672-640

Location: I-90, exit 25; 0.3 mi w. 2161 Coffeen Ave 82801. Fax: 307/672-6401. **Terms:** Reserv deposi weekly/monthly rates. **Facility:** 45 rooms. Cozy rooms in converted historic flour mill. Some with view of mountains. 2 tw bedroom units. 2 stories; interior/exterior corridors; designated smoking area. **Dining:** Restaurant nearby. **Services:** winte plug-ins. **Some Rooms:** kitchen, whirlpools. **Cards:** AE, DS, MC, VI. *(See color ad below)*

ROCK TRIM MOTEL LLC
◇◇◇ SAVE
◆
Motel

		1P:	$38- 45	2P/1B:	$42-	50	2P/2B:	$48- 56	XP: $4-6	D1
5/1-10/1										
3/1-4/30 & 10/2-2/29		1P:	$30- 36	2P/1B:	$32-	40	2P/2B:	$34- 44	XP: $4-6	D1

Phone: (307)672-246

Location: I-90, exit 25; w to Coffeen Ave; 1.3 mi n. 449 Coffeen Ave 82801. **Terms:** Handling fee impose weekly rates, in winter; small pets only. **Facility:** 18 rooms. Some basement rooms. 1 story; exterior corridor **Services:** winter plug-ins. **All Rooms:** combo or shower baths. **Some Rooms:** 4 efficiencies, no utensil **Cards:** AE, DS, MC, VI. **Special Amenities:** Free local telephone calls.

RESTAURANT

GOLDEN STEER   **Lunch:** $6-$11   **Dinner:** $7-$19   **Phone:** 307/674-9334
    Location: 0.8 mi s from I-90, exit 20; on I-90 business loop. 2071 N Main St 82801. **Hours:** 11 am-2 & 4-9
    pm, Sat 4 pm-10 pm, Sun 4 pm-9 pm. Closed major holidays. **Features:** casual dress; children's menu;
    cocktails & lounge. Contemporary dining room. **Cards:** AE, DI, DS, MC, VI.
American

SUNDANCE—1,100

LODGINGS

ARROWHEAD MOTEL   Rates Subject to Change   **Phone:** 307/283-3307
5/15-9/15		2P/1B:	$50- 55	2P/2B:	$60	XP:	$4
3/1-5/14 & 12/2-2/29		2P/1B:	$36- 45	2P/2B:	$40- 50	XP:	$4
9/16-12/1		2P/1B:	$36- 45	2P/2B:	$45- 48	XP:	$3

    Location: I-90 business loop & US 14. 214 Cleveland 82729 (PO Box 191). **Terms:** Handling fee imposed.
    Facility: 12 rooms. Clean, cozy rooms. 1 story; exterior corridors; designated smoking area.
Motel
Dining: Restaurant nearby. **Services:** winter plug-ins. **Cards:** AE, DI, DS, MC, VI. Budget Host. *(See color ad p 264)*

BEAR LODGE MOTEL   **Phone:** (307)283-1611
6/1-8/20	1P: $56	2P/1B:	$56	2P/2B:	$64	XP: $4	F16
8/21-11/5	1P: $44- 48	2P/1B:	$44- 48	2P/2B:	$50- 54	XP: $4	F16
3/1-5/31 & 11/6-2/29	1P: $34- 38	2P/1B:	$34- 38	2P/2B:	$40- 48	XP: $4	F16

    Location: I-90 business loop & US 14. 218 Cleveland Ave 82729 (PO Box 912). Fax: 307/283-2537.
    Terms: Reserv deposit; small pets only. **Facility:** 33 rooms. 2 two-bedroom units. 2 stories; exterior corridors;
Motel
whirlpool. **Dining:** Restaurant nearby. **Services:** winter plug-ins. **Cards:** AE, CB, DI, DS, MC, VI. IMA.
(See color ad p 320)

BEST WESTERN INN AT SUNDANCE   **Phone:** (307)283-2800
5/29-9/5 [CP]	1P: $59- 89	2P/1B:	$64- 99	2P/2B:	$79- 99	XP: $5	F17
9/6-9/30 [CP]	1P: $54- 66	2P/1B:	$59- 69	2P/2B:	$66- 76	XP: $5	F17
3/1-5/28 & 10/1-2/29 [CP]	1P: $44- 54	2P/1B:	$49- 59	2P/2B:	$49- 59	XP: $5	F17

    Location: I-90, exit 189; just n, then just w on I-90 business loop. 2719 E Cleveland 82729.
    Fax: 307/283-2727. **Terms:** Pets, $25 dep req. **Facility:** 44 rooms. Brand new motel. Gift items in lobby. Sun
Motel
patio. 2 stories; interior corridors; designated smoking area; small heated indoor pool. **Services:** winter plug-ins.
All Rooms: extended cable TV. **Cards:** AE, DI, DS, MC, VI. **Special Amenities:** Free breakfast and free local telephone
calls. *(See color ad below)*

SUNDANCE MOUNTAIN INN   **Phone:** (307)283-3737
5/29-9/5 [EP]	1P: $49- 79	2P/1B:	$54- 89	2P/2B:	$69- 99	XP: $5	F17
9/6-9/30 [EP]	1P: $49- 59	2P/1B:	$54- 69	2P/2B:	$59- 69	XP: $5	F17
3/1-5/28 & 10/1-2/29 [CP]	1P: $39- 49	2P/1B:	$44- 54	2P/2B:	$44- 54	XP: $5	F17

    Location: I-90, exit 187; 0.4 mi n on SR 585. 26 SR 585 82729 (PO Box 947). Fax: 307/283-3738.
    Terms: Small pets only, $25 dep req. **Facility:** 40 rooms. 1 two-bedroom unit. 1-2 stories; exterior corridors;
Motel
designated smoking area; small heated indoor pool, sauna, whirlpool. **Dining:** Restaurant nearby. **Services:** winter plug-ins.
All Rooms: extended cable TV. **Cards:** AE, DI, DS, MC, VI. **Special Amenities:** Free breakfast and free local telephone
calls.

RESTAURANT

ARO FAMILY RESTAURANT   **Lunch:** $5-$10   **Dinner:** $7-$16   **Phone:** 307/283-2000
    Location: I-90 business loop & US 14. 205 Cleveland Ave 82729. **Hours:** 5:30 am-10 pm, in summer; 6
    am-9 pm, in winter. Closed: 11/25 & 12/25. **Features:** casual dress; children's menu; carryout; cocktails; a la
    carte. Informal & congenial. Homestyle cooking. **Cards:** AE, CB, DI, DS, MC, VI.
American

TETON VILLAGE—300—See also GRAND TETON NATIONAL PARK.

LODGINGS

ALPENHOF
(AAA)

	Guaranteed Rates						Phone: (307)733-3242
3/1-3/27 & 12/17-2/29	1P: $128- 278	2P/1B: $128- 278	2P/2B: $178- 238	XP: $10			F6
7/13-8/21	1P: $109- 198	2P/1B: $109- 198	2P/2B: $141- 198	XP: $10			F6
4/5-7/12 & 8/22-12/2	1P: $79- 178	2P/1B: $79- 178	2P/2B: $98- 198	XP: $10			F6
3/28-4/4 & 12/3-12/16	1P: $98- 188	2P/1B: $98- 188	2P/2B: $118- 148	XP: $10			F6

◆◆◆
Resort Lodge

Location: 12.5 mi nw of Jackson; on SR 390, 7 mi n of SR 22. 3255 McCollister Dr 83025 (PO Box 288). Fax: 307/739-1516. **Terms:** Reserv deposit, 45 day notice, in winter, 7 day in summer; handling fee imposed; package plans, in winter. **Facility:** 38 rooms. At base of Jackson Hole Ski Area. 5 units with fireplace. Closed 4/4-5/21 & 10/14-12/3. 3 luxury rooms, some with fireplace or whirlpool, $275-$350; 4 stories; interior corridors; mountain view; heated pool, sauna, whirlpool. **Dining:** Restaurant; 7 am-11 pm; cocktails; also, Alpenhof Dining Room, The Alpenhof Bistro, see separate listing. **Services:** giftshop; complimentary evening beverages. Fee: massage. **Recreation:** hiking trails, game room. Fee: downhill skiing; bicycles, horseback riding, hot air balloon, air tram. **All Rooms:** extended cable TV. **Some Rooms:** whirlpools. **Cards:** AE, CB, DI, DS, JC, MC, VI. *(See color ad p 292)*

**BEST WESTERN JACKSON HOLE RESORT HOTEL
AND CONFERENCE CENTER**   **Phone: (307)733-3657**
(AAA) (SAVE)

	All Year	1P: $89- 279	2P/1B: $89- 279	2P/2B: $89- 279	XP: $10-20	F14

◆◆◆
Motor Inn

Location: SR 390, 7 mi nw of jct SR 22; at the base of Teton Village ski area, 12.5 mi nw of Jackson. 3245 W McCollister 83025 (PO Box 348). Fax: 307/733-9543. **Terms:** Check-in 4 pm; reserv deposit; handling fee imposed. **Facility:** 101 rooms. Some compact rooms. Closed 4/15-5/15 & 10/15-12/1. Closed 10/16-11/30 & 4/6-5/14; 4-5 stories; interior corridors; heated pool, sauna, whirlpools. **Dining:** Dining room; 7 am-10 pm; $9-$19; cocktails. **Services:** giftshop. **Recreation:** Fee: bicycles, horseback riding. **Some Rooms:** kitchen. **Cards:** AE, DI, DS, MC, VI. **Special Amenities:** Free local telephone calls.

BEST WESTERN INN AT JACKSON HOLE   **Phone: (307)733-2311**
(AAA) (SAVE)

	All Year	1P: $89- 279	2P/1B: $89- 279	2P/2B: $89- 279	XP: $10-20	F14

◆◆◆
Motor Inn

Location: SR 390, 7 mi nw of jct SR 22, 12.5 mi nw of Jackson. 3345 W McCollister Dr 83025 (PO Box 328). Fax: 307/733-0844. **Terms:** Check-in 4 pm; reserv deposit; handling fee imposed; package plans, in winter; 4 night min stay, 12/1-3/31. **Facility:** 83 rooms. At base of Teton Mountain ski area. Efficiency units with fireplace. 3-4 stories; exterior corridors; designated smoking area; heated pool, sauna, whirlpools. **Dining:** Dining room, restaurant; sushi bar; $9-$22. **Services:** Fee: massage. **Recreation:** hiking trails. Fee: bicycles, horseback riding. **Some Rooms:** kitchen. **Cards:** AE, DI, DS, MC, VI. **Special Amenities:** Free local telephone calls. Best Western Rewards. *(See color ad p 291)*

SASSY MOOSE INN OF JACKSON HOLE   Rates Subject to Change   **Phone: 307/733-1277**
◆◆

	3/1-3/26, 5/13-10/2, 12/17-1/8 & 1/28-2/29 [BP]	1P: $109- 119	2P/1B: $119- 139	2P/2B: $119- 139	XP: $20	F12
	3/27-5/12, 10/3-12/16 & 1/9-1/27 [BP]	1P: $85	2P/1B: $85- 110	2P/2B: $85- 110	XP: $20	F12

Bed & Breakfast

Location: 2 mi n on SR 390 from jct SR 22, 5 mi s from Teton Village, 6 mi nw from Jackson. 3859 Miles Rd 83014. Fax: 307/739-0793. **Terms:** Check-in 4 pm; reserv deposit, 30 day notice. **Facility:** 5 rooms. Rooms in newly built log house in natural mountain meadow with view of Tetons. Next to golf course. 2 stories; interior corridors; smoke free premises. **Services:** winter plug-ins. **All Rooms:** combo or shower baths. **Cards:** AE, DS, MC, VI.

VILLAGE CENTER INN   **Phone: (307)733-3155**
(AAA) (SAVE)

	All Year	1P: $76- 110	2P/1B: $76- 110	2P/2B: $76- 110	XP: $10	F5

◆
Motel

Location: SR 390, 7 mi nw of jct SR 22, 12.5 mi nw of Jackson. 3275 W McCollister Dr 83025 (PO Box 310). Fax: 307/733-3183. **Terms:** Check-in 4 pm; reserv deposit, 30 day notice; handling fee imposed. **Facility:** 16 rooms. Modest accommodations next to ski lift. Register at Teton Village Property Management. Rooms on top of shops & ski rental store. 2 two-bedroom units $98-$139 for up to 2 persons; 3 stories; no elevator; exterior corridors; designated smoking area. **Dining:** Restaurants nearby. **Services:** giftshop. Fee: massage. **Recreation:** cross country skiing; hiking trails. Fee: downhill skiing, snowmobiling; bicycles, horseback riding. **All Rooms:** kitchens, extended cable TV. **Cards:** MC, VI. **Special Amenities:** Free local telephone calls.

RESTAURANTS

THE ALPENHOF BISTRO   **Lunch: $4-$9**   **Dinner: $6-$12**   **Phone: 307/733-3242**
◆◆
American

Location: 12.5 mi nw of Jackson; on SR 390, 7 mi n of SR 22; in Alpenhof. 3255 McCollister Drive 83025 **Hours:** 11:30 am-10:30 pm. Closed: 4/4-5/15 & 10/12-12/4. **Features:** casual dress; carryout; cocktails & lounge. Casual atmosphere with lighter family dining. **Cards:** AE, CB, DI, DS, MC, VI.

ALPENHOF DINING ROOM   **Dinner: $19-$38**   **Phone: 307/733-3462**
◆◆◆
Continental

Location: 12.5 mi nw of Jackson; on SR 390, 7 mi n of SR 22; in Alpenhof. 3255 McCollister Drive 83025 **Hours:** 7:30 am-10:30 & 6-10 pm. Closed: 4/4-5/15 & 9/28-12/4. **Reservations:** suggested **Features:** casual dress; children's menu; health conscious menu; carryout; cocktails & lounge; a la carte European atmosphere. Tableside offerings some game specialties. Smoke free premises. **Cards:** AE, CB, DI, DS, MC, VI.

THERMOPOLIS—3,200

LODGINGS

BEST WESTERN MOONLIGHTER MOTEL   **Phone: (307)864-2321**
(AAA) (SAVE)

	7/8-8/31 [CP]	1P: $58- 60	2P/1B: $61- 63	2P/2B: $67- 71	XP: $3	F12
	6/1-7/7 [EP]	1P: $53- 55	2P/1B: $56- 58	2P/2B: $61- 65	XP: $3	F12
	5/15-5/31 & 9/1-2/29 [EP]	1P: $44- 46	2P/1B: $47- 49	2P/2B: $51- 55	XP: $3	F12
	3/1-5/14 [EP]	1P: $38	2P/1B: $38- 40	2P/2B: $42- 46	XP: $3	F12

◆◆
Motel

Location: Downtown; on US 20. 600 Broadway 82443. Fax: 307/864-5100. **Terms:** Weekly/monthly rates small pets only. **Facility:** 26 rooms. 1-2 stories; exterior corridors; designated smoking area; small heated pool. **Dining:** Restaurant nearby. **Services:** winter plug-ins. **All Rooms:** extended cable TV. **Cards:** AE, DI, DS, JC, MC, VI.

HOLIDAY INN OF THE WATERS
◆◆◆
Motor Inn

6/18-8/21	1P:	$80- 102	2P/1B:	$80- 108	2P/2B:	$80- 108	XP:	$6	F19
5/28-6/17 & 8/22-9/5	1P:	$66- 86	2P/1B:	$66- 92	2P/2B:	$66- 92	XP:	$6	F19
3/1-5/27 & 9/6-2/29	1P:	$52- 69	2P/1B:	$52- 77	2P/2B:	$52- 75	XP:	$6	F19

Rates Subject to Change   Phone: (307)864-3131

Location: In Hot Springs State Park. 115 E Park St 82443 (PO Box 1323, Hot Springs State Park). Fax: 307/864-3131. **Facility:** 80 rooms. On shaded grounds, within walking distance of park attractions. 2 stories; interior/exterior corridors; heated pool. Fee: racquetball courts. **Services:** winter plug-ins. Fee: massage. **Recreation:** jogging. **Cards:** AE, CB, DI, DS, JC, MC, VI. *(See color ad below & opposite title page)*

HOT SPRINGS SUPER 8
◆◆
Motel

5/16-9/15 [CP]	1P:	$68- 108	2P/1B:	$72- 120	2P/2B:	$74- 102	XP: $5-25	F10
3/1-5/15 & 10/1-2/29 [CP]	1P:	$47- 67	2P/1B:	$52- 80	2P/2B:	$52- 92	XP: $5-25	F10
9/16-9/30 [CP]	1P:	$55- 75	2P/1B:	$57- 77	2P/2B:	$61- 81	XP: $5-25	F10

Rates Subject to Change   Phone: 307/864-5515

Location: US 20, s of town. Lane 5, Hwy 20 S 82443 (PO Box 569). Fax: 307/864-5447. **Facility:** 52 rooms. New property with attractive public areas & very clean rooms. Mini-fridge avail, extra charge. Weekends rates, $10 extra charge; 2 stories; interior corridors; designated smoking area; small heated indoor pool. **All Rooms:** combo or shower baths. **Cards:** AE, DS, JC, MC, VI.

QUALITY INN & SUITES (THE PLAZA HOTEL)
FYI
Motel

6/1-8/31 [CP]	1P:	$90- 105	2P/1B:	$90- 105	2P/2B:	$90- 105	XP:	$5	F12
5/1-5/31 [CP]	1P:	$65- 76	2P/1B:	$65- 76	2P/2B:	$65- 76	XP:	$5	F12
3/1-4/30 & 9/1-2/29 [EP]	1P:	$55- 75	2P/1B:	$55- 75	2P/2B:	$55- 75	XP:	$5	F12

Rates Subject to Change   Phone: (307)864-2939

Too new to rate. **Location:** Just s of US 20; in Hot Springs State Park. 116 E Park St 82433. Fax: 307/864-2939. **Terms:** Reserv deposit. **Facility:** 35 rooms. Across the street from Thermopolis Hot Springs State Park. Scheduled to open November 15, 1998; 2 stories; interior corridors; smoke free premises. **Services:** winter plug-ins. **Cards:** AE, MC, VI.

RESTAURANT

THE SAFARI CLUB   **Lunch:** $5-$9   **Dinner:** $6-$19   Phone: (307)864-3131
◆◆
American

Location: In Hot Springs State Park; in Holiday Inn of the Waters. 115 E Park St 82443. **Hours:** 6 am-10 pm. **Features:** casual dress; children's menu; early bird specials; salad bar; cocktails & lounge; area transportation; a la carte. Sun breakfast & buffet 7 am-2 pm. Hundreds of different types of mounted fish, birds & animals decorate the restaurant & lounge. **Cards:** AE, DI, DS, JC, MC, VI.

TORRINGTON—5,700

LODGINGS

KINGS INN
AAA SAVE
◆◆
Motor Inn

| All Year | 1P: | $45- 50 | 2P/1B: | $50- 55 | 2P/2B: | $54 | XP: | $5 | D |

Phone: (307)532-4011

Location: Downtown; on US 85. 1555 Main St 82240. Fax: 307/532-7202. **Terms:** Weekly rates; pets, $4 extra charge, in designated rooms. **Facility:** 52 rooms. Quiet rooms, economy lodging. 2 stories; interior corridors; heated indoor pool, whirlpool. **Dining:** Restaurant; 7 am-10 pm; cocktails. **Recreation:** exercise equipment. **All Rooms:** extended cable TV. **Cards:** AE, CB, DI, DS, MC, VI. **Special Amenities:** Free local telephone calls and preferred room (subject to availability with advanced reservations).

MAVERICK MOTEL
AAA SAVE
◆
Motel

| All Year | 1P: | $36 | 2P/1B: | $38 | 2P/2B: | $40 | XP: | $4 | D21 |

Phone: (307)532-4064

Location: 1.5 mi w on US 26 & 85. (Rt 1, Box 354, 82240). Fax: 307/532-2577. **Terms:** Small pets only. **Facility:** 11 rooms. Excellent housekeeping. 1 story; exterior corridors. **Services:** winter plug-ins. **All Rooms:** extended cable TV. **Some Rooms:** kitchen, no utensils. **Cards:** AE, CB, DI, DS, MC, VI.

SUPER 8 MOTEL
◆◆
Motel

| All Year | 1P: | $46 | 2P/1B: | $52 | 2P/2B: | $58 | XP: | $5 | |

Rates Subject to Change   Phone: 307/532-7118

Location: Just s on US 85. 1548 S Main 82240 (PO Box 1213). Fax: 307/532-7118. **Terms:** Reserv deposit, 30 day notice. **Facility:** 57 rooms. First floor rooms at garden level. 2 stories; interior corridors; heated indoor pool. **Services:** winter plug-ins. **Some Rooms:** kitchen. **Cards:** AE, CB, DI, DS, MC, VI.

UCROSS

LODGING

THE RANCH AT UCROSS
Phone: (307)737-228█

(AAA) (SAVE)   5/1-9/30 [BP]   1P: $130- 150   2P/1B: $140- 160   2P/2B: $140- 160   XP: $10   D1█
         3/1-4/30 & 10/1-2/29 [BP]   1P: $100- 110   2P/1B: $100- 110   2P/2B: $100- 110   XP: $10   D1█
◆ ◆ ◆   **Location:** Jct US 14/16, 0.5 mi w on US 14. 2673 US Hwy 14E 82835. Fax: 307/737-2211. **Terms:** Rese█
Resort Ranch   deposit; AP avail. **Facility:** 31 rooms. Once a private resort. Various room types from bed & breakfast to mot█
style to duplex cottages. Quiet ranch setting. 1-2 stories; interior/exterior corridors; heated pool; 2 tennis court█
Dining: Dining room; breakfast from 7 am, dinner from 7 pm; cocktails. **Services:** giftshop. **Recreation:** fishin█
Fee: horseback riding. **Some Rooms:** whirlpools. **Cards:** DS, MC, VI. **Special Amenities:** Early check-in/late check-o█
and free breakfast. *(See ad p 314)*

WAPITI—See also YELLOWSTONE NATIONAL PARK.

LODGINGS

ABSAROKA MOUNTAIN LODGE
Phone: (307)587-396█

(AAA) (SAVE)   6/1-9/30   1P: $87- 97   2P/1B: $87- 97   2P/2B: $112- 125   XP: $7
         5/1-5/31   1P: $79- 88   2P/1B: $79- 88   2P/2B: $103- 111   XP: $7
◆ ◆   **Location:** 19 mi w on US 14/16/20. 1231 E Yellowstone Hwy 82450. Fax: 307/527-9628. **Terms:** Ope█
Cottage   5/1-9/30; reserv deposit, 30 day notice; handling fee imposed; AP avail; package plans. **Facility:** 16 room█
Cabins along mountain stream in national forest; 12 mi e of Yellowstone Park. Tues night barbecue. 2 two█
bedroom units, $108-$135 for up to 6 persons;1 kitchen unit, $120; 1 story; exterior corridors; smoke free premises; pla█
ground. **Dining:** Dining room; 7:30 am-9:30 & 6-8:30 pm; $8-$19; cocktails. **Recreation:** naturalist programs Mon, Wed █
Fri evenings; nightly campfires; fishing; volleyball net, horseshoe pits. Fee: horseback riding. **All Rooms:** combo or showe█
baths. **Some Rooms:** kitchen. **Cards:** DS, MC, VI. **Special Amenities:** Early check-in/late check-out and preferred roor█
(subject to availability with advanced reservations). *(See color ad p 280)*

BILL CODY RANCH
Rates Subject to Change   **Phone:** 307/587-627█

(AAA)   6/10-8/31   1P: $105   2P/1B: $105   2P/2B: $105- 125   XP: $10
       5/15-6/9 & 9/1-9/30   1P: $78   2P/1B: $78   2P/2B: $78- 98   XP: $10
◆ ◆ ◆   **Location:** 6 mi w on US 14/16/20. 2604 Yellowstone Hwy 82414 (2604 Yellowstone Hwy, CODY█
Cottage   Fax: 307/587-6272. **Terms:** Open 5/15-9/30; check-in 4 pm; reserv deposit, 30 day notice; handling fe█
imposed; weekly rates; AP, BP, MAP avail; package plans. **Facility:** 14 rooms. In Shoshone National Forest i█
East Yellowstone Valley. Beautiful mountain area. Log cabins in wooded setting, Western decor. 26 mi e of Yellowstone Park█
7 two-bedroom units. 1-2 stories; interior/exterior corridors; designated smoking area; enclosed whirlpool; playground█
Dining: Dining room; 7 am-9:30 & 6-8 pm; $9-$19; cocktails. **Recreation:** naturalist program Tues, Thurs & Sat evenings█
cowboy campfire one night a week; fishing; hiking trails, basketball hoop, horseshoes. Fee: horseback riding, guided tra█
rides. **Cards:** DS, MC, VI. *(See color ad p 279)*

ELEPHANT HEAD LODGE
Phone: (307)587-398█

(AAA) (SAVE)   6/2-9/20   1P: $75- 100   2P/1B: $75- 100   2P/2B: $85- 100
       5/15-6/1 & 9/21-10/15   1P: $68- 90   2P/1B: $68- 90   2P/2B: $77- 90
◆ ◆   **Location:** 19.8 mi w on US 14/16/20. 1170 Yellowstone Park Hwy 82450. Fax: 307/527-7922. **Terms:** Ope█
Cottage   5/15-10/15; reserv deposit, 30 day notice; AP avail; package plans; pets. **Facility:** 10 rooms. Cozy cabins i█
wilderness setting. 3 rooms with lofts. 12 mi e of Yellowstone Park. 2 two-bedroom units. 3 kitchen units, $120█
$150 for 8 persons. Historic cabin prices reflect sleeping capacity. Features fireplace, suites & lofts; 1 story; exterior corridors█
smoke free premises. **Dining:** Dining room; 7:30 am-9:30, noon-1 & 3:30-8:30 pm; $7-$19; cocktails. **Recreation:** fishing█
movies shown 5 nights a week; 1 portable TV/VCR avail; forest service presentations Mon, Tues & Sat, Swingse█
Fee: horseback riding. **All Rooms:** combo or shower baths. **Some Rooms:** 3 kitchens. **Cards:** AE, DS, MC, VI█
Special Amenities: Early check-in/late check-out and preferred room (subject to availability with advance█
reservations). *(See color ad p 165 & p 320)*

GOFF CREEK LODGE
Phone: (307)587-375█

(AAA) (SAVE)   6/20-8/20   1P: $90- 100   2P/1B: $90- 100   2P/2B: $100- 110   XP: $6
       5/1-6/19 & 8/21-11/1   1P: $72- 80   2P/1B: $72- 80   2P/2B: $81- 90   XP: $6
◆ ◆   **Location:** 21.4 mi w on US 14/16/20. 995 E Yellowstone Hwy 82414 (Box 155, CODY). Fax: 307/587-3753█
Cottage   **Terms:** Open 5/1-11/1; reserv deposit, 30 day notice; handling fee imposed; weekly rates; package plans█
small pets only, $5 extra charge. **Facility:** 17 rooms. Log cabin units nestled along pine shaded stream█
Evening campfire. 10 mi e of Yellowstone Park. 1 story; exterior corridors; smoke free premises. **Dining:** Dining room█
am-9:30 & 6-9 pm; $6-$18; cocktails; Thurs evening cookouts. **Recreation:** fishing; hiking trails, nightly camp fires█
Fee: horseback riding. **All Rooms:** combo or shower baths. **Some Rooms:** 2 kitchens. **Cards:** MC, VI.
(See color ad p 282)

WISE CHOICE INN
Phone: (307)587-500█

(AAA) (SAVE)   6/7-8/31   1P: $45   2P/1B: $50   2P/2B: $55   XP: $5   F1█
       4/15-6/6 & 9/1-11/15   1P: $25   2P/1B: $30   2P/2B: $35   XP: $5   F1█
◆   **Location:** 2.8 mi w on US 14/16/20. 2908 Yellowstone Hwy 82450. **Terms:** Open 4/15-11/15; reserv deposi█
Motel   handling fee imposed; weekly rates; pets, $3 extra charge. **Facility:** 17 rooms. Nestled between ranches i█
beautiful Wapiti Valley. Simple, well kept rooms. Some family units with bunk beds. Some rooms with mountai█
view. 29 mi e of Yellowstone Park. 1 story; exterior corridors; designated smoking area; playground. **Cards:** AE, DS, MC, VI█
Special Amenities: Early check-in/late check-out and free local telephone calls. *(See color ad p 282)*

RESTAURANT

WAPITI LODGE STEAKHOUSE
Dinner: $12-$19   **Phone:** 307/587-6659█

(AAA)   **Location:** US 14, 16 & 20. 3189 Yellowstone Hwy 82450. **Hours:** 5 pm-10 pm 5/1-8/31; 5 pm-10 pm█
    Tues-Sat 9/1-4/30. Closed: 11/25 & 12/25. **Reservations:** accepted. **Features:** casual dress; children'█
◆ ◆   menu; cocktails & lounge. Specializing in steak & seafood. Located in beautiful Wapiti Valley. **Cards:** MC, VI.
American

WHEATLAND—3,300

LODGINGS

BEST WESTERN TORCHLITE MOTOR INN   Phone: (307)322-4070

	7/23-8/1 [EP]	1P:	$75			2P/2B:	$75	XP: $5
	6/1-7/22 & 8/2-8/15 [CP]	1P:	$51	2P/1B:	$56	2P/2B:	$56	XP: $5
	3/1-5/31 & 8/16-2/29 [EP]	1P:	$41	2P/1B:	$46	2P/2B:	$46	XP: $5

Motor Inn   **Location:** I-25, between exits 78 & 80; on frontage road. 1809 N 16th St 82201 (PO Box 637). Fax: 307/322-4072. **Terms:** Reserv deposit; pets dep req. **Facility:** 50 rooms. Modern rooms. Truck parking. 2 stories; exterior corridors; designated smoking area; heated pool, whirlpool. **Dining:** Restaurant; 5:30 am-10 pm; $8-$19; cocktails. **Services:** winter plug-ins. **All Rooms:** extended cable TV. **Cards:** AE, CB, DI, DS, MC, VI. **Special Amenities:** Early check-in/late check-out and free local telephone calls.

MOTEL WEST WINDS   Rates Subject to Change   Phone: 307/322-2705

	7/17-7/26	1P:	$43	2P/1B:	$48	2P/2B:	$58	XP: $5
Motel	5/1-7/16 & 7/27-9/30	1P:	$33	2P/1B:	$38	2P/2B:	$43	XP: $5
	3/1-4/30 & 10/1-2/29	1P:	$28	2P/1B:	$33	2P/2B:	$38	XP: $5

Location: 1 mi n of I-25, exit 78. 1756 South Rd 82201. **Terms:** Reserv deposit. **Facility:** 30 rooms. Spacious, budget oriented rooms. 2 stories; exterior corridors. **Services:** winter plug-ins. **All Rooms:** combo or shower baths. **Cards:** AE, CB, DI, DS, MC, VI.

VIMBO'S MOTEL   Phone: (307)322-3842

	7/16-7/24	1P:	$68	2P/1B:	$73	2P/2B:	$75	XP: $4
	7/1-7/15 & 7/25-8/15	1P:	$48	2P/1B:	$53	2P/2B:	$55	XP: $4
	6/1-6/30 & 8/16-8/31	1P:	$43	2P/1B:	$45	2P/2B:	$49	XP: $4
Motor Inn	3/1-5/31 & 9/1-2/29	1P:	$38	2P/1B:	$43	2P/2B:	$45	XP: $4

Location: 0.3 mi from I-25, exit 78. 203 16th St 82201 (PO Box 188). **Terms:** Small pets only. **Facility:** 38 rooms. Very clean rooms. 2 stories; interior/exterior corridors; designated smoking area. **Dining:** Restaurant, see separate listing. **Services:** giftshop; winter plug-ins. **All Rooms:** extended cable TV. **Cards:** AE, DS, MC, VI. **Special Amenities:** Free local telephone calls.

RESTAURANT

VIMBO'S RESTAURANT   **Lunch:** $4-$9   **Dinner:** $4-$17   Phone: 307/322-3725

   Location: 0.3 mi n from I-25, exit 78; beside Vimbo's Motel. 203 16th St 82201. **Hours:** 5:30 am-9 pm, Fri & Sat-10 pm, Sun 6:30 am-9 pm; 5:30 pm-9 pm, Sun 6:30 am-9 pm, in summer. Closed: 11/25 & 12/25.

Features: casual dress; children's menu; cocktails & lounge; a la carte. Family dining offering varied menu. American   Gift shop. **Cards:** AE, DS, MC, VI.

WORLAND—5,700

LODGINGS

BEST WESTERN SETTLERS INN   Phone: (307)347-8201

	All Year [CP]	1P:	$44- 54	2P/1B:	$49- 58	2P/2B:	$49- 58	XP: $6 F12

Location: 1 mi e on US 16. 2200 Big Horn Ave 82401. Fax: 307/347-9323. **Terms:** Pets. **Facility:** 44 rooms. Small lobby with comfortable rooms. 2 stories; interior corridors. **Dining:** Restaurant nearby. **Services:** winter plug-ins. **All Rooms:** extended cable TV. **Cards:** AE, DI, DS, MC, VI.

DAYS INN   Phone: (307)347-4251

	6/1-8/31	1P:	$42- 48	2P/1B:	$48- 58	2P/2B:	$48- 62	XP: $6 F12
	9/1-10/16	1P:	$42- 46	2P/1B:	$46- 52	2P/2B:	$48- 56	XP: $6 F12
Motel	3/1-5/31 & 10/17-2/29	1P:	$42- 45	2P/1B:	$42- 48	2P/2B:	$48- 52	

Location: 0.5 mi n on US 20. 500 N 10th St 82401. Fax: 307/347-6500. **Terms:** Reserv deposit; small pets only, $5 extra charge. **Facility:** 42 rooms. Some newly constructed modern rooms. All rooms with voice mail. 1 story; exterior corridors; designated smoking area. **Services:** winter plug-ins. **All Rooms:** combo or shower baths, extended cable TV. **Cards:** AE, CB, DI, DS, MC, VI. **Special Amenities:** Free breakfast and free local telephone calls.

SUPER 8 MOTEL   Rates Subject to Change   Phone: 307/347-9236

	7/1-8/14 [CP]	1P:	$45	2P/1B:	$49	2P/2B:	$56	XP: $4
	6/1-6/30 & 8/15-8/30 [CP]	1P:	$41	2P/1B:	$45	2P/2B:	$53	XP: $4
Motel	8/31-10/31 [CP]	1P:	$33	2P/1B:	$37	2P/2B:	$45	XP: $2
	3/1-5/31 & 11/1-2/29 [CP]	1P:	$31	2P/1B:	$34	2P/2B:	$36	XP: $2

Location: US 16, 0.9 mi w. 2500 Big Horn Ave 82401. Fax: 307/347-9236. **Facility:** 35 rooms. Economy lodging with modern rooms & furnishings. Very clean rooms. 2 stories; interior corridors. **Services:** winter plug-ins. **Cards:** AE, CB, DI, DS, JC, MC, VI.

RESTAURANTS

HARRY'S STEAK HOUSE   **Lunch:** $6-$8   **Dinner:** $10-$27   Phone: 307/347-9261

   Location: 0.5 mi e on US 16. 1620 Big Horn Ave 82401. **Hours:** 11 am-10 pm. Closed major holidays & Steakhouse   Sun. **Features:** casual dress; carryout; cocktails & lounge; a la carte. Prime rib nightly, steak & seafood. Family dining. **Cards:** AE, CB, DI, DS, MC, VI.

RAM'S HORN CAFE   **Lunch:** $5-$15   **Dinner:** $5-$15   Phone: 307/347-6351

   Location: City center; on US 16. 629 Big Horn Ave 82401. **Hours:** 6 am-10 pm. Closed: 12/25. **Features:** casual dress; children's menu; cocktails & lounge; street parking; a la carte. Wide menu selection. American   Coffee shop operation on one side & dining room & lounge on the other. **Cards:** AE, DI, MC, VI.

GIVE A WHOLE YEAR OF AAA MEMBERSHIP.

In addition to the peace of mind of emergency road service, AAA members enjoy expert travel planning, exclusive discounts, and more. All year long, as recipients use their AAA benefits, they'll appreciate your thoughtfulness.

- 24-Hour Road Services
- Member Discounts
- Travel Services

Celebrate the special people in your life with the gift that shows you care. Lavish them with a whole year of AAA membership benefits and services.

Gift purchase includes festive card holder and envelope.

CALL OR VISIT YOUR **AAA** OFFICE TODAY.

1-800-JOIN-AAA

Need a tow? Call AAA.

We'll give you a tow, boost your battery, change a flat, or deliver fuel. When you're a member, the answer to your car problems is as simple as that.

Contact your local AAA Club for more information.

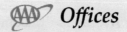

Offices

Cities with main offices are listed in **BOLD TYPE** and toll-free member service numbers in *ITALIC TYPE*.
All are closed Saturdays, Sundays and holidays unless otherwise indicated.

The type of service provided is designated below the name of the city where the office is located:

Auto travel services, including books/maps, marked maps and on-demand Triptik maps ✛
Auto travel services, including books/maps, marked maps, but no on-demand Triptik maps ●
Provides books/maps only. No marked maps or on-demand Triptik maps available ■
Travel agency services ▲

IDAHO

BOISE—AAA OREGON/IDAHO, 3040 ELDER ST, 83705. MON-FRI 8:30-5:30. (208) 342-9391, *(800) 999-9391.*✛▲

COEUR D'ALENE—INLAND AUTOMOBILE ASSOCIATION, 296 W SUNSET AVE #26, 83814-8330. MON-FRI 8:30-5. (208) 664-5868.✛▲

IDAHO FALLS—AAA OREGON/IDAHO, 660 S WOODRUFF AVE, 83401-5299. MON-FRI 8:30-5:30. (208) 522-8495, *(800) 283-8495.*✛▲

LEWISTON—INLAND AUTOMOBILE ASSOCIATION, 2116 12TH AVE, 83501-3595. MON-FRI 8:30-5. (208) 746-0407, *(800) 356-2228.*✛▲

TWIN FALLS—AAA OREGON/IDAHO, 870 BLUE LAKES BLVD #3, 83301. MON-FRI 8:30-5:30. (208) 734-6441, *(800) 999-6441.*✛▲

MONTANA

BILLINGS—AAA MONTANA, 3220 4TH AVE N, 59101-1203. MON-FRI 8-5:30. (406) 248-7738, *(800) 391-4222.*✛▲

BOZEMAN—AAA MONTANA, 711 W MAIN, 59715. MON-FRI 8-5:30. (406) 586-6156, *(800) 391-4222.*✛▲

GREAT FALLS—AAA MONTANA, 505 10TH AVE S, 59405-4046. MON-FRI 8:30-5:30. (406) 727-2900, *(800) 391-4222.*✛▲

HELENA—AAA MONTANA, 2100 11TH AVE, 59601-4876. MON-FRI 8-5:30, SAT 9-1. (406) 447-8100, *(800) 332-6119.*✛▲

KALISPELL—AAA MONTANA, 440 W IDAHO, 59901-3945. MON-FRI 8-5:30. (406) 755-5511, *(800) 391-4222.*✛▲

MISSOULA—AAA MONTANA, 1200 S RESERVE SUITE B, 59801. MON-FRI 8-5:30. (406) 549-5181, *(800) 391-4222.*✛▲

WYOMING

CHEYENNE—AAA WYOMING, 1450 STILLWATER AVE, 82009. MON-FRI 8-5:30, SAT 9-1. (307) 634-8861, *(800) 391-4222.*✛▲

SHERIDAN—AAA WYOMING, 52 E BRUNDAGE, 82801. MON-FRI 8-5:30. (307) 672-3447, *(800) 391-4222.*▲

Temperature Averages - Maximum/Minimum
From the records of the National Weather Service

	JAN	FEB	MAR	APR	MAY	JUN	JUL	AUG	SEP	OCT	NOV	DEC
IDAHO												
Boise	36/21	42/26	52/31	62/37	71/45	79/51	90/59	88/57	78/49	65/40	48/30	39/25
Idaho Falls	28/3	33/8	42/18	58/29	68/38	76/44	88/50	86/47	75/38	62/28	43/17	33/9
Lewiston	38/24	44/28	53/33	63/39	71/46	78/52	90/58	88/56	78/49	64/40	48/32	42/28
Pocatello	32/13	37/18	46/26	60/33	69/41	78/48	90/55	87/53	77/44	64/34	45/25	36/19
MONTANA												
Billings	33/13	36/15	43/23	57/34	68/43	76/51	89/58	86/55	75/46	63/37	46/26	39/19
Great Falls	32/14	34/15	41/21	55/33	66/42	72/49	84/56	81/54	70/46	59/38	44/26	37/20
Havre	26/6	29/8	40/18	57/32	69/43	75/51	86/57	83/54	72/44	60/35	42/21	33/12
Kalispell	26/9	32/12	40/19	55/30	65/39	72/46	83/49	80/46	69/39	55/31	37/21	29/16
Miles City	27/6	32/9	42/19	59/33	71/44	79/53	90/60	88/58	75/47	62/36	44/22	34/13
WYOMING												
Casper	33/14	37/16	43/21	56/31	66/40	77/49	87/56	85/55	74/45	61/36	44/23	37/18
Cheyenne	38/14	40/15	44/20	55/29	64/39	76/48	84/54	82/53	73/43	62/33	47/22	42/18
Lander	31/8	36/12	45/20	56/31	66/40	76/48	86/55	84/54	73/45	60/34	43/19	35/12
Sheridan	34/9	36/11	43/19	56/31	67/40	75/48	87/56	86/53	74/43	62/33	46/21	39/14
Yellowstone Nat. Pk.	26/10	30/11	37/17	48/26	57/33	67/41	76/47	74/45	64/37	52/29	38/20	28/12

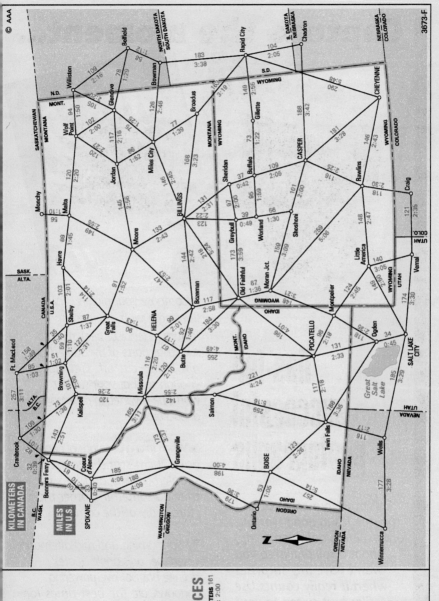

© AAA

IDAHO
MONTANA
WYOMING
DRIVING DISTANCES

U.S. IN MILES 100 · CANADA IN KILOMETERS 161
AVERAGE TIME (EXCLUDING STOPS): 2:00

KILOMETERS
IN CANADA

MILES
IN U.S.

3673-F

Capture the moment...

Tips for successful photographs

Know your camera, and be sure it's in good working order. Before going on a trip, shoot a roll of film so you won't have any surprises when it really counts. Use film best suited to your purpose; camera shop personnel can help you choose the right kind. Then, follow the instructions that come with it.

- Compose your picture. Try framing it with a foreground feature (a fence or tree), making sure that parts of the subject are not being cut off. Get close enough so that your subject won't be dwarfed in an expanse of background.

- When taking close-ups of people, have them stand against a simple backdrop, and be sure they do something other than stare stiffly at the camera.

- Mid-morning and mid-afternoon, when the sun's angle creates definite but not overpowering shadows, are the best times for general photography. Pictures taken during the shadowless high noon hours tend to be flat.

- If the weather turns bad, take pictures anyway. Rain and fog can add a special magic to your efforts.

Savings for all Seasons

Hertz rents Fords and other fine cars.
® REG. U.S. PAT. OFF. © HERTZ SYSTEM INC., 1998/2004-98.

No matter the season, Hertz offers AAA members exclusive discounts and benefits.

With a fleet of more than 500,000 vehicles and over 5,500 rental locations worldwide, Hertz makes traveling more convenient and efficient wherever and whenever you go. Hertz offers AAA members discounts up to 20% on car rentals worldwide.

To receive your exclusive AAA member discounts and benefits, mention your AAA membership card at time of reservation and present it at time of rental.

For reservations and program details, call your AAA travel office or the Hertz/AAA Desk at **1-800-654-3080**.

AAA
Show Your Card & Save ®

Hertz®
exactly.

Border Information

FOR CANADIAN RESIDENTS

Entering the United States

UNITED STATES CUSTOMS permits you to bring, free of duty, for personal use and not intended for sale: clothing, personal effects and equipment appropriate to the trip. Personal effects may include 200 cigarettes, 50 cigars or 4.4 pounds (2 kgs) of tobacco or proportionate amounts of each, and 1 liter of alcoholic beverage.

If you are planning to be in the United States at least 72 hours, you may bring gifts up to a fair retail value of $100 (U.S.), provided you have not claimed this exemption within the preceding 6 months. Perfume containing alcohol and valued at more than $5 retail, tobacco products and alcoholic beverages are excluded from the gift provision.

Radio Communication Equipment: You may use your General Radio Service Station (CB) and cellular phone in the United States without any restrictions.

Returning to Canada

CANADIAN CUSTOMS allows you to bring, free of duty and taxes, goods valued up to $200 (Canadian) any number of times per year, provided you have been in the United States **48 hours or more.** All goods must accompany you; a written declaration *may* be required.

You may claim a $50 (Canadian) exemption on goods, excluding alcoholic beverages and tobacco products, if you are returning after an absence of **24 hours or more** and are not using any other exemption. If more than $50 worth of goods is brought back, the regular rate of duty and taxes will be levied on the entire value. This exemption may apply any number of times in a year.

If you are returning after **7 days or more** in the United States (not counting the day of departure from Canada), you may claim an exemption on goods valued up to $500 (Canadian). Goods, other than alcohol and tobacco products, are not required to accompany you; a written declaration *may* be required.

Permitted within the $200 and $500 exemptions are up to 50 cigars, 200 cigarettes, 200 tobacco sticks and 7 ounces (200 gm) of tobacco and up to 40 ounces (1.14 L) of wine or liquor, or 9 qts. (8.5 L) of beer and/or ale (or its equivalent of 24 bottles or cans). You must meet the minimum age requirement of the province entered to claim alcohol or tobacco products.

There is nothing to prevent you from importing any quantity of goods, even if you do not qualify for any kind of personal exemption, provided the goods you are importing are not restricted and the full rate of duty and taxes is paid.

Special Tariff: When you exceed your $200 or $500 exemptions, a special rate of 7 percent combined duty and taxes is levied on the next $300 value in goods (except tobacco and alcohol) in excess of maximum exemptible amounts, provided the goods are of U.S. origin. Regular duties apply on any amount over that. For detailed information concerning specific duty rates, consult Canadian Customs before leaving on your trip.

All exemptions are individual and may not be combined with those of another person. You may be asked to verify the length of your visit; dated receipts normally constitute proof.

GIFTS to the value of $60 (Canadian) may be sent from abroad, free of duty or taxes. These may not include alcoholic beverages, tobacco products or advertising matter. Gifts valued at over $60 (Canadian) are subject to duty and taxes on the amount in excess of $60. Gifts *sent* from abroad do not count against your personal exemption, but gifts brought back *must* be included as part of your exemption.

Points of Interest Index

INDEX ABBREVIATIONS

RECREATION-WINTER ACTIVITIES

RESEARCH ORGANIZATIONS

RESTORED VILLAGES & SETTLEMENTS

ROCKS

SCENIC DRIVES

SCHOOL BUILDINGS

SCHOOLS

SCHOOLS-COLLEGES & UNIVERSITIES

SCHOOLS-INSTITUTES

SELF-GUIDING TOURS

SHIPS & BOATS

SHOPS, FIRMS & STORES

SIGHTSEEING-AIRCRAFT RIDES & TOURS

SIGHTSEEING TOURS

WALKING TOURS

WATERFALLS

WATER PARKS

WILDERNESS AREAS

WILDLIFE SANCTUARIES

SAVE *Attraction Admission Discount Index*

Bed & Breakfast Lodgings Index

Some bed and breakfasts listed below might have historical significance. Those properties are also referenced in the Historical index. The indication that continental [CP] or full breakfast [BP] is included in the room rate reflects whether a property is a Bed-and-Breakfast facility.

Country Inns Index

Some of the following country inns can also be considered as bed-and-breakfast operations. The indication that continental [CP] or full breakfast [BP] is included in the room rate reflects whether a property is a Bed-and-Breakfast facility.

We'll never leave you alone.

Historical Lodgings & Restaurants Index

Some of the following historical lodgings can also be considered as bed-and-breakfast operations. The indication that continental [CP] or full breakfast [BP] is included in the room rate reflects whether a property is a Bed-and-Breakfast facility.

Resorts Index

Many establishments are located in resort areas; however, the following places have extensive on-premises recreational facilities:

Comprehensive City Index

Here is an alphabetical list of all cities appearing in this TourBook. Cities are presented by state/province. Page numbers under the POI column indicate where points of interest text begins. Page numbers under the L&R column indicate where lodging and restaurant listings begin.

COMPREHENSIVE CITY INDEX (CONT'D)

Photo Credit Index

NOTES